CONTEMPORARY LINGUISTICS

An Introduction

Second Edition

CONTEMPORARY LINGUISTICS

An Introduction

Second Edition

William O'Grady
University of Hawaii at Manoa

and

Michael Dobrovolsky
University of Calgary

U.S. Edition prepared by
Mark Aronoff
State University of New York at Stony Brook

St. Martin's Press
New York

Senior editor: Catherine Pusateri
Development editor: Joyce Hinnefeld
Development associate: Kristin Bowen
Manager, publishing services: Emily Berleth
Project management: Omega Publishing Services, Inc.
Art director: Sheree L. Goodman
Cover design and art: Marjory Dressler

For information, write:
St. Martin's Press, Inc.
175 Fifth Avenue
New York, NY 10010

ISBN: 0-312-06780-1

Acknowledgments

Copyright © 1991 by Douglas Campbell Coupland. From the
book *Generation X.* By Douglas Campbell Coupland. Reprinted
by permission of St. Martin's Press, Incorporated.

International Phonetic Alphabet reprinted by permission of the
publisher.

Map and key depicting regional dialects of American English,
from *The Structure of American English* by W. Nelson Francis,
copyright © 1958 The Ronald Press. Reprinted by permission of
John Wiley & Sons, Inc.

Spectrographs on pp. 535–536 first appeared in Peter Ladefoged's
A Course on Phonetics, Harcourt Brace Jovanovich, Inc.
Reprinted by permission.

"Tiff and I" by Lesléa Newman is reprinted from *Sweet Dark
Places,* © 1991 by Lesléa Newman, published by HerBooks,
1991, with permission of the author.

PREFACE

This is the second American edition of a textbook originally published in Canada and now in its second Canadian edition. As with the first U.S. edition, I have strived to retain all that was so praiseworthy in the Canadian original, while incorporating new material to make a genuinely American textbook. To that end, some of the specifically Canadian factual material has been deleted or replaced (though not where a Canadian example served its pedagogical purpose as well as another might), and some specifically American material has been added, especially in the chapter on language in social contexts, where American dialects and social phenomena have been given center stage.

New to this edition

Because of its editorial history, though, this second American edition is a revision not of one book, but of two: the 1989 American edition and the second (1992) Canadian edition. I would like to believe that this mixed ancestry only gives it greater strength, but that is for the reader to judge. In any case, in each chapter I have tried to select the best of both originals, along with many of the changes suggested by reviewers and colleagues. No chapter has gone unscathed, though some have been more affected than others. The *core chapters* (Chapters 1 through 6) have all been revised and updated to reflect new developments and discoveries. In addition, I have taken from the second Canadian edition almost entirely *new chapters* on historical linguistics (Chapter 7), neurolinguistics (Chapter 9), and writing (Chapter 13), along with the much improved chapter on animal communication (Chapter 14).

On a more global level, the *exercise sections* at the ends of each chapter have been expanded substantially; topical sections, labeled *For the Student Linguist,* written from a student's perspective by Amy Schafer, a graduate student at the University of Massachusetts, have been added to many chapters; the *glossary* has been enlarged to the point where it contains all the technical terms discussed in the book; the *advanced sections* have been marked with an asterisk in the contents and the word "advanced" in the text.

More than any other introductory linguistics textbook, this one results from a cooperative effort: it has sixteen authors and three editors. In addition, this second edition incorporates many of the suggestions and corrections of a large number of colleagues. For the American revision, five reviewers provided extensive comments on the entire text of the first edition: Dee Holisky, George Mason University; Kostas Kazazis, University of Chicago; Yutaka Ohno, University of Massachusetts; Amy Schafer, University of Massachusetts; Valdis J. Zeps, University of Wisconsin, Madison; and Joseph Malone, Barnard College, who also reviewed the book in *Language*. In addition, a number of users of the first American edition sent suggestions and information directly to me, for which I am very grateful. Let me specifically thank Barbara Abbott, K. Boot, Alice Harris, Leanne Hinton, A. Huettner, Kostas Kazazis, Yukata

Ohno and John Street. I would also like to acknowledge Virginia Clark, Kyle Johnson, and Jennifer Peterson, reviewers for the first American edition, for their valuable suggestions during the formative stages of this project.

On the editorial side, here at Stony Brook, preparing this edition would have been much more difficult without the help of two students, Eriko Sato-Zhu and Ekyoung Kim. I am grateful to William O'Grady and Yutaka Sato for their heroic efforts in the copy-editing stage. At St. Martin's, Cathy Pusateri, Kristin Bowen, and Emily Berleth have been very helpful. Mostly, though, I was in almost daily contact with Joyce Hinnefeld, development editor, for close to six months: I will miss the phone calls.

Mark Aronoff

FROM THE PREFACES
TO THE CANADIAN EDITIONS

Thanks to the application of rigorous analysis to familiar subject matter, linguistics provides students with an ideal introduction to the kind of thinking we call "scientific." Such thinking proceeds from an appreciation of problems arising from bodies of data, to hypotheses that attempt to account for those problems, to the careful testing and extension of these hypotheses. But science is more than a formal activity. One of the great pleasures offered introductory students of linguistics is the discovery of the impressive body of subconscious knowledge that underlies language use. This book attempts to emphasize the extent of this knowledge as well as to introduce the scientific methodology used in linguistic analysis.

As the title suggests, we have attempted an introduction to linguistic analysis as it is practised at this stage in the development of our discipline. While we do not ignore or reject other fruitful approaches to linguistics, we have taken the generative paradigm as basic for two reasons. First, generative linguistics provides a relatively coherent and integrated approach to basic linguistic phenomena. Phonetics, phonology, morphology, syntax, and semantics are viewed within this framework as perhaps in no other as fully integrated and interrelated. Secondly, the generative approach has been widely influential in its application to a broad range of other linguistic phenomena over the past twenty years.

No textbook can be all things to all users. We hope that this book will provide students not only with a springboard to the realm of scientific linguistic analysis, but with a greater appreciation for the wonder of human language, the variety and complexity of its structure, and the subtlety of its use.

Colleagues from Canada and the United States have read and commented upon individual chapters and sections of the textbook. In addition to those who responded anonymously to our questionnaire and those whose contributions are acknowledged in the first edition, we would like to express our gratitude to Peter Seyffert (for his assistance on several occasions), Mark Aronoff, Howard Aronson, Byron Bender, Derek Bickerton, Vit Bubenik, Andrew Carnie, Vanna Condax, Eung-Do Cook, John DeFrancis, Sheila Embleton, Paula Erlichman, Alice Harris, Brian Henderson, Joyce Hildebrand, Ricky Jacobs, Kazue Kanno, Brian King, Anatole Lyovin, Barry Meislin, Jeff Miller, Yves-Charles Morin, Michael O'Grady, Terry Pratt and the students in his introductory linguistics course at the University of Prince Edward Island, Ken Rehg, Laurie Reid, Lorna Rowsell, Patricia Shaw, Albert Schütz, Stanley Starosta, Theo Vennemann, Tim Vance, Douglas Walker, and Nava Zvaig.

William O'Grady/Michael Dobrovolsky

CONTENTS

Note: * indicates advanced section.

1 LANGUAGE
A Preview

*The gift of language is the single human trait
that marks us all genetically, setting us
apart from the rest of life.*
Lewis Thomas, *The Lives of a Cell*

Language is many things—a system of communication, a medium for thought, a vehicle for literary expression, a social institution, a matter for political controversy, a factor in nation building. All normal human beings speak at least one language, and it is hard to imagine much significant social or intellectual activity taking place in its absence. Each of us, then, has a stake in understanding how language is organized and how it is used. This book provides a basic introduction to **linguistics**, the discipline that studies these matters.

1.1 CREATIVITY

What is human language? What does it mean to "know" a language? To answer these questions, it is first necessary to understand the resources that a language makes available to its **native speakers**, those who have acquired it as children in a natural setting. The scope and diversity of human thought and experience place great demands on language. Because communication is not restricted to a fixed set of topics, language must do something more than provide a package of ready-made messages. It must enable us to produce and understand new words, phrases, and sentences as the need arises. In short, human language must be **creative**—allowing novelty and innovation in response to new experiences, situations, and thoughts.

Underlying the creative aspect of language is an intricate mental system that defines the boundaries within which innovation can take place. The operation of this system can be illustrated by a relatively simple phenomenon in English: the process that creates verbs (roughly, words naming actions) from nouns (roughly, words naming things). As the following sentences show, there is a great deal of freedom to innovate in the formation of such verbs.

1. *a*) He *wristed* the ball over the net.
   b) She would try to *stiff-upper-lip* it through.
   c) She *Houdini'd* her way out of the locked closet.

However, there are also constraints on this freedom. For instance, a new verb is rarely coined if a word with the intended meaning already exists. Although

Table 1.1 Nouns used as verbs

Noun use	Verb use
leave the boat on the *beach*	*beach* the boat
keep the airplane on the *ground*	*ground* the airplane
crush the aspirin into *powder*	*powder* the aspirin
stab the man with a *knife*	*knife* the man
catch the fish with a *spear*	*spear* the fish
make the child an *orphan*	*orphan* the child

we may say *carton the eggs* to mean 'put the eggs in the carton', we do not say *hospital the patient* to mean 'put the patient in the hospital'. This is presumably because the well-established verb *hospitalize* already has the meaning that the new form would have.

There are also narrow constraints on the meaning and use of particular subclasses of these verbs. One such constraint involves verbs that are created from time expressions such as *summer* and *holiday*.

2. *a*) Julia *summered* in Paris.
   b) Kent *wintered* in Mexico.
   c) Martine *holidayed* in France.
   d) They *honeymooned* in Hawaii.

While the sentences in *2* are all acceptable, not all time expressions can be used in this way. (Throughout this book an asterisk is used to indicate that a sentence is unacceptable.)

3. *a*) *Jerome *midnighted* in the streets.
   b) *Andrea *nooned* at the restaurant.
   c) *Philip *one o'clocked* at the airport.

These examples show that when a verb is created from a time expression, it must be given a very specific interpretation—roughly paraphrasable as 'to be somewhere for the period of time X'. Thus, *to summer in Paris* is 'to be in Paris for the summer,' *to holiday in France* is 'to be in France for the holidays', and so on. Since *noon* and *midnight* express points in time rather than periods of time, they cannot be used to create verbs of this new class.

Constraints are essential to the viability of the creative process. If well-established words were constantly being replaced by new creations, the vocabulary of English would be so unstable that communication could be jeopardized. A similar danger would arise if there were no constraints on the meaning of new words. If *winter in Hawaii* could mean 'make it snow in Hawaii' or 'wish it were winter in Hawaii' or any other arbitrary thing, the production and interpretation of new forms would be chaotic and would subvert rather than enrich communication.

This rule-governed creativity characterizes all levels of language, including the way in which sounds are combined to form words. The forms in *4*, for instance, are recognizable as possible names for new products or inventions.

4. *a*) prasp
   b) flib
   c) traf

Such forms contrast with the patterns in *5,* which simply do not have the "sound" of English words.

   5. *a)* psarp
      b) bfli
      c) ftra

The contrast shows that our subconscious knowledge of English includes a set of constraints on possible sequences of sounds.

   Still other constraints determine how new words can be created from already existing forms with the help of special endings. Imagine, for example, that you learn that there is a word *soleme* (used perhaps for a newly discovered atomic particle). As a speaker of English, you then automatically know that something with the properties of a soleme can be called *solemic.* You also know that to make something solemic is to *solemicize* it, and you call this process *solemicization.* Further, you know that the *c* is pronounced as *s* in *solemicize* but as *k* in *solemic.* Without hesitation, you also recognize that *solemicize* is pronounced with the stress on the second syllable. (You would say *soLEmicize,* not *SOlemicize* or *solemiCIZE.*)

   Nowhere is the ability to deal with novel utterances in accordance with rules more obvious than in the production and comprehension of sentences. Apart from a few fixed expressions and greetings, much of what you say, hear, and read in the course of a day consists of sentences that are novel to you. In conversations, lectures, newscasts, and textbooks you are regularly exposed to novel combinations of words, the expression of unfamiliar ideas, and the presentation of new information. Such is the case with the sentences you have just read. While each of these sentences is no doubt perfectly comprehensible to you, it is extremely unlikely that you have ever seen any of them before.

   This ability to deal with novel utterances does not ensure that you can understand or use any imaginable combination of words. You would not ordinarily say a sentence such as *6a,* although *6b* would be perfectly acceptable.

   6. *a)* *He brought a chair in order to sit on.
      b) He brought a chair to sit on.

Or, to take another example, *7a* is well formed—if bizarre—but *7b* is gibberish.

   7. *a)* The pink kangaroo hopped over the talking lamp.
      b) *Pink the the talking hopped kangaroo lamp over.

As with other aspects of language, your ability to produce and comprehend sentences is subject to limitations.

1.2 GRAMMAR AND LINGUISTIC COMPETENCE ====

As we have seen, speakers of a language are able to produce and understand an unlimited number of utterances, including many that are novel and unfamiliar. This ability, which is often called **linguistic competence,** constitutes the central subject matter of linguistics and of this book.

   In investigating linguistic competence, linguists focus on the mental system that allows human beings to form and interpret the words and sentences of their language. This system is called a **grammar**. For the purposes of this book, we will divide the grammar into the following components.

Table 1.2 The components of a grammar

Component	Responsibility
Phonetics	the articulation and perception of speech sounds
Phonology	the patterning of speech sounds
Morphology	word formation
Syntax	sentence formation
Semantics	the interpretation of words and sentences

Linguists use the term *grammar* in a rather special and technical way. Because this usage may be unfamiliar, we will devote some time to considering several properties of the system that linguists call a grammar.

Generality: All Languages Have a Grammar

One of the most fundamental claims of modern linguistic analysis is that all languages have a grammar. This can be verified by considering a few simple facts. Since all languages are spoken, they must have phonetic and phonological systems; since they all have words and sentences, they also must have a morphology and a syntax; and since these words and sentences have systematic meanings, there obviously must be semantic principles as well. As these are the very things that make up a grammar, it follows that all human languages have this type of system.

It is not unusual to hear the remark that some language—Acadian French, Navaho, or Chinese—"has no grammar." (This is especially common in the case of languages that are not written or have not yet been analyzed by Western scholars.) Unfamiliar languages sometimes appear to an untrained observer to have no grammar simply because their grammatical systems are different from those of better-known languages. In Walbiri (an aboriginal language of Australia), for example, the relative ordering of words is so free that the English sentence *The two dogs now see several kangaroos* could be translated by the equivalent of any of the following sentences.

8. *a*) Dogs two now see kangaroos several.
   b) See now dogs two kangaroos several.
   c) See now kangaroos several dogs two.
   d) Kangaroos several now dogs two see.
   e) Kangaroos several now see dogs two.

Whereas Walbiri may not restrict the order of words in the way English does, its grammar imposes other types of requirements. For example, in the sentence types we are considering, Walbiri speakers must place the ending *lu* on the word for 'dogs' to indicate that it names the animals that do the seeing rather than the animals that are seen. In English, by contrast, this information is conveyed by placing *two dogs* in front of the verb and *several kangaroos* after it.

Rather than showing that Walbiri has no grammar, such differences simply demonstrate that it has a grammar unlike that of English in certain respects. This important point is applicable to all differences among languages: although no two languages have exactly the same grammar, there are no languages without a grammar.

A similar point can be made about different varieties of the same language. As you are probably already aware, English is the language of many different communities around the world. The particular variety of English found within each of these communities has its own characteristic pronunciation, vocabulary, and sentence patterns. This is just another way of saying that each variety of English has its own grammar. Just as it is impossible to have a language without a grammar, so no variety of language could exist if it did not have a grammar.

Equality: All Grammars Are Equal

Whenever there is more than one variety of a particular language, questions arise as to whether one is somehow better or more correct than another. From the point of view of modern linguistics, it makes no more sense to say that one variety of English is better than another than it does to say that the grammar of English is better (or worse) than the grammar of Thai.

All languages and all varieties of a particular language have grammars that enable their speakers to express any proposition that the human mind can produce. In terms of this all-important criterion, then, all varieties of language are absolutely equal as instruments of communication and thought. The goal of contemporary linguistic analysis is not to rank languages on some imaginary scale of superiority. Rather, linguists seek to understand the nature of the grammatical systems that allow people to speak and understand a language.

This same point is sometimes made by noting that linguistics is **descriptive**, not **prescriptive**. This means that linguists seek to *describe* human linguistic ability and knowledge, not to *prescribe* one system in preference to another. A parallel point of view is adopted in other scientific disciplines as well. The first concern of all scientists is to describe and explain the facts that they observe, not to change them.

Even though it rejects prescriptivism, modern linguistic analysis does not deny the importance of clear expression in writing and speech. Such skills are quite rightly an object of concern among educators. However, the difficulties that arise in these areas typically result from the inconsistent or careless use of one's linguistic knowledge, not from any inherent flaw in the grammar itself.

Linguists also acknowledge that certain patterns (*I seen that, They was there, He didn't do nothing, He ain't here*) may be restricted to particular socioeconomic groups within the English-speaking community. As discussed in more detail in chapter 12, the use of these patterns may therefore have negative social consequences: it may be harder to win a scholarship, to get a job, to be accepted in certain circles, and so forth. From a purely linguistic point of view, however, there is absolutely nothing wrong with grammars that permit such structures. Like grammars for other variants of English (and other languages), they permit their users to express and understand the same unlimited range of thoughts and ideas.

Changeability: Grammars Change over Time

It is a well-established fact that the grammars of all languages are constantly changing. Some of these changes are relatively minor and occur very quickly (for example, the addition of new words such as *glasnost, yuppie, fax, cursor,* and *attrit* to the vocabulary of English). Other changes have a more dramatic effect on the overall form of the language and typically take place over a long period of time. The formation of negative structures in English has undergone this type of change. Prior to 1200, English formed negative constructions by placing *ne* before the verb and a variant of *not* after it.

9. *a*) Ic ne seye not. ('I don't say.')
   b) He ne speketh nawt. ('He does not speak.')

By 1400 or thereabouts, *ne* was used infrequently and *not* (or *nawt*) typically occurred by itself after the verb.

10. *a*) I seye not the wordes.
    b) We saw nawt the knyghtes.

It was not until several centuries later that English developed its current practice of allowing *not* to occur after only certain types of verbs (such as *do, have, will,* and so on).

11. *a*) I will not say the words. (versus *I will say not the words.)
    b) He did not see the knights. (versus *He saw not the knights.)

These modifications illustrate the extent to which grammars can change over time. The structures exemplified in *10* are archaic by today's standards and those in *9* sound completely foreign to most speakers of modern English.

Through the centuries, individuals and organizations who believe that certain varieties of language are better than others have frequently expressed concern over what they perceive to be the deterioration of English. In 1710, for example, the writer Jonathan Swift (author of *Gulliver's Travels*) lamented "the continual Corruption of our English Tongue." Among the corruptions to which Swift objected were contractions such as *he's* for *he is*, although he had no objection to *Tis* for *It is*.

In the nineteenth century, Edward S. Gould, a columnist for the New York *Evening Post*, published a book entitled *Good English; or, Popular Errors in Language,* in which he accused newspaper writers and authors of "sensation novels" of ruining the language by introducing "spurious words" like *jeopardize, leniency,* and *underhanded.* To this day, the tradition of prescriptive concern about the use of certain words continues in the work of such popular writers as Edwin Newman and John Simon, who form a kind of self-appointed language police.

Linguists reject the view that languages attain a state of perfection at some point in their history and that subsequent changes lead to deterioration and corruption. As noted above, there are simply no grounds for claiming that one system of grammar is somehow superior to another. There is therefore no reason to think that language change can or will undermine the adequacy of English (or any other language) as a medium of communication.

Universality: Grammars Are Alike in Basic Ways

There are many differences among languages, as even a superficial examination of their sound patterns, vocabularies, and word order reveals. But this does not mean that there are no limits on the type of grammars that human beings can acquire and use. Quite to the contrary, current research suggests that there are important grammatical principles and tendencies shared by all human languages.

One such principle involves the manner in which sentences are negated. With unlimited variation, one would expect the equivalent of English *not* to occur in different positions within the sentence in different languages. Thus, we might predict that each of the following possibilities should occur with roughly equal frequency.

12. *a*) Not Pat is here.
    b) Pat not is here.
    c) Pat is not here.
    d) Pat is here not.

As it happens, the first and fourth patterns are very rare. In virtually all languages, negative elements such as *not* either immediately precede or immediately follow the verb.

The relative ordering of other elements is also subject to constraints. To see this, we need only consider the six logically possible orders for a simple three-word statement such as *Canadians like hockey.*

13. *a*) Canadians like hockey.
    b) Canadians hockey like.
    c) Like Canadians hockey.
    d) Like hockey Canadians.
    e) Hockey like Canadians.
    f) Hockey Canadians like.

Interestingly, more than 95 percent of the world's languages adopt one of the first three orders for basic statements. Only a handful of languages use any of the last three orders as basic. This once again reflects the existence of constraints and preferences that limit variation among languages.

These are not isolated examples. As later chapters will show, some grammatical categories and principles are universal. And where there is variation (as in the case of word order), there is typically a very limited set of options. Contrary to first appearances, then, the set of grammars learned and used by human beings is limited in significant ways.

Tacitness: Grammatical Knowledge Is Subconscious

Because the use of language to communicate presupposes a grammar, it follows that all speakers of a language must have knowledge of its grammar. However, this knowledge differs from knowledge of arithmetic, traffic safety, and other subjects that are taught at home or in school. Unlike these other types of knowledge, grammatical knowledge is acquired without the help of instruction when one is still a child and it remains largely subconscious throughout life. As an example of this, consider your pronunciation of the past tense ending written as *ed* in the following words.

14. *a*) hunted
    b) slipped
    c) buzzed

Notice that whereas you say *id* in *hunted,* you say *t* in *slipped* and *d* in *buzzed.* Moreover, if you heard the new verb *flib,* you would form the past tense as *flibbed* and pronounce the ending as *d.* Although it is unlikely that you have ever been aware of this phenomenon before now, you make these distinctions automatically if you are a native speaker of English. This is because the grammatical subsystem regulating this aspect of speech was acquired when you were a child and now exists subconsciously in your mind.

Even more subtle phonological patterning can be found in language, as the following contrasts help illustrate.

15. pint   *paynk
      fiend   *fiemp
      locked   *lockf
      wronged   *wrongv
      next   *nexk
      glimpse   *glimpk

The words in the left-hand column obey an obscure constraint on the selection of consonant sequences in word-final position: when a vowel is long and followed by two consonants (*pint*) or when a vowel is short and followed by three consonant sounds (*next,* pronounced 'nekst'), the final consonant must always be one made with the tongue tip raised. (The consonants *t, d, s,* and *z* are made in this manner, but consonants such as *p, f, v,* and *k* are not.) Words that do not adhere to this phonological constraint (the right-hand column) are unacceptable to speakers of English. Even linguists have to dig deeply to uncover such patterning, but in everyday language use, we routinely make decisions about the acceptability of forms based on subconscious knowledge of such constraints.

Consider one final example. Speakers of English know that there are certain structures in which the word *he* can refer to each member of a group or to a single individual outside that group.

16. Each boy who the woman interviewed thinks that he is a genius.

Sentence *16* can mean either that each boy in the group that the woman interviewed thinks that he himself is a genius or that each boy thinks that a particular person not mentioned in the sentence (say, the teacher) is a genius. However, only one of these interpretations is possible in the following sentence.

17. The woman who each boy interviewed thinks that he is a genius.

In *17,* *he* can refer only to someone not mentioned in the sentence. In contrast with what happens in sentence *16,* *he* cannot refer to each individual in the group designated by the phrase *each boy.* Since speakers are able to make this contrast, they must have knowledge of the relevant grammatical principle even though they are not consciously aware of it.

Summary

Linguists use the term *grammar* to refer to a subconscious linguistic system of a particular type. Consisting of several components (phonetics, phonology, morphology, syntax, and semantics), a grammar makes possible the production and comprehension of a potentially unlimited number of utterances. Because no language can exist without a grammar and no one can use a language without knowledge of its grammar, the study of grammatical systems has come to be the focus of contemporary linguistic analysis.

As noted above, the grammatical knowledge needed to use and understand language is acquired without the benefit of instruction and is for the most part subconscious. Since we therefore cannot investigate grammar by simply recalling prior training or by self-consultation, the study of human linguistic systems requires considerable effort and ingenuity. As is the case in all science, information about facts that can be observed (the pronunciation of words, the interpretation of sentences, and so on) must be used to draw inferences about the sometimes invisible mechanisms (atoms, cells, or grammars, as the case may be) that are ultimately responsible for these phenomena. A good deal of this book is concerned with the findings of this research and with what they tell us about the nature and use of human language.

1.3 SPECIALIZATION

As far as can be determined, the languages spoken in the world today cannot be traced to a common source. Rather, they seem to belong to a number of distinct families whose histories can be traced back no more than a few thousand years. Archaeological evidence suggests that language existed prior to that time for perhaps as long as 100,000 years, but virtually nothing is known about this period of linguistic prehistory or about how language originated in the first place.

There is every reason to believe, though, that humans have a special capacity for language that is not shared by other creatures. The evolutionary adaptation of certain physiological mechanisms for linguistic ends has occurred only in humans. The so-called speech organs (the lungs, larynx, tongue, teeth, lips, palate, and nasal passages) did not originally evolve for speech; rather, they were—and still are—directly concerned with ensuring the physical survival of the organism. But each nonlinguistic use of these organs is paralleled by a linguistic use unique to humans. Table 1.3 compares the linguistic uses of the major speech organs with their primary survival functions in humans and other mammals.

In humans, these organs have all become highly specialized for linguistic ends. The vocal folds, for example, are more muscular and less fatty in humans than in nonhuman primates such as chimpanzees and gorillas. Because of a highly

Table 1.3 Dual functions of the speech organs

Organ	Survival function	Speech function
Lungs	to exchange CO_2, oxygen	to supply air for speech
Vocal folds	to create seal over passage to lungs	to produce voice for speech sounds
Tongue	to move food back to throat	to articulate vowels and consonants
Teeth	to break up food	to provide place of articulation for consonants
Lips	to seal oral cavity	to articulate vowels and consonants

developed network of neural pathways, they also respond more precisely to commands from the brain. The same extensive set of neural pathways allows a high degree of control over other speech organs, such as the tongue, palate, and lips. Such control exceeds anything found in even our closest primate relatives.

There are additional indications of the evolution of linguistic vocalization. Unlike the breathing of survival respiration, speech breathing shows higher lung pressure and a longer exhalation time than respiration. Abdominal muscles that are not normally employed for respiration are brought into play in a systematic and refined manner in order to maintain the air pressure needed for speech. Again, a specialized, extensive set of neurological controls exclusive to humans makes this type of breathing possible.

In other words, the human capacity for speech is superimposed on already existing biological structures. Evolution has produced a refinement both in degree and in kind through a long interplay between the demands of language and the development of the human speech-producing apparatus.

We know considerably less about the evolutionary specialization for nonvocal aspects of language such as word formation, sentence formation, and the interpretation of meaning. Nonetheless, it is clear that some sort of evolutionary specialization must have occurred. As we will see in Chapter 9, specific parts of the brain are associated with each of these linguistic activities. Moreover, the brain areas in question have no counterparts in other species. These facts suggest that the human brain is specially structured for language, and that species with different types of brains will not be able to acquire or use the types of grammars associated with human language. After devoting most of this book to the study of grammatical phenomena in human language, we will, in Chapter 14, return to the question of whether comparable linguistic systems occur in other species.

Summing Up

Human language is characterized by **rule-governed creativity**. Speakers of a language possess a **grammar**, a mental system of elements and rules that allows them to form and interpret familiar and novel utterances. The grammar governs the articulation, perception, and patterning of speech sounds, the formation of words and sentences, and the interpretation of utterances. Contrary to popular belief, all languages have grammars that are roughly equal in complexity and are acquired subconsciously by their speakers. The existence of such linguistic systems in humans is the product of unique anatomical and cognitive specialization.

Key Terms

creative	phonetics
descriptive	phonology
grammar	prescriptive
linguistic competence	semantics
native speakers	syntax

Sources

The discussion of word creation is based on an article by Eve Clark and Herb Clark, "When Nouns Surface As Verbs" in *Language* 55 (1979). The Walbiri data are based on K. Hale's article "Person Marking in Walbiri" in *A Festschrift for Morris Halle,* edited by S. Anderson and P. Kiparsky (New York: Holt, Rinehart and Winston, 1973). The Gould book is cited in Dennis Baron's *Grammar and Good Taste* (New Haven: Yale University Press, 1982). The data on the positioning of negative elements within sentences in human language come from an article by O. Dahl, "Typology of Sentence Negation" in *Linguistics* 17:79–106 (1979).

Recommended Reading

Clark, Eve and Herb Clark. 1979. "When Nouns Surface As Verbs." *Language* 55:767–811.

Farb, Peter. 1975. *Word Play: What Happens When People Talk.* New York: Bantam Books.

Matthei, Edward and Thomas Roeper, 1983. *Understanding and Producing Speech.* Glasgow: Fontana.

Questions

1. We can create verbs from nouns as discussed in section 1.1.

   i) Describe the meanings of the new verbs in the following sentences.

      a) We punk-rocked the night away.
      b) He dog-teamed his way across the arctic.
      c) We MG'd to Oregon.
      d) We Concorded to London.
      e) He Khaddafi'd the American Embassy.
      f) He Gretzky'd his way to the net.
      g) We Greyhounded to Toronto.
      h) We'll have to Ajax the sink.
      i) She Windexed the windows.
      j) You should Clairol your hair.
      k) Let's carton the eggs.

   ii) Create five verbs from nouns. Make a sentence using each new verb you created.

2. Imagine that you are an advertising executive and that your job involves inventing new names for products.

   i) Which of the following forms would be acceptable to native speakers of English? Discuss them with your friends.

      a) mbood   e) sproke
      b) frall   f) flube
      c) coofp   g) worpz
      d) ktleem   h) bsarn

  ii) Create four new forms that would be accepted by native speakers of English and four that would not.

3. Part of linguistic competence involves the ability to recognize whether novel utterances are acceptable. Consider the following sentences and determine which are possible sentences in English. For each unacceptable sentence, describe the reason for its unacceptability and change the sentence to make it acceptable.

    a) Jason's mother left himself with nothing to eat.
    b) Miriam is eager to talk to.
    c) This is the man who I took a picture of.
    d) Colin made Jane a sandwich.
    e) Is the dog sleeping the bone again?
    f) Wayne prepared Zena a cake.
    g) Max cleaned the garden up.
    h) Max cleaned up the garden.
    i) Max cleaned up it.
    j) I desire you to leave.
    k) That you likes liver surprises me.

4. Consider the following sentences, each of which is acceptable to some speakers of English, but not to others. Try to identify the prescriptive rules that are violated in each case.

    a) He don't know about the race.
    b) You was out when I called.
    c) Me and Peter walked to school.
    d) There's twenty horses registered in the show.
    e) That window's broke, so be careful.
    f) Jim and me are gonna go campin' this weekend.
    g) Who did you come with?
    h) I seen the parade last week.
    i) He been lost in the woods for ten days.
    j) My car needs cleaned 'cause of all the rain.
    k) Julie ain't got none.
    l) Somebody left their book on the train.
    m) Murray hurt hisself in the game.

2 PHONETICS
The Sounds of Language

Heavenly labials in a world of gutturals
Wallace Stevens

We do not need to speak in order to use language. Language can be written, recorded mechanically, and even produced by computers in limited ways, but speech remains the primary way we encode it. As we saw in Chapter 1, humans are anatomically specialized to speak, and our species spoke long before we began to write language down. Because language and speech are so closely linked, we begin our study of language by examining the inventory and structure of the sounds of language. This branch of linguistics is called **phonetics**.

Human languages display a wide variety of sounds, called **phones** or **speech sounds**. There are a great many speech sounds, but not an infinite number of them. The class of possible speech sounds is not only finite, it is universal. A portion of the total set will be found in the inventory of any human language. Any human, child or adult, can learn how to pronounce these sounds, regardless of racial or cultural background.

Certain sounds that humans are capable of producing with the vocal tract do not occur in speech—the sound made by inhaling through one corner of the mouth, for instance, or the "raspberry" produced by sticking out the tongue and blowing hard across it. Equally "exotic-seeming" sounds do occur in human languages, such as the clicking made by drawing the tongue hard away from the sides of the upper molars or the sound made by constricting the sides of the throat while breathing out.

There are two ways of approaching phonetics. One way studies the physiological mechanism of speech production. This is known as **articulatory phonetics**. The other, known as **acoustic phonetics**, deals with the physics of speech sounds. It examines the physical properties of speech sounds as they are determined and measured by machines, and attempts to deduce the acoustic basis of speech production and perception. Both approaches are indispensable to an understanding of phonetics. This chapter focuses on articulatory phonetics, but also makes some reference to the acoustic properties of sounds and to acoustic analysis.

2.1 PHONETIC TRANSCRIPTION

Since the sixteenth century, efforts have been made to devise a universal system for transcribing the sounds of speech. The best-known system, the **International Phonetic Alphabet (IPA)**, has been developing since 1888 (see Table 2.1).

The goal of this system of transcription is to represent each sound of human speech with a single symbol. These symbols are enclosed in brackets [ ] to indicate that the transcription is phonetic and does not represent the spelling system of a particular language. For example, the sound spelled *th* in English *this* is transcribed as [ð] (the symbol is called *eth*, as in *weather*). IPA transcription uses this symbol to write the sound in whichever language it is heard, whether it is English, Spanish, Turkmen (a Turkic language spoken in Central Asia and written with the Cyrillic alphabet), or any other. The use of a standardized international phonetic alphabet enables linguists to transcribe languages consistently and accurately. In common North American usage, though, some phonetic symbols differ from those employed by IPA transcription. For example, the sound heard at the beginning of the English word *shark* is transcribed as [ʃ] in IPA, but usually as [š] in North America. These differences will be noted where relevant, but we will follow IPA in most cases.

Table 2.1 Use of [ð] in the International Phonetic Alphabet

Language	Spelling	IPA
English	<u>th</u>is	[ðɪs]
Spanish	bo<u>d</u>a	[bɔða] 'wedding'
Turkmen	а<u>д</u>ak	[aðak] 'foot'

Segments

A phonetic alphabet represents speech in the form of **segments**, or individual speech sounds like [p], [s], or [m]. This may seem to be a natural thing to do, but anyone who hears a new language for the first time finds it hard to break up the flow of speech into the individual sounds that make up words. Even when we hear our own language spoken, we do not focus our attention on individual sounds as much as we do on the meanings of words, phrases, and sentences. Still, all speakers of a language can identify the sounds of their language. Linguistic knowledge makes it possible to break down a stream of speech into its component parts, one of which is sound segments.

Errors in speech production provide one kind of evidence for the existence of segments. Slips of the tongue such as *Ko<u>l</u>aco<u>d</u>or* for *Ko<u>d</u>aco<u>l</u>or* and *<u>m</u>elcome <u>w</u>at* for *<u>w</u>elcome <u>m</u>at* show segments shifting and reversing position within words. This suggests that segments are individual units of linguistic structure and should be represented individually in a system of transcription. Using segments, however, is only one way to represent speech. The **syllable**, presented in chapter 3, is also represented in some writing systems (see chapter 15). In one form of Japanese writing, for example, signs such as か [ka], と [to], and み [mi] represent syllables without recourse to segmental transcription.

Segments can be analyzed into smaller subunits called **features**. Even though features are not represented in most writing systems, they are important elements of linguistic representation. Features reflect individual aspects of articulatory control or acoustic effects produced by articulation. This chapter presents segmental transcription, since it is the most widely used way of representing speech. Features and syllables are introduced in the following chapter.

What makes segmental phonetic transcription a "natural" way of transcribing speech is the relative invariance of speech sounds. It is impossible to represent all variants of human speech sounds, since no one says the same sound in exactly the same way twice. Nonetheless, the sounds of speech remain invariant enough from language to language for us to transcribe them consistently. A *p* sound is much the same in English, Russian, or Uzbek. The fact that when producing a *p* sound, English speakers press their lips together but Russian speakers draw theirs slightly inward does not make the sounds different enough to warrant separate symbols. But the sounds *p* and *t* are distinct enough from each other in languages the world over to be consistently transcribed with separate symbols.

2.2 THE SOUND-PRODUCING SYSTEM

Sound is produced when air is set in motion. The speech production mechanism consists of an air supply, a sound source that sets the air in motion, and a set of filters and resonators that modifies the sound in various ways. The air supply is provided by the lungs. The sound source is in the **larynx**, where the vocal cords are located. The filters are the organs above the larynx: the tube of the throat between the oral cavity and the larynx, which is called the **pharynx**; the oral cavity; and the nasal cavity. These passages are collectively known as the **vocal tract** and are depicted in Figure 2.1.

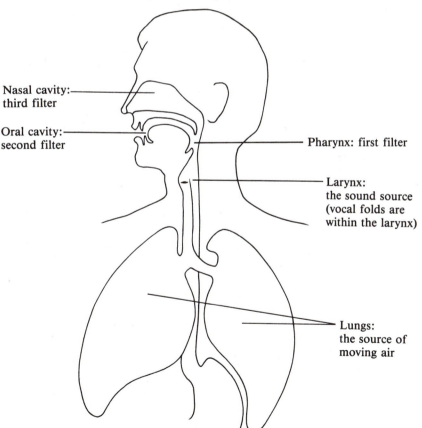

Figure 2.1 The sound producing system

The Lungs

In order to produce the majority of sounds in the world's languages, we take air into the lungs and then expel it during speech. (A small number of sounds are made with air as it flows into the vocal tract.) A certain level of air pressure is needed to keep the speech mechanism functioning steadily. The pressure is maintained by the action of various sets of muscles coming into play during the course of an utterance. The muscles are primarily the **intercostals** (the muscles between the ribs) and the **diaphragm** (the large sheet of muscle that separates the chest cavity from the abdomen).

The Larynx

As air flows out of the lungs up the **trachea** (windpipe), it passes through a boxlike structure made of cartilage and muscle, the larynx (commonly known as the voice box or Adam's apple). The main portion of the larynx is formed by the *thyroid cartilage*, which spreads outward like the head of a plow. The thyroid cartilage rests on the ring-shaped *cricoid cartilage*. Fine sheets of muscle flare from the inner sides of the larynx, forming the paired vocal folds

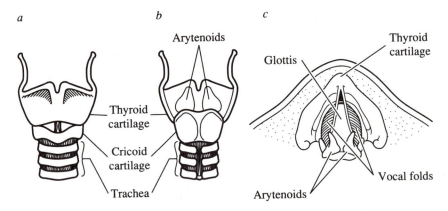

Figure 2.2 The larynx *a* from the front; *b* from the back; *c* from above, with the vocal folds in the open position. The striated lines indicate muscles, a number of which have been eliminated from the drawings to show the cartilages more clearly.

(vocal cords). The vocal folds can be pulled apart or drawn closer together, especially at their back or posterior ends, where each is attached to one of two small cartilages, the *arytenoids*. As air passes through the space between the vocal folds, which is called the **glottis**, different glottal states are produced, depending on their positioning.

Glottal States

The vocal folds may be positioned in a number of ways to produce different glottal states. The first two glottal states presented in Figure 2.3 are commonly encountered in most of the world's languages. The third describes the glottal state that underlies a common speech phenomenon, and the fourth illustrates one of a number of glottal states not encountered in English.

Voicelessness When the vocal folds are pulled apart as illustrated in Figure 2.3, air passes directly through the glottis. Any sound made with the vocal folds in this position is said to be **voiceless**. You can confirm a sound's voicelessness by touching your fingers to the larynx as you produce it. You will not feel any vibration from the vocal folds being transmitted to your fingertips. The initial sounds of *fish*, *sing*, and *house* are all voiceless.

Voicing When the vocal folds are brought close together, but not tightly closed, air passing between them causes them to vibrate, producing sounds that are said to be **voiced**. (See Figure 2.3, where the movement of the vocal folds during voicing is indicated by the wavy lines.) You can determine whether a sound is voiced in the same way you determined voicelessness. By lightly touching the fingers to the larynx as you produce an extended version of the initial sounds of the words *zip* or *vow*, or any vowel, you can sense the vibration of the vocal folds within the larynx.

Whisper Another glottal state produces a **whisper**. Whispering is voiceless, but, as shown in Figure 2.3, the vocal folds are adjusted so that the anterior (front) portions are pulled close together, while the posterior (back) portions are apart.

Murmur Yet another glottal state produces a **murmur**, also known as **whispery voice**. Sounds produced with this glottal configuration are voiced, but the vocal folds are relaxed to allow enough air to escape to produce a simultaneous whispery effect.

These four glottal states represent only some of the possibilities of sound production at the glottis. Combined with various articulations made above the larynx, they produce a wide range of phones. Before examining these in more detail, we will first consider the three major classes of phone.

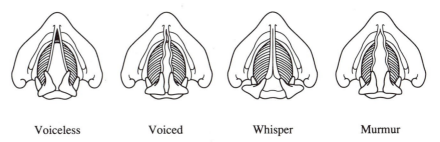

Voiceless   Voiced   Whisper   Murmur

Figure 2.3 Four glottal states: the stylized drawing represents the vocal folds and glottis from above; its anterior portion is towards the top. The small triangles represent the cartilages that spread and close the vocal folds.

2.3 SOUND CLASSES ===============

The sounds of language can be grouped into classes, based on the phonetic properties that they share. You have already seen what some of these properties can be. All voiced sounds, for example, form a class, as do all voiceless sounds. The most basic division among sounds is into two major classes, **vowels** and **consonants**. Another class of sounds, the **glides**, shares properties of both vowels and consonants. Each of these classes of sounds has a number of distinguishing features.

Vowels and Consonants

Vowels and consonants can be distinguished on the basis of differences in articulation, as well as acoustically and functionally.

Consonantal sounds, which may be voiced or voiceless, are made with a narrow or complete closure in the vocal tract. The airflow is either blocked momentarily or restricted so much that noise is produced as air flows past the constriction. Vowels are produced with little obstruction in the vocal tract and are generally voiced.

As a result of the difference in articulation, consonants and vowels differ in the way they sound. Vowels are more sonorous than consonants—that is, we perceive them as louder and longer lasting than consonants.

The greater sonority of vowels allows them to form the basis of **syllables**. A syllable can best be understood as a peak of sonority surrounded by less sonorous segments. For example, the words, *a* and *go* each contain one syllable, the word *water* two syllables, and the word *telephone* three syllables. In counting the syllables in these words, we are in effect counting the vowels. A vowel is thus said to form the **nucleus** of a syllable. "Syllabic Liquids and Nasals" (page 26) will show that certain types of consonants can form syllabic nuclei as well.

In *1*, the initial sounds of the words in the left column are all consonants; those on the right are all vowels.

1. take   above
    cart   at
    feel   eel
    jump   it
    think   ugly
    bell   open

Table 2.2 sums up the differences between the two classes presented here.

Table 2.2 The major differences between consonants and vowels

Vowels	Consonants
• Are produced with relatively little obstruction in the vocal tract	• Are produced with a narrow or complete closure in the vocal tract
• Are more sonorous	• Are less sonorous
• Are syllabic	• Are generally not syllabic

Glides

A type of sound that shows properties of both consonants and vowels is called a glide. Glides may be thought of as rapidly articulated vowels; this is the auditory impression they produce. Glides are produced with an articulation like that of a vowel. However, they move quickly to another articulation, as do the initial glides in *yet* or *wet*, or quickly terminate, as do the word-final glides in *boy* and *now*.

Even though they are vowellike in articulation, glides function as consonants. For example, glides can never form the nucleus of a syllable. Since glides show properties of both consonants and vowels, it is no wonder that the terms semivowel or semiconsonant are used interchangeably with the term glide.

2.4 CONSONANT ARTICULATION

Airflow is modified in the oral cavity by the placement of the tongue and the positioning of the lips. These modifications occur at specific places or points of articulation. The major places of articulation used in speech production are outlined in this section. Figure 2.4 provides a midsagittal section or cutaway view of the vocal tract, on which each place of articulation has been indicated.

The Tongue

The primary articulating organ is the tongue. It can be raised, lowered, thrust forward or drawn back, and even rolled back. The sides of the tongue can also be raised or lowered.

Phonetic description refers to five areas of the tongue. The **tip** is the narrow area at the front. Just behind the tip lies the **blade**. The main mass of the tongue is called the **body**, and the hindmost part of the tongue that lies in the mouth is called the **back**. The **root** of the tongue is contained in the upper part of the throat.

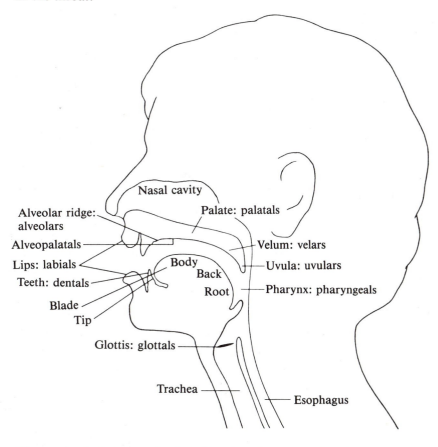

(Places of articulation are listed, followed by the term used to describe sounds made at the place. Areas of the tongue are also designated.)

Figure 2.4 The vocal tract

Places of Articulation

Each point at which the airstream can be modified to produce a different sound is called a **place of articulation**. Places of articulation are found at the lips, within the oral cavity, in the pharynx, and at the glottis.

Labial Any sound made with closure or near closure of the lips is said to be **labial**. Sounds involving both lips are termed **bilabial**; sounds involving the lower lip and upper teeth are called **labiodentals**. English includes the bilabials heard word-initially in _peer_, _bin_, and _mouth_, and the labiodentals heard initially in _fire_ and _vow_.

Dental Some phones are produced with the tongue placed against or near the teeth. Sounds made in this way are called **dentals**. If the tongue is placed between the teeth, the sound is said to be **interdental**. Interdentals in English include the initial consonants of the words _this_, _thy_, and _thing_. (Some English speakers produce _s_ and _z_ as dentals although for most speakers they are alveolars.)

Alveolar Within the oral cavity, a small ridge protrudes from just behind the upper front teeth. This is called the **alveolar ridge**. The tongue may touch or be brought near this ridge. Alveolar sounds are heard at the beginning of the following English words: _top_, _deer_, _soap_, _zip_, _lip_, and _neck_.

Alveopalatal and Palatal Just behind the alveolar ridge, the roof of the mouth rises sharply. This area is known as the **alveopalatal** area (**palatoalveolar** in some books). Alveopalatal consonants are heard in the following English words: _show_, _measure_, _chip_, and _judge_. The highest part of the roof of the mouth is called the **palate**, and sounds produced with the tongue on or near this area are called **palatals**. The glide heard word-initially in _yes_ is a palatal.

Velar The soft area toward the rear of the roof of the mouth is called the **velum**. Sounds made with the tongue in this position are called **velars**. Velars are heard in English at the beginning of the words _call_ and _guy_, and at the end of the word _hang_. The glide heard word-initially in _wet_ is called a **labiovelar**, since the back of the tongue is raised near the velum and the lips are rounded at the same time.

Uvular The small fleshy flap of tissue known as the **uvula** hangs down from the velum. Sounds made with the tongue near or touching this area are called **uvulars**. English has no uvulars, but the _r_ sound of standard French is uvular.

Pharyngeal The area of the throat between the uvula and the larynx is known as the pharynx. Sounds made through the modification of airflow in this region by retracting the tongue or constricting the pharynx are called **pharyngeals**. Pharyngeals can be found in many dialects of Arabic, but not in English.

Glottal Sounds produced by adjusting the glottal opening to states other than voicing or voicelessness are called **glottals**. The sound at the beginning of the English words _heave_ and _hog_ is made at the glottis.

2.5 MANNERS OF ARTICULATION

The lips, tongue, velum, and glottis can be positioned in different ways to produce different sound types. These various configurations are called **manners of articulation**.

Oral versus Nasal

A basic distinction in manners of articulation is between **oral** and **nasal** phones. Oral sounds are produced with air flowing through only the mouth. The velum, however, can be lowered to allow air to pass through the nasal passages, producing a sound that is nasal. Both consonants and vowels can be nasal, in which case they are generally voiced. The consonants at the end of the English words *sun*, *sum*, and *sung* are nasal. For many speakers of English, the vowels of words such as *can't* and *wink* are also nasal.

Stops

Stops are made with a complete and momentary closure of airflow through the oral cavity. In the world's languages, stops are found at bilabial, dental, alveolar, palatal, velar, uvular, and glottal points of articulation.

In English, bilabial, alveolar, and velar oral and nasal stops are found. Most speakers also have a glottal stop. The glottal stop is commonly heard in English in the expression *uh-uh*, meaning 'no'. The two vowels in this utterance are each preceded by a momentary closing of the airstream at the glottis. The *t* before [n] in words like *button* and *written* is pronounced as a glottal stop by most American English speakers. In some dialects, the glottal stop is also commonly heard in place of the [t] in a word like *bottle*. The glottal stop is often spelled with an apostrophe (*bo'l*); its standard phonetic transcription is [ʔ]. The phonetic symbols for English stops are given in Table 2.3, grouped according to point of articulation. As you can see, the stops, with one exception, occur in voiced and voiceless pairs accompanied by a nasal. The glottal stop is always voiceless. It is produced with the vocal folds drawn firmly together, and since no air can pass through the glottis, the vocal folds cannot be set in motion.

Table 2.3 English stops and their transcription

Bilabial	Transcription		
Voiceless	span	[p]	
Voiced	ban	[b]	
Nasal	man	[m]	
Alveolar			
Voiceless	stun	[t]	
Voiced	dot	[d]	
Nasal	not	[n]	
Velar			
Voiceless	scar	[k]	
Voiced	gap	[g]	
Nasal	wing	[ŋ]	
Glottal			
Voiceless	button	[ʔ]	(see above)

Fricatives

Fricatives are consonants produced with a continuous airflow through the mouth. They belong to a large class of sounds called **continuants** (a class that also includes vowels and glides), all of which share this property. The fricatives form a special class of continuants; during their production, they are accompanied by a continuous audible noise. The air used in their production passes through a very narrow opening, resulting in turbulence, which causes the noise.

English Fricatives English has voiceless and voiced labiodental fricatives at the beginning of the words _fat_ and _vat_, voiceless and voiced interdental fricatives word-initially in the words _thin_ and _those_, alveolar fricatives word-initially in _sing_ and _zip_, and a voiceless alveopalatal fricative word-initially in _ship_. The voiced alveopalatal fricative is rare in English. It is the first consonant in the word _azure_, and is also heard in the words _pleasure_ and _rouge_. The voiceless glottal fricative of English is heard in _hotel_ and _hat_.

Special note must be taken of the alveolar fricatives [s] and [z]. There are two ways that English speakers commonly produce these sounds. Some speakers raise the tongue tip to the alveolar ridge and allow the air to pass through a grooved channel in the tongue. Other speakers form this same channel using the blade of the tongue; the tip is placed behind the lower front teeth. Still others pronounce these sounds as dentals. The symbols for English fricatives are given in Table 2.4. Dentals are not distinguished from alveolars, since most languages have sounds with either one or the other point of articulation, but not both.

Table 2.4 The transcription of English fricatives

Glottal state	Point of articulation	Transcription
	Labiodental	
Voiceless	fan	[f]
Voiced	van	[v]
	Interdental	
Voiceless	thin	[θ]
Voiced	then	[ð]
	Alveolar	
Voiceless	sun	[s]
Voiced	zip	[z]
	Alveopalatal	
Voiceless	ship	[ʃ]
Voiced	azure	[ʒ]
	Glottal	
Voiceless	hat	[h]

Affricates

When a stop is released, the tongue moves rapidly away from the point of articulation. Some noncontinuant consonants show a slow release of the closure; these sounds are called **affricates**. English has only two affricates, both of which are alveopalatal. They are heard word-initially in _church_ and _jump_, and are transcribed as [tʃ] and [dʒ], respectively. Table 2.5 presents the two English affricates.

Table 2.5 English affricates

	Alveopalatal
Voiceless	[tʃ]
Voiced	[dʒ]

Stridents and Sibilants At the beginning of this chapter we noted that acoustic as well as articulatory criteria are sometimes used in describing speech sounds. An acoustic criterion comes into play to describe fricatives and affricates. These sounds are subdivided into two types, some of which are distinctly noisier than others as they are articulated. The noisier fricatives and affricates are called **stridents** (see Table 2.6). Their less noisy counterparts, which have the same or nearly the same place of articulation, are labeled nonstrident.

Strident sounds are relatively higher in pitch than other sounds and have a hissing quality. In English, these sounds are [s], [z], [ʃ], [ʒ], [tʃ], and [dʒ]. [s] and [z] are also known as **sibilants**.

Table 2.6 Strident and nonstrident fricatives and affricates in English

Articulation	Strident	Nonstrident
Alveolar	[s], [z]	[θ], [ð] (Interdental)
Alveopalatal	[ʃ], [ʒ] [tʃ], [dʒ]	(none in English)

Voice Lag and Aspiration (advanced)

After the release of some voiceless stops in English, you can sometimes hear a lag or brief delay before the voicing of a following vowel. Since the lag in the onset of vocalic voicing is accompanied by the release of air, the traditional term for this phenomenon is **aspiration**. It is transcribed with a small raised [ʰ] after the aspirated consonant. Table 2.7 provides some examples of aspirated and unaspirated consonants in English. Note that the sounds that show both aspirated and unaspirated varieties are all voiceless stops. In other languages, fricatives and affricates may also be aspirated or unaspirated. (Some vowel symbols are introduced here as well.)

Table 2.7 Aspirated and unaspirated consonants in English

Aspirated		Unaspirated	
[pʰæt]	pat	[spæt]	spat
[tʰʌb]	tub	[stʌb]	stub
[kʰowp]	cope	[skowp]	scope

Figure 2.5 shows how aspiration of a voiceless consonant takes place, using the aspirated consonant [pʰ] as an example. Though the sequence of articulations takes places continuously, the figure illustrates only certain moments.

a) As articulation of the voiceless consonant is begun, the glottis is open.

b) The closure for the consonant is released and the vowel articulation begins; however, the glottis is not yet closed enough to permit voicing to begin. Because of this, the vowel is briefly voiceless, giving the impression of an extra release of air that we call *aspiration*.

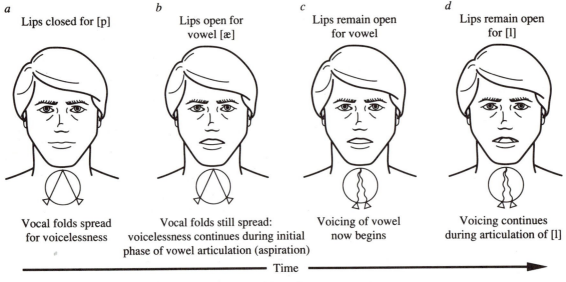

a
Lips closed for [p]

b
Lips open for
vowel [æ]

c
Lips remain open
for vowel

d
Lips remain open
for [l]

Vocal folds spread
for voicelessness

Vocal folds still spread:
voicelessness continues during initial
phase of vowel articulation (aspiration)

Voicing of vowel
now begins

Voicing continues
during articulation of [l]

—————————————— Time ——————————————▶

Figure 2.5 Aspirated consonant production (English *pal*)

c) After a short delay, measurable in milliseconds, voicing of the vowel begins.

d) The lips remain open and voicing continues during the articulation of the final consonant of the word.

Figures 2.6 and 2.7 show the relation between articulation and voicing for unaspirated and voiced consonants. The unaspirated consonant, such as the [p] of English *spill*, shows voicing of the vowel starting very soon after release of the consonant articulation. The voiced initial [b] of English *bill* shows voicing starting just before the release of the bilabial articulation.

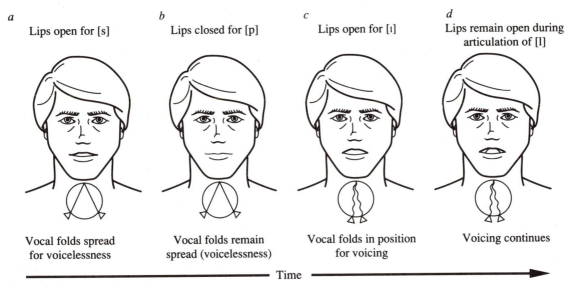

a
Lips open for [s]

b
Lips closed for [p]

c
Lips open for [ɪ]

d
Lips remain open during
articulation of [l]

Vocal folds spread
for voicelessness

Vocal folds remain
spread (voicelessness)

Vocal folds in position
for voicing

Voicing continues

—————————————— Time ——————————————▶

Figure 2.6 Unaspirated consonant production (English *spill*)

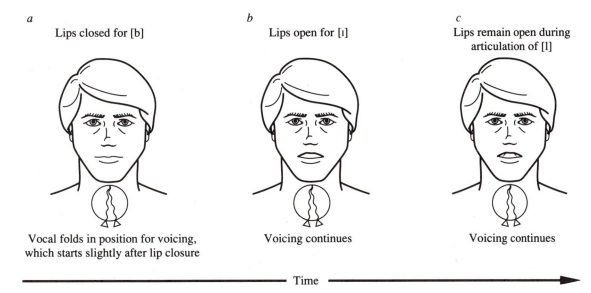

a
Lips closed for [b]

Vocal folds in position for voicing,
which starts slightly after lip closure

b
Lips open for [ɪ]

Voicing continues

c
Lips remain open during
articulation of [l]

Voicing continues

Time →

Figure 2.7 Voiced consonant release (English *bill*)

Liquids

Among the sounds commonly found in the world's languages are *l* and *r* and their numerous variants. They form a special class of consonants known as **liquids**. Liquids are continuants, but the vocal tract obstruction formed when producing them is not as great as it is for the fricative consonants.

Laterals Varieties of *l* are called **laterals**. As laterals are articulated, air escapes through the mouth along the lowered sides of the tongue. When the tongue tip is raised to the dental or alveolar position, the dental or alveolar laterals are produced. Both may be transcribed as [l].

Because laterals are generally voiced, the term *lateral* used alone usually means 'voiced lateral'. Still, there are instances of voiceless laterals in speech. The voiceless dental or alveolar lateral is written with an additional phonetic symbol, called a diacritic. In this case, the diacritic is a circle beneath the symbol: [l̥]. Voiceless laterals can be heard in the pronunciation of the English words *pl̥ease* and *cl̥ear*.

English *r*'s Numerous varieties of *r* are also heard in the world's languages. This section describes the types found in English.

The *r* of English, as it is spoken in the United States and Canada, is made either by curling the tongue tip back into the mouth or by bunching the tongue upward and back in the mouth. This *r* is known as a **retroflex** *r* and is heard in *ride* and *car*. It is transcribed as [r] in this book. IPA transcription favors [ɹ] for this sound, though it also offers the symbol [r].

Another sound commonly identified with *r* is the **flap**. The flap is produced when the tongue tip strikes the alveolar ridge as it passes across it. It is heard in the North American English pronunciation of *bitter* and *butter*, and in some British pronunciations of *very*. It is commonly transcribed as [D] and is generally voiced. The IPA symbol is ɾ.

Table 2.8 presents the laterals, *r*, and flap of English.

Table 2.8 English liquids

	Dental/alveolar			
Laterals	voiced	[l]	[lɪp]	lip
	voiceless	[l̥]	[pl̥ijz]	please
R's	retroflex voiced	[r]	[rɪd]	rid
	voiceless	[r̥]	[pr̥ej]	pray
	flap voiced	[D]	leDɪŋ]	letting

Syllabic Liquids and Nasals

Liquids and nasals are more resonant than other consonants and in this respect are more like vowels than are the other consonants. In fact, they are so vowel-like in their resonance that they can function as syllabic nuclei. When they do so, they are called **syllabic liquids** and **syllabic nasals** (see Table 2.9). Syllabic liquids and nasals are found in many of the world's languages, including English. In transcription, they are usually marked with a short diacritic line underneath. Unfortunately for beginning linguistics students, North American transcription is not always consistent here. The syllabic *r* sound heard in words like *bir̲d* and *he̲r* is usually transcribed as a vowel-*r* sequence: [ər]. This is because many linguists hear this sound not as a consonant but as a vowel with '*r*-coloring'. (The vowel symbol is presented in "Basic Parameters for Describing Vowels" on page 28.) The IPA symbol for this sound is [ɚ]. For reasons of symmetry, in this book we will use the diacritic line to mark syllabic *r* rather than the more common North American [ər] or IPA [ɚ].

Table 2.9 Syllabic liquids and nasals in English

Syllabic		Nonsyllabic	
bottle	[bɑDl̩]	lift	[lɪft]
funnel	[fʌnl̩]	pill	[pʰɪl]
bird	[br̩d]	rat	[ræt]
her	[hr̩]	car	[kʰɑr]
button	[bʌt?n̩]	now	[naw]
rhythm	[rɪðm̩]	mat	[mæt]

American Glides

Recall that a glide is a very rapidly articulated non-syllabic segment. The two glides of English are the *y*-glide [j] of *ye̲s* and *bo̲y*, and the *w*-glide [w] of *we̲t* and *no̲w*. (The [j] in IPA transcription corresponds to [y] in North American transcription.)

The [j] is a palatal glide whose articulation is virtually identical to that of the vowel [i] of *se̲e*. You can verify this by pronouncing a [j] in an extended manner; it will sound very close to an [i]. The glide [w] is made with the tongue raised and pulled back near the velum and with the lips protruding, or **rounded**. For this reason, it is sometimes called a labiovelar. The [w] corresponds closely in articulation to the vowel [u] of *who̲*. This can be verified by extending the pronunciation of a [w]. Some speakers of English also have a voiceless labiovelar glide, transcribed [ʍ], for *wh* in words like *whi̲ch* (but not in *witch*), *whe̲n*, *whe̲re*, and *whe̲el*.

English Consonants Table 2.10 provides a summary of the places and manners of articulation of English consonants.

Table 2.10 English consonants: places and manners of articulation

			Labial	Labiodental	Interdental	Alveolar	Alveopalatal	Velar	Glottal
		Place of articulation							
Stop	voiceless		p			t		k	ʔ
	voiced		b			d		g	
Fricative	voiceless			f	θ	s	ʃ		h
	voiced			v	ð	z	ʒ		
Affricate	voiceless						tʃ		
	voiced						dʒ		
Nasal	voiced		m			n		ŋ	
Liquid	voiced lateral					l			
	voiced retroflex					r, D			
Glide	voiced						j (palatal)	w	
	(voiceless)							(ʍ)	

Manner of articulation (vertical label on left)

2.6 VOWELS

Vowels are sonorous, syllabic sounds made with the vocal tract more open than it is for consonant articulations. Different vowels are produced by varying the placement of the body of the tongue and shaping the lips. The shape of the cavity can be further altered by protruding the lips to produce rounded vowels, or by lowering the velum to produce a nasal vowel. Finally, vowels may be tense or lax, depending on the degree of vocal tract constriction during their articulation.

Simple Vowels and Diphthongs

English vowels are divided into two major types, **simple vowels** and **diphthongs**. Simple vowels do not show a noticeable change in quality. The vowels of *pit*, *set*, *cat*, *dog*, *but*, *put* and the first vowel of *suppose* are all simple vowels. Diphthongs are vowels that exhibit a change in quality within a single syllable. English diphthongs show changes in quality that are due to tongue movement away from the initial vowel articulation toward a glide position. This change in vowel quality is clearly perceptible in words such as *say*, *buy*, *cow*, *ice*, *lout*, *go*, and *boy*. The change is less easy to hear, but present nonetheless, in the vowels of words such as *heat* and *lose*. Table 2.11 presents the simple vowels and diphthongs of English. The diphthongs are transcribed as a vowel-glide sequence.

Table 2.11 Simple vowels and diphthongs of American English

Simple vowel		Diphthong	
pit	[ɪ]	heat	[ij]
set	[ɛ]	say	[ej]
cat	[æ]	buy	[aj]
pot	[ɑ]	cow	[aw]
but	[ʌ]	lose	[uw]
bought	[ɔ]	grow	[ow]
put	[ʊ]	boy	[ɔj]
suppose	[ə]		

Basic Parameters for Describing Vowels

Vowel articulations are not as easy to feel as consonant articulations at first, since the vocal tract is not narrowed as much. To become acquainted with vowel articulation, alternately pronounce the vowels of *he* and *pot*. You will feel the tongue move from a **high front** to a **low back** position. Once you feel this tongue movement, alternate between the vowels of *pot* and *pat*. You will feel the tongue moving from the low back to low front position. Finally, alternate between the vowels of *he* and *who*. You will notice that in addition to a tongue movement between the high front and high back position, you are also rounding your lips for the [uw]. Figure 2.8 shows a midsagittal view of the tongue position for the vowels [ij], [ɑ], and [uw] based on X-ray studies of speech.

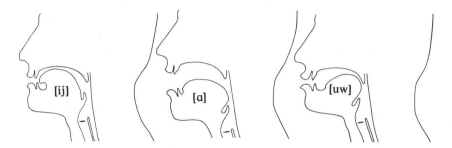

Figure 2.8 Tongue position and transcription for three English vowels

Vowels for which the tongue is neither raised nor lowered are called **mid** vowels. The front vowel of English *made* or *fame* is mid, front, and unrounded. The vowel of *code* and *soak* is mid, back, and rounded. In the case of diphthongs, the articulatory descriptions refer to the tongue position of the vowel nucleus. The vowels presented so far are summed up in Table 2.12. Note that in describing the vowels the articulatory parameters are presented in the order *height*, *backness*, *rounding*.

Table 2.12 Basic phonetic parameters for describing American English vowels

heat	[ij]	high, front, unrounded
fate	[ej]	mid, front, unrounded
mad	[æ]	low, front, unrounded
sun	[ʌ]	mid, back, unrounded
Sue	[uw]	high, back, rounded
boat	[ow]	mid, back, rounded
cot	[ɑ]	low, back, unrounded

Tongue positions for these vowels are illustrated in Figure 2.9. The trapezoid corresponds roughly to the space within which the tongue moves, which is wider at the top of the oral cavity and more restricted at the bottom. Since many books distinguish between central and back vowels, the traditional term *central* is supplied in parentheses.

Tense and Lax Vowels

All the vowels illustrated in Figure 2.9 except [æ] and [ʌ] are tense: they are produced with a greater degree of constriction of the tongue body or tongue root than are certain other vowels. Some vowels of English are made with roughly the same tongue position but with a less constricted articulation: they

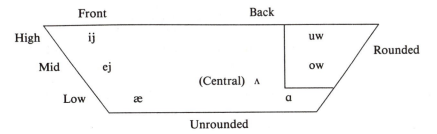

Figure 2.9 Basic tongue positions for English vowels

are called lax vowels. Table 2.13 provides examples from English comparing tense and lax vowels. Note that not all vowels come in tense/lax pairs.

Table 2.13 Tense and lax vowels in English

	Tense		Lax
heat	[ij]	hit	[ɪ]
mate	[ej]	met	[ɛ]
(no tense partner)	—	mat	[æ]
(no tense partner)	—	cut	[ʌ]
(no tense partner)	—	Canada	[ə]
shoot	[uw]	should	[ʊ]
coat	[ow]	(caught	[ɔ] in some dialects)

The difference between two of the vowels illustrated in Table 2.13 is not obvious at first. Both the vowel [ʌ] in *cut, dud, pluck,* and *Hun,* and the vowel [ə] of *Canada, about, tomahawk,* and *sofa* are lax. The vowel of the second set, called **schwa**, is called a **reduced** vowel; it is characterized by very brief duration as well as being lax, and it never receives stress.

The vowel [ɔ] is heard before *r,* as in the words *more* and *torn,* and is heard in the diphthong of *boy.* It is also heard in some American dialects and is widespread in British, Australian, and New Zealand English in words like *caught* and *law.* In other American and most Canadian dialects, both members of pairs like *caught* and *cot* are pronounced with the vowel [ɑ] or [a] (see below).

There is a test that helps determine whether vowels are tense or lax. In English, monosyllabic words spoken in isolation do not end in lax vowels, (except for [ɔ]). We find *see, say, Sue, so,* and *saw* in English, but not *s*[ɪ], *s*[ɛ], *s*[æ], *s*[ʊ], or *s*[ʌ].

The representation of vowels and their articulatory positions (Figure 2.9) is expanded in Figure 2.10 to include both tense and lax vowels.

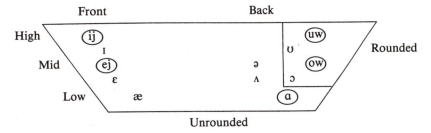

Figure 2.10 Tense and lax vowels (Tense vowels are circled.)

We have represented the tense vowels in Table 2.13 as diphthongs. In these diphthongs, there is little or no difference in tongue position between the vowel and the following glide. However, there are three diphthongs in which the difference between the two is considerable. In [aj], as in *buy*, and in [aw], as in *mouse*, the first component of the diphthong is the low unrounded vowel [a]. In [ɔj], as in *boy*, the first component is the lax mid back rounded vowel [ɔ]. Like all English diphthongs, these are tense; however, they have no lax counterparts.

Figure 2.11 places these diphthongs on the articulation chart, completing the inventory of English vowels.

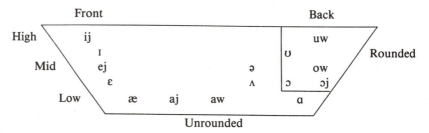

Figure 2.11 English Vowels

The difference between the two low unrounded vowels [a] and [ɑ] is quite subtle. [a] is more front, while [ɑ] is more back, usually tense and sometimes slightly rounded. Most speakers have [a] only in the diphthongs [aj] and [aw], but [ɑ] in words like *top* and *cot*. Dialects differ fairly widely, however, in the exact quality of these vowels. In a few New England dialects and in British English, [a] occurs by itself as a distinct vowel in a small set of words: *aunt*, *bath*, *calf*, *can't*, *half*, and *laugh*, where other dialects have the vowel [æ]. In this book we follow the majority of American speakers in using [a] in the diphthong and [ɑ] elsewhere, but listen carefully to your own speech and the speech of those around you before you decide which of these symbols to use.

This rather formidable crowd of vowels should not intimidate you. If you are a native speaker of English, you have been using these vowels (and others, some of which you will be introduced to in the next chapter) most of your life. Learning to hear them consciously and transcribe them is not a difficult task. The next section provides more examples of the transcription of English consonants and vowels.

2.7 PHONETIC TRANSCRIPTION OF AMERICAN ENGLISH CONSONANTS AND VOWELS

Tables 2.14 and 2.15 show the phonetic symbols for consonants and vowels commonly used to transcribe American English. To show how each symbol is used, one word is transcribed completely, and then some other words in which the same sound is found are given. You will notice that in the example words, the spelling of the sound may vary. Be careful of this when you transcribe words phonetically—the sound of a word, not its spelling, is what is transcribed! Remember also that most speakers do not use all these different sounds.

Table 2.14 Consonants

Symbol	Word	Transcription	More examples
[pʰ]	pit	[pʰɪt]	pain, upon, apart
[p]	spit	[spɪt]	spar, crispy, upper, Yuppie, culprit, bumper
[tʰ]	tick	[tʰɪk]	tell, attire, terror, Tutu
[t]	stuck	[stʌk]	stem, hunter, nasty, mostly
[kʰ]	keep	[kʰijp]	cow, kernel, chord
[k]	skip	[skɪp]	scatter, uncle, blacklist, likely
[tʃ]	chip	[tʃɪp]	lunch, lecher, ditch, belch
[dʒ]	judge	[dʒʌdʒ]	germ, journal, budge, wedge
[b]	bib	[bɪb]	boat, liberate, rob, blast
[d]	dip	[dɪp]	dust, huddle, sled, draft
[D]	butter	[bʌDr̩]	madder, matter, hitting, writer, rider
[g]	get	[gɛt]	gape, mugger, twig, gleam
[f]	fit	[fɪt]	flash, coughing, proof, phlegmatic, gopher
[v]	vat	[væt]	vote, oven, prove
[θ]	thick	[θɪk]	thought, ether, teeth, three, bathroom
[ð]	though	[ðow]	then, bother, teethe, bathe
[s]	sip	[sɪp]	psychology, fasten, lunacy, bass, curse, science
[z]	zap	[zæp]	Xerox, scissors, desire, zipper, fuzzy
[ʃ]	ship	[ʃɪp]	shock, nation, mission, glacier, wish
[ʒ]	azure	[æʒr̩]	measure, rouge, visual, garage (for some speakers)
[h]	hat	[hæt]	who, ahoy, forehead, behind, José
[j]	yet	[jɛt]	use, few
[w]	witch	[wɪtʃ]	wait, weird, queen
[ʍ]	which	[ʍɪtʃ]	what, where, when (not all speakers have this sound)
[l]	leaf	[lijf]	loose, lock, alive, hail
[r]	reef	[rijf]	prod, arrive, tear
[r̩]	bird	[br̩d]	early, hurt, stir, purr, doctor
[m]	moat	[mowt]	mind, humor, shimmer, sum, thumb
[n]	note	[nowt]	now, winner, angel, sign, wind
[ŋ]	sing	[sɪŋ]	singer, longer, bank, twinkle

Table 2.15 Vowels

Symbol	Word	Transcription	More examples
[ij]	fee	[fij]	she, cream, believe, receive, serene, amoeba, highly
[ɪ]	fit	[fɪt]	hit, income, definition, been (for some speakers)
[ej]	fate	[fejt]	they, clay, grain, gauge, engage, great, sleigh
[ɛ]	let	[lɛt]	led, lead, says, said, sever, guest, air
[æ]	bat	[bæt]	panic, racket, laugh, Vancouver
[uw]	boot	[buwt]	to, two, loose, brew, Louise, Lucy, through
[ʊ]	book	[bʊk]	should, put, hood
[ow]	note	[nowt]	no, throat, though, slow, toe, oaf, O'Conner
[ɔj]	boy	[bɔj]	loyal, coin
[ɔ]	bore	[bɔr]	oral, normal, caught, bought
[ɑ]	pot	[pʰɑt]	cot, father, rob
[ə]	roses	[rowzəz]	collide, afford, hinted, telegraph, (to) suspect
[ʌ]	shut	[ʃʌt]	other, udder, tough, lucky, was, flood
[aw]	crowd	[krawd]	(to) house, plow, bough
[aj]	lies	[lajz]	my, tide, thigh, buy

2.8 OTHER VOWELS AND CONSONANTS (advanced)

Up to this point, we have considered only the vowels and consonants of English. Many speech sounds found in English are heard in other languages. There are also many speech sounds found in the world's languages that are not heard in English. Since phonetic descriptions are universally valid, once you have mastered the basic articulatory parameters, it is not too difficult to describe and even to pronounce less familiar sounds. This section presents a number of speech sounds found in other languages.

Vowels

Front vowels, which in English are always unrounded, can also be rounded. A high front tense rounded vowel is heard in French *pur* 'pure', German *Bücher* 'books', and Turkish *düğme* 'button'. It is transcribed as [ü] in North America, but as [y] in IPA transcription—a difference that sometimes leads to confusion. A rounded high front lax vowel, [ʏ], is heard in Canadian French *lune*, 'moon' and *duc* 'duke'. A rounded mid front tense vowel, transcribed [ø], is found in French *peu* 'few' and German *schön* 'beautiful'. A rounded mid front lax vowel, transcribed [œ], is heard in French *oeuf* 'egg' and *peur* 'fear', German *örtlich* 'local', and Turkish *göl* 'lake'. Finally, an unrounded high back vowel, transcribed as [ɨ], is heard in Russian words like *byl* 'was', and Rumanian *mînă* 'hand'. These vowels, as well as other "exotic" ones, are found in many other languages as well. Table 2.16 illustrates the vowels presented in this chapter (UR = unrounded, R = rounded). Note carefully that the tense vowels are presented without glides. This is intentional; whereas English tense vowels include glides, the tense vowels of the languages cited here (and many others) do not.

Table 2.16 Articulatory grid of vowels presented in this chapter

	Front		Back	
	UR	R	UR	R
High	i	y	ɨ	u tense
	ɪ	ʏ		ʊ lax
Mid	e	ø	ə (lax)	o tense
	ɛ	œ	ʌ	ɔ lax
Low	æ		ɑ (tense)	
			a (lax)	

Nasal Vowels Nasal vowels, like nasal consonants, are produced with a lowered velum. Air passes simultaneously through the oral and nasal cavities. Nasal vowels can be heard in English, French, Portuguese, Hindi, and a wide variety of other languages. They are often transcribed with a tilde [˜] over the vowel symbol as shown in Table 2.17.

Table 2.17 Some nasal vowels

English: win [wĩn]
French: pain [pɛ̃] 'bread'
Portuguese: sento [sẽntu] 'one hundred'
Polish: ząb [zɔ̃p] 'tooth'

Consonants

The same consonants found in English are widespread in other languages. A few additional consonants are introduced in this section.

Stops In many European languages, we find not alveolar [t], [d], and [n], but dental [t̪], [d̪], and [n̪]. Although this seems like a very slight difference in articulation, it can be readily observed in the speech of French, Spanish, or Italian speakers. Bilingual English/Spanish speakers will switch between dental and alveolar positions when moving back and forth between languages.

Other stop positions are common in the world's languages. Retroflex stops [ṭ] and [ḍ], pronounced with the tongue curled back as in English [r], are common in the languages of India. Serbo-Croatian has both a voiceless and voiced palatal stop in words like *ćasa* 'dish', and *đak* 'pupil'. These are transcribed as [c] and [ɟ], respectively. Eskimo dialects show a voiceless and voiced uvular stop pair in words like *imaq* 'sea', and *ugsik* 'cow'. These are transcribed as [q] and [G], respectively. A nasal stop is also made at the palatal point of articulation, as in Spanish *año* 'year' (transcribed as [ñ] in North American and as [ɲ] in IPA) and at the uvula as well, transcribed as [N].

We now turn to the glottal state known as *whispery voice* or *murmur*. In Hindi there is a series of stops sometimes incorrectly referred to as voiced aspirated stops that make use of whispery voice (murmur). These stops can be represented with double underdots.

In the next table, examples of non-English stop articulations and glottal states are laid out. Sounds found in English are set off in boxes in Table 2.18.

Table 2.18 Stops

	Bilabial	Dental	Alveolar	Retroflex	Palatal	Velar	Uvular	Glottal
Voiceless	[p]	[t̪]	[t]	[ṭ]	[c]	[k]	[q]	[ʔ]
Voiced	[b]	[d̪]	[d]	[ḍ]	[ɟ]	[g]	[G]	
Nasal	[m]	[n̪]	[n]	[ṇ]	[ɲ]	[ŋ]	[N]	
Murmured	b̤		d̤			g̤		

Fricatives A bilabial fricative, produced by drawing the lips almost together and forcing the airstream through the narrow opening, is found in many languages. The voiceless bilabial fricative [ɸ] is heard word-initially in the Japanese word *Fuji* (the mountain). The voiced bilabial fricative [β] is found in Spanish in words like *deber* 'to owe'. A voiceless palatal fricative [ç] is found in Standard German; the word *ich* 'I' contains this sound. Velar fricatives are not found in English but are widespread in the world's languages. The voiceless velar fricative [x] is common in German and Russian. The composer Bach's name, pronounced in German, has a final voiceless velar fricative. A voiced velar fricative [ɣ] is commonly heard in Spanish words such as *agua* 'water'.

Table 2.19 presents a grid on which some common fricative consonants are ranged according to point and manner of articulation. Dentals are not distinguished from alveolars, as most languages have fricatives with either one or the other point of articulation, but not both. Sounds found in English are set off in boxes.

Table 2.19 Fricatives

	Bilabial	Labio-dental	Inter-dental	Dental or Alveolar	Alveo-palatal	Palatal	Velar	Glottal
Voiceless	[ɸ]	[f]	[θ]	[s]	[ʃ]	[ç]	[x]	[h]
Voiced	[β]	[v]	[ð]	[z]	[ʒ]	[j]	[ɣ]	

Affricates Affricates are found at most points of articulation. In German, a voiceless labiodental affricate, transcribed [pf], is heard at the beginning of the word *pferd* 'horse'. Some New York speakers have voiceless and voiced dental (or alveolar) affricates [ts] and [dz] in words like *time* and *dime*.

Table 2.20 presents a grid including the two English affricates and some others commonly found in languages. Sounds found in English are again set off in a box.

Table 2.20 Affricates

	Labiodental	Alveolar	Alveopalatal	Velar
Voiceless	[pf]	[ts]	[tʃ]	[kx]
Voiced	[bv]	[dz]	[dʒ]	[gɣ]

Liquids As with the stops, laterals may be dental as well as alveolar. Laterals can also be made with the tongue body raised to the palate. Such a sound is called a palatal lateral and is transcribed with the symbol [ʎ]. It is heard in some pronunciations of the Spanish words *caballo* 'horse' and *calle* 'street', and in the Serbo-Croatian words *dalje* 'farther' and *ljudi* 'people'. The palatal lateral may also be voiceless, in which case it is transcribed as [ʎ̥].

Lateral fricatives are produced when a lateral is made with a narrow enough closure to be classified as a fricative. This sound is transcribed as [lʒ] when voiced and [ɬ] when voiceless. Lateral fricatives can be heard in many American Indian languages, in Welsh, and in many languages spoken in the Caucasus. Table 2.21 shows some examples of voiceless alveolar lateral fricatives from Welsh.

Table 2.21 Voiceless alveolar lateral fricatives in Welsh

llan	[ɬan]	'clan'
ambell	[ambɛɬ]	'some'

Other types of *r* besides the retroflex and flap are also found. One is called a **tap**. Unlike the flap, which is made as the tongue rapidly passes across a point of articulation, the tap is made by rapidly touching the tongue tip to the back of the teeth or the alveolar ridge. (The point of articulation is language-specific.) It should not be confused with a [d], which is a true stop. Stops are made with a brief articulatory closure, while a tap is a very rapid gesture of striking the point of articulation and pulling away. The tap is transcribed as [ɾ] in IPA, though it is often found transcribed as [r] on a language-specific basis. The tap is the variety of *r* heard in Spanish *pero* 'but' and *pájaro* 'bird'.

Other *r*-like sounds are widely heard in the world's languages. The **trill** is made by passing air over the raised tongue tip and allowing it to vibrate. Trills are commonly transcribed as [r̃] (IPA [r]). They can be heard in the Spanish words *perro* 'dog' and *río* 'river', and the Italian words *carro* 'wagon' and *birra* 'beer'. A similar trilling effect can be made with the uvula, and is called a uvular trill. Its IPA transcription is [R].

A uvular *r* made without trilling is more commonly heard. This is the voiced *r* of Standard European French; it is also widespread in German. IPA transcription classifies this sound along with the fricatives. It is transcribed as [χ] when voiceless and as [ʁ] when voiced.

Table 2.22 presents the liquids. As before, sounds found in English are set off in boxes. The flaps, taps, and trills, though usually voiced, can be voiceless as well. Voicelessness for these sounds is usually indicated by a small open circle beneath the symbol, as in [r̥] or [R̥].

Table 2.22 Liquids

		Dental/Alveolar	Palatal	Uvular
Laterals:	voiced	[l]	[ʎ]	
	voiceless	[l̥]	[ʎ̥]	
Lateral fricatives:	voiced	[lʒ]		
	voiceless	[ɫ]		
R's:	retroflex	[r]		
	flap	[D]		
	tap	[ɾ]		
	trill	[r̃]		[R]

Glides The schwa [ə] appears as a glide in "r-less" dialects of English. In these varieties, words like *here* and *door* are pronounced [hijə̯] and [dɔə̯]. The curved line diacritic indicates that the schwa is a nonsyllabic glide.

Other glides are found in the world's languages. The most commonly heard one is a glide made with the tongue position of [j] but with the lips rounded. It is transcribed as [ɥ] and can be heard in French words such as [ɥit] *huit* 'eight', [ɥil] *huile* 'oil', and [ɥitχ] *huitre* 'oyster'.

2.9 SUPRASEGMENTALS

All sounds have certain inherent **suprasegmental** or **prosodic** properties that form part of their makeup no matter what their place or manner of articulation. These properties are **pitch**, **loudness**, and **length**. Pitch is the auditory property of a sound that enables us to place it on a scale that ranges from low to high. All sounds give a subjective impression of being relatively higher or lower in pitch. Pitch is especially noticeable in sonorous sounds like vowels, glides, liquids, and nasals. Even stop and fricative consonants convey different pitches. This is particularly obvious among the fricatives, as you can hear by extending the pronunciation of [s] and then of [ʃ]; the [s] is clearly higher pitched. All sounds have some degree of intrinsic loudness as well or they could not be heard. Moreover, all sounds occupy a certain stretch of time—they give the subjective impression of length.

Pitch

Speakers of any language have the ability to control the pitch of vowels and sonorant consonants. This is accomplished by controlling the tension of the vocal folds and the amount of air that passes through the glottis. The combination of tensed vocal folds and greater air pressure results in higher voice pitch, while less tense vocal folds and lower air pressure results in lower voice pitch. Two kinds of controlled pitch movement found in human language are called **tone** and **intonation**.

Tone Languages A language is said to have tone or be a **tone language** when differences in word meaning are signaled by differences in pitch. Pitch on forms in tone languages functions very differently from the movement of pitch in a nontone language. When a speaker of English says *a car?* with a rising pitch, the form *car* does not mean anything different from the same form pronounced on a different pitch level or with a different pitch contour. In contrast, when the speaker of a tone language such as Mandarin pronounces the form *ma* [ma] with a falling pitch, it means 'scold', but when the same form [ma] is pronounced with a rising pitch, the meaning is 'hemp'. There is no parallel to anything like this in nontone languages, such as English and French.

While tones may seem exotic to native speakers of Western European languages, they are very widespread. Tone languages are found throughout North and South America, Sub-Saharan Africa, and the Far East.

Some tone languages have distinct level tones. Sarcee, an Athapaskan language spoken in Canada, shows tones at high, mid, and low pitch levels. In Figure 2.12, the uppercase letters H, M, and L stand for high, mid, and low tones, respectively. A line drawn from the letter to the vowel indicates the pitch at which the vowel is spoken.

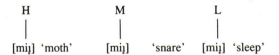

Figure 2.12 Sarcee level tones

Level tones that signal meaning differences are called **register tones**. Two or three register tones are the norm in most of the world's register tone languages, although as many as four have been reported for Mazatec (a language spoken in Mexico).

In some languages, tones change pitch on single syllables. Moving pitches that signal meaning differences are called **contour tones**. In Mandarin, both register and contour tones are heard. Contour tones are shown by pitch level notation lines that converge above the vowel, as shown in Figure 2.13. In Figure 2.13, there is one (high) register tone. The other tones are all contour tones.

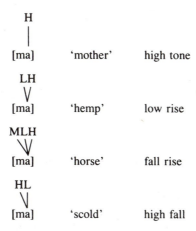

```
H
|
[ma]        'mother'      high tone

LH
\/
[ma]        'hemp'        low rise

MLH
\\/
[ma]        'horse'       fall rise

HL
\/
[ma]        'scold'       high fall
```

Figure 2.13 Register and contour tones in Mandarin

A single tone may also be associated with more than one syllabic element. In Mende, a language spoken in West Africa, there are certain polysyllabic forms that show the same tone on each syllable (here, the diacritic ´ indicates a high tone and the diacritic ` indicates a low tone).

Table 2.23 High-tone and low-tone words in Mende

pélé	'house'
háwámá	'waistline'
kpàkàlì	'tripod chair'

Our notation allows us to represent one tone as characteristic of more than one vowel. The single underlying tone unit is associated with all vowels.

Figure 2.14 Tone as a word feature

In some languages, tone may mark grammatical categories. In Bini, a language spoken in Nigeria, tone can signal differences in the tense of a verb (such as past versus present), as Figure 2.15 shows.

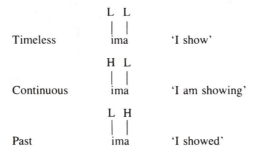

```
              L L
              | |
Timeless      ima        'I show'

              H L
              | |
Continuous    ima        'I am showing'

              L H
              | |
Past          ima        'I showed'
```

Figure 2.15 Tense and tone in Bini

Phonetic transcription for tones varies a great deal. In addition to the notation given above, tones can be marked by diacritics. Often the symbol [´] represents a high tone and [`] a low tone, so that the Bini words in Figure 2.15 are transcribed as [ìmà], [ímà], and [ìmá], respectively. Contour tones are sometimes marked with a combination of the two, so that a word like Mandarin *horse* from Figure 2.13, which has a fall-rise, is represented as [mǎ].

Intonation Pitch movement in spoken utterances that is not related to differences in the word meaning is called intonation. It makes no difference to the meaning of the word *seven*, for example, whether it is pronounced with a rising pitch or a falling pitch. Intonation often serves to convey information of a broadly meaningful nature. For example, the falling pitch we hear at the end of a statement in English such as *Fred parked the car* signals that the utterance is complete. For this reason, falling intonation at the end of an utterance is called a terminal intonation contour. Rising or level intonation, on the other hand, often signals incompleteness. Rising or level intonations are heard in the nonfinal forms found in lists and telephone numbers as in Figure 2.16. In questions,

e e n y m e e n y m i n e y m o e

two eight f o u r two f i v e one t h r e e

Figure 2.16 Rising nonterminal intonations

as in Figure 2.17, final rising intonations also signal a kind of incompleteness in that they indicate that a conversational exchange is not finished. However, English sentences that contain question words like *who*, *what*, *when*, and *how* (for example, *What did you buy?*) ordinarily do not have rising intonation. It is as if the question word itself is enough to indicate that an answer is expected.

Did you have a n i c e t i m e

Figure 2.17 Rising intonation in a question

Intonation can be represented graphically as in Figures 2.16 and 2.17. A more formal way of representing intonation is shown in Figure 2.18. Here, as in tonal representation, L and H are relative terms for differences in pitch. The letters H and L are placed above the syllabic elements on which the pitch change occurs. The diagonal lines indicate that the lowering pitch spreads across the remaining pitch-bearing elements.

L HL

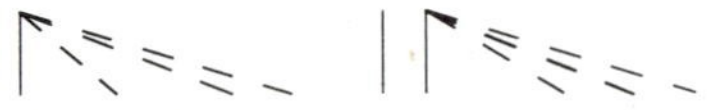

Sam bought a new vacuum cleaner bag.

Figure 2.18 A terminal contour

Rising intonation on names or requests is commonly heard in addressing people. Its use indicates that the speaker is opening a conversation or that some further action is expected from the listener.

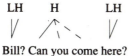

Bill? Can you come here?

Figure 2.19 Two non-terminal contours

The complex uses of intonation have just been touched on here. Consider, for example, that rising intonation is often used to express politeness, as in *Please sit down*. Some linguists think that this use is an extension of the 'open-ended mode' of intonation, and that since a rising intonation indicates that further response is expected (but not demanded) of the hearer, a sentence uttered with a rising intonation sounds less like an order and so is more polite.

Intonation and Tone (advanced) Tone and intonation are not mutually exclusive. Tone languages show intonation of all types. This is possible since the tones are not absolute but relative pitches. A tone is perceived as high if it is high relative to the pitches around it. As long as this relative difference is maintained, the pitch distinctions will also be maintained. Figure 2.20 shows this graphically. It represents the overall pitch of a declarative sentence in Igbo, a West African language with register tones. Note how an Igbo speaker clearly maintains the distinction among the pitch registers even as the overall pitch of the utterance falls. Each high tone is lower than the preceding high tone, but higher than the low tone that immediately precedes it. This phenomenon is known as **downdrift**.

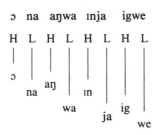

'He is trying to ride a bicycle.'

Figure 2.20 Tone and intonation—downdrift in Igbo

Length

In many languages, there are vowels or consonants whose articulation is held longer relative to that of other vowels and consonants. This phenomenon, known as length, is widespread in the world's languages. Length is indicated in phonetic transcription by the use of a colon [:] placed after the long segment.

Hungarian, German, Cree, and Finnish are a few of the many languages that show long and short vowels. Yap, a language spoken on the island of Yap in the Western Pacific, shows short and long vowels in pairs of words such as those in Table 2.24. Italian shows short and long consonants in pairs of words such as those in Table 2.25. Long and short consonants are found in many other languages, including Finnish, Turkish, and Hungarian.

Table 2.24 Short and long vowels in Yap

[θis]	'to topple'	[θi:s]	'(a) post'
[pul]	'to gather'	[pu:1]	'moon'
[ʔer]	'near you'	[ʔe:r]	'part of a lagoon'

Table 2.25 Short and long consonants in Italian

fato	[fatɔ]	'fate'	fatto	[fat:ɔ]	'fact'
fano	[fanɔ]	'grove'	fanno	[fan:ɔ]	'they do'
casa	[kasa]	'house'	cassa	[kas:a]	'box'

Stress

In any utterance, some vowels are perceived as more prominent than others. In a word such as *telegraphic* [tʰɛləgræfɪk], the two vowel nuclei that are more prominent than the others are [ɛ] and [æ]. Vowels perceived as relatively more prominent are **stressed**. Stress is a cover term for the combined effects of pitch, loudness, and length—the result of which is vowel prominence. In each language, the effect of these prosodic features varies. In general, English stressed vowels are higher in pitch, longer, and louder than unstressed ones. But this is not always the case. The example word *telegraphic* might just as well be pronounced with the stressed syllables lower than the unstressed ones. The important thing is that they be prominent with respect to the syllables around them, and this is usually accomplished by a relatively large shift in one or all of the three parameters—pitch, loudness, and length.

In some languages, the impression of vowel prominence results from an interaction of the prosodic parameters that is different from that found in English. In modern Greek, for example, syllables tend to be of equal length. Stress, therefore, is manifested mostly by a change in pitch and loudness and not in syllable length. Tone languages do not change the pitch level or contour of tones to mark stress. In many of these languages, relative prominence is marked by exaggerating the vowel length or pitch contour.

There are various ways to mark stress in phonetic transcription. North American transcription commonly uses an acute accent [´] placed over the vowel nucleus in question to mark the most prominent or **primary** stress, and a grave accent [`] to mark the second more prominent or **secondary** stress. (This should not be confused with the use of the same diacritics to mark tone in tone languages.) Stress can also be marked by placing numbers above the stressed vowels, usually [1] for a primary stress and [2] for a secondary stress. The word *telegraphic* is transcribed as either of the following:

2.   [tʰɛ̀ləgræfɪk]   or   [tʰɛləgrǽfɪk]

Since it is debatable whether any degrees of stress less than primary, secondary, and tertiary exist, this book will mark only primary and secondary stresses. Unmarked vowels have tertiary stress. Table 2.26 shows some differences in

English stress placement. In the last four examples in the table, you can see that the quality of certain vowels varies depending on whether they are stressed or unstressed. This is common in English, Russian, and many other languages, but it is not universal.

Table 2.26 Differing stress placement in English

(an)	éxport	[ékspɔrt]	(to) expórt	[ekspɔ́rt]
(a)	présent	[prézənt]	(to) presént	[prijzént]
	télegràph	[tʰéləgræf]		
	telégraphỳ	[təlégrəfij]		
	tèlegráphic	[tʰèləgrǽfɪk)		

2.10 COARTICULATION

Speech production is not a series of isolated events. The process of articulation is a complex one, and many fine adjustments are carried out very rapidly as we speak. As a consequence, speech production often results in the articulation of one sound affecting that of another sound, or **coarticulation**.

You have seen how nasal sounds are produced with the velum lowered to allow air to pass through the nasal cavities. Raising and lowering the velum is not always precisely coordinated with other speech production activity. Speakers often anticipate lowering the velum for nasal consonants and, consequently, produce a nasal vowel before a nasal consonant. Many English speakers do this when they pronounce words such as *bank* [bæ̃ŋk] or *him* [hɪ̃m] (see Figure 2.21). Another typical articulatory adjustment occurs when we pronounce the sound [k] before the vowel [ij] in English words such as *keys* and *keel*. The [k] we articulate before [ij] is pronounced with the back of the tongue so far forward it nearly touches the palate. It is scarcely a velar articulation at all for many speakers. The [k] we pronounce before the vowels [ɑ] and [ow] in words such as *call* and *cold* is articulated further back and is a true velar. These adjustments are made in anticipation of the tongue position that will be needed for the vowel in question: front for [iy] and back for the [ɑ] and [ow]. The [k] pronounced before the vowel [uw] in a word such as *cool* also shows lip rounding in anticipation of the following (back) rounded vowel.

```
Stop released,
velum begins
to lower for [ŋ].
  ↓
[ b æ̃ ŋ k ]
       ↑
     Velum rises.
```

Figure 2.21 Coarticulation resulting in a nasal vowel

Articulatory adjustments that occur during the production of speech are called **processes**. Their cumulative effect often results in making words easier to articulate, and in this sense they are said to make speech more efficient. When speakers of English nasalize the vowel of *bank*, they do not delay lowering the velum until the exact moment the nasal consonant articulation is reached. Most English speakers begin lowering the velum for a nasal consonant almost as soon as they articulate the vowel that precedes it. In a parallel manner, when speakers pronounce [k] as more palatal in a word such as *key*, they are speaking more efficiently from the point of view of articulation since they are making a less drastic adjustment in moving from the articulation of a more palatal [k] to that of a high front vowel than they would make in moving from a velar [k] to a high front vowel. Even more drastically, a speaker of English who says [pṛejd] for *parade* is making a major adjustment that results in a more efficient articulation. The two syllables of a careful pronunciation of *parade* are reduced to one by dropping the unstressed vowel of the first syllable. The voicelessness of the initial stop is then carried on through the [ṛ].

Articulatory Processes

Only a finite number of processes operate in language, though their end result is to produce a great deal of linguistic variability. This section surveys some of the most common of these processes.

Assimilation A number of different processes collectively known as **assimilation** result from the influence of one segment on another. Assimilation always results from a sound becoming more like another nearby sound in terms of one or more of its phonetic characteristics.

Progressive and Regressive Assimilation Nasalization of a vowel before a nasal consonant is caused by speakers anticipating the lowering of the velum in advance of a nasal segment. The result is that the preceding segment takes on the nasality of the following consonant. This type of assimilation is known as anticipation or **regressive assimilation**, since the nasalization is, in effect, moving *backwards* to a preceding segment. The nasalization of vowels following nasal consonants by contrast is an example of lag or **progressive assimilation**, since the nasality moves *forward* from the nasal consonant onto the vowel (see Table 2.27). It results from speakers not immediately raising the velum after the production of a nasal stop.

Table 2.27 Progressive nasalization of vowels in Scots Gaelic

[mõ:r]	'big'
[nĩ]	'cattle'
[mũ]	'about'
[nẽ:l]	'cloud'

Voicing assimilation is also widespread. For many speakers of English, voiceless liquids and glides occur after voiceless stops in words such as *please* [pl̥ijz], *proud* [pr̥awd], and *pure* [pj̥ur]. These sounds are said to be devoiced in this environment. Devoicing is a kind of assimilation. Here, the vocal folds are not set in motion immediately after the release of the voiceless consonant closure. The opposite of devoicing is voicing. In Dutch, fricatives assimilate to the voicing of the stops that follow them, in anticipation of the voiced consonant. The element *af* [af] 'off, over' is pronounced with a [v] in the words *afbellen* 'to ring off' and *afdekken* 'to cover over'.

Assimilation for place of articulation is also widespread in the world's languages. Nasal consonants are very likely to undergo this type of assimilation, as shown in Table 2.28. The negative forms of each of these words is made with either *im* or *in*. In both cases, the form shows a nasal consonant that has the same place of articulation as the stop consonant that follows it: labial in the case of *possible* and *potent*, and alveolar in the case of *tolerable* and *tangible*. In informal speech, many English speakers pronounce words such as *inconsequential* and *inconsiderate* with an [ŋ] where the spelling shows *n*. Assimilation can also be heard in pronunciations such as *Va*[ŋ]*couver* and *i*[ɱ]*fant*. Occasionally, it even crosses the boundaries between words. In rapid speech, it is not uncommon to hear people pronounce a phrase such as *in code* as [ɪŋkʰówd].

Table 2.28 Assimilation for place of articulation

possible	impossible
potent	impotent
tolerable	intolerable
tangible	intangible

The preceding English example shows regressive assimilation in place of articulation. The example in Table 2.29, taken from German, shows progressive assimilation that again affects nasal consonants. In careful speech, certain German verb forms are pronounced with a final [ən], as in *laden* 'to invite', *loben* 'to praise', and *backen* 'to bake'. In informal speech, the final [ən] is reduced to a syllabic nasal, which takes on the point of articulation of the preceding consonant. The diacritic line under the phonetically transcribed nasals indicates that they are syllabic.

Table 2.29 Progressive assimilation in German

Careful speech		Informal speech	
laden	[la:dən]	[la:dn̩]	'to invite'
loben	[lo:bən]	[lo:bm̩]	'to praise'
backen	[bakən]	[bakŋ̩]	'to bake'

Flapping is a type of assimilatory process in which an alveolar stop is pronounced as a voiced flap between vowels, the first of which is generally stressed. This process is characteristic of American English in words such as *butter*, *writer*, *fatter*, *udder*, *wader*, *waiter*, and even phrases such as (*I*) *caught her*. The sound heard intervocally in these forms is the voiced flap [D] (discussed on page 25) and not the voiced stop [d]. Flapping is considered a type of assimilation since it results in voicing and sonority being maintained throughout a sequence of segments.

Dissimilation, the opposite of assimilation, results in two sounds becoming less alike in articulatory or acoustic terms. The resulting sequence of sounds is easier to articulate and distinguish. It is a much rarer process than assimilation. One commonly heard example of dissimilation in English occurs in words ending with three consecutive fricatives, such as *fifths*. Many speakers dissimilate the final [fθs] sequence to [fts], apparently to break up the sequence of three fricatives with a stop.

Deletion is a process that removes a segment from certain phonetic contexts. Deletion occurs in everyday rapid speech in many languages. In English, a schwa [ə] is often deleted when the next vowel in the word is stressed (see Table 2.30). Deletion also occurs as an alternative to dissimilation in a word such as *fifths*. Many speakers delete the [θ] of the final consonant cluster and say [fɪfs]. In very rapid speech, both [f] and [θ] are sometimes deleted, resulting in [fɪs].

Table 2.30 Deletion of [ə] in English

Slow speech	Rapid speech	
[pəréjd]	[pr̥éjd]	parade
[kərówd]	[kr̥ówd]	corrode
[səpʰówz]	[spówz]	suppose

Epenthesis is a process that inserts a syllabic or a nonsyllabic segment within an existing string of segments. For example, in careful speech, the words *warmth* and *something* are pronounced [warmθ] and [sʌmθɪŋ]. It is common in casual speech for speakers to insert a [p] between the *m* and the *th* and pronounce the words [warmpθ] and [sʌmpθɪŋ]. Consonant epenthesis of this type is another example of a coarticulation phenomenon. In English, the articulatory transition from a sonorant consonant to a nonsonorant appears to be eased by the insertion of a consonant that shares properties of both segments. Notice that the epenthesized consonants are nonsonorant, all have the same place of articulation as the sonorant consonant to their left, and all have the same voicing as the nonsonorant consonant to their right.

Table 2.31 Some examples of English consonant epenthesis

Word	Nonepenthesized pronunciation	Epenthesized pronunciation
something	[sʌmθɪŋ]	[sʌmpθɪŋ]
warmth	[warmθ]	[warmpθ]
length	[lɛŋθ]	[lɛŋkθ]
prince	[prɪns]	[prɪnts]
tenth	[tɛnθ]	[tɛntθ]

Vowels may also be epenthesized. In Turkish, a word may not begin with two consonants. When words are borrowed into Turkish, an epenthetic vowel is inserted between certain sequences of two initial consonants, creating a new and permissible sequence. (The reason for the differences among the vowels need not concern us here; note, though, that the vowel is always high; see Section 2.8 for further presentation of [ɨ] and other unfamiliar symbols.)

Table 2.32 Vowel epenthesis in Turkish

Source word	Turkish form
train	t[i]ren
club	k[u]lüb
sport	s[ɨ]por

Metathesis is a process that reorders a sequence of segments. Metathesis often results in a sequence of phones that is easier to articulate. It is common to hear metathesis in the speech of children, who often cannot pronounce all the consonant sequences that adults can. For example, English-speaking children pronounce *spaghetti* as *pesghetti* [pəskɛDij]. In this form, the initial sequence [spə], which is often difficult for children to pronounce, is metathesized to [pəs]. Another example found in many dialects is the form [æks] for [æsk].

The pronunciations of *prescribe* and *prescription* as *perscribe* and *perscription* are often-cited examples of metathesis in adult speech. In these cases, metathesis may facilitate the pronunciation of the two consonant-*r* sequences in each word.

Summing Up

The study of the sounds of human language is called **phonetics**. These sounds are widely transcribed by means of the **International Phonetic Alphabet**. The sounds of language are commonly described in **articulatory** and **acoustic** terms; they fall into three major types: **consonants, vowels,** and **glides**. Sounds may be **voiced** or **voiceless**, and **oral** or **nasal**. Consonants are produced at various **places of articulation: labial, dental, alveolar, alveopalatal, palatal, velar, glottal,** and **pharyngeal**. At the places of articulation, the airstream is modified by different **manners of articulation** and the resulting sounds are **stops, fricatives,** or **affricates**. Vowels are produced with less drastic closure and are described with reference to tongue position (**high, low, back,** and **front**), tension (**tense** or **lax**), and lip rounding (**rounded** or **unrounded**). Language also shows **suprasegmental** phenomena such as **tone, intonation,** and **stress**. A number of phonetic **processes** act on **natural classes** of sounds in speech.

Key Terms

acoustic phonetics	diphthong
affricates	dorsum
alveolar ridge	downdrift
alveopalatal	feature
articulatory phonetics	flap
aspiration	flapping
assimilation	fricative
back	front
bilabial	glide
blade of tongue	glottal
body of tongue	glottis
coarticulation	high
continuant	intercostals
contour tones	interdental
dental	intonation
diaphragm	IPA

labiodentals

larynx

lax

length

loudness

low

manner of articulation

metathesis

murmur

nasal

nucleus

oral

palate

pharyngeals

pharynx

phone

pitch

place of articulation

primary stress

processes

progressive assimilation

prosodic

register tone

regressive assimilation

retroflex

root

rounded

secondary stress

segment

sibilant

speech sounds

stop

strident

suprasegmental

syllabic consonants

syllable

tense

terminal (intonation) contour

tip of tongue

tone

tone language

trachea

uvula

uvular (sound)

velum

vocal folds

vocal tract

voice

voiceless (sound)

voicing assimilation

vowel

whispery voice

Sources

Information on the International Phonetic Alphabet can be obtained from the International Phonetic Association, University College, Gower Street, London WC1E 6BT, England. Sarcee data are from E.-D. Cook, "Vowels and Tones in Sarcee" in *Language* 47:164–79; Gaelic data are courtesy of James Galbraith. Bini data are adapted from Ladefoged (cited below). More detailed reading on the phonetics of English and other languages is reported below.

Recommended Reading

Catford, J.C. 1977. *Fundamental Problems in Phonetics.* Bloomington: Indiana University Press.

Cruttenden, Alan. 1986. *Intonation.* Cambridge: Cambridge University Press.

Fromkin, V.A., ed. 1978. *Tone: A Linguistic Survey.* New York: Academic Press.

Ladefoged, P. 1982. *A Course in Phonetics*. 2d ed. Toronto: Harcourt Brace Jovanovich.

Pullum, G.K., and W.A. Ladusaw. 1986. *Phonetic Symbol Guide*. Chicago: University of Chicago Press.

Rogers, H. 1991. *Theoretical and Practical Phonetics*. Toronto: Copp Clark Pitman Ltd.

Shearer, William M. 1968. *Illustrated Speech Anatomy*. Springfield, Illinois: Charles C. Thomas.

Appendix A: Articulatory Representation of English Consonants

Place of articulation		Labial	Interdental	Alveolar	Alveopalatal	Velar	Glottal
Manner of articulation	*Glottal state*						
STOP	− voice	p		t		k	ʔ
	+ voice	b		d		g	
FRICATIVE	− voice	f	θ	s	ʃ		h
	+ voice	v	ð	z	ʒ		
AFFRICATE	− voice				tʃ		
	+ voice				dʒ		
NASAL	+ voice	m		n		ŋ	
LIQUID							
Lateral	+ voice			l			
Retroflex	+ voice			r			
GLIDE	+ voice	w			j*	(w)	
	− voice	ʍ				(ʍ)	
Major manner features	The glides [w] and [ʍ] are represented in parentheses as velars since they are both labial and velar (labiovelar). The features of labials are assigned to them. *The glide [j] is a palatal.						

Appendix B: The International Phonetic Alphabet (Condensed)

CONSONANTS

	Bilabial	Labiodental	Dental	Alveolar	Postalveolar	Retroflex	Palatal	Velar	Uvular	Pharyngeal	Glottal
Plosive	p b			t d		ʈ ɖ	c ɟ	k g	q ɢ		ʔ
Nasal	m	ɱ		n		ɳ	ɲ	ŋ	N		
Trill	ʙ			r					R		
Tap or Flap				ɾ		ɽ					
Fricative	ɸ β	f v	θ ð	s z	ʃ ʒ	ʂ ʐ	ç j	x ɣ	χ ʁ	ħ ʕ	h ɦ
Lateral fricative				ɬ lʒ							
Approximant		ʋ		ɹ		ɻ	j	ɰ			
Lateral approximant				l		ɭ	ʎ	L			
Ejective stop	p'			t'		t'	c'	k'	q'		

Where symbols appear in pairs, the one to the right represents a voiced consonant. Shaded areas denote articulations judged impossible.

VOWELS

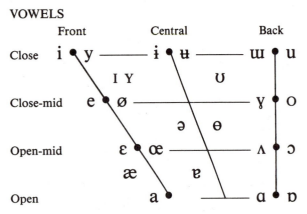

Where symbols appear in pairs, the one to the right represents a rounded vowel. The symbols for vowels used in this book sometimes differ from IPA usage.

Questions

1. In order to become more aware of the differences between spelling and pronunciation, answer the following questions about English spelling.

    a) Find four words that show four different spellings of the sound [f].
    b) Find six words that have the letter *a* pronounced differently.
    c) Find four words in which different groups of letters represent only one sound.

2. How many segments are there in the following words?

    a) at   e) psychology
    b) math   f) knowledge
    c) cure   g) mailbox
    d) hopping   h) awesome

3. Pronounce the following words.

    a) though   e) zoom   i) huge   m) when
    b) thought   f) silk   j) choose   n) ghetto
    c) form   g) pan   k) judge   o) pneumatic
    d) view   h) boat   l) buns   p) winced

    i) Is the first sound in each word voiced or voiceless?
    ii) Is the last sound in each word voiced or voiceless?

4. For each of the following pairs of sounds, state whether they have the same or different place of articulation. Then identify the place of articulation for each sound.

    a) [s] : [l]   e) [m] : [n]   i) [b] : [f]
    b) [k] : [ŋ]   f) [dʒ] : [ʃ]   j) [tʃ] : [dʒ]
    c) [p] : [g]   g) [f] : [h]   k) [s] : [v]
    d) [l] : [r]   h) [w] : [j]   l) [θ] : [t]

5. For each of the following pairs of sounds, state whether they have the same or different manners of articulation. Then identify the manner of articulation for each sound.

    a) [s] : [θ]   e) [l] : [t]   i) [r] : [w]
    b) [k] : [g]   f) [ð] : [v]   j) [tʃ] : [dʒ]
    c) [w] : [j]   g) [tʃ] : [s]   k) [h] : [ʔ]
    d) [f] : [ʃ]   h) [m] : [ŋ]   l) [z] : [ʒ]

6. Give the phonetic transcription that corresponds to each of the following articulatory descriptions.

    a) voiceless velar stop   e) voiced velar nasal
    b) voiced labiodental fricative   f) voiceless interdental fricative
    c) voiced alveopalatal affricate   g) high back rounded lax vowel
    d) voiced palatal glide   h) low front unrounded vowel

7. Which of the following pairs of words show the same vowel quality? Mark each pair as *same* or *different*. Then transcribe each word.

    a) back   sat   h) hide   height
    b) cot   caught   i) least   heed
    c) bid   key   j) drug   cook
    d) luck   flick   k) sink   fit
    e) ooze   deuce   l) oak   own
    f) cot   court   m) pour   port
    g) fell   fail   n) mouse   cow

8. Using descriptive terms like sibilant, fricative, and so on, provide a single phonetic characteristic that all the segments in each group shares. Try to avoid over-obvious answers such as 'consonant', or 'vowel'.
    Example: [b d g œ m j] are all voiced.

    a) [p t k g ʔ]   f) [h ʔ]
    b) [i e ɛ æ]   g) [u o ɔ ɨ]
    c) [tʃ dʒ ʃ ʒ]   h) [s z tʃ dʒ ʃ ʒ]
    d) [p b m f v]   i) [l r m n ŋ j w]
    e) [ʌ ə ɔ ʊ a]   j) [t d l r n s z]

9. Give the phonetic transcription of the following words including aspiration.

    a) tog   g) juice   m) sigh   s) accord
    b) kid   h) thimble   n) hulk   t) astound
    c) attain   i) peel   o) explode   u) pure
    d) despise   j) stun   p) tube   v) wheeze
    e) elbow   k) Oscar   q) spell   w) remove
    f) haul   l) cooler   r) cord   x) clinical

10. Using H, L, and lines, transcribe the intonation of the following English phrases. Compare your results with the transcriptions of several classmates. Are they the same? If they aren't, discuss what aspects of intonation (such as emotion or speech context) might account for the differences in transcription.

    a) 'Hi, Alice.'
    b) 'Allen got a trumpet and a flute for Christmas.'
    c) 'Soccer and swimming are Judy's favorite sports.'

11. Mark primary and secondary (where present) stresses on the following words. Follow the example in Table 2.26, but it is not necessary to transcribe the words.

    a) sunny   f) arrive   k) secret
    b) banana   g) defy   l) exceed
    c) blackboard   h) summary   m) summery
    d) Canada   i) Canadian   n) Canadianize
    e) (to) reject   j) (a) reject   o) difficult

12. Find a fluent speaker of a language other than English and transcribe phonetically ten words of that language. If you encounter any sounds for which symbols are not found in this chapter (including Section 2.8), attempt to describe them in phonetic terms and then invent diacritics to help you transcribe them.

13. Using Figure 2.21 as your model, provide coarticulation diagrams for the following words. Be sure that your diagrams capture the movement of the lips, tongue, velum, and glottis as in the model.

   a) had   b) snap   c) please   d) dome

14. Compare the careful speech and rapid speech pronunciations of the following English words and phrases. Then, name the process or processes that make the rapid speech pronunciation different from the careful speech in each case. (Stress is omitted here.)

		Careful speech	*Rapid speech*
a)	in my room	[ɪn maj ruwm]	[ɪm maj ruwm]
b)	I see him	[aj sij hɪm]	[aj sijɪm]
c)	within	[wɪθɪn]	[wɪðɪn]
d)	balloons	[bəluwnz]	[bluwnz]
e)	sit down	[sɪt dawn]	[sɪDawn]
f)	my advice	[maj ədvajs]	[maj əvajs]
g)	Scotch tape	[skɑtʃ tʰejp]	[kʰɑtʃ stejp]
h)	protection	[pɹowtʰɛkʃən]	[pɹ̩tʰɛkʃən]
i)	hand me that	[hænd mij ðæt]	[hæ̃mijðæt]
j)	Pam will miss you	[pæm wɪl mɪs juw]	[pæm̩mɪʃjə]

For the Student Linguist

DON'T WORRY ABOUT SPELLING

What if you had to choose: either nobody would read and write ever again, or nobody would speak or hear language. This is a total nonchoice for me—I'd pitch out liner notes and lyric sheets in a second, but would be really upset about losing all my Ella Fitzgerald CDs. Not that it would be easy to function without reading and writing. Road signs, for example, are pretty important, and even linguistics textbooks have their uses. But the point is, I think spoken language is more fundamental than reading or writing. Let's assume it is, but let's also assume that writing is pretty important to modern society. The question, then, is how closely writing should resemble speaking.

Current spelling is much closer to the way English *used* to be spoken than the way it's spoken today, and for years various folks have been proposing spelling reforms. Would learning to read be easier if you didn't have to deal with spelling nightmares like *night, though, tough, cough, two, due, who, threw, shoe, through,* or *answer*? Some of these words are already being changed, informally, in advertising, pop music, and casual writing. For example, when my best friend sends me letters, she always writes *nite, tho, tuff, cough, 2, due, who, threw, shoe, thru,* and *anser*. Are these spellings any better? For someone who's learning to read English, it could be hard to figure out that *tho* and *who* aren't supposed to rhyme but *2, due, who, threw, shoe* and *thru* are supposed to rhyme, although there's now a difference in spelling for the nonrhyming *tho* and *tuff*.

Phonetic transcription—using the IPA—is unambiguous about what rhymes with what. For every sound there's exactly one symbol (except for a couple substitutions for different keyboards), and for every symbol there's exactly one sound. Thus the word list becomes: najt, ðow, tʰʌf, kʰɔf, tuw, duw, huw, θruw, ʃuw, θruw, and ænsər. Making the change-over from standard spelling to IPA would be a nightmare, though. We'd have to reconfigure our keyboards, for starters. Instead of five vowel symbols (and many combinations of them) and twenty-one consonants we'd have about eighteen vowels and twenty-five consonants.

Imagine all the changeover details could be taken care of (including instantly teaching everyone the IPA). Think about how much richer writing could be if it included all the information you get from hearing someone speak. You'd have information about the writer's regional background and class plus information about the level of formality of the piece you were reading. Depending on how detailed the writing system was, you would be able to read all sorts of nuances of stress and intonation.

I've transcribed the same piece of dialogue in several different systems below. The first system is probably the hardest to read, and the following systems get progressively easier. Try to figure out the dialogue from the first system, checking the later ones for clarification if you get stuck. Also try to figure out the stylistic differences among the different versions of the dialogue.

1. ʃijləʔejtʰejlardʒpʰʌmpkʰɪnpʰaj ʔəwɛrðæt ʔælənwəzwatʃɪŋ ọːw̥ ʔælən ʃijsɛdbrɛθilij pʰæsm̥ij ðij wɪptʰ kʰrịm̥ ʃijlə hijwajnd ʔajmtʃrajiŋ tʰuwfɪnɪʃgrajndɪŋðijkɔfij

2. ʃijləʔejDəlaːdʒpʰʌmpkʰɪnpʰaj   ʔəwɛrðæʔæln̩wəzwatʃn̩   oːw ʔæln̩ ʃijsɛʔbrɛθlij pʰæsmijðəwɪpkʰrijm   ʃijlə hijwajnd ʔajmtʃrajn̩tʰəfɪnɪʃgrajndn̩ðəkɔfij

3. ʃíjləʔejDəlaːdʒpʰʌmpkʰɪnpʰáj   ʔəwɛrðæʔæln̩wəzwátʃn̩   oːw ʔæln̩ ʃijsɛʔbréθlij pʰæsmijðəwɪpkʰríjm   ʃíjlə hijwájnd ʔajmtʃrájn̩tʰəfɪnɪʃgrájndn̩ðəkɔ́fij

4. ʃijlə ejt ej lardʒpʰʌmpkʰɪn pʰaj ʔəwɛr ðæt ʔælən wəz watʃɪŋ oːw ʔælən ʃij sɛd brɛθilij pʰæs mij ðij wɪptʰ kʰrijm ʃijlə hij wajnd ʔajm tʃrajiŋ tʰuw fɪnɪʃ grajndɪŋ ðij kɔfij

5. ʃijlə ejt ej lardʒ pʰʌmpkʰɪn pʰaj, ʔəwɛr ðæt ʔælən wəz wa tʃɪŋ. "oːw ʔælən," ʃij sɛd brɛθɪlij, "pʰæs mij ðij wɪptʰ kʰrijm." "ʃijlə," hij wajnd, "ʔajm tʃrajɪŋ tʰuw fɪnɪʃ grajndɪŋ ðij kɔfij."

The downside of this type of writing is that there'd be so much variability. For instance, you might care about the accent or tone of a character in a novel, but do you really need to know where the journalist who wrote this morning's article on the economy was raised? And what if his or her editor were from someplace else? Whose accent would get printed? Not to mention the difficulties of something like a GRE exam or SAT test written in someone else's dialect.

Of course, the degree of variability depends on how extreme the system is. There's a wide gap between standard spelling and the fairly narrow (detailed) transcription system used in examples *1* through *3*. Writing could be more phonetic than it is now, but we don't have to force people to include every minor variation in pronunciation. We could forget about stress marks and anything to show intonation—except for a few simple things like question marks and exclamation points. We could also leave off fairly predictable things like aspiration (you'll discover how predictable aspiration is in the next chapter). Examples *4* and *5* are probably a lot easier to understand than *1* through *3*, since *4* and *5* are not as detailed (broad transcription) and, most importantly, because they have spaces between the words. Putting in spaces makes the writing less like the actual pronunciation, but it also takes away the ambiguity of figuring out whether something like [ʃijla] is supposed to be *she lo* . . . (as in *she locked the door* . . .) or *Sheila*.

In fact, the new writing system could keep punctuation, keep word spaces, and have nothing but the bare minimum to distinguish the way one word sounds from the way other words sound. The trick, then, is to figure out what the bare minimum is. It's a pretty difficult question, and before you can answer it you'll need to read about phonology and morphology. You'll also need to figure out what exactly a word *is*, anyway. So, read the next two chapters and then come back to this section and read it again. Then devise the perfect writing system, use it for your senior thesis, patent it, market it, make a fortune off of it, and retire to a lovely little tropical island (with good food) where they don't speak English.

3 PHONOLOGY
The Function and Patterning of Sounds

My voice goes after what my eyes cannot reach,
With the twirl of my tongue I encompass
words and volumes of words.

Walt Whitman

When we speak of linguistic knowledge, we often mean subconscious or implicit knowledge that speakers of a language cannot readily put into words. As pointed out in Chapter 1, English speakers know that forms like *slish* and *screnk* are acceptable, while forms like *srish* and *screpk* are not. Few people could state without considerable reflection what pattern, if any, governs the acceptability of some sequences and the unacceptability of others. This chapter deals with **phonology**, the component of a grammar made up of the elements and principles that determine how sounds pattern in a language. Phonologists attempt to make explicit statements about the sound patterns of individual languages in order to discover something about the linguistic knowledge that people must have in order to use these patterns. Even more broadly, the study of phonology attempts to discover general principles that underlie the patterning of sounds in human language.

The search for sound patterns in language implies the existence of some basic elements or units that combine to make up these patterns. Three major units of analysis will be presented in this chapter. The smallest of these units is the **feature**. Features may be thought of as the smallest building blocks of phonological structure, corresponding as they do to articulatory or acoustic categories such as [voice] or [strident]. A second element of phonological structure is the segment. In this chapter, we investigate the patterned variation of segments. We will also learn more about the makeup of segments from features and how this fact is connected with phonological patterning. Segments, in turn, are combined to produce **syllables** such as *in*, *duc*, or *tion*. A syllable is a unit of linguistic structure that consists of a syllabic element and any segments that are associated with it. These units—feature, segment, and syllable—all form part of a speaker's linguistic knowledge.

Phonological structure is composed of hierarchical levels of elements; each level is composed of elements at the level beneath it. In Figure 3.1, the word-level unit *induction* is represented by the abbreviation *Wd*. This word consists of three syllables, each of which is represented with the Greek letter σ (*sigma*). Each syllable is made up of a number of segments (the internal structure of syllables is also hierarchical, and is treated in Section 3.5). Each segment, in turn, is composed of features. A representation of *induction* is given in Figure 3.1. (For purposes of illustration, only a few features are provided for each segment.)

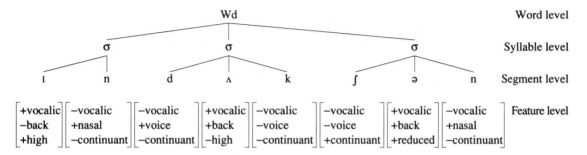

Figure 3.1 Partial phonological representation of *induction*

In the next sections, we look at the phonological knowledge that enables speakers to distinguish among forms and to deal with the considerable phonetic variation found in the pronunciation of speech segments.

3.1 SEGMENTS IN CONTRAST

All speakers know which segments of their language **contrast**. Segments are said to contrast (or to be distinctive or be in opposition) when their presence alone may distinguish forms with different meanings from each other. The segments [s] and [z] contrast in the words *sip* and *zip*, as do the vowels of *hit*, *hate*, and *hot*.

Minimal Pairs

A basic test for a sound's distinctiveness is called a minimal pair test. A minimal pair consists of two forms with distinct meanings that differ by only one segment found in the same position in each form. The examples [sɪp] *sip* and [zɪp] *zip* given previously form a minimal pair and show that the sounds [s] and [z] contrast in English.

A number of minimal pairs that demonstrate consonant contrasts for English are given in Table 3.1. Remember it is on the basis of sound and not spelling that minimal pairs are established. In displaying contrasts, contrasting words are often placed along the horizontal axis with respect to their place of articulation, reading from left to right (labial, alveolar, and so on), and vertically with respect to manner of articulation, in order to show which places and manners of articulation are exploited by the language in question. The phonetic context in which a sound occurs is called its **environment**. Pairs that show segments in nearly identical environments, such as *azure/assure* or *author/either*, are called near-minimal pairs. They help to establish contrasts where no minimal pairs can be found.

Table 3.1 Contrasts among consonants in English

Stops and affricates (non-continuants)

Labial		Alveolar		Alveopalatal		Velar		Glottal
tap	[p]	pat	[t]	chug	[tʃ]	pick	[k]	
tab	[b]	pad	[d]	jug	[dʒ]	pig	[g]	

Continuants

		Interdental						
fat	[f]	thigh	[θ]	sip	[s]	mesher	[ʃ]	hug [h]
vat	[v]	thy	[ð]	zip	[z]	measure	[ʒ]	

Nasals

sum	[m]			sun	[n]	sung	[ŋ]	

Liquids and glides

wet	[w]					yet	[j] (palatal)	
				leer	[l]			
				rear	[r]			

You may assume that two segments contrast once a minimal pair or a near-minimal pair has been established. It is in fact rare to find minimal pairs for all distinctive sounds in all environments in a language, since the historical evolution of every language has led to some sounds being utilized more frequently than others, or being eliminated from some environments. For example, you will find no minimal pairs involving [h] and [ŋ] in word-initial or word-final position in English, because there are no words that begin with [ŋ] or end in [h]. It is also difficult to find minimal pairs in English that involve the sound [ʒ], which occurs for the most part in words borrowed from French such as *azure* and *mirage*.

Vowel Contrasts in English Contrasts among English vowels can be established with a few sets of examples. For now, we will continue to assume that English vowel-glide sequences like [ij], [uw], [ow], and so on are single vowels. From this perspective, we can say that the vowels [ij] and [ɪ], [ej] and [ɛ], and so on, contrast.

Table 3.2 Vowel contrasts in American English

beet	[bijt]	[ij]
bit	[bɪt]	[ɪ]
bait	[bejt]	[ej]
bet	[bɛt]	[ɛ]
bat	[bæt]	[æ]
cooed	[kʰuwd]	[uw]
could	[kʰʊd]	[ʊ]
code	[kʰowd]	[ow]
caught	[kʰɔt]	[ɔ]
cot	[kʰɑt]	[ɑ]
cut	[kʰʌt]	[ʌ]
lewd	[luwd]	[uw]
loud	[lawd]	[aw]
lied	[lajd]	[aj]
Lloyd	[lɔjd]	[ɔj]

Language-Specific Contrasts

Contrasts are language-specific; sounds that are distinctive in one language will not necessarily be distinctive in another. For example, the difference between the two vowels [ɛ] and [æ] is crucial to English, as we can see from minimal pairs like *Ben* [bɛn] and *ban* [bæn]. But in Turkish, this difference in pronunciation is not distinctive. A Turkish speaker may pronounce the word for 'I' as [bɛn] or [bæn], and it will make no difference to the meaning.

Table 3.3 Language-specific vowel contrasts: English versus Turkish

English		Turkish	
[bɛn]	Ben	[bɛn]	I
[bæn]	ban	[bæn]	I

Conversely, sounds that do not contrast in English, such as long and short vowels, may be distinctive in another language. There are no minimal pairs of the type [hɑt]:[hɑ:t] or [luws]:[lu:ws] in English. But in Serbo-Croatian, the following pairs contrast.

Table 3.4 Serbo-Croatian short/long vowel contrasts

[grad]	'city'	[gra:d]	'hail'
[duga]	'stave'	[du:ga]	'rainbow'

Establishing the contrasting segments in a language is a first step in phonological analysis. But in any language, there are many sounds that never contrast. The following section deals with this major subject of phonological analysis.

3.2 PHONETICALLY CONDITIONED VARIATION: PHONEMES AND ALLOPHONES

Everyday speech contains a great deal of phonetic variation. Some of it is due to variation in articulation that arises from extralinguistic factors such as orthodontic work, fatigue, excitement, gum chewing, and the like. Such variation is not part of the domain of phonology. Much phonetic variation, however, is systematic. It occurs most often among phonetically similar segments and is conditioned by the phonetic context (environment) in which the segments are found. This variation occurs because segments are affected and altered by the phonetic characteristics of neighboring elements or the larger phonological context in which they occur. Every speaker has the ability to factor out this variation in order to focus attention on only the relevant contrasts of the language.

Complementary Distribution

When first learning phonetic transcription, English speakers are often surprised that all the *l*'s they pronounce are not identical. In Table 3.5, the *l*'s in column A are voiced, while those in column B are voiceless (indicated here by a subscript). Most speakers of English are unaware that they routinely produce this difference in articulation, which can be heard clearly when the words in column B are pronounced slowly.

Table 3.5 Voiced and voiceless *l* in English

A		B	
blue	[bluw]	plow	[pl̥aw]
gleam	[glijm]	clap	[kl̥æp]
slip	[slɪp]	clear	[kl̥ijr]
flog	[flɑg]	play	[pl̥ej]
leaf	[lijf]		

The voicelessness of the *l*'s in column B is an automatic consequence of their phonetic environment. Voiced and voiceless *l* vary systematically in that all of the voiceless *l*'s occur predictably after the class of voiceless stops. Since no voiced [l] ever occurs in the same phonetic environment as a voiceless one (and vice versa), we say that the two variants of *l* are in **complementary distribution**.

Table 3.6 Complementary distribution of [l] and [l̥] in English

	[l]	[l̥]
After voiceless stops	no	yes
Elsewhere	yes	no

The term *elsewhere* is used in Table 3.6 to indicate the wider distribution (occurrence in a greater number of different phonetic environments) of voiced [l]. It occurs after voiced stops, voiceless fricatives, and in word-initial position.

In spite of these phonetic differences, native speakers consider the two English *l*'s to be instances of the same segment, since they are phonetically similar, and the differences between them are systematic and predictable. This perception of sameness is supported by the fact that the two *l*'s never contrast in English. There are no minimal pairs like [plej] and [pl̥ej]. We can sum up the relationship that the two *l*'s bear to each other by stating that, for speakers of English, the two *l*'s are phonetically different but in the sound system of English, given their phonetic similarity, predictable distribution, and noncontrastiveness, they are phonologically the same.

Phonemes and Allophones

The ability to group phonetically different sounds together into one class is shared by all speakers of all languages. This phonological knowledge is represented formally on a level of phonological representation that is distinct from phonetic representation. Predictable variants of non-contrastive segments are grouped together into a phonological unit called a **phoneme**. These variants, which are referred to as **allophones**, are usually phonetically similar and are frequently found in complementary distribution. A representation of this relationship is shown in Figure 3.2. The phonemic symbol for the class—

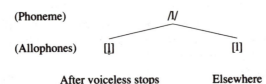

Figure 3.2 The phoneme /l/ and its allophones [l̥] and [l] in English

generally the same symbol as the elsewhere variant—is placed between slashes, and the symbols for allophones are enclosed in phonetic brackets. Allophonic variation is found throughout language. In fact, every speech sound we utter is an allophone of some phoneme and can be grouped together with other phonetically similar sounds into a class that is represented by a phoneme on a phonological level of representation. An important part of phonological analysis deals with discovering the phonemes of languages and accounting for allophonic variation.

Some Other Considerations Before we go on to examine in more detail the patterning of phonemes and allophones, some other considerations in determining their status in a language must be taken into account. So far, we have seen that a minimal pair test is a quick and direct way of establishing that two sounds belong to separate phonemes in a language. If the sounds contrast, they are members of different phonemes. We have also seen that if certain phonetically similar sounds are non-contrastive and in complementary distribution, they may be considered allophones of one phoneme. In some cases, however, we must go beyond these procedures to discover the phonological inventory of a language.

As noted in Section 3.1, certain patterns of distribution prevent some sounds in a language from ever contrasting with each other. In cases like these, we can establish the phonemic status of a sound by default. If the sound cannot be grouped together with any other phonetically similar sounds as an allophone of a phoneme, we may assume it has phonemic status. The following data from English help to illustrate this point.

1. *[ŋowp]   (does not exist)   [howp]   'hope'
    *[ŋejt]   (does not exist)   [hejt]   'hate'

We can see here that [h] and [ŋ] do not contrast in initial position in English. The following examples show that they do not contrast in final position either.

2. [lɔŋ]   'long'   *[lɔh]   (does not exist)
    [sɪŋ]   'sing'   *[sɪh]   (does not exist)
    [klæŋ]   'clang'   *[klæh]   (does not exist)

These lists could be extended for pages, but a minimal pair involving [h] and [ŋ] could never be found in English. It is also the case that [h] and [ŋ] are in complementary distribution. Nevertheless, these facts taken together do not lead us to conclude that [h] and [ŋ] are allophones of one phoneme. Since they are so distinct phonetically, we assume that each one is a member of a separate phoneme.

Minimal pairs or near-minimal pairs help us establish which sounds contrast in a language; phonetic similarity and complementary distribution help us decide which sounds are allophones of one phoneme. But not all examples of variation among sounds can be dealt with through these approaches.

In some cases, phonetically similar sounds are neither in complementary distribution nor are they found to contrast. It is still possible, nevertheless, to determine which phonemes these sounds belong to. A case in point is the variation in English voiceless stops when they are found in word-final position, as in the word *stop*. Sometimes an English speaker releases the articulation of these sounds rather forcefully. Let us represent this with a diacritic sign [!]. At other times, the same speaker may keep the articulators closed for a moment after the articulation; the diacritic [¬] can represent this. Some speakers may even coarticulate a glottal closure (represented here with the symbol for a glottal stop preceding the consonant in question) and produce the word as [stɑʔp]. Thus we can find at least three pronunciations of *stop*: [stɑp!], [stɑp¬], and [stɑʔp]. Since there is no difference in the meaning of these forms and since the final consonants are phonetically similar, we say that these sounds are in **free variation**, and that they are all allophones of the phoneme /p/. The same pattern holds for the other voiceless stops of English.

The Reality of Phonemes

Phonemes are more than convenient symbols for groups of allophones. Phonemes represent a form of linguistic knowledge. Even though we never pronounce a phoneme, only its allophones, there is evidence that speakers mentally store the phonological system of their language in terms of phonemes. It is not surprising, for example, that English spelling uses only one letter for both [l] and [l̥], since there is only one /l/ phoneme. Generally, spelling systems all over the world ignore phonetic variation that is non-distinctive.

Another demonstration of the reality of phonological versus phonetic distinctions lies in speech perception. Speakers of English often have a hard time hearing the phonetic difference between the voiced and voiceless allophones of /l/, because the difference is not contrastive. Allophonic differences are easily ignored in perception, even though they are systematically produced in the appropriate context. Phonologically relevant distinctions, such as that between /l/ and /r/ in the English words *lift* and *rift*, are never missed. Speakers of languages other than English sometimes find it difficult to distinguish between [r] and [l] when learning English if these two sounds are not contrastive in their language. In Japanese, for example, [l] and [r] are allophones of the same phoneme. It is not surprising that speakers of Japanese sometimes have difficulty making this distinction in English. Conversely, English speakers may have a difficult time perceiving and producing the long versus short vowel contrasts of Japanese, since long and short vowels do not contrast in English.

Classes and Generalization in Phonology

Phonological analysis permits us to account for the great amount of phonetic variation in everyday speech. This systematic variation is widely extended within languages. Compare the English data in Table 3.5 with those in Table 3.7.

Table 3.7 Voiced and voiceless allophones of English /r/

A		B	
brew	[bruw]	prow	[pr̥aw]
green	[grijn]	trip	[tr̥ɪp]
drip	[drɪp]	creep	[kr̥ijp]
frog	[frɔg]	pray	[pr̥ej]
shrimp	[ʃrɪmp]		

The data shows that the allophones of English /r/ pattern like those of English /l/. Based on this information, we can state that there is an /r/ phoneme in English with (at least) two allophones—one voiced, the other voiceless. But if we were to stop there, we would overlook an important point. The phonemes /r/ and /l/ belong to the same class of sounds: both are *liquids*. By taking this information into account, we can state a general fact about English.

3. In English, liquids have voiceless allophones after voiceless stops and voiced allophones elsewhere.

A major goal of phonological description is the formulation of the most general statements possible about sound patterns. Reference to classes of segments helps accomplish this. Additional data from English illustrate this point.

Table 3.8 Voiced and voiceless allophones of English glides

A		B	
beauty	[bjuwDij]	putrid	[pj̥uwtr̥ɪd]
Duane	[dwejn]	twin	[tw̥ɪn]
Gwen	[gwɛn]	quick	[kw̥ɪk]
view	[vjuw]	cute	[kj̥uwt]
swim	[swɪm]		
thwack	[θwæk]		

These forms demonstrate that the contrasting glides /j/ and /w/ each pattern like the liquids. We can now extend our general statement even further.

4. In English, liquids and glides have voiceless allophones after voiceless stops, and voiced allophones elsewhere.

Clearly, allophones do not pattern piecemeal, but rather according to their class membership.

Canadian Raising

Another example of allophonic variation is taken from English. In most Canadian and some American dialects, pronunciations like those illustrated in Table 3.9 are common.

Table 3.9 Low and central vowel allophones in Canadian English

[ajz]	eyes	[ʌjs]	ice
[lajz]	lies	[lʌjs]	lice
[tr̥ajd]	tried	[tr̥ʌjt]	trite
[tr̥ajb]	tribe	[tr̥ʌjp]	tripe
[hawz]	(to) house (verb)	[hʌws]	house (noun)
[lawd]	loud	[lʌwt]	lout
[kʰaw]	cow	[skʌwt]	scout
[flaj]	fly	[flʌjt]	flight

In Table 3.9, the vowels [aj] and [ʌj] are in complementary distribution. The [aj] occurs before the class of voiced consonants or in word-final position, and the [ʌj] occurs before the class of voiceless consonants. The two are allophones of a single phoneme /aj/. The same relationship holds between the vowels [aw] and [ʌw], which are allophones of /aw/.

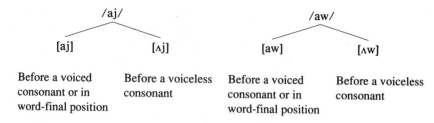

Figure 3.3 Allophones of /aj/ and /aw/ in Canadian English

Again, we see this phonological fact reflected in everyday language use. Most speakers of Canadian English find it difficult to distinguish between these allophones, even when the difference is pointed out to them. This is because the difference is not contrastive. On the other hand, many people who speak varieties of English that do not have the [ʌj] or [ʌw] allophones are very much aware of their presence in Canadian English. To them, a Canadian speaker sounds markedly different, even though they may be confused about the nature of the difference.

> I don't agree he was an American. . . . Where all other English-speaking people pronounce OU as a diphthong, the Canadian . . . makes a separate sound for each letter. The word *about*, for instance, he pronounces as ab-oh-oot.
>
> Philip MacDonald, *The List of Adrian Messenger*

This phenomenon is sometimes referred to as Canadian Raising, since the allophone [ʌj] has a higher vowel component than the elsewhere [aj].

English Vowels and Glides

A final example of predictable variation that refers to classes of segments is again taken from English. Table 3.2 showed contrasts among English vowels. In English, the non-low, tense vowels [ij], [ej], [uw], and [ow], always contain one of the two glides [j] and [w]. Note that the labiovelar glide [w] occurs with the back rounded vowels [u] and [o] and the palatal glide [j] occurs with the front unrounded vowels [i] and [e]. Stated in other words, we can say that the back round vowels predictably co-occur with the back (labiovelar) glide and the front vowels co-occur with the non-back unrounded glide. These facts are summed up in Table 3.10.

Table 3.10 Tense vowel-glide combinations in English

Vowel	Glide (both non-back and unrounded)			Vowel	Glide (both back and rounded)		
i	j	[fijt]	feat	u	w	[buwt]	boot
e	j	[fejt]	fate	o	w	[bowt]	boat

This data shows parallels with the allophonic distribution we have considered so far: certain elements are predictable under certain systematically statable phonetic conditions. Here, however, instead of a number of variants of a phoneme, we have two sounds whose distribution is statable in a specific environment (after non-low tense vowels) once we know they belong to a certain class of sounds (glides). We can thus draw from the data in Table 3.10 the following generalization about the English vowel system.

5. The non-low tense vowels of English are predictably followed by a glide that has the same backness and roundedness as the vowel.

Given the variation in English vowels that we have examined, we are now able to summarize what we have discovered about the English vowel system.

The English Vowel System We have already seen that certain elements of phonemes, such as voicing, vowel height, etc., are not present in phonological representation because they are predictable from the phonetic context in which the allophone is found. Since the presence of the appropriate glides following the class of non-low tense vowels is predictable, they need not be present in the phonological representation of the English vowels either.

These generalizations enable us to represent the contrasts between words like *heat* and *hit*, *late* and *let*, *cooed* and *could* purely as tense versus lax vowel contrasts, and not as contrasts that also involve the presence of glides. We can also represent the vowel found in words like *code* and *snow* without a following glide. Figure 3.4 sums up the differences between phonetic and phonological representations for the vowels of English.

heat	[ij]	/i/				cooed	[uw]	/u/
hit	[ɪ]	/ɪ/				could	[ʊ]	/ʊ/
late	[ej]	/e/	luck	[ʌ]	/ʌ/	code	[ow]	/o/
let	[ɛ]	/ɛ/				boy	[ɔj]	/ɔj/
sat	[æ]	/æ/				caught	[ɔ]	/ɔ/
						cot	[ɑ]	/ɑ/
			tide	[aj]	/aj/			
			loud	[aw]	/aw/			

Figure 3.4 Phonetic and phonological representations of English vowels

Language-Specific Patterns

Although the phenomenon of allophonic variation is universal, the patterning of phonemes and allophones is language-specific. What we discover for one language may not hold true for another.

Language-Specific Variation in Allophonic Nasalization It is not unusual for nasal vowel allophones to occur near a nasal consonant, but, as table 3.11

Table 3.11 Nasal vowels in Scots Gaelic

[mõːr]	'big'
[nĩ]	'cattle'
[nẽːl]	'cloud'
[mũ]	'about'
[rũːn]	'secret'

shows, the patterning may vary from language to language. Scots Gaelic has oral and nasal vowel allophones. Here we can state the following.

6. Vowels are nasal in Scots Gaelic when preceded or followed by a nasal consonant.

Malay, a language spoken in Malaysia and Singapore, presents another variation on the theme of nasal allophones.

Table 3.12 Nasalization in Malay

[mẽw̃ãh]	'luxurious'
[mãjãŋ]	'stalk'
[mãrah]	'scold'
[nãɛ̃ʔ]	'ascend'
[mɔ̃laraŋ]	'forbid'
[mãkan]	'eat'
[rumãh]	'house'
[kəreta]	'car'

Here, all vowels and glides following a nasal are predictably nasalized until an obstruent, liquid, or glottal ([h], [ʔ]) is reached. For Malay the generalization is as follows.

7. In Malay, all vowels and glides following a nasal consonant and not separated from it by a nonnasal consonant are nasalized.

Language-Specific Variation in Allophonic Distribution As was shown in Section 3.1, a phonemic contrast in one language may not prove to be a phonemic contrast in another. This means that the relationship of phonemes to allophones may vary. A comparison of the contrasts among stops in English and Khmer (Cambodian) illustrates this point. In both languages, aspirated and unaspirated phones can be heard.

Table 3.13 Stop phones in English and Khmer

English		Khmer	
[p]	[pʰ]	[p]	[pʰ]
[t]	[tʰ]	[t]	[tʰ]
[k]	[kʰ]	[k]	[kʰ]

In English, aspirated and unaspirated stops are allophonic; there are no contrasting forms like [pɪk] and [pʰɪk]. In Khmer, unaspirated and aspirated voiceless stops contrast.

Table 3.14 Khmer contrastive voiceless stops

[pɔ:ŋ]	'to wish'	[pʰɔ:ŋ]	'also'
[tɔp]	'to support'	[tʰɔp]	'be suffocated'
[kat]	'to cut'	[kʰat]	'to polish'

The phonological contrasts of the two languages are different, even though the phones are not.

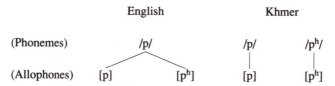

Figure 3.5 English and Khmer voiceless bilabial stop phonemes and allophones

These distributions are the same for the other voiceless stops in both languages. (Section 3.5 deals with the distribution of the English voiceless stop allophones, the aspirated stops in particular.)

3.3 PHONETIC AND PHONEMIC TRANSCRIPTION

Having seen how nondistinctive properties of segments are factored out by phonological analysis, we can now compare the type of transcription used for segmental phonological representation with phonetic transcription. The following examples show this difference for the classes of sounds in English that we have examined so far.

Table 3.15 Phonetic and phonemic transcription

Phonetic transcription	Phonemic transcription	Word	Predictable property(s) not represented in phonemic transcription
[pl̥aw]	/plaw/	plow	voicelessness of liquid
[kr̥ijp]	/krip/	creep	voicelessness of liquid; glide after non-low tense vowel
[kwɪk]	/kwɪk/	quick	voicelessness of glide
[lejt]	/let/	late	glide after non-low tense vowel
[lɛt]	/lɛt/	let	—
[tʰajd]	/tajd/	tied	aspiration

The contrast between phonetic and phonemic representation is even more striking for the Malay forms given earlier, as shown in Table 3.16.

Table 3.16 Phonetic and phonemic transcription of Malay nasal vowels

Phonetic transcription	Phonemic transcription	Word	Predictable property(s) not represented in phonemic transcription
[mẽw̃ãh]	/mewah/	'luxurious'	nasalization
[mãj̃ãn]	/majan/	'stalk'	nasalization
[nãɛ̃ʔ]	/naɛʔ/	'ascend'	nasalization

Here, nasalization on all vowel and glide segments is predictable and is therefore omitted from the phonological representation.

Although the phonetic and phonemic transcription up to this point has employed segments, segmental notation is itself a kind of shorthand, since segments are ultimately composed of features. The next section takes up this aspect of phonology.

3.4 FEATURES

Current linguistic practice does not assume that segments are the ultimate units of phonological structure. Instead, linguists view segments as composed of smaller elements. This section deals with **features**—the units of phonological structure that make up segments.

Why We Use Features

There are a number of reasons why linguists have settled on features as the most basic phonological unit.

Features as Independent and Coordinated Elements We have already seen in Chapter 1 that speech is produced by a number of coordinated articulatory activities such as voicing, tongue position, lip rounding, and so on. Features such as [voice], [high], [round] (features are written in square brackets) directly reflect this activity, in that each feature is rooted in an independently controllable aspect of speech production. The representation of a segment by features captures this coordinated activity by placing features in an array called a **matrix**. Each feature or group of features defines a specific property of the segment. This representation is in binary terms: [+] means that a feature is present, and [−] means that it is absent. Figure 3.6 shows a feature matrix for the English vowel [ɑ].

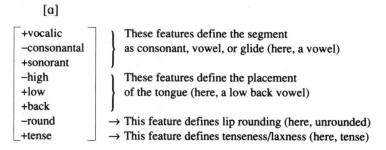

Figure 3.6   Feature matrix for the English vowel /ɑ/

Features and Natural Classes   A second reason for viewing segments as composed of features is that each feature may represent a phonologically relevant characteristic of segments. To understand what is meant by this, we first examine how features enable us to distinguish among classes of sounds with many members. For example, the set of sounds /p/, /t/, /tʃ/, and /s/ can be readily distinguished from the set /b/, /d/, /dʒ/, and /z/ by the feature [voice] alone. In phonological terms, features express **natural classes**, which are classes of sounds that share a feature or features, such as voiceless stops, glides, high vowels, nasal consonants, and so on. Any natural class requires fewer features to define it than to define any one of its members. In Table 3.17, for example, fewer features are needed to define the class of English front vowels than to define the vowel /æ/.

Table 3.17   Two natural classes: front and back vowels in English

⎡− consonantal⎤ ⎪+ vocalic⎪ ⎪+ sonorant⎪ ⎣− back⎦	⎡− consonantal⎤ ⎪+ vocalic⎪ ⎪+ sonorant⎪ ⎣+ back⎦	⎡− consonantal⎤ ⎪+ vocalic⎪ ⎪+ sonorant⎪ ⎪− back⎪ ⎪− high⎪ ⎪+ low⎪ ⎣− round⎦
/i/	/u/	
/ɪ/	/ʊ/	
/e/	/o/	
/ɛ/	/ʌ/	
/æ/	/ɑ/	/æ/

Because features define natural classes, we can now see their relevance to phonological analysis. It is not individual phonemes such as /p/, /b/, /k/, and /g/ that contrast in English; rather, the entire class of voiced stops contrasts with the class of voiceless stops. It is the feature [voice] that is contrastive, not the individual segments, since we can define the contrast between each pair of segments with otherwise identical articulations as residing in the feature [voice]. Since this single feature is employed in all voiced-voiceless contrasts, we say that [voice] is a **distinctive feature** of English.

Other features provide for other contrasts. For example, we can express the contrast between /t/ and /s/ in English with the feature [continuant]. Both /t/ and /s/ are voiceless and have an alveolar point of articulation. (The fact that the tongue tip is used in the production of one sound and the tongue blade is used in the other is not relevant to this phonological distinction in English, and can therefore be ignored.) By viewing the relevant distinctive feature as [continuant], we can use the same feature to distinguish between /p/ and /f/, /b/ and /v/, and /d/ and /z/.

Table 3.18 Stop-fricative contrasts as a feature

p [−continuant]	f [+continuant]
b	v
t	s
d	z

By systematically examining the phonemic contrasts of a language, we can extract the phonologically distinctive features and state the phonemic inventory in terms of these irreducible linguistic elements.

Finally, certain features define classes of sounds that are not always reflected in traditional descriptive terminology but that are also relevant to phonological patterning. The feature [coronal], for example, refers to the class of sounds made with the tongue tip or blade raised. It turns out that just this feature is required to state the constraint on the selection of consonant sequences in coda position in English presented in Chapter 1: when a vowel is tense and followed by two consonants (*pint*), or when a vowel is lax and followed by three consonants (*next*), the final consonant must always be [+coronal] (t, d, s, z, θ, ð, ʃ, ʒ, tʃ, or dʒ). Features are thus more than phonetic descriptions in a different guise.

Features, Processes, and Allophonic Variation Reference to features also enables us to understand the nature of allophonic variation more exactly. Viewed from the perspective of features, allophonic variation is not simply the substitution of one sound for another, but rather the environmentally conditioned change or specification of a feature or features. Processes like those presented in Chapter 2 are the primary factors in the changing of features. Liquid-glide devoicing in English, for example, is the change of the value of the feature [voice] from [+voice] to [−voice] after voiceless consonants. Vowel nasalization in Malay is the change of the value of the nasal feature from [−nasal] to [+nasal] under just the conditions stated in *7*.

Since features are considered to be the ultimate building blocks of phonology, linguists have attempted to state all possible phonological facts about language with the fewest number of features possible. Only a limited number of features—currently around twenty-four—are used. Features thus constitute an important part of a theory of what is possible (and what is not possible) in the phonological behavior of human beings.

The next section presents the features of English. Tables 3.19 and 3.20 present the consonant and vowel segments of English along with the features needed to represent them in matrix form. It is a good idea to look these figures over before going on to read about individual features.

Table 3.19 Feature matrix for English consonants

		p	pʰ	b	t	tʰ	d	k	kʰ	g	f	v	s	z	θ	ð	ʃ	ʒ	tʃ	dʒ	m	n	ŋ	l	r	j	w	ʍ	h	ʔ
Major class features	[consonantal]	+	+	+	+	+	+	+	+	+	+	+	+	+	+	+	+	+	+	+	+	+	+	+	+	−	−	−	−	−
	[sonorant]	−	−	−	−	−	−	−	−	−	−	−	−	−	−	−	−	−	−	−	+	+	+	+	+	+	+	+	−	−
	[vocalic]	−	−	−	−	−	−	−	−	−	−	−	−	−	−	−	−	−	−	−	−	−	−	−	−	−	−	−	−	−
Laryngeal features	[voice]	−	−	+	−	−	+	−	−	+	−	+	−	+	−	+	−	+	−	+	+	+	+	+	+	+	+	−	−	−
	[CG]	−	−	−	−	−	−	−	−	−	−	−	−	−	−	−	−	−	−	−	−	−	−	−	−	−	−	−	−	+
	[SG]	−	+	−	−	+	−	−	+	−	−	−	−	−	−	−	−	−	−	−	−	−	−	−	−	−	−	−	+	−
Place features	[labial]	+	+	+	−	−	−	−	−	−	+	+	−	−	−	−	−	−	−	−	+	−	−	−	−	−	+	+	−	−
	[round]	−	−	−	−	−	−	−	−	−	−	−	−	−	−	−	−	−	−	−	−	−	−	−	−	−	+	+	−	−
	[coronal]	−	−	−	+	+	+	−	−	−	−	−	+	+	+	+	+	+	+	+	−	+	−	+	+	−	−	−	−	−
	[anterior]	−	−	−	+	+	+	−	−	−	−	−	+	+	+	+	−	−	−	−	−	+	−	+	+	−	−	−	−	−
	[strident]	−	−	−	−	−	−	−	−	−	+	+	+	+	−	−	+	+	+	+	−	−	−	−	−	−	−	−	−	−
Dorsal features	[high]	−	−	−	−	−	−	+	+	+	−	−	−	−	−	−	−	−	−	−	−	−	+	−	−	+	+	+	−	−
	[back]	−	−	−	−	−	−	+	+	+	−	−	−	−	−	−	−	−	−	−	−	−	+	−	−	−	+	+	−	−
Manner features	[nasal]	−	−	−	−	−	−	−	−	−	−	−	−	−	−	−	−	−	−	−	+	+	+	−	−	−	−	−	−	−
	[continuant]	−	−	−	−	−	−	−	−	−	+	+	+	+	+	+	+	+	−	−	−	−	−	+	+	+	+	+	+	−
	[lateral]	−	−	−	−	−	−	−	−	−	−	−	−	−	−	−	−	−	−	−	−	−	−	+	−	−	−	−	−	−
	[delayed release]	−	−	−	−	−	−	−	−	−	−	−	−	−	−	−	−	−	+	+	−	−	−	−	−	−	−	−	−	−

Table 3.20 Feature Matrix for English Vowels

		i	ɪ	e	ɛ	æ	ʌ	ə	ɑ	u	ʊ	o	ɔ
Major class features	[consonantal]	−	−	−	−	−	−	−	−	−	−	−	−
	[sonorant]	+	+	+	+	+	+	+	+	+	+	+	+
	[vocalic]	+	+	+	+	+	+	+	+	+	+	+	+
Laryngeal features	[voice]	+	+	+	+	+	+	+	+	+	+	+	+
Place features	[round]	−	−	−	−	−	−	−	−	+	+	+	+
Dorsal features	[high]	+	+	−	−	−	−	−	−	+	+	−	−
	[back]	−	−	−	−	−	+	+	+	+	+	+	+
	[low]	−	−	−	−	+	−	−	+	−	−	−	−
	[tense]	+	−	+	−	−	−	−	+	+	−	+	−
	[reduced]	−	−	−	−	−	−	+	−	−	−	−	−
Manner feature	[continuant]	+	+	+	+	+	+	+	+	+	+	+	+

The Features of English

Most features have labels that reflect traditional articulatory terms such as [voice], [consonantal], and [nasal]. These features require little further description. A few features have less familiar labels, such as [coronal] and [anterior]. From this point on, features will be used to describe classes of sounds. At the same time, we will continue throughout the book to use time-honored terms such as *consonant*, *glide*, and *obstruent* (a fricative, affricate, or nonnasal stop) in phonetic description. The traditional terminology will be maintained because it is still widely used in phonetic description.

Features are not ranged haphazardly in a matrix. Rather, they are organized into groups that reflect natural classes. The following headings indicate what these classes are and how the features represent them.

Major Class Features These features represent the classes consonant, obstruent, nasal, liquid, glide, and vowel.

[consonantal] Produced with a major obstruction in the oral cavity. All nonsonorant consonants are [+ consonantal]. *Examples*: [p] [b] [s] [z] [tʃ] [ʒ].

[vocalic] Vowels and syllabic liquids. *Examples*: [i] [ɑ] [l̩] [r̩].

[sonorant] All and only the "singables": vowels, glides, liquids, and nasals (even when they are voiceless).

Table 3.21 Use of major class features

	Obstruents	Vowels	Glides	Liquids	Nasals
[consonantal]	+	−	−	+	+
[vocalic]	−	+	−	−	−
[sonorant]	−	+	+	+	+
Examples:	p b z θ	i ɑ	j w	l r	m n

Laryngeal Features These features represent laryngeal states.

[voice] All voiced sounds are [+ voice]; all voiceless sounds are [− voice].

[spread glottis] ([SG]) This feature distinguishes unaspirated from aspirated consonants. Aspirated consonants are [+SG].

[constricted glottis] ([CG]) Made with the glottis closed. In English, only the glottal stop [ʔ] is [+CG].

Place Features These features represent place of articulation.

[labial] Any sound articulated with one or both lips is [+labial]. In English: [p] [b] [f] [v] [w]. See [round].

[round] Rounded vowels and the rounded labiovelar glide [w]. Sounds that are [+round] are made by protruding the lips; therefore, all [+round] sounds are also [+labial]. Sounds that are [+labial], however, are not necessarily [+round], since sounds like [p] or [f] can be produced without necessarily rounding the lips. The labiovelar glide [w] is both [+labial] and [+round].

[coronal] Any sound articulated with the tongue tip or blade raised is [+coronal]. *Examples*: [t] [d] [θ] [ð] [s] [z] [tʃ] [dʒ] [ʃ] [ʒ] [n] [l] [r].

[anterior] Any sound articulated in front of the alveopalatal region is considered to be [+anterior]. *Examples*: [p] [b] [t] [d] [s] [z] [θ] [ð].

[strident] The 'noisy' fricatives and affricates only. In English, [s], [z], [ʃ], [ʒ], [tʃ], and [dʒ] are [+strident].

Table 3.22 Use of place of articulation features

	Labials	Dentals/ alveolars	Alveopalatals	Palatals/ velars
[anterior]	+	+	−	−
[coronal]	−	+	+	−
Examples:	p b m	t d ð θ s z n l r	ʃ ʒ tʃ dʒ	k g ŋ

Dorsal Features These features represent placement of the body of the tongue.

[high] Sounds produced with the tongue body raised are considered [+high]. This applies to both vowels and consonants. *Examples*: [ij] [uw] [j] [k] [g].

[low] Vowels made with the tongue body distinctly lowered from a central position in the oral cavity are [+low]. *Examples*: [æ] [ɑ]; [h] and [ʔ] are *not* [+low] since they are not made in the oral cavity.

[back] Any sound articulated behind the palatal region in the oral cavity. *Examples*: [uw] [ow] [ɑ] [k] [g].

[tense] Expresses the tense-lax distinctions among vowels.

[reduced] Only the schwa ([ə]) is [+reduced].

Manner Features These features represent manner of articulation.

[nasal] Any sound made with the velum lowered is [+nasal].

[continuant] Free or nearly free airflow through the oral cavity: vowels, fricatives, glides, and liquids. *Examples*: [ɛ] [j] [r].

[lateral] All and only varieties of *l* are [+ lateral].

[delayed release] All and only affricate consonants such as [tʃ] and [dʒ] are [+ delayed release].

Feature notation does not provide a convenient way to distinguish the diphthongs [aj], [aw], and [oj] from the other vowels. These diphthongs may be treated as vowel-glide sequences when using features.

While feature representation may at first look more complex and clumsy than strictly segmental representation, it is in the long run very advantageous. Instead of listing individual sets of contrastive phonemes, we express contrasts at the level of the feature, as in English, where we can say that the feature [voice] is contrastive. Much allophonic variation can now be represented as the addition, loss, or change of a few features. The influence of the conditioning environment is also made more obvious with this type of representation, as shown in Section 3.7.

3.5 ABOVE THE SEGMENT: SYLLABLES

We have established a segmental unit of phonological analysis called the phoneme, which is composed of phonological elements called features. The examples of allophonic variation used thus far all result from conditioning by neighboring segments. The examples of allophonic variation in this section depend on conditioning that involves another level of phonological representation, the **syllable**.

Defining the Syllable

The syllable is composed of a nucleus (usually a vowel) and its associated non-syllabic segments. Native speakers of a language demonstrate their awareness of this unit of phonological structure whenever they count syllables in a word. No English speaker would hesitate to say that the word *accident* has three syllables, and most speakers would feel confident that it could be broken up into the syllables /æk . sə . dənt/ (the '.' marks syllable divisions informally). As we will see later on in this chapter, speakers also demonstrate knowledge that syllables have internal structure as well. The organization of a syllable is shown in Figure 3.7 with the monosyllabic English word *sprint*.

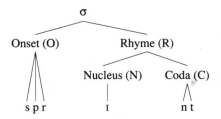

Figure 3.7 Internal structure of a syllable

A complete description of the internal structure of a syllable requires four subsyllabic units. The **nucleus** (abbreviated **N**) is the syllable's only obligatory member; it is a vocalic segment that forms the core of a syllable. The **coda** (**C**) consists of those segments that follow the nucleus in the same syllable. The **rhyme** (**R**) is made up of the nucleus and coda. The **onset** (**O**) is made up of those segments that precede the rhyme in the same syllable.

We assume the existence of subsyllabic units for a number of reasons. One of them is the fact that speakers do not syllabify words in random or variable ways. The word *extreme* /ɛkstrim/ would never be syllabified as /ɛ . kstrim/. Instead, syllables comply with certain constraints that prohibit them (in English) from beginning with a sequence like *kstr* and so result in the syllabification /ɛk . strim/.

Table 3.23 Some syllable-initial sequences in English

/ə . plɔd/	applaud
/di . klajn/	decline
/ɛk . splen/	explain
/ɪm . prə . vajz/	improvise

Constraints can be stated for each of the terminal subsyllabic units O, N, and C. To illustrate this, we turn to the constraints that govern the phonological shape of onsets in English.

Onset Constraints and Phonotactics

Native speakers of any language intuitively know that certain words that come from other languages sound unusual. They often adjust the segment sequences of these words to conform with the pronunciation requirements of their own language. These speaker intuitions are based on a tacit knowledge of the permissible syllable structures of the speaker's own language. For example, English-speaking students learning Russian have difficulty pronouncing a word like *vprog* [fprɔk] 'value, good', since the sequence [fpr] is never found in English onsets. Since speakers typically adjust an impermissible sequence by altering it to a permissible one, many English speakers would pronounce the Russian word [fprɔk] as [fəprɔk], or even delete the initial /f/ and say [prɔk] in order to adjust the impermissible sequence *fpr* to a permissible English onset. **Phonotactics**, the set of constraints on how sequences of segments pattern, forms part of a speaker's knowledge of the phonology of his or her language.

Some English Onsets The following table contains examples of the possible syllable-initial consonant sequences of English that contain a voiceless stop consonant. These sequences are all illustrated in word-initial position to make them easier to pick out. (Stress marking and phonetic details such as liquid-glide devoicing that are not relevant to the present discussion are omitted here.)

Table 3.24 Initial consonant clusters in English containing a voiceless stop

Labial + sonorant		Coronal + sonorant		Velar + sonorant	
[pl]	please	[tl]	—	[kl]	clean
[pr]	proud	[tr]	trade	[kr]	cream
[pw]	—	[tw]	twin	[kw]	queen
[pj]	pure	[tj]	tune (Southern)	[kj]	cute
[spl]	splat	[stl]	—	[skl]	sclerosis
[spr]	spring	[str]	strip	[skr]	scrap
[spw]	—	[stw]	—	[skw]	squeak
[spj]	spew	[stj]	stew (Southern)	[skj]	skewer

The foregoing examples show that the first segment of a word-initial three-consonant cluster in English is always *s*; the second consonant in the series is always a voiceless stop, and the third is either a liquid or a glide. These sound patterns can be formally represented as follows:

$$\sigma \quad [\; s \quad \begin{Bmatrix} p \\ t \\ k \end{Bmatrix} \quad \begin{Bmatrix} (l) \\ r \\ (w) \\ j \end{Bmatrix} \quad \text{Nucleus}$$

Figure 3.8 Possible three-consonant onset clusters in English

In this formalization, σ indicates the boundary of a syllable, and the curly braces designate 'either/or'. The sounds in parentheses are not found in all combinations. Although there are twenty-four possible two- and three-consonant syllable-initial sequences in English containing a voiceless stop, not all of these combinations are exploited in the vocabulary of the language.

Accidental and Systematic Gaps

Some gaps in the inventory of possible English words include *snool*, *splick*, *sklop*, *flin*, *trob*, and *krid*, although none of these forms violates any constraints on onset combinations found in English. Gaps in a language's inventory of forms that correspond to nonoccurring but possible forms are called **accidental gaps**. Occasionally, an accidental gap will be filled in by the invention of a new word. The word *Kodak* is one such invented word. Borrowed words such as *perestroika* (from Russian), *taco* (from Spanish), and *Zen* (from Japanese) are readily accepted by English speakers as long as their syllable structures conform to the phonotactic patterns of the language.

Table 3.24 has shown which syllable-initial consonant clusters involving voiceless stops are permissible in English. Gaps in the occurring syllable structures of a language that result from the exclusion of certain sequences are called **systematic gaps**. Certain onset sequences like /bz/, /pt/, and /fp/ are systematic gaps in the pattern of English and are outright unacceptable to English speakers. Such sequences will ordinarily be adjusted phonologically when they are pronounced in spontaneous speech. This can be seen in the case of borrowings from other languages into English. Many Greek words beginning with /ps/ and /pt/ have been absorbed into English, as the spellings of *psychology*, *psoriasis*, and *pterodactyl* attest. In all of them, the impermissible onset clusters */ps/ and */pt/ have been reduced to /s/ or /t/ in onsets. However, when these same forms occur word-internally, where their syllabification is different, the 'lost' segments may resurface. For example, the *pter* of *pterodactyl* means 'wing'; both consonants are heard in the word *helicopter*, where English syllabification has resulted in the structure *heli.cop.ter*.

There are many other words that violate phonotactic conditions and that nonetheless do commonly appear in spoken English, such as *pueblo* [pweblow], *Tlingit* [tl̩ŋɪt], and Elmer Fudd's *stweet* [stwijt] 'street' (which results from a persistent replacement of /r/ by /w/). The Southern pronunciation of 'Tuesday' as [tjuwzdej] is also not difficult for other American speakers. This appears to be the case because these sequences are not absolutely excluded from the onset phonotactics of English as are such sequences as */ps/ and */bz/. As Figure 3.8 shows, onsets like */pw/ and */stw/ are possibilities that are not exploited due to language-specific restrictions on the sequencing of certain features. For example, a labiovelar glide does not usually occur in an onset after a labial consonant, and an alveolar stop such as /t/ is not followed by /l/; in both cases there is a restriction (in English) on stop-sonorant onset sequences with the same place of articulation. Such restrictions are nonetheless relatively easy to overcome in pronunciation.

Language-Specific Phonotactics It is important to emphasize that certain aspects of the particular constraints discussed in the previous section are universal (form part of human linguistic ability), whereas others are language-specific. An onset like /pl/ is found in many languages besides English (for example, in Russian, Thai, and French), while an onset sequence like /lp/ is rarely if ever found. We may therefore say that no restrictions against an onset like /pl/ appear to exist as part of human linguistic capacity, while the virtual nonexistence of onsets like */lp/ suggest that something in their articulatory makeup disqualifies them from occurring in language. Language-specific constraints, on the other hand, hold true for individual languages such as English, and they may or may not be found in other languages. Each language has its own set of restrictions on the phonological shapes of its syllable constituents. Speakers of Russian, for example, are quite accustomed to pronouncing onset sequences such as /pt/, /ps/, and /fsl/, which are not found in English.

Table 3.25 Some onset sequences in Russian

[psa]	'dog's'
[fslux]	'aloud'
[pt^{j}itsə]	'bird'

Phonotactic constraints represent one kind of phonological knowledge. You might wonder what prevents English words like *extreme*, *applaud*, *decline*, *explain*, and *improvise* from being syllabified as /ɛks.trim/, /əp.lɔd/, /dik.lajn/, /ɛks.plen/, and ɪmp.rəv.ajz/, since these divisions do not violate any phonotactic constraints either. The next section answers this question by providing a procedure for establishing the association of consonants and vowels in syllables.

Setting Up Syllables (advanced)

Each language defines its own syllable structure, although there are universal principles that interact with language-specific factors. The process for setting up syllables in a given language involves the following steps.

Step a Since the syllabic nucleus is the only obligatory constituent of a syllable, it is constructed first. Each vowel segment in a word makes up a syllabic nucleus. To represent this, link a vowel to an N above it by drawing an association line. Above each nucleus symbol, place an R (for rhyme), which is filled out in step c below. Above each R, place a σ symbol; link all with association lines.

Figure 3.9

Step b Onsets before codas: the longest sequence of consonants to the left of each nucleus that does not violate the phonotactic constraints of the language in question is called the **onset** of the syllable. Link these consonants to an O and join it to the same syllable as the vowel to the right. Note that there is no onset in the first syllable of *extreme*.

Figure 3.10

Step c Any remaining consonants to the right of each nucleus form the **coda** and are linked to a C above them. This C is associated with the syllable nucleus to its left in the rhyme. A syllable with a coda is called a **closed syllable**.

Figure 3.11

Step d Syllables that make up a single form (usually a word) branch out from the representation *Wd* (this step is frequently omitted from phonological representations to save space; the complete representation is understood even when *Wd* is not written out).

Figure 3.12

Given this procedure, it is clear why words such as *applaud* and *explain* in Table 3.23 are syllabified the way they are. The permissible consonant clusters make up the onset of the second syllable, and not the coda of the first syllable.

Some Further Syllabification This procedure is used to syllabify forms in any language. An example from Turkish demonstrates in more detail how this universal syllabification procedure works. Turkish has different syllable structure constraints than English. As in English, onsets are optional in Turkish, but when present, may consist of no more than one segment—a constraint not found in English. A nucleus may consist of a long vowel (which is equivalent to two short vowels in length) or a short vowel. Codas can be no more than two segments long, and are largely limited to the following combinations: fricative-stop (for example, -ft$_o$), or sonorant-obstruent (for example, -rp$_o$).

The following words can be syllabified in the steps given above (steps c and d have been collapsed here). Note how the procedure leads to a different syllabification of the word *cift* 'plow' in steps b and c of the examples.

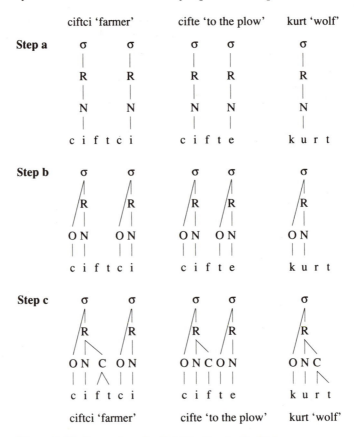

Figure 3.13 Examples of syllabification in Turkish

In these examples, the *t* of *ciftci* 'farmer' is assigned to the coda of the first syllable, since the following *c* has already taken up the sole consonant position permitted in a Turkish onset. However, the *t* of *cifte* 'to the plow' is assigned to the onset of the second syllable since it is not followed by another consonant.

Because of language-specific differences in phonotactic constraints, applying the same procedure to syllabify English words yields different syllabifications. The following figure demonstrates the syllabification of the English words *slim*, *decline*, and *scrap*.

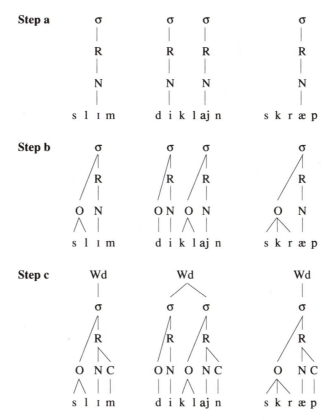

Figure 3.14 Examples of syllabification in English

With this method in mind, we can now consider the relevance of syllables to phonological description.

Syllabic Phonology

One reason that syllables are treated as units of phonological structure is because they are relevant to stating generalizations about the distribution of allophonic features. The next sections provide examples of the role of syllables in phonological analysis.

Aspiration in English As Table 3.26 shows, the voiceless stops of English each have an aspirated and an unaspirated allophone.

Table 3.26 English aspiration

A		B		C	
[pʰǽn]	pan	[spǽn]	span	[slǽp]	slap
[pʰéjn]	pain	[spéjn]	Spain	[slát]	slot
[pʰówk]	poke	[spowk]	spoke	[blák]	block
[tʰówn]	tone	[stówn]	stone		
[kʰín]	kin	[skín]	skin		
[pʰərspájr]	perspire	[splǽt]	splat		
[tʰəméjDow]	tomato	[ʌpsét]	upset		
[kʰənúw]	canoe				
[əpʰán]	upon				
[ətʰǽk]	attack				
[tʰəkʰíjlə]	tequila				

The distribution of the feature [aspiration] can be stated generally by referring to syllable structure.

Table 3.27 Distribution of aspirated stops in English

Aspirated stops	Unaspirated stops
• syllable-initially	Elsewhere: • in a syllable onset preceded by *s* (whether another C follows or not) • before a consonant

The phonemic representations of the three English stops are unaspirated, since aspiration is a predictable feature. The environments where aspiration occurs can be stated very generally by referring to syllable structure.

> *8.* English voiceless stops are aspirated syllable-initially.

This statement accounts for all the data in column A of Table 3.26, where voiceless stops appear syllable-initially. No aspiration is found in the forms in columns B and C since the voiceless stops appear either as the second member of the syllable onset (in *span, Spain, spoke, stone,* and *skin*), or in a coda, as in *upset*.

Ambisyllabicity (advanced) Some English words, such as *upper, happy,* and *walking,* do not show aspiration where it is expected, given that the syllabification procedure results in the following: /ʌ . pər/, /hæ . pi/, and /wɔ . kɪŋ/. This fact is accounted for by assuming that the voiceless stops in these forms are simultaneously in both syllables, a phenomenon known as **ambisyllabicity**. These consonants are all found preceded by a stressed syllable; in contrast, the aspirated stops in words like *upon* [ʌpʰán] and *attack* [ətʰǽk] (Table 3.26, column A) show aspiration, but are all found as the onset of a stressed syllable. In words with ambisyllabic voiceless stops, it is assumed that the stress attracts the voiceless stop into the preceding syllable. This requires us to assume further that a word is resyllabified after stress has applied to the appropriate syllable. Figure 3.15 shows this process in stages. Figure 3.15a shows initial syllabification of the word *happy*; Figure 3.15b shows stress placement on the first syllable; in Figure 3.15c, the dotted line shows the ambisyllabicity of the voiceless stop that is caused by the stress. The now ambisyllabic consonant cannot undergo aspiration since it is (at least partly) in the preceding syllable.

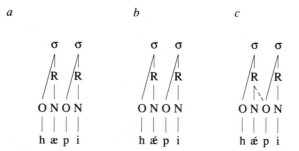

Figure 3.15 Ambisyllabicity in English: *a.* initial syllabification; *b.* stress; *c.* resyllabification with ambisyllabic consonant

Ambisyllabicity is not as arbitrary as it might appear at first. Its presence not only accounts for the lack of aspiration in these forms, but also helps explain why the first syllables of *upper*, *happy*, and *kicking* might otherwise appear to end in stressed lax vowels, a distribution that is otherwise not frequent in English (except in expressive/onomatopoeic words like *baa* /bæ/). The simultaneous presence of the voiceless stop in the coda of the first syllable and the onset of the second means not only that we do not expect aspiration, but also that the first syllable is closed and so the presence of a lax vowel is normal.

Phonetic Length in English Vowels English offers a second example of the phonological relevance of syllables. Phonetic length is predictable in English vowels, as the next examples show.

Table 3.28 Phonetic length in English

A		B	
bad	[bæ:d]	bat	[bæt]
Abe	[e:jb]	ape	[ejp]
phase	[fe:jz]	face	[fejs]
leave	[li:jv]	leaf	[lijf]
tag	[tʰæ:g]	tack	[tʰæk]
brogue	[bro:wg]	broke	[browk]
		tame	[tʰẽjm]
		meal	[mijl]
		soar	[sɔr]
		show	[ʃow]

English vowels are shorter before voiceless consonants, before sonorant consonants, and in word-final position; they are longer before voiced non-sonorant consonants. As the next examples show, this distribution is determined by syllable structure. The first-syllable vowels all precede voiced, non-sonorant consonants, but they are short since the voiced consonant is in the following syllable.

Table 3.29 Short vowels before voiced consonants in English

obey	[ow . bej]	/obe/
redo	[rij . duw]	/ridu/
regard	[rij . gɑrd]	/rigɑrd/
ogre	[ow . gr̩]	/ogr̩/

In order for an English vowel to be long, it must be followed by a voiced consonant in the same syllable. The following generalization can now be made.

> *9.* English vowels are long when followed by a voiced obstruent in the same syllable.

As the analyses of the distribution of aspiration and vowel length in English have shown, the use of syllabic representations in phonology permits us in some cases to make more general statements about allophonic patterns in language than if we use only statements that do not make reference to syllable structure.

In the next section we turn our attention to the way in which statements of phonological patterning and distribution are formalized.

3.6 DERIVATIONS AND RULE ORDERING

At this point, we have established the existence of three hierarchically related levels of phonological structure. In this model, phonological elements from a lower level are organized and grouped into higher-level elements. Thus, *features* are grouped into (segmental) *phonemes*, which in turn are organized into *syllables*. We have also seen how general statements that refer to natural classes and syllable structure account for the presence of non-contrastive elements. Current linguistics also provides a way to link phonological and phonetic representations in a formal manner.

The relationship between phonological and phonetic representation is formalized by assuming that the unpredictable features of the phonemic segment are basic or **underlying**. For our purposes, the terms *phonemic* and *underlying* mean the same thing. Phonetic representations are then **derived** by the use of **phonological rules**. (For now, we will refer to general statements such as *7*, *8*, and *9* as rules; in Section 3.7 we will see how these statements are formalized.) Underlying and derived representations are given in segmental transcription; nevertheless, keep in mind that all segments are understood to be composed of features.

Derivations

Phonetic forms are derived by setting up the underlying representation (also called an *underlying form*) and then allowing the rule or rules in question to operate in those contexts where they are relevant.

The derivation of three phonetic representations (PRs) from underlying representations (URs) is presented in Figure 3.16. Here, the underlying representation is on the top line (the cross hatch [#] symbolizes a word boundary); reading downward, each rule applies in sequence, and the underlying representation is adjusted as required. Where a rule fails to apply, the form remains unchanged; this information is conveyed by dashes. The resulting output then serves as the input to the following rule. Finally, when all rules relevant to the derivation in question have applied, a phonetic representation is provided. The two rules presented in the following example are aspiration and vowel lengthening (see Section 3.5).

UR	#slæp#	slap	#tæp#	tap	#pæd#	pad
Aspiration	—		#tʰæp#		#pʰæd#	
V-length	—		—		#pʰæ:d#	
PR	[slæp]		[tʰæp]		[pʰæ:d]	

Figure 3.16 The phonological derivation of three English words

In this example, two rules are applied (since the words being derived are all monosyllabic, the syllable boundaries are equivalent to word boundaries and so are not indicated here). The first accounts for aspiration. Since the initial consonant of the URs #tæp# and #pæd# are voiceless stops found in onset position, they fulfill the conditions under which English stops become aspirated. We therefore indicate that aspiration occurs by providing an intermediate form on a new line.

We have also seen that in English, vowels are predictably long when they occur before a voiced stop in the same syllable. In Figure 3.16, the /æ/'s of *slap* and *tap* occur before voiceless stops and so are not lengthened. The vowel of *pad*, however, occurs in just the environment associated with long vowels and so is predictably lengthened.

The use of such derivations underscores the fact that allophonic variation is the result of processes that apply in the course of language use. Underlying representations capture the knowledge that speakers have about the nature of their phonological system, and rules reflect the application of allophonic processes.

Rule Application (advanced)

We have seen that more than one rule may be employed in a derivation. Consequently, we must now ask how several rules are applied to a given underlying form when these rules interact.

Unordered and Free Rule Application   In Figure 3.16, we saw the application of the rules of English aspiration and vowel lengthening, which apply to voiceless stops and vowels, respectively. Note that the environments in which each of these rules apply (onset and precoda position, respectively) are entirely different. Therefore, these rules do not interact or affect each other in any way; the order in which they are applied makes no difference to the outcome of a derivation. Figure 3.17 shows the same rules applied in reverse order; there is no difference in the outcome.

UR	#slæp# slap	#tæp# tap	#pæd# pad
V-length	—	—	#pæ:d#
Aspiration	—	#tʰæp#	#pʰæ:d#
PR	[slæp]	[tʰæp]	[pʰæ:d]

Figure 3.17 Unordered rule application

We therefore say that the rules of aspiration and vowel lengthening are *unordered* with respect to each other.

It is frequently the case that the prior application of one rule will create an environment that allows another rule to apply later on in the derivation. Such a relationship between rules is called *feeding*. The rules of English stress and schwa-deletion (Figure 3.18) are in a feeding relationship. Since the presence of stress is a crucial condition of the schwa-deletion rule, stress must first be applied to an underlying form so that the schwa-deletion rule can work. The stress rule, therefore, feeds the schwa-deletion rule.

The rules of English schwa-deletion and liquid-glide devoicing, given in example *4* (page 61), are also in a feeding relation in the casual speech pronunciation of a word like *parade*. After a schwa has been lost through schwa-deletion, a liquid or glide that follows the schwa in the underlying representation is now directly after a voiceless stop, and therefore subject to liquid-glide devoicing, as the next example shows. The arrows, which are normally not written in derivations, here indicate feeding relationships.

UR	#pəred# parade
Stress	#pəréd#
Schwa-deletion	#préd#
Liquid-glide devoicing	#pred#
Diphthongization	#préjd#
Vowel lengthening	#pré:jd#
PR	[pré:jd]

Figure 3.18 Feeding order in a derivation

Notice now that no incorrect forms would result if, say, the schwa-deletion rule attempted to apply before the stress rule. Because its environment is not present, the schwa-deletion rule would simply fail to apply. However, once the stress rule was applied, the schwa-deletion rule could then follow in its turn, ultimately leading to a correct phonetic representation. What these facts suggest is that rules in a feeding relation may apply in *free order,* each attempting to apply wherever the required conditions are met. The result will be the desired phonetic output.

UR	#pəred# parade
Schwa-deletion	(required conditions not met)
Stress	#pəréd#
Schwa-deletion	#préd#
Liquid-glide devoicing	#préd#
(Other rules)	#pré:jd#
PR	[#pré:jd#]

Figure 3.19 Free rule application in a derivation

As a second example of free rule ordering, we now consider the rules of aspiration and stress in English.

As we saw in Section 3.5, the rule that aspirates stop consonants contains syllable boundaries as part of its environment. The voiceless stops of *connect* and *upon* are aspirated because they are in syllable-initial position.

However, the voiceless stop in *happy* is not aspirated because it is ambisyllabic (as was shown in Section 3.5, it becomes ambisyllabic when the preceding syllable is stressed). It follows that the stress rule (and resulting resyllabification procedure) must apply in a derivation before the aspiration rule can apply. As was shown in Figure 3.15, syllabification occurs automatically to underlying forms and resyllabification takes place if necessary after a rule applies. Here again, by allowing rules to apply whenever conditions for their application are met, we can derive the correct forms like *connect* [kʰənɛ́kt], *upon* [əpʰán], and *happy* [hǽpij]. Diphthongization is unordered here and so placed last. Here again, the dot indicates a syllable boundary; boldface type indicates ambisyllabicity.

UR	#kə.nɛkt#	connect	#ə.pɑn#	upon	#hæ.pi#	happy
Aspiration	(required conditions not met)					
Stress	#kə.nɛ́kt#		#ə.pán#		#hǽ.pi#	
Resyllabification	—		—		#hǽpi#	
Aspiration	#kʰənɛ́kt#		#ə.pʰán#		—	
Dipththongization	—		—		#hǽpij#	
PR	[kʰənɛ́kt]		[əpʰán]		[hǽpij]	

Figure 3.20 Free rule application in a derivation: another example

Extrinsic Rule Ordering   There are cases in language to suggest that rule application can be more complex. In English, there is a rule of flapping that creates a voiced flap from underlying /t/ or /d/ between two vowels, the first of which is stressed. Thus, we find [hít] *hit*: [híDɾ] *hitter*, [bǽt] *bat*: [bǽDɾ] *batter*, and [sǽd] *sad*: [sǽDɾ] *sadder*. As you have seen in Section 3.2, in some dialects there is also a rule that raises the diphthong /aj/ to [ʌj] before a voiceless consonant.

The flapping and raising rules interact in a very specific way. Since the flapping rule creates a voiced segment, its application removes the context that allows the raising rule to apply. (This kind of rule interaction is called a *bleeding* relation.) Now, if the flapping rule applied first (as might be the case if all rule ordering were free), the raising rule would then fail to apply, resulting in the phonetic form [rájDɾ] shown in Figure 3.21 on the right. But in much Canadian speech (and some U.S. dialects as well), the word *writer* is characteristically pronounced [rʌjDɾ]. In order to provide this output, we must guarantee that the rules apply in the order Raising before Flapping.

UR	#rajtɾ#	writer			#rajtɾ#	writer
Stress	#rájtɾ#			Stress	#rájtɾ#	
Raising	#rʌ́jtɾ#			Flapping	#rájDɾ#	
Flapping	#rʌ́jDɾ#			Raising	—	
PR	[rʌ́jDɾ]			PR	[rájDɾ]	

Figure 3.21 Different orders of rule application in a derivation

Such rule ordering is called **extrinsic ordering**, since it must be set up by the analyst independently of a general principle like free rule application. The need for extrinsic rule ordering contradicts the notion that speakers simply apply the phonological rules of their language whenever possible.

3.7 THE FORM AND NOTATION OF RULES

General statements about allophonic distribution are formalized as rules, which reflect the dynamic nature of processes (Chapter 2, Section 10).

Rules

Rules take the following form.

10. A → B/X ___ Y

In this notation, *A* stands for an element in the underlying representation, *B* for the change it undergoes, and *X* and *Y* for the conditioning environment. Either *X* or *Y* may be absent (null) if the conditioning environment is found only on one side of the allophone. The ___ (focus bar) indicates the position of the segment undergoing the rule. The slash separates the statement of the change from the statement of the conditioning environment. This rule is read as *A becomes B between X and Y.*

As an example of rule writing, we return to the distribution of liquid-glide devoicing in English (Section 3.2): in English, liquids and glides have voiceless allophones after syllable-initial voiceless stops, voiced allophones elsewhere. The rule statement operates on the voiced allophones of liquids and glides as basic (underlying) and changes the feature [+ voice] to [− voice] in the appropriate environment.

Figure 3.22 Liquid-glide devoicing in English expressed as a rule

This rule is read as follows.

11. Liquids and glides become voiceless after syllable-initial voiceless stops.

Rule and feature notation formally represents the origin of allophones in phonetic processes that arise in the course of speech. For example, the devoicing of liquids and glides in English is a typical process of assimilation. The rule notation in Figure 3.22 shows explicitly how this change of [+ voice] to [− voice] occurs in a specific class of sounds following the class of sounds that is [− voice].

Deletion as a Rule We have already seen that English speakers (optionally) drop a schwa [ə] in an open syllable when it is followed by a stressed syllable, as in *police* [pl̥ijs] and *parade* [pr̥ejd]. The rule can be formalized as follows. Here, Cø is an abbreviation for any number of successive consonants from zero on up.

$$[\text{ə}] \rightarrow \emptyset \,/\, \text{C}\emptyset \underline{\quad\quad} \sigma \text{ C}\emptyset \quad \begin{array}{c} \text{V} \\ \text{[+stress]} \end{array}$$

Figure 3.23 Schwa-deletion in English

The English schwa-deletion rule interacts with the constraint on possible consonant sequences. It automatically fails to apply when an impermissible sequence would result. Since ₀pt^h and ₀dl are impermissible onsets in English, there are no forms like *[pt^héjDow] *potato* or *[dlíjt] *delete* (except in very, very fast speech).

Epenthesis and Alpha Rules Recall that epenthesis involves the insertion of a segment into a sequence of other segments. In Section 3.2 we saw that the glides following English tense non-low vowels are predictable by a general rule: the tense non-low [−back] vowels /i/ and /e/ are followed by the [−back], glide /j/; the tense non-low [+back] vowels /u/ and /o/ are followed by the [+back] glide /w/.

In order to represent this epenthesis, we can make use of a type of notation called *alpha notation*. Here, the Greek letter α is a variable (like x in algebra) that can stand for either feature value. For example, a feature statement like [α round] can be read as either [+round] or [−round], but the alpha variable or variables used in a rule must match. When the alpha is used in a rule, it must have the same value wherever it occurs. For example, an alpha may be read as '+'. If it is, all other alphas in the same rule are to be read as '+'.

With alpha notation, we can capture the variability of the glide insertion in English as follows.

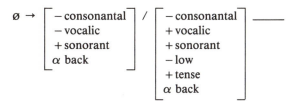

Figure 3.24 Alpha notation in English glide epenthesis

In reading an alpha, you are reading a rule twice, once with the plus value for the alpha feature, and once with the minus value. The rule in Figure 3.24 states that a [+back] glide is inserted after a [+back] non-low tense vowel and that a [−back] glide is inserted after a [−back] non-low tense vowel. Since there are only two glides in the phonological inventory of English, [+back] /w/ and [−back] /j/, the correct glide will be inserted by the rule.

Rules That Refer to Syllable Structure The rule of vowel lengthening in English makes reference to syllable structure. The boundary of the syllable may be represented by a bracket and a subscript σ. Recall the rule of vowel lengthening in English.

    12. English vowels are long when followed by a voiced obstruent consonant in the same syllable.

Presented as a rule, an underlying short vowel is lengthened in the appropriate context.

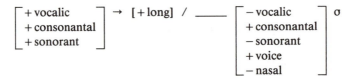

Figure 3.25 Vowel lengthening in English

Notice here that the onset of the syllable is irrelevant to the statement of the rule and so is not included in the formalization.

Vowel Epenthesis Vowel epenthesis is frequently triggered when an impermissible phonotactic structure is encountered in a borrowed word, as in the English pronunciation of the name *Dmitri*. It is also the case that in some dialects of English, a coda consisting of *l* and another consonant is not permitted. In these dialects, *milk* is pronounced [mɪlək] and *film* [fɪləm]. This change can be represented in rule format as follows.

$$\emptyset \;\rightarrow\; [\text{ə}] \;/\; [\,+\text{lateral}] \underline{\hspace{2cm}} \begin{bmatrix} -\text{vocalic} \\ +\text{consonantal} \end{bmatrix}_\sigma$$

Figure 3.26 Schwa epenthesis in English as a rule

A more complete representation of this process requires showing the change of syllable structure, as in Figure 3.27.

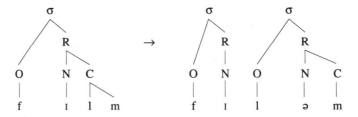

Figure 3.27 Syllabic representation of schwa epenthesis in English

Processes: A Last Word

The combined use of features and processes in phonological description reflects the dynamic nature of linguistic behavior. First, the use of features reflects a basic level of phonological activity—contrasts take place on the feature level, not on the level where segments are represented. Secondly, the use of process notation and rule formalization reflects the realities of linguistic production, in which sounds are affected by the context in which they are pronounced.

In Section 3.8, we will see how the wide range of stress patterns found in human language emerges from the interaction of a small number of processes specific to the phenomenon of stress.

Represen-
tations
(advanced)

In recent years, the formalization of rules has become more graphic. This change has taken place because certain types of processes have been viewed as the spreading of features from one segment (represented as a feature matrix) to another one. These graphic presentations of feature changes are referred to as **representations**. Tones and certain assimilation processes are particularly amenable to this kind of representation.

Tonal Assimilation as a Representation In Chapter 2, you saw how tone is represented on separate levels or tiers of phonological description. Association lines link the tone to the appropriate vowel. A representation of the word *tunko* 'sheep' from Duwai, a language spoken in West Africa, is as follows, where L indicates low tone, and H high.

Figure 3.28 Representing tone

This type of representation has the advantage of being able to show explicitly certain facts about tone languages. Tones, like other phonological phenomena, are subject to contextually conditioned variation. A good example of this comes from Duwai. In Duwai, many words show the tonal pattern LH (low-high).

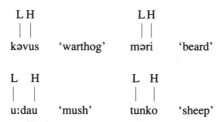

Figure 3.29 Low-high tonal patterns in Duwai

When a word with an LH tonal pattern is followed by a word with a H tone, such as the form *bái* '(is) not', the H tone of the first word becomes L: *kə̀vús* 'warthog' becomes *kə̀vùs bái* 'it's not a warthog'; *mə̀rí* 'beard' becomes *mə̀rì bái* 'it's not a beard', and so on.

This tonal change is represented as spreading of the L tone of the first vowel of the word to the final vowel of the word, and is shown by drawing a dotted association line (which represents the change in tone) and breaking the original association line from the vowel to the former tone value (the short double lines indicate the loss of association).

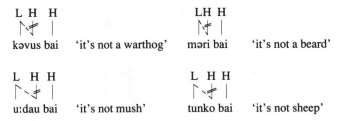

kəvus bai   'it's not a warthog'   məri bai   'it's not a beard'

u:dau bai   'it's not mush'   tunko bai   'it's not sheep'

Figure 3.30 Tone assimilation in Duwai

Seeing how a tone feature-changing process is represented leads us now to reconsider the presentation of features.

Representation and the Feature Hierarchy We have seen that segments are composed of smaller elements called features. We have also seen that features are organized into groupings that reflect natural classes. Figure 3.31 presents the grouping of features into a **feature hierarchy**, which is a representation of how features are related to each other.

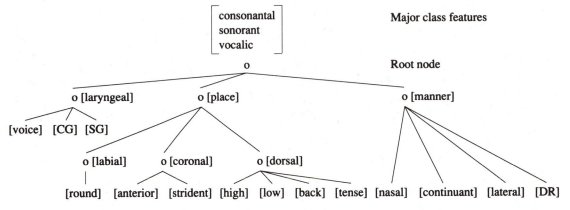

Figure 3.31 The feature hierarchy

Reading the Feature Hierarchy: Nodes and Tiers Each feature grouping in the feature hierarchy is represented by a label called a **class node** or simply **node** (the node symbol is a small circle: o). Beneath each node are grouped the feature or features that make up that subclass.

Nodes and features are ranked on levels or **tiers** that reflect their relation to each other. For example, all major class features are grouped together at the highest node, called the **root node**. The root node thus defines whether a segment in question is a vowel, consonant, or glide.

On the first tier under the root node are placed the nodes and features that specify all the remaining articulatory properties of a segment. From the **laryngeal node** branch out the features that express voicing states. The **place node** branches out into the major place features. The **manner node** branches out into features that relate to general manner of articulation.

Nodes serve a dual purpose in the hierarchy. First, they function as labels for natural classes of features—hence labels like *laryngeal node*, *place node*, and *manner node*. At the same time, nodes, like features themselves, may be referred to directly when making statements about processes. The next section shows examples of how this is done.

Assimilation and the Feature Hierarchy   Aside from the fact that they reflect natural articulatory classes, a major justification for these groupings claims that they directly reflect the operation of processes.

Figure 3.30 illustrates the spreading of a tone. The same type of representation is well suited to capturing assimilatory processes involving segmental features. This is the case because features frequently spread from segment to segment in the same manner as tones.

Nasal Assimilation   In English, a vowel nasalizes when it is immediately followed by a nasal consonant in the same syllable. One or more consonants may follow the nasal consonant. (For some speakers, the vowels must also be stressed.) The words *banks*, *shunted*, and *nimble*, for example, are pronounced [bæ̃ŋks], [ʃʌ̃ntəd], and [nɪ̃mbl̩]. This regressive nasalization in English can be represented as follows (the subscript σ following the square bracket indicates the boundary of the syllable, that is, that the nasal consonant is in the coda; the change undergone by the word *bank* is provided in phonetic transcription below the representation).

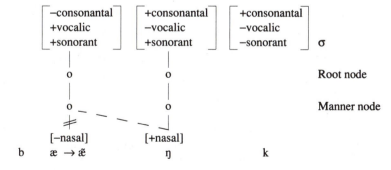

Figure 3.32 Vowel nasalization in English (regressive assimilation)

Laryngeal Assimilation: English Liquid-Glide Devoicing Revisited   We have already seen (Figure 3.22) how English liquid-glide devoicing is stated in rule format. Since this particular variation is in fact assimilatory, it lends itself well to statement as a representation.

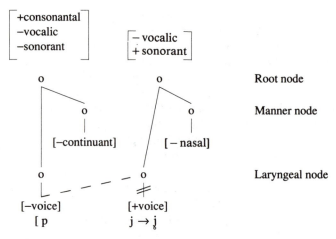

Figure 3.33 Liquid-glide devoicing in English as a representation

The root and manner node features represent the leftmost class as stops and the class to its right as liquids or glides. The place node is not represented since the place of articulation of both the stops and the liquids and glides is irrelevant to the process in question here. The dotted line represents the spreading of the laryngeal node feature [−voice] from the voiceless stop to the liquid or glide, and the breaking of the association line that links the [+voice] feature of the liquid or glide to the laryngeal node indicates its disassociation.

3.8 STRESS AND METRICS (advanced)

Many languages exhibit stress, which is defined as the perceived prominence of one or more syllabic elements over others in a word. Recall that stress is easily perceived in English in pairs of semantically related words such as the contrasting noun and verb pairs *présent/presént*, and *éxport/expórt*.

This section is concerned with stress whose placement can be predicted by general linguistic principles. The study of stress placement is referred to as **metrics**. Properly speaking, it is the rhyme of a syllable that bears stress; however, current notation refers directly to syllables in representing stress.

Unbounded Feet

The formalization of stress in much current analysis rests on the use of units called **metrical feet** (often referred to simply as *feet*), which are elements of metrical structure consisting of a stressed syllable and an associated unstressed syllable (or syllables). To see how this works, we begin with an example from French.

Table 3.30 Stress placement in French

oú	'or'
amí	'friend'
emportér	'carry off'
amicalemént	'amicably'
hospitalisatión	'hospitalization'

In French, the last vowel of a word receives primary stress. Metrical feet express this final stress by placing an x directly over the rightmost (final) syllable nucleus of a word at a level of representation called the **foot level**. Unstressed syllables within the foot are represented by dots; the foot is enclosed in parentheses. Details of syllable structure are not given unless it is necessary.

```
(.      .     .     .     x)          (.     x)          (x)  Foot level
 σ      σ     σ     σ     σ            σ     σ            σ
 a m i c a l e m e n t                a m i               ou
```

Figure 3.34 French stress: right-headed unbounded foot

The x represents the stressed element, or **head**, of the metrical foot (students will have to forgive linguists for employing terminology in which a foot has a head). The head is the obligatory element of a metrical foot—no foot can be without a stress. Since there is only one primary stress in each French word, only one foot is represented. We can also see from the data provided that any number of unstressed syllables may be a part of a metrical foot in French. This type of foot, consisting of a head and any number of unstressed syllables, is called an **unbounded foot**. French specifically requires a **right-headed unbounded foot** in each word—a foot in which the head is located over the rightmost syllable. We can also see that monosyllabic words have only the obligatory element of a foot on them (the head). A metrical foot that consists only of a head is called a **degenerate foot** (or **minimal foot**).

Some languages predictably stress the initial syllable of each word. Figure 3.35 shows a **left-headed unbounded foot** (a foot in which the head is located over the leftmost syllable), which is needed to represent the initial stressing pattern of the Hungarian words for 'mixed', 'keep stirring', and 'unstirred'.

```
(x   .)              (x    .     .)            (x    .    .    .)     Foot level
 σ   σ                σ    σ     σ              σ    σ    σ    σ
 k e v e r t          k e v e r g e t          k e v e r e t l e n
```

Figure 3.35 Hungarian stress: left-headed unbounded foot

Bounded Feet

Frequently, more than one stress is heard in a word. In many languages, words with multiple stresses fall on alternating syllables. Alternating stresses can be heard in English words like *ànecdótal* and *Mìssissáuga*. In Chemehuevi (an Amerindian language spoken in California), the word *ha?ísutùivì* 's/he likes' is a typical example of alternating stress. In alternating stress languages, the stresses fall exactly two syllables apart (degenerate feet excepted), and only one stress is primary in each word. Alternating stress is expressed by employing a constituent called a **bounded foot**, which is a unit of metrical representation that consists of a stressed syllable and no more than one unstressed syllable.

Bounded feet can be left-headed or right-headed. You may already be familiar with such traditional terms as **trochaic** and **iambic**. A trochaic foot is equivalent to a bounded, left-headed foot. An iambic foot is equivalent to a bounded, right-headed foot.

Trochaic foot   Iambic foot
(bounded, left-headed)   (bounded, right-headed)
(x   .   )   (.   x)   Foot level
σ   σ   σ σ
promise   collect

Figure 3.36 Two traditional bounded foot types and their metrical representations

Building in Either Direction Since alternating stress languages show more than one foot on each word, we have to assign feet to the words in some systematic manner. It seems reasonable to assume that feet are assigned to a word by starting at the beginning of the word, and working through it from left to right. The next example shows both left-headed and right-headed bounded feet built from left-to-right over words in two different languages. Note the presence of degenerate feet in two of the examples; remember that these result because a head is required on each foot, and whenever binary feet are constructed over an odd number of syllables, one syllable will be left over at the end of the procedure. In the example, words are given with primary stresses only; how secondary stresses are represented is shown later on in this section. The arrows are placed before the feet simply as a reminder of directionality of application; they are not ordinarily written. The syllable numbers are also provided for the sake of clarity and are also not usually written.

Left-headed bounded foot,   Right-headed bounded foot,
left-to-right application   left-to-right application
Language: Maranungku (Australia)   Language: Chemehuevi (California)

$\rightarrow$(x   .)(x .)(x) $\rightarrow$(.   x) (.   x)(x)   Foot level
   σ_1 σ_2 σ_3 σ_4 σ_5 σ_1 σ_2 σ_3 σ_4 σ_5
   l a ŋ k a r a t e t i   'prawn'   u n i n u p i r u   'make'

$\rightarrow$ (x .) (x .) (x   .) $\rightarrow$ (. x) (. x)(.   x)   Foot level
   σ_1 σ_2 σ_3 σ_4 σ_5 σ_6 σ_1 σ_2 σ_3 $\sigma_4$$\sigma_5$ σ_6
   w e l e p e l e m a n t a   'kind of duck'   h a ʔ i s u t u i v i   's/he liked'

Figure 3.37 Two types of alternating stress, left-to-right application

As these examples show, left-headed bounded feet ordinarily result in stresses on odd-numbered syllables, while right-headed bounded feet result in stresses on even-numbered syllables.

A curious fact about the assigning of bounded feet is that in some languages it appears to start at the ends of words and work its way 'backwards' from right to left. Figure 3.38 provides examples of right-to-left foot building in two languages. Here again, the bounded, left-headed foot results in stress on odd-numbered syllables, and the bounded, right-headed foot assigns stress to even numbered syllables.

A strange thing about these examples, however, is that there seems to be no reason to assume that stressing was applied from right-to-left, since the same results can be obtained by building the appropriate bounded feet from left-to-right. Stress on the word *warawara*, for example, will also fall on the first and third syllables with left-to-right application. How can we tell that stress is applied right-to-left in these languages?

Left-headed bounded foot,
right-to-left application
Language: Warao (Venezuela)

(x .) (x .) ←
σ₁ σ₂ σ₃ σ₄
w a r a w a r a   'kind of fish'

Right-headed bounded foot,
right-to-left application
Language: Weri (New Guinea)

(. x)(.   x) ←   Foot level
σ₁ σ₂σ₃ σ₄
u l u a m i t   'mist'

Figure 3.38 Two types of alternating stress, right-to-left application

The answer to this question lies in the fact that the words in Figure 3.38 above all consist of an even number of syllables. The stress pattern of words in these same languages with odd numbers of syllables will not work out unless stress is applied in the correct direction. Figure 3.39 shows the correct stressing for two forms with an odd number of syllables.

Left-headed bounded foot,
right-to-left application
Language: Warao

(x) (x .) (x .) ←
σ₁ σ₂ σ₃ σ₄σ₅
j i w a r a n a e   'he found it'

Right-headed bounded foot,
right-to-left application
Language: Weri

(x) (. x)(. x) ←   Foot level
σ₁ σ₂ σ₃ σ₄ σ₅
a k u n e t e p a l   'times'

Figure 3.39 Right-to-left application in words with an odd number of syllables. The result is the correct stress pattern required in these languages.

However, if we try to apply stress from left-to-right in these forms, incorrect patterns result, as Figure 3.40 shows.

Left-headed bounded foot,
incorrect left-to-right application
Language: Warao

→ (x .) (x .)(x)
σ₁ σ₂ σ₃ σ₄σ₅
*j i w a r a n a e

Right-headed bounded foot,
incorrect left-to-right application
Language: Weri

→ (. x) (. x) (x) Foot level
σ₁ σ₂ σ₃ σ₄ σ₅
*a k u n e t e p a l

Figure 3.40 Incorrectly applied left-to-right application. Compare this figure with the required correct result shown in Figure 3.38.

Therefore, in order to know whether alternating stresses are being applied left-to-right or right-to-left in a language, we must be sure to compare words with both odd- and even-numbered syllables.

It is important to note that it is rare to find a pure alternating stress language, since other factors may intervene to complicate the stress pattern. Nevertheless, the basic principle of alternating stress assignment holds in a great many of the world's languages.

Primary and Secondary Stresses

To understand the basis of secondary stress assignment, we return briefly to the stressing of the words *promise* and *collect* in Figure 3.36, where we were left with the appearance that stress had been assigned to the words. In fact, this was not the case. Stress had only been assigned to feet. The placement of stress on the word is represented by assigning an x on a new level, not surprisingly called the **word level**, over the existing stress on the foot level. Two word-level feet are illustrated in Figure 3.41.

```
(x  )                           (   x)      Word level
(x  .)                          (.  x)      Foot level
 σ  σ                            σ  σ
promise                         collect
```

Figure 3.41 Foot- and word-level stress representation

This same principle accounts for the placement of secondary stresses, which are derived from the initial placement of stresses by the basic metrical pattern. On the word level, we build another foot (usually an unbounded one) over the syllable-level foot that takes the primary word stress. The result will be that one of the stresses initially assigned by foot building will be the head of the word-level foot and will be interpreted as the primary stress. The remaining stresses are considered to be secondary stresses.

As an example, let us take the Chemehuevi word *haʔisutuivɨ* 's/he liked' from Figure 3.37. Its complete stress pattern is *haʔɨsutùivɨ*. To represent this pattern, we begin as above by building right-headed bounded feet from left-to-right over the word form at the foot level.

```
(.  x) (.  x)(.  x)   Foot level
 σ  σ  σ  σσ  σ
ha ʔ i s u t u i v ɨ
```

Figure 3.42 Initial foot building in Chemehuevi: right-headed bounded feet, left-to-right application

On the word level, we build (for Chemehuevi) a left-headed unbounded foot over the leftmost foot-level stress. This captures the fact that the first stress in a Chemehuevi word is the primary one. In this way, we represent both primary and secondary stresses: the syllable with the greatest number of x's over it is taken to be the most prominent, or primary stressed syllable; the syllables with only one x have secondary stress; the remaining syllables are unstressed.

```
(   x          )    Word level:  left-headed unbounded foot
(.  x)(.  x)(.  x)   Foot level:  right-headed bounded feet, L→R
 σ  σ  σ  σσ  σ
ha ʔ i s u t u i v ɨ
```

Figure 3.43 Word-level foot building in Chemehuevi. Both primary and secondary stresses are now represented.

The formal generalization for Chemehuevi stress is as follows—foot level: right-headed bounded feet, applying from left-to-right; word level: left-headed unbounded foot.

Complexity from Simplicity: Stress Parameters

Stress patterns in language can be highly intricate, but linguists believe that their complexity, like so much other linguistic complexity, arises from interaction among a set of universally available options. These options are called **parameters**. Table 3.31 lists the stress parameters we have explored in this chapter.

Table 3.31 Some stress parameters

1. bounded/unbounded feet
2. left-/right-headed feet
3. directionality: left-to-right/right-to-left

Interaction among the setting of these three parameters, along with a fourth parameter, extrametricality, accounts for a wide variety of the stress patterns found in human language. All of the examples of stress patterning that have been presented in this section resulted from the setting of just these three parameters, as Table 3.32 shows. Note that the directionality parameter is not relevant for languages with unbounded feet. Primary stress is excluded from the table.

Table 3.32 Stress parameter setting for languages presented in this section

Language	Bounded/unbounded feet	Headedness	Directionality
French	unbounded	right	
Hungarian	unbounded	left	
Maranungku	bounded	left	left-to-right
Chemehuevi	bounded	right	left-to-right
Warao	bounded	left	right-to-left
Weri	bounded	right	right-to-left

Extra-metricality

There are exceptions to the requirement that all syllables are associated with some foot for the purposes of stress assignment. In some languages, we find that a single syllable at the beginning or end of a word is never stressed. Because it falls outside the effects of stress rules, such a syllable is said to be **extrametrical**. To represent this fact formally, an extrametrical syllable is formally excluded from the foot-building procedure. To see how extrametricality interacts with foot structure, consider the following data from Kusaiean, a language spoken in the Caroline Islands.

Table 3.33 Penultimate stress in Kusaiean

kʌta:	'some'
kɔ́:kɔ:	'to lead'
pʌlákfɔ:n	'stupid'
miní:ni:	'thin'
mʌlǽlæ	'light'
mʌlælǽjak	'become light'

In Kusaiean, stress always falls on the penultimate (next-to-last) syllable of a word. The data in Table 3.33 show this clearly; stress may be found on first, second, third, and even fourth syllables, since stress is always on the penultimate syllable of polysyllabic words. The final syllable, however, is never stressed. This regularity is expressed by representing word-final syllables as extrametrical, as in Figure 3.44. The angled brackets represent the fact that final syllables are invisible to stress assignment, which otherwise proceeds as usual, here building a right-headed unbounded foot over the word.

```
(.   x )                                    (.   .   x )        Foot level
 σ  σ< σ>                                    σ   σ   σ  <σ>
m ʌ l æ <l æ>                               m ʌ l æ l æ <y a k>
```

Figure 3.44 Kusaiean stress assignment using extrametricality

You may wonder what happens to extrametrical syllables after stress has been assigned. Since all syllables must belong to a foot, it is assumed that extrametrical syllables are joined to the metrical foot after stress placement. This process is called **stray syllable adjunction**.

Stress universally falls towards the margins (beginning or end) of words. Since stress falls toward the left or right margin of a word, it is rare to find a primary stress landing more than one syllable from the margin of a form. Extrametrical syllables capture this fact in that they are limited to a single occurrence as the initial or final syllable of words; they are not found word-internally. The careful use of extrametricality allows us to adhere to the basic principles that account for all stressing in terms of either unbounded or bounded feet. The next section provides additional justification for the use of extrametricality in stress assignment, and shows how it interacts with the building of bounded feet.

Bounded Feet and Extrametricality   In Swahili, stress falls on alternating syllables; the penultimate (next-to-last) syllable receives the strongest stress.

Table 3.34 Stress in Swahili

tʃúra	'toad'
tʃakúla	'food'
sìkuzóte	'always'
uʃikamáno	'adhesion'

To assign primary and secondary stresses in Swahili, we first tentatively assume that final syllables are extrametrical, since they are never stressed. Since stresses are alternating, we know that they must be assigned using bounded feet. Applying the principles presented earlier, we can arrive at a decision about the headedness of the bounded feet. Left-headed feet, whether applied from left-to-right or right-to-left, are excluded, since they would result in the first syllable of a word like *uʃikamano* being stressed. Given that the bounded feet needed to assign stress in Swahili are right-headed, we must then decide on the direction of application. The words *tʃakúla* and *uʃikamáno* provide no definitive answer, since their stresses would be correct (still assuming extrametricality) whether the right-headed feet were assigned from left-to-right or from right-to-left. The word *sìkuzóte* is crucial; still assuming extrametricality, applying bounded, right-headed feet from left-to-right will produce the wrong pattern of stresses (**sikúzóte*: remember that all feet, unless extrametrical, must have a stress). By employing extrametricality and building from right-to-left, we can come up with the right stress pattern (see Figure 3.45). We therefore employ bounded, right-headed feet assigned from right-to-left in conjunction with extrametricality since these settings will provide all and only correct stresses.

```
(x) (.   x)                              (.   x)        Foot level
 σ   σ   σ  <σ>                           σ   σ  <σ>
 s i k u z o <t e>                       t ʃ a k u <l a>
```

Figure 3.45 Swahili stress assignment using right-headed bounded feet and right-to-left application

On a second line of the metrical representation we build a right-headed unbounded foot. Since primary stress assignment on the word level is sensitive only to the x's on the foot level, the result will be main stress on the penultimate syllable and secondary stresses on any preceding stressed syllables.

```
(        x)                              (    x)        Word level
(x) (.   x)                              (.   x)        Foot level
 σ   σ   σ  <σ>                           σ   σ  <σ>
 s i k u z o <t e>                       t ʃ a k u <l a>
```

Figure 3.46 Swahili word-level stress assignment

Summing Up

Phonology deals with the sequential and phonetically conditioned patterning of sounds in language. To account for this patterning, three units of phonological representation have been established: the **feature**, the **phoneme**, and the **syllable**. Phonemes are contrastive segmental units composed of distinctive features. Phonetically conditioned variants of phonemes are called **allophones**. Phonology makes use of **underlying forms**, **derivations**, **phonological rules**, and **representations** in its formal notation. Rules apply in **free** or **extrinsic** order to guarantee that correct phonetic representations are derived from underlying representation.

The chapter also reviews the **processes** that are the basis of this patterned variation, and shows how the patterning of phonological units is based upon general elements and principles that are applicable to the study of any human language. Interacting with features and segmental processes, a limited set of **parameters** accounts for the phenomenon of **stress** in human language.

Key Terms

accidental gaps	anterior
allophone	assimilation
alpha rules	association lines
alternating stress	back
ambisyllabicity	bleeding

bounded foot
closed syllable
coda
complementary distribution
consonantal
contrast
coronal
degenerate foot
deletion
directionality
distinctive features
dorsal features
elsewhere
environment
epenthesis
extrametricality
extrinsic rule ordering
feature
feature hierarchy
feeding
free (unordered) rule application
iambic
labial
laryngeal features
low
major class features
manner features
matrix
metrical feet
metrics
minimal foot

minimal pair
natural class
node
onset
open syllable
ordered rule application
phoneme
phonemic transcription
phonetic transcription
phonological rules
place features
reduced
representations
rhyme
root node
rounded
sonorant
spread glottis
spreading
stray syllable adjunction
stressed (syllable)
strident
syllable
systematic gaps
tense
tiers
tonal assimilation
trochaic
unbounded foot
underlying (form)
vocalic

Sources

A classic and still valuable presentation of phonemic analysis is found in H. A. Gleason, Jr.'s *An Introduction to Descriptive Linguistics* (New York: Holt, Rinehart and Winston, 1961). Tone data on Mende are from W. R. Leben's "The Representation of Tone" and on Duwai from R. G. Schuh's "Tone Rules," both in *Tone: A Linguistic Survey*, edited by V.A. Fromkin (New York: Academic Press, 1978). The approach to stress is inspired by Hayes (cited below), whereas the representations used follow both the direction of M. Halle and J.-R. Vergnaud, *An Essay on Stress* (Cambridge, Mass.: MIT Press, 1987) and B. Hayes, "A Revised Parametric Metrical Theory," *Proceedings of NELS* 17 (1): 1987. Syllabification, tone , and autosegmental analysis are drawn from numerous sources, all summarized recently in Goldsmith (cited below). The Malay data are adapted from Kenstowicz and Kisseberth (cited below); additional examples were provided by S.L. Lee (personal communication).

Kusaiean material is drawn from K-d Lee, *Kusaiean Reference Grammar* (Honolulu: University of Hawaii Press, 1975); Chemehuevi data is from Margret L. Press, *Chemehuevi: A Grammar and Lexicon*, *University of California Publications in Linguistics* 92 (Berkeley, Calif.: University of California Press, 1980).

Data sources for questions are as follows: for Inuktitut, B. Harnum (personal communication); for Mokilese, S. Harrison's *Mokilese Reference Grammar* (Honolulu: University of Hawaii Press, 1976); for Tamil, R. Radhakrishnan (personal communication); for Gascon, R. C. Kelley's *A Descriptive Analysis of Gascon* (Amsterdam: Mouton, 1978); for Plains Cree, Y. Carifelle and M. Pepper (personal communication); for Tzutujil, John R. Dayley, *Tzutujil Grammar* (Berkeley, Calif.: University of California Press, 1985); for Huallaga Quechua, David John Weber, *A Grammar of Huallaga (Huánuco) Quecha* (Berkeley, Calif.: University of California Press, 1989); for Maung, A. Capell and H.E. Hinch, *Maung Grammar*, *Texts and Vocabulary* (The Hague: Mouton, 1970); for Mende, L. Hyman and D. Pulleyblank, "The Basics of Autosegmental Phonology Applied to Tone"; for Moru, A.N. Tucker, *The Eastern Sudanic Languages*, pp. 112, 271 (London: Dawsons, 1967/1940).

Recommended Reading

Anderson, Stephen R. 1985. *Phonology in the Twentieth Century*. Chicago: University of Chicago Press.

Clements, George N., and Samuel Jay Keyser. 1983. *CV Phonology*. Cambridge, Mass.: MIT Press.

Goldsmith, John. 1990. *Autosegmental and Metrical Phonology*. Cambridge, Mass.: Blackwell.

Hayes, Bruce. 1981. *A Metrical Theory of Stress Rules*. Bloomington: Indiana University Linguistics Club.

Hogg, Richard, and C.B. McCully. 1987. *Metrical Phonology: A Coursebook*. London: Cambridge University Press.

Hyman, Larry M. 1975. *Phonology: Theory and Analysis*. New York: Holt, Rinehart and Winston.

Keating, Patricia. 1988. "The Phonology-Phonetics Interface." In *Linguistics: The Cambridge Survey*. Vol. 1. Edited by F. Newmeyer, 281–302. New York: Cambridge University Press.

Katamba, Francis. 1989. *An Introduction to Phonology*. London: Longman.

Kenstowicz, Michael, and Charles Kisseberth. 1979. *Generative Phonology*. New York: Academic Press.

Stampe, David. 1980. *A Dissertation on Natural Phonology*. New York: Garland.

Appendix: Hints for Solving Phonology Problems ==

The task of solving a phonology problem is made easier if certain facts presented in this chapter and summarized here are kept in mind.

1. Begin by looking for minimal pairs. These establish which segments are contrastive. For example, in the following data from Tagalog (Philippines), minimal pairs in items a) and e) and c) and f), and the near minimal pair b) and d) show that the phones [h and [ʔ] contrast and therefore belong to separate phonemes, /h/ and /ʔ/, respectively.

a) kahon	'box'	d) ʔari	'property'
b) hariʔ	'king'	e) kaʔon	'to fetch'
c) ʔumagos	'to flow'	f) humagos	'to paint'

2. Allophones of a given phoneme are usually phonetically similar. Look for sounds that are phonetically similar, and check to see whether they are in complementary distribution. The best way to do this is to list the environments. In the following data, also from Tagalog, [d] and [r], both voiced alveolars, should be considered as possible allophones. List the environments in which these sounds are found. Are they in complementary distribution?

a) datiŋ	'to arrive'	f) daraʔiŋ	'will complain'
b) dami	'amount'	g) marumi	'dirty'
c) dumi	'dirt'	h) marami	'many'
d) daratiŋ	'will arrive'	i) daʔiŋ	'to complain'
e) mandurukot	'pickpocket'	j) mandukot	'to go pickpocketing'

3. If two potential allophones of one phoneme are in complementary distribution, you can be reasonably sure they are allophones of the same phoneme. Try to make a general statement about their distribution in terms of some natural phonological class. For example:

> Tagalog [d] and [r] are in complementary distribution and are allophones of one phoneme. The allophone [r] occurs between vowels; [d] occurs elsewhere—here, word-initially, as in items a), b), c), f), and so on, and after nasal consonants, as in items e) and j).

4. Select one allophone as basic. This is usually the allophone with the widest distribution (the elsewhere variant). It may be helpful to set up a traditional phoneme-allophone diagram (See Figure 3.3.)

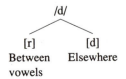

5. Write a phonological rule or provide a representation that accounts for the predictable features of the other allophones. Your rule (or representation) is probably correct if it describes a common linguistic process in terms of natural classes of sounds interacting with neighboring segments and/or syllable structure.

For example, for the above: d → r/V ___ V

Here, the process that leads to the allophony is a form of assimilation, in that an underlying stop consonant becomes a continuant when found between two continuants (the vowels).

You can assume that any segments are phonemic if there are no minimal pairs for them and if they cannot be shown to be allophones of a phoneme. The data simply did not provide minimal pairs.

Questions

Assume phonetic transcription of the data in all exercises.

1. *Inuktitut* (Eastern) (Native Canadian)

a)	iglumut	'to a house'	h)	pinna	'that one up there'
b)	ukiaq	'late fall'	i)	ani	'female's brother'
c)	aiviq	'walrus'	j)	iglu	'(snow)house'
d)	aniguvit	'if you leave'	k)	panna	'that place up there'
e)	aglu	'seal's breathing hole'	l)	aivuq	'she goes home'
f)	iglumit	'from a house'	m)	ini	'place, spot'
g)	anigavit	'because you leave'	n)	ukiuq	'winter'

i) List all the minimal pairs in this data. Based on the minimal pairs you have found, list all the contrastive pairs of vowels.

ii) Using the vowel charts in Figure 2.9 and 2.10 as your models, make a chart of Inuktitut vowel phonemes.

2. *Hindi* (Hindi is a language of the Indo-European family spoken in India) Consider the segments [b] and [ḅ] in the data below and answer the questions that follow. The segment transcribed [ḅ] is a murmured voiced stop; it was presented in Chapter 2, Section 8.

a)	bara	'large'	f)	ḅɛd	'disagreement'
b)	ḅari	'heavy'	g)	bais	'twenty-two'
c)	bina	'without'	h)	ḅəs	'buffalo'
d)	ḅir	'crowd'	i)	bap	'father'
e)	bori	'sackcloth'	j)	ḅag	'part'

i) Are the segments [b] and [ḅ] allophones of the same phoneme or do they belong to separate phonemes? If you believe they belong to separate phonemes, give evidence from the data to support your analysis. If you believe they are allophones of the same phoneme, list the conditioning environments.

3. *Mokilese* (Mokilese is an Austronesian language of the South Pacific)
Examine the following data from Mokilese carefully, taking note of where voiceless vowels occur.

a)	pi̥san	'full of leaves'	g)	uduk	'flesh'
b)	tu̥pu̥kta	'bought'	h)	kaskas	'to throw'
c)	pu̥ko	'basket'	i)	poki	'to strike something'
d)	ki̥sa	'we two'	j)	pil	'water'
e)	su̥pwo	'firewood'	k)	apid	'outrigger support'
f)	kamwɔki̥ti	'to move'	l)	ludʒuk	'to tackle'

i) The vowel phonemes of Mokilese are /i e ɛ u o ɔ a/. In Mokilese, [i̥] is an allophone of /i/, and [u̥] is an allophone of /u/. No other vowels have voiceless allophones. State in words the conditioning factors that account for this. Be as general as possible in referring to classes of sounds.

ii) Using features, formulate a rule that accounts for the derived allophones.

4. *Gascon* (Gascon is spoken in southwest France)
The phones [b], [β], [d], [ð], [g], and [ɣ] are all found in Gascon, as the following examples show.

a)	bux	'you'	m)	gat	'cat'
b)	bako	'cow'	n)	lũ̃g	'long'
c)	ũmbro	'shadow'	o)	salıβo	'saliva'
d)	brẽn	'endanger'	p)	noβı	'husband'
e)	dilys	'Monday'	q)	aβe	'to have'
f)	dĩŋko	'until'	r)	ʃıβaw	'horse'
g)	duso	'sweet'	s)	buðet	'gut'
h)	fred	'cold'	t)	eʃaðo	'hoe'
i)	pũnde	'to lay eggs'	u)	bıɣar	'mosquito'
j)	dudze	'twelve'	v)	rıɣut	'he laughed'
k)	guteʒa	'flow'	w)	agro	'sour'
l)	ẽŋgwãn	'last'	x)	darıɣa	'pull out'

i) Which pairs among the phones [b], [β], [d], [ð], [g], and [ɣ] are the most phonetically similar? Support your claim with phonetic descriptions of the similar pairs.

ii) List the environments in which the phones [b], [β], [d], [ð], [g], and [ɣ] are found.

iii) Is there any evidence for grouping these pairs of sounds into phonemes? State the evidence for each pair.

iv) Make a general statement about the patterning of the phonemes you have established.

v) Following your analysis, write the following forms in phonemic transcription.

    (1) [puɣo]   (2) [deðat]   (3) [ʃıβaw]   (4) [ambud]

5. *Plains Cree* (Plains Cree is a Native Canadian language of the Algonquian family)

The following data from Plains Cree shows a number of different voiced and voiceless consonantal segments.

a)	niska	'goose'	l)	nisto	'three'
b)	kodak	'another'	m)	tʃi:gahigan	'axe'
c)	asaba:p	'thread'	n)	a:dim	'dog'
d)	wasko:w	'cloud'	o)	mi:bit	'tooth'
e)	paskwa:w	'prairie'	p)	pime:	'lard'
f)	ni:gi	'my house'	q)	mide	'heart'
g)	ko:gos	'pig'	r)	o:gik	'these'
h)	tahki	'often'	s)	tʃihtʃij	'finger'
i)	namwa:tʃ	'not at all'	t)	wa:bos	'rabbit'
j)	ospwa:gan	'pipe'	u)	na:be:w	'man'
k)	midʒihtʃij	'hand'	v)	mi:dʒiwin	'food'

i) Do [p] and [b] belong to separate phonemes, or can they be allophones of one phoneme? If you think they belong to separate phonemes, list data to support your case. If you think they are allophones, first state the conditioning factors in words, and then, using features, formulate a rule that accounts for their distribution.

ii) Do the same for [t] and [d], [k] and [g], and [tʃ] and [dʒ].

iii) Can you make a general statement about the relationship among all the consonantal pairs whose distribution you have examined?

iv) Using Figure 3.16 as your model, provide complete derivations of the forms for k) *hand*, m) *axe*, and o) *tooth*.

6. There are a number of natural classes in the vowel and consonant data below. Circle three natural classes in each set of data. Indicate which feature or features define the class, as in the example.

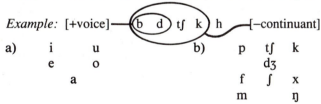

Example: [+voice] — (b d) tʃ k) h — [−continuant]

a)
i		u	
	e	o	
		a	

b)
p	tʃ	k
	dʒ	
f	ʃ	x
m		ŋ

7. Name the single feature that distinguishes the following pairs of sounds.

a)	[θ] : [ð]	e)	[b] : [m]	i)	[ʌ] : [ə]
b)	[p] : [f]	f)	[s] : [ʃ]	j)	[s] : [θ]
c)	[u] : [ʊ]	g)	[ɪ] : [i]	k)	[e] : [ɛ]
d)	[i] : [e]	h)	[k] : [x]	l)	[u] : [o]

8. Complete the feature matrix for each of the sounds indicated. The V abbreviates the features [+ vocalic, − consonantal], and the C abbreviates the features [− vocalic, + consonantal].

a) [e]   V
$$\begin{bmatrix} +\text{sonorant} \\ -\text{high} \\ -\text{low} \end{bmatrix}$$

b) [tʃ]   C
$$\begin{bmatrix} -\text{sonorant} \\ -\text{voice} \end{bmatrix}$$

c) [m]   C
$$\begin{bmatrix} +\text{sonorant} \\ +\text{anterior} \\ +\text{nasal} \end{bmatrix}$$

d) [s]   C
$$\begin{bmatrix} -\text{sonorant} \\ +\text{strident} \\ +\text{coronal} \end{bmatrix}$$

e) [l]   C
$$\begin{bmatrix} +\text{sonorant} \end{bmatrix}$$

f) [j]
$$\begin{bmatrix} -\text{vocalic} \\ -\text{consonantal} \\ +\text{high} \end{bmatrix}$$

i) Using the appropriate features from Figure 3.31, represent each segment on a feature hierarchy tree.

9. *English/Korean*

As we have seen, phonological adaptation of loanwords may reflect facts about syllable structure. Recently, the Korean automobile name *Hyundai* has been adapted into English in various ways, one of which follows. Given the Korean form and the English adaptation provided, state two reasons based on syllable structure conditions that explain why the English form is pronounced the way it is.

Korean form		*English form*
/hjʌndæ/	→	/hʌnde/ [hʌndej]

10. *English*

Some speakers of English have two types of [l]. One, called *clear l*, is transcribed as [l] in the following data. The other, called *dark l*, is transcribed with [ɫ]. Examine the data, and answer the questions that follow.

a) lajf	life	g) pʰɪɫ	pill
b) lijp	leap	h) fijɫ	feel
c) lu:wz	lose	i) hɛɫp	help
d) ijlowp	elope	j) bʌɫk	bulk
e) dijlajt	delight	k) soɫd	sold
f) slijp	sleep	l) fʊɫ	full

Do [l] and [ɫ] belong to separate phonemes or are they allophones of the same phoneme? If you believe they belong to separate phonemes, answer question *i*). If you believe they are allophones of the same phoneme, answer the remaining questions.

i) List the evidence that makes your case for considering [l] and [ɫ] as separate phonemes.

ii) State the distribution of [l] and [ɫ] in words.

iii) Which variant makes the best underlying form? Why?

iv) Can you make reference to syllable structure in your distribution statement? If you can, do so in rule form.

11. *Turkish*

As you saw in Section 3.5, Turkish syllables have the following structure:
- maximum number of consonants in an onset: 1
- maximum number of vowels in a nucleus: 1
- maximum number of consonants in a coda: 2, of which the first is a fricative or sonorant

With these stipulations in mind, syllabify the following forms:

a) k u r t t e n   b) m e l ε k c ı k   c) k e m ε n d   d) k e m ı k t e n

In this further data from Turkish, the phones [i] and [ı] are in complementary distribution and form one phoneme, and the phones [e] and [ε] are also in complementary distribution and form another (separate) phoneme. Examine the data and answer the questions that follow.

a)	gεldık	'we arrived'	f)	cıkcεk	'flower'	k)	liman	'harbor'
b)	ıʃ	'work'	g)	cıft	'plow'	l)	emın	'sure'
c)	elın	'your hand'	h)	εl	'hand'	m)	didık	'shredded'
d)	ıp	'thread'	i)	memεr	'passage'	n)	bıt	'louse'
e)	sεs	'voice'	j)	sεksεn	'eighty'	o)	silah	'weapon'

i) Provide a statement of the distribution of [i] and [ı] and [e] and [ε] in words. Make your statement as general as possible, but be precise!

ii) State a rule that derives the allophones of both phonemes from the underlying form. Use features! Be sure to give your rule a mnemonic name; use this name in the answer to question *iii)*.

iii) Provide underlying representations and derivations for the following forms.

UR	#	#	'cord'	#	#	'lasso'
PR	[siɲɪm]			[kemεnd]		

12. You saw in Section 3.6 how the characteristic Canadian pronunciation of *writer* [rʌjDɾ] differs from the American pronunciation [rajDɾ] due to the ordering of the rules of raising and flapping. It is also the case that both Canadians and Americans pronounce the word *rider* the same: [raːjDɾ]. These facts provide evidence that the rule of vowel lengthening is ordered with respect to flapping in both Canadian and American English.

a) What is the order of rule application needed to derive the form *rider* in Canadian and American English? State in words the reason for your answer.

b) Provide derivations of the forms for *writer* and *rider* in both Canadian and American English (four forms in all). Be sure to show the appropriate order for raising, flapping, and stress rules. These rules need not be presented in formal notation.

13. State each of the following rules in English, making reference to natural classes and common linguistic processes.

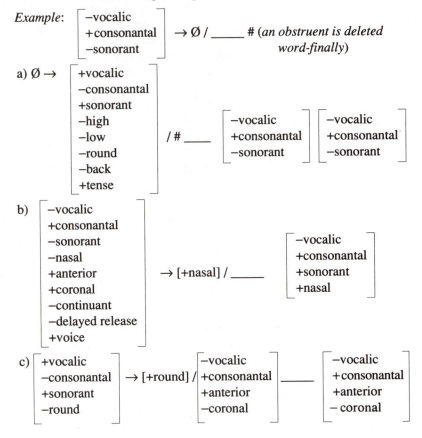

14. Change the following statements into rule notation. Be sure to name the process in question for each case.

   a) Voiceless stops become corresponding fricatives between vowels.
   b) A schwa is inserted after a voiced stop word-finally.
   c) Low unrounded vowels become rounded before *m*.

15. *Tamil* (Tamil is a Dravidian language spoken in South India and Sri Lanka) In the following Tamil data, some words begin with glides while others do not. The symbol [ḍ] represents a voiced retroflex stop and the diacritic [̯] indicates dentals.

Initial j-glide		*Initial w-glide*		*No initial glide*	
a) jeli	'rat'	f) wodi	'break'	k) arivu	'knowledge'
b) ji:	'fly'	g) wo:laj	'palm leaf'	l) aintu	'five'
c) jilaj	'leaf'	h) wu:si	'needle'	m) a:saj	'desire'
d) jeŋge:	'where'	i) wujir	'life'	n) a:ru	'river'
e) jiḍuppu	'waist'	j) wo:ram	'edge'	o) a:di	'origin'

i) The occurrence of these glides is predictable. Using your knowledge of natural classes, make a general statement about the distribution of the glides.

ii) Assuming the glides are not present in the underlying representations, name the process that accounts for their presence in the phonetic forms.

iii) Using features, write a rule using alpha notation that formalizes this process. Show the derivation of the forms for *fly* and *break*.

16. *Mende* (Mende is spoken in Liberia and Sierra Leone)

In Mende, the forms that mean 'on' (*ma*) and 'in' (*hu*) are suffixes (they are attached to a preceding word; see Chapter 4). Notice in the data below that suffixes all bear tone, but that the tone varies on different words. In the examples, ´ indicates a high tone, ` a low tone, and ^ a falling (high-to-low) tone.

a) kɔ́   'war'   kɔ́má   'on war'   kɔ́hú   'in war'
b) pélé   'house'   pélémá   'on (the) house'   péléhú   'in (the) house'
c) bɛ̀lɛ̀   'trousers'   bɛ̀lɛ̀mà   'on trousers'   bɛ̀lɛ̀hù   'in trousers'
d) ngílà   'dog'   ngílàmà   'on (the) dog'   ngílàhù 'in (the) dog'

i) Can you account for the differences in tone on the suffixes for 'on' and 'in' in Mende? State your solution with autosegmental notation such as that illustrated in Figure 3.28 to 3.30. (*Hint*: Assume that the suffixes have no tone to begin with, but that the words to which they are attached do have tone.)

ii) Assuming that you have answered question *i*) successfully, account for the tones of the suffixes meaning 'on' and 'in' in the remaining examples.

e) mbû   'owl'   mbúmà   'on (the) owl'   mbúhù   'in (the) owl'
f) njàhâ   'woman'   njàhámà   'on (the) woman'   njàháhù 'in (the) woman'

17. *Moru* (Miza dialect; Moru is a Sudanic language)

In Moru, contour tones are not found on short vowels in underlying representations. However, phonetic forms of combined lexical items do show contour tones. Can you represent this using autosegmental notation? (*Hint*: A segmental process is involved as well as a typical suprasegmental process and the two processes must be ordered.) In the data provided, ´ indicates a high tone, ` a low tone, and ^ a falling (high-to-low) tone. Vowels with no tone mark need not be considered.

a) màá   →   [mǎ]   'we'
   we

b) ká ùmu   →   [kûmu]   'he runs'
   he runs

c) ká ɔ̀nga   →   [kɔ̂nga]   'he jumps'
   he jumps

d) njá àdì ùzi ja → [njâdùzi ja] 'who are you calling?'
   you call who?

18. Consider the stress patterns in the language data below. Using Table 3.31 as your model, state which parameters are necessary to account for stress placement and what the settings for the necessary parameters are for each set of data.

Latvian (Latvia)
a) víens   'I'
b) mázga:t   'to wash'
c) mázga:ties   'to wash oneself'
d) némazga:ties   'not to wash oneself'
e) pá:rka:rtoʃana:s   'reorganization'

Maung (Goulburn Islands, Australia)
a) ŋábi   'I'
b) bàládʒi   'bag'
c) wùyíba   'mangrove worm'
d) jìniwúnjan   'he cooked it'
e) àwùniláŋuŋ   'he was eating them'
f) gùniyába   'you must give it to him'

Tzutujil (Guatemala)
a) sá   'white'
b) waʔnáq   'eaten'
c) ʃwaʔí   'he ate'
d) ʃtʃʔɛjo:ní   'he hit'
e) tatʃʔejáʔ   'hit it'
f) atʃaxiló:m   'husband'

Hiligaynon (Philippines): not all Hiligaynon words are assigned stress in the same way; only one class of words is represented here (*Hint*: Note in this language that foot building is limited to a maximum of two feet. You need not formalize this fact in your answer.)

a) pamàŋkután   'problem'
b) kàwatán   'thief'
c) bulág   'blind'
d) palaŋitaʔún   'highly sought after'
e) nagapaŋitaʔáj   'to look for each other'

Huallaga Quechua (Peru) (*Hint*: This answer will require reference to Section 3.8.)

a) umá:ta   'to my head'
b) uma:píta   'from my head'
c) uma:pitámi   'from my head (assertive)'
d) tʃajlláraq   'just a moment ago'
e) ajwajkánmi   'they are going'
f) ajwashajkikáma   'hit it'
g) ájwaj   'go'

For the Student Linguist

THE FEATURE PRESENTATION

You've already read that features are the fundamental building blocks of phonemes. By writing rules with features, you can describe simply a change that happens to an entire class of sounds. You also make a stronger statement when you use features in a rule. For example, rule *1* says something about all the stops in a language, but rule *2* only says something about a list of sounds.

1. [−continuant] → [−voice] / __ #
   (stops become voiceless at the end of a word)
2. {p,t,k,b,d,g} → {p,t,k,p,t,k} / __ #
   (p "becomes" p at the end of a word;
   b becomes p at the end of a word; etc.)

If you're just listing sounds, nothing requires them to have anything in common with each other. The sounds in the list could be a totally random selection of sounds turning into another totally random selection of sounds, as in rule *3,* and you'd have no way of predicting that *3* should be less common than *2*.

3. {e,t,w,b,n,h} → {ʃ,p,tʃ,g,a,m} / __ #
   (e becomes ʃ at the end of a word, etc.)

If you use features, you can predict that the set of changes described by rule *2* should be common (because once the rule is translated to features, it's merely rule *1,* a delightfully simple rule), but the set of changes described by rule *3* should be weird and unlikely. To describe rule *3* with features you'd have to write six different rules, and each rule would be ugly and complicated. (I'm assuming that the more features you have to include in a rule, the more complicated it is.) For example, the first rule, changing [e] to [ʃ], would be:

4.
$$\begin{bmatrix} -\text{consonantal} \\ +\text{voice} \\ -\text{high} \\ -\text{low} \\ -\text{back} \\ +\text{tense} \end{bmatrix} \rightarrow \begin{bmatrix} +\text{consonantal} \\ -\text{voice} \\ +\text{coronal} \\ +\text{continuant} \\ +\text{strident} \\ -\text{anterior} \\ -\text{del.rel.} \end{bmatrix} / \_\_ \#$$

However, you can accept the brilliance of features without buying the idea of using a matrix of binary features (like you've done so far), or a hierarchy of binary features (as shown in Section 3.5, Representing Processes). Features could have only one value (these are called "monovalent" or "privative" features). So instead of, say, [−nasal] and

[+ nasal], there'd only be [nasal]. Sounds that had [nasal] in the matrix/representation would be nasal; everything else would be oral. How is that any different from using a binary feature? The difference is that with a binary feature, you can write rules about things that are [− nasal]. You could write a rule like:

5. $\begin{bmatrix} - \text{continuant} \\ - \text{nasal} \end{bmatrix} \rightarrow [- \text{voice}] \; / \underline{\quad} \#$

    (oral stops become voiceless at the end of a word).

But if [− nasal] didn't exist, the only rule you could write would be:

6. $[- \text{continuant}] \rightarrow [- \text{voice}] \; / \underline{\quad} \#$

    (all stops, including nasal stops, become voiceless at the end of a word).

If [− nasal] did exist, you could write rule *5* or rule *6*. Monovalent features, then, give you fewer possible rules. That's great if you can still write all the rules you need for every language, but awful if you can't write every rule you need.

Having fewer possible rules isn't important just because it would make this unit of linguistics easier. It's also important because, theoretically, if there are fewer possible rules in a language, it's easier for a child trying to learn the language to figure out how the sound system in that language works. He or she has fewer options to consider.

What if features could have three values? Or four? Or an infinite number of values? For example, there could be four features for the different laryngeal states: [A laryngeal], for glottal stops; [B laryngeal], for voiced sounds; [C laryngeal], for voiceless unaspirated sounds; and [D laryngeal], for voiceless aspirated sounds. Just like nothing can be both [+ voice] and [− voice] at the same time, nothing could be [A laryngeal] and [B laryngeal] at the same time (or [A laryngeal] and [C laryngeal], etc.). Place of articulation could be handled the same way: [A place] for labials, [B place] for dentals, [C place] for alveolars, etc.

With this type of multivalued system, none of the subgroups (like dentals and alveolars) could be lumped together in a rule. Thus, for the place system I described, you couldn't talk about all of the coronals at once—you could only talk about the dentals or the alveolars or the alveo-palatals and so forth. Once again, whether this is good or bad depends on how well it describes actual languages. (You might want to try out a multivalued feature system for place on some of the phonology problems you've already solved for homework or in class discussions, and see if they're harder or easier to do this way than with a binary feature system.)

These are just a couple of the possible variations on feature systems. I haven't even begun to question the merit of these *features*—i.e., do we *really* need [voice]? Or [strident]? Or [delayed release]? Think about this as you work on a few phonology problems, and see if you can come up with a better feature system. There's a lot of room for change here.

4 MORPHOLOGY
The Study of Word Structure

Llanfairpwllgwyngyllgogerychwyhndrobwllllantysiliogogogoch

(a town name in Wales)

How is it that we can use and understand words in our language that we have never encountered before? This is the central question of **morphology**, the component of a grammar that deals with the internal structure of words. If we are watching a television program about homelessness in American cities, for example, we may hear that many of the homeless are former mental patients who were released because of a policy of deinstitutionalization. An expert interviewed on the program may advocate reinstitutionalization as the only recourse for many of these people. Even if we have never heard these terms before, we understand quite effortlessly that they refer to the practices of releasing patients from hospitals for the mentally ill (*deinstitutionalization*) and returning them to these institutions (*reinstitutionalization*). We know this because we know what the word *institution* means, and we have an unconscious command of English morphology.

As with any other area of linguistic theory, we must distinguish between general morphological theory that applies to all languages and the morphology of a particular language. General morphological theory is concerned with delimiting exactly what types of morphological rules can be found in natural languages. The morphology of a particular language, on the other hand, is a set of rules with a dual function. First, these rules are responsible for **word formation**, the formation of new words. Second, they represent the speakers' unconscious knowledge of the internal structure of the already existing words of their language.

In this chapter, we examine both word structure and word formation. We begin by identifying the minimal meaningful units of language.

4.1 THE MINIMAL MEANINGFUL UNITS OF LANGUAGE

In any science, one of the basic problems is to identify the minimal units, the basic parts out of which more complex units are constructed. Cells, molecules, atoms, particles—each is the minimal unit of some science. In language, we must distinguish the basic units of sound, which in themselves are meaningless, from the basic meaningful units, which are made up of individually meaningless sounds.

Words

Most people, if asked what the minimal meaningful units of language are, would have a ready answer—words. Indeed, of all the units of linguistic analysis, the **word** is the most familiar. In fact, its existence is taken for granted by most of us. We rarely have difficulty picking out the words in a stream of speech sounds or deciding where to leave spaces when writing a sentence. But what, precisely, is a word? A word need not have any special phonetic properties: some words bear stress but others do not; some words are set off by intonational cues but others are not. The two syllables in the following examples have exactly the same pronunciation even though they are separate words in the first case but part of the same word in the second case.

>   *1.* a door   adore

It is also difficult to distinguish words from other linguistic units in terms of the types of meaning they express. *Bachelor* and *unmarried adult male*, for example, seem to have the same meaning, even though one is a word and the other a phrase. Similarly, *builder* and *someone who builds* mean about the same thing even though one is a word and the other a phrase.

Free Forms

Most linguists believe that the word is best defined in terms of the way in which it patterns syntactically. One widely accepted definition of this type is as follows:

>   *2.* A word is a minimal free form.

A **free form** is an element that can occur in isolation and/or whose position with respect to neighboring elements is not entirely fixed. Thus, we would say that *hunters* is a word since it can occur in isolation (as in answer to the question, *Who are they*?) and can occur in different positions within the sentence, as *3* shows.

>   *3.* *a*) The hunters pursued the bear.
>   *b*) The bear was pursued by the hunters.

In contrast, the units *-er* and *-s* do not count as words here since they cannot occur in isolation and their positioning with respect to adjacent elements is completely fixed. Thus, we cannot say **erhunts* or **serhunt*, only *hunters*.

   The reference to *minimal* in *2* is necessary to ensure that we do not identify phrases such as *the hunters* as a single word. Although this unit can occur in isolation and can occupy different positions, it is not a minimal free form since it consists of two smaller free forms—*the* and *hunter*. (We know that *the* is a separate word because its positioning with respect to *hunters* is not entirely fixed; thus, another word can appear between the two, as in *the courageous hunters*.)

Signs and Morphemes

Words, though they may be definable as minimal free forms, are not the minimal meaningful units of language we are looking for, since they can often be broken down further. The word *hunters*, which as we have just seen can stand alone and is thus a free form, nonetheless consists of three meaningful parts: *hunt*, *er*, and *s*. The traditional term for these minimal meaningful units is **sign**. A more common term in linguistics is **morpheme**.

   Most linguistic signs are **arbitrary**, which means that the connection between the sound of a given sign and its meaning is purely conventional, not rooted in some property of the object for which the sign stands. For example, there is nothing about the sound of the word *frog* that has anything to do with frogs. We could just as appropriately use the word *gorf* to refer to those little green creatures, or [tʃiŋwa], which is the Mandarin Chinese word, or [plava] the Sanskrit word. The minimal meaningful units of language are not words, but arbitrary signs or morphemes.

4.2 MORPHOLOGY

There are two basic types of words in human language—simple and complex. **Simple** words are those that cannot be broken down into smaller meaningful units while **complex** words can be analyzed into constituent parts. The word *houses*, for example, is made up of the form *house* and the plural marker -*s*, neither of which can be divided into smaller morphemes. While many English words consist of only one morpheme, others can contain two, three, or more (see Table 4.1).

Table 4.1 Words consisting of one or more morphemes

One morpheme	Two	Three	More than three
and			
boy	boy-s		
hunt	hunt-er	hunt-er-s	
hospital	hospital-ize	hospital-iz-ation	hospital-iz-ation-s
gentle	gentle-man	gentle-man-ly	gentle-man-li-ness

Morphology deals with the internal structure of complex words. The words of any language can be divided into two broad types of categories, **closed** and **open**, of which the latter are most relevant to morphology. The closed categories are the **function words: pronouns** like *you* and *she*; **conjunctions** like *and*, *if*, and *because*; **determiners** like *a* and *the*; and a few others. Newly coined or borrowed words cannot be added to these categories, which is why we say that they are closed. The categories of words that are open are the **major lexical categories: noun (N), verb (V), adjective (A),** and **adverb (Adv).** It is to these categories that new words may be added. Because the major problem of morphology is how people make up and understand words that they have never encountered before, morphology is concerned largely with major lexical categories.

Each word that is a member of a major lexical category is called a **lexical item**. A lexical item can best be thought of as an entry in a dictionary or **lexicon**. The entry for each lexical item will include, in addition to its pronunciation (phonology), information about its meaning (semantics), to what lexical category it belongs, and in what syntactic environments it may occur (subcategorization).

Identifying Morphemes and Allomorphs

A major problem for morphological analysis is how to identify the morphemes that make up words. Given our definition of the morpheme as the minimal meaning-bearing unit of language, this will involve matching strings of sounds with co-occurring features of meaning. As an example of this procedure, consider the small set of data from Turkish in Table 4.2. In Table 4.2, there is

Table 4.2 Some Turkish plurals

Turkish	
/mumlar/	'candles'
/toplar/	'guns'
/adamlar/	'men'
/kitaplar/	'books'

only one feature of meaning, plurality, that is present in all four cases. There is also only one string of sounds, /lar/, that is found in all four words. This suggests that /lar/ is the morpheme marking plurality in Turkish while /mum/ means 'candle', /top/ means 'gun', and so on. We would therefore predict that a single candle would be designated by the morpheme /mum/, without /lar/. This is correct.

This is an unusually simple case, and many complications can arise. One such complication involves the fact that morphemes do not always have an invariant form. The morpheme used to express indefiniteness in English, for instance, has two forms—*a* and *an*.

4. an orange   a building
    an accent   a car
    an eel   a girl

The form *a* is used before words beginning with a consonant and the form *an* before words beginning with a vowel. The variant forms of a morpheme are called its **allomorphs**.

As another example of allomorphic variation, consider the manner in which you pronounce the plural morpheme *-s* in the following words.

5. cats
    dogs
    judges

Whereas the plural is pronounced as [s] in the first case, it is realized as [z] in the second, and as [əz] in the third. Here again, selection of the proper allomorph is dependent on phonetic facts. We will examine this phenomenon in more detail in Section 4.5.

Free and Bound Morphemes

The analysis of morphological structure is based on a number of fundamental contrasts. The first involves the distinction between a **free** morpheme, which can constitute a word by itself, and a **bound** morpheme, which must be attached to another element. The morpheme *house*, for example, is free since it can be used as a word on its own; plural *-s*, on the other hand, is bound.

The morphemes that are free or bound in English do not necessarily have the same status in other languages. For example, in Hare (an Athapaskan language spoken in Canada's Northwest Territories), words that indicate body parts are always bound to a morpheme designating a possessor. Table 4.3 shows the morphemes *fí* ('head'), *bé* ('belly'), and *dzé* ('heart'), each of which must be attached to a morpheme naming the possessor. (A high tone is marked by the diacritic ´.)

Table 4.3 Some bound forms in Hare

Hare		
sefí	'my head'	(never *fí)
nebé	'your belly'	(never *bé)
ʔedzé	'his heart'	(never *dzé)

Just as there are some free forms in English that are bound in other languages, so there are some bound forms in English that are free in other languages. Past tense, for example, is expressed by a bound morpheme (usually *-ed*) in English, but by the free morpheme *le* in Mandarin. (To simplify, tone is not marked in these examples.)

6. *a*) Ta chi   le fan.
        He eat past meal
        'He ate the meal.'
   b) Ta chi   fan   le.
        He eat meal past
        'He ate the meal.'

As you can see from these examples, *le* is apparently not attached to the verb since it is separated from it by the direct object in *6b*.

Word Structure

Like sentences, complex words such as *builder* and *gentlemanly* have an internal structure. In this section, we will consider the categories and representations that are relevant to the analysis of word structure.

What sort of structure do complex words have? Let's look in some detail at the word *denationalization*. This word contains five morphemes: *de nation al ize ation*. *Nation* is a free morpheme, since it can stand alone as a word, while the rest are bound morphemes. But simply listing the parts of the word and whether they are free or bound does not tell us all there is to know about the structure of this word. The parts have to be put together in a particular way, with a particular arrangement and order. For example, none of these possible orders of the same five morphemes constitutes an English word:

7. *ationizalnationde
   *alizdeationnation
   *nationdeizational

In fact, of the 120 possible arrangements of these five morphemes, only one, *denationalization*, could be an English word. The order is so strict because each of the bound morphemes is an **affix**, a morpheme which not only must be bound, but must be bound in a particular position. Furthermore, each affix attaches only to a particular lexical category (either N or V or A), called its **base**, and results in a word of another particular lexical category. The negative affix *de-*, for example, attaches to verbs and forms other verbs:

8. ionize → deionize
   segregate → desegregate

Similarly, the affix *-al* forms adjectives from nouns, *-ize* forms verbs from adjectives or nouns, and *-ation* forms nouns from verbs.

CHAPTER FOUR

116

Given these restrictions, the structure of the word *denationalization* can best be seen as the result of beginning with the simple form *nation*, which we may call the **root** of the word, and adding affixes successively, one at a time, as follows:

> *9.* nation
> national
> nationalize
> denationalize
> denationalization

The structure of the entire word may be represented by means of either a **set of labeled brackets** or a **tree diagram**. (Brackets and trees are also used to represent the structures of sentences, and are discussed more fully in Chapter 5.) The two types of notation are for the most part interchangeable. Both are shown in Figure 4.1. The diagram reveals how the word begins at its **root**,

$[[de[[[nation]_N al]_A ize]_V]_V ation]_N$

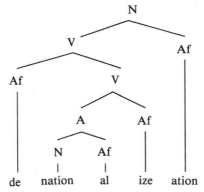

Figure 4.1

which cannot be broken down any further by morphological analysis, and is built up one affix at a time. The abbreviation Af stands for *affix*.

Some other representations of structures of English words are given in Figure 4.2. Such representations indicate the details of morphological structure. Where these details are irrelevant to the point being considered, it is traditional to use a much simpler system of representation that indicates only the location of the morpheme boundaries: *il-legal*, *hospital-ize*, and so on.

a
$[[hunter]_N s]_N$

b
$[[[hospital]_N ize]_V ed]_V$

c
$[[[hope]_N less]_A]ness]_N$

d
$[mis[under[stand]_V]_V]_V$

Figure 4.2

Stems A **stem** is the actual form to which an affix is added. In many cases, the stem will also be a root. In *books*, for example, the element to which the affix *-s* is added is the root. In other cases, however, an affix can be added to a unit larger than a root. This happens in words such as *hospitalized*, in which the past tense affix *-ed* is added to the stem *hospitalize*—a unit consisting of the root morpheme *hospital* and the suffix *-ize* (see Figure 4.3). In this case, *hospital* is not only the root for the entire word but also the stem for *-ize*. The unit *hospitalize*, on the other hand, is simply the stem for *-ed*.

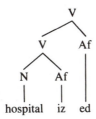

Figure 4.3

Types of Affixes It is possible to distinguish among several types of affixes in terms of their position relative to their stem. An affix that is attached to the front of its stem is called a **prefix** while an affix that is attached to the end of its stem is termed a **suffix**. Both types of affix occur in English, as Table 4.4 shows.

Table 4.4 Some English prefixes and suffixes

Prefixes	Suffixes
disappear	vividly
replay	government
illegal	hunter
inaccurate	distribution

A far less common type of affix, known as an **infix**, occurs within another morpheme. The data in Table 4.5, from the Philippine language Tagalog, contain two infixes, *-um-* and *-in-*. Often word-internal vowel or consonant replacement is confused with infixing. A change such as the one found in English *foot-feet* is not an example of infixing since there is no morpheme **ft*. As you see in Table 4.5, the form to which the Tagalog infix is added actually exists as a separate morpheme.

Table 4.5 Some Tagalog infixes

Stem		Infixed form	
takbuh	'run'	tumakbuh	'ran'
lakad	'walk'	lumakad	'walked'
pili?	'choose'	pinili?	'chose'

In English, although infixing is not part of the normal morphological system, it does occur quite commonly with expletives, providing a kind of extra emphasis, as in the following examples:

10. guaran-damn-tee
abso-bloody-lutely

Still another kind of affix varies according to the stem with which it occurs. It is called a **reduplicative** affix since its form duplicates all or part of the stem. Once again, Tagalog provides examples of this type of affixation (see Table 4.6). The reduplicative affix here is a copy of the first consonant-

Table 4.6 Some reduplicative affixes

Stem		Reduplicated form	
takbuh	'run'	tatakbuh	'will run'
lakad	'walk'	lalakad	'will walk'
pili?	'choose'	pipili?in	'will choose'

vowel sequence of the root. This is an example of **partial reduplication**. Full reduplication is the repetition of the entire word, as in the data in Table 4.7, from Turkish and Indonesian, respectively.

Table 4.7 Some examples of full reduplication

Turkish			
tʃabuk	'quickly'	tʃabuk tʃabuk	'very quickly'
javaʃ	'slowly'	javaʃ javaʃ	'very slowly'
iji	'well'	iji iji	'very well'
gyzel	'beautifully'	gyzel gyzel	'very beautifully'

Indonesian			
oraŋ	'man'	oraŋ oraŋ	'all sorts of men'
anak	'child'	anak anak	'all sorts of children'
maŋga	'mango'	maŋga maŋga	'all sorts of mangoes'

Structure without Affixes When one word is formed from another, the structural relation between the two words is usually marked by means of an affix, as we have seen, but it is possible for one word to be formed from another without any affix.

Conversion, or **zero-derivation**, is probably the most frequent single method of forming words in English. It is especially common in the speech of children. Conversion creates a new word without the use of affixation by simply assigning an already existing word to a new syntactic category. In the case of the derived verbs in Table 4.8, there is no modification, whereas in the case of the derived nouns, there is a stress shift. Structurally, the derived forms remain simple in both instances even though they are new lexical items belonging to a syntactic category different from that of the source form. In the case of *father* and *butter*, for instance, the derived form is a verb capable of taking the normal past tense ending.

Table 4.8 Some examples of conversion

Noun	Derived verb	Verb	Derived noun
father	father	subjéct	súbject
butter	butter	contést	cóntest
ship	ship	survéy	súrvey
nail	nail	permít	pérmit
brush	brush	condúct	cónduct

11. He fathered three children.
He buttered the bread.

Conversion is usually restricted to unsuffixed words, although there are a few exceptions such as *propos-ition* (noun to verb), *refer-ee* (noun to verb), and *dirt-y* (adjective to verb).

Another device is **ablaut**, the replacement of a vowel with a different vowel (see Table 4.9). Ablaut was frequent in earlier stages of English and in related ancient languages. Vestiges remain in Modern English, though the process is no longer productive (used in forming new words).

Table 4.9 Some examples of ablaut

Verb stem	Ablaut noun
sing	song
abide	abode
shoot	shot
sell	sale

Stress shift is used in English to mark the difference between related nouns and verbs. We have already seen some examples of this in Table 4.8. Generally, the verbs have final stress, while the nouns have initial stress, as the further examples in Table 4.10 illustrate.

Table 4.10 Nouns and verbs that differ only in stress

Noun	Verb
cómbine	combíne
tórment	tormént
ímplant	implánt
rétest	retést

Nonaffixal morphology is common in other languages and may involve vocalic patterns or tone and other suprasegmental phonological features, sometimes in complex ways.

Word-Based Morphology In English, the stem of a new word is almost invariably an already existing word. For this reason, we say that English morphology is **word-based**: words are built on words. As we saw in the case of the complex word *denationalization*, each affix is added successively to an English word.

There are, however, many English words whose stems, when the outer affixes are removed, are not existing English words. Consider the words *recalcitrant*, *horrible*, and *uncouth*. These are all English words, but when the affixes *re-*, *-ible*, and *un-* are removed, we are left with the stems **calcitrant*, **horr*, and **couth*, which are not English words. In all three cases, the reasons for the anomaly are historical. *Recalcitrant* and *horrible* were borrowed in their entirety from Latin and French. Because the affixes *re-* and *-ible* were also borrowed, these words appear to have been formed by means of English morphology, although they were not. English has many words like these two, borrowed from the Romance languages, from which many productive English affixes have also been borrowed. Many of them have nonword stems for the same reason. *Uncouth* is not borrowed, but was formed many centuries ago from the then existing word *couth* (historically related to *can* and *know* and still found in some British dialects). Some time after *uncouth* was formed, *couth* disappeared from most dialects, including the standard, leaving *uncouth* stranded without a stem. *Grateful* is another example of the same phenomenon. Words like *grateful* and *horrible* may be described as having bound stems; in any case, they can be explained as cases of historical accident. When we understand how such exceptional words arose, it remains true that all productive English word formation is word-based. Whether all languages are like English in this respect is still an open question.

Some Problematic Cases It is not always easy to determine a word's internal structure. In the case of words such as *cranberry* and *huckleberry*, it is tempting to assume that the root is *berry*, but this leaves us with the morphemes *cran-* and *huckle-*. These elements are obviously not affixes like *un-* or *re-* since they occur with only one root. At the same time, however, neither *cran-* nor *huckle-* can be considered a free morpheme since neither ever stands alone as an independent word. The status of such morphemes continues to be problematic for linguists, who generally classify them as exceptional cases (or refer to them as **cranberry morphemes**).

A slightly different problem arises in the case of words such as *receive*, *deceive*, *conceive*, and *perceive* or *remit*, *permit*, *submit*, and *commit*. The apparent affixes in these words do not express the same meaning as they do when they are attached to a free morpheme. Thus, the *re-* of *receive*, for example, does not have the sense of 'again' that it does in *redo* ('do again'). Nor does the *de-* of *deceive* appear to express the meaning 'reverse the process of' associated with the affix in *demystify* or *decertify*. Moreover, the other portions of these words (*ceive* and *mit*) have no identifiable meaning either.

Because they have no meaning, *ceive* and *mit* are not morphemes of a normal sort. However, they do have some interesting properties. For example, when certain suffixes are added to words ending in *ceive*, *ceive* quite regularly becomes *cept* (as in *receptive* and *deception*); similarly, *mit* becomes *miss* when the same suffixes are added (*permissive*, *admission*). These changes are not phonologically determined, since the *ss* does not occur before these suffixes in other words ending in *t* (*prohibitive*, *edition*). The changes must therefore be due to idiosyncratic properties of *mit* and *ceive*, similar to those of the morpheme *man*, whose plural is always *men* rather than the expected *mans* (*postmen*, *brakemen*, and so on). *Mit* and *ceive* are thus very similar to morphemes.

4.3 WORD FORMATION

A characteristic of all human languages is the potential to create new words. The categories of noun, verb, adjective, and adverb are open in the sense that new members are constantly being added. The two most common types of word formation are **derivation** and **compounding**, both of which create new words from already existing morphemes. Derivation is the process by which a new word is built from a **base**, usually through the addition of an affix. Compounding, on the other hand, is a process involving the combination of two words (with or without accompanying affixes) to yield a new word. The noun *helper*, for example, is related to the verb *help* via derivation; the compound word *mailbox*, in contrast, is created from the words *mail* and *box*.

Derivation

Derivation creates a new word by changing the category and/or the meaning of the base to which it applies. The derivational affix *-er*, for instance, combines with a verb to create a noun with the meaning 'one who does X', as shown in Figure 4.4.

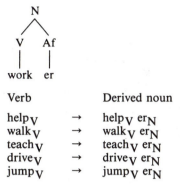

Verb		Derived noun
help$_V$	→	help$_V$ er$_N$
walk$_V$	→	walk$_V$ er$_N$
teach$_V$	→	teach$_V$ er$_N$
drive$_V$	→	drive$_V$ er$_N$
jump$_V$	→	jump$_V$ er$_N$

Figure 4.4

English Derivational Affixes English makes very widespread use of derivation. Table 4.11 lists some examples of English derivational affixes, along with

Table 4.11 Some English derivational affixes

Affix	Change	Semantic effect	Examples
Suffixes			
-able	V → A	able to be X'ed	fixable
-ation	V → N	the result of X'ing	realization
-er	V → N	one who X's	worker
-ing	V → N	the act of X'ing	the shooting
	V → A	in the process of X'ing	the sleeping giant
-ion	V → N	the result or act of X'ing	protection
-ive	V → A	having the property of doing X	assertive
-ment	V → N	the act or result of X'ing	adjournment
-al	N → A	pertaining to X	national
-ial	N → A	pertaining to X	presidential
-ian	N → A	pertaining to X	Canadian
-ic	N → A	having the property of X	organic
-ize	N → V	put in X	hospitalize
-less	N → A	without X	penniless
-ous	N → A	the property of having or being X	poisonous
-ate	A → V	make X	activate
-ity	A → N	the result of being X	stupidity, priority
-ize	A → V	make X	modernize
-ly	A → Adv	in an X manner	quietly
-ness	A → N	the state of being X	happiness, sadness
Prefixes			
ex-	N → N	former X	ex-president
in-	A → A	not X	incompetent
un-	A → A	not X	unhappy
	V → V	reverse X	untie
re-	V → V	X again	rethink

information about the type of base with which they combine and the type of category that results. The first entry states that the affix *-able* applies to a verb base and converts it into an adjective with the meaning 'able to be X'ed'. Thus, if we add the affix *-able* to the verb *fix*, we get an adjective with the meaning 'able to be fixed'.

Derivational Rules Each line in Table 4.11 can be thought of as a **word formation rule** that predicts how words may be formed in English. Thus, if there is a rule whereby the prefix *un-* may be added to an adjective *X*, resulting in another adjective, *unX*, with the meaning 'not X', then we predict that an adjective like *harmonious* may be combined with this prefix to form the adjective *unharmonious*, which will mean 'not harmonious'. The rule also provides a structure to the word, given in Figure 4.5.

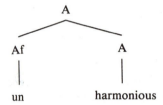

Figure 4.5

These rules have another function: they may be used to analyze words as well as to form them. Suppose, for example, that we come across the word *unharmonious* in a book on architecture. Even though we may never have encountered this word before, we will probably not notice its novelty, but simply use our unconscious knowledge of English word formation to process its meaning. In fact, many of the words that we encounter in reading, especially in technical literature, are novel, but we seldom have to look them up, relying instead on our morphological competence.

Sometimes beginning students have trouble determining the category of the base to which an affix is added. In the case of *worker*, for instance, the base (*work*) is sometimes used as a verb (as in *they work hard*) and sometimes as a noun (as in *the work is time-consuming*). This may then make it difficult to know which category occurs with the suffix *-er* in the word *worker*. The solution to this problem is to consider the use of *-er* (in the sense of 'one who X's') with bases whose category can be unequivocally determined. In the words *teacher* and *writer*, for instance, we see this affix used with bases (*teach* and *write*) that are clearly verbs. Moreover, we know that *-er* can combine with the verb *sell* (*seller*) but not the noun *sale* (*saler). These facts allow us to conclude that the base with which it combines in the word *worker* must be a verb rather than a noun.

Multiple Derivations Derivation can create multiple levels of word structure, as shown in Figure 4.6. Although complex, *organizational* has a structure consistent with the word formation rules given in Table 4.11. Starting with the outermost affix, we see that *-al* forms adjectives from nouns, *-ation* forms nouns from verbs, and *-ize* forms verbs from nouns.

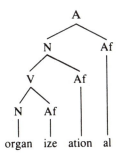

Figure 4.6

In some cases, the internal structure of a complex word is not obvious. The word *unhappiness*, for instance, could apparently be analyzed in either of the ways indicated in Figure 4.7. By considering the properties of the affixes *un-* and *-ness*, however, it is possible to find an argument that favors Figure 4.7a

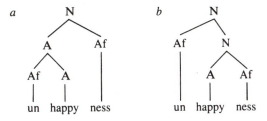

Figure 4.7

over 4.7b. The key observation here is that the prefix *un-* combines quite freely with adjectives, but not with nouns as shown in Table 4.12. (The advertiser's *uncola* is an exception to this rule and therefore attracts the attention of the reader or listener.) This suggests that *un-* must combine with the adjective

Table 4.12 Distribution of *un-*

un + A	un + N
unable	*unknowledge
unkind	*unintelligence
unhurt	*uninjury

happy before it is converted into a noun by the suffix *-ness*—exactly what the structure in Figure 4.7a depicts. The derivation of this word therefore proceeds in two steps. First, the prefix *un-* is attached to the adjective *happy*, resulting in another adjective (see Figure 4.8). The second step is to add the suffix *-ness* to this adjective (see Figure 4.9). We see, then, that complex words have structures consisting of hierarchically organized constituents. The same is true of sentences, as we will see in the next chapter.

A phonological constraint (advanced) Derivation does not always apply freely to the members of a given category. Sometimes, for instance, a particular derivational affix is able to attach only to stems with particular phonological prop-

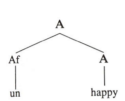

Figure 4.8

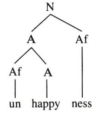

Figure 4.9

erties. A good example of this involves the English suffix *-en*, which combines with adjectives to create verbs with a causative meaning ('cause to become X'). As the following examples illustrate, however, there are many adjectives with which *-en* cannot combine.

Table 4.13 Restrictions on the use of *-en*

Acceptable	Unacceptable
whiten	*abstracten
soften	*bluen
madden	*angryen
quicken	*slowen
liven	*greenen

The suffix *-en* is subject to a phonological constraint. In particular, it can only combine with a monosyllabic stem that ends in an obstruent. Hence it can be added to *white*, which is both monosyllabic and ends in an obstruent, but not to *abstract*, which has two syllables, or to *blue*, which does not end in an obstruent.

Compounding

In derivational word formation, we take a single word and change it somehow, usually by adding an affix, to form a new word. The other way to form a new word is by combining two already existing words in a **compound**. *Blackbird*, *doghouse*, *seaworthy*, and *blue-green* are examples of compounds.

Compounding is highly productive in English and in related languages such as German. It is also widespread throughout the languages of the world. In English, compounds can be found in all the major lexical categories—nouns (*doorstop*), adjectives (*winedark*), and verbs (*stagemanage*)—but nouns are by far the most common type of compounds. Verb compounds are quite infrequent. Among noun compounds, most are of the form noun + noun (N N), but A N compounds are also found quite frequently; V N compounds are rare. An example of each type is given in Figure 4.10. Compound adjectives are of the type A A or N A, as shown in Figure 4.11.

Figure 4.10 Types of noun compounds

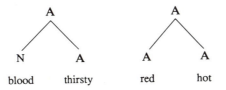

Figure 4.11 Types of adjective compounds

Although there are very few true compound verbs in English, this does not seem to be due to any general principles. In other languages, compound verbs are quite common.

Structurally, two features of compounds stand out. One is the fact that the constituent members of a compound are not equal. In all the examples given thus far, the lexical category of the last member of the compound is the same as that of the entire compound. Furthermore, the first member is always a modifier of the second: steamboat is a type of boat; red-hot is a degree of hotness. In other words, the second member acts as the **head** of the compound, from which most of the syntactic properties of the compound are derived, while the first member is its **dependent**. This is generally true in English and in many other languages, although there are also languages in which the first member of a compound is the head.

The second structural peculiarity of compounds, which is true of all languages of the world, is that a compound never has more than two constituents. This is not to say that a compound may never contain more than two words. Three-word (*dog food box*), four-word (*stone age cave dweller*), and longer compounds (*trade union delegate assembly leader*) are easy to find. But in each case, the entire compound always consists of two components, each of which may itself be a compound, as shown in Figure 4.12. The basic compounding

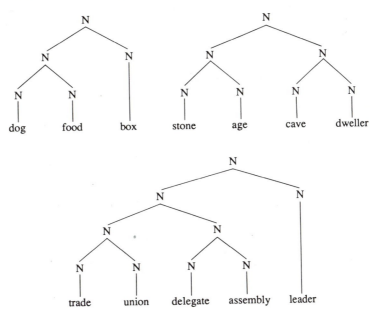

Figure 4.12

operation is therefore always binary, although repetition of the basic operation may result in more complex individual forms.

Compounding and derivation may also feed each other. The members of a compound are often themselves derivationally complex, and sometimes, though not often, a compound may serve as the base of a derivational affix. An example of each of these situations is given in Figure 4.13.

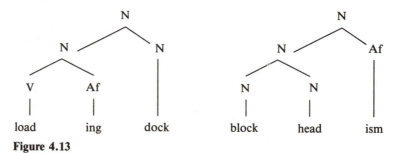

Figure 4.13

English orthography is not consistent in representing compounds since they are sometimes written as single words, sometimes with an intervening hyphen, and sometimes as separate words. However, it is usually possible to recognize noun compounds by their stress pattern since the first component is pronounced more prominently than the second. In noncompounds, conversely, the second element is stressed (see Table 4.14).

Table 4.14 Compounds versus noncompounds

Compound word		Non-compound expressions	
greénhoùse	an indoor garden	greèn hoúse	a house painted green
bláckboàrd	a chalkboard used in classrooms	blàck boárd	a board that is black
wét sùit	a diver's costume	wèt suít	a suit that is wet

Although the exact types of compounds differ from language to language, the practice of combining two existing words to create a new word is very widespread, as Table 4.15 indicates.

Other Word Formation

Compounding and derivation through affixation are the most common word formation processes in English, but they are not the only ones. As the examples in this section indicate, there are various other ways to create new words.

Clipping is a process whereby a new word is created by shortening a polysyllabic word. This process, which seems especially popular among students, has yielded forms such as *prof* for *professor*, *phys-ed* for *physical education*, *ad* for *advertisement*, and *poli-sci* for political science. A number of such abbreviations have been accepted in general usage: *doc, auto, lab, sub, bike, porn, burger, condo,* and *prep.* The most common abbreviations occur in names—such as *Liz, Ron, Kathy,* and *Lyn.*

Table 4.15 Compounds from various languages

Mandarin		
tian-liang sky brightens 'dawn'	tou-teng head aches 'headache'	di-zhen earth quakes 'earthquake'

French		
timbre-poste stamp mail 'postage stamp'	grand'mère great mother 'grandmother'	coffre-fort box strong 'safe'

German	
Haus-friedens-bruch house peace break 'trespass'	Wort-bedeutungs-lehre word meaning theory 'semantics'

Finnish	
lammas-nahka-turkki sheep skin coat 'sheepskin coat'	elin-keino-tulo-vero-laki life's means income tax law 'income tax law'

Tagalog		
basag-ulo break-head 'a brawl/trouble'	agaw-buhaj snatch-life 'near death/dying'	hampas-lupaʔ strike-ground 'a vagabond'

Acronyms are formed from the initial sounds or letters of a string of words, such as the name of an organization or a scientific expression. Some examples of acronyms include AIDS for acquired immune deficiency syndrome, NASA for National Aeronautics and Space Administration, radar for radio detecting and ranging, and snafu for situation normal all fouled up. Where the combined initial letters follow the pronunciation patterns of English, the string can be pronounced as a word, such as NATO (North Atlantic Treaty Organization). However, if it happens to be unpronounceable, then each letter is sounded out separately (RBI for run batted in, UNH for University of New Hampshire, NFL for National Football League). In other cases, even if the combined initials can be pronounced, it may be customary to sound out each letter, as in NIV for New International Version (of the Bible) or UCLA for the University of California at Los Angeles.

Blends are words that are created from parts of two already existing lexical items. Well-known examples of blends include *motel* from *motor hotel*, *brunch* from *breakfast* and *lunch*, *selectric* from *select* and *electric*, *telethon* from *telephone* and *marathon*, *dancercise* from *dance* and *exercise*, and *chortle*, coined by Lewis Carroll as a blend of *chuckle* and *snort*. Usually, the first part of one word and the last part of a second one are combined to form a blend. Sometimes, though, only the first word is clipped, as in *perma-press* for 'permanent-press'.

Backformation is a process whereby a word whose form is similar to that of a derived form undergoes a process of deaffixation. *Resurrect* was originally formed in this way from *resurrection*. Other backformations in English include *enthuse* from *enthusiasm*, *donate* from *donation*, and *orient* or *orientate* from *orientation*. A major source of backformations in English has been words that end with *-or* or *-er* and have meanings involving the notion of an agent, such as *editor*, *peddler*, *swindler*, and *stoker*. Because hundreds of words ending in these affixes are the result of affixation, it was assumed that these words too had been formed by adding *-er* or *-or* to a verb. By the process of backformation, this led to the conclusion that *edit*, *peddle*, *swindle*, and *stoke* exist as simple verbs.

Backformation continues to produce new words in modern English. Two relatively recent products of this process are the verbs *liaise* from *liaison* and *self-destruct* from *self-destruction*. The even more striking backformation *attrit*, from *attrition*, was often used by military officials during the recent Gulf War to refer to the decimation of Iraqi troops (as in *The enemy is 50 percent attritted*). It is not difficult to imagine new instances of backformation in English yielding forms such as *cush* (from *cushy*), *cessant* (from *incessant*), *sipid* (from *insipid*), *hairdress* (from *hairdresser*), *burgle* from *burglar*, and so on. Indeed the verb *tuit*, a backformation from *intuition*, was recently heard on the radio!

Other Sources It is sometimes possible to create new words from names. For example, brand names sometimes become so widely used that they are accepted as generic terms (*kleenex* for 'facial tissue' or *xerox* for 'photocopy'). Scientific terms such as *watt*, *curie*, and *fahrenheit* provide examples of words derived from the names of individuals associated with the things to which they refer.

Finally, all languages have words that have been created to sound like the thing to which they refer. Examples of such **onomatopoeic** words in English include *buzz*, *hiss*, *sizzle*, and *cuckoo*. Since these words are not exact phonetic copies of the things to which they refer, onomatopoeic words with the same referents can differ from language to language (see Table 4.16).

Table 4.16 Onomatopoeia across languages

English	Japanese	Tagalog
cock-a-doodle-doo	kokekokko	kuk-kukauk
meow	njaa	ŋijaw
chirp	pii-pii	tiririt
bow-wow	wan-wan	aw-aw

4.4 INFLECTION

Virtually all languages have contrasts such as singular and plural, and past and present. These contrasts are often marked with the help of **inflection**. Instead of creating a new word as derivation or compounding does, inflection modifies a word's form in order to mark the grammatical subclass to which it belongs. In the case of English nouns, for instance, inflection marks the plural subclass by adding the affix *-s* (see Table 4.17). In the case of verbs, on the other hand, inflection marks a distinction between past and nonpast subclasses—usually by adding the suffix *-ed* to indicate the past tense (see Table 4.18).

Table 4.17 Plural inflection

Singular	Plural
apple	apple s
car	car s
dog	dog s

Table 4.18 Tense inflection

Present	Past
work	work ed
jump	jump ed
hunt	hunt ed

Because inflection applies after all word formation rules, the plural affix can be added to the output of derivation and compounding as well as to a simple noun (see Table 4.19). Similarly, tense affixes can be attached to the output of derivation and compounding as well as to simple verbs (see Table 4.20).

Table 4.19 Inflection of derived or compound nouns

Derived form	Compound
worker s	football s
creation s	outlaw s
kingdom s	blackboard s

Table 4.20 Inflection of derived or compound verbs

Derived form	Compound
hospitalize d	babysit s
activate d	manhandle d

Inflection versus Derivation

As the preceding examples show, inflection is expressed primarily by means of affixation. Thus, in English the plural is marked by the suffix *-s* (barring a few exceptions such as *man/men*) while the past is generally marked by the suffix *-ed* (although a number of verbs use ablaut, as in *sink/sank* and *ride/rode* or suppletion, as in *go/went*).

Because inflection and derivation are both marked by affixation, the distinction between the two can be a subtle one and it is sometimes unclear which function a particular affix has. Three criteria are commonly used to help distinguish between inflectional and derivational affixes.

Category change First, inflection does not change either the grammatical category or the type of meaning found in the word to which it applies.

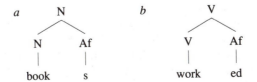

Figure 4.14

The word to which the plural suffix *-s* is attached in Figure 4.14a is still a noun and still has the same type of content or meaning. Even though *books* differs from *book* in referring to several things rather than just one, the type of thing(s) to which it refers remains the same. Similarly, a past tense suffix such as the one in Figure 4.14b indicates that the action took place in the past, but it does not change the word's category (which remains a V), nor does it modify the type of meaning. The verb continues to denote an action regardless of whether the tense is past or non-past.

In contrast, derivational affixes characteristically change the category and/or the type of meaning of the form to which they apply and are therefore said to create a new word. Consider the following examples of derivation.

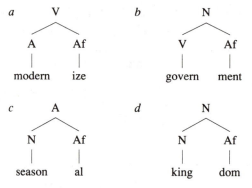

Figure 4.15

As Figure 4.15a shows, *-ize* makes a verb out of an adjective, changing the type of meaning it expresses from a property (*modern*) to an action (*modernize*). Parallel changes in category and type of meaning are brought about by *-ment* (V to N) and *-al* (N to A). Matters are a little different in the case of *-dom*, which does not bring about a category change (since both the base and the resulting word are Ns). However, *-dom* does modify the type of meaning from 'person' (for *king*) to 'place' (for *kingdom*).

A second property of inflectional affixes has to do with their positioning within the word. As the examples in *12* illustrate, a derivational affix must be closer to the root than an inflectional affix. (IA = inflectional affix; DA = derivational affix.)

12. neighbor hood   s   *neighbor   s   hood
     root   DA   IA   root   IA   DA

The positioning of inflectional affixes outside derivational affixes reflects the fact that inflection takes place after all word formation processes, including derivation.

A third criterion for distinguishing between inflectional and derivational affixes has to do with **productivity**, the relative freedom with which they can combine with stems of the appropriate category. Inflectional affixes typically have very few exceptions. The suffix *-s*, for example, can combine with virtually any noun that allows a plural form (aside from a few exceptions such as *oxen* and *feet*). In contrast, derivational affixes characteristically apply to restricted classes of stems. Thus, *-ize* can combine with only certain nouns to form a verb.

13. hospitalize   *clinicize
     terrorize   *horrorize
     crystalize   *glassize

In the case of verbs, matters are somewhat more complicated, since many English verbs have irregular or idiosyncratic past tense forms (*saw, left, went,* and so on). Nonetheless, the distribution of the inflectional affix *-ed* is still considerably freer than that of a derivational affix such as *-ment*, which combines with only certain verbs to give nouns. While all the verbs in Table 4.21 can take the regular past tense ending, only those in the first three rows are able to take the *-ment* suffix. With only eight inflectional affixes, English is not a highly inflected language. In some languages, inflectional affixes number in the dozens and encode many contrasts not represented in English. We will see examples of such languages in the next section. Table 4.22 gives a complete list of productive English inflectional affixes.

Table 4.21 Compatibility with *-ment*

Verb ⟶ Past		Verb ⟶ Noun	
confine	confined	confine	confinement
align	aligned	align	alignment
treat	treated	treat	treatment
arrest	arrested	arrest	*arrestment
straighten	straightened	straighten	*straightenment
cure	cured	cure	*curement

Table 4.22 English inflectional affixes

Nouns	
plural *-s*	the book<u>s</u>
possessive *-'s*	John<u>'s</u> book
Verbs	
third person singular present *-s*	John read<u>s</u> well.
progressive *-ing*	He is work<u>ing</u>.
past tense *-ed*	He work<u>ed</u>.
past participle *-ed*	He has stud<u>ied</u>.
Adjectives and adverbs	
comparative *-er*	This one is small<u>er</u>. He arrived earl<u>ier</u>.
superlative *-est*	This one is the small<u>est</u>. He arrived earl<u>iest</u>.

Nominal Inflection (advanced)

In this section, we will consider three common types of contrasts that are expressed with the help of inflectional affixes on nouns.

Number is the morphological category that expresses contrasts involving countable quantities. The simplest number contrast consists of a two-way distinction between the **singular** (one) and the **plural** (more than one). This is the contrast found in the English inflectional system, where a noun takes the suffix *-s* if it refers to two or more entities. Even this basic distinction is not found in all languages, however. In Nancowry (spoken in India's Nicobarese Islands), for example, number is not marked on nouns at all. A sentence such as *14* is therefore ambiguous since *nɔ́t* 'pig' can refer to one or more pigs.

14. sák   nɔ́t   ʔin   ciʔɔ́j.
   spear pig   the   we
   'We speared the pig(s).'

In Inuktitut, on the other hand, there is an obligatory three-way number contrast involving singular, dual (two and only two), and plural (more than two).

15. iglu   'a house'
   igluk   'two houses'
   iglut   'three or more houses'

Noun Class Some languages divide nouns into classes based on shared semantic and/or phonological properties. A well-known example of this involves what is sometimes called **gender classification**. In French, Italian, and Spanish, for example, nouns are either masculine or feminine while in German there are three subclasses: masculine, feminine, and neuter. In general, there is a correlation between the inherent sex of living things and the grammatical gender of the noun designating them. For example, in Italian, *fratello* 'brother' is masculine while *sorella* 'sister' is feminine. However, most inanimate nouns in gender languages are classified more or less arbitrarily. Thus, *lune* 'moon' is feminine in French while the corresponding German word *Mond* is masculine. Even some nouns referring to animate entities seem to be classified arbitrarily since German *Mädchen* 'young girl' is neuter, not feminine, and French *victime* 'victim' is feminine regardless of whether the person it refers to is male or female. Facts like these have led many linguists to use the more neutral term **noun class** rather than gender to refer to this type of contrast.

Some languages have extremely elaborate systems of noun classification. The Bantu language Swati, for instance, makes use of prefixes to distinguish among more than a dozen noun classes, some of which are given in Table 4.23. (Tone is not represented in these examples.)

Table 4.23 Noun classification in Swati

Prefix	Example		Description of class
um(u)	um-fana	'boy'	persons
li	li-dvolo	'knee'	body parts, fruit
s(i)	si-tja	'plate'	instruments
in	in-dʒa	'dog'	animals
bu	bu-bi	'evil'	abstract properties
pha	pha-ndle	'outside'	locations

Noun class or gender can be marked in a variety of ways. In some languages, the form of the determiner varies depending on the class of the noun. Thus, Spanish uses the definite determiner *el* for masculine nouns and *la* for feminine ones; French uses *le* for the masculine subclass and *la* for the feminine subclass. In other languages, inflectional affixes rather than determiners can be used to indicate the gender subclass of the noun. Russian, for instance, uses one set of affixes for most nouns in the feminine subclass and another set for most nouns in the masculine subclass. The examples in Table 4.24 show the gender endings for nouns that head subject phrases.

Table 4.24 Russian gender endings

Noun		Ending	Class
dom	'house'	Ø	masculine
ulica	'street'	-a	feminine
tʃuvstvo	'sensation'	-o	neuter

The class of a noun may be revealed in a variety of ways. It often appears as a marker on the noun itself, as in the Swati examples in Table 4.23. Russian uses distinct sets of affixes for most masculine, feminine, and neuter nouns. But the major effect of noun class is not on the nouns themselves. Instead, the gender of a noun can be detected most reliably on other words of the sentence that **agree** with the noun: adjectives, verbs, and pronouns. To pick a simple example, in Spanish nouns may be either masculine or feminine, as we have noted. The typical feminine marker is -*a* and the typical masculine marker -*o*. Many nouns, however, are irregular and therefore have the "wrong" marker, or no marker at all. So, the word *mapa* 'map' is masculine, though it ends in -*a,* and the feminine word *mujer* 'woman' has no suffix. But, we can tell the gender of these nouns from the adjectives that agree with them: *el mapa pequeño* 'the small map'; *una mujer alta* 'a tall woman'. In each case, the adjective shows the normal marker for the gender of the noun. In English, there are no gender markers at all on nouns. Nonetheless, the different pronouns (masculine *he*; feminine *she*; neuter *it*) that agree with them tell us that nouns in English are divided into three genders.

Case Still another type of inflectional contrast associated with nouns in many languages involves **case**—a category that encodes information about the syntactic role (subject, direct object, and so on) of a noun. In Modern English, this information is expressed largely through word order and the use of prepositions.

16. Bette composed a song on the bus.

In this sentence, the subject *Bette* occurs before the verb and the direct object *a song* appears after it, while the element expressing location (*the bus*) is preceded by the preposition *on*. In many languages, however, these distinctions are marked by inflectional affixes. As an illustration of this, consider Table 4.25,

Table 4.25 Turkish case

Case	Form
Nominative	ev
Accusative	ev-i
Dative	ev-e
Genitive	ev-in
Locative	ev-de
Ablative	ev-den

which presents the set of related nominal forms (called a **nominal paradigm** or **declension**) for the Turkish word *ev* 'house'. In general, the **nominative (Nom)** case (which is not overtly marked in Turkish) indicates the subject of the sentence; the **accusative (Ac)** the direct object; the **dative (Dat)** the indirect object or recipient; and the **genitive (Gen)** the possessor. The **locative (Loc)** marks place or location, and the **ablative (Abl)** marks direction away from. The following sentences illustrate the use of these forms.

17. *a*) Adam   ev-i   Ahmed-e   gøster-di.
       man-Nom house-Ac Ahmed-Dat showed
       'The man showed the house to Ahmed.'
   b) Ev   -in   rengi   māvidir.
       house-Gen color-Nom blue
       'The house's color is blue.'
   c) Adam   ev-de   kaldɨ.
       man-Nom house-Loc stayed
       'The man stayed in the house.'
   d) Adam   ev-den   tʃɨktɨ.
       man-Nom house-Abl went
       'The man went from the house.'

The contrasts represented in the Turkish case system are intermediate in complexity compared to languages like Finnish, which has fifteen distinct case categories, and languages like Rumanian, which has only two contrasts. It is sometimes suggested that nouns in Modern English exhibit a maximally simple two-way contrast between the genitive (marked by -'*s*) and all other grammatical functions.

In many languages, number, gender, and case contrasts are combined into one ending, as the nominal paradigm for Russian in Table 4.26 shows. In this

Table 4.26 Russian nominal paradigms

Masculine nouns (*dom* 'house')

	Singular	Plural
Nominative	dom	dom-a
Genitive	dom-a	dom-ov
Accusative	dom	dom-a
Dative	dom-u	dom-am
Locative	dom-e	dom-ax
Instrumental	dom-om	dom-ami

Feminine nouns (*ulica* 'street')

	Singular	Plural
Nominative	ulic-a	ulic-ɨ
Genitive	ulic-ɨ	ulic
Accusative	ulic-u	ulic-ɨ
Dative	ulic-e	ulic-am
Locative	ulic-e	ulic-ax
Instrumental	ulic-oj	ulic-ami

Neuter nouns (*tʃuvstvo* 'sensation')

	Singular	Plural
Nominative	tʃuvstv-o	tʃuvstv-a
Genitive	tʃuvstv-a	tʃuvstv
Accusative	tʃuvstv-o	tʃuvstv-a
Dative	tʃuvstv-u	tʃuvstv-am
Locative	tʃuvstv-e	tʃuvstv-ax
Instrumental	tʃuvstv-om	tʃuvstv-ami

paradigm, a single ending is used to indicate the noun's number, gender, and case. Thus *-ov*, for example, is used to indicate that the noun belongs to the masculine gender, that it is plural, and that it functions as a genitive. A morpheme that encodes more than one grammatical contrast is called a **portmanteau** morpheme.

Some languages make use of case marking to encode grammatical contrasts quite unlike those found in familiar European languages. In the Australian language Yidin, for instance, the case-marking pattern groups together the subject of an intransitive verb and the direct object of a transitive verb (both of which receive a zero ending) while using a special marker (*-ngu*) for the subject of a transitive verb (see Figure 4.16). In this type of system, the case associated with the subject of the transitive verb (such as *-ngu* in Figure 4.16a) is called the **ergative**, while the case associated with the direct object (*tree*) and with the subject of an intransitive verb (*man* in Figure 4.16b) is called the **absolutive**.

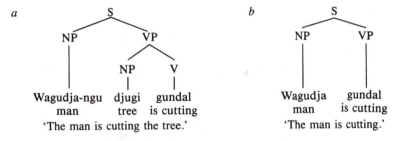

Figure 4.16 Case marking in Yidin

Ergative case marking is found in a small but varied set of languages, including Basque (Spain), Tagalog (in the Philippines), Avar (in the Caucasus), Inuktitut (in northern Canada and Greenland), and Halkomelem (on the west coast of Canada). Ergative case marking is far less common than the nominative-accusative pattern, which groups together the subjects of transitive and intransitive verbs, distinguishing them from direct objects. This is the pattern found in German, Russian, Turkish, Japanese, Korean, and many other languages. In the examples in Figure 4.17 from Tamil (a language spoken in South India and Sri Lanka), the subject of both a transitive and an intransitive verb takes the zero ending, while the direct object has the suffix *-ai*. (The internal structure of the NPs is not represented here.)

English nouns do not use case contrasts to distinguish between subjects and direct objects, although the genitive suffix *-'s* is used to mark the possessor role. However, pronouns exhibit a more elaborate set of contrasts.

18. Nominative: *They* laughed. *They* read the billboard.
    Accusative: Sue saw *them*.
    Genitive: Sue took *their* car.

Since the same form of the pronoun is used for the subject of a transitive verb as for the subject of an intransitive verb, we can say that these contrasts follow the nominative-accusative pattern.

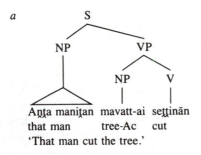

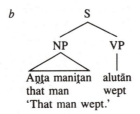

a
‘That man cut the tree.’

b
‘That man wept.’

Figure 4.17 Nominative-accusative marking in Tamil

Verbal Inflection (advanced)

In this section, we consider some of the more common inflectional categories associated with verbs in the world's languages.

Person and Number Agreement A widely attested type of verbal inflection in human language involves **person**—a category that typically distinguishes among the first person (or speaker), the second person (or addressee), and the third person (anyone else). In many languages, the verb is marked for both the person and number (singular or plural) of the subject. A clear illustration of this is found in Finnish, which exhibits the contrasts in the present tense shown in Table 4.27. (The complete set of inflected forms associated with a verb is

Table 4.27 Finnish verbal paradigm

	Singular		Plural	
First person	puhun	'I speak'	puhumme	'we speak'
Second person	puhut	'you speak'	puhutte	'you speak'
Third person	puhuu	'he, she, or it speaks'	puhuvat	'they speak'

called a **verbal paradigm** or a **conjugation**.) Because the inflectional markers provide so much information about the person and number of the subject phrase, this element need not be overtly present in Finnish.

19. *a*) As-uu tässä.
    live - 3rd sg. here
    '[He] lives here.'
   b) As-un tässä.
    live - 1st sg. here
    '[I] live here.'

The optionality of the subject phrase is a common feature of languages with rich verbal inflection.

English has a much more impoverished system of person and number agreement in the verb, and an inflectional affix is used only for the third person singular in the present tense (see Table 4.28). Except for commands, formal English does not tolerate sentences without overtly expressed subjects.

20. *Spoke English.

Table 4.28 English verbal paradigm

	Singular	Plural
First person	I speak	we speak
Second person	you speak	you speak
Third person	he, she, or it speaks	they speak

Tense is the category that encodes the time of a situation with reference to the moment of speaking. Thus, the past tense is used with verbs denoting an action that occurs prior to the moment of speaking.

There are many different types of tense systems in the languages of the world. In terms of inflection, for example, English makes a two-way contrast between past (marked by the inflectional suffix -ed in regular verbs) and the non-past (unmarked). Notice that the non-past form of the verb can be used for both present and future events.

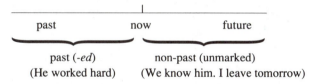

Figure 4.18

In the Australian language Dyirbal, in contrast, there is a two-way distinction between future and non-future. As the following examples show, the latter form can be used for both present and past events.

21. a) Future: b) Non-future:
   bani-ɲ   bani-ɲu
   'will come'   'came, is coming'

In Spanish and Lithuanian, on the other hand, inflectional endings are used to express a three-way past-present-future contrast.

22.   Spanish: Lithuanian:
   a) Juan habl-ó bien.   Dirb-au.
      'John spoke well.'   'I worked.'
   b) Juan habl-a bien.   Dirb-u.
      'John speaks well.'   'I work.'
   c) Juan habl-ar-á bien.   Dirb-siu.
      'John will speak well.' 'I will work.'

A still richer system of contrasts is found in the Bantu language Chi-Bemba, which uses its inflectional system to distinguish degrees of pastness and futurity. (In the following examples, the diacritics mark tone; affixes expressing tense contrasts are underlined.)

Table 4.29 Tense in ChiBemba

Past	Future
Remote past (before yesterday) ba-àlí-bomb-ele 'They worked.'	Remote future (after tomorrow) ba-ká-bomba 'They'll work.'
Removed past (yesterday) ba-àlíí-bomba 'They worked.'	Removed future (tomorrow) ba-kà-bomba 'They'll work.'
Near past (earlier today) ba-àcí-bomba 'They worked.'	Near future (later today) ba-léé-bomba 'They'll work.'
Immediate past (just happened) ba-á-bomba 'They worked.'	Immediate future (very soon) ba-áláá-bomba 'They'll work.'

Voice Still another grammatical contrast in verbal systems involves what has traditionally been called **voice**. The major function of this system is to indicate the role of the subject in the action described by the verb. In English, there are two voices. In the active voice, the subject denotes the actor or agent (in sentence *23,* the one who writes). In the passive voice, in contrast, the subject denotes a nonactor. As the following sentences indicate, the English passive voice is expressed with the help of the verb *be* and a past participle.

    23. An author writes books.
    24. *a*) Books are written by an author.
        b) The author was given a royalty by the company.

In many languages, the passive voice is marked by a special bound morpheme rather than by an auxiliary verb. The following example is from Turkish, in which *-il* marks the passive.

    25. Pendʒere Hasan tarafindan atʃ -il   -di.
        window Hasan   by   open Pass Past
        'The window was opened by Hasan.'

4.5 MORPHOLOGY AND PHONOLOGY

Chapter 3 of this book dealt with allophonic variation in terms of rules that derive allophones from underlying (phonemic) representations. A second type of variation in language involves morphemes and their contextual variants, allomorphs. An example of allomorphic variation can be seen in the English plural morpheme, which has different allomorphs in the words *cat*[s], *dog*[z], and *match*[əz]. Like allophonic variation, this phenomenon is analyzed with the help of a single underlying representation from which the allomorphs can be derived. The rules that account for both allophonic and allomorphic variation make reference to phonetic environments, including syllable structure. There are, however, differences between allophonic and allomorphic variation, two of which are outlined in the following section.

Morpho-phonemic Rules

Rules that account for alternations among allomorphs (morphophonemic alternations) are called **morphophonemic** rules. The major differences between allophonic and morphophonemic rules can be summed up under two major points.

- Allophonic rules are exceptionless—they apply in the appropriate environment to all classes and forms in a language. There are, for example, no exceptions to a rule such as aspiration in English. In contrast, morphophonemic rules often show exceptions. They may, for example, apply to a limited class of forms, as in the case of the rule that changes final *f* to *v* in the plural of a few English words such as *knife* and *thief*. (We will examine this rule in more detail later in this section.)
- Morphophonemic rules often (but do not always) make reference to particular morphemes or morphological structures. This does not occur with allophonic rules.

Deriving Allomorphs

We treat allomorphs in much the same way as we treat allophones. An underlying representation (UR) is set up, and rules apply to derive all phonetic variants from the same underlying representation. Often, the underlying representation of the morpheme is the elsewhere allomorph—the one that occurs with the widest distribution.

The allomorphs of the English plural morpheme provide a good example of phonologically conditioned allomorphs.

English Plural Allomorphs   The plural morpheme in English shows three-way variation in its allomorphs. The three allomorphs, /-s/, /-z/, and /-əz/, are distributed in a systematic manner, as Table 4.30 illustrates. The phonetic form

Table 4.30 English plural allomorphs

Allomorph /-s/		Environment
tops	/tɑps/	Stems end in a voiceless
mitts	/mɪts/	consonant that is not
backs	/bæks/	both strident and
puffs	/pʌfs/	coronal.
baths	/bæθs/	(p, t, k, f, θ)

Allomorph: /-z/		Environment
cobs	/kɑbz/	Stems end in a vowel or a
lids	/lɪdz/	voiced consonant that is
lads	/lædz/	not both strident and
doves	/dʌvz/	coronal.
lathes	/leðz/	
pins	/pɪnz/	(b, d, g, v, ð, m, n, ŋ, r, l, w, j)
bums	/bʌmz/	
wings	/wɪŋz/	
teas	/tiz/	
days	/dez/	

Allomorph /-əz/		Environment
hisses	/hɪsəz/	Stems end in a consonant
buzzes	/bʌzəz/	that is both strident
crutches	/krʌtʃəz/	and coronal.
judges	/dʒʌdʒəz/	(s, z, ʃ, ʒ, tʃ, dʒ)
wishes	/wɪʃəz/	

of these allomorphs is determined by the segment that precedes them. Stems that end in a strident coronal consonant always appear with the /-əz/ allomorph. Stems that end in a vowel or a voiced consonant that is not both strident and coronal take the /-z/ allomorph, and stems that end in a voiceless consonant that is not both strident and coronal take the /-s/ allomorph.

A fundamental strategy of the linguist in selecting the underlying representation of an allomorph is to choose the one with the widest distribution. Since the /-z/ allomorph occurs after all vowels as well as after most voiced consonants, it is chosen as basic. This choice results in underlying representations that show /-z/ after all stems, as in Table 4.31.

Table 4.31 Underlying representations of some English plurals

tops	tɑp-z	cobs	kɑb-z	hisses	hɪs-z
mitts	mɪt-z	lids	lɪd-z	buzzes	bʌz-z
				judges	dʒʌdʒ-z

Derivation Once the underlying representations have been set up, the phonetic forms (PFs) can be derived. We can account for the allomorph /-əz/ by noting that whenever the underlying /-z/ appears after a stem that ends in a strident coronal consonant, a schwa is present. This reflects a general phonotactic constraint of English: a word cannot contain a sequence of strident coronals in the same syllabic coda. Such a sequence may occur across word boundaries in compound forms, such as *buzz saw* /bʌz sɔ/. It may even occur across syllable boundaries, as in *posture* /pɑstʃr̩/ (/pɑʃtʃr̩/ for some speakers). But when a sequence of two coronal stridents occurs in a coda, it is broken up by the epenthesis of a schwa. (In effect, a new syllable is created.) It is possible to write a rule that inserts a schwa and breaks up the succession of a stem-final strident coronal consonant and the strident coronal /-z/ of the underlying representation, as in Figure 4.19. At this point, we can derive forms such as *matches*, *judges*, and so on. This is shown in Figure 4.20.

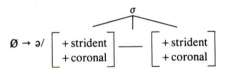

Figure 4.19 English schwa epenthesis

	UF	# m æ tʃ - z #
Schwa epenthesis		# m æ tʃ - ə z #
	PF	[mætʃəz]

Figure 4.20 Derivation of English *matches*

It is now necessary to account for the appearance of [s] after voiceless consonants and [z] elsewhere. This is formalized in Figure 4.21. No rule is necessary for the /-z/ allomorph, which will now appear only in words where the rules of voicing assimilation and schwa epenthesis have not applied. It is the

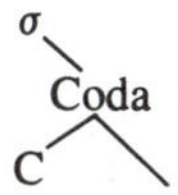

$$C \rightarrow [-\text{voice}] / [-\text{voice}]\_\_\_\_\_$$

Figure 4.21 Voicing assimilation

elsewhere variant, the allomorph that appears where none of the restricted, rule-derived allomorphs appear. Figure 4.22 shows derivations of all three plural allomorphs. The ordering of the rules is crucial here. If voicing assimilation applied first, the plural ending of forms such as *match* and *hiss* would incorrectly end up as [mætʃəs] and [hɪsəs], since the suffix would assimilate in voicing before epenthesis could apply. In the next section we see how these same rules for determining the plural allomorphs of English interact with another type of morphophonemic rule.

	UF	# b ʊ k - z #	# f ɪ b - z #	# m æ tʃ - z #
Schwa epenthesis		---	---	# m æ tʃ - ə z #
Voicing assimilation		# b ʊk - s #	---	---
	PF	[bʊks]	[fɪbz]	[mætʃəz]

Figure 4.22 Derivations of English plural forms

Conditioning by Morphological Class

A second type of morphophonemic rule refers to a subclass of forms, rather than applying to all members of a class of forms. English plurals again provide the example.

Irregular English Plurals As Table 4.32 illustrates, English includes a limited class of words that show an alternating /f/ and /v/ in their plural forms. The

Table 4.32 Alternating stem-final /f/ and /v/ in English

The /f/ — /v/ alternation (irregular forms)		No alternation (regular forms)	
wife	wives	whiff	whiffs
thief	thieves	chief	chiefs
leaf	leaves	fife	fifes
knife	knives	laugh	laughs

alternating class is unproductive; new words with final /f/ entering English will not show this alternation. For example, speakers would pluralize a hypothetical new word *nif* as [nɪfs], not [nɪvz]. This suggests that each word in this class needs to be marked as undergoing a rule that voices its stem-final segment when the form is pluralized. Such a rule takes the form shown in Figure 4.23,

Rule PL: f → v / ____] - z$_{\text{plural}}$

Figure 4.23 The f → v alternative rule for English

in which it is labeled *Rule PL*. Information about rules that a form must undergo is included in its dictionary entry. A form that undergoes Rule PL is marked as [+ Rule PL]. Forms that are not so marked are automatically assumed to be [− Rule PL]. Following a stem-changing rule such as Rule PL, the morphophonemic rule of voicing assimilation introduced in Figure 4.21 applies. Other relevant rules such as vowel lengthening apply as well. (Stress is not shown in Figure 4.24.) The allophonic rule of vowel lengthening presented in Chapter 3 has also applied here to give the correct form of *thieves*.

	UF	# θif - z #[+ Rule PL]	# tʃif - z #
f→v (Rule PL)		# θijv - z #	---
Voicing assimilation		---	# tʃif - s #
Vowel lengthening		# θi:v - z #	---
	PF	[θi:jvz]	[tʃijfs]

Figure 4.24 Derivation of English *thieves* and *chiefs*

The underlying forms presented so far in this chapter are all very much unlike their phonetic representations. The next section takes up the implications of this kind of representation in more detail.

Abstract Underlying Represen- tations

Underlying representations generally show some degree of difference from phonetic representations. There are no phonetic forms like [mɪtz], [pæθz], or [wajfz] in English, although such forms are found as underlying representations. Underlying representations are therefore said to be **abstract**. By an abstract representation, we mean one that is distinct from its phonetic realization. The greater the difference between the phonological and the phonetic representations, the more abstract the phonological representation is said to be.

Although morphophonemic URs can be very abstract, there is an advantage to this kind of representation. Employing abstract underlying representations enables us to make greater generalizations about the relationship among allomorphs. For example, we have just seen how two phonetically distinct forms of the root morpheme *thief* are derived from the same UR.

Abstraction and English Stems In English, we can derive the root of both *electri*[k] and *electri*[s]*ity* from one underlying form. This approach expresses the fact that English speakers recognize the two phonetic forms as variants of the same morpheme. Assuming that the underlying representation ends in *k*, we can write a morphophonemic rule that changes *k* to *s* before the suffix *-ity*, as in Figure 4.25. The variant of the stem that ends in *k* is chosen as underlying

k → s / ___ + ɪti

Figure 4.25 English *k* to *s* fronting

for two reasons. First, the stem *electri*[k] has a wider distribution than the allomorph *electri*[s]; it occurs in words such as *electrical* as well as in the unsuffixed form. Second, our proposed rule has the advantage of reflecting a natural process of fronting of final /k/ to [s] before the high front vowel of the suffix. It would be more difficult to find phonetic motivation for a rule that changes an /s/ to [k] in final position or before the suffix -*al*.

It is also significant that the rule must include morphological information—the identity of the suffix that triggers the change—since /k/ is not pronounced as [s] whenever it appears before the vowel [ɪ] in English. If it were, English speakers would automatically pronounce *kill* as *sill*, and *kick* as *sick*. Since they do not, we assume that the morphological information is a crucial determining factor in this rule.

The derivations of *electric* and *electricity* are given in Figure 4.26. The allophonic rule of flapping and the stress rule are also involved in this deri-

	UR	# ijlɛktrɪk #	# ilɛktrɪk - ɪti #
Stress		# ijlétrɪk #	# ilɛktrík - ɪti #
k→s rule		---	# ilɛktrís - ɪti #
Flapping		---	# ilɛktrís - ɪDi #
	PR	[ijléktrɪk]	[ijlɛktrísɪDij]

Figure 4.26 Derivation of *electric* and *electricity* in English

vation but are not formalized here. Our underlying form is rather abstract in the case of #ilɛktrɪk + ɪti#, but our rule has allowed us to represent an English speaker's knowledge that the stems *electri*[k] and *electri*[s] are allomorphs of the same morpheme.

Summing Up

This chapter is concerned with the structure of **words** in human language. Many words consist of smaller formative elements, called **morphemes**. These elements can be classified in a variety of ways (**free** vs. **bound**, **root** vs. **affix**, **prefix** vs. **suffix**) and can be combined in different ways to create new words. Two basic processes of word formation in English are **derivation** and **compounding**. Words may also be **inflected** to mark grammatical contrasts in **person**, **number**, **gender**, **case**, **tense**, and **voice**.

Although the processes of word formation may differ, all languages have the means to create new words and therefore exhibit the rule-governed creativity that is typical of human language.

Interaction between the phonological and morphological components of the grammar is reflected by the presence of allomorphs. The use of underlying representations and derivation by **morphophonemic** rule accounts for these morphophonemic alternations. In some cases, allomorphy is determined by the fact that only certain classes of forms undergo a given morphophonemic rule. Dealing with allomorphy leads to underlying representations, which in many instances are **abstract**.

Key Terms

ablaut	morpheme
absolutive	morphophonemic
abstract	nominative
accusative	noun class
acronyms	number
affix	onomatopoeic
agreement	partial reduplication
allomorph	person
backformation	phonological constraint
base	plural
blend	portmanteau
bound	prefix
case	reduplicative (affix)
clipping	replacement
coinage	root
complex	second person
compounding	simple
conjugation	singular
conversion	stem
dative	suffix
derivation	suppletion
ergative	tense
first person	third person
free form	tone
full reduplication	transitive
head	tree structures
infix	word
inflection	word manufacture
intransitive	word-based morphology
lexicon	zero derivation

Sources

The discussion of words and morphemes draws heavily on the classic treatments found in Gleason's *An Introduction to Descriptive Linguistics* (cited below) and C. F. Hockett's *A Course in General Linguistics* (New York: Macmillan, 1958). The problem of an underlying form for the plural suffix and of morphophonemic variation in general is discussed in Arnold Zwicky's article "Settling on an Underlying Form: The English Inflectional Endings" in *Testing Linguistic Hypotheses*, edited by D. Cohen and J. Wirth (New York: John Wiley and Sons, 1975).

Recommended Reading

Aronoff, M. 1976. *Word Formation in Generative Grammar*. Cambridge, Mass.: MIT Press.

Bauer, Laurie. 1983. *English Word-formation*. London: Cambridge University Press.

Gleason, H. 1955. *An Introduction to Descriptive Linguistics*. New York: Holt, Rinehart and Winston.

Matthews, P. H. 1991. *Morphology*. London: Cambridge University Press.

Spencer, Andrew. 1991. *Morphological Theory*. Oxford: Blackwell.

Appendix: How to Identify Morphemes in Unfamiliar Languages

One part of morphological analysis involves identifying morphemes in unfamiliar languages and determining the nature of the information that they carry. (A number of the problems in the set of exercises that follow this chapter will give you an opportunity to practice this type of analysis.) The key procedure to follow in working on this sort of problem can be stated simply as follows:

• Identify recurring forms and match them with recurring meanings.

Consider again the following small sample of data from Turkish, consisting of four words along with their English translations. (In actual practice, of course, a data sample would also include sentences and it might well be unclear at first where the word boundaries should be placed.)

Table 4.33 Some Turkish words

/mumlar/	'candles'
/toplar/	'guns'
/adamlar/	'men'
/kitaplar/	'books'

As you can see, the form /lar/ occurs in all four items in our sample. From the translations of these items, we can see that there is also a feature of meaning—namely, plurality—that is present in all four cases. Using the procedure just stated, we therefore hypothesize that /lar/ is the morpheme marking plurality in Turkish. Once this has been determined, we can then infer that /mum/ in /mumlar/ is also a morpheme (presumably with the meaning 'candle'), that /top/ in /toplar/ is a morpheme (with the meaning 'gun'), and so on. A larger sampling of Turkish data would confirm the correctness of these inferences.

In doing morphological analysis in unfamiliar languages, there are a number of pitfalls to avoid. For the type of exercise normally used at the introductory level, the following guidelines should prove especially useful.

• Do not assume that the morpheme order in the language you are analyzing is the same as in English. In Korean, for example, morphemes indicating location (the rough equivalent of 'at', 'in', and so forth) follow rather than precede the noun (hence, *hakkjo-ejse* is literally 'school at').

• Do not assume that every semantic contrast expressed in English will also be manifested in the language you are analyzing. In Turkish, for example, there is no equivalent for English *the* and *a*. In Mandarin Chinese, the same pronoun form can be used to refer to a male or a female (there is no *he-she* distinction).

- Do not assume that every contrast expressed in the language you are analyzing is manifested in English. For example, some languages distinguish more than two number categories (Inuktitut distinguishes singular, dual, and plural) and some languages make multiple tense contrasts (ChiBemba has an eight-way distinction).
- Remember that a morpheme can have more than one form (allomorph). Just as the English plural suffix can be realized as /s/, /z/, or /əz/, so morphemes in other languages can have more than one realization. For example, further study of Turkish would reveal that the plural suffix in this language can also be realized as /ler/, depending on the vowel in the stem to which the suffix is attached.

Questions

1. Consider the following words and answer the questions below.

a) fly	f) reuse	k) spiteful	p) preplan
b) desks	g) triumphed	l) suite	q) optionality
c) untie	h) delight	m) fastest	r) prettier
d) tree	i) justly	n) deform	s) mistreat
e) dislike	j) payment	o) disobey	t) premature

i) For each word, determine whether it is simple or complex.

ii) Circle all of the bound morphemes. Underline all of the roots.

2. All but one of the following Persian words consist of more than one morpheme. (*Note*: There is no overt morpheme for the third person singular pronoun 'he', so the word [xarid] contains only one morpheme.)

a) [xaridam]	'I bought'
b) [xaridi]	'you (sg) bought'
c) [xarid]	'(he) bought'
d) [naxaridam]	'I did not buy'
e) [namixaridand]	'they were not buying'
f) [naxaridim]	'we did not buy'
g) [mixarid]	'(he) was buying'
h) [mixaridid]	'you (pl) were buying'

i) Try to match each of the following notions with a morpheme in the Persian data.

a) I	e) they
b) you (sg)	f) not
c) we	g) was/were + *-ing* (continuous)
d) you (pl)	h) buy

ii) How would you say the following in Persian?

a) They were buying.

b) You (sg) did not buy.

c) You (sg) were buying.

3. The following Turkish data involves allomorphic variation.

a) [lokanta] 'a restaurant'   [lokantada] 'in/at a restaurant'
b) [kapɨ] 'a door'   [kapɨda] 'in/at a door'
c) [randevu] 'an appointment'   [randevuda] 'in/at an appointment'
d) [baʃ] 'a head'   [baʃta] 'in/at a head'
e) [kitap] 'a book'   [kitapta] 'in/at a book'
f) [koltuk] 'an armchair'   [koltukta] 'in/at an armchair'
g) [taraf] 'a side'   [tarafta] in/at a side'

i) Identify the Turkish morpheme meaning 'in/at'.
ii) Does this morpheme have more than one allomorph?
iii) If so, what are the allomorphs? Describe their distribution as generally as possible.

4. Consider the following words.

a) desks   e) triumphed   i) preplan (V)   m) optionality
b) untie   f) ageless   j) fastest   n) prettier
c) invalid (A)   g) justice   k) reuse   o) mistreat
d) dislike (V)   h) payment   l) disobey   p) preview (V)

i) Draw a tree structure for each word.
ii) For the word *optionality*, what is the base for the affix *-ion*? What is
the base for the suffix *-ity*? Are either of these bases also the root for
the entire word? If so, which one?

5. Each of the following columns illustrates a different morphological process.

Column 1   *Column 2*
a) mouse/mice   f) récord/recórd
b) dive/dove   g) ímport/impórt
c) take/took   h) cónvict/convíct
d) goose/geese   i) ímprint/imprínt
e) eat/ate   j) óutrage/outráge

i) What morphological process is at work in column 1? column 2?
ii) Describe in your own words the difference between the process exemplified in column 1 versus that in column 2.
iii) Think of at least one more English example to add to each column.

6. The following words can be either nouns or verbs.

a) record   f) outline   k) report
b) journey   g) convict   l) outrage
c) exchange   h) imprint   m) answer
d) remark   i) reprint   n) import
e) surprise   j) retreat   o) cripple

i) For each word, determine whether stress placement can be used to
make the distinction between noun and verb.

ii) Think of two more English examples illustrating the process of stress shift to mark a category distinction.

7. The following Samoan data illustrates one of the morphological processes discussed in this chapter.

a)	[mate]	'he dies'	[mamate]	'they die'
b)	[nofo]	'he stays'	[nonofo]	'they stay'
c)	[galue]	'he works'	[galulue]	'they work'
d)	[tanu]	'he buries'	[tatanu]	'they bury'
e)	[alofa]	'he loves'	[alolofa]	'they love'
f)	[taoto]	'he lies'	[taooto]	'they lie'
g)	[atamaʔi]	'he is intelligent'	[atamamaʔi]	'they are intelligent'

i) What morphological process is illustrated by these data?
ii) Describe how this process works.
iii) If 'he is strong' in Samoan is *malosi*, how would you say 'they are strong' in Samoan?

8. The following data from Agta (spoken in the Philippines) illustrates a specific type of affix.

a)	[dakal]	'big'	[dumakal]	'grow big, grow up'
b)	[darág]	'red'	[dumarág]	'redden'
c)	[ɾuráw]	'white'	[ɾumuráw]	'become white'

i) What is the affix in Agta meaning 'become X'?
ii) What type of affix is it?
iii) Describe its placement.

9. The following words from Chamorro, spoken in Guam and the Mariana Islands, illustrate some of the morphological processes described in this chapter.

I. *Root*		*Derived word*
a)	[adda] 'mimic'	[aadda] 'mimicker'
b)	[kanno] 'eat'	[kakanno] 'eater'
c)	[tuge] 'write'	[tutuge] 'writer'

II. *Root*		*Derived word*
d)	[atan] 'look at'	[atanon] 'nice to look at'
e)	[saŋan] 'tell'	[saŋanon] 'tellable'
f)	[guaija] 'love'	[guaijajon] 'lovable'
g)	[tulaika] 'exchange'	[tulaikajon] 'exchangeable'
h)	[chalek] 'laugh'	[chalekon] 'laughable'
i)	[ngangas] 'chew'	[ngangason] 'chewable'

III. *Root*		*Derived word*
j)	[nalang] 'hungry'	[nalalang] 'very hungry'
k)	[dankolo] 'big'	[dankololo] 'very big'
l)	[metgot] 'strong'	[metgogot] 'very strong'
m)	[bunita] 'pretty'	[bunitata] 'very pretty'

     i) What morphological process is involved in I? in II? in III?

     ii) Do any changes in lexical category take place in I? in II? in III?

     iii) Formulate a general statement as to how the derived words in I are formed. Does the same apply to the derived words in III? If not, how would you change the statement to account for the forms in III?

     iv) Does the affix in II have more than one allomorph? If so, what are the allomorphs? What is their distribution?

10. In this chapter, an argument was presented in favor of the following structure for the word *unhappiness*.

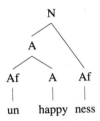

Using the same type of argument, justify tree structures for the words *unforgiving*, *replacement*, and *redefinable*. (*Hint*: This will involve determining the type of syntactic category with which the affixes in these words can combine; see Table 4.11.)

11. In English, the suffix *-er* can be added to a place name. Examine the words in the two columns below.

Column 1	*Column 2*
Winnipeger	*Denverer
Yellowknifer	*Victoriaer
New Yorker	*Vancouverer
Newfoundlander	*Torontoer
Londoner	*Ganderer

    a) In general terms, what does the suffix *-er* mean in these words?

    b) How is this *-er* different in meaning from the *-er* found in the words *skater* and *walker*?

    c) As shown in Column 2, the distribution of *-er* in the above data is restricted in some way. State the constraint illustrated above in your own words.

    d) Does this constraint also apply to the type of *-er* used in the word *skater*? (*Hint*: What would you call 'one who discovers' or 'one who ploughs'?)

12. The following words have all been formed by compounding. Draw a tree structure for each word. If you are in doubt as to the lexical category of the compound, remember that the category of the head determines the category of the word.

a) football   m) city center
b) billboard   n) air bag
c) sunbather   o) potato peel
d) in-crowd   p) bitter-sweet
e) fastfood   q) hockey match
f) software   r) coffee table
g) freeze-dry   s) flower-power
h) overbook   t) blueprint
i) tree trunk   u) Greenpeace
j) leadfree   v) space ship
k) shortstop   w) brain dead
l) girlfriend   x) kill-joy

13. The words in column 2 have been created from the corresponding word in column 1. Indicate the word formation process responsible for the creation of each word in column 2.

Column 1		*Column 2*
a) automation	→	automate
b) humid	→	humidifier
c) stagnation, inflation	→	stagflation
d) love, seat	→	loveseat
e) énvelope	→	envélop
f) typographical error	→	typo
g) aerobics, marathon	→	aerobathon
h) act	→	deactivate
i) curve, ball	→	curve ball
j) perambulator	→	pram
k) (a) comb	→	comb (your hair)
l) beef, buffalo	→	beefalo
m) random access memory	→	RAM
n) megabyte	→	meg
o) teleprinter, exchange	→	telex
p) influenza	→	flu

14. Here are five instances where a new word is needed. Create a word for each of these definitions using the word formation process suggested. Fill in the blanks with your new words.

   a) Use an acronym . . . . for your uncle's second oldest brother.
      "We visited my _____ at Christmas."
   b) Use onomatopoeia . . . . for the sound of a coffee percolator at work.
      "I can't concentrate because my perc is _____ ing."
   c) Use conversion . . . . for wrapping something breakable in bubbles.
      "You'd better _____ that ornament or else it might break."

d) Use a compound . . . . for the annoying string of cheese stretching from a slice of hot pizza to one's mouth.

"As the _____ hung precariously from my lips, our eyes met!"

e) Use backformation . . . . for the action of backformation.

"We had to _____ words in Linguistics today."

15. Create new words for each of the following situations.

a) Use a product name . . . . for the act of scrubbing with Ajax.

"I _____ed the tub after giving Fido a bath."

b) Use a proper name . . . . for the act of breaking dishes, which Jonathan does regularly.

"He's going to _____ all of my best dishes."

c) Use clipping . . . . for a course in ovinology (the study of sheep).

"Have you done your _____ assignment yet?"

d) Use derivation . . . . for being able to be contacted.

"The counsellor is not very _____."

e) Use a blend . . . . for a hot drink made with milk and nutmeg.

"I'll have a _____ and two peanut butter cookies, please."

16. Determine whether the words in each of the following groups are related to one another by processes of inflection or derivation.

a) go, goes, going, gone
b) discover, discovery, discoverer, discoverable, discoverability
c) lovely, lovelier, loveliest
d) inventor, inventor's, inventors, inventors'
e) democracy, democrat, democratic, democratize

17. The following sentences contain both derivational and inflectional affixes. Underline all of the derivational affixes and circle the inflectional affixes.

a) The farmer's cows escaped.
b) It was raining.
c) Those socks are inexpensive.
d) Jim needs the newer version.
e) The strongest rower won.
f) The pitbull has bitten the cyclist.
g) She quickly closed the book.
h) The alphabetization went well.

18. (*Advanced*) Each of the following corpora of data illustrates inflection of some type.

I. GERMAN

a) Der Mann ist krank.
'The man is sick.'

b) Die Frau ist krank.
'The woman is sick.'

II. GREEK

c) o eryatis fonazi ton andra
'The worker calls the man.'

d) o andras plironi ton eryati
'The man pays the worker.'

e) o andras ine afstiros
'The man is strict.'

III. BASQUE

f) Aitak bazuen fabrike aundi.
father owned factory big
'Father owned a big factory.'

g) Aite izango da.
'Father will be (there).'

IV. ITALIAN

h) le ziè sono americanè.
'The aunts are American.'

i) gli zii sono studiosi.
'The uncles are studious.'

j) la zia è studiosa.
'The aunt is studious.'

k) lo zio è americano.
'The uncle is American.'

V. ENGLISH

l) I am biting my tongue.

m) You are biting your tongue.

n) She is biting her tongue.

  i) What type of nominal inflection do the German sentences illustrate?

  ii) What type of nominal inflection is exemplified in the Greek data? It is marked morphologically in two ways. Identify both ways.

  iii) Of the two patterns of case-marking discussed in the chapter, which does the Greek data show?

  iv) How is the pattern of case-marking different in Basque from that of Greek?

  v) In the Italian data, there are four different forms of the word meaning 'the'. Name two inflectional contrasts that are present in each of those four forms.

  vi) What type of verbal inflection is illustrated in the Italian sentences?

  vii) Examine the English data in V. What types of verbal inflection are present on the verb 'to be'? What types of nominal inflection are present on the six pronouns in these sentences?

19. The following data provides the possible forms of the regular past tense morpheme of English.

a)	walked	/wɔkt/	l)	heaved	/hivd/
b)	cracked	/krækt/	m)	wheezed	/wizd/
c)	flipped	/flɪpt/	n)	fined	/fajnd/
d)	hissed	/hɪst/	o)	flitted	/flɪtəd/
e)	huffed	/hʌft/	p)	butted	/bʌtəd/
f)	hushed	/hʌʃt/	q)	padded	/pædəd/
g)	munched	/mʌntʃt/	r)	loaded	/lodəd/

h) drubbed /drʌbd/   s) collided /kʌlajdəd/
i) dragged /drægd/   t) allowed /ʌlawd/
j) jogged /dʒɑgd/   u) sowed /sod/
k) fudged /fʌdʒd/

i) List the alternate forms of the past tense morpheme.
ii) Which alternate makes the best underlying form? Why?
iii) State in words the conditioning factors that account for the presence of the alternate forms of the past tense morpheme.

20. Vowel harmony is a process that results in all vowels of a word sharing a certain feature or features. Morphophonemic rules of vowel harmony are found in many languages.

		Singular	*Plural*
a)	'eye'	gøz	gøzler
b)	'candle'	mum	mumlar
c)	'gun'	top	toplar
d)	'horse'	at	atlar
e)	'sheath'	kın	kınlar
f)	'thread'	ip	ipler
g)	'rose'	gyl	gyller
h)	'hand'	el	eller

i) List the allomorphs of the plural morpheme in the preceding data from Turkish.
ii) What phonological feature is shared by the vowels of both allomorphs of the plural?
iii) What phonological feature distinguishes the vowels of the allomorphs?
iv) Is it possible in this case to pick one allomorph as the best underlying form?
v) If it is possible, explain why it is so and provide a representation of the underlying representation using the feature hierarchy.

For the Student Linguist

BAMBIFICATION

Well of course language is productive. You can't possibly read this chapter without being completely convinced of how very easy it is to make up new words. Morphological productivity is mildly interesting when you're creating transparent new words, such as when you have a verb like *fax* and create a new verb like *refax* (fax again) or *speed-fax* (fax fast) or an adjective like *faxable* (can be faxed), but it's not exactly earth-shattering.

What amazes me, though, is running across a new word, knowing it's a perfectly good word in English, knowing exactly how to pronounce it, and not having a clue about what it means. I'm not talking about knowing *frete* could be a word because it doesn't break any phonological rules of English. I'm talking about a word whose meaning remains mysterious even though that word can be broken down into recognizable, meaningful parts. Take the word *Brazilification,* which appears in Douglas Coupland's novel *Generation X. Brazilification* might appear in a sentence like "The recent Brazilification seen in the U.S. will have a large impact on tax reform plans." *Brazilification* could mean "the replacement of forests with cattle ranches," or "the improved quality of coffee," or a many other things; it actually means "the widening gulf between the rich and the poor and the accompanying disappearance of the middle classes" (p.11). From this, the meaning of *Brazilify* is transparent: make the gulf between the rich and the poor wider, thereby causing the disappearance of the middle classes.

Now consider *Bambification,* another morphologically complex word from Coupland's book. It means "make like X", where X is a variable which can be replaced by *Brazil*, or *Bambi*, or some other noun. *Bambification* doesn't mean "make like Bambi's economic system," although theoretically it could. It means "the mental conversion of flesh and blood living creatures into cartoon characters possessing bourgeois Judeo-Christian attitudes and morals" (p. 48).

Morphology is even more interesting when you look at compounds. The four words below, also gleaned from *Generation X*, could each be interpreted in a few ways. For each word, I've given the real definition and my own, made-up definition (Coupland's are made-up too, but his were first, so I count them as the real definitions). I've also given the morphological structure that matches one of the definitions. Your task is to figure out how the structure would be different (if it is) for the other definition.

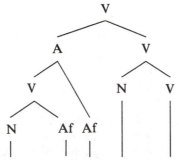

VACCINATED TIME TRAVEL
To fantasize about traveling backward in time, but only with the proper vaccinations. (p. 11)

VACCINATED TIME TRAVEL
To travel freely in time, but only to times and places worth going to.

GREEN DIVISION
Sorting waste into chic recycling bins, showing how environmentally aware you are to all your friends.

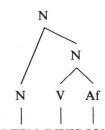

GREEN DIVIS ION
Knowing the difference between envy and jealousy. (p. 150)

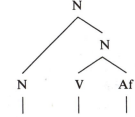

DUMPSTER CLOCK ING
The tendency when looking at objects to guesstimate the amount of time they will take to eventually decompose: *"Ski boots are the worst. Solid plastic. They'll be around till the sun goes supernova."* (p. 162)

DUMPSTER CLOCKING
Reckoning time by the amount and nature of the contents of the dumpster. *"An old couch, three textbooks, and twenty pounds of notebooks beneath a case of empties. Must be late May."*

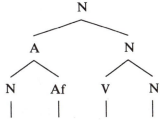

TERMINAL WANDERLUST
The inescapable urge, when seated at a computer, to do *anything* else as long as it involves getting away from the machine. Often involves coffee and cigarettes.

TERMIN AL WANDER LUST
A condition common to people of transient middle-class upbringings. Unable to feel rooted in any one environment, they move continually in the hopes of finding an idealized sense of community in the next location. (p. 171)

5 SYNTAX
The Analysis of Sentence Structure

. . . [T]he game is to say something new with old words
Ralph Waldo Emerson, *Journals* (1849)

One of the main themes of this book is that language use involves an intricate system of largely subconscious grammatical knowledge. Nowhere is this more obvious than in the study of how words are combined to produce sentences. In this chapter we will consider the system of rules and categories that underlies sentence formation in human language. This component of the grammar is called **syntax**.

Like the other linguistic systems considered in this book, the syntactic component of the grammar is both creative and systematic. As noted in chapter 1, speakers of a language are able to combine words in novel ways, forming sentences that they have neither heard nor seen before. However, not just any combination of words will give a well-formed sentence. English speakers recognize that the pattern in *1* is not permissible even though the same words can be combined in a different way to form the acceptable structure in *2*.

1. *House painted student a the.
2. A student painted the house.

We say that an utterance is **grammatical** if speakers judge it to be a possible sentence of their language. Thus, example *2* is a grammatical sentence of English, but *1* is not.

This chapter will focus on the 'architecture' of grammatical sentences, with an emphasis on the manner in which words are combined to form various types of sentence structure. Section 5.1 introduces some of the most common categories of words found in language as well as some simple rules that govern the organization of these categories into larger structural units. Subsequent sections describe other aspects of sentence structure, using examples and phenomena drawn from English and other languages.

Contemporary linguistic research has yet to reach a consensus about precisely how sentence structure should be analyzed, and a variety of quite different possibilities are currently being explored. This chapter will introduce a simple version of **transformational syntax**, currently the most popular and best known approach to syntactic analysis. Although many linguists disagree with various features of this approach, it is very widely used in linguistics and other disciplines concerned with language (psychology, anthropology, speech pathology). For this reason, it is the usual point of departure for introductions to the study of sentence structure. Section 5.6 provides a brief discussion of some alternatives to transformational analysis.

5.1 CATEGORIES AND STRUCTURE

A fundamental fact about words in all human languages is that they can be grouped together into a relatively small number of classes, called **syntactic categories**. This classification reflects a variety of factors, including the type of meaning that words express, the type of affixes that they take, and the type of structures in which they can occur.

Word-Level Categories

Table 5.1 provides examples of the word-level categories that are most central to the study of syntax.

Table 5.1 Syntactic categories

Lexical categories	Examples
Noun (N)	Harry, boy, wheat, policy
Verb (V)	arrive, discuss, melt, hear, remain
Adjective (A)	good, tall, silent, old, expensive
Preposition (P)	to, in, on, near, at, by
Adverb (Adv)	silently, slowly, quietly, quickly, now

Non-lexical categories	Examples
Determiner (Det)	the, a, this, these
Auxiliary (Aux)	will, can, may, must, be, have
Conjunction (Con)	and, or, but
Degree word (Deg)	too, so, very, almost, more, quite

The four most studied syntactic categories are **noun (N)**, **verb (V)**, **adjective (A)**, and **preposition (P)**. These elements, which are often called **lexical** categories, play a very important role in sentence formation, as we will soon see. A fifth and less studied lexical category consists of **adverbs (Adv)**, most of which are derived from adjectives.

Languages may also contain **non-lexical** or **functional** categories, including **determiners (Det)**, **auxiliary verbs (Aux)**, **conjunctions (Con)** and **degree words (Deg)**. Such elements generally have meanings that are harder to define and paraphrase than those of lexical categories. For example, the meaning of the noun *hill* is easier to describe than the meaning of a determiner such as *the* or an auxiliary such as *would*.

A potential source of confusion in the area of word classification stems from the fact that some forms are ambiguous in terms of their category.

3. *a) comb* used as a noun:
   The woman found a comb.
   b) comb used as a verb:
   The boy should comb his hair.

4. *a*) *near* used as a preposition:
      The child stood near the fence.
   b) *near* used as a verb:
      The runners neared the finish line.
   c) *near* used as an adjective:
      The end is nearer than you might think.

How then can we determine a word's category?

Meaning One criterion involves meaning. Nouns, for instance, typically name entities such as individuals (*Harry*, *Sue*) and objects (*book*, *desk*). Verbs, on the other hand, characteristically designate actions (*run*, *jump*), sensations (*feel*, *hurt*), and states (*be*, *remain*). In 3, for example, the noun *comb* refers to an object whereas the verb *comb* denotes an action.

The meanings associated with nouns and verbs can be elaborated in various ways. The typical function of an adjective, for instance, is to designate a property or attribute that is applicable to the types of entities denoted by nouns. Thus, when we say *That tall building*, we are attributing the property 'tall' to the building designated by the noun.

In a parallel way, adverbs typically denote properties and attributes that can be applied to the actions designated by verbs. In the following sentences, for example, the adverb *quickly* indicates the manner of Janet's leaving and the adverb *early* specifies its time.

5. *a*) Janet left quickly.
   b) Janet left early.

Unfortunately, a word's meaning does not always provide a clear indication of its category membership. For example, there are 'abstract' nouns such as *difficulty*, *truth*, and *likelihood*, which do not name entities in the strict sense. Moreover, even though words that name actions tend to be verbs, some action-naming words can also be used as nouns (*push* and *shove* are nouns in *give someone a push/shove*). Matters are further complicated by the fact that in some cases, words with very similar meanings belong to different categories. For instance, the words *like* and *fond* are very similar in meaning (as in *Mice like/are fond of cheese*), yet *like* is a verb and *fond* an adjective.

Inflection Most linguists believe that meaning is only one of several criteria that enter into determining a word's category. A second criterion, compatibility with various types of inflectional affixes (see Chapter 4, Section 4), is summarized in Table 5.2.

Table 5.2 Lexical categories and their inflectional affixes

Category	Inflectional affix	Examples
N	plural -*s*	books, chairs, doctors
	possessive -'*s*	John's, (the) man's
V	past tense -*ed*	hunted, watched, judged
	progressive -*ing*	hunting, watching, judging
A	comparative -*er*	taller, faster, smarter
	superlative -*est*	tallest, fastest, smartest

Although helpful, inflection does not always provide the information needed to determine a word's category. In English, for example, not all adjectives can take the comparative and superlative affixes (*intelligenter, *beautifulest) and some nouns do not normally take the plural suffix (*moistures, *braveries).

A third—and more reliable—criterion for determining a word's category involves the type of elements with which it can combine to form larger utterances. This topic constitutes the focus of the next section of this chapter.

Phrase Structure

Sentences are not formed by simply stringing words together like beads on a necklace. Rather, sentences have hierarchical structures consisting of groups of words that may themselves consist of smaller groups of words, and so on. This section will focus on the internal structure of syntactic units built around Ns, Vs, As, and Ps, with an emphasis on the organizational properties that they have in common. Such units are called **phrases**.

Heads Phrases are built around a 'skeleton' consisting of two levels, as depicted below. (The symbol P in the upper level stands for 'phrase'.)

```
NP      VP      AP      PP     ← Phrase level
|       |       |       |
N       V       A       P      ← Word level
```

Figure 5.1 The organization of phrase structure

Each level of phrase structure can be thought of as a sort of 'hook' (like a hook on a pole) to which elements of different types can be attached.

The lowest level is reserved for the word around which the phrase is built—an N in the case of NPs, a V in the case of VPs, and so on. This element is called the **head** of the phrase. As the following examples show, it is possible to have a phrase in which only the head position is filled. (The material in parentheses provides a context in which these one-word phrases might occur.)

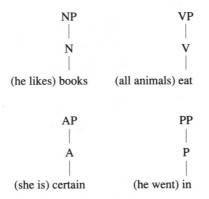

Figure 5.2 Phrases in which only the head position is filled

Although phrases can consist of just one word, they often contain other elements as well. For example:

6. *a*) [_{NP} the <u>books</u>]
   b) [_{VP} will <u>eat</u>]
   c) [_{AP} quite <u>certain</u>]
   d) [_{PP} almost <u>in</u>]

In addition to a head (the underlined element), each of these phrases includes a second word that has a special semantic and syntactic role.

Specifiers These words (determiners such as *the*, auxiliaries such as *will*, and degree words such as *quite* or *almost*) are said to function as **specifiers**. Semantically, specifiers help to make more precise the meaning of the head. Hence, the Det *the* in *6a* indicates that the speaker has in mind specific books, the Aux *will* in *6b* indicates a future event, and the Deg words *quite* and *almost* in *6c*, *d* indicate the degree to which a particular property or relation is manifested.

Syntactically, specifiers typically mark a phrase boundary. In English, specifiers occur at the left boundary (the beginning) of their respective phrases. They are attached to the top level of phrase structure, to the left of the head. Together, these two elements form the phrase structures depicted in the following tree diagrams.

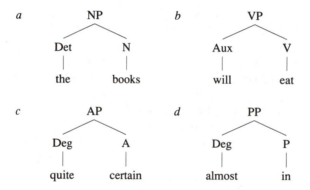

Figure 5.3 Phrases consisting of a specifier and a head

As we will see in Section 5.4, other languages (Thai, for example) place specifiers at the right boundary (the end) of phrases.

The syntactic category of the specifier differs depending on the category of the head. As the examples in Figure 5.3 help show, determiners serve as the specifiers of Ns, auxiliaries as the specifiers of Vs, and degree words as the specifiers of As and (some) Ps.

Table 5.3 Some specifiers

Category	Function	Examples
Det	specifier of N	the, a, this, those
Aux	specifier of V	will, can, have, be
Deg	specifier of A or P	very, quite, more, almost

Put another way, a positional property of nouns is that they can appear with a determiner specifier, a positional property of verbs is that they can appear with an auxiliary specifier, and so forth. This is an example of how a word's combinatorial properties can help one to identify its category.

7. *a*) verb with a determiner:
    *the destroy
  b) noun with an auxiliary:
    *will destruction

Question 3 at the end of the chapter provides practice in identifying specifiers and heads.

Complements Consider now some examples of slightly more complex phrases.

8. *a*) [NP the <u>books</u> about the war]
  b) [VP may <u>eat</u> the hamburger]
  c) [AP quite <u>certain</u> about the answer]
  d) [PP almost <u>in</u> the house]

In addition to a specifier and a head, the phrases in *8* also contain a **complement**. These elements, which are themselves phrases, provide information about entities and locations whose existence is implied by the meaning of the head. For example, the meaning of *eat* implies an object that is eaten, the meaning of *in* implies a location, and so on.

9. (The customer) may eat [the hamburger].
                               ↑
          Complement naming the thing eaten

10. almost in [the house]
          ↑
    Complement naming a location

Complements are attached to the right of the head in English (but to the left in many other languages—see Section 5.4). Figure 5.4 illustrates the structure of a VP and a PP consisting of a specifier, a head, and a complement.

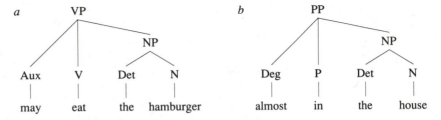

Figure 5.4 Phrases with an NP complement

As noted above, complements are themselves phrases. Thus, the complement of the V *eat* is an NP that itself consists of a determiner (*the*) and a head (*hamburger*). This phrase then combines with the verb and its auxiliary specifier to form a still larger structural unit.

Still more complex phrases are illustrated in Figure 5.5. Here, the NP and AP each consists of a specifier, a head, and a PP complement. This PP in turn consists of a P head and an NP complement composed of a determiner and an N head. (The triangle over the NPs in these examples indicates that in order to save space we do not depict their internal structure.)

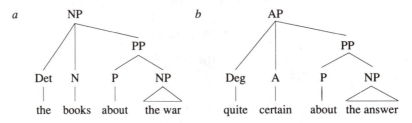

Figure 5.5 Phrases with a PP complement

Question 4 at the end of the chapter provides practice in identifying complements.

The Rules How does the grammar ensure that specifiers, heads, and complements occupy the appropriate positions in phrase structure? The arrangement of the elements that make up a phrase is regulated by a special type of grammatical mechanism called a **phrase structure rule**. The following phrase structure rules stipulate the position of specifiers, heads, and complements in the various types of phrases that we have been considering. (The arrow can be read as 'consists of' or 'branches into'. The three dots in each rule indicate that other complement options are available; these will be discussed in Section 5.2.)

11. *a*) NP→(Det) N (PP) . . .
    b) VP→(Aux) V (NP) . . .
    c) AP→(Deg) A (PP) . . .
    d) PP→(Deg) P (NP) . . .

The first of these rules states that an NP can consist of a determiner, an N head, and a PP complement (as in Figure 5.5a); the second rule captures the fact that a VP can be composed of an auxiliary, a V, and an NP complement (as in Figure 5.4a); and so on.

As the parentheses in our rules indicate, both specifiers and complements are optional. Thus, in accordance with what we have already seen, a phrase may consist of a specifier, a head, and a complement; a head and a complement; a specifier and a head; or just a head (see Figure 5.6).

Generalizing the Rules By now, you will have noticed that there are very obvious structural similarities among NPs, VPs, APs, and PPs. In all four phrase types, the specifier is attached at the top level to the left of the head while the complement is attached to the right. These similarities can be summarized with the help of the template in Figure 5.7, in which X stands for N, V, A, or P.

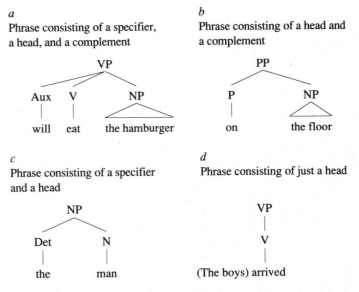

a
Phrase consisting of a specifier,
a head, and a complement

b
Phrase consisting of a head and
a complement

c
Phrase consisting of a specifier
and a head

d
Phrase consisting of just a head

Figure 5.6 Some phrase types (only the head is present in all patterns)

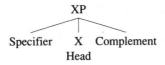

Figure 5.7 The phrase structure template

Instead of having four separate phrase structure rules to capture the placement of specifiers, heads, and complements, we now can formulate the single general rule in *12*.

12. **The XP Rule:**
   XP→(Specifier) X (Complement)

Because the symbol X stands for N, V, A, or P, this rule is an abbreviation for the four separate phrase structure rules given in *11* above.

   The rule in *12* is more abstract than the four more specific rules that were initially proposed since it makes use of the special symbol X. However, it is also more economical and is able to express the structural properties shared by the four different phrase types. For these reasons, rules formulated in terms of the X notation are widely used in contemporary syntactic analysis.

Sentences

Traditionally, the largest unit of syntactic analysis is the sentence (S). It is formed by combining an NP and a VP in accordance with the rule stated in *13*. (The NP that combines with the VP in this way is called the **subject**.)

13. **The S Rule:**
   S→NP VP

A complete sentence structure is illustrated in Figure 5.8.

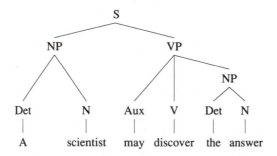

Figure 5.8 Syntactic representation of a complete sentence

Each phrase in Figure 5.8 complies with the previously given rules. Thus, the S consists of a subject NP and a VP (consistent with the S rule). In accordance with the XP rule, the NP consists of a specifier (the Det *a*) and an N head. For its part, the VP consists of a specifier (the Aux *may*), a V head (*discover*), and a complement NP (often called a **direct object**). The internal structure of this NP is likewise consistent with the XP rule since it is composed of a determiner specifier (*the*) and an N head (*answer*).

Tree diagrams such as Figure 5.8 capture a fundamental insight about the architecture of sentence structure. That insight is that sentences do not simply consist of strings of words. Rather, within any sentence, words are grouped together to form phrases, which then combine with each other to form still larger phrases, and so on. As we will see shortly, even very complex sentence structures can be built by following the simple rules outlined here.

Table 5.4 Summary of phrase structure rules

The S Rule	S→NP VP
The XP Rule	XP→(Specifier) X (Complement)

The appendix at the end of the chapter outlines a procedure that can be used to assign sentences an appropriate tree structure. Question 5 provides an opportunity to practice this procedure.

A Look Ahead Thus far in this chapter, we have been concentrating on phrases that consist of specifiers, heads, and complements. However, human language contains other types of syntactic patterns as well. For example, some phrases—called **coordinate structures**—are formed by joining two (or more) elements of the same type with the help of a conjunction such as *and* or *or*.

   14. Coordinate structures:
      a) [_{NP} a pencil] and [_{NP} a notebook]
      b) [_N hamburgers] or [_N hotdogs]

Still another type of pattern includes a **modifier**, an optional element that describes a property of the head. The most common types of modifiers in English are adjectives (which modify N heads) and adverbs (which modify verb heads).

   15. a) Adjective modifying an N head:
         a *good* book

b) Adverb modifying a V head:
He slept *soundly*.

We can form sentences containing coordinate structures and modifiers by making relatively small and simple adjustments to our system of phrase structure rules. These adjustments are discussed in Section 5.5. They can be read now or later at the discretion of the course instructor. This textbook postpones discussion of these matters in favor of some topics in syntactic analysis that go beyond the simple elaboration of phrase structure rules.

Tests for Phrase Structure (advanced)

According to the syntactic analysis being presented here, the words that make up a sentence form intermediate structural units called phrases. How do linguists using this approach to syntax determine which words should be grouped together into phrases? The existence of the syntactic units, or **constituents**, that make up tree structures can be independently verified with the help of special tests. Although we cannot consider all of these tests here, it is possible to give some examples.

The Substitution Test Evidence that NPs are syntactic units comes from the fact that they can often be replaced by a single word such as the pronoun *they* or *it*. This is illustrated in *16*, where *they* replaces the NP *the citizens*. (This is called a **substitution test**.)

16. [NP The citizens] rebelled after *they* discovered the truth.
(they = the citizens)

The substitution test also confirms that a PP such as *at the corner* is a unit since it can be replaced by a single word in sentences such as *17*.

17. They stopped [PP at the corner] and we stopped *there* too.
(there = at the corner)

The Movement Test A second indication that *at the corner* forms a constituent is that it can be moved as a single unit to a different position within the sentence. (This is called a **movement test**.) In *18*, for instance, *at the corner* can be moved from a position after the verb to the beginning of the sentence.

18. They stopped [PP at the corner] → [PP At the corner], they stopped.

The Coordination Test Finally, we can conclude that a group of words forms a constituent if it can be joined to another group of words by a conjunction such as *and* or *or*. (This is labelled the **coordination test** since patterns built around a conjunction are called coordinate structures; see Section 5.5.) Thus, we know that the VP *will sweep the floor* in *19* is a constituent because it can be joined to *will make the beds* by the conjunction *and*.

19. Harry [VP will sweep the floor] and [VP will make the beds].

X′ Categories (advanced)

Thus far, we have been assuming that the architecture of phrase structure complies with the blueprint in Figure 5.9, repeated from above. However, this is somewhat of a simplification since there is reason to believe that complements

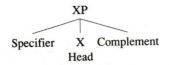

Figure 5.9 The phrase structure template

and heads may actually be attached to a level of phrase structure midway between the word level and the phrase level, as depicted in Figure 5.10. The intermediate level of structure is represented by the symbol X′ (pronounced 'X-bar').

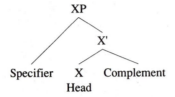

Figure 5.10 The phrase structure template (revised)

According to this viewpoint, then, all phrases have the tri-level structures shown below, in which the head and its complement form an X′-level constituent and the specifier is attached at the higher XP level. (These examples illustrate the internal structure of a VP and an NP only, but APs and PPs have a parallel structure.)

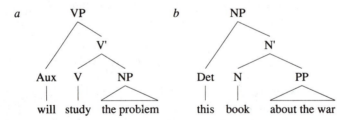

Figure 5.11 A VP and an NP with an intermediate X′ level

The existence of X′ categories can be verified with the help of the same sort of syntactic tests discussed in the previous section. Consider, for example, the V′ in the phrase *will study the problem* in Figure 5.11a. As the following sentence shows, this unit can be replaced by *do so* and should therefore be a constituent according to the substitution test.

> 20. The students will [_{V′} study the problem] and their parents may *do so* too.
> (do so = study the problem)

Now consider the N′ *book about the war* in Figure 5.11b. As the next sentence shows, this unit can be replaced by the element *one*.

> 21. This [_{N′} book about the war] is simpler than that *one*.
> (one = book about the war)

The fact that *one* can replace *book about the* war in this manner confirms that it is a syntactic unit, consistent with the structure in Figure 5.11b.

In order to accommodate these new three-level structures, it is necessary to replace our original XP rule by the two phrase structure rules in *22*.

> *22.* **The XP Rule:**
> XP→(Specifier) X′
> **The X′ Rule:**
> X′→X (Complement)

The first of these rules stipulates that XP categories such as NP and VP consist of an optional specifier (a determiner, an auxiliary, and so forth) and an X′. The second rule then states that an X′ (be it an N′, a V′, or whatever) consists of a head, X, and any complements. Taken together, these two rules form the three-level structures illustrated in Figure 5.11, as desired.

Because three-level structures take up a considerable amount of space and can be tedious to draw, it is common practice to eliminate the intermediate level of phrase structure unless it is absolutely essential to the point being discussed. Since none of the phenomena that we will be discussing requires an intermediate level of phrase structure, we will not make further use of it here. In order to do more advanced syntactic analysis, though, you will need to be familiar with the X′ level.

5.2 COMPLEMENT OPTIONS

The simple rules outlined in Section 5.1 can form a very wide variety of phrases and sentences. Much of this variety stems from the fact that human language allows many different complement options. For example, in addition to the structures considered in Section 5.1, in which each head took at most one complement, there are also structures in which a head takes two (or more) complements. The verb *put* is a case in point. As the following examples show, it requires both an NP complement and a PP complement.

> *23.* *a*) *put* with an NP complement and a PP complement:
>   The librarian put [NP the book] [PP on the shelf].
> *b*) *put* without an NP complement:
>   *The librarian put [PP on the shelf].
> *c*) *put* without a PP complement:
>   *The librarian put [NP the book].

The VP *put the book on the shelf* has the structure depicted in Figure 5.12, in which the VP consists of the head *put* and its two complements—the NP *the book* and the PP *on the shelf*.

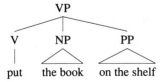

Figure 5.12 A verb with two complements

We can therefore revise our earlier XP rule as follows, using an asterisk to indicate that one or more complements can occur.

24. **The XP Rule** (revised):
     XP→(Specifier) X (Complement*)

This rule also expresses the simple but important fact that complements (however many there are) occur to the right of the head in English.

Complement Options for Verbs

Information about the complements permitted by a particular word is included in its entry in a speaker's **lexicon**, or mental dictionary. Thus, the lexicon for English includes an entry for *slam* that indicates its syntactic category (V), its phonological representation, its meaning, and the fact that it takes an NP complement (as in *She slammed the door*).

25. *slam*: category: V
             phonological representation: /slæm/
             meaning: CLOSE LOUDLY, . . .
             complement: NP

Table 5.5 illustrates some of the more common complement options for verbs in English. The subscripted prepositions indicate the subtype of PP complement, where this is relevant. *Loc* stands for any preposition expressing a location (such as *near*, *on*, *under*).

Table 5.5 Some examples of verb complements

Complement option	Sample heads	Example
Ø	vanish, arrive, die	The child arrived.
NP	devour, cut, prove	The professor proved [$_{NP}$ *the theorem*].
AP	be, become	The man became [$_{AP}$ *very angry*].
PP$_{to}$	dash, talk, refer	The dog dashed [$_{PP}$ *to the door*].
NP NP	spare, hand, give	We handed [$_{NP}$ *the man*] [$_{NP}$ *a map*].
NP PP$_{to}$	hand, give, send	He gave [$_{NP}$ *a diploma*] [$_{PP}$ *to the student*].
NP PP$_{for}$	buy, cook, reserve	We bought [$_{NP}$ *a hat*] [$_{PP}$ *for Andy*].
NP PP$_{loc}$	put, place, stand	He put [$_{NP}$ *the muffler*] [$_{PP}$ *on the car*].
PP$_{to}$ PP$_{about}$	talk, speak	I talked [$_{PP}$ *to a doctor*] [$_{PP}$ *about Sue*].
NP PP$_{for}$ PP$_{with}$	open, fix	We opened [$_{NP}$ *the door*] [$_{PP}$ *for Andy*] [$_{PP}$ *with a crowbar*].

According to this table, the verbs in the first line (*vanish*, *arrive*, and *die*) can occur without any complement, those in the second line occur with an NP complement, and so on.

A word can belong to more than one subcategory. The verb *eat*, for example, can occur either with or without an NP complement and therefore belongs to both of the first two subcategories in our table.

26. After getting home, they ate (the sandwiches).

However, not all verbs exhibit this flexibility. Although *devour* is similar in meaning to *eat*, it requires an explicitly stated complement NP and therefore belongs only to the second subcategory in our table.

27. a) *devour* without a complement:
        *After getting home, they devoured.

b) *devour* with a complement:
After getting home, they devoured the sandwiches.

The classification of words in terms of their complement options is called **subcategorization**. Subcategorization interacts with the phrase structure rules to ensure that lexical items appear in the appropriate types of tree structures. Thus, because *devour* belongs to the subcategory of verbs that require an NP complement, it is permitted in the tree structure depicted in Figure 5.13a (where there is an NP complement) but not in the tree structure in Figure 5.13b.

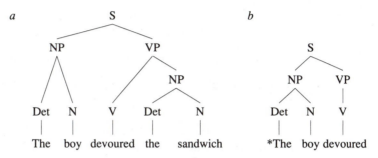

Figure 5.13 Subcategorization determines the type of syntactic structure in which *devour* can occur

Thanks to subcategorization, then, heads occur only in tree structures where they have compatible complement phrases.

Complement Options for Other Categories

Various complement options are also available for Ns, As, and Ps. The following tables provide examples of various possibilities.

Table 5.6 Some examples of noun complements

Complement option	Sample heads	Example
$\emptyset$	car, boy, electricity	the car
PP_{of}	memory, failure, death	the memory [$_{PP}$ *of a friend*]
PP_{of} PP_{to}	gift, description, donation	the gift [$_{PP}$ *of a prize*] [$_{PP}$ *to the winner*]
PP_{with} PP_{about}	argument, discussion, conversation	an argument [$_{PP}$ *with Stella*] [$_{PP}$ *about politics*]

Table 5.7 Some examples of adjective complements

Complement option	Sample heads	Example
$\emptyset$	tall, green, smart	very tall
PP_{about}	curious, glad, angry	curious [$_{PP}$ *about China*]
PP_{to}	apparent, obvious	obvious [$_{PP}$ *to the student*]
PP_{of}	fond, full, tired	fond [$_{PP}$ *of chocolate*]

Table 5.8 Some examples of preposition complements

Complement option	Sample heads	Example
$\emptyset$	near, away, down	(he got) down
NP	in, on, by, near	in [$_{NP}$ *the house*]
PP	down, up, out	down [$_{PP}$ *into the cellar*]

Here again, subcategorization ensures that particular heads can appear in tree structures only if there is an appropriate type of complement. Thus, the adjective *curious* can occur with an '*about* PP', but the adjective *fond* cannot.

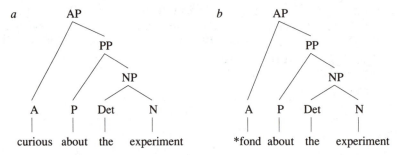

Figure 5.14 Subcategorization permits *curious*, but not *fond*, to take an '*about* PP' as complement.

Complement Clauses

In addition to the complement options considered to this point, all human languages allow sentence-like constructions to function as complements. A simple example of this from English is given in *28*.

 28. [The psychic knows [that/whether/if the contestant will win]].

The smaller bracketed phrase in *28* is called a **complement clause** or **embedded clause** while the larger phrase in which it occurs is called a **matrix clause**.

 Words such as *that*, *if*, and *whether* are known as **complementizers (Cs)**. They take an S complement, forming the CP (complementizer phrase) structure depicted in Figure 5.15.

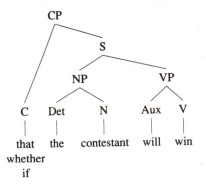

Figure 5.15 Syntactic structure for a CP

Although Cs are non-lexical categories, they fit into structures parallel to those found with lexical categories. Thus, the head (C) and its complement (S) together make up an XP category (CP). In Section 5.3, we will see that there is even a type of element that can occur in the specifier position under CP.

 When a CP occurs in a sentence such as *28,* in which it serves as complement of the verb *know*, the entire sentence has the structure in Figure 5.16.

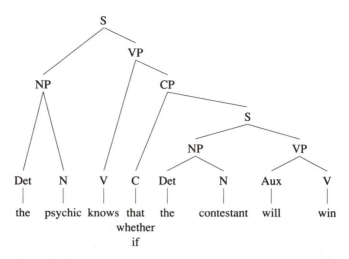

Figure 5.16 Syntactic structure for a sentence with an embedded CP

Of course, not all verbs can take a CP complement. The following table provides examples of some of the verbs that are commonly found with a complement of this type.

Table 5.9 Some verbs permitting CP complements

Complement(s)	Sample heads	Example
CP	believe, know, think, remember	They believe [$_{CP}$ *that Eric left*].
NP CP	persuade, tell, convince, promise	They told [$_{NP}$ *Mary*] [$_{CP}$ *that Eric had left*].
PP$_{to}$ CP	concede, admit	They admitted [$_{PP}$ *to Mary*] [$_{CP}$ *that Eric had left*].

There is no limit on the number of embedded clauses that can occur in a sentence. As Figure 5.17 shows, we can easily put together a long string of complement clauses.

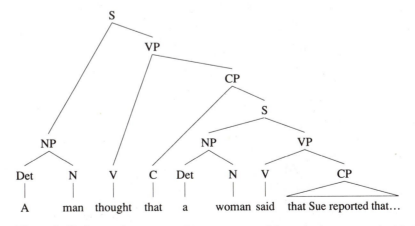

Figure 5.17 Syntactic structure for a sentence with more than one embedded CP

This structure is made possible by the fact that each CP complement can contain a verb that itself permits a complement CP. Hence the topmost clause contains the verb *think*, whose complement clause contains the verb *say*, whose clausal complement contains *report*, and so on.

Other Categories with CP Complements A CP may serve as a complement to an A, an N, or a P in addition to a V.

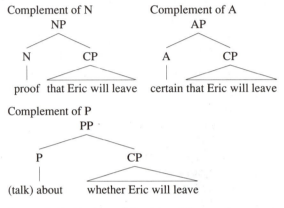

Figure 5.18 N, A, and P with a CP complement

Table 5.10 gives examples of some other adjectives, nouns, and prepositions that can take CP complements.

Table 5.10 Some As, Ns, and Ps permitting CP complements

Items	Example with CP complement
Adjectives	
afraid, certain, aware, confident	They are afraid [$_{CP}$ *that Eric left*].
Nouns	
claim, belief, fact, knowledge, proof, conclusion	They lack proof [$_{CP}$ *that Eric left*].
Prepositions	
over, about	They argued over [$_{CP}$ *whether Eric had left*].

Although structures of this sort are common in English and other languages, we will restrict our attention in the remainder of this chapter to embedded clauses that are complements of Vs.

5.3 TRANSFORMATIONS

Although phrase structure rules interact with the set of complement options permitted by individual heads to form a very wide range of patterns, there are syntactic phenomena that they cannot describe in an entirely satisfactory way. This section considers two such phenomena and discusses the changes that must be made in order to accommodate them.

Inversion in Yes-No Questions

To begin, let us consider the English *yes-no* questions exemplified in *29*. (These structures are called *yes-no* questions because the expected response is usually '*yes*' or '*no*'.)

> *29.* *a*) Will the boy leave?
> *b*) Can the cat climb this tree?

These sentences have an auxiliary verb to the left of the subject rather than in the specifier position of the VP, as in *30*.

> *30.* *a*) The boy [will leave].
> *b*) The cat [can climb this tree].

Our phrase structure rules place the auxiliary in the appropriate position in *30*, but not in *29*. How does the word order found in the former sentences come about?

The question structures that we are considering are built in two steps. In the first step, the usual phrase structure rules are used to form a structure in which the Aux occupies its normal position within the VP. This allows us to express the fact that even in question structures it functions as a specifier, making more precise the meaning of the verb.

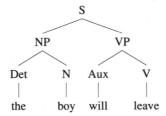

Figure 5.19 Aux occurring as a specifier of V

The second step in the formation of question structures requires a **transformation**, a special type of rule that can move an element from one position to another. In the case we are considering, a transformation known as **Inversion** moves the Aux from its position within the VP to a position to the left of the subject. For now, we can formulate this transformation as follows.

> *31.* **Inversion:**
> Move Aux to the left of the subject NP.

Inversion applies to the structure depicted in Figure 5.19, yielding the sentence in *32* with the auxiliary verb to the left of the subject NP—the position appropriate for a question structure. (The arrow shows the movement brought about by Inversion. For now, we will not try to draw a tree diagram for structures that have undergone a transformation.)

> *32.* Will the boy leave?

The transformational analysis has at least two advantages. First, we do not have to say that there are two types of auxiliary verbs in English: those that occur at the beginning of the sentence and those that occur next to the verb as its specifier. Rather, we can say that all auxiliaries function as specifiers of the verb, consistent with the simple analysis in Section 5.1. Those sentences that have an auxiliary verb to the left of the subject simply undergo an 'extra' process—the Inversion transformation that moves the auxiliary from its position within the VP in order to signal a question.

Second, the transformational analysis automatically expresses the fact—known to all speakers of English—that the sentence *Will the boy leave* is the question structure corresponding to *The boy will leave*. According to the analysis presented here, both sentences have exactly the same structure after the application of the phrase structure rules. They differ only in that Inversion has applied to move the auxiliary verb in the question structure.

Deep Structure and Surface Structure

The preceding examples show that at least some sentences must be analyzed with the help of two distinct rule systems—phrase structure rules, which determine the internal structure of phrasal categories, and transformations, which can modify these tree structures by moving an element from one position to another. If we think about this in terms of the architecture of sentence structure, the transformational analysis is claiming that there are two levels of syntactic structure. The first, called **deep structure**, is formed by the phrase structure rules in accordance with the head's subcategorization properties. As we will see in the chapter on semantics, deep structure plays a special role in the interpretation of sentences.

The second level of syntactic structure corresponds to the final syntactic form of the sentence. Called **surface structure**, it results from applying whatever transformations are appropriate for the sentence in question.

The deep structure for both the sentence *The boy will leave* and the corresponding question structure *Will the boy leave?* is given in Figure 5.20.

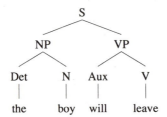

Figure 5.20 The deep structure for the question *Will the boy leave* and the statement *The boy will leave*

The surface structure for the question pattern is then formed by applying the Inversion transformation, yielding *33*.

33. Will the boy␣leave?

In contrast, the statement pattern *The boy will leave* has a surface structure (final syntactic form) that looks just like its deep structure since no transformations apply.

The following diagram depicts the organization of the syntactic component of the grammar as it has just been outlined.

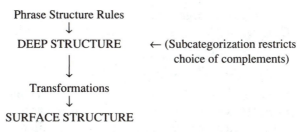

Figure 5.21 The syntactic component of the grammar

As this diagram shows, the grammar makes use of different syntactic mechanisms. Some of these mechanisms are responsible for the architecture of phrases (phrase structure rules), others for the determination of a head's possible complements (subcategorization), and still others for the movement of categories within syntactic structure (transformations).

Wh Movement

Consider now the set of question constructions exemplified in *34*. These sentences are called **wh questions** because of the presence of a question word beginning with *wh*.

34. a) Which car should the man fix?
   b) What can the child sit on?

Do the deep structures associated with *34a* and *34b* resemble the surface form of these sentences or are they quite different? Within the system of syntactic analysis we are using, the sentences in *34* have the deep structures illustrated in Figure 5.22. (We treat the *wh* words *who* and *what* as simple nouns and *which* as a determiner.)

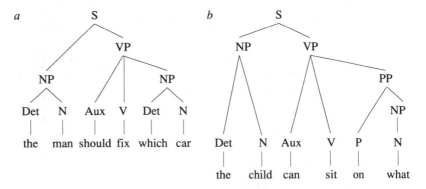

Figure 5.22 Deep structures for two *wh* questions

According to these deep structures, *which car* occurs as complement of the verb *fix* in Figure 5.22a while *what* appears as complement of the preposition *on* in Figure 5.22b. This expresses an important fact about the meanings of these sentences since *which car* asks about the thing that was fixed in the first case while *what* asks about the location where the child can sit in the second case.

A second argument in favor of this analysis involves subcategorization. Consider in this regard the following sentences.

35. *a*) *The man should fix.
    b) *The child can sit on.

Notice that these sentences are somehow incomplete without an NP complement. However, there is no such problem with the *wh* questions in *34*, which suggests that the *wh* phrases must be fulfilling the complement function in these sentences. The deep structures in Figure 5.22 express this fact by treating the *wh* phrase as complement of the verb in the first pattern and complement of the preposition in the second.

In order to convert these deep structures into the corresponding surface structures, we need a transformation that will move the *wh* phrase from its position in deep structure to a position at the beginning of the sentence. The transformation in question, called **Wh Movement**, can be formulated as follows.

36. **Wh Movement**:
    Move the *wh* phrase to the beginning of the sentence.

By applying *Wh* Movement and Inversion to the deep structure in Figure 5.22a, we can form the desired question structure.

37. Which car should the man fix?

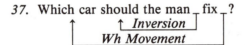

Application of the same two transformations to the deep structure in Figure 5.22b yields the *wh* question in *38*.

38. What can the child sit on?

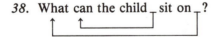

Wh Movement of PPs Sometimes, more than one *wh* question can be formed from the same deep structure. Consider in this regard the deep structure in Figure 5.22b above, repeated here.

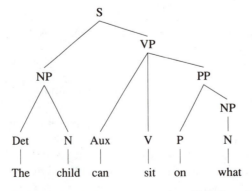

Figure 5.23 A deep structure in which the *wh* word is a complement of a P

We have already seen that we can form the sentence *What can the child sit on?* by fronting the *wh* word *what* and applying Inversion. However, this is not the only sentence that can be formed from this deep structure. By treating the PP *on what* as a *wh* phrase and moving it to the front of the sentence, it is possible to form the slightly different sentence in *39*.

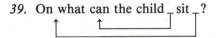

> *39.* On what can the child ⌐ sit ⌐?

We see, then, that by allowing *Wh* Movement to apply to either an NP or a PP that contains a *wh* word, it is possible to form two distinct grammatical sentences from the same deep structure.

A More Detailed Look at Transformations (advanced)

Up until now, our discussion of transformations has left unsettled an interesting technical issue. Reconsider in this regard the simple *yes-no* question exemplified in *40*.

> *40.* Will the boy ⌐ leave?

In what position does the auxiliary verb 'land' when it is moved by Inversion to the left of the subject? If we assume that sentences such as *40* are simple Ss, no position is available for the fronted auxiliary to the left of the subject since the S rule (S → NP VP) says that an S should consist just of an NP and a VP.

Another Look at Inversion This problem can be solved if we assume that all Ss occur within larger CPs, as depicted in Figure 5.24.

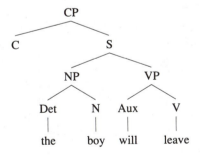

Figure 5.24 S with a CP shell

By adopting this structure, we take the position that *all* Ss occur within a CP, whether they are embedded or not. It may help to think of the CP category as a 'shell' that forms an outer layer of structure around an S. When embedded within a larger sentence, the CP can contain an overt complementizer such as *that* or *whether*. Elsewhere, the C position in the CP shell is present but is simply left empty.

It is into this empty position that the auxiliary verb is moved in *yes-no* questions. Thus, the Inversion transformation can be reformulated as follows.

> *41.* **Inversion** (revised):
>   Move Aux to C.

According to this proposal, then, the sentence *Will the boy leave?* is formed by applying the Inversion transformation to the deep structure in Figure 5.24 above to give the surface structure in Figure 5.25.

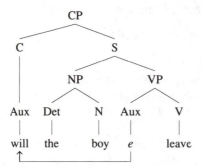

Figure 5.25 Movement of Aux to the C position

A transformation can do no more than change an element's position. It does not change the categories of any words and it cannot eliminate any part of the structural configuration created by the phrase structure rules. Thus, *will* remains an Aux even though it is moved into the C position, and the specifier position that it formerly occupied remains in the tree structure. Marked by the symbol *e* (for 'empty') and called a **trace**, it records the fact that the moved element comes from the specifier position within the VP.

Why do we attach a moved Aux to the C position rather than some other part of sentence structure? The answer lies in the embedded CPs in sentences such as the following.

42. *a*) The coach wonders [CP <u>if</u> the girl should stay].
     b) A fan asked [CP <u>whether</u> the team will win].

The underlined elements in these CPs are complementizers and therefore occur in the C position. Assuming that there can be only one element in each position in a tree structure, there should be no room for the moved Aux under the C label in the embedded CPs in *42*. We therefore predict that Inversion should not be able to apply in these cases. The ungrammaticality of the sentences in *43* shows that this is correct.

43. Inversion in embedded CPs that include complementizers:
     a) *The coach wonders [CP if-should the girl ⌐ stay].
     b) *A fan asked [CP whether-will the team ⌐ win].

Interestingly, the acceptability of Inversion in embedded CPs improves quite dramatically when there is no complementizer (and the C position is therefore open to receive the moved Aux).

44. Inversion in embedded CPs that do not have complementizers:
     a) The coach wondered [CP would the team ⌐ win].

b) A fan asked [_{CP} will the team ⌐ win].

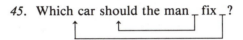

Although some speakers prefer not to apply Inversion in embedded clauses at all (especially in formal speech), most speakers of English find the sentences in *44* to be much more natural than those in *43*. This is just what we would expect if Inversion must move the Aux to an empty C position, as required by our analysis.

To summarize before continuing, we have introduced two changes into the system of syntactic analysis used until now. First, we assume that all Ss occur inside CPs. Second, we assume that the Inversion transformation moves the auxiliary from its position within VP to an empty C position to the left of the subject NP. This not only gives the correct word order for question structures, it helps explain why Inversion sounds so unnatural when the C position is already filled by another element, as in *43*.

Another Look at *Wh* Movement Now reconsider the *wh* question pattern in *45*.

45. Which car should the man ⌐ fix ⌐?

We have already seen that the transformation of *Wh* Movement moves the *wh* phrase to the beginning of the sentence, to the left even of the fronted Aux, but we have not attempted to determine its precise place in the tree structure.

Given that the moved Aux is located in the C position (see above), it seems reasonable to conclude that the fronted *wh* phrase is in the specifier position of CP (this being the only position to the left of the C). Certainly, we know that this position is available to receive the moved *wh* phrase: because there is no class of words that serves as specifier of C, this position will always be empty in deep structure prior to the application of *Wh* Movement.

We therefore reformulate the *Wh* Movement transformation as follows.

46. ***Wh* Movement** (revised):
    Move a *wh* phrase to the specifier position under CP.

The sentence *Which car should the man fix?* can now be analyzed in steps, the first of which involves formation of the deep structure depicted in Figure 5.26. Consistent with our earlier assumption, the S here occurs within a CP shell.

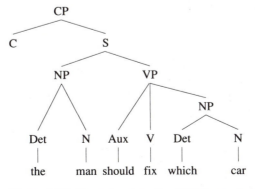

Figure 5.26 Deep structure for *Which car should the man fix?*

Wh Movement and Inversion then apply to this deep structure, yielding the surface structure in Figure 5.27. Note that the Aux has moved to the C position and the *wh* phrase to the specifier position within CP.

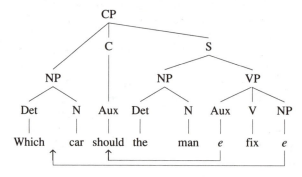

Figure 5.27 Movement of Aux to C and of the *wh* phrase to the specifier of CP

Like other transformations, *Wh* Movement cannot eliminate any part of the structural configuration formed by the phrase structure rules. The position occupied by the *wh* phrase in deep structure is therefore not lost. Rather, it remains as a trace (an empty category), indicating that the moved element corresponds to the complement of the verb *fix*.

Constraints on Transformations (advanced)

Interestingly, there are certain contexts in which transformations are unable to operate. As a preliminary illustration of this, consider the following two pairs of sentences.

47. *a*) Carl should see [a picture of Dracula].
    b) Who should Carl see [a picture of ＿]?

48. *a*) [A picture of Dracula] could frighten John.
    b) *Who could [a picture of ＿] frighten John?

In the first example, the *wh* word is extracted from a complement phrase and the result is acceptable. In *48*, in contrast, the *wh* word is extracted from the subject NP. The ungrammaticality of the resulting sentence suggests that it is not possible to move an element out of a subject phrase. We can express this fact by formulating the following constraint on transformations.

49. **The Subject Constraint**:
    No element may be removed from a subject phrase.

A constituent (such as the subject) that does not permit extraction of a component part is called an **island**.

Subject NPs are not the only type of island found in English. As the following examples show, it is also not possible to remove a *wh* word from a coordinate structure. (The coordinate structure is placed in brackets; as outlined in detail in Section 5.5, a coordinate structure is a phrase in which a word such as *and* or *or* joins together categories of the same type.)

50. a) The author might write [a story or a poem].
   b) *What might the author write [a story or ⌐]?

51. a) Sue will talk [to Tom and to Mary].
   b) *Who will Sue talk [to Tom and to ⌐]?

We can account for these facts by formulating the following constraint.

52. **The Coordinate Structure Constraint**:
   No element may be removed from a coordinate structure.

There are many different types of islands in language, and a good deal of current research focusses on how they should be described, what properties they have in common, and how they differ from language to language. However, since most of this work is too complex to discuss in an introductory textbook, we can do no more than mention this important phenomenon here.

5.4 UNIVERSAL GRAMMAR AND PARAMETRIC VARIATION

Thus far, our discussion has focussed on English. There are many other syntactic phenomena in our language that are worthy of consideration and we will examine some of them in Section 5.5. First, however, it is important to extend the scope of our analysis to other languages.

The syntactic devices presented in earlier sections of this chapter are not found only in English. Indeed, recent work suggests that all languages share a small set of syntactic categories and that these categories can be combined to form phrases whose internal structure includes heads, complements, and specifiers. Moreover, it appears that transformational operations are subject to highly similar constraints in all languages. (For example, the prohibition against extraction from coordinate structures discussed in Section 5.3 holds cross-linguistically, so that sentences like *50b* and *51b* in the previous section are not found in any language.) The system of categories, mechanisms, and constraints shared by all human languages is called **Universal Grammar**.

The fact that certain syntactic properties are universal does not mean that there are no differences among languages. This is because Universal Grammar leaves room for specific types of variation. Quite often, for example, Universal Grammar will make available a small number of alternatives for a particular system, allowing individual languages to differ in these specific ways. (The set of alternatives permitted for a particular phenomenon is often called a **parameter**.) In this section, we will consider a few phenomena of this type, beginning with variation in the inventory of syntactic categories.

Variation in Syntactic Categories

Of the syntactic categories considered in this chapter, only nouns and verbs are found in all human languages. The adjective category, while very common, is not universal. In many languages (such as Hausa, Korean, Telugu, Swahili, Hua, and Bemba), there are no adjectives and no direct translation for English sentences such as *53.*

53. The cat is hungry.

Instead, the concept 'hungry' is expressed with the help of a noun in structures such as *54a* or a verb in structures such as *54b*.

54. a) The cat has hunger.
    b) The cat hungers.

Some examples of this phenomenon in Korean follow. (Nom = nominative, the subject marker)

55. Use of a noun where English uses an adjective:
  a) Ku chayk-i   <u>caymi</u> issta.
       that book-Nom interest exist
       'That book is interesting.'
  b) Ku pap-i   <u>mas</u> issta.
       that food-Nom taste exist
       'That food is tasty.'
56. Use of a verb where English uses an adjective:
  a) Ku pap-i   <u>maypta</u>.
       that food-Nom be-spicy
       'That food is spicy.'
  b) Cip-i   <u>khuta</u>.
       house-Nom be-big
       'The house is big.'

Despite their English translation, the words *maypta* 'spicy' and *khuta* 'big' in the latter two examples are a type of verb in Korean and take tense markers and other types of inflectional endings used for verbs in that language.

Still other languages seem to lack the P category. Where English has a preposition, the Mayan language Jacaltec, for example, either uses no morpheme at all (see *57a*) or employs a noun (such as *s-wi'* 'head' as in *57b*).

57. a) xto   naj <u>conob</u>.
        went he town
        'He went to town.'
    b) ai naj <u>s-wi'</u> witz.
        is he   head hill
        'He is on the hill.'

There are even languages that lack both As and Ps. For example, the Nootkan languages of Vancouver Island and northwest Washington State apparently have only two lexical categories—N and V.

These facts suggest that there is a lexical category parameter that allows at least the following alternatives.

Table 5.11 Parametric variation in lexical categories

Language	Categories used
Nootkan	N, V
Jacaltec	N, V, A
Korean	N, V, P
English	N, V, A, P

Variation in Phrase Structure Rules

As you can see, the N and V categories are universal, with languages differing from each other in terms of whether they use A and P.

Even where languages have the same categories, the precise rules for sentence formation may differ. In Thai, for example, determiners follow rather than precede the noun. (Tones have been omitted here.)

58. sii   nii
color this
'this color'

This order reflects the fact that in Thai the head uniformly appears at the beginning of the phrase, so that Ns appear at the beginning of NPs, Ps at the beginning of PPs, Vs at the beginning of VPs, and so on.

Still another word order pattern is found in Japanese, which consistently places heads in the final position within their phrase. Thus, the noun comes at the end of the NP, the verb at the end of the VP, and so on. Because Ps occur at the end of the PP, they are called **postpositions** rather than prepositions. (Ac = accusative, the direct object marker)

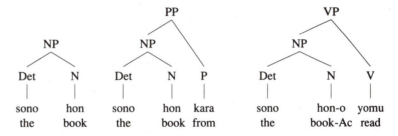

Figure 5.28 Phrase structure in Japanese

These word order differences reflect the positioning of heads with respect to the other elements in their phrases, not the presence of an entirely new type of syntactic system. We can account for these facts by assuming that there is an XP parameter that allows the three alternatives outlined below.

59. *a*) Thai (uniformly head-initial):
S → NP VP
XP → X (Complement*) (Specifier)
b) Japanese (uniformly head-final):
S → NP VP
XP → (Specifier) (Complement*) X
c) English (mixed):
S → NP VP
XP → (Specifier) X (Complement*)

As these rules indicate, the head either uniformly precedes or uniformly follows its complements and specifiers in Thai and Japanese. In English, on the other hand, the head follows its specifier but precedes any complements. The important thing to recognize here is that despite these differences, Thai, Japanese and English still have phrases and these phrases include a head in addition to optional specifiers and complements. Beneath the obvious word order differences, then, there is a more fundamental similarity in the categories and rule types needed to build syntactic structure.

Variation in the Choice of Transformations

Languages often differ from each other in the kinds of rules they use to form a particular sentence type. In Tamil (a language of India), for example, *yes-no* questions are formed without an Inversion transformation by simply adding the particle *-ā* to the end of the sentence. This is illustrated in *60*. (The diacritic ‿ indicates a dental point of articulation; the diacritic ‾ marks a long vowel; ḷ is a retroflex liquid.)

60. *a*) Muṭṭu paḷam pariṭṭān.
   Muttu fruit picked
   'Muttu picked the fruit.'
   b) Muṭṭu paḷam pariṭṭān-ā.
   Muttu fruit picked -Q
   'Did Muttu pick the fruit?'

Instead of positing a question-forming transformation for Tamil, then, we simply formulate the following phrase structure rule. (*Q* stands for the question particle *-ā*.)

61. S → NP VP (Q)

Rule *61* helps form the tree structure depicted in Figure 5.29, corresponding to sentence *60b*.

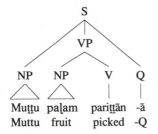

Figure 5.29 A Tamil question structure

Examples like this show that languages can use very different means to express the same type of meaning. Whereas English can use a movement transformation (Inversion) to form *yes-no* questions, the corresponding sentence type in Tamil is formed by the phrase structure component of the grammar. An intermediate system is found in Yiddish, which uses Inversion together with a pre-sentential particle to indicate a *yes-no* question.

62. *a*) Statement:
   Mojʃe hot gekojft a hunt.
   'Moses has bought a dog.'
   b) Question:
   Ci hot Mojʃe gekojft a hunt?
   'Q has Moses bought a dog?'

Just as many languages form *yes-no* questions without the help of the Inversion transformation, many languages do not make use of *Wh* Movement in the formation of *wh* questions. Languages of this type include Japanese, Korean, Tamil, Chinese, and Thai. The following example is from Thai.

63. Khun ʔaan ʔaray?
    you read what
    'What did you read?'

Notice that, unlike English, Thai does not front the question word in its *wh* questions.

Variation in the Formulation of Transformations

Languages may also differ from each other by adopting slightly different forms of the same basic transformational rule. A major difference between French and English, for instance, relates to the nature of the Inversion rule used in *yes-no* questions. Like English, French can form a question by moving an auxiliary leftward, as *64* illustrates.

64. Inversion of an Aux:
    a) Tu as essayé.
        'You have tried.'
    b) As-tu essayé?
        'Have you tried?'

However, unlike English, French also allows inversion of regular (non-auxiliary) Vs.

65. Inversion of a V:
    a) Il sait.
        'He knows.'
    b) Sait-il?
        knows he
        'Does he know?'

Crucially, though, Inversion in French is possible only if the subject is a pronoun (such as *tu* 'you' or *il* 'he'). A sentence derived by movement of a V or Aux to the left of a non-pronominal subject, as in *66b*, is ungrammatical.

66. Inversion over a non-pronominal subject:
    a) Jean sait.   Jean a essayé.
        'John knows.'   'John has tried.'
    b) *Sait Jean?   *A Jean essayé?
        'Knows John?'   'Has John tried?'

In order to question a sentence such as *66a*, French must use one of the following two structures.

67. *a*) Est-ce que Jean sait?
        'Is it that John knows?'
    b) Jean sait-il?
        'John knows-he?'

In the first of these sentences, the special structure *est-ce que* 'is it that' is used to signal a question while in the second the pronoun *il* 'he' is added and the verb appears to the left of this pronoun. In neither structure does Inversion move a verb over a non-pronominal subject.

Still a different type of Inversion rule is found in Spanish, where a V can be moved to the left of any type of subject to form a question.

68. Inversion over a pronominal subject:
  a) Él partió
      'He left.'
  b) Partió él?
      'Left he?'
69. Inversion over a non-pronominal subject:
  a) Juan partió.
      'John left.'
  b) Partió Juan?
      'Left John?'

However, only a V can undergo inversion; an Aux cannot.

70. Inversion of an Aux:
  a) Juan ha partido.   Él ha partido.
      'John has left'   'He has left'
  b) *Ha Juan partido?   *Ha él partido?
      'Has John left?'   'Has he left?'

The differences just outlined are reflected in the type of Inversion transformation used by each of these languages.

71. Inversion (English):
    Aux moves to the left of the subject.
72. Inversion (French):
    Aux or V moves to the left of a pronoun subject.
73. Inversion (Spanish):
    V moves to the left of the subject.

Inversion provides an example of how languages can differ from each other by adopting slightly different versions of essentially the same rule. Thus, English allows only auxiliaries to undergo Inversion, but places no restriction on the type of subject NP involved in this process. French, on the other hand, permits any type of verb to be inverted but only if the subject is a pronoun. Spanish, in contrast, places restrictions on the types of verbs that can undergo Inversion, but not on the subjects.

5.5 SOME EXTENSIONS (advanced)

Now that we have considered the basic rule systems used by the syntactic component of the grammar in human language, it is possible to broaden our treatment of English syntax by briefly examining a number of additional structural patterns. We focus in this section on three such patterns—coordinate structures, modifier constructions, and relative clauses.

Coordination

A common syntactic pattern in English and other languages is formed by grouping together two or more categories of the same type with the help of a conjunction such as *and* or *or*. This phenomenon is known as **coordination**.

74. Coordination of NPs:
    [NP the man] and [NP a child]
75. Coordination of VPs:
    [VP go to the library] and [VP read a book]
76. Coordination of PPs:
    [PP down the stairs] and [PP out the door]
77. Coordination of APs:
    [AP quite beautiful] and [AP very expensive]
78. Coordination of Ss:
    [S The man entered the building] and [S the woman waited in the car].

Coordination exhibits four important properties. First, there is no limit on the number of coordinated categories that can appear prior to the conjunction. Thus, the grammar can form structures such as *79*, in which the subject NP contains four smaller NPs prior to the underlined conjunction and one after it.

79. [NP A man, a boy, a cat, a dog, <u>and</u> a hamster] got into the car.

Second, a category at any level (a head or an entire XP) can be coordinated. The preceding examples illustrate coordination of XPs; following are examples involving word-level categories.

80. *a*) Coordination of N:
    The [N book] and [N magazine]
    b) Coordination of P:
    [P up] and [P down] the stairs
    c) Coordination of V:
    [V repair] and [V paint] the deck.

Third, coordinated categories must be of the same type. Thus, the coordinated categories are both NPs in *74*, VPs in *75*, and so on. As *81* shows, coordination of different category types generally gives a quite unnatural result.

81. *a*) Coordination of an NP and a PP:
    *He read [PP in the library] and [NP the book]
    b) Coordination of an NP and an AP:
    *He left [NP the house] and [AP very angry]

Finally, the category type of the coordinate phrase is identical to the category type of the elements being conjoined. Hence, if VPs are coordinated, the coordinate structure is a VP; if NPs are coordinated, the coordinate structure is an NP; and so on.

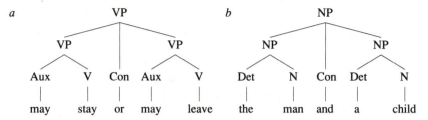

Figure 5.30 Coordinate structures

How does the grammar form coordinate structures? One possibility is that there is a separate rule for each coordinate structure. For categories of the N-type, for example, the following two rules could be formulated. (The * symbol indicates that one or more categories can occur to the left of the conjunction, as in example *79*; Con = conjunction.)

82. *a*) NP → NP* Con NP
    b) N → N* Con N

A set of parallel rules for verbal categories could also be formulated.

83. *a*) VP → VP* Con VP
    b) V → V* Con V

Similar rules can be devised for other categories (S, AP, PP, and so on) as well, but you can probably see that the result will be a rather long list of new rules.

Fortunately, we can avoid these complications by using the 'X notation' employed throughout this chapter to formulate a single general statement that can take the place of the more specific rules exemplified above. (As before, X stands for N, V, A, or P.)

84. **The Coordination Rule**:
    $X^n \rightarrow X^n*$ Con X^n

The symbol X^n in this rule stands for 'a category at any structural level', indicating that either an X or an XP can be coordinated. As before, the asterisk (*) indicates that one or more categories can occur to the left of the conjunction. Thus, we can not only form structures such as *a man and a boy*, in which just two elements are coordinated, but also structures such as *a man*, *a boy*, *a cat*, *a dog and a hamster*, in which a much larger number of items undergoes coordination. By adding just one more rule to the grammar, then, we can form a very broad range of coordination structures.

Modifiers

Thus far, our treatment of phrase structure has ignored **modifiers**, a class of elements that encode optionally expressible properties of heads. Although all lexical categories can have modifiers, we will focus here on the types of categories that can modify Ns and Vs.

Adjective phrases (APs) make up the single most commonly used class of modifiers in English. As the following examples show, APs serve as modifiers of Ns. (This is not the only function of APs: they can also function as complements of verbs such as *become* and *seem*, as in *He became/seemed* [*very angry*]; see Table 5.5.)

85. APs serving as modifiers of N:
A *very tall* man walked into the room.
She made *exceptional* progress.

The most common modifiers of Vs are adverb phrases (AdvPs) and PPs that describe manner or time.

86. AdvPs serving as modifiers of V:
Describing manner: Ellen proceeded *carefully*.
                     Ellen *carefully* proceeded.
Describing time: We arrived *early*.
87. PPs serving as modifiers of V:
Describing manner: Ellen proceeded *with care*.
Describing time: He stayed *for three days*.

As these examples show, English modifiers vary in terms of their position with respect to the head. Thus, APs precede the N while PPs follow the verb. Many AdvPs can occur either before or after the verb that they modify, as the first examples in *86* illustrate.

Table 5.12 Modifier position in English

Modifier	Position
AP	precedes the head
PP	follows the head
AdvP	precedes or follows the head

A Rule for Modifiers How do modifiers fit into phrase structure? For the purposes of this introduction to syntax, we will attach modifiers at the XP level of phrase structure, as depicted below.

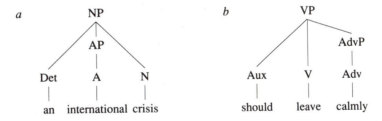

Figure 5.31 Phrases containing modifiers

In order to account for the placement of modifiers, we must expand our original XP rule so that it allows the various options shown in *88*.

88. **The Expanded XP Rule**:
XP → (Spec) (Mod) X (Complement*) (Mod)

This rule allows a modifier to occur before the head (as in Figure 5.31a) and/or after it (see Figure 5.31b). Where there is a complement, a modifier that occurs after the head will normally occur to the right of the complement as well. This is illustrated in Figure 5.32.

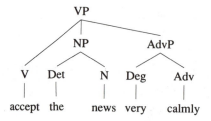

Figure 5.32 A phrase in which both the complement and the modifier occur after the head (the modifier occurs after the complement)

In this example, the XP rule gives a phrase consisting of a head (the verb *accept*), a complement (the NP *the news*), and a modifier (the AdvP *very calmly*)—in that order.

Relative Clauses (advanced)

Consider now the structure exemplified in *89.*

89. *a*) Sue knows the man [who Bob criticized __].
     b) Harry visited the village [which Sue walked to __].

The bracketed phrases in *89* are **relative clauses**, CP-sized modifiers that provide information about the N head to their left. In sentence *89a*, for example, the relative clause helps identify the man by indicating that he is the person criticized by Bob.

Like other modifiers, relative clauses occur within the same phrase as the head that they modify. Thus, the bracketed relative clause in *89a* should be part of the NP headed by the N *man*. This can be verified with the help of the substitution test illustrated in *90*, which shows that the sequence *the man who Bob criticized* is a syntactic unit since it can be replaced by the pronoun *him*.

90. Sue knows [_NP_ the man who Bob criticized __] and I know *him* too.
     (him = the man who Bob criticized)

***Wh* Movement Again**   Relative clause structures resemble embedded *wh* questions in two respects. First, they begin with a *wh* word such as *who* or *which*. Second, there is an empty position within the sentence from which the *wh* phrase has apparently been moved. In sentences *89a* and *89b*, for instance, the NP positions following the transitive verb *criticize* and the preposition *to* are unfilled in surface structure.

The first step in the formation of the relative clause in *89a* involves the deep structure in Figure 5.33. Here, the *wh* word *who* occurs as complement of the verb *criticize* since it corresponds to the person who is criticized. (The relative clause itself is in the usual position for a post-head modifier; see the preceding section.)

The next step involves the application of the *Wh* Movement rule (as outlined in Section 5.3) to give the structure in Figure 5.34. (Recall that *wh* phrases move to the specifier position under CP.) Notice that no new transformations are required to form relative clause structures such as these. Rather, relative clauses can be formed with the help of the same *Wh* Movement transformation that is independently required for *wh* questions.

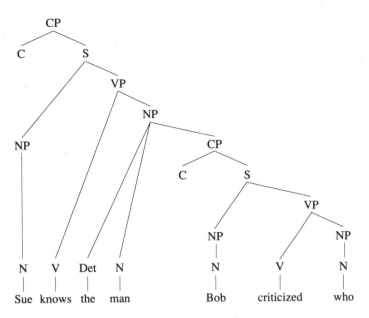

Figure 5.33 Deep structure of a relative clause structure

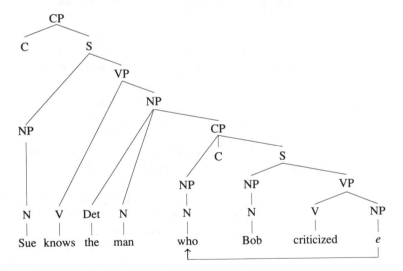

Figure 5.34 Surface structure of a relative clause: the *wh* phrase has moved to the specifier position within CP

Now consider a relative clause structure in which the *wh* word originates in the subject position.

91. Sue knows the man [who criticized Bob].

Here *who* corresponds to the person who does the criticizing, not the person who gets criticized, as in the previous example. The deep structure for this sentence therefore corresponds to Figure 5.35, in which the *wh* word appears in the subject position.

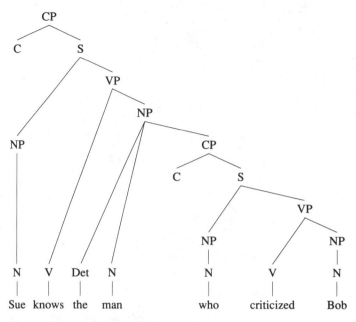

Figure 5.35 Deep structure for a relative clause structure with a *wh* phrase in subject position

Like other *wh* words, the *who* here subsequently moves to the specifier position within CP even though the actual order of the words in the sentence does not change as a result of this movement.

5.6 OTHER TYPES OF SYNTACTIC ANALYSIS

Thus far in this chapter, we have focused our attention on the analysis of sentence structure employed by practitioners of transformational syntax. As mentioned at the outset, however, this is not the only type of syntactic analysis used in contemporary linguistics. In this section, we will briefly consider two other types of syntactic analysis, one focusing on grammatical relations such as subject and direct object, and the other focusing on the way in which syntactic structure is used to communicate information. In order to illustrate how these analyses work, we will make use of a sentence type that has played a very important role in the development of syntactic theory over the last several decades.

Passive Structures

Consider the pair of sentences in *92*, which are virtually identical in meaning despite obvious structural differences.

> 92. *a*) The thieves took the painting.
>   *b*) The painting was taken by the thieves.

In order to describe the differences and similarities between these two sentences, it is necessary to distinguish between the **agent** (the doer of the action designated by the verb) and the **theme** (the entity directly affected by that action). (These notions are discussed in more detail in Chapter 6.)

93. *a*) Active sentence:
    The thieves took the painting.
    Agent   *Theme*
  b) Passive sentence:
    The painting was taken (by the thieves).
    Theme   *Agent*

The *a* sentence is called **active** because the agent is encoded as subject of the sentence while the *b* sentence is called **passive** in recognition of the fact that the theme is encoded as subject. There are many other such pairs in English.

94. *a*) The dog chased the truck.
  b) The truck was chased by the dog.
95. *a*) The teacher praises Ginette frequently.
  b) Ginette is praised by the teacher frequently.
96. *a*) The child broke the dishes.
  b) The dishes were broken by the child.

The transformational analysis of passive sentences cannot be adequately discussed until we have considered some issues in the study of semantics (see Section 2 of Chapter 6). However, it is possible to consider two other perspectives on the analysis of this important syntactic pattern.

Relational Analysis

The key point of **relational** analysis is that at least some syntactic phenomena are best described in terms of grammatical relations such as subject and direct object rather than morphological patterns or the order of words. This can be seen by comparing the passive structure in English with the equivalent construction in some other languages.

In terms of morphology and word order, the English passive has two distinctive properties. First, the VP contains some form of the auxiliary *be* (*was*, *is*, and so on) together with a verb in the so-called 'past participle form', which is normally marked by the suffix *-ed* or *-en* (hence *was taken*, *was chased*, and so on). Second, the relative order of the agent and theme in passive sentences is the reverse of that found in active sentences. Thus, whereas the theme precedes the agent in passive sentences, the opposite order is found in active sentences, as sentence *93* demonstrated.

Table 5.13 Properties of the English passive

Morphology	Word order
Some form of Aux *be* Past participle form of the V	the theme comes before the agent

Interestingly, however, none of these structural features is universally associated with passive structures. In Tzotzil (a Mayan language of Mexico), for instance, the relative order of the agent and the theme is the same in active and passive constructions.

97. *a*) Active sentence:
     Lá snákan ti vĩnike ti xpétule.
                 Theme   Agent
     seated   the man the Peter
     'Peter seated the man.'
    b) Passive sentence:
     Inákanat ti vĩnike juʔun ti xpétule.
             Theme   Agent
     was seated the man by   the Peter
     'The man was seated by Peter.'

Here the passive is signalled by a change in the form of the verb and the appearance of the preposition *juʔun* 'by' before the agent, not by a change in the relative order of the agent and theme.

In Mandarin Chinese, on the other hand, passivization changes the positioning of the agent and the theme, but does not affect the form of the verb and does not include an auxiliary such as *be*.

98. *a*) Active sentence:
     Zhu laoshi piyue le wode kaoshi.
     Agent   *Theme*
     Zhu professor marked my test
     'Professor Zhu marked my test.'
    b) Passive sentence:
     Wode kaoshi bei Zhu laoshi piyue le.
     Theme   *Agent*
     my test by Zhu professor marked.
     'My test was marked by Professor Zhu.'

Here, the passive is marked by a change in word order and by the appearance of the preposition *bei* 'by' before the agent, but the verb has exactly the same form in both patterns.

What then do the passive sentences of English, Tzotzil, Chinese, and other languages have in common? According to proponents of relational analysis, the crucial facts involve a correspondence between the grammatical relations found in a passive sentence and those in its active counterpart.

99. *a*) Active sentence: The thieves took the painting.
           Subject   *Direct object*

           Subject   *Oblique*
    b) Passive sentence: The painting was taken (by the thieves).

Notice that the direct object in the active *99a* (*the painting*) is the subject in the passive *99b* while the subject in *99a* (*the thieves*) occurs as part of a PP in *99b*. (An NP that occurs with a preposition is said to be **oblique**.)

It is now possible to think of passive sentences as the product of the following two changes to the corresponding active pattern.

Table 5.14 Properties of passive structures

Active pattern		Passive pattern
Subject	→	oblique
Direct object	→	subject

Since the criteria used to identify subjects and direct objects differ from language to language, these changes are compatible with a variety of different structural effects. In English, where the direct object appears after the verb and the subject before it, a change in an NP's grammatical relation will also involve a change in its linear position. Thus a theme NP that serves as subject (as in the passive) rather than direct object (as in the active) will appear to the left of the verb rather than to the right.

> 100. *a*) Active sentence:
>   The thieves took the painting.
>   ↑
>   *Theme serving as direct object*
>   *b*) Passive sentence:
>   The painting was taken (by the thieves).
>   ↑
>   *Theme serving as subject*

In other languages, changes in grammatical relations may be marked by something other than a change in word order. In the Tzotzil passive, for example, addition of the preposition *juʔun* is enough to indicate that the agent is no longer the subject. As in English, however, passive structures in Tzotzil exhibit the pair of relational changes stated in Table 5.14.

Many other syntactic phenomena can be analysed in terms of processes that affect subjects and direct objects. As our study of passivization illustrates, these concepts are especially useful when comparing syntactic phenomena in languages with different word order and/or morphological patterns.

Functional Analysis

Syntactic analysis can also focus on the way in which different syntactic structures are used to communicate information. Such analyses are often called **functional** since they seek to understand syntactic phenomena in terms of their communicative function. The contrast between active and passive sentences is especially instructive in this regard. Although both sentence types have the same basic meaning, they differ from each other in the way in which they present the situation that they describe. Put another way, they differ from each other in the way in which they 'package' the information to be communicated. Two differences can be noted here.

First, passive sentences tend to de-emphasize the role of the agent in the situation being described. In fact, the vast majority of passive structures do not mention the agent at all. Hence, we can say simply *The painting was taken* or *The dishes were broken*, without attributing responsibility for these events to any particular person.

Second, passive sentences foreground the theme by making it the subject of the sentence. As a result, the situation is presented from the perspective of that individual. (As we will see in Chapter 6, the subject usually introduces the entity that the rest of the sentence is about.) Consider in this regard the following passage.

> *101.* MacGregor is a pretty lucky guy. Last night, he went out, got drunk, and started rolling around in the street. Before too long, *he was hit by a car*. But he wasn't even injured. In fact, he got up and walked home.

The italicized passive sentence in this passage sounds completely natural since it brings to the foreground the pronoun *he*, which refers to the person (MacGregor) from whose perspective the entire series of events is being described. In contrast, the passive is not nearly so natural in the following context.

> *102.* MacGregor is a pretty lucky guy. Last night, he went out, got drunk and started rolling around in the street. Before too long, **a car was hit by MacGregor*. But his hand wasn't even injured . . .

Here the passive sentence seems quite out of place. This is because it foregrounds the car even though the rest of the passage is clearly about MacGregor. This in turn creates a discontinuity in the flow of information, making the passage quite unnatural.

In sum, then, the functional analysis of the passive pattern focuses on the way in which it packages information compared to active sentences. The key claim is that the function of this structure is to de-emphasize the agent (often deleting it entirely) and to draw attention to the theme NP.

By analyzing syntactic structures functionally, it is often possible to gain insights into why a language has the particular syntactic patterns that it does and how these patterns contribute to the larger task of communication. For this reason, the functional method is being used by a growing number of linguists to analyze the sentence structures of human language.

Summing Up

In this chapter we have been concerned with some of the fundamental devices involved in forming sentences in human language. As we have seen, **phrase structure rules** determine the architecture of a sentence's **deep structure**, **subcategorization** information ensures a match between **heads** and the **complements** with which they appear in syntactic structure, and **transformations** can modify deep structures in various ways to produce **surface structures**. Taken together, these devices make up an important part of our overall linguistic competence in that they provide the means to combine words into sentences in novel ways.

Although the precise rules for sentence formation differ from language to language, **Universal Grammar** provides all languages with the same general types of mechanisms (syntactic categories, phrase structure rules, and transformations). Many of the differences among languages can be traced to the existence of a small set of **parameters**, each of which makes available a variety of alternatives.

Key Terms

active	oblique
adjective	parameter
adverbs	passive
agent	phrase structure rule
auxiliary verbs	phrase structure
complement	predicate
complement clause	preposition
conjunctions	relative clauses
constituent	specifiers
coordinate structures	subcategorization
coordinate structure constraint	subject constraint
coordination test	subject
deep structure	substitution test
degree word	surface structure
determiner	syntactic categories
direct object	theme
head	trace
inversion	transformation
island	universal grammar
lexical category	verb
matrix clause	*wh* movement
modifier	*wh* question
movement test	X′ rule
noun	XP rule

Sources

Transformational syntax is the most popular of the half dozen major syntactic theories used in contemporary linguistics. Traditionally, it is the theory taught in introductory linguistics courses in North America, both because it is so widely used and because many of the other approaches that exist today have developed in response to it. The particular system outlined here involves a variety of simplifications to make it appropriate for presentation in an introductory course.

The treatment of auxiliary verbs as specifiers involves a simplification similar to the one used in *The Language Lottery* by D. Lightfoot (Cambridge, Mass.: MIT Press, 1982) and, to some extent, the book by Radford cited below. The system of subcategorization employed here is loosely based on the one outlined in *Generalized Phrase Structure Grammar* by G. Gazdar, E. Klein, G. Pullum, and I. Sag (Cambridge, Mass.: Harvard University Press, 1985), which describes a non-transformational approach to syntax. The theory of transformations presented here is essentially the one employed throughout the 1980s by the vast majority of people working within transformational grammar.

The status of adjectives in Universal Grammar is discussed by R. M. W. Dixon in *Where Have All the Adjectives Gone?* (The Hague: Mouton, 1982). The data on Jacaltec is from *The Jacaltec Language* by C. Day (Bloomington: Indiana University Press, 1973). The claim that the Nootkan languages have only two lexical categories is based on the discussion in "Noun and Verb in Nootkan" by W. Jacobsen, Jr. in *The Victoria Conference on Northwestern Languages,* 83–155 (Heritage Record No. 4. Vancouver: British Columbia Provincial Museum, 1979). A similar system is described for the now extinct Yana by E. Sapir in *Language* (New York: Harcourt Brace, 1921). Variation in question structures is discussed in "Speech Act Distinctions in Syntax" by J. Sadock and A. Zwicky in *Language Typology and Syntactic Description*, Vol. 1 (cited below), from which the Yiddish example in Section 5.4 is taken.

The discussion of the relational analysis of passive sentences is intended to be neutral between Lexical Functional Grammar as outlined in *The Mental Representation of Grammatical Relations*, edited by Joan Bresnan (Cambridge, Mass.: MIT Press, 1982) and Relational Grammar as described in "Toward a Universal Characterization of Passivization" by D. Perlmutter and P. Postal in *Studies in Relational Grammar I*, edited by D. Perlmutter (Chicago: University of Chicago Press, 1983). The functional analysis of passives draws on the discussion in *Functional Syntax* by Susumu Kuno (Chicago: University of Chicago Press, 1987) and *Functional Syntax and Universal Grammar* by W. Foley and R. Van Valin (New York: Cambridge University Press, 1986).

The exercises for this chapter were prepared by Joyce Hildebrand.

Recommended Reading

Baker, C. L. 1989. *English Syntax*. Cambridge, Mass.: MIT Press.

Blake, Barry. 1990. *Relational Grammar*. New York: Routledge & Kegan Paul.

Givón, Talmy. 1984. *Syntax: A Functional Typological Approach*. Vol. 1. Philadelphia: John Benjamins Publishing Co.

Radford, Andrew. 1988. *Transformational Grammar: A First Course*. New York: Cambridge University Press.

Sells, Peter. 1985. *Lectures on Contemporary Syntactic Theories*. Stanford, Calif.: Center for the Study of Language and Information.

Shopen, Timothy, ed. 1985. *Language Typology and Syntactic Description*. Vols. 1–3. New York: Cambridge University Press.

Appendix: How to Build Tree Structures

Although it is relatively easy to check a tree structure to see if it complies with the relevant phrase structure rules, it is somewhat harder to build a tree structure from scratch when trying to analyze a new phrase or sentence. In such cases, you will probably find it easiest to proceed in steps, working from the bottom up and from right to left. As an illustration, let us first consider the phrase *near the door*.

The first step involves assigning each word to the appropriate category, as depicted in Figure 5.36.

Figure 5.36 The first step: determining the word-level categories

Then, working from right to left, the XP levels are added above each N, V, A, or P. Thus, we first add an NP label above the N *door*. There is clearly no complement here, but there is a specifier (the determiner *the*), which can be attached at the NP level in accordance with the XP rule.

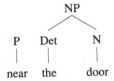

Figure 5.37 Building the NP

Next, we carry out the same procedure for the P *near*, adding the required PP level.

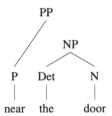

Figure 5.38 Adding the PP level above the P head

The NP to the right of the P clearly functions as its complement (since it names the location entailed by the meaning of *near*). This element is therefore attached at the PP level in accordance with the XP rule, giving the complete structure depicted in Figure 5.39.

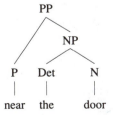

Figure 5.39 The complete PP

A Sentential Example Consider now how we proceed in the case of a complete sentence such as *The apple might hit the man*. Assignment of each word to the appropriate category gives the structure depicted in Figure 5.40.

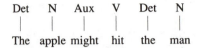

Figure 5.40 The categories for each word in the sentence

Working from right to left, it is easy to see that the noun *man* heads an NP that contains a specifier but no complement.

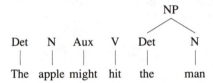

Figure 5.41 The structure of the rightmost NP

Next, we focus on the V *hit*, adding the required VP level.

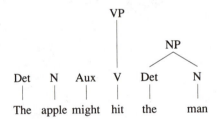

Figure 5.42 Adding the VP level above the V head

As specifier, the auxiliary *might* clearly attaches to the VP. But what of the NP *the man*? It occurs to the right of the V and names an entity entailed by the meaning of *hit* (the person who is hit). As such, it is the complement of the V and must also be attached to the VP in accordance with the XP rule.

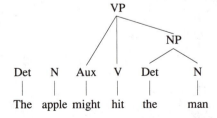

Figure 5.43 The structure of the VP

Finally, we can form the phrase built around the N *apple* and combine this NP with the already formed VP in accordance with the S rule (S → NP VP). This yields the complete sentence illustrated in Figure 5.44.

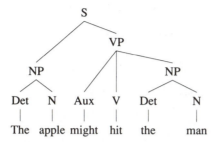

Figure 5.44 The complete sentence

Transformations As explained in Section 5.3, the syntactic analysis of some sentences involves transformations in addition to the usual phrase structure rules. Recognizing that one of the transformations used in this chapter has applied is relatively simple: if a sentence contains an auxiliary verb to the left of the subject, then Inversion has applied; if it begins with a *wh* word, then *Wh* Movement has applied. In the sentence *What has the customer purchased?*, then, both of these transformations have applied.

In order to determine the deep structure, we must 'return' the auxiliary verb to its position within the specifier of VP and we must determine the position from which the *wh* word has been moved. Since the *wh* word in the sentence *What has the customer purchased?* asks about the complement of the verb (the thing that is purchased), we place *what* in the verbal complement position in deep structure. This gives the deep structure depicted in Figure 5.45, consistent with the phrase structure rules we have been discussing.

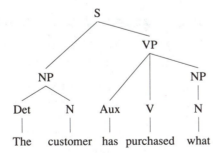

Figure 5.45 Deep structure for *What has the customer purchased*

If you are using the more detailed system outlined in Section 5.3, the deep structure will be slightly more complex. As depicted below, it must also include a CP category, so that there will be empty positions to which the auxiliary and the *wh* word can be moved.

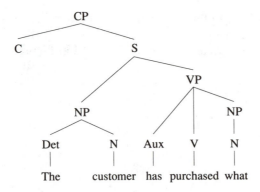

Figure 5.46 Deep structure with the CP shell

The auxiliary *has* then moves to the C position (Inversion) and *what* to the specifier position under CP (*Wh* Movement), yielding the complete surface structure depicted in Figure 5.47.

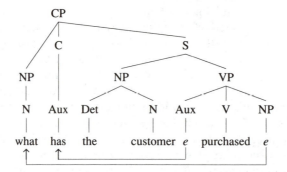

Figure 5.47 The surface structure: the *wh* phrase has moved to the specifier position within CP and the Aux has moved to the C position

Questions

1. Place an asterisk next to any of the sentences that are ungrammatical for you. Can you figure out what makes these sentences ungrammatical?

    a) The instructor told the students to study.
    b) The instructor suggested the students to study.
    c) The customer asked for a cold beer.
    d) The customer requested for a cold beer.
    e) He gave the Red Cross some blood.
    f) He donated the Red Cross some blood.
    g) The pilot landed the jet.
    h) The jet landed.
    i) A journalist wrote the article.
    j) The article wrote.
    k) Jerome is bored of his job.
    l) Jerome is tired of his job.

2. Indicate the category of each word in the following sentences. (*Hint*: It may help to refer back to Sections 5.1 and 5.2.)

   a) That glass suddenly broke.
   b) A jogger ran toward the end of the lane.
   c) These dead trees must be removed.
   d) Sam hurriedly searched through the garbage.
   e) The peaches are quite ripe.
   f) Jeremy will play the trumpet and the drums in the orchestra.

3. Each of the following phrases consists of a specifier and a head. Draw the appropriate tree structure for each example.

   a) the zoo   f) this house
   b) was writing   g) very competent
   c) so witty   h) quite near
   d) will pass   i) should eat
   e) less bleak   j) those books

4. The following phrases includes a head, a complement and (in some cases) a specifier. Draw the appropriate tree structure for each example. For now, there is no need to depict the internal structure of complements. (*Hint*: See the tree diagrams in Figures 5.4 and 5.5.)

   a) into the house
   b) fixed the telephone
   c) make the mistakes
   d) more towards the window
   e) stop the pollution
   f) have studied this material
   g) could earn the money

5. After carefully reading the first two sections of the appendix, draw phrase structure trees for each of the following sentences.

   a) Those guests have left.
   b) Maria ate the brownie.
   c) That shelf will fall.
   d) The glass broke.
   e) The student lost the debate.
   f) The manager has offered a raise.
   g) The judge sentenced that shoplifter.
   h) The teacher organized a discussion.
   i) A psychic will speak to this group.

6. Apply the substitution test to determine which of the bracketed sequences in the following sentences form constituents.

   a) [The tragedy] upset the entire family.
   b) They hid [in the cave].

   c) The [computer was very] expensive.

   d) [The town square and the civil building] will be rebuilt.

   e) Jane has [left town].

   f) The goslings [swam across] the lake.

7. Apply the movement test to determine which of the bracketed sequences in the following sentences form constituents.

   a) We ate our lunch [near the river bank].

   b) Steve looked [up the number] in the book.

   c) The [island has been] flooded.

   d) I love [peanut butter and bacon sandwiches].

   e) The environmental [movement is gaining momentum].

8. Lexical categories are divided into subcategories on the basis of their complements. For each of the following words, two potential complement options are given.

Verb	*Options*	*Verb*	*Options*
a) bark	ø *or* NP NP	e) clean	NP PP_{for} *or* NP NP
b) destroy	NP *or* ø	f) mumble	NP *or* NP NP
c) observe	NP *or* PP_{to} PP_{about}	g) throw	ø *or* NP PP_{loc}
d) discuss	NP *or* ø	h) make	NP PP_{to} *or* NP PP_{for}

Noun	*Options*
a) debate	PP_{of} PP_{to} *or* PP_{with} PP_{about}
b) hammer	ø *or* PP_{with} PP_{about}
c) success	PP_{of} PP_{to} *or* PP_{of}
d) transfer	PP_{with} PP_{about} *or* PP_{of} PP_{to}
e) sickness	ø *or* PP_{with} PP_{about}

Adjective	*Options*
a) strong	ø *or* PP_{about}
b) sick	NP *or* PP_{of}
c) bored	PP_{with} *or* PP_{of}
d) knowledgeable	PP_{to} *or* PP_{about}
e) thin	PP_{of} *or* ø

For each of the words:

  i) Determine which one of the two options matches the verb's subcategorization requirements.

  ii) Justify your choice by creating a sentence using that complement option.

9. The following sentences all contain embedded clauses that function as complements of a verb. Draw a tree structure for each sentence.

   a) The reporter said that an accident injured a woman.

   b) The fishermen think that the company polluted the bay.

   c) Bill reported that a student had asked whether the eclipse would occur.

The following sentences all contain embedded clauses that function as complements of an adjective, a preposition, or a noun. Draw a tree structure for each sentence.

d) The police were happy that the criminal had surrendered.
e) That officer was sure that Gerry was speeding down the highway.
f) Ray wondered about whether the exam would cover that section.
g) The jury believed the claim that the driver had totalled the Porsche.

10. The derivations of the following sentences involve the Inversion transformation. Give the deep structure and the surface structure for each sentence.

a) Will the owner of the company hire Hilary?
b) Can the dog fetch the frisbee?
c) Should the student report the incident?
d) Must the musician play that music?
e) Is that player leaving the team?

11. The following sentences involve the rules of *Wh* Movement and Inversion. Give the deep structure and the surface structure for each of these sentences.

a) Who should the director call?
b) What is Joanne eating?
c) Who will those immigrants live with?
d) What might Terry bake?
e) What was Anne bringing?
f) Who will the jury blame?

12. The following data is from Igbo, a language spoken in Nigeria.

a) Nwáànjì áhừ   b) ū̃ló̃   à
   woman   that   house this
   'that woman'   'this house'

i) Assuming that this data is typical, what is the order of specifiers and heads in Igbo?
ii) Draw the phrase structure trees for the two Igbo phrases.

13. The following data is from Malagasy, spoken on the island of Madagascar.

a) Entin' kafe   Dan.   b) Mankany amin' ny restauranta Dan.
   brings coffee Dan   goes   to   the restaurant Dan
   'Dan brings coffee.'   'Dan goes to the restaurant.'

i) Based on this data, what are the phrase structure rules for Malagasy?
ii) Draw the tree structure for each of the Malagasy sentences.

14. Consider the following data from Selayarese (spoken in Indonesia).

a) Laʔallei doeʔ   injo i-Baso.
   took   money the Baso
   'Baso took the money.'

     b) nraʔbai   sapon injo.
       collapsed house the
       'The house collapsed.'

     c) Lataroi doeʔ injo ri lamari   injo i-Baso.
       put   money the in cupboard the Baso
       'Baso put the money in the cupboard.'

     i) Write the phrase structure rules required to form these sentences.

     ii) How do they differ from English phrase structure rules?

15. The following data is from Korean. You may ignore the nominative (subject) and accusative (direct object) markers for the purposes of this exercise.

     a) Terry-ka   ku yeca-lul coahanta.
       Terry-Nom that girl-Ac likes
       'Terry likes that girl.'

     b) I   noin-i   hakkyo ey kassta.
       this man-Nom school to went
       'This man went to school.'

     c) Sue-ka   chinkwu eykey chayk-ul ilkessta.
       Sue-Nom friend   to   book-Ac read
       'Sue read the book to a friend.'

     i) Write the phrase structure rules required to form these sentences.

     ii) Draw the tree structure for each of the Korean sentences.

16. The following data is from Swati, a Bantu language spoken in Swaziland. Answer the questions that follow.

     a) Inja ijahamba.   d) Umfana unika umlimi imali.
       dog leaves   boy   gives farmer money
       'The dog leaves.'   'The boy gives money to the farmer.'

     b) Sipho ushaja inja.   e) Umfana unika bani imali.
       Sipho hits   dog   boy   gives who money
       'Sipho hits the dog.'   'Who did the boy give money to?'

     c) Sipho ushaja ini?
       Sipho hits   what
       'What does Sipho hit?'

     i) Give the phrase structure rule for S and XP in Swati.

     ii) What are the major differences between these rules and the ones required for the Korean data in the preceding problem?

     iii) Is there a *Wh* Movement transformation in Swati?

17. The following data illustrates the Inversion transformation in German.

     a) Das Kind wird die Schwester lehren.
       the child will the sister   teach
       'The child will teach the sister.'

     b) Wird das Kind die Schwester lehren?
       will the child the sister   teach
       'Will the child teach the sister?'

c) Der Mann liebt die Frau.
'The man loves the woman.'

d) Liebt der Mann die Frau?
loves the man the woman
'Does the man love the woman?'

e) Liebt er die Frau?
loves he the woman
'Does he love the woman?'

i) State the Inversion rule that applies in German to produce *yes-no* questions.

ii) How is the German Inversion rule different from its English counterpart?

18. The following sentences all contain conjoined categories. Draw a tree structure for each of the sentences.

a) The cyclist drank a gallon of water and a liter of Coke.
b) The airplane has landed at the airport and will taxi to the terminal.
c) The dog went down the stairs and out the door.
d) Crusoe landed on an island and ate a goat.
e) Jill will recycle that book and magazine.
f) Anya thinks that spring will come and that gardens will flourish.
g) Mary is fond of dogs but tired of the fleas.

19. The following sentences contain modifiers of various types. For each sentence, first identify the modifier(s), then draw the tree structures.

a) A large iguana suddenly appeared.
b) The principal made an important announcement after the class.
c) An unusual event occurred before the game.
d) The very hazardous waste seeped into the ground quickly.
e) A huge moon hung in the black sky.
f) Timothy bought an enormous map yesterday.

20. Each of the following sentences contains a relative clause. Draw the deep structure and the surface structure trees for each of these sentences.

a) The animals which Sam saw in the zoo had come from Kenya.
b) Kyle likes the girl who June introduced to the class.
c) The woman who Clyde lives with recycles plastic.
d) Helen recited the poem which Wordsworth had written.
e) The canoe which Crusoe carved was too heavy.

21. In each of the following sentences, indicate above each NP whether it is subject, direct object, or oblique, and indicate below each NP whether it is agent or theme.

a) Marie purchased a present.
b) The class was conducted by an expert.
c) Those books were read by young children.
d) An expert conducted the class.
e) A present was purchased by Marie.

For the Student Linguist

BACKWARDS

Sometimes poetry frustrates me because of all the seemingly non-sensical sentence bits I get after my brain automatically inserts a dramatic pause at the end of each line. Because I'm stuck, waiting for my eyes to get to the next line, as I try to figure out what's so incredibly significant about a line consisting of "Eskimo" or "his amber eyes" or "detritus" and nothing else. But I really like Lesléa Newman's work because the line divisions actually seem meaningful and because she seems to be having so much fun arranging these sentence bits.

Tiff and I[1]

Tiff and I sit
in Tompkins Square Park
reading poetry
under a sky
full of clapping pigeons.
He calls them flying rats
but I think
the pink and green circles
around their necks
like greasy oil puddles are
beautiful.
Tiff says
all my poems sound better
backwards.

Backwards
all my poems sound better
Tiff says.
Beautiful
like greasy oil puddles
around their necks are
the pink and green circles
but I think
he calls them flying rats.
Full of clapping pigeons
under a sky
reading poetry
in Tompkins Square Park
Tiff and I sit.

If you read the poem as if it were prose, I think the first half sounds pretty bland and the second half is just plain loopy:

Tiff and I sit in Tompkins Square Park reading poetry under a sky full of clapping pigeons. He calls them flying rats but I think the pink and green circles around their necks like greasy oil puddles are beautiful. Tiff says all my poems sound better backwards.

Backwards all my poems sound better Tiff says. Beautiful like greasy oil puddles around their necks are the pink and green circles but I think he calls them flying rats. Full of clapping pigeons under a sky reading poetry in Tompkins Square Park Tiff and I sit.

In fact, I can't read the second half in prose format without imagining flying poems that have greasy pink and green circles around their necks, a sky that is reading poetry, and two people who've spent the afternoon eating live pigeons.

What is it about the change from prose to poetry that makes this string of words interesting and meaningful? (We've got to drudge through some syntax here, but trust me, it's relatively painless and worth it.) Assume that the first half of the poem has three untransformed sentences, and the second half has sentences that have undergone transformations. Also notice that one word—*are*—gets switched into a different line in the second stanza. It shouldn't be too hard to draw tree structures for the sentences in the first stanza *if* you do it line-by-line (i.e., first draw the tree for "Tiff and I sit," then for "in Tompkins Square Park," etc., and then hook them together).

The sentences in the second stanza will be harder to draw trees for, but if you do the first stanza line-by-line, those parts will be the same, except for where the word *are* is switched. So all you really need to do is figure out which parts of the trees got moved, and in which order. Actually, that's not even too hard to do, since only constituents can be moved.

You've probably figured out by now why this poem is in the syntax chapter: it does a good job of showing off what constituents are and of showing how the same words, even the same phrases, can have a different meaning when they're moved. However, this poem does more than show off constituents. I also like the rhythm of the poem—the way some of the lines seem to invite me to pause after them, and other lines lead me quickly on to the next line. Take a look at the subcategorizations of the last word of each line. Some of them lead you to expect a complement and others don't. Try reading the poem again and see if the subcategorization frames make a difference in how much emphasis you put on each line.

Finally, look at some other poetry that you love or hate and see what sort of match there is between grouping in lines or stanzas and grouping into constituents. Look at some different types of writing and their phrase structures; since punctuation is sadly limited in how well it can show pauses or emphasis or any sort of complex tone, the actual structure of the sentence can be crucial if the sentence is to be read with the right emphasis. And look in particular at some of your own writing and at how transformations of sentences could make a difference in their clarity. All of this theory might actually improve your writing.

[1]Newman, Lesléa (1991) "Tiff and I" in *Sweet Dark Places* HerBooks: Santa Cruz, CA.

6 SEMANTICS
The Study of Meaning

*Indeed, it is well said, in every object there is
inexhaustible meaning.*

Thomas Carlyle

Up to now, this book has focused on the form of utterances—their sound pattern, morphological structure, and syntactic organization. But there is more to language than just form. In order for language to fulfill its communicative function, utterances must also convey a message; they must have content. Speaking very generally, we can call this message or content the utterance's **meaning**.

This chapter is concerned with **semantics**, the study of meaning in human language. Because some work in this complicated area of linguistic analysis presupposes considerable knowledge of other disciplines (particularly logic, mathematics, and philosophy), not all aspects of contemporary semantics are suitable for presentation in an introductory linguistics textbook. We will restrict our attention here to four major topics in semantics: (1) the nature of meaning, (2) some properties of the conceptual system underlying meaning, (3) the contribution of syntactic structure to the interpretation of sentences, and (4) the role of nongrammatical factors in the understanding of utterances.

6.1 MEANING

Long before linguistics existed as a discipline, thinkers were speculating about the nature of meaning. For thousands of years, this question has been considered central to philosophy. More recently, it has come to be important in psychology as well. Contributions to semantics have come from a diverse group of scholars, ranging from Plato and Aristotle in ancient Greece to Bertrand Russell in the twentieth century. Our goal in this section will be to consider in a very general way what this research has revealed about the meanings of words and sentences in human language.

Semantic Relations among Words

By virtue of their meaning, words and phrases are able to enter into a variety of semantic relations with other words and phrases in the language. Because these relationships help identify those aspects of meaning relevant to linguistic analysis, they constitute a good starting point for this chapter.

Synonymy **Synonyms** are words or expressions that have the same meanings in some contexts. The following pairs of words provide plausible examples of synonymy in English.

Table 6.1 Some synonyms in English

youth	adolescent
automobile	car
remember	recall
purchase	buy
big	large

Although it is easy to think of contexts in which both words in each pair have essentially the same meaning, there are also contexts in which their meanings diverge at least slightly. For example, although *youth* and *adolescent* both refer to people of about the same age, only the latter word has the meaning of 'immature' in a phrase such as *He's such an adolescent!* Many linguists believe that it would be inefficient for a language to have two words or phrases whose meanings are absolutely identical in all contexts, and that complete synonymy is therefore rare or nonexistent.

Antonymy **Antonyms** are words or phrases that are opposites with respect to some component of their meaning. The following pairs of words provide examples of antonymy.

Table 6.2 Some antonyms in English

dark	light
boy	girl
hot	cold
up	down
in	out
come	go

In each of these pairs, the two words contrast with respect to at least one component of their meaning. Thus, the meanings of *boy* and *girl* are opposites with respect to sex, although they are alike with respect to species (both are human). Similarly, *come* and *go* are opposites with respect to direction, although both involve the concept of movement.

Polysemy and Homophony **Polysemy** occurs where a word has two or more related meanings. The following table contains some examples of polysemous words in English.

Table 6.3 Some polysemy in English

Word	Meaning A	Meaning B
bright	'shining'	'intelligent'
to glare	'to shine intensely'	'to stare angrily'
a deposit	'minerals in the earth'	'money in the bank'

If you consult a reasonably comprehensive dictionary for any language, you will find numerous examples of polysemy. The ease with which words acquire additional related meanings allows language to accommodate the new concepts and perspectives that accompany cultural change.

Homophony exists where a single form has two or more entirely distinct meanings. In such cases, it is assumed that there are two (or more) separate words with the same pronunciation rather than a single word with different meanings.

Table 6.4 Some homophones in English

Word	Meaning A	Meaning B
bat	'a winged rodent'	'a piece of equipment used in baseball'
bank	'a financial institution'	'the edge of a river'
club	'a social organization'	'a blunt weapon'
pen	'a writing instrument'	'a small cage'

Polysemy and homophony create **lexical ambiguity** in that a single form has two or more meanings. Thus, a sentence such as *1* could mean either that Liz purchased an instrument to write with or that she bought a small cage.

1. Liz bought a pen.

Of course, in actual speech the surrounding words and sentences usually make the intended meaning clear. The lexical ambiguity in sentences such as the following therefore normally goes unnoticed.

2. He got a loan from the *bank*.
3. Because Liz needed a place to keep her guinea pig, she went downtown and bought a *pen* for $10.

Semantic Relations Involving Sentences

Like words, sentences have meanings that can be analyzed in terms of their relation to other meanings. We consider three such relations here—paraphrase, entailment, and contradiction.

Paraphrase Two sentences that can have the same meaning are said to be **paraphrases** of each other. The following pairs of sentences provide examples of complete or near paraphrases.

4. a) The police chased the burglar.
   b) The burglar was chased by the police.
5. a) I gave the summons to Erin.
   b) I gave Erin the summons.
6. a) It is unfortunate that the team lost.
   b) Unfortunately, the team lost.
7. a) Paul bought a car from Sue.
   b) Sue sold a car to Paul.
8. a) The game will begin at 3:00 P.M.
   b) At 3:00 P.M., the game will begin.

The *a* and *b* sentences in each of the above pairs are obviously very similar in meaning. Indeed, it would be impossible for one sentence in any pair to be true without the other also being true. Thus, if it is true that the police chased the burglar, it must also be true that the burglar was chased by the police. Similarly, if it is false that the police chased the burglar, then it must also be false that the burglar was chased by the police. (Sentences whose meanings are related to each other in this way are said to have the same **truth conditions**.)

For some linguists, this is enough to justify saying that the two sentences have the same meaning. However, you may notice that there are subtle differences in emphasis between the *a* and *b* sentences in *4* to *8*. For instance, it is natural to interpret *4a* as a statement about what the police did and *4b* as a statement about what happened to the burglar. Similarly, *8b* seems to place more emphasis on the starting time of the game than *8a* does. As is the case with synonymy, many linguists feel that languages do not permit two or more structures to have absolutely identical meanings and that paraphrases are therefore never perfect.

Entailment A relation in which the truth of one sentence necessarily implies the truth of another, as happens in examples *4* to *8* above, is called **entailment**. In the cases we have been considering, the entailment relation between the *a* and *b* sentences is mutual since the truth of either sentence guarantees the truth of the other. In some cases, however, entailment is asymmetrical. The following examples illustrate this.

    9. *a*) The park wardens killed the bear.
       b) The bear is dead.
  10. *a*) Robin is a man.
      b) Robin is human.

The *a* sentences in *9* and *10* entail the *b* sentences. If it is true that the park wardens killed the bear, then it must also be true that the bear is dead. However, the reverse does not follow since the bear could be dead without the park wardens having killed it. Similarly, if it is true that Robin is a man, then it is also true that Robin is human. Once again though, the reverse does not hold: even if we know that Robin is a human, we cannot conclude that Robin is a man rather than a woman or a child.

Contradiction Sometimes, it turns out that if one sentence is true, then another sentence must be false. This is the case with the examples in *11*.

  11. *a*) Charles is a bachelor.
      b) Charles is married.

If it is true that Charles is a bachelor, then it cannot be true that he is married. When two sentences cannot both be true, we say that there is a **contradiction**.

What Is Meaning?

Although it is relatively easy to determine whether two words or sentences have identical or different meanings, it is much more difficult to determine precisely what meaning is in the first place. In fact, despite many centuries of study, we still know very little about the nature of meaning or how it is represented in the human mind. Nonetheless, it is worthwhile to review briefly some of the better known proposals and the problems that they encounter.

Connotation One notion that is closely linked with the concept of meaning is **connotation**, the set of associations that a word's use can evoke. For people living in the north, for example, the word *winter* evokes thoughts of snow, bitter cold, short evenings, frozen fingertips and the like. These associations make up the word's connotation, but they cannot be its meaning (or at least not its entire meaning). This is because *winter* is still used for the season stretching from December to March even if none of these other things are present (for example, if one lives further to the south). We must therefore look beyond connotation for our understanding of what meaning is.

Word Meaning

The basic repository of meaning within the grammar is the lexicon, which provides the information about the meaning of individual words relevant to the interpretation of sentences.

Referents One well-known approach to semantics attempts to equate a word's meaning with the entities to which it refers—its **referents**. According to this theory, the meaning of the word *dog* corresponds to the set of entities (dogs) that it picks out in the real world. Although not inherently implausible, this idea encounters certain serious difficulties. For one thing, there is a problem with words such as *unicorn* and *dragon*, which have no referents in the real world even though they are far from meaningless. A problem of a different sort arises with expressions such as *the Prime Minister of Great Britain* and *the leader of the Conservative Party*, both of which refer (in 1993 at least) to John Major. Although these two expressions may have the same referent, we would not say that they mean the same thing. No one would maintain that the phrase *Prime Minister of Great Britain* could be defined as 'the leader of the Conservative Party' or vice versa.

Extension and Intension The impossibility of equating a word's meaning with its referents has led to a distinction between **extension** and **intension**. Whereas a word's extension corresponds to the set of entities that it picks out in the world, its intension corresponds to its inherent sense, the concepts that it evokes. Some examples are given in Table 6.5. Thus, the extension of *woman*

Table 6.5 Extension versus intension

Phrase	Extension	Intension
Prime Minister of Great Britain	John Major	leader of the majority party in Parliament
World Series champions (1992)	Toronto Blue Jays	winners of the baseball championship
capital of California	Sacramento	city containing the state legislature

would be a set of real world entities (women) while its intension would involve notions like 'female' and 'human'. Similarly, the phrase *Prime Minister of Great Britain* would have as its extension an individual ('John Major'), but its intension would involve the concept 'leader of the majority party in Parliament'. The distinction between a word's intension and its extension does not allow us to resolve the question of meaning. It simply permits us to pose it in a new way: what is the nature of a word's inherent sense or intension?

One suggestion is that word meanings (intensions) correspond to mental images. This is an obvious improvement over the referential theory since it is conceivable that one might have a mental image of a unicorn or a dragon even if there are no such entities in the real world. Unfortunately, this idea encounters serious difficulties of another sort. For one thing, it is hard to conceive of a mental image for words like *nitrogen*, *522,101*, *if*, *very*, and so on. Moreover, there seems to be no mental image for the meaning of the word *dog* that could be general enough to include Chihuahuas and Irish wolfhounds, yet still exclude foxes and wolves.

Semantic Features Still another approach to meaning tries to equate a word's intension with an abstract concept consisting of smaller components called **semantic features**. This **componential analysis** is especially effective when it comes to representing similarities and differences among words with related meanings. The feature analysis in Figure 6.1 for the words *man*, *woman*, *boy*,

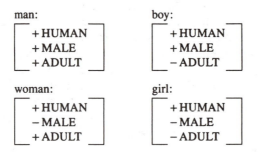

man:
```
┌            ┐
│ + HUMAN    │
│ + MALE     │
│ + ADULT    │
└            ┘
```

boy:
```
┌            ┐
│ + HUMAN    │
│ + MALE     │
│ − ADULT    │
└            ┘
```

woman:
```
┌            ┐
│ + HUMAN    │
│ − MALE     │
│ + ADULT    │
└            ┘
```

girl:
```
┌            ┐
│ + HUMAN    │
│ − MALE     │
│ − ADULT    │
└            ┘
```

Figure 6.1 Semantic feature composition for *man, woman, boy, girl*

and *girl* illustrates this. An obvious advantage of this approach is that it allows us to group entities into natural classes (much as we do in phonology). Hence, *man* and *boy* could be grouped together as [+ HUMAN, + MALE], while *man* and *woman* could be put in a class defined by the features [+ HUMAN, + ADULT].

Componential analysis gives its most impressive results when applied to sets of words referring to classes of entities with shared properties. As illustrated above, a few simple features will allow us to distinguish among subclasses of people—men, women, boys, and girls. Unlike phonological features, however, semantic features do not seem to make up a small, well-defined class, and it is often very hard to reduce word meanings to smaller parts. Can we say, for example, that the meaning of *blue* consists of the feature [+ COLOR] and something else? If so, what is that other thing? Isn't it blueness? If so, then we still have not broken the meaning of *blue* into smaller features, and we are back where we started.

In other cases, it is unclear whether semantic features really provide any insights into the nature of the meaning they are supposed to represent. What value is there, for instance, in characterizing the meaning of *dog* in terms of the feature complex [+ ANIMAL, + CANINE] so long as there is no further analysis of the concept underlying the feature [CANINE]? A similar objection could be made to the use of features like [HUMAN] and [MALE] to define *man* and *woman*.

Meaning and Concepts What, then, can we say about meaning? From the preceding survey, it seems that meaning must be something that exists in the mind rather than the world and that it must be more abstract than pictures and more complex than features. The seventeenth-century philosopher John Locke suggested that words are "marks of ideas in the mind." This proposal is typical of a wide range of traditional and modern approaches to semantics, all of which try to relate meaning to mental concepts of some sort. Since concepts don't have to correspond to objects in the world and need not be images or sets of features, these approaches can avoid the problems outlined above. However, they face a serious problem of their own. Unless it is possible to determine what a concept is, it does little good to equate the meaning of linguistic forms with concepts in the mind. In the next section of this chapter, we will consider the human conceptual system from the point of view of linguistic meaning and try to determine some of its basic properties.

6.2 THE CONCEPTUAL SYSTEM

Underlying the use of words and sentences to express meaning in human language is a conceptual system capable of organizing and classifying every imaginable aspect of our experience, from inner feelings and perceptions, to cultural and social phenomena, to the physical world that surrounds us. This section focuses on what the study of this conceptual system reveals about how meaning is expressed through language. We will begin by considering some examples that illustrate the way in which these concepts are structured, extended, and interrelated.

Fuzzy Concepts

We tend to think that the concepts expressed by the words and phrases of our language have precise definitions with clear-cut boundaries that distinguish them from other concepts. Some concepts may indeed be like this. For example, the concept expressed by the phrase *Member of Congress* seems to be clear-cut enough: one is a Member of Congress if and only if one is duly elected to a particular legislative body; no other person can be truthfully called a Member of Congress.

But are all concepts so straightforward? Consider the concept associated with the word *rich*. How much does one have to be worth to be called rich? Five hundred thousand dollars? Eight hundred thousand? A million? Is there any figure that we can give that would be so precise that a person who was short by just five cents would not be called rich? It seems not. While one could miss out on being a Member of Congress by five votes, it does not seem possible to miss out on being rich by just five cents. Moreover, while some people clearly qualify as rich and others uncontroversially qualify as nonrich, an indefinitely large number of people fall into the unclear area at the borderline of the concept and it is just not possible to say definitively whether or not they count as rich. This is because the notion of 'richness' does not have clear-cut boundaries; it is what we call a **fuzzy concept**.

Many linguists believe that this type of fuzziness pervades the human conceptual system. Certainly, it is not hard to think of everyday concepts whose boundaries are fuzzy in the same way as the preceding example—*tall*, *old*, *playboy*, *strong*, *grey-haired*, *genius*, *clean*, *bargain*, and so on.

Graded Membership A second important fact about concepts is that their members can be graded in terms of their typicality. Consider first a fuzzy concept such as 'basketball star'. Even within the set of people who we can agree are basketball stars, some provide better examples of this concept than others. At the time of writing, for instance, Michael Jordan is a better example of a basketball star than is Patrick Ewing. Although basketball fans agree that both players are stars, Michael Jordan has scored more points, won more awards, set more records, endorsed more products on TV, received more media attention, and so on. This makes him a better example of a star than Patrick Ewing.

Even concepts whose boundaries can be scientifically defined exhibit this type of graded membership. A good example of this involves the concept 'bird'. Even assuming that English speakers all think of birds as 'warm-blooded, egg-laying, feathered vertebrae with forelimbs modified to form wings' (the dictionary definition), they still feel that some of these creatures are more bird-like than others. Thus, robins and magpies, for example, are intuitively better examples of birds than are hummingbirds, ostriches, or penguins.

Examples like these suggest that concepts have an internal structure, with the best or **prototypical** exemplars (Michael Jordan in the case of 'basketball stars', robins in the case of 'birds') close to the core and less typical members arranged in successively more peripheral regions.

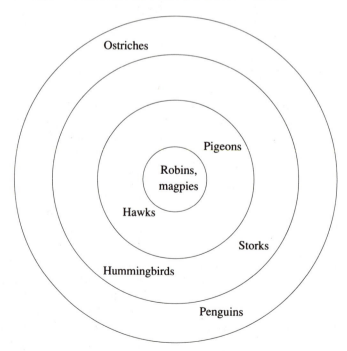

Figure 6.2 Possible internal structure of the concept 'bird'

The existence of fuzzy concepts and of graded membership in concepts provides important insights into the nature of the human conceptual system. In particular, it seems that many (perhaps even most) concepts expressed in language are not rigid all-or-nothing notions with precise and clear-cut boundaries. Rather, they are characterized by an internal structure that recognizes degrees of typicality as well as by fuzzy boundaries that make categorization uncertain in some cases.

Metaphor

The concepts expressed through language are not isolated from each other. Rather, they make up a giant network, with many interconnections and associations among the various subparts. A good example of these interconnections involves **metaphor**, the understanding of one concept in terms of another.

We have a tendency to think of metaphor as a literary device reserved for the use of authors and poets. In fact, however, there is reason to think that it has a prominent place in the conceptual system shared by all human beings. The effects of this prominence are seen in the way in which we use language to talk about various abstract notions.

A simple example of this involves the concept of time, which we analyze metaphorically by treating it as if it were a concrete commodity. Consider in this regard the following sentences, which illustrate how we talk about time.

12. *a*) You're *wasting* my time.
    b) This gadget will *save* you hours.
    c) How do you *spend* your time these days?
    d) I have *invested* a lot of time in that project.
    e) You need to *budget* your time.
    f) Is that *worth* your while?
    g) He's living on *borrowed* time.
    g) You don't use your time *profitably*.

The words that we use in speaking about time suggest that it is conceptualized as something concrete—a commodity that can be saved, wasted, and invested just like other valuable things can.

What is the basis for the metaphor that determines how we talk about time? There is apparently no objective, inherent similarity between time and commodities such as gold or money. What brings these two concepts together is the *perception*, based in part on culture and in part on the subjective feeling that the passing of time is like the passage of valuable commodities from one hand to another.

A Spatial Metaphor Another very prevalent metaphor in our language involves the use of words that are primarily associated with spatial orientation to talk about physical and psychological states. The basis for these metaphors appears to lie in our physical experience. Unhappiness and ill health tend to be associated with lethargy and inactivity, which often involve being on one's back (physically down). In contrast, happiness and good health are often correlated with energy and movement, which involve being on one's feet (physically up).

Table 6.6 Metaphorical use of spatial terms

Emotions: happy is up, sad is down

I'm feeling *up*.	I'm feeling *down*.
That *boosted* my spirits.	He *fell* into a depression.
My spirits *rose*.	Her spirits *sank*.
You're in *high* spirits.	He's feeling *low*.
the *height* of ecstasy	the *depths* of depression
That gave me a *lift*.	

Physical health: up is health and life, down is sickness and death

He's at the *peak* of health.	He's *sinking* fast.
Lazarus *rose* from the dead.	He *fell* ill.
He's in *top* shape.	He came *down* with the flu.
	His health is *declining*.
	He's feeling *under* the weather.

These few examples illustrate a more general point about language and meaning. The innumerably many concepts that we express through language do not all exist independent of each other. Rather, many concepts are structured and understood metaphorically in terms of notions more basic to our physical and cultural experience. Thus, time is understood in terms of a commodity metaphor, health and happiness in terms of a spatial metaphor, and so on. By studying how concepts are represented in language, we can gain valuable insights into the role of experience and metaphor in the human conceptual system.

The Lexicalization of Concepts

Do all human beings share the same conceptual system? Do all languages express concepts in the same way? These are questions that have fascinated and puzzled researchers for many decades. At the present time, there is no reason to believe that human beings in different linguistic communities have different conceptual systems. But there is ample evidence that languages can differ from each other in terms of how they express concepts.

Lexicalization The classic and frequently distorted example of how languages can differ from each other in the expression of concepts involves the words for 'snow' in Eskimo (Inuktitut). Sometimes estimated in the hundreds by unknowledgeable commentators, the set of simple words for 'snow' in Eskimo is in fact much smaller. For example, one well-known dictionary gives only the following four items (although other dictionaries give several more for at least some varieties of Eskimo).

Table 6.7 Words for 'snow' in Eskimo

aput	'snow on the ground'
qana	'falling snow'
piqsirpoq	'drifting snow'
qimuqsuq	'snow drift'

As you can see, there is nothing particularly startling about this list of words. In fact, even in English there is more than just one word to describe snow in its various forms—*snow*, *slush*, *blizzard*, and *sleet* come to mind, for example.

The types of differences we are considering involve **lexicalization**, the process whereby concepts are encoded in the words of a language. Thus, Eskimo lexicalizes the concepts 'falling' and 'snow' in a single word (*qana*) while English uses two separate words. While some lexicalization differences may correlate with cultural factors (the relative importance of types of snow in traditional Eskimo culture), this is not always so. For example, English has an unusually rich set of vocabulary items pertaining to the perception of light.

Table 6.8 Some verbs pertaining to light in English

glimmer	glisten
gleam	glow
glitter	flicker
shimmer	shine
flare	glare
flash	

Although most English speakers know and use the words in this list, it is hard to see how the variety found in this particular area of vocabulary can be correlated with any identifiable feature of our culture or society.

The lexicalization differences just illustrated are generally not considered by linguists to have any special importance. As we have tried to emphasize throughout this book, the focus of linguistic analysis is on the *system* of knowledge that makes it possible to speak and understand a language. The fact that a particular language has more words pertaining to snow or light does not in and of itself provide any insight into the nature of the human linguistic system, and therefore does not merit special attention. However, as we will see in the next subsection, there are lexicalization differences whose properties can shed light on how linguistic systems express meaning.

Motion Verbs All languages have words that can describe motion through space (in English, *come*, *go*, and *move*, among many others). However, recent work suggests that there may be systematic differences in terms of how languages express motion and the concepts related to it. In English, for example, there are many verbs that simultaneously express both the concept of motion and the manner in which the motion occurs.

Table 6.9 Some verbs expressing motion and manner in English

The rock *rolled* down the hill.
The puck *slid* across the ice.
She *limped* through the house.
The smoke *swirled* through the opening.

Notice how each of these verbs expresses both the fact that something moved and the manner in which it moved (by rolling, sliding, limping, and so on).

Interestingly, Romance languages (descendents of Latin) cannot express motion events in this way. Thus, while Spanish has a verb *rodar* with the meaning 'to roll', it does not use this verb to express both manner and motion as English does.

13. *La botella rodó en la cueva.*
'The bottle rolled into the cave.'

Instead, the motion and its manner have to be expressed separately.

14. La botella entró en la cueva, rodando.
'The bottle entered the cave, rolling.'

However, Spanish *does* have a series of verbs that jointly express the concept of motion and the path along which it occurs.

Table 6.10 Some verbs expressing motion and path in Spanish

El globo *bajó* por la chimenea.
'The balloon moved-down through the chimney.'

El globo *subió* por la chimenea.
'The balloon moved-up through the chimney.'

La botella *volvió* a la orilla.
'The bottle moved-back to the bank.'

La botella *cruzó* el canal.
'The bottle moved-across the canal.'

La botella *salió* de la cueva.
'The bottle moved-out from the cave.'

As the English translations show, Spanish verbs of motion express both the concept of movement and the direction of its path—down, up, back, across, out, and so forth. (English, too, has verbs that can express both motion and path—*descend*, *ascend*, *return*, and so on—but these words are not part of its native vocabulary. Rather they were borrowed into English from latinate sources, usually through French.)

Another lexicalization option is found in the Amerindian language Atsugewi, in which verbs can express both motion and the type of thing that moves.

Table 6.11 Some verb roots expressing motion and the thing moving in Atsugewi

lup	for movement of a small, shiny spherical object (a hailstone)
t	for movement of a smallish, flat object that can be attached to another (a stamp, a clothing patch, a shingle)
caq	for movement of a slimy, lumpish object (a toad, a cow dropping)
swal	for movement of a limp linear object, suspended by one end (a shirt on a clothesline, a hanging dead rabbit)
qput	for movement of loose, dry dirt
staq	for movement of runny, unpleasant material (manure, guts, chewed gum, rotten tomatoes)

We learn two things from these facts. First, the concept of motion is associated with a number of other concepts, including 'path', 'manner of movement', and 'moving thing'. Second, the way in which these concepts are grouped together for purposes of lexicalization can differ systematically from language to language. Languages such as English have verbs that simultaneously lexicalize motion and manner while other languages have verbs that simultaneously lexicalize motion and path (Spanish) or motion and the type of thing that moves (Atsugewi).

The general picture that is emerging from this type of work is that within particular semantic domains, there may be a small universal set of concepts (motion, manner, path, thing that moves, and so on) and a small set of options for how these concepts can be combined for purposes of lexicalization. Unlike the lexicalization differences involving snow and light discussed earlier, these differences appear to be highly systematic and to reveal some general tendencies about the way in which meaning can be expressed in human language. Further work of this type should provide additional insights into the organization of the human conceptual system as well as the ways in which its component notions can be lexicalized in human language.

The Grammaticization of Concepts

Of the indefinitely large set of concepts expressible in human language, a relatively small subset enjoys a special status. These are the concepts that are lexicalized as affixes and nonlexical (functional) categories in one language or another. Some of the concepts that are treated this way in English are listed in Table 6.12.

Table 6.12 Some concepts associated with affixes and non-lexical categories in English

Concept	Affix
Past	*-ed*
More than one	*-s*
Again	*re-*
Negation	*in-*, *un-*

Concept	Nonlexical category
Obligation	*must*
Possibility	*may*
Definite, specific	*the*
Indefinite, non-specific	*a*
Disjunction	*or*
Negation	*not*
Conjunction	*and*

Concepts that are expressed as affixes or nonlexical categories are said to have been **grammaticized**.

Some concepts tend to be highly grammaticizable in that most, if not all, languages lexicalize them as affixes or special nonlexical categories. Negation and conjunction are possible examples of concepts that are grammaticized in all languages. Contrasts involving singular versus plural and past versus non-past are encoded by special affixes in many languages, but not all. Still other concepts are grammaticized in a smaller number of languages, as the following example from the Siouan language Hidatsa illustrates.

Hidatsa Assertion Morphemes In Hidatsa, each statement is accompanied by a morpheme to indicate which of the following five categories it exemplifies. (Still other markers are used for questions, commands, and wishes.)

Table 6.13 Assertion morphemes in Hidatsa

ski *The speaker is certain of the statement's truth*	

Waceo iikipi kure heo-<u>ski</u>
'The man (definitely) carried the pipe.'

c *The speaker believes the statement to be true*	

Waceo iikipi kure heo-<u>c</u>.
'The man (supposedly) carried the pipe.'

wareac *The speaker regards the statement to be common knowledge*	

Waceo iikipi kure heo-<u>wareac</u>.
'The man carried the pipe (they say).'

rahe *The statement is based on an unverified report from someone else*	

Waceo wiira rakci heo-<u>rahe</u>.
'The man roasted the goose (it is rumored).'

toak *The truth of the statement is unknown to both speaker and listener*	

Waceo cihpa rakci heo-<u>toak</u>.
'The man roasted the prairie dog (perhaps).'

Choice of the appropriate assertion morpheme is extremely important in Hidatsa. A speaker who utters a false sentence marked by the morpheme *-ski* is considered to be a liar. Had he used the morpheme *-c*, on the other hand, it would be assumed that he simply made a mistake.

While English has ways of indicating these contrasts (by using expressions such as *perhaps*, *I heard that*, and *I guess*), it does not have a grammatical system of morphemes that obligatorily encodes this information in every sentence. By investigating the grammaticization options found in different languages, it may eventually be possible to identify the factors that determine which concepts are singled out for association with affixes and nonlexical categories.

6.3 SYNTACTIC STRUCTURE AND INTERPRETATION

The preceding sections have focused on the meaning conveyed by the individual words and phrases that make up a sentence. In this section, we turn to the problem of sentence interpretation, with an emphasis on how the positioning of words and phrases in syntactic structure helps determine the meaning of the entire sentence, consistent with the following principle.

15. **The Principle of Compositionality**:
The meaning of a sentence is determined by the meaning of its component parts and the manner in which they are arranged in syntactic structure.

There are many different ideas about precisely how the meaning of a sentence's component words and their arrangement in syntactic structure determine sentence meaning. For purposes of illustration, we will consider the relevance of syntactic structure to three aspects of sentence interpretation—the representation of structural ambiguity, the assignment of thematic roles, and the interpretation of pronouns.

Structural Ambiguity

Some sentences are ambiguous because their component words can be arranged into phrases in more than one way. This is called structural ambiguity and is to be distinguished from lexical ambiguity, which is the result of homophony or polysemy. Structural ambiguity is exemplified by phrases like *old men and women*, where we can take old to be a property of both the men and the women or of the men alone. These two interpretations or readings can be linked to separate tree structures, as Figure 6.3 shows. (C = conjunction.)

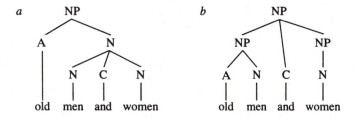

Figure 6.3

Figure 6.3a corresponds to the reading in which *old* modifies *men* as well as *women*. This is shown by making the adjective a sister of the category that dominates both nouns. In Figure 6.3b, on the other hand, the adjective is a sister of only the N *men*, and this structure corresponds to the reading in which 'old' applies only to the men.

Another case of structural ambiguity is found in sentences such as *16*.

16. Nicole saw the people with binoculars.

In one interpretation of *16*, the people had binoculars when Nicole noticed them (the phrase *with binoculars* modifies the noun *people*), while in the other interpretation, Nicole saw the people by using the binoculars (the PP modifies the verb). These two readings can be represented as in Figure 6.4. In Figure 6.4a, the PP *with binoculars* combines with the N *people*, reflecting the first reading for this sentence. In Figure 6.4b, on the other hand, the PP combines with the verb and its direct object and is not linked in any special way to the N *people*.

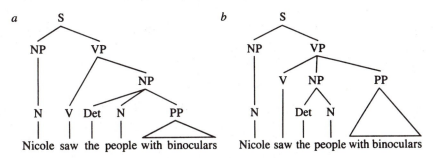

Figure 6.4

As a final example of this type of structural ambiguity, consider the compound *French history teacher*, which can refer either to a history teacher who is French or to a teacher of French history. These two readings can be associated with the trees depicted in Figure 6.5a and 6.5b, respectively.

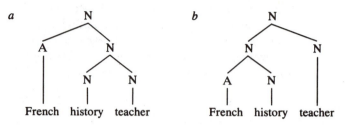

Figure 6.5

The three cases of structural ambiguity just outlined all have in common the fact that the two interpretations can be related to differences in the surface structure tree. Sometimes, however, ambiguity can be properly characterized only with the help of deep structure. Consider in this regard a sentence such as the following:

17. Who do you expect to play?

On one reading, *17* can be interpreted as a question about who your opponent will be (who you will play against) while on another, it asks who will be playing. Although it is difficult to see how the grouping of constituents in surface structure could reflect these different interpretations, consideration of the relevant deep structures provides the needed insight. The first reading corresponds to *18a*, in which *who* appears as direct object of *play*. The second interpretation, on the other hand, is associated with the deep structure depicted in *18b,* in which the *wh* word is subject of *play*. In both cases, *Wh* Movement will yield the sentence in *17*. (See Section 3 of Chapter 5.)

18. a) You expect to play who.
      b) You expect who to play.

The fact that deep structure is needed to represent certain types of ambiguity provides interesting additional evidence for the view that there are at least two levels of syntactic structure—deep structure and surface structure.

Thematic Roles (advanced)

Part of semantic interpretation involves determining the roles that the referents of NPs play in the situation described by sentences. Consider in this regard the simple sentence in *19*.

19. The senator sent the lobster from Maine to Nebraska.

It would be impossible to understand this sentence if we could not identify the senator as the person who is responsible for sending something, the lobster as the thing that is sent, and so on. The term **thematic role** or **semantic role** is used to describe the part played by a particular entity in an event. In most linguistic analyses, at least the thematic roles in Table 6.14 are recognized. (These

Table 6.14 Thematic roles

The senator sent the lobster from Maine to Nebraska		
Agent:	the entity who deliberately performs an action	*the senator*
Theme:	the entity undergoing a change of state or transfer	*the lobster*
Source:	the starting point for a transfer	*Maine*
Goal:	the end point for a transfer	*Nebraska*

definitions have been simplified somewhat.) The notion of transfer used in the definition of theme, source, and goal is intended to involve not only actual physical movement, but also changes in possession, as in *20*, and identity, as in *21*.

> *20.* Terry gave the skis to Mary.
>   agent   theme   goal
> *21.* The magician changed the handkerchief into a rabbit.
>   agent   theme   goal

Many semantic analyses recognize various other thematic roles, as shown in Table 6.15, to describe the NPs in sentences such as the following:

> *22.* The astronomer saw the comet with a new telescope at the observatory.

Table 6.15 Some additional thematic roles

The astronomer saw the comet with a new telescope at the observatory.		
Experiencer:	the entity perceiving something	*the astronomer*
Stimulus:	the entity perceived	*the comet*
Instrument:	the entity used to carry out an action	*a new telescope*
Location:	the place at which an entity or action is located	*the observatory*

Thematic Role Assignment Where do thematic roles come from, and how does the grammar ensure that the appropriate thematic role is associated with each NP in a sentence? Thematic roles originate in word meaning. Thus, if the sentence *Harry hit the ball* contains an agent and a theme, it is because the verb *hit* has the type of meaning that implies an entity that does the hitting (an agent) and an entity that gets hit (a theme). Similarly, if we understand Maine as a source and Nebraska as a goal in sentence *19*, it is because of the difference in the meaning of the prepositions *from* and *to* that occur with these NPs.

Table 6.16 Some words and the thematic roles implied by their meanings

hit	V, < agent, theme >
walk	V, < agent >
to	P, < goal >
from	P, < source >
near	P, < location >

These roles are then assigned to NPs based on their position in syntactic structure, with each NP receiving one and only one role.

    As a first example of this, let us consider the complement of a preposition. In such cases, the process of thematic role assignment can be summarized as follows.

> *23.* A P assigns a thematic role to its complement NP.

The operation of this convention is illustrated in Figure 6.6.

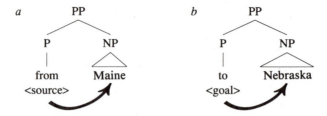

Figure 6.6

Matters are slightly more complicated in the case of Vs. Here we must distinguish between the theme role, which is assigned to the V's complement, and the agent role, which is assigned to its subject (the NP immediately under S).

24. A V assigns a theme role (if it has one) to its complement NP.
     A V assigns an agent role (if it has one) to its subject NP.

This is exemplified in the following structures.

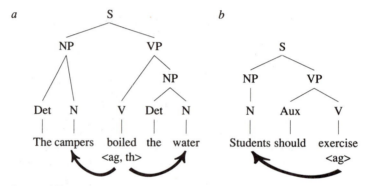

Figure 6.7

In accordance with *24*, the theme role (where present) is assigned to the V's NP complement while the agent role is assigned to the subject.

The structure in Figure 6.8 illustrates the assignment of thematic roles in a sentence that contains a P in addition to a V.

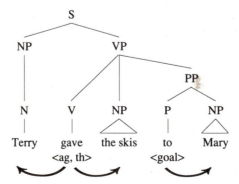

Figure 6.8

Here, the P *to* assigns its goal role to its complement NP *Mary* while the verb *give* assigns its theme role to the complement *the skis* and its agent role to the subject *Terry*.

Deep Structure and Thematic Roles In the examples considered to this point, it is unclear whether an NP receives its thematic role on the basis of its position in deep structure or surface structure. This is because our example sentences are all formed without the help of movement transformations, so that each NP occupies the same position in both deep structure and surface structure. But now consider a sentence such as *25*, which is formed with the help of *Wh* Movement.

> 25. What should the man bring?

This sentence has the deep structure depicted in Figure 6.9.

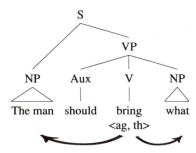

Figure 6.9

Since the theme role is assigned to the complement of V (see *24* and Figure 6.8 above), it follows that the NP *what* in the above example receives this role by virtue of its position in deep structure, not surface structure (where it occurs at the beginning of the sentence). This allows us to draw the following conclusion.

> 26. An NP's deep structure position determines its thematic role.

The relevance of deep structure to the assignment of thematic roles is important for two reasons. First, it shows that syntactic structure not only represents the way in which words are organized into phrases, but also is relevant to semantic interpretation. Second, the fact that an NP's position in deep structure determines its thematic role provides additional support for the existence of this underlying level of syntactic structure. This, in turn, lends support to the claim that there must be at least two types of syntactic rules: phrase structure rules, which form the deep structure, and transformations, which convert it into surface structure.

Passives (advanced) Now let us reconsider the passive structures first discussed in Chapter 5.

> 27. The thief was arrested (by the police).
>   *Theme*   *Agent*

From the point of view of thematic role assignment, this sentence is strange in two respects. First, the NP that occurs in subject position in this sentence (*the thief*) bears the theme role since it refers to the person who is placed in custody. As we saw earlier, the theme role should be assigned to the complement of the verb, not its subject. Second, instead of being assigned to the subject position, the agent role (corresponding to the person doing the arresting) is assigned to an NP that occurs in an optional PP headed by the P *by*. How are we to account for these facts?

The first of these facts follows straightforwardly from the type of deep structure assigned to passive sentences. (For the time being, we ignore the PP *by the police*.)

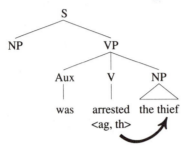

Figure 6.10 Deep structure for *The thief was arrested*

Since the NP *the thief* appears as complement of the verb *arrest* in deep structure and since an NP's deep structure position determines its thematic role, it follows that it will be assigned the theme role, as desired.

But what of the agent role? The crucial assumption is that the passive form of a verb loses the ability to assign an agent role. This is why passive sentences are perfectly acceptable even when there is no agent NP (for example, *The thief was arrested*). When an NP bearing the agent role does appear, it occurs not in the subject position but rather as complement of the preposition *by*. Because the verb is unable to assign an agent role, some other element must do this job if the agent role is to be assigned. *By* is that element, being unique among prepositions in having the type of meaning that assigns an agent role. Thus, the sentence *The thief was arrested by the police* has the deep structure depicted in Figure 6.11. (This *by* should not be confused with the *by* in *He stood by the tree*, which assigns a location role.)

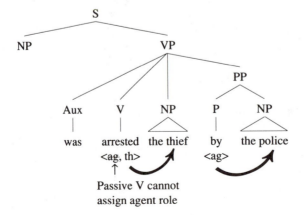

Figure 6.11

In this structure, the passive verb (*was*) *arrested* assigns its theme role to its complement (the NP *the thief*) while the special preposition *by* assigns its agent role to its complement (the NP *the police*). This ensures that the sentence has the correct interpretation, with the police doing the arresting and the thief getting arrested.

In order to form the correct surface structure for passive sentences, we need a transformation that will move the NP bearing the theme role from the direct object position to the subject position when the latter is empty.

28. **NP Movement**:
   Move NP into the subject position.

This transformation applies to the deep structure in Figure 6.11 to give the surface structure depicted in Figure 6.12.

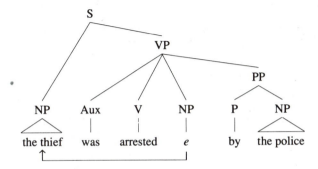

Figure 6.12

In sum, then, the transformational analysis of passives makes use of both deep structure and surface structure. In order to account for thematic role assignment, the NP that receives the theme role occurs as complement of the verb in deep structure, while the NP that receives the agent role, if present, occurs as complement of the special preposition *by*. A transformation then moves the NP bearing the theme role from its deep structure position to the subject position in surface structure, giving the correct final form of the sentence.

The Interpretation of Pronouns (advanced)

The category of **pronouns** includes words such as *he*, *she*, *himself*, and *herself*. These words are characterized by the fact that their interpretation can be determined by another element in the same sentence. (This other element is called the **antecedent**.) Consider in this regard the following two sentences.

29. a) Jim's new car cost *him* a lot of money.
   b) Jim hurt *himself*.

In the first of these sentences, the pronoun *him* can have the same referent as the NP *Jim* or can be taken to refer to someone not mentioned in the sentence (say, Jim's father). In the second sentence, in contrast, the pronoun *himself* must have the same referent as *Jim*; no other interpretation is possible. The former type of pronoun is called a **pronominal** and the latter type a **reflexive pronoun**.

The interpretation of pronominals and reflexive pronouns also differs in the following sentences.

30. *a*) [_S Clare knew that [_S Alexis trusted *herself*]].
    b) [_S Clare knew that [_S Alexis trusted *her*]].

Notice that *herself* in *30a* can refer only to Alexis, but that *her* refers to either Clare or someone not mentioned in the sentence. This is because the interpretation of reflexive pronouns, but not ordinary pronominals, is subject to the following principle.

31. A reflexive pronoun must have an antecedent in the smallest S containing it.

Since *Alexis*, but not *Clare*, occurs in the smallest S containing the reflexive pronoun in *30*, only it is an eligible antecedent for *herself*.

Principle A A somewhat more abstract feature of syntactic structure enters into the interpretation of the reflexive pronouns in sentences such as *32*, which has the tree structure in Figure 6.13. (Pronouns are treated as N-type categories that head NPs; to save space, some word-level category labels are omitted. Possessor NPs occur in the specifier position within larger NPs.)

32. The boy's uncle admired himself.

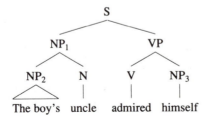

Figure 6.13

Although there are two NPs in the same S as *himself* (namely, *the boy* and *the boy's uncle*), only one (*the boy's uncle*) can serve as antecedent for the reflexive pronoun. Thus, the person who was admired in *32* must have been the boy's uncle, not the boy.

The principle needed to ensure this interpretation makes use of the notion **c-command**, which is defined as follows.

33. NP_a c-commands NP_b if the first category above NP_a contains NP_b.

Although c-command might appear to be a rather technical notion, the underlying idea is very simple. Figure 6.14 illustrates the type of configuration in which c-command occurs. When trying to determine c-command relations, you can either use the definition in *33* or apply the template in Figure 6.14 to the tree structure being analyzed.

We can now formulate the constraint on the interpretation of reflexives, called **Principle A,** as follows. In order to keep the discussion at an introduc-

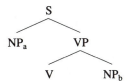

Figure 6.14 The c-command configuration

tory level, we consider only the version of this principle required for simple, one-clause sentences.

>   *34.* **Principle A**:
>   A reflexive pronoun must have an antecedent that c-commands it.

When using Principle A, the key step involves determining whether a potential antecedent c-commands the reflexive pronoun. Compare in this regard the status of the NPs *the boy* and *the boy's uncle* in figure 6.13.

Since the first category above *the boy's uncle* (namely, S) contains the reflexive, this NP c-commands *himself* according to our definition and can therefore serve as its antecedent. As we have already seen, the sentence has this interpretation.

In contrast, the first category above NP_2 (*the boy*) is NP_1, as illustrated in Figure 6.15.

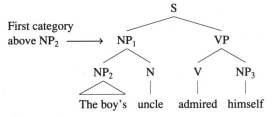

Figure 6.15

Since NP_1 does not contain the reflexive, there is no c-command relationship between NP_2 and *himself* according to our definition. It is therefore not possible for *the boy* to serve as antecedent for *himself*.

Principle B Now let us consider the interpretation of pronominals. As the following example shows, the interpretation of the pronominal *him* contrasts sharply with that of the reflexive *himself* in the structure that we have been considering. Thus, *him* can refer to the boy, but not to the boy's uncle—the opposite of what we observed for *himself*.

>   *35.* The boy's uncle admired him.

How are we to account for these facts? The relevant constraint, called **Principle B**, is stated in *36*. (As with Principle A, we present only the version of this principle relevant to simple one-clause sentences.)

>   *36.* **Principle B**:
>   A pronominal must not have an antecedent that c-commands it.

To see how this principle works, consider the following structure.

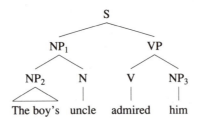

Figure 6.16

In this structure, NP$_1$ (*the boy's uncle*) c-commands *him* since the first category above it (namely, S) also contains *him*. Principle B therefore prevents NP$_1$ from serving as antecedent for *him*. In contrast, NP$_2$ (*the boy*) does not c-command *him* since the first category above it (namely, NP$_1$) does not contain the pronoun. Thus, nothing prevents the interpretation in which *him* and *the boy* refer to the same person.

There is much more that can and should be said about the interpretation of pronouns. A more detailed examination of this very complex phenomenon would reveal the need for even more abstract principles referring to additional properties of syntactic structure. However, the examples we have already considered suffice to illustrate the crucial point in all of this, which is that syntactic structure plays an important role in the interpretation of both pronominals and reflexive pronouns.

6.4 OTHER FACTORS IN SENTENCE INTERPRETATION

Syntactic structure provides only part of the information needed to determine the meaning of a sentence. Other necessary information comes from **pragmatics**, which includes the speaker's and addressee's background attitudes and beliefs, their understanding of the context in which a sentence is uttered, and their knowledge of how language can be used to inform, to persuade, to mislead, and so forth. This section focuses on the role of pragmatics in sentence interpretation.

The Role of Beliefs and Attitudes

As we saw in the preceding section, the grammar includes a structural principle (Principle B) that regulates the interpretation of pronominals such as *he* and *they*. However, as the following sentences show, nonlinguistic knowledge and beliefs can also play an important role in selecting the antecedent for a pronominal.

37. *a*) The judge denied the prisoner's request because he was cautious.
    b) The judge denied the prisoner's request because he was dangerous.

These two sentences have identical syntactic structures, differing only in the choice of the adjective in the second clause (*cautious* in the first sentence versus *dangerous* in the second). Yet, most people feel that *he* refers to the judge in *37a* but to the prisoner in *37b*.

These preferences seem to have nothing to do with structural principles. Rather, the crucial factor involves our beliefs about different groups within society. In particular, since most people believe that a judge is more likely to be cautious than dangerous, they take the pronoun to refer to the judge in the first sentence but the prisoner in the second.

Presupposition There are many other ways in which a speaker's beliefs can be reflected in language use. Compare in this regard the following two sentences.

38. *a*) Have you stopped exercising regularly?
    b) Have you tried exercising regularly?

Use of the verb *stop* implies a belief on the part of the speaker that the listener has been exercising regularly. No such assumption is associated with the verb *try*.

The assumption or belief implied by the use of a particular word or structure is called a **presupposition**. The following two sentences provide another example of this.

39. *a*) Nick admitted that the team had lost.
    b) Nick said that the team had lost.

Choice of the verb *admit* in *39a* indicates that the speaker is presupposing the truth of the claim that the team lost. No such presupposition is associated with choice of the verb *say* in *39b*. The speaker is simply reporting Nick's statement without taking a position on its accuracy.

Still another type of presupposition is illustrated in *40*.

40. *a*) Abraham Lincoln was assassinated in 1865.
    b) Abraham Lincoln was murdered in 1865.

Notice that use of the verb *assassinate* in *40a* involves the assumption that Abraham Lincoln was a prominent political figure, but that no such presupposition is associated with the verb *murder*.

Setting

As noted at the beginning of this section, the pragmatic factors relevant to sentence interpretation can include knowledge of the context in which a sentence is uttered. Two types of contextual information are involved here, the first having to do with the physical environment in which a sentence is uttered (the **setting**), and the second having to do with the other utterances in the speech event (the **discourse**). In this subsection we will consider an example of how information about the setting enters into language use; the role of discourse will be examined in the next subsection. Both these issues are examined from a slightly different perspective in Chapter 12.

Deictics All languages have forms whose use and interpretation depend on the location of the speaker and/or addressee within a particular setting. Called spatial **deictics**, these forms are exemplified in English by words such as *this* and *here* (proximity to the speaker) versus *that* and *there* (proximity to the addressee and/or distance from the speaker). Thus, if Steve and Brian are sitting across from each other at a table, each would refer to a plate directly in front of him as *this plate* and to a plate in front of the other person or a plate distant from both as *that plate*. Without an understanding of how the setting in which a sentence is uttered can influence the choice of words such as *this* and *that*, it would be impossible for speakers of English to use or interpret these forms correctly.

As the preceding examples show, English makes a two-way distinction in its expression of deictic contrasts. However, many languages use a third set of forms in this part of their grammar.

Table 6.17 A three-way deictic distinction

Language	'this'	'that'	'that over there'
Spanish	este	ese	aquel
Korean	i	ku	ce
Japanese	kono	sono	ano
Palauan	tia	tilecha	se
Turkish	bu	ʃu	o

An even more complex system is found in the Amerindian language Tlingit, which makes a four-way distinction: *jáa* 'this one right here', *héi* 'this one nearby', *wée* 'that one over there', and *jóo* 'that one far off'.

Determiners are not the only type of element whose use and interpretation require reference to features of the setting. In English, for example, deictic contrasts are also crucial to the understanding of such commonly used verbs as *come* and *go*. Notice in this regard the striking difference in perspective found in the following two sentences.

41. *a*) The bear is coming into the tent!
    b) The bear is going into the tent!

Whereas *come* with a third person subject implies movement towards the speaker (hence we know that the person who utters *41a* must be in the tent), *go* with the same type of subject suggests movement away from the speaker. Use of *come* with a first person subject (*I*) is different again. Hence the sentence *I'm coming over* implies that the speaker is about to go to where the addressee is. As was the case with deictic determiners, we could not fully understand these sentences without reference to the physical setting in which they are uttered.

Discourse

Properties of other utterances in the same speech event (the discourse) are also crucial to understanding a sentence. A very simple example of this involves the interpretation of elements such as *he*, *it*, and *there*, whose referent is often determined by a word or phrase in a preceding utterance. Consider in this regard the following passage.

42. A child went for a walk in the park. While *there, he* saw a rabbit. Since *it* was injured, *he* took *it* home.

Each of the italicized words in this passage relies for its interpretation on information encoded in a preceding sentence. Thus, we interpret *there* with reference to *in the park, he* with reference to *a child*, and *it* with reference to *a rabbit*.

Old and New Information One of the most important contrasts in the study of discourse is the distinction between new and old information. **Old** (or **given**)

information consists of the knowledge that the speaker assumes is available to the addressee at the time of the utterance, either because it is shared by both or because it has already been introduced into the discourse. In contrast, **new information** involves knowledge that is introduced into the discourse for the first time. Consider the contrast between the following two sentences.

43. *a*) The man is at the front door.
    b) A man is at the front door.

Choice of *the* as the determiner for *man* in *43a* suggests that the referent of the phrase is someone who has been mentioned in the previous discourse and is therefore already known to the addressee (old information). In contrast, choice of the determiner *a* in *43b* implies that the referent is being introduced into the discourse for the first time (new information).

Notice that both sentences in *43* use *the* as the determiner for *front door*. This is because the setting for the conversation presumably includes only one front door, whose identity and location is known to both speaker and addressee. As noted, old information can consist of shared knowledge such as this and need not always be explicitly stated in the previous discourse.

Topics Another important notion for the study of discourse is that of **topic**, which corresponds to what a sentence or group of sentences is about. Consider the following passage.

44. Once upon a time there was a merchant with two sons. The older son wanted to be a scholar. He spent his time reading and studying. As for the younger son, he preferred to travel and see the world.

The first sentence in this passage introduces a merchant and his two sons as new information. A topic (the older son) is selected in the second sentence and maintained in the third, in which *he* refers back to *the older son*. The final sentence then switches to a new topic (the younger son), providing some information about him. This switch is facilitated by the expression *as for*, which is often used in English as a marker of new topics.

In English, the subject of the sentence tends also to be the topic. This is why it is natural to interpret the active sentence in *45a* as being about the police and the passive sentence in *b* as being about the burglar.

45. *a*) The police chased the burglar.
    b) The burglar was chased by the police.

In some languages, a special affix is used to identify the topic. The following sentences from Japanese illustrate this phenomenon. (Nom = nominative, the subject marker; Top = topic marker; Q = question marker)

46. *Speaker A*: Dare-ga kimasita-ka?
                Who-Nom came -Q?
    Speaker B: John-ga kimasita.
                John-Nom came.
    Speaker A: John-wa dare-to kimasita-ka?
                John-Top who-with came -Q?
                'Who did John come with?'

The topic marker in Japanese (the suffix *-wa*) is distinguished from the subject marker (*-ga*) by its use to mark old or background information. This is why speaker B responds to A's first question by using the subject marker on the NP *John*. Because this NP provides new information here (an answer to A's question), the topic marker would be inappropriate. However, once it has been established that John is the person who came, the corresponding NP can then bear the topic marker. This is precisely what happens in Speaker A's final utterance, wherein the NP *John* (which is now associated with previously established information) is marked by the topic suffix *-wa*.

Conversational Strategies

In addition to background beliefs, the setting, and the discourse context, there is at least one other major type of information that enters into the interpretation of utterances. This information has to do with the 'rules for conversation', our understanding of how language is used in particular situations to convey a message. If, for example, I ask someone, '*Would you like to go to a movie tonight?*' and I receive as a response '*I have to study for an exam*', I know that the other person is declining my invitation even though there is nothing in the literal meaning of the sentence that says so. Moreover, even though the response does not contain a literal answer to my invitation, I recognize it as a perfectly appropriate way to respond to my question. (Notice that the same could not be said of a response like '*I have to comb my hair*' or '*I enjoy reading books*'.)

As speakers of a language, we are able to draw inferences about what is meant but not actually said. Information that is conveyed in this way is called a **conversational implicature**. The ease with which we recognize and interpret implicatures stems from our knowledge of how people in our linguistic community use language to communicate with each other.

The general overarching guideline for conversational interactions is often called the **Co-operative Principle**.

47. **The Co-operative Principle**:
Make your contribution appropriate to the conversation.

More specific **maxims** or guidelines ensure that conversational interactions actually satisfy the Co-operative Principle.

Table 6.18 Some conversational maxims

The Maxim of Relation:
Be relevant.

The Maxim of Quality:
Try to make your contribution one that is true. (Do not say things that are false or for which you lack adequate evidence.)

The Maxim of Quantity:
Do not make your contribution more or less informative than required.

The Maxim of Manner:
Avoid ambiguity and obscurity; be brief and orderly.

These maxims are responsible for regulating normal conversation but, as we will see directly, each can be suspended under certain circumstances to create particular effects.

Relation The Maxim of Relation is crucial to evaluating the appropriateness of responses to the question *'Would you like to go to a movie tonight?'* (the example given at the beginning of this section). Because we assume that the conversational contributions of others are relevant to the topic at hand, we are able to infer from the response *'I have to study for an exam'* that the speaker is unable or unwilling to go to the movie. Similarly, because it is hard to see a connection between combing one's hair and being able to go to a movie, we judge the response *'I have to comb my hair'* to be irrelevant and hence inappropriate.

Of course, the Maxim of Relation can sometimes be suspended by a speaker who wants to create a particular impression. For example, if someone asks you *'Have you finished that term paper yet?'*, and you respond *'It's been raining a lot lately, hasn't it?'*, you violate the Maxim of Relation by not responding in a relevant way. On the other hand, by giving this response you signal to the other person that you want to move away from the topic of conversation that has been raised.

Quality The Maxim of Quality requires that the statements used in conversations have some factual basis. If, for example, I ask *'What's the weather like?'* and someone responds *'It's snowing'*, I will normally assume that this statement provides reliable information about the current weather.

In order to achieve irony or sarcasm, however, it is sometimes possible to abandon the Maxim of Quality and say something that one knows to be false. Thus, if two people live in the middle of a sweltering desert and one person insists on asking every morning *'What's the weather like?'*, it might be appropriate for the other person to respond sarcastically *'Oh, today it's snowing, as usual'*, perhaps with a particular facial expression or intonation to indicate that the statement was not intended as a true report of the facts.

Quantity The Maxim of Quantity introduces some very subtle guidelines into a conversation. If, for example, someone asks me where a famous American author lives, then the nature of my response will depend in large part on how much information I believe to be appropriate for that point in the conversation. If I know that the other person is simply curious about which part of the country the author lives in, it might suffice to respond *'in Michigan'*. On the other hand, if I know that the person wants to visit the author, then much more specific information (perhaps even an address) is appropriate.

The Maxim of Quantity can be suspended in order to mislead a conversational partner. For example, if someone asks me where Mary is and I know that Mary does not want to see this person, I might respond by saying *'I think she went downtown or something'* even though I know precisely where in the downtown area she is. In responding in this way, I am not being untruthful since I have said nothing false, but by giving less information than is appropriate I am violating the Maxim of Quantity and hence being misleading.

Manner The Maxim of Manner imposes several constraints on language use, two of which will be exemplified here. First, imagine that I refer to a particular person as *the man who Mary lives with*. A listener would be justified in concluding that the man in question is not Mary's husband. This is because, by the Maxim of Manner, a briefer and less obscure description, *Mary's husband*, would have been used if it could have correctly described Mary's companion.

Second, imagine that I am writing a letter of recommendation to an employer and I say about a former student of mine '*You will be fortunate indeed if you can get Henry to work for you*'. By using a sentence that can be interpreted in two dramatically different ways ('You will be glad to have Henry on your staff' versus 'It is not easy to get Henry to do any work'), I violate the Maxim of Manner by using an ambiguous structure. Since the maxims are violated only for specific purposes (as when the Maxim of Quality is suspended to yield sarcasm), the person to whom the letter is written would be justified in concluding that my choice of language constitutes a veiled warning about Henry.

The Maxims in Other Societies The preceding maxims represent constraints on conversation that may well be an integral part of language use in all cultures. This is not to say that the maxims are employed in exactly the same way in all linguistic communities, however. In fact, we know that the circumstances under which it is appropriate to suspend a maxim can differ. A good example of this involves the Maxim of Quantity as it is used in rural areas of the Malagasy Republic (formerly called Madagascar), the large island off the east coast of Africa.

Because rural villages in the Malagasy Republic form small, tightly integrated societies, new information is rare and considerable prestige accrues to its holder. Speakers are therefore often reluctant to impart it to just anyone. When asked about a particular event, then, they may reply evasively, avoiding mention of the information being sought by their conversational partner. Thus, a visit to the market might be described by saying simply '*there were many people there*' rather than giving any specific details. This suggests not only that the Maxim of Quantity can be overridden, but that the conditions under which this happens may be intertwined with the cultural practices of a particular society.

Speech Acts

Still another set of factors that must be taken into account in semantic analysis involves the type of act associated with the utterance of a sentence. According to one influential proposal, there are three basic speech acts: the **locutionary act**, which corresponds to the utterance of a sentence with a particular meaning; the **illocutionary act**, which reflects the intent of the speaker in uttering that sentence (to praise, criticize, warn); and the **perlocutionary act**, which involves the effect that the speaker has on his or her addressees in uttering the sentence. Suppose, for example, that a teacher who is having trouble maintaining order in the classroom utters the sentence *I'll keep you in after class*. In uttering such a sentence, the teacher is simultaneously producing three speech acts—a locutionary act (involving utterance of a sentence with the meaning 'I'll make you stay in school later than usual'), an illocutionary act (a warning), and a perlocutionary act (silencing the students).

There is no one-to-one relationship between syntactic structure and speech acts. An illocutionary act of warning, for example, could involve (1) a declarative sentence (a statement), (2) an imperative (a command), (3) a *yes-no* question, or (4) a *wh* question.

> 48. *a*) There's a bear behind you.
>   *b*) Run!
>   *c*) Did you know there's a bear behind you?
>   *d*) What's that bear doing in here?

Similarly, a perlocutionary act aimed at getting someone to open the window could be expressed in a variety of ways.

> 49. *a*) I wish you'd open the window.
>   *b*) Open the window.
>   *c*) Could you open the window?
>   *d*) Why don't you open the window?
>   *e*) It's awfully hot in here.

Because of the perlocutionary act associated with these utterances, the appropriate response on the part of the listener should be to open the window. Speakers of English therefore know that *49c* is not to be interpreted as a simple request for information. Only as a joke would someone respond by saying *Yes, I could* and then not do anything about opening the window.

Despite the indirect relationship between sentence structure and speech acts, there is a small set of verbs whose use makes explicit the illocutionary force of a sentence. Common examples of these verbs include *promise*, *bet*, *warn*, and *agree*.

> 50. *a*) I promise that I'll be there.
>   *b*) I bet that the Yankees will lose.
>   *c*) I warn you that's not a good idea.
>   *d*) I agree that you should do it.

The verbs in *50* indicate the type of illocutionary act involved in uttering the sentence—an act of promising, an act of warning, and so on. Such verbs are called **performatives** since the very act of producing them involves the performance of an illocutionary act. Thus, in saying *I promise that I'll be there*, I automatically carry out an illocutionary act of promising. Such is not the case with a sentence like *I'll be there*, which could be a simple prediction, a warning, or a threat.

When a verb is used performatively, it always has a first person subject (*I* or *we*) and occurs in the present tense. Some performative verbs are subject to an additional restriction: they can only be appropriately uttered by speakers with a certain social status or authority. Only a clergyman or a similarly qualified person can appropriately utter the sentence *I pronounce you man and wife* while only a judge can properly say *I sentence you to five years in prison*.

6.5 LANGUAGE, MEANING, AND THOUGHT

As we examine the way in which words and structures are used to express meaning, it is natural to wonder about the possibility that language might play a role in shaping how we think. While it is certainly plausible to believe that language facilitates reasoning and problem solving by providing a way to represent complex thoughts, it has sometimes been proposed that linguistic systems might have a considerably more fundamental effect on cognition. Indeed, it has even been suggested that the particular language people speak shapes the way in which they think and perceive the world.

The Sapir-Whorf Hypothesis

The best-known and most influential version of this idea has come to be known as the **Sapir-Whorf Hypothesis** in honor of Edward Sapir and Benjamin Lee Whorf, the two linguists who articulated it most clearly. Sapir, for instance, wrote in 1929:

> Human beings . . . are very much at the mercy of the particular language which has become the medium of expression for their society . . . the 'real world' is to a large extent unconsciously built upon the language habits of the group.

Several years later, Whorf expressed essentially the same sentiment when he made the following claim.

> We dissect nature along lines laid down by our native language. The categories and types that we isolate from the world of phenomena we do not find there because they stare every observer in the face; on the contrary, the world is presented in a kaleidoscopic flux of impressions which has to be organized by our minds—this means largely by the linguistic systems in our minds.

Two types of linguistic phenomena are commonly cited in support of the Sapir-Whorf Hypothesis: cross-linguistic differences in vocabulary, and variation in the type of grammatical contrasts a language encodes. The first type of phenomenon is exemplified by the claim discussed on page 220 that Eskimo has far more words for snow than does English, or that Arabic has more words for sand. From this, it is sometimes concluded that Eskimo and Arabic allow their speakers to make perceptual distinctions pertaining to snow and sand that English speakers cannot.

A more plausible explanation is that language is shaped by the need to adapt to the cultural and physical environment. According to this alternate view, if a language has a large vocabulary in a particular area, it is because subtle distinctions of that type are important to its speakers. Even speakers of a language without an extensive vocabulary in that area should be able to make the relevant contrasts if they become important to them. This is presumably why skiers, for instance, are able to distinguish among many different types of snow, even though their language may not have a separate word for each. Where necessary, they can then use the resources of their language to describe these distinctions by creating expressions such as *powder snow*.

Consider now cross-linguistic differences in the expression of grammatical contrasts—the type of phenomenon on which Whorf concentrated. Whorf attempted to link the apparent lack of tense contrasts in Hopi (an Amerindian language spoken in the American Southwest) with different cultural attitudes toward time and the future. According to Whorf, time for the Hopi does not consist of the passage of countable units (like days), but rather the successive reappearance of the same entity. There is no 'new day' for the Hopi, Whorf claimed, just the return of the same day. Whorf believed that this is reflected in the Hopi belief that the future is best dealt with by working on the present situation (which will return as the future).

Here again, innumerable problems arise. For one thing, Whorf was apparently mistaken in his belief that Hopi does not have tense; such a category is, in fact, found in this language. Moreover, even if there were no tense contrasts in Hopi or if they were radically different from those found in English, it is unlikely that they could be correlated with speakers' attitudes toward time. There are doubtlessly many individual speakers of English who share the Hopi philosophy for dealing with the future (and some Hopi speakers who do not).

The problem of Hopi tense aside, there are many grammatical phenomena that it would be absurd to correlate with the ability to make distinctions in the real world. Finnish, for instance, has no grammatical contrasts that reflect natural gender (or sex), but one would hardly conclude that the absence of a distinction between *he* and *she* impedes the ability of Finns to distinguish between males and females. Likewise, it is hard to believe that speakers of French believe that women, tents, and shirts are somehow alike even though the words for all three entities (*femmes*, *tentes*, and *chemises*) are assigned to the same gender class (feminine).

An Experiment There have been various attempts to verify the Sapir-Whorf Hypothesis by experimental means. The most famous of these experiments was conducted in 1958. The basic idea was to determine the effect of English and Navaho on the perception of color, size, and shape. In Navaho, verbs expressing handling actions vary in form depending on the shape of the object being handled. Thus, a long flexible object (a snake) requires the verbal form *fánléh*, a long rigid object (a spear) requires the verbal form *fántúh* while flat flexible material requires *fánilcóós*. Since there is no such contrast in English, it was thought that children speaking these two languages might group objects in different ways. An experiment was designed to test this.

The children participating in the experiment were presented with a pair of objects such as a piece of rope and a stick, and then shown a third object and asked to tell the experimenter which of the pair went best with the new object. It was thought that the responses of the Navaho-speaking children might reflect the classification imposed by the verb system of their language rather than similarities in size or color. However, it was found that the responses of the forty-seven white English-speaking children (from Boston) were very similar to those of the fifty-nine monolingual speakers of Navaho. Given the differences between the two languages, this is not the result predicted by the Sapir-Whorf Hypothesis.

The repeated failure of experimental attempts to uncover systematic shaping effects for language has drastically reduced the credibility of the Sapir-Whorf Hypothesis. This is not to say that languages do not represent reality in different ways. Clearly, they do. Thus, French distinguishes between knowing someone (*connaître*) and knowing something (*savoir*), a distinction that is not made in the verb system of English. On the other hand, as noted earlier, English has an extremely fine set of contrasts involving light (*glimmer, glitter, glow*, *gleam*, and *glisten*) that are not found in other languages. What is in doubt is whether such differences in the linguistic description of reality reflect deeper, language-induced differences in patterns of thought or perception.

Summing Up

The study of **semantics** is concerned with a broad range of phenomena including the nature of **meaning**, the role of syntactic structure in the interpretation of sentences, and the effect of **pragmatics** on the understanding of utterances. Although serious problems and obstacles remain in all these areas, work in recent years has at least begun to identify the type of relations and principles involved in the understanding of language. These include the notions of **extension** and **intension** in the case of word meaning, **thematic role** assignment in the case of sentence interpretation, and **c-command** in the case of pronoun interpretation. Other factors known to be involved in an utterance's interpretation include the speaker's and addressee's background beliefs (as manifested, for example, in **presuppositions**), the context provided by the **setting** and the **discourse**, and the **maxims** associated with the **Co-operative Principle**.

Key Terms

agent	motion verbs
antecedent	non-lexical categories
antonyms	old information
c-command	paraphrases
Co-operative principle	polysemy
componential analysis	pragmatics
connotation	presupposition
conversational implicature	principle A
conversational maxim	principle B
denotation	principle of compositionality
discourse	pronominal
entailment	pronouns
extension	prototypical
functional categories	reflexive pronoun
fuzzy concepts	semantic feature
goal	semantics
graded membership	setting
grammaticized	source
homophones	spatial metaphor
lexical ambiguity	spatial deictics
lexicalization	structurally ambiguous
location	synonyms
maxim of manner	thematic roles
maxim of quality	theme
maxim of quantity	topic
maxim of relation	truth conditions

Sources

Surveys of the nature of word meaning and semantic relations can be found in many sources, including the book by Allen cited below. The discussion of fuzzy categories and graded membership in Section 6.2 draws from Part 1 of *Women, Fire, and Dangerous Things* by G. Lakoff (Chicago: University of Chicago Press, 1987) and the references cited there. The discussion of metaphor takes as its starting point the book *Metaphors We Live By*, cited below. The four Eskimo words for snow in Table 6.7 are from *The Handbook of American Indian Languages* by F. Boas (Washington: Smithsonian Institute, 1911) and are also cited on p. 123 of the book by Allen referenced below; for a longer list of words for snow, see *Dictionnaire français-eskimau du parler de l'Ungava* (Québec: Presses de l'Université Laval, 1970); see also "The Great Eskimo Vocabulary Hoax" by G. Pullum in *Natural Language and Linguistic Theory* 7: 275–81 (1989). The discussion of verbs of motion is based on the paper "Lexicalization Patterns: Semantic Structure in Lexical Form" by L. Talmy in *Language Typology and Syntactic Description*, Vol 3, edited by T. Shopen, 57–149 (New York: Cambridge University Press, 1985). The definition of grammaticization used in Section 6.2 is based on D. Slobin's "Crosslinguistic Evidence for the Language-Making Capacity" in The *Crosslinguistic Study of Language Acquisition*, Vol. 2, edited by D. Slobin, 1172–73 (Hillsdale, N.J.: Erlbaum, 1985). The data on Hidatsa assertion morphemes in the same section is from *Hidatsa Syntax* by G.H. Matthews (The Hague: Mouton, 1965).

The treatment of structural ambiguity, thematic role assignment, and pronoun interpretation in this chapter presents slightly simplified versions of views widely held within generative grammar in the last half of the 1980s. For a simple summary of the last two issues, see *Lectures on Contemporary Syntactic Theories* by P. Sells (Stanford, Calif.: Center for the Study of Language and Information, 1985).

The data used in the discussion of deixis comes from "Deixis" by S. Anderson and E. Keenan in *Language Typology and Syntactic Description*, Vol. 3, edited by T. Shopen, 259–308 (New York: Cambridge University Press, 1985). The discussion of topicalization draws on the "Major Functions of the Noun Phrase" by A. Andrews in *Language Typology and Syntactic Description*, Vol. 1, edited by T. Shopen, 62–154 (New York: Cambridge University Press, 1985). The discussion of the Cooperative Principle and the maxims of conversation is based primarily on "Logic and Conversation" by Paul Grice in *Syntax and Semantics*, Vol. 3, edited by P. Cole and J. Morgan, 41–58 (New York: Academic Press, 1975) and the paper by L. Horn cited below. The discussion of Malagasy conversation is based on "The Universality of Conversational Postulates" by E. Ochs in *Language in Society* 5:67–80 (1976).

Speech act theory is introduced in J. Austin's classic work *How to Do Things with Words* (Oxford: Clarendon Press, 1962). The quote from Edward Sapir on language and thought comes from a passage cited in Whorf's article "The

Relation of Habitual Thought and Behavior to Language" reprinted in *Language, Thought and Reality*, edited by J. Carroll (Cambridge, Mass.: MIT Press, 1956). The quote from Whorf is taken from his article "Science and Linguistics," also reprinted in *Language, Thought and Reality*. The attempt to verify the Sapir-Whorf Hypothesis experimentally is reported in an article by J. Carroll and J. Casagrande, "The Function of Language Classification in Behavior" in *Readings in Social Psychology*, edited by E. Maccoby et al. (New York: Henry Holt, 1958).

Recommended Reading

Allen, Keith. 1986. *Linguistic Meaning*. Vols. 1 and 2. New York: Routledge & Kegan Paul.

Fodor, Janet Dean. 1978. *Semantics: Theories of Meaning in Generative Grammar*. Cambridge, Mass.: Harvard University Press.

Horn, Laurence. 1988. "Pragmatic Theory." In *Linguistics: The Cambridge Survey*. Vol. 1. Edited by F. Newmeyer, 113–45. New York: Cambridge University Press.

Hurford, James, and Brendan Heasley. 1983. *Semantics: A Coursebook*. New York: Cambridge University Press.

Kempson, Ruth. 1977. *Semantic Theory*. London: Cambridge University Press.

Ladusaw, William. 1988. "Semantic Theory." In *Linguistics: The Cambridge Survey*. Vol. 1. Edited by F. Newmeyer, 89–112. New York: Cambridge University Press.

Lakoff, George, and Mark Johnson. 1982. *Metaphors We Live By*. Chicago: University of Chicago Press.

Lyons, John. 1977. *Semantics*. Vols. 1 and 2. London: Cambridge University Press.

McCawley, James, 1981. *Everything That Linguists Have Always Wanted to Know About Logic*. Chicago: University of Chicago Press.

Prince, Ellen. 1988. "Discourse Analysis: A Part of the Study of Linguistic Competence." In *Linguistics: The Cambridge Survey*. Vol. 2. Edited by F. Newmeyer, 164–82. New York: Cambridge University Press.

Questions

1. Two relations involving word meanings are antonymy and synonymy. Which relation is illustrated in each of the pairs of words below?

    a) flourish-thrive   e) uncle-aunt
    b) intelligent-stupid   f) intelligent-smart
    c) casual-informal   g) flog-whip
    d) young-old   h) drunk-sober

2. It was noted in this chapter that a single form can have two or more meanings. Depending on whether these meanings are related to each other, this phenomenon involves polysemy or homophony. Which of these two relations is exemplified by the forms below?

   a) grass   herbage used for grazing animals; marijuana
   b) leech   a bloodsucking worm; a hanger-on who seeks advantage
   c) range   a cooking stove; a series of mountains
   d) key   an instrument used to open a lock; an answer sheet for a test or assignment
   e) reel   a spool for photographic film; round device at the butt end of a fishing rod for the line
   f) race   the act of running competitively; people belonging to the same genetic grouping
   g) /flawər/   a blossom; finely ground wheat

3. Three semantic relations among sentences were covered in this chapter: paraphrase, entailment, and contradiction. Which of these relations is exemplified in each of the following pairs of sentences?

   a) I saw Terry at the anniversary party.
      It was Terry that I saw at the anniversary party.
   b) Jules is Mary's husband.
      Mary is married.
   c) My pet cobra likes the taste of chocolate fudge.
      My pet cobra finds chocolate fudge tasty.
   d) Vera is an only child.
      Olga is Vera's sister.
   e) It is fifty miles to the nearest service station.
      The nearest service station is fifty miles away.
   f) My cousin Bryan teaches at the community college for a living.
      My cousin Bryan is a teacher.

4. In discussing the nature of meaning, we noted that it is necessary to distinguish between intension and extension. Describe the intensions and the extensions of each of these phrases.

   a) the President of the United States
   b) the Queen of England
   c) the capital of Canada
   d) women who have walked on the moon
   e) the Prince of Wales
   f) Princess Diana's husband

5. In our discussion of semantic decomposition, we noted that at least some words have meanings that can be represented in terms of smaller semantic features. Four such words are *dog*, *puppy*, *cat*, and *kitten*.

   i) Attempt to provide the semantic features associated with each of these words.

ii) How are the pairs *dog-puppy* and *cat-kitten* different from *man-boy* and *woman-girl*?

iii) Try to provide semantic features for the words *circle*, *triangle*, and *quadrangle*? What problems do you encounter?

6. Each of the following words is associated with a concept.

a) island   e) whisper
b) soft   f) husband
c) white   g) baseball bat
d) wristwatch   h) mountain

i) Determine which of these examples are fuzzy concepts.

ii) Choose one of the fuzzy concepts above. Name one prototypical member of that concept and one member that is closer to the concept boundary.

iii) Draw a diagram for the concept 'dwelling' similar to that of Figure 6.2 in this chapter. Do the same for the concept 'vehicle'.

7. Examine the following sets of sentences, each of which include words or phrases used metaphorically.

a) She gave him an icy stare.
   He gave her the cold shoulder.
   He exudes a lot of warmth towards people.
   They got into a heated argument.

b) He drops a lot of hints.
   The committee picked up on the issue.
   She dumps all her problems on her friends.
   Although he disagreed, he let it go.

c) the eye of a needle
   the foot of the bed
   the hands of the clock
   the arm of a chair
   the table legs

d) I'm looking forward to it.
   She can foretell the future.
   I can remember back to when I was two years old.
   He drags up old conflicts.
   You must plan ahead for retirement.

e) This lecture is easy to digest.
   He just eats up the lecturer's words.
   Chew on this thought for a while.
   Listen to this juicy piece of gossip.

For each set of sentences:

i) Identify the words or phrases that are used metaphorically in each sentence.

ii) Determine the basis for each of these metaphor sets.

Use the pattern: 'The metaphors in (x) describe _____ in terms of _____.'

Example: The metaphors in (a) describe human relationships in terms of temperature.

8. The section on lexicalization of concepts discussed how some languages simultaneously express motion and path, motion and movement, and/or motion and thing moving in motion verbs. Can you change the sentence *He moved the goods by truck to the warehouse* so that both movement and vehicle used to move are lexicalized in one verb? What other verbs express a similar combination of concepts?

9. Consider the following Fijian pronouns.

a)	au	1st person singular 'I'
b)	iko	2nd person singular 'you'
c)	koja	3rd person singular 'he/she/it'
d)	kedaru	1st person dual 'I and you'
e)	keiru	1st person dual 'I and one other (not you)'
f)	kemudrau	2nd person dual 'you two'
g)	rau	3rd person dual 'they two'
h)	kedatou	1st person trial 'I and two others, including you'
i)	keitou	1st person trial 'I and two others, excluding you'
j)	kemudou	2nd person trial 'you three'
k)	iratou	3rd person trial 'they three'
l)	keda	1st person plural 'we (more than three), including you'
m)	keimami	1st person plural 'we (more than three), excluding you'
n)	kemuni	2nd person plural 'you (more than three)'
o)	ira	3rd person plural 'they (more than three)'

i) Some concepts are grammaticized in the Fijian pronoun system which are not grammaticized in the English pronoun system. Can you identify them?

ii) Which concept is grammaticized in the English pronoun system but not in the Fijian system?

10. Each NP in the following sentences has a thematic role that represents the part that its referent plays in the situation described by the sentence.

a) The man chased the intruder.
b) The cat jumped from the chair onto the table.
c) Aaron wrote a letter to Marilyn.
d) The governor entertained the guests in the lounge.
e) Henry mailed the manuscript from Atlanta.

Using the terms described in this chapter, label the thematic role of each NP in these sentences and identify the assigner for each thematic role.
Example: <u>Bill</u> wrote <u>a novel</u>   in <u>the park</u>.

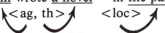

11. Each of the following sentences has undergone a movement transformation.

    a) What has Larry given to the bride?
    b) Who will Liane kiss?
    c) Which house will the group leave from?
    d) What has Marvin forgotten on the bus?
    e) The necklace was stolen by the burglar.
    f) The ball was thrown to Evan by Louise.

    Write out the deep structure string for each of these sentences and mark all thematic roles and thematic role assigners.

    Example: a) <u>Larry</u> has given <u>what</u> to <u>the bride</u>

    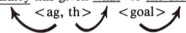

12. One of the relations involved in the interpretation of pronouns is that of c-command. Examine the following tree structure for the sentence *Jack's brother gave himself a haircut.*

    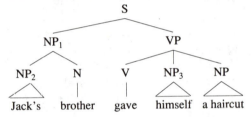

    i) Who does *himself* refer to in this sentence?
    ii) Does NP$_2$ c-command NP$_3$?
    iii) Are questions *i)* and *ii)* relevant to each other? If they are, explain how your answer to *ii)* supports your answer to *i)*.
    iv) Does the antecedent change if you change *himself* to *him*? Why?

13. In the following sentence, the pronoun *she* could, according to Principle B, refer to either *the architect* or *the secretary*, because both of them are outside of the smallest *S* that contains the pronoun.

    The architect gave the secretary a raise after she typed the report.

    i) Which interpretation comes to mind first?
    ii) Why? (For most people, there are two reasons.)
    iii) What happens to the pronoun's interpretation if you change the word *secretary* to *janitor*?
    iv) What prevents *she* from having the NP *a raise* as an antecedent?

14. In the following pairs of sentences, one of the two sentences contains a presupposition relating to the truth of the complement clause.

    a) John regrets that Maria went to the graduation ceremony.
       John believes that Maria went to the graduation ceremony.
    b) The captain thought that the ship was in danger.
       The captain realized that the ship was in danger.

c) It is significant that the criminal was sentenced.
It is likely that the criminal was sentenced.

For each pair:
i) Identify the sentence that contains this presupposition, and state the presupposition it contains.
ii) Locate the word that implies the presupposition.

15. In Malagasy, the use of the deictics *ety* 'here' and *aty* 'there' depend on whether the object in question is visible to the speaker. How does this differ from the English use of *here/there*?

a) Ety ny tranony. 'Here is his house (visible to the speaker)'
b) Aty ny tranony. 'There is his house (not visible to the speaker)'

16. The syntactic construction *It was ____ that ____* is called a cleft construction and is used in certain discourse contexts. Consider the following conversations involving cleft constructions.

a) *A*: Did Sally claim that she saw a flying saucer last night?
B: No, it was <u>a meteorite</u> that <u>Sally claimed she saw last night</u>.
b) *A*: Did Sally claim that she saw a flying saucer last night?
B: No, it was <u>Sally</u> that <u>claimed she saw a meteorite last night</u>.
c) *A*: Did Sally claim that she saw a flying saucer last night?
B: No, it was <u>last week</u> that <u>Sally claimed she saw a flying saucer</u>.

i) Is B's response equally acceptable in all three interactions?
ii) Choose one of the discourses in which B's response is appropriate. How do the underlined parts correspond to new and old information?
iii) For the discourse in which B's response is unacceptable, can you now explain why it is unacceptable?
iv) In addition to the cleft construction, identify the way in which new information is marked phonetically in B's responses.

For the Student Linguist

A teller said "Someone came in a truck. I heard some screams coming from inside. People were rolling on the floor. Then it was over and I smoked a pack of cigarettes on the way home."

By the time the Bureau had been hauled in, the local pigs had decided someone else had done it. But the tip-off, by Oneida Otters star center Billie Jones, was about her partner. "Everyone thought two people were involved from the beginning," Jones claimed. "But it was when I saw the suds in the record store behind the pizzeria that it all came together."

The King could not be reached for comment by press time.

It's surprisingly easy to write an article in which every sentence is ambiguous. It's much harder—maybe even impossible—to write one that isn't ambiguous, or to write anything that isn't ambiguous. Maybe this explains why legal language is so tedious in its attempt to be unambiguous and why our court system is so clogged (obstructed, that is, not filled with Dutch wooden shoes), and why multiple-choice exams are so awful.

To show that the sentences in this article really are ambiguous, I'll attempt to disambiguate the first couple of paragraphs of Blanche's story in painstaking detail. By the time I'm done, you'll probably be able to see ambiguity everywhere you go.

Blanche VanBuren is an elderly Elvis aficionado who resides in Oneida, Illinois. And she's just plain old, all would agree (see tree *1B*). Or, when considering Elvis fans from Oneida, she's getting up in years (see tree *1A*), but in some other context she'd be considered pretty young (because most of the Elvis fans in Oneida are teenyboppers, whereas Blanche is pushing thirty.) Maybe Blanche has been an Elvis fan for a long time (*1B*). Or maybe, just maybe, most Oneidan Elvis fans are new to their admiration of him (it began with the postage stamp), but Blanche has loved Elvis since 1984, when she encountered him on a spaceship, and is therefore, comparatively speaking, an old Elvis-fan-from-Oneida (tree *1A*). Of course, she could also be a fan of only the *old* Elvis—that is, she liked his Vegas days but hated the early stuff. You can figure out the tree for this reading.

Let's assume Blanche is elderly. And a neat freak, because she washed the Peoria Institution for Savings from top to bottom (taking the shotgun to teach a lesson to litterbugs.) Then again, she might be an incredibly compulsive cleaner in her own house and spend so much money on lemon-scented antiseptics that she robbed the P.I.S. and took along that sawed-off broom because she was delirious from inhaling ammonia all day. Let's consider her implements. The shotgun was old. The broom was sawed-off. Was the broom old? We don't know; the story doesn't provide information on its age. Was the shotgun sawed-off? This is a classic case of structural ambiguity, made famous by the example "the old men and women" and the answer should be obvious by now (but see trees *2A* and *2B* for confirmation).

The article does make clear that the event of interest took place yesterday, but I'm wondering whether Blanche habitually cleans out banks, and it just happened to be the P.I.S. yesterday, or if this was an out-of-the-blue cleaning or what. Could be that she cleans the P.I.S. every day, but usually she has more equipment than a broom and a gun.

Then there's the possibility that Blanche is an early model electric cooling device (or an antique paper and balsa wood construction), once owned (and affectionately named) by Elvis, which either: (a) blew all the dirt out of the bank or (b) was brought to life and performed the robbery. You never know.

What about Darrel Apley? If the writer of this article had any ethics, he (Darrel) is not the person who owns Union Electric, nor is he (Darrel) a shocked witness who preferred to remain anonymous. If the writer had ethics there would have to have been three different people who all said "Blanche should be at home . . ." and one of them is Darrel, one's the owner of U.E., and the third is shocked and prefers anonymity (tree *3A*). However, sloppy writing and broken promises are everywhere, and it's quite possible that *the owner of Union Electric* and *a shocked witness who preferred to remain anonymous* are actually intended to describe Darrel (tree *3B*).

"Blanche should be at home at this time of the day." Should? As in, given her normal patterns, the most likely case is that Blanche is at home? Or *should* as in if that lowdown, bank-thieving woman knew what was good for her she'd be at home watching *All My Children*?

"Her favorite soap is on the TV." This one's easy; it's nothing but lexical ambiguity. Her favorite soap could be Ivory Family Size or the aforementioned *All My Children*. If this were spoken instead of written, we'd have to explore the option that her favorite soap is called "On the TV.", and actually, considering the doubts you might have about the writer's integrity, that could have been what Darrel (and maybe two others) meant. Of course, "on" is ambiguous between "being broadcast" or "on top of" but enough is enough.

The rest of the article you can disambiguate on your own. It's useful to draw trees for the structurally ambiguous parts and make sure the different interpretations match the trees. Every *written* sentence—every portion of material from one period to another—is ambiguous, but not every *S* in the technical, linguistic sense is ambiguous. Be sure to look for lexical ambiguity, structural ambiguity, and pronouns that could refer to a few different people. Also look carefully at Jones's quote—this one is hard but interesting. Finally, check out your local newspaper. I predict that many of the sentences in it are as ambiguous as the ones in this article. You could even examine the instructions for your next linguistics homework assignment, and (politely) tease your instructor if they're not crystal clear. Be careful, though—he or she might hold you to the same standard in your writing.

TREES:

(1A)

an old Elvis fan from Oneida

(elderly?)   (aficionado?)
(longtime?) (cooling device?)
[She's an old fan compared to
Oneidan Elvis fans.]

(1B)

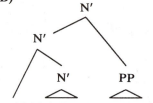

an old Elvis fan from Oneida

(elderly?)   (aficionado?)
(longtime?) (cooling device?)
[She's an old fan compared to all
Elvis fans.]

(2A)

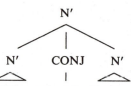

sawed-off broom and old shotgun
[Only the broom is sawed-off.]

(2B)

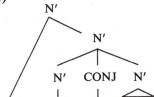

sawed-off broom and old shotgun
[Both the broom and the shotgun
are sawed-off.]

(3A)

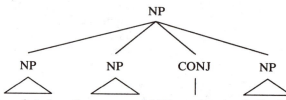

Darrel Apley, the owner of U.E. and a shocked witness . . .
[three different people]

(3B)

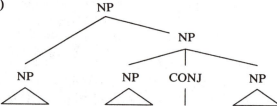

Darrel Apley, the owner of U.E. and a shocked witness . . .
[One person: "Darrell Apley, (who is) the owner . . . .", after "who is"
has been deleted. Don't worry about the details of this structure.]

7 HISTORICAL LINGUISTICS
The Study of Language Change

Many men sayn that in sweveninges
Ther nys but fables and lesynges;
But men may some swevenes sene
Whiche hardely that false ne bene,
But afterwarde ben apparaunt.
Chaucer, *The Romance of the Rose* (c. 1370)

Language change is both obvious and rather mysterious. The English of the late fourteenth century, for example, is so different from Modern English that without special training it is difficult to understand the opening lines to *The Romance of the Rose* cited above. Not only would these sentences have a foreign sound, but words and structures such as *sweveninges*, *lesynges*, and *false ne bene* are unfamiliar. The existence of such differences between early and later variants of the same language raises questions as to how and why languages change over time.

Historical linguistics is concerned with both the description and explanation of language change. In this chapter we examine the nature and causes of language change and survey in some detail phonological, morphological, syntactic, lexical, and semantic change. We also explore techniques used to reconstruct linguistic prehistory and briefly discuss interrelated research into language acquisition and linguistic universals.

7.1 THE NATURE OF LANGUAGE CHANGE

All languages undergo change over time. English has undergone continuous and dramatic change throughout its three major periods: Old English (roughly from 450 to 1100), Middle English (from 1100 to 1500), and Modern English (from 1500 to the present). While Chaucer's Middle English is at least partially comprehensible today, Old English looks like a completely foreign language. The following is an extract from an eighth century Old English document, a translation of Bede's Latin history of England. (The letter þ, called 'thorn', represented the phoneme /θ/ in Old English; here and elsewhere in this chapter the diacritic ¯ marks a long vowel in the orthography.)

1. and Seaxan þā sige geslōgan.
and Saxons the victory won
'And the Saxons won the victory.'

þā sendan hī hām ǣrenddracan.
then sent they home messenger
'Then they sent home a messenger.'

These Old English sentences differ from their Modern English counterparts in many respects. In terms of pronunciation, for instance, the Old English word *hām* [ha:m] 'home' in the second sentence became [hɔ:m] in Middle English, and then [howm] in Modern English. In its morphology, Old English differed significantly from Modern English. The suffix *-an* on the Old English word for 'sent' indicates both past tense and plurality of the subject (*hī* 'they'). Differences in word order are also readily apparent, with the verb following both the subject and the object in the first sentence and preceding both the subject and the object in the second. Neither of these word orders would be acceptable in the Modern English forms of these sentences.

In addition, some Old English words have disappeared from use, as the unfamiliar *ǣrenddracan* 'messenger' and *sige* 'victory' indicate. Still other words have been maintained, but with a change in meaning. For example, the Old English word *geslōgan* (which we translated as 'won') is the past tense of the verb *slēan*, the Old English predecessor of our word *slay*. Although the Modern English meaning of this word in normal usage is restricted to the act of killing, the Old English verb could also mean 'to strike, beat, coin (money), and forge (weapons)'. As these examples imply, all components of the grammar from meaning (semantics) to individual sounds (phonology) are subject to change.

Systematicity of Language Change

A striking fact about language change in general is its regularity and systematicity. For example, the development of a fixed subject-verb-direct object (SVO) basic word order in English did not affect just a few verbs; all verbs in Modern English appear before rather than after the direct object. Similarly, the changes affecting the vowel in the word *hām* did not occur in that word only; they represent the regular development of the Old English vowel *ā* ([a:]).

Table 7.1 Changes affecting Old English [a:]

Old English	Middle English	Modern English	
[ba:t]	[bɔ:t]	[bowt]	'boat'
[a:θ]	[ɔ:θ]	[owθ]	'oath'
[sta:n]	[stɔ:n]	[stown]	'stone'

Causes of Language Change

The inevitability of language change is guaranteed by the way in which language is handed down from one generation to the next. Children do not begin with an intact grammar of the language being acquired but rather must construct a grammar on the basis of the available data (see Chapter 10). In such a situation it is hardly surprising that differences will arise, even if only subtle ones, from one generation to the next. Moreover, since all children use the same physiological and cognitive endowment in learning language, it is to be expected that the same patterns of change will be consistently and repeatedly manifested in all languages. Following is a brief overview of the principal causes of language change.

Articulatory Simplification As might be expected, most sound changes have a physiological basis. Since such sound changes typically result in articulatory simplification, they have traditionally been related to the idea of 'ease of articulation'. Although this notion is difficult to define precisely, we can readily identify cases of articulatory simplification in our everyday speech such as the deletion of a consonant in a complex cluster or, in some dialects, the insertion of a vowel to break up a complex cluster.

Table 7.2 Simplification of complex clusters

Deletion of a consonant			
[fɪfθs]	→	[fɪfs]	'fifths'

Insertion of a vowel			
[æθlijt]	→	[æθəlijt]	'athlete'

Spelling Pronunciation Not all changes in pronunciation have a physiological motivation. A minor, but nevertheless important, source of change in English and other languages is **spelling pronunciation**. Since the written form of a word can differ significantly from the way it is pronounced, a new pronunciation can arise which seems to reflect more closely the spelling of the word. A case in point is the word *often*. Although this word was pronounced with a [t] in earlier English, the voiceless stop was subsequently lost resulting in the pronunciation [ɔfən] (compare *soften*). However, since the letter *t* was retained in the spelling, [t] has been reintroduced into many speakers' pronunciation of this word.

Another case in point is the pronunciation of [s] in words such as *assume* and *consume*. Although in earlier English such words were pronounced with [s], sound change resulted in a pronunciation with [ʃ] (as in *assure*). Similar to the case of *often*, a pronunciation with [s] has been reintroduced into many dialects on the basis of the spelling (which remained unchanged even after the sound change took place). Since spelling tends to remain stable even though sound changes have occurred (English spelling began stabilizing more than three hundred years ago), spelling pronunciation can reintroduce a pronunciation that was earlier altered through sound change.

Analogy and Reanalysis Cognitive factors also play a role in change in all components of the grammar. Two sources of change having a cognitive basis are **analogy** and **reanalysis**. Analogy reflects the preference of speakers for regular patterns over irregular ones. It typically involves the extension or generalization of a regularity on the basis of the inference that if elements are alike in some respects, they should be alike in others as well. Both phonological and semantic characteristics can serve as a basis for analogy. For example, on the basis of its phonological similarity with such verbs as *sting/stung* and *swing/swung*, in some dialects *bring* has developed a form *brung*, as in *I('ve) brung it into the house*. Children create forms such as *goed* by analogy with regular past tense forms like *played*. As we will see, analogy plays a very important role in morphological change.

Reanalysis is particularly common in morphological change. Morphological reanalysis often involves an attempt to attribute a compound or root + affix structure to a word that formerly was not broken down into component morphemes. A classic example in English is the word *hamburger*, which originally referred to a type of meat patty deriving its name from the city of Hamburg in Germany. This word has been reanalysed as consisting of two components, *ham + burger*. The latter morpheme has since appeared in many new forms including *fishburger*, *chickenburger*, and even as a free morpheme *burger*. Note that the resulting reanalysis must not necessarily be correct. (There is usually no ham in a burger!)

Language Contact Another cause of linguistic change is **language contact**, which occurs when speakers of one language frequently interact with the speakers of another language or dialect. As a consequence, extensive **borrowing** can occur, particularly where there are significant numbers of bilinguals or multilinguals. Although borrowing can affect all components of the grammar, the lexicon is typically most affected. English, for example, has borrowed many Amerindian words including *Canada*, *moccasin*, *totem*, *tomahawk*, *muskrat*, *moose*, and *skunk*.

Among the effects that borrowing can have on the sound system are the introduction of new phonemes or allophones and changes in their distribution. For example, some English speakers pronounce the name of the classical composer, *Bach*, with the final velar fricative [x] found in the German pronunciation. If there is a significant number of borrowings from another language, the borrowed foreign segment can eventually become a new phoneme. In the early Middle English period, the London dialect had [f] but not [v] in word-initial position. The [v] was later introduced as a result of contact with other English dialects and with French, in which it did occur word-initially. As a result of this contact, a contrast developed between /f/ and /v/ word-initially, as found in Modern English pairs such as *file* and *vile*.

Language (as well as dialect) contact also results in another minor but nevertheless important source of language change, **hypercorrection**. Hypercorrection occurs when a speaker who is attempting to speak another dialect or language overgeneralizes particular rules. For example, most Americans speak a dialect in which no distinction is made between intervocalic [t] and [d] so that words such as *latter* and *ladder* are both pronounced with an intervocalic flap [D] (see Chapter 2). If a speaker from such a dialect attempts to emulate the pronunciation of a speaker from another dialect who does distinguish the two stops intervocalically, hypercorrection could result in the use of intervocalic [t] in words where [d] should be used; for example, the pronunciation *pro*[t]*igy* for *prodigy*.

Another example of hypercorrection is the use of *I* in constructions such as *He saw John and I*. This usage is an overgeneralization of the rule that only *I* should be used in subject position, never *me*. According to this rule, *John and I are going* is correct but *John and me/me and John are going* is incorrect. For some speakers, hypercorrection has resulted in the inference that all coordinate phrases with *me* (such as *John and me*) are incorrect even when they serve as the direct object (complement) of the verb. Note that the person who says *He saw John and I* would not say *He saw I*.

7.2 SOUND CHANGE

Although all components of the grammar are susceptible to change over time, some types of change yield more obvious results than others. Variation and change are particularly noticeable in the phonology of a language. Several common types of sound change can be distinguished.

Most sound changes begin as subtle alterations in the sound pattern of a language in particular phonetic environments. The linguistic processes underlying such **phonetically conditioned** sound change are identical to the ones found in the phonology of currently spoken languages (see Chapter 2, Section 10). The application of such processes usually brings about an articulatory simplification and over time significant changes in the phonology of a language can result.

Although all aspects of phonology (for example, tone, stress, and syllable structure) are subject to change over time, we will restrict our attention here to change involving segments. Since most sound changes involve sequences of segments, the main focus will be on **sequential change**. However, we will also discuss one common type of **segmental change**, involving the simplification of an affricate. In addition, in order to indicate that more than just articulatory factors play a role in sound change, we will discuss a case of sound change based on auditory factors. All important sound changes discussed in this section and referred to in this chapter are found in the following catalogue.

Table 7.3 Catalogue of sound changes

Sequential change
Assimilation
Place and/or manner of articulation
Palatalization/affrication
Nasalization
Umlaut
Dissimilation
Epenthesis (segment addition)
Metathesis (segment movement)
Weakening and deletion
Vowels
Vowel reduction
Syncope
Apocope
Consonants
Degemination
Voicing
Frication
Rhotacism
Deletion
Consonant strengthening
Glide strengthening
Segmental change
Deaffrication
Auditorily-based change
Substitution

Assimilation The most common type of phonetically conditioned change is **assimilation**, which has the effect of increasing the efficiency of articulation through a simplification of articulatory movements. We will focus here on the four main types indicated in the catalogue.

Partial assimilation involving **place** or **manner of articulation** is a very common change which, over time, can result in total assimilation. In the Spanish and Latin examples in Table 7.4, the place of articulation of the nasal assimilated to the following consonant.

Table 7.4 Assimilation (place of articulation) in Spanish and Latin

| Old Spanish | semda | Modern Spanish | senda | 'path' |
| Early Latin | inpossibilis | Later Latin | impossibilis | 'impossible' |

The first of the Old English examples in Table 7.5 shows voicing assimilation and the second shows the assimilation of nasality.

Table 7.5 Assimilation in manner of articulation in Old English

Early Old English	Later Old English	
slæpde	slæpte	'slept'
stefn	stemn	'stem (of a tree)'

In the Italian examples in Table 7.6, a stop assimilates totally to a following stop.

Table 7.6 Total assimilation in Italian

Latin	Italian	
octo (c = [k])	otto	'eight'
septem	sette	'seven'
damnum	danno	'damage'

Another type of assimilation is **palatalization**—the effect that front vowels and the palatal glide [j] typically have on velar, alveolar, and dental stops, making their place of articulation more palatal. If you compare your pronunciation of *keep* as opposed to *cot*, you will notice that the pronunciation of [k] in the former is much more palatal than in the latter due to the influence of [i]. Palatalization is often the first step in **affrication**, a change in which palatalized stops become affricates, either [ts] or [tʃ] if the original stop was voiceless or [dz] or [dʒ] if the original stop was voiced.

Table 7.7 Palatalization/affrication induced by front vowels and [j]

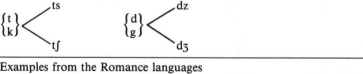

Examples from the Romance languages				
Latin	centum [k]	Old French	cent	[ts]	'one hundred'
Latin	centum [k]	Italian	ciento [tʃ]	'one hundred'
Latin	medius	Italian	mezzo [dz]	'half'
Latin	gentem	Old French	gent	[dʒ]	'people'

Nasalization refers to the nasalizing effect that a nasal consonant can have on an adjacent vowel. This change occurred in both French and Portuguese, with the subsequent loss of the nasal consonant. (The pronunciation of the vowels in our examples underwent additional changes in height and backness in French.)

Table 7.8 Nasalization in Portuguese and French

Latin	Portuguese	French	
bon-	bon [bõ]	bon [bɔ̃]	'good'
un-	um [ũ]	un [œ̃]	'one'

Although assimilation is probably most common in the case of adjacent segments, it can also apply at a distance. A case in point is **umlaut**, the effect a vowel or sometimes a glide in one syllable can have on the vowel of another syllable, usually a preceding one. Umlaut (resulting in front rounded vowels [y] and [ø]) played an important role in Old English and is the source of irregular plurals such as *goose/geese* and *mouse/mice* in Modern English. For example, the plural of the pre-Old English words *gōs* 'goose' and *mūs* 'mouse' was formed by adding a suffix -[i]. As a result, umlaut of the vowel in the preceding syllable occurred in the plural forms (see pre-Old English stages 1 and 2 in Table 7.9) but not in the singular forms. By early Old English, the suffix -[i] had been lost in a separate change, leaving the umlauted vowel as the marker of the plural form. (Subsequent changes included the derounding of the umlauted vowels [ȳ] and [ø̄] yielding [ī] and [ē] respectively by Middle English, and the Great Vowel Shift as described on page 268).

Table 7.9 Umlaut in English

Pre-Old English 1		Pre-OE 2		Early OE		Subsequent changes	
[gōs]	>	[gōs]	>	[gōs]	>	[guws]	'goose'
[gōsi]	>	[gø̄si]	>	[gø̄s]	>	[gijs]	'geese'
[mūs]	>	[mūs]	>	[mūs]	>	[maws]	'mouse'
[mūsi]	>	[mȳsi]	>	[mȳs]	>	[majs]	'mice'

Dissimilation The process whereby one segment is made less like another segment in its environment, **dissimilation**, is much less frequent than assimilation. This type of change typically occurs when it would be difficult to articulate or perceive two similar sounds in close proximity. The word *anma* 'soul' in Late Latin, for example, was modified to *alma* in Spanish, thereby avoiding two consecutive nasal consonants. Like assimilation, dissimilation can also operate at a distance to affect non-adjacent segments. For instance, the Latin word *arbor* 'tree' became *arbol* in Spanish and *alboro* in Italian, thereby avoiding two instances of [r] in neighboring syllables. (By contrast, dissimilation did not occur in French where *arbre* has retained both instances of [r].)

Epenthesis Another common sound change, **epenthesis**, involves the insertion of a consonant or vowel into a particular environment. In some cases, epenthesis results from the anticipation of an upcoming sound.

Table 7.10 Epenthesis in Old English

Earlier form	Change	Later form	
ganra	VnrV > VndrV	gandra	'gander'
simle	VmlV > VmblV	simble	'always'
æmtig	VmtV > VmptV	æmptig	'empty'

In these examples, the epenthetic [b], [d], or [p] has the place of articulation of the preceding nasal but agrees with the following segment in terms of voice and nasality. The epenthetic segment therefore serves as a bridge for the transition between the segments on either side.

Table 7.11 The nature of epenthesis

[m]	[b]	[l]	[m]	[p]	[t]
labial	labial	non-labial	labial	labial	non-labial
nasal	non-nasal	non-nasal	nasal	non-nasal	non-nasal
voiced	voiced	voiced	voiced	voiceless	voiceless

In other cases, vowel epenthesis serves to break up a sequence of sounds which would otherwise be difficult to pronounce or even inconsistent with the phonotactic patterns of the language. As mentioned, some English speakers avoid [θl] clusters by inserting an epenthetic [ə] in their pronunciation of words such as *athlete* as *ath*[ə]*lete*. In the history of Spanish, word-initial [sk] clusters were avoided by inserting a vowel.

Table 7.12 Examples of epenthesis

| Latin | schola [sk] | Spanish | escuela [esk] | 'school' |
| Latin | scrībere [sk] | Spanish | escribir [esk] | 'write' |

Metathesis A change in the relative positioning of segments is called **metathesis**. This change, like assimilation and dissimilation, can affect adjacent segments or segments at a distance.

Table 7.13 Metathesis of adjacent segments in Old English

Earlier form	Later form	
wæps	wæsp	'wasp'
þridda	þirdda	'third'

Metathesis at a distance is found in the change from Latin *mīrāculum* 'miracle' to Spanish *milagro*, in which [r] and [l] have changed places although they were not adjacent.

Figure 7.1 Metathesis of non-adjacent segments in Spanish

Weakening and Deletion Both vowels and consonants are also susceptible to outright **deletion** as well as to various **weakening** processes. We will first treat the effects of these processes on vowels and then turn to their effects on consonants.

Vowel deletion may involve a word-final vowel (**apocope**) or a word-internal vowel (**syncope**). A vowel in an unstressed syllable is particularly susceptible to deletion, especially when a nearby neighboring syllable is stressed.

Table 7.14 Vowel deletion in French

Apocope

Latin	French	
cúra	cure [kyr]	'cure'
ōrnáre	orner	'decorate'

Syncope

Latin	French	
pérdere	perdre	'lose'
vívere	vivre	'live'

The effects of syncope are also apparent in the loss of the medial vowel in Modern English words such as *vegetable*, *interest*, and *family*, which are frequently pronounced as [védʒtəbl̩], [íntrɛst], and [fǽmlij].

Vowel deletion is commonly preceded by **vowel reduction** in which a full vowel is reduced to a short central vowel [ə]. Vowel reduction typically affects short vowels in unstressed syllables and may affect all or only a subset of the full vowels.

Figure 7.2 Vowel reduction

Vowel reduction with subsequent deletion (syncope and apocope) occurred in Middle English and Early Modern English.

Table 7.15 Vowel reduction and deletion in English

Syncope

Old English		Middle English (vowel reduction)		Early Modern English (syncope)	
stanas	[a]	stones	[ə]	stones	ø
stanes	[e]	stones	[ə]	stone's	ø

Apocope

Old English		Middle English (vowel reduction)		Early Modern English (apocope)	
nama	[a]	name	[ə]	name	ø
talu	[u]	tale	[ə]	tale	ø

Consonant deletion is also a very common sound change. For example, the word-initial cluster [kn] was found in Old and Middle English, as the spelling of such words as *knight*, *knit*, *knot*, and *knee* implies, but the [k] was subsequently lost giving us our modern pronunciation. The loss of word-final consonants has played a major role in the evolution of Modern French. The final letters in the written forms of the following words reflect consonants which were actually pronounced at an earlier stage of the language.

Table 7.16 Consonant loss in French

French spelling (masculine form)	Current pronunciation	
gros	[gro]	'large'
chaud	[ʃo]	'warm'
vert	[ver]	'green'

Just as vowel reduction can be identified as a weakening process since it represents an intermediate step on the pathway from a full vowel to deletion of the vowel, so too can pathways of **consonant weakening** be identified. The following scale of **consonantal strength** can be helpful in identifying cases of weakening.

Consonantal strength

stronger ↑ voiceless stops
voiceless fricatives, voiced stops
voiced fricatives
nasals
liquids
weaker ↓ glides

(*Note*: Geminate consonants are stronger than their non-geminate counterparts.)

Figure 7.3 Scale of consonantal strength

Accordingly, geminates weaken to non-geminates (**degemination**), stops weaken to fricatives (**frication**), and voiceless stops or voiceless fricatives weaken to voiced stops or voiced fricatives respectively (**voicing**). Weakening can ultimately result in the deletion of the consonant. Following is a typical pathway of weakening.

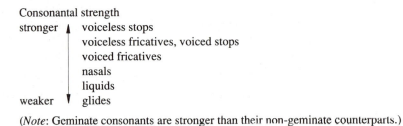

Figure 7.4 Typical pathway of consonant weakening

Consonants are particularly subject to weakening in an intervocalic environment. Parts of the pathway of consonantal weakening are exemplified with developments from the Romance languages shown in Table 7.17.

Table 7.17 Consonantal weakening in Romance

Degemination (tt > t)	Latin	mi**tt**ere	Spanish	me**t**er	'to put'
Voicing (t > d)	Latin	mā**t**ūrus	Old Spanish	ma**d**uro	'ripe'
Frication (d > ð)	Old Spanish	ma**d**uro	Spanish	ma**d**uro [ð]	'ripe'
Deletion (ð > ø)	Old French	[ma**ð**yr]	French	mûr	'ripe'

Rhotacism is a relatively common type of weakening that typically involves the change of [z] to [r]. Often rhotacism is preceded by a stage involving the voicing of [s] to [z]. Within the Germanic family of languages for instance,

[s] first became [z] in a particular intervocalic environment. This [z] remained in Gothic but became [r] in other Germanic languages such as English, German, and Swedish. The effects of the latter part of this change can be seen in the standard spellings of the following words.

Table 7.18 Rhotacism in English, German, and Swedish

Gothic	English	German	Swedish
maiza	more	mehr	mera
diuzam	deer	Tier	djur
huzd	hoard	Hort	—

In Modern English, rhotacism is the source of the alternation between [z] and [r] in *was* and *were*. The [r] resulted from earlier [z] which was originally intervocalic.

Consonantal Strengthening Just as consonants weaken, they can also strengthen. **Glide strengthening** (the strengthening of a glide to an affricate) is particularly common, especially in word-initial position. In the following Italian examples, the glide [j] has been strengthened to [dʒ].

Table 7.19 Glide strengthening in Italian

Latin	iūdicium	[j]	Italian	giudizio	[dʒ]	'justice'
Latin	iuvenis	[j]	Italian	giovane	[dʒ]	'young'

Segmental Change

Segments such as affricates are considered phonologically complex because they represent the fusing of a stop plus a fricative into a single segment, for example, [dʒ] or [ts]. Such complex segments are commonly subject to simplification. A very common type of segmental simplification is **deaffrication,** which has the effect of turning affricates into fricatives by eliminating the stop portion of the affricate.

Table 7.20 Deaffrication in French

Old French	cent [ts]	French	cent [s]	'one hundred'
Old French	gent [dʒ]	French	gent [ʒ]	'people, tribe'

Since deaffrication of [tʃ] (as well as [dʒ]) has not occurred in English, early borrowings from French maintain the affricate, while later borrowings have a fricative.

Table 7.21 Borrowings from French

Early borrowings (before deaffrication occurred in French)	
Old French [tʃ]	**English [tʃ]**
chaiere	chair
chaine	chain
(Compare Modern French [ʃ] in chaire 'throne, seat' and chaîne 'chain'.)	

Later borrowings (after deaffrication occurred in French)	
Modern French [ʃ]	**English [ʃ]**
chandelier	chandelier
chauffeur	chauffeur

Auditorily-based Change

Although articulatory factors (particularly relating to 'ease of articulation') are of central importance in sound change as indicated in the preceding discussion, auditory factors also play a role. **Substitution** is a type of auditorily-based change involving the replacement of one segment with another similar sounding segment. A common type of substitution involves [f] replacing either [x] or [θ]. Earlier in the history of English, [f] replaced [x] in some words while [f] replaced [θ] in the Cockney, non-standard dialect spoken in London.

Table 7.22 Auditorily-based substitution

[x] > [f]	Middle English	laugh [x]	English	laugh [f]
[θ] > [f]	English	thin [θ]	Cockney	[fɪn]

So far we have treated sound changes without consideration of their effect on the sound pattern of the particular language as a whole. All of the foregoing sound changes can lead both to new types of allophonic variation and to the addition or loss of phonemic contrasts. Examples of such cases are presented in the next section.

Phonetic versus Phonological Change

The sound changes outlined in the previous sections can affect the overall sound pattern (phonology) of a language in different ways. Commonly, the first stage of a sound change results in the creation of a new allophone of an already existing phoneme. The term **phonetic sound change** can be used to refer to this stage.

A good example of phonetic sound change involves the laxing of short high vowels that has developed in Canadian French. This change can be seen in closed word-final syllables, among other environments.

Table 7.23 Vowel laxing in Canadian French

European French	Canadian French	
Closed syllable		
[vit]	[vɪt]	'quick'
[libr]	[lɪbr]	'free'
[ekut]	[ekʊt]	'listen'
[pus]	[pʊs]	'thumb'
Open syllable		
[vi]	[vi]	'life'
[li]	[li]	'bed'
[vu]	[vu]	'you'
[lu]	[lu]	'wolf'

Whereas Canadian French has the lax vowels [ɪ] and [ʊ] in closed final syllables, European French has kept the tense vowels [i] and [u]. Both dialects of French retain [i] and [u] in open syllables. This suggests that Canadian French has developed the following rule.

$$
\begin{bmatrix} V \\ +\text{high} \\ -\text{long} \end{bmatrix} \rightarrow [-\text{tense}] / \_\_\_ C(C) \#
$$

Figure 7.5 Vowel laxing rule in Canadian French

While this rule did introduce an allophone not present in European French, it did not create any new phonemes since there is no contrast between lax vowels and their tense counterparts in Canadian French.

Sometimes sound change can lead to changes in a language's phonological system by adding, eliminating, or rearranging phonemes. Such **phonological change** can involve **splits**, **mergers**, or **shifts**.

Splits In a phonological split, allophones of the same phoneme come to contrast with each other due to the loss of the conditioning environment, with the result that one or more new phonemes are created. The English phoneme /ŋ/ was the result of a phonological split. Originally, [ŋ] was simply the allophone of /n/ that appeared before a velar consonant. During Middle English, consonant deletion resulted in the loss of [g] in word-final position after a nasal consonant, leaving [ŋ] as the final sound in words such as *sing*.

Table 7.24 Phonological split resulting in /ŋ/

Original phonemic form	/sɪng/
Original phonetic form	[sɪŋg]
Deletion of [g]	[sɪŋg] > [sɪŋ]
New phonemic form	/sɪŋ/

The loss of the final [g] in words created minimal pairs such as *sin* (/sɪn/) and *sing* (/sɪŋ/), in which there is a contrast between /n/ and /ŋ/. This example represents a typical phonological split. When the conditioning environment of an allophonic variant of a phoneme is lost through sound change, the allophone is no longer predictable and thus itself becomes phonemic. The original phoneme (in our example /n/) splits into two phonemes (/n/ and /ŋ/).

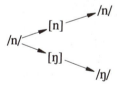

Figure 7.6 A phonological split

Mergers In a phonological merger, two or more phonemes collapse into a single one, thereby reducing the number of phonemes in the language. The case of auditorily-based substitution discussed above has this effect in Cockney English, where all instances of the interdental fricative /θ/ have become /f/. Consequently, the phonemes /θ/ and /f/ have merged into one (/f/) and words such as *thin* and *fin* have the same phonological form (/fɪn/). Similarly, /v/ and /ð/ have merged (for example, /smuv/ for *smooth*).

Figure 7.7 A phonological merger

Shifts A phonological shift is a change in which a series of phonemes is systematically modified so that their organization with respect to each other is altered. A well-known example of such a change is called the Great English Vowel Shift. Beginning in the Middle English period and continuing into the eighteenth century, the language underwent a series of modifications to the long vowels.

Table 7.25 The Great English Vowel Shift

Middle English	Great Vowel Shift			Later glide addition	Modern English	
[ti:d]	[i:]	>	[aj]		[tajd]	'tide'
[lu:d]	[u:]	>	[aw]		[lawd]	'loud'
[ge:s]	[e:]	>	[i:]	> [ij]	[gijs]	'geese'
[sɛ:]	[ɛ:]	>	[i:]	> [ij]	[sij]	'sea'
[go:s]	[o:]	>	[u:]	> [uw]	[guws]	'goose'
[brɔ:kən]	[ɔ:]	>	[o:]	> [ow]	[browkən]	'broken'
[na:mə]	[a:]	>	[e:]	> [ej]	[nejm]	'name'

Figure 7.8 illustrates the effect of these changes on English long vowels.

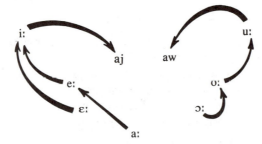

Figure 7.8 Changes brought about by the Great English Vowel Shift

These changes took place gradually, and the diphthongization of [i:] and [u:] involved an intermediate stage during which the vowel nucleus in the diphthong was [ʌ] rather than [a]. In some variants of English, this pronunciation has been retained before voiceless consonants (for example, [ʌwt] *out* and [wʌjf] *wife*).

Explaining Phonological Shift

The causes and even the details of the Great English Vowel Shift still remain unclear. In fact, the causes of phonological shift in general are not well understood. A possible motivation in some cases appears to involve the notion of phonological space within phonemic systems. As in the case of 'ease of articulation', phonological space is difficult to define precisely. For our purposes, and focusing on vowels only, we can consider the vowel quadrangle (a schematicization of the oral cavity) as the phonological space that vowels must occupy. Although the vowel systems of languages can be arranged in various ways (see Chapter 8), there is a tendency for languages to maximize the use of space in the quadrangle. Accordingly, if a language has only three vowel phonemes, they will likely be /i/, /a/, and /o/ or /u/, not (for example) /i/,

/e/, /ɛ/. Similarly, if a language has five vowels, they will be distributed throughout the phonological space, typically as /i/, /e/, /a/, /o/, /u/ rather than /u/, /ʊ/, /a/, /o/, /ɔ/ for example.

a Typical distribution of vowels in phonological space

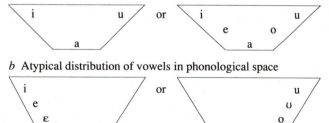

b Atypical distribution of vowels in phonological space

Figure 7.9 Vowel distribution

Languages with seven (or more) vowels (the case in English at the starting point of the Great English Vowel Shift in Figure 7.8) often undergo **diphthongization**. This can be seen as a reaction to the overcrowding of the phonological space. Its effect is to reduce the seven vowel system to a five vowel system. (Think of the two diphthongs as not infringing on the space of the simple vowels.)

Overcrowding appears to have resulted in diphthongization in many languages, including Old High German and Spanish.

Table 7.26 Diphthongization in Old High German and Spanish

Old High German diphthongization			Spanish diphthongization		
i:		u:	i		u
	ia	ua	e	je we	o
e: ↗		↖ o:	ɛ ↗	↖ ɔ	
ɛ:		ɔ:		a	
	a:				

Old High German			Latin	Spanish	
Earlier	Later				
hēr	hiar	'here'	petra	piedra	'stone'
flōt	fluat	'flood'	mortem	muerte	'death'

The diphthongization in these two languages differs from that of the Great English Vowel Shift in two ways. The mid vowels and not the high vowels are affected, and different sets of diphthongs result. Nevertheless, in terms of phonological space all these cases of diphthongization achieve the same result: namely, the reduction of an overcrowded seven vowel system to a five vowel system. (Of course, the Great English Vowel Shift is further complicated by other developments.)

Sound Change and Rule Ordering

In describing language change, it is often crucial to identify the relative chronology, or times at which different changes have occurred. Three important changes in the history of English can be given as the following (somewhat simplified) rules.

1) Voicing
   C   →   [+voice] / [+voice] ___ [+voice]

2) Syncope
   V   →   Ø / ___ C #
   [−stress]

3) Assimilation
   C   →   [+voice] /   C ___
                            [+voice]

Figure 7.10 Three rules in the history of English

These changes have played an important role in the evolution of English plural forms such as *hooves* (versus *hoof*) and *wolves* (versus *wolf*). Of the possible orderings of these three rules, only one will derive the contemporary pronunciation from the earlier (Old English) phonemic form. Two of the possible orderings are as follows.

Table 7.27 Rule ordering in the history of English

Hypothesis A	
Original phonemic form	wulfas
Voicing	wulvas
Syncope	wulvs
Assimilation	wulvz

Hypothesis B	
Original phonemic form	wulfas
Voicing	wulvas
Assimilation	(cannot apply)
Syncope	wulvs (incorrect)

If we assume hypothesis A with the ordering voicing, syncope, and assimilation, we can account for the [vz] in the modern pronunciation of a word such as *wolves*. By contrast, the ordering proposed in hypothesis B would not account for the present pronunciation.

7.3 MORPHOLOGICAL CHANGE

In this section we discuss morphological changes resulting from analogy and reanalysis as well as changes involving the addition or loss of affixes.

Addition of Affixes

Borrowing has been a very important source of new affixes in English. During the Middle English period, many French words containing the suffix *-ment* (for example, *accomplishment*, *commencement*) made their way into the language. Eventually, *-ment* established itself as a productive suffix in English and was used with bases that were not of French origin (for example, *acknowledge-*

ment, merriment). The ending *-able*, which converts a verb into an adjective (for example, *readable, lovable*, etc.), followed a similar pattern. Although words with this ending (for example, *favorable, conceivable*) were initially borrowed into English as whole units, eventually the suffix became productive and was used with new bases.

Not all new affixes are the result of borrowing. Words themselves can develop into affixes in a process called **fusion**. If two words are frequently adjacent, over time they can become fused together to form a single unit consisting of a stem and an affix. Fusion can result in either prefixes or suffixes.

Table 7.28 Fusion

word word	>	stem + affix (suffixation)
word word	>	affix + stem (prefixation)

A number of Modern English suffixes are derived from earlier words by means of fusion.

Table 7.29 English suffixes resulting from fusion

Suffix	Old English word	
-hood (childhood)	hād	'state, condition, rank'
-dom (freedom)	dōm	'condition, power'
-ly (fatherly)	(ge-)līc	'similar, equal, like'

Another case of fusion is the development of the future tense affixes in Italian which are derived from various forms of the Latin word *habere* 'to have'.

Table 7.30 Fusion resulting in a future tense affix in Italian

Latin	Italian	
amāre + habē<u>o</u>	amer<u>ò</u>	'I will love'
amāre + hab<u>ē</u>mus	amer<u>emo</u>	'we will love'

Loss of Affixes

Just as affixes can be added to the grammar, they can also be lost. Sometimes affixes simply fall into disuse for no apparent reason. For example, a number of Old English derivational affixes, including *-bǣre* and *-bora*, are no longer used.

Table 7.31 Affixes no longer found in English

N + bǣre	>	A	*lustbǣre*	'pleasant, agreeable' from *lust* 'pleasure'	
N + bora	>	N	*mundbora*	'protector' from *mund* 'protection'	

It is also very common for affixes to be lost through sound change. For example, Old English had a complex system of affixes marking case and gender. Nouns were divided into three gender classes—masculine, neuter, and feminine. Assignment to a class was not based on sex (natural gender) but on grammatical gender; for example, the word for *stone* (Old English *stān*) and even a word for *woman* (*wīfmann*) were masculine, the word for *sun* (*sunne*) was feminine, and another word for *woman* (*wīf*) was neuter. Each gender class was associated with a different set of case endings.

The following Old English sentence contains all four case categories.

2. Se cniht   geaf gief-e þæs hierd-es   sun-e
the youth-Nom gave gift-Acc the shepherd-Gen son-Dat
'The youth gave a gift to the shepherd's son.'

Table 7.32 Old English case affixes

	Masculine	Neuter	Feminine
Singular			
	hund 'dog'	dēor 'animal'	gief 'gift'
Nominative	hund	dēor	gief-u
Accusative	hund	dēor	gief-e
Genitive	hund-es	dēor-es	gief-e
Dative	hund-e	dēor-e	gief-e
Plural			
Nominative	hund-as	dēor	gief-a
Accusative	hund-as	dēor	gief-a
Genitive	hund-a	dēor-a	gief-a
Dative	hund-um	dēor-um	gief-um

By the fifteenth century, English case endings had changed radically. Consonant deletion resulted in the loss of the earlier [m] of the dative plural suffix and through vowel reduction all the unstressed vowels of the case endings were reduced to the central vowel [ə] (which was later lost through vowel deletion). Consequently, many of the earlier case and gender distinctions were obliterated. (The following examples also include changes to the stem-internal vowels as the result of various processes, including the Great English Vowel Shift.)

Table 7.33 The loss of case affixes through sound change (in English *hound*)

	Old English	Middle English (e = [ə])	Modern English
Singular			
Nominative	hund	hund	hound
Accusative	hund	hund	hound
Genitive	hund-es	hund-(e)s	hound's
Dative	hund-e	hund-(e)	hound
Plural			
Nominative	hund-as	hund-(e)s	hounds
Accusative	hund-as	hund-(e)s	hounds
Genitive	hund-a	hund-(e)	hounds'
Dative	hund-um	hund-(e)	hounds

Whereas Old English had five distinct affixes for cases, Middle English had only two suffixes, *-e* and *-es* which, with the loss of schwa, were ultimately reduced to a single suffix *-s*, still used in Modern English for the plural and the possessive. This represents a typical example of how sound change can result in modification to the morphological component of the grammar.

From Synthetic to Analytic to Synthetic

Since languages vary greatly in the complexity of their morphology, linguists often make a distinction between analytic and synthetic languages (see Chapter 8). Whereas analytic languages have very few affixes (for example, Modern English), synthetic languages have many (for example, Latin, Old English).

Even in the absence of borrowing, sound change and fusion ensure that there is an endless transition in the morphology of a language over time. As we have seen, due to the loss of case endings through sound change English has developed from a synthetic language with many inflectional affixes to an analytic one with very few, as the above discussion of nouns such as *hound* indicates.

By contrast, fusion ensures the rise of new synthetic forms. Fusion can be observed in some Modern English dialects in forms such as *coulda* (for example, *I coulda won*) which represents the fusion of *could* and *have*. For many speakers, the *-a* is treated as a suffix that is no longer related to *have*, as evident in spellings such as *could of* which result from confusion over how to represent the pronunciation of *coulda* in written English. Through fusion, a language with an analytic morphology can become much more synthetic over time.

Analogy

The drastic effects that sound change can have on the morphology of a language are often alleviated through analogy. For example, the plural of Old English *hand* 'hand' was *handa*. Vowel reduction and apocope applying to *handa* would have yielded a Modern English plural form identical to the singular form, namely *hand*.

Table 7.34 Sound changes applied to Old English *handa* 'hands'

handa	
handə	vowel reduction
hand	apocope

Obviously, then, the Modern English plural *hands* cannot be the direct consequence of sound change. Rather, it is the result of earlier analogy with words such as Middle English *hund* 'hound' (see Table 7.33) which did form the plural with the suffix *-s*. This suffix, whose earlier form *-as* was predominant even in Old English, was extended by analogy to all English nouns with a few exceptions (*oxen*, *men*, *geese*, etc.). Other plural forms besides *hands* that were created on the basis of analogy include *eyes* (*eyen* in Middle English) and *shoes* (formerly *shooen*).

Continuing analogy along these lines is responsible for the development of the plural form *youse* (from *you*) in some English dialects. Each generation of English-speaking children temporarily extends the analogy still further by producing forms such as *sheeps*, *gooses*, and *mouses*. To date, however, these particular innovations have not been accepted by adult speakers of Standard English and are eventually abandoned by young language learners.

Reanalysis

As mentioned in Section 1, reanalysis can result in a new morphological structure for a word. It can affect both borrowed words and, particularly in cases where the morphological structure of the word is no longer transparent, native words. Reanalysis can result in new productive patterns, as in the case of *(-)burger*, or it can remain quite isolated, affecting perhaps only one word. Since the type of reanalysis exemplified by *hamburger* is not based on a correct analysis of a word (at least from a historical perspective) and does not usually involve a conscious or detailed study of the word on the part of the speaker, it is often called **folk etymology**.

Although in the case of *hamburger*, the only evidence of folk etymology is the productive uses of *(-)burger* (for example, as an independent word and in compounds of the type *fishburger*), folk etymology commonly involves changes in pronunciation reflecting the new morphological analysis. For example, our word *earwig* derives from Old English *ēarwicga* [ǽərwidʒa], a compound consisting of 'ear' and 'insect'. Taking into consideration sound change alone, the expected Modern English pronunciation of this word would be *earwidge* [irwɪdʒ]. However, the second part of the compound was lost as an independent word by Middle English, so speakers could no longer associate it with the meaning of 'insect'. Subsequently, reanalysis related the second part of the compound to the verb 'wiggle' resulting in Middle English *arwygyll* (literally 'ear + wiggle'). The end result is Modern English *-wig* and not *-widge*. More examples of folk etymology are found in the following table.

Table 7.35 Folk etymology in English (native words and borrowings)

Modern word	Source
belfry	Middle English *berfrey* 'bell tower' (unrelated to *bell*)
bridegroom	Middle English *bridegome* (unrelated to *groom*) (compare Old English *brȳd* 'bride' and *guma* 'man')
muskrat	Algonquian *musquash* (unrelated to either *musk* or *rat*)
woodchuck	Algonquian *otchek* (unrelated to either *wood* or *chuck*)

Although reanalysis of individual words is common, affixes can also be affected, sometimes with new productive morphological rules developing as a result. This is the case of the Modern English adverbial suffix *-ly* (developing from Old English *-lic(e)*). In Old English, adjectives could be derived from nouns by adding the suffix *-lic*. Adverbs, in turn, could be derived by adding the suffix *-e* to adjectives (including those derived with *-lic*).

Table 7.36 The derivation of Old English adjectives and adverbs

Formation of an adjective from a noun				
[dæg]$_N$	+ lic	→	[dæglic]$_A$	'daily' (as in 'daily schedule')
Formation of an adverb from an adjective				
[dēop]$_A$	+ e	→	[dēope]$_{Adv}$	'deeply'
Formation of an adverb from a derived adjective with -lic				
[dæg + lic]$_A$	+ e	→	[dæglice]$_{Adv}$	'daily' (as in 'she ran daily')

At some point, the entire complex suffix *-lic + e* was reanalysed as an adverbial suffix (rather than as an adjectival suffix *-lic* plus an adverbial suffix *-e*). It was then used by analogy to derive adverbs from adjectives in forms where it was not used before, resulting in Modern English *deeply* and other such words.

7.4 SYNTACTIC CHANGE

Like other components of the grammar, syntax is also subject to change over time. Syntactic changes can involve modifications to phrase structure rules or transformations, as the following examples illustrate.

Word Order

All languages make a distinction between the subject and direct object. This contrast is typically represented through case marking or word order. Since Old English had an extensive system of case marking, it is not surprising that its word order was somewhat more variable than that of Modern English. The most common word order in unembedded clauses was subject-verb-object (SVO).

3. S   V   O
    Hē   geseah   Þone mann.
    'He   saw   the   man.'

However, when the clause began with an element such as *Þa* 'then' or *ne* 'not', the verb occurred in second position and preceded the subject.

4.   V   S   O
    Þa   sende   sē cyning   Þone disc
    then sent   the king   the   dish
    'Then the king sent the dish.'

Although this word order is still found in Modern English, its use is very limited and subject to special restrictions, unlike the situation in Old English.

5.   V   S   O
    Rarely has   he ever deceived   me.

When the direct object was a pronoun, the subject-object-verb order was typical.

6. S   O   V
    Hēo hine   lǣrde.
    She him   advised
    'She advised him.'

The subject-object-verb order also prevailed in embedded clauses, even when the direct object was not a pronoun.

7.   S   O   V
    Þa   hē   Þone cyning   sōhte,   hē bēotode.
    when he   the king   visited, he boasted
    'When he visited the king, he boasted.'

Since case markings were lost during the Middle English period through sound change, fixed subject-verb-object order became the means of marking grammatical relations. As Table 7.37 shows, a major change in word order took place between 1300 and 1400, with the verb-object order becoming dominant.

Table 7.37 Word order patterns in Middle English

Year (A.D.)	1000	1200	1300	1400	1500
Direct object before the verb (%)	53	53	40	14	2
Direct object after the verb (%)	47	47	60	86	98

From SOV to SVO Just as languages can be classified in terms of their morphology, they can also be grouped on the basis of the relative order of subject

(S), object (O), and verb (V) in basic sentences. Almost all languages of the world fall into one of three types: SOV, SVO, or VSO, with the majority being one of the first two types. Just as languages change through time from one morphological type to another, they can also change from one syntactic type to another. A case in point is found in the history of English, which shows the development from SOV to SVO syntax.

Evidence indicates that the earliest form of Germanic (from which English descended), was an SOV language. One of the earliest recorded Germanic sentences, for example, has this word order. The sentence in *8* was inscribed on a golden horn (now called the Golden Horn of Gallehus) about sixteen hundred years ago.

8. Horn of Gallehus

	S		O	V
	ek HlewagastiR	HoltijaR	horna	tawido
	I Hlewagastir	of Holt	horn	made

'I, Hlewagastir of Holt, made the horn.'

Another type of evidence for an earlier SOV order is found in morphological fusion (see Section 3). Since fusion depends on frequently occurring syntactic patterns, it can sometimes serve as an indicator of earlier syntax. The OV compound, very common in Old English (as well as in Modern English), likely reflects an earlier stage of OV word order.

Table 7.38 Old English compounds with OV structure

manslæht	'man' + 'strike'	'manslaughter, murder'
æppelbære	'apple' + 'bear'	'apple-bearing'

If the earliest Germanic was SOV and Modern English is firmly SVO, then Old English represents a transitional syntactic type. In developing from SOV to SVO syntax, languages seem to follow similar pathways. For example, Modern German, which developed from the same Germanic SOV source as English, shares two of Old English's distinguishing characteristics. First, the verb is typically placed in the second position of the sentence in main clauses, preceded by the subject or some other element (such as an adverb). Secondly, the SOV order is employed for embedded clauses.

9. Modern German word order
   a) Verb in second position in unembedded clauses:
   (Compare the Old English sentence in *4*.)

	V	S	O
Gestern	hatte	ich	keine Zeit.
yesterday	had	I	no time

   'I had no time yesterday'
   b) SOV in embedded clauses:
   (Compare the Old English sentence in *7*.)

	S	O	V
Als	er	den Mann	sah . . .
when	he	the man	saw

   'When he saw the man . . .'

The change from SOV to SVO is not restricted to English and other Germanic languages. The same change is evident, for example, in completely unrelated languages such as those of the Bantu family of Africa. Since linguists are still not sure why languages change from one syntactic type to another, the causes of such change will undoubtedly remain an important area of investigation, especially since the relative order of verb and object (OV versus VO) has been closely linked with other word order patterns (see Chapter 8).

Inversion in the History of English

In Old and Middle English the Inversion transformation (see Chapter 5) involved in the formation of *yes-no* questions could apply to all verbs, not just auxiliaries, yielding forms that would be unacceptable in Modern English.

> *10.* Speak they the truth?

During the sixteenth and seventeenth centuries, the Inversion rule was changed to apply solely to auxiliary verbs.

> *11.* Inversion (old form):
> The V moves to the left of the subject.
> They speak→Speak they?
> They can speak→Can they speak?
>
> Inversion (new form):
> The Aux moves to the left of subject.
> They speak→*Speak they?
> They can speak→Can they speak?

With this change, structures such as *Speak they the truth?* were no longer possible. The corresponding question came to be formed with the auxiliary *do* as in *Do they speak the truth?*

7.5 LEXICAL AND SEMANTIC CHANGE

Another obvious type of language change involves modifications to the lexicon. Since we have already dealt with some changes relating to derivational and inflectional morphology in Section 3, the main focus here will be on lexical change involving entire words. Simply stated, there are two possible types of lexical change, addition and loss. The addition or loss of words often reflects cultural changes that introduce novel objects and notions and eliminate outmoded ones.

Addition of Lexical Items

Addition is frequently the result of technological innovations or contact with other cultures. Such developments result in **lexical gaps** which can be filled by adding new words to the lexicon. New words are added either through the word formation processes available to the language or through borrowing.

Word Formation Compounding and derivation have always been available to English speakers for the creation of new words. In fact, much of the compounding and derivation in Old English seems very familiar.

Table 7.39 Compounding and derivation in Old English

Noun compounds

| N + N | sunbēam | 'sunbeam' |
| A + N | middelniht | 'midnight' |

Adjective compounds

| N + A | blōdrēad | 'bloodred' |
| A + A | dēadboren | 'stillborn' |

Derived nouns

| [bæc]$_V$ + ere | → | bæcere | 'baker' |
| [frēond]$_N$ + scip | → | frēondscipe | 'friendship' |

Derived adjectives

| [wundor]$_N$ + full | → | wundorfull | 'wonderful' |
| [cild]$_N$ + isc | → | cildisc | 'childish' |

Just as speakers of Modern English can use compounding and derivation to create new words (for example, the N + N compound *airhead*), so could Old English speakers create new words such as the poetic N + N compound *hwœlweg*, literally 'whale' + 'path' to mean 'sea'.

Note, however, that even though many Old English compounding and derivational rules have been maintained in Modern English, words which were acceptable in Old English are not necessarily still in use in Modern English, even though many of them are quite understandable.

Table 7.40 Old English compound and derived forms no longer used

Noun compounds

| N + N | bōccræft ('book' + 'craft') | 'literature' (compare *witchcraft*) |
| A + N | dimhūs ('dim' + 'house') | 'prison' |

Adjective compounds

| N + A | ælfscīene ('elf' + 'beautiful') | 'beautiful as a fairy' |
| A + A | eallgōd ('all' + 'good') | 'perfectly good' |

Derived nouns

| [sēam]$_V$ + ere | → | sēamere | 'tailor' (compare *seamster*, *seamstress*) |
| [man]$_N$ + scipe | → | manscipe | 'humanity' (compare *friendship*) |

Derived adjectives

| [word]$_N$ + full | → | wordfull | 'wordy' (compare *wonderful*) |
| [heofon]$_N$ + isc | → | heofonisc | 'heavenly' (compare *childish*) |

However, not all word formation processes available to Modern English speakers were also found in Old English. For example, conversion (as in Modern English [summer]$_N$→[summer]$_V$) was not possible in Old English. In fact, conversion is typically not available to (synthetic) inflectional languages such as Old English since change in a word category in such languages is usually indicated morphologically and conversion, by definition, does not involve the use of affixes.

Borrowing As discussed in Section 1, language contact over time can result in an important source of new words, borrowing. Depending on the cultural relationship holding between languages, three types of influence of one language on the other are traditionally identified: **substratum**, **adstratum**, and **superstratum**.

Substratum influence is the effect of a politically or culturally non-dominant language on a dominant language in the area. Both North American English and Canadian French, for instance, have borrowed vocabulary items from Amerindian languages (see examples in Section 1). From a much earlier period in the history of English, the influence of a Celtic substratum is also evident, particularly in place names such as *Thames*, *London*, and *Dover*. Substratum influence does not usually have a major impact on the lexicon of the borrowing language. Borrowed words are usually restricted to place names and unfamiliar items or concepts. This situation reflects the fact that it is usually the speakers of the substratum language who inhabited the area first.

Superstratum influence is the effect of a politically or culturally dominant language on another language or languages in the area. For example, the Athapaskan language Gwich'in (Loucheux) (spoken in Canada's Northwest Territories), has borrowed a number of governmental terms and expressions from English, including *bureaucratic*, *constituents*, *program*, *business*, *development*, and *political*.

In the case of English, Norman-French had a superstratum influence. The major impact of French on the vocabulary of English is related to a historical event—the conquest of England by French-speaking Normans in 1066. As the conquerors and their descendants gradually learned English over the next decades, they retained French terms for political, judicial, and cultural notions. These words were in turn borrowed by native English speakers who, in trying to gain a place in the upper-middle class, were eager to imitate the speech of their social superiors. Not surprisingly, borrowing was especially heavy in the vocabulary areas pertaining to officialdom: government, the judiciary, and religion. Other areas of heavy borrowing include science, culture, and warfare.

Table 7.41 Some French loanwords in English

Government	tax, revenue, government, royal, state, parliament, authority, prince, duke, slave, peasant
Religion	prayer, sermon, religion, chaplain, friar
Judiciary	judge, defendant, jury, evidence, jail, verdict, crime
Science	medicine, physician
Culture	art, sculpture, fashion, satin, fur, ruby
Warfare	army, navy, battle, soldier, enemy, captain

In some cases, French loanwords were used in conjunction with native English words to convey distinctions of various sorts. For a minor crime, for example, the English word *theft* was employed, but for a more serious breach of the law the French word *larceny* was used. The English also kept their own words for domesticated animals, but adopted the French words for the meat from those creatures.

Table 7.42 French loanwords used in conjunction with native English words

English origin	French origin
cow	beef
calf	veal
sheep	mutton
pig	pork

Adstratum influence refers to the situation where two languages are in contact and neither one is clearly politically or culturally dominant. In a city such as Montreal with its large number of bilingual speakers, English and French inevitably influence each other.

Table 7.43 French influence on Montreal English

Montreal English	
subvention	'subsidy'
metro	'subway'
autoroute	'highway'

Earlier in the history of English, when the Scandinavians settled part of England beginning in 800 A.D., there was substantial contact between the speakers of English and Scandinavian resulting in an adstratum relationship. As evident in the examples in Tables 7.43 and 7.44, adstratum contact usually results in the borrowing of everyday words. In fact, without consulting a dictionary, most English speakers could not distinguish between borrowings from Scandinavian and native English words.

Table 7.44 Some loanwords from Scandinavian

anger, cake, call, egg, fellow, gear, get, hit, husband, low, lump, raise, root, score, seat, skill, skin, take, their, they, thrust, ugly, window, wing

Borrowed words from many other languages attest to various types of cultural contact and serve often to fill the lexical gaps such contact inevitably brings.

Table 7.45 Some lexical borrowings into English

Italian	motto, artichoke, balcony, casino, mafia, malaria
Spanish	comrade, tornado, cannibal, mosquito, banana, guitar, vigilante, marijuana
German	poodle, kindergarten, seminar, noodle, pretzel
Dutch	sloop, cole slaw, smuggle, gin, cookie, boom
Slavic languages	czar, tundra, polka, intelligentsia, robot
Amerindian languages	toboggan, opossum, wigwam, chipmunk, Ottawa, Toronto
Hindi	cummerbund, thug, punch, shampoo, chintz

Although borrowing has been a very rich source of new words in English, it is noteworthy that the most frequently used vocabulary items have been the least susceptible to replacement by loanwords. This reflects a general tendency for highly frequent words to be relatively resistant to loss or substitution.

Table 7.46 Origin of the 5000 most frequent words in English

Degree of frequency	Source language (%)			
	English	French	Latin	Other
First 1000	83	11	2	4
Second 1000	34	46	11	9
Third 1000	29	46	14	11
Fourth 1000	27	45	17	11
Fifth 1000	27	47	17	9

Loss of Lexical Items

Just as words can be added to the lexicon, they can also be lost. Loss of a word frequently occurs as a result of changes in society, particularly in the case where the object or notion a word refers to has become obsolete.

Table 7.47 Some Old English words lost through cultural change

dolgbōt	'compensation for wounding'
Þeox	'hunting spear'
eafor	'tenant obligation to the king to convey goods'
flȳtme	'a blood letting instrument'

Semantic Change

Although changes in word meaning take place continually in all languages, words rarely jump from one meaning to an unrelated one. Typically, the changes are step by step and involve one of the following phenomena.

Semantic broadening is the process in which the meaning of a word becomes more general or more inclusive than its historically earlier form.

Table 7.48 Semantic broadening

Word	Old meaning	New meaning
bird	'small fowl'	'any avian'
barn	'place to store barley'	'any agricultural building'
aunt	'father's sister'	'father or mother's sister'

Semantic narrowing is the process in which the meaning of a word becomes less general or less inclusive than its historically earlier meaning.

Table 7.49 Semantic narrowing

Word	Old meaning	New meaning
hound	'any dog'	'a hunting breed'
meat	'any type of food'	'flesh of an animal'
fowl	'any bird'	'a domesticated bird'
disease	'any unfavorable state'	'an illness'

In **amelioration** the meaning of a word becomes more positive or favourable. The opposite change, **pejoration**, also occurs.

Table 7.50 Amelioration

Word	Old meaning	New meaning
pretty	'tricky, sly, cunning'	'attractive'
knight	'boy'	'a man of honorable military rank'

Table 7.51 Pejoration

Word	Old meaning	New meaning
silly	'happy, prosperous'	'foolish'
wench	'girl'	'wanton woman, prostitute'

Given the propensity of human beings to exaggerate, it is not surprising that the **weakening** of meaning frequently occurs. For example, our word *soon* used to mean 'immediately' but now simply means 'in the near future'. Other examples include the following.

Table 7.52 Weakening

Word	Old meaning	New meaning
wreak	'avenge, punish'	'to cause, inflict'
quell	'kill, murder'	'to put down, pacify'

Semantic shift is a process in which a word loses its former meaning taking on a new, but often related, meaning.

Table 7.53 Semantic shift

Word	Old meaning	New meaning
immoral	'not customary'	'unethical'
bead	'prayer'	'prayer bead, bead'

Sometimes a series of semantic shifts occurs over an extended period of time, resulting in a meaning which is completely unrelated to the original sense of a word. The word *hearse*, for example, originally referred to a triangular harrow. Later, it denoted a triangular frame for church candles and later still was used to refer to the device which held candles over a coffin. In a subsequent shift it came to refer to the framework on which curtains were hung over a coffin or tomb. Still later, *hearse* was used to refer to the coffin itself before finally taking on its current sense of the vehicle used to transport a coffin.

One of the most striking types of semantic change is triggered by **metaphor**, a figure of speech based on a perceived similarity between distinct objects or actions. (See Chapter 6 for a discussion of metaphor.) Metaphorical change usually involves a word with a concrete meaning taking on a more abstract sense, although the word's original meaning is not lost. The meanings of many English words have been extended through metaphor.

Table 7.54 Some examples of metaphor in English

Word	Metaphorical meaning	Word	Metaphorical meaning
grasp	'understand'	down	'depressed'
yarn	'story'	sharp	'smart'
high	'on drugs'	dull	'stupid'

7.6 THE SPREAD OF CHANGE

Up to this point, we have been concerned with the causes and description of linguistic change. Still to be dealt with is the question of how linguistic innovations spread. This section focuses on two types of spread, one involving the way in which an innovation is extended through the vocabulary of a language and the other the way in which it spreads through the population.

Diffusion through the Language

Some linguistic change first manifests itself in a few words and then gradually spreads through the vocabulary of the language. This type of change is called **lexical diffusion**. A well-attested example in English involves an ongoing change in the stress pattern of words such as *convert*, which can be used as either a noun or a verb. Although the stress originally fell on the second syllable regardless of lexical category, in the latter half of the sixteenth century three such words, *rebel*, *outlaw*, and *record*, came to be pronounced with the stress on the first syllable when used as nouns. As Figure 7.11 illustrates, this stress shift was extended to an increasing number of words over the next decades.

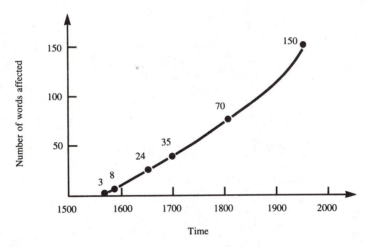

Figure 7.11 Diffusion of stress shift in English

This change has still not diffused through the entire vocabulary of English. There are about a thousand nouns of the relevant sort which still place the stress on the second syllable (for example, *report*, *mistake*, and *support*). The following table illustrates the spread of this change to date.

Table 7.55 Stress shift in English (nouns)

Before the 16th century	During the 16th century	During the 18th century	Today
rebél	rébel	rébel	rébel
affíx	affíx	áffix	áffix
recéss	recéss	recéss	récess
mistáke	mistáke	mistáke	mistáke

This ongoing change can be observed in progress today. The noun *address*, for example, is pronounced by many people with stress on the first syllable as [ǽdrɛs], although the older pronunciation [ədrés] is still heard. Some speakers alternate between the two. This change may continue to work its way through the language until all nouns in the class we have been considering are stressed on the first syllable.

The changes discussed in the section on analogy also spread word by word. For example, the transition of strong (irregular) verbs (the *sing/sang/ sung* type) to the weak verb class (regular verbs with past tense *-ed*) is an ongoing change. Both strong and weak past tense forms of original strong verbs such as *dive* and *shine* are heard in current English: *dove/dived* and *shone/shined*.

However, not all linguistic change involves gradual diffusion through the vocabulary of a language. Sound changes typically affect all instances of the segment(s) involved. For example, in some Caribbean dialects of Spanish the consonant weakening of [s] to [h] in syllable-final position affects all instances of word-internal *s* in all words. The relevant rule can be stated as follows.

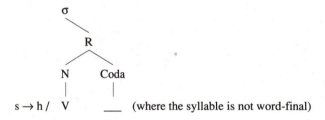

Figure 7.12 Consonant weakening of [s] to [h] in certain Spanish dialects

This rule has resulted in changes such as those exemplified in Table 7.56.

Table 7.56 The effects of the [s] to [h] change in some Spanish dialects

Standard pronunciation	New pronunciation	
[felismente]	[felihmente]	'happily'
[estilo]	[ehtilo]	'type'
[españa]	[ehpaña]	'Spain'

This change is entirely regular, affecting all instances of a word-internal syllable-final [s] in the speech of individuals who adopt it.

Accordingly, two types of language change can be identified. One, exemplified by the stress shifts in bisyllabic English nouns of the type we have discussed, affects individual words one at a time and gradually spreads through the vocabulary of the language. The other, exemplified by the consonant weakening of syllable-final [s] to [h] in some dialects of Spanish, involves an across the board change that applies without exception to all words.

Spread through the Population

For a language change to take place, the particular innovation must be accepted by the linguistic community as a whole. For example, although as mentioned, children acquiring English typically form the past tense of *go* as *goed* instead of *went*, *goed* has never received widespread acceptance. Doubtless the verb form in *he throve on fame* would be equally unacceptable to most speakers today. In earlier English, however, *throve* was the past tense form of *thrive* (compare *drive/drove*). At some point in the past, then, the novel form *thrived* did receive general acceptance.

Just as change sometimes begins with a small number of words, effects of a change often appear first in the speech of a small number of people. Social pressures play an important role in determining whether a particular innovation will spread through the entire linguistic community. Since speakers can consciously or unconsciously alter the way they speak to approximate what they perceive to be a more prestigious or socially acceptable variety of speech, once a change has taken hold in the speech of a high prestige group it may gradually spread to other speakers and ultimately affect the entire linguistic community.

There have been numerous examples of this in the history of English, notably the loss of postvocalic [r] along the east coast of the United States. This change, which resulted in an 'r-less' pronunciation of words such as *far* as [fɑ:], originated in parts of England in the seventeenth and eighteenth centuries. At that time, postvocalic [r] was still pronounced throughout English-speaking settlements in North America. Two factors accounted for its loss in parts of this continent. First, the children of the New England gentry picked up the new pronunciation in British schools and subsequently brought it back to the colony. Second, the speech of newly arrived immigrants, including colonial administrators and church officials who enjoyed high social status in the colony, typically lacked the postvocalic [r]. As a result, the innovation was widely imitated and ultimately spread along much of the east coast and into the south.

Social pressures were also involved in limiting the spread of this innovation. It did not penetrate Pennsylvania or the other Midland states since the most prestigious group of settlers there were Quakers from northern England, an area which retained the postvocalic [r]. More recently the 'r-less' pronunciation has become stigmatized, even in areas where it was previously firmly entrenched, and we now see a trend to restoration of [r] in environments where it had been deleted.

7.7 LANGUAGE RECONSTRUCTION

When we compare the vocabulary items of various languages, we cannot help but notice the strong resemblance certain words bear to each other. By systematically comparing languages, we can establish whether two or more languages descended from a common parent and are therefore **genetically related** (see Chapter 8). It is also possible through such **comparative reconstruction** to reconstruct properties of the parent language with some degree of certainty.

Comparative Reconstruction

The most reliable sign of family relationships is the existence of **systematic phonetic correspondences** in the vocabulary items of different languages. Many such correspondences can be found in the following sample of vocabulary items from English, Dutch, German, Danish, and Swedish, all of which are members of the Germanic family of languages.

Table 7.57 Some Germanic cognates

English	Dutch	German	Danish	Swedish
man	man	Mann	mand	man
hand	hand	Hand	hånd	hand
foot	voet	Fuß (β = [s])	fod	fot
bring	brengen	bringen	bringe	bringa
summer	zomer	Sommer	sommer	sommar

Since the relationship between the phonological form and meaning of a word is mostly arbitrary, the existence of systematic phonetic correspondences in the forms of two or more languages must point toward a common source. Conversely, where languages are not related, their vocabulary items fail to show systematic similarities. This can be seen by comparing words from Turkish, which is not related to the Germanic languages, with their counterparts in the languages cited in Table 7.58.

Table 7.58 Some words in Turkish, a non-Germanic language

adam	'man'
el	'hand'
ajak	'foot'
getir	'bring'
jaz	'summer'

Words that have descended from a common source (as shown by systematic phonetic correspondences and, usually, semantic similarities) are called **cognates**. Cognates are not always as obvious as the Germanic examples in Table 7.57. Where languages from the same family are only distantly related, the systematic correspondences may be considerably less striking. This is exemplified in the following data from English, Russian, and Hindi, all of which are distantly related to each other. Forms from the unrelated Turkish are included to emphasize the similarities among the first three languages.

Table 7.59 Some distantly related cognates compared to non-related Turkish

English	Russian	Hindi	Turkish
two	dva	dō	iki
three	tri	tīn	ytʃ
brother	brat	bhāji	kardeʃ
nose	nos	nāk	burun

Once the existence of a relationship between two or more languages has been established, an attempt can be made to reconstruct the common source. This reconstructed language, or **proto-language**, is made up of **proto-forms**, which are written with a preceding * (for example, *hand*) to indicate their hypothetical character as reconstructions of earlier forms that have not been recorded or are not directly observable.

Techniques of Reconstruction

Reconstruction can be undertaken with some confidence because (as discussed in the previous sections) the processes underlying language change are systematic. Once the processes are uncovered by linguists, they can be reversed, allowing us to infer earlier forms of the language. Although it is possible to reconstruct all components of a proto-language (its phonology, morphology, syntax, lexicon, and semantics), we will focus in the following on phonological reconstruction, the area in which linguists have made the most progress.

Reconstruction Strategies Reconstruction of a proto-form makes use of two general strategies. The most important one is the **phonetic plausibility strategy**, which requires that any changes posited to account for differences between the proto-forms and later forms must be phonetically plausible. Secondarily, the **majority rules strategy** stipulates that if no phonetically plausible change can account for the observed differences, then the segment found in the majority of cognates should be assumed. It is important to note that the first strategy always takes precedence over the second; the second strategy is a last resort.

Consider the following cognates (somewhat simplified) from members of the Muskogean family (Amerindian).

Table 7.60 Muskogean cognates

Choctaw	Koasati	Hitchiti	Creek	
haʃi	ha:si	ha:si	hasi	'sun'

The data exemplify a correspondence between [s] and [ʃ] before the vowel [i]. To account for this, we could assume either that Choctaw underwent a change that converted [s] to [ʃ] before [i] or that the other three languages underwent a change converting [ʃ] to [s] before [i].

Hypothesis A
Proto-form for 'sun':   *hasi
Sound change (Choctaw only):   *s > ʃ/___i

Hypothesis B
Proto-form for 'sun':   *haʃi
Sound change (Koasati, Hitchiti, and Creek):   *ʃ > s/___i

Figure 7.13 Muskogean cognates

Both reconstruction strategies favor hypothesis A. Most importantly, the phonetic change needed to account for the Choctaw form involves palatalization before [i]. Since palatalization in this context is a very common phenomenon in human language, it is reasonable to assume that it occurred in Choctaw. It would be much more difficult to argue that the proto-language contained [ʃ] before [i] and that three languages underwent the change posited by hypothesis B since depalatalization before [i] would be an unusual phonetic process. (The reconstructed *s posited in hypothesis A is also compatible with the majority rules strategy since three of the four languages in the data have [s] before [i].)

Reconstruction and the Catalogue of Sound Changes Although there are factors that can confound our attempt to determine the relative plausibility of various sound changes, the changes listed in the catalogue in Table 7.3 can generally be considered highly plausible. The following table lists some plausible versus less plausible or even implausible changes based on that catalogue.

Table 7.61 Different rules in terms of their plausibility based on catalogue of sound changes

Rule	Name of sound change in catalogue
High probability	
t>tʃ/___i	palatalization/affrication
n>m/___b	assimilation (place of articulation)
t>d/V___V	voicing
k>ø/V___st	consonant deletion
Low probability	
tʃ>t/___i	(does not correspond to any listed change)
m>n/___b	(does not correspond to any listed change)
d>t/V___V	(does not correspond to any listed change)
ø>k/V___st	(does not correspond to any listed change)

Reconstructing Proto-Romance Consider now a slightly more complex example involving data from several languages of the Romance family.

Table 7.62 Some Romance cognates

Spanish	Sardinian	French	Portuguese	Rumanian	Original meaning
riba [β]	ripa	rive [ʁiv]	riba	rîpă	'embankment'
amiga [ɣ]	amica	amie [ami]	amiga	—	'female friend'
copa	cuppa	coupe [kup]	copa	cupă	'cup, goblet'
gota	gutta	goutte [gut]	gôta	gută	'drop'

(*Note*: Orthographic *c* represents [k] in all the above examples and Rumanian ă represents [ə]. [β] is a voiced bilabial fricative and [ɣ] a voiced velar fricative. Some details of vowel quality have been ignored.)

Our goal here is to reconstruct the proto-forms for these words in Proto-Romance, the parent language of the Modern Romance languages, which stands very close to Latin.

Let us first consider the reconstruction of the Proto-Romance form for 'embankment'. Since the first two segments are the same in all the cognate languages, we can reconstruct Proto-Romance *r and *i on the basis of the majority rules strategy. In the case of the second consonant, however, there are differences between the cognates.

Table 7.63 Systematic correspondences in the second consonant of the cognates for 'embankment'

Spanish	Sardinian	French	Portuguese	Rumanian
-β-	-p-	-v	-b-	-p-

It is most important that we first think in terms of phonetic plausibility. In the absence of evidence to the contrary, we will assume that one of the segments found in the cognates ([p], [b], [v], or [β]) should be reconstructed for Proto-Romance. Logically possible changes ranked with respect to their phonetic plausibility are found in the following table.

Table 7.64 Changes based on phonetic plausibility

Change in V___V	Name of change based on catalogue	Phonetic plausibility
p > b	voicing	high
p > v	voicing (p > b) and frication (b > v)	high
p > β	voicing (p > b) and frication (b > β)	high
b > p	—	low
β > p	—	low
v > p	—	low

In terms of plausibility, the only possible reconstruction for Proto-Romance is
*p. Proto-Romance *p undergoes no change in Sardinian and Rumanian, but
in Portuguese it underwent intervocalic voicing and in Spanish it underwent
both voicing and frication (that is, weakening). (We assume that voicing
preceded frication since Portuguese shows voicing but no frication.) If we
assume that the final vowel of the proto-form was still present in French when
the consonant changes took place, we can conclude that voicing and frication
occurred in this language as well. (In its written form, *rive* retains a sign of the
earlier reduced vowel [ə].) These changes are phonetically plausible and thus
expected.

Table 7.65 Summary of the changes affecting Proto-Romance *p

*p > p/V___V	no change in Sardinian or Rumanian
*p > b/V___V	voicing in Portuguese
*p > b > β/V___V	voicing and frication in Spanish
*p > b > v/V___V	voicing and frication in French

Turning now to the final vowel, we note that three languages have full
vowels, Rumanian has [ə], and French has no vowel. Since vowel reduction and
apocope are identified as phonetically plausible changes in the catalogue, it is
appropriate to posit a full vowel for the proto-language. Furthermore, since
the three languages with a full vowel all have [a], we can posit this vowel on the
basis of the majority rules strategy. Accordingly, the reconstructed proto-form
is *ripa.

Table 7.66 Summary of the changes affecting Proto-Romance *a

Language	Change (word-final)	Name of change(s)
*Rumanian	*a > ə	vowel reduction
*French	*a > ə > ø	vowel reduction and deletion

We can now outline the development of the word in French, which has the
most complicated history of the five languages.

Table 7.67 Evolution of French *rive* from *ripa

Change	*ripa	Name of change
p > b/V___V	riba	voicing
b > v/V___V	riva	frication
a > ə/___#	rivə	vowel reduction
ə > ø/___#	riv	apocope

In the case of the cognates for 'female friend' (the second row of Table 7.62), the first three segments are the same in all the languages in the data. According to the majority rules strategy, we can reconstruct the first three segments as *ami-. In the reconstruction of the second consonant, however, we must appeal to our strategy of phonetic plausibility.

Table 7.68 Systematic correspondences in the second consonant of the cognates for 'female friend'

Spanish	Sardinian	French	Portuguese	Rumanian
-ɣ-	-k-	-ø	-g-	—

Once again, since intervocalic voicing, frication, and deletion are phonetically plausible changes, it is most appropriate to posit *k for the proto-form.

Table 7.69 Summary of the changes affecting Proto-Romance *k

Language	Change (in V___V)	Name of change(s)
Portuguese	*k > g	voicing
Spanish	*k > g > ɣ	voicing and frication
French	*k > g > ɣ > ø	voicing, frication, and deletion

In the case of the final vowel, we have the same situation we had in the previous form. The full vowel is found in Spanish, Sardinian, and Portuguese, but there is no vowel in French. We can therefore assume the full vowel *a for the proto-form, with subsequent vowel reduction and apocope in French. Consequently, we arrive at the proto-form *amika.

Finally, applying the same procedure to the cognates in the final two rows of Table 7.62 yields the proto-forms *kuppa 'cup' and *gutta 'drop'. All the languages in the data retain the initial consonant of both proto-forms. The vowel *u is reconstructed on the basis of the majority rules strategy, since we have no phonetic grounds for choosing either [u] or [o] as the older vowel. The systematic correspondences involving the intervocalic consonants are given in the following table.

Table 7.70 Systematic correspondences of the medial consonants of *kuppa and *gutta

Spanish	Sardinian	French	Portuguese	Rumanian
-p-	-pp-	-p	-p-	-p-
-t-	-tt-	-t	-t-	-t-

Regardless of whether we are dealing with original *pp or *tt, the same pattern is evident in the case of both geminate types. There is a geminate stop consonant in Sardinian and a single consonant in Spanish, French, Portuguese, and Rumanian. Since degemination is an expected sound change (see the catalogue), we assume that the proto-forms contained geminate consonants which underwent degemination except in Sardinian. This is an example of a case where the phonetic plausibility strategy overrules the majority rules strategy (since four of the five languages have [p]/[t] whereas only one language has [pp]/[tt]). As far as the final vowels are concerned, the same pattern found in the previous examples is once again evident. Proto-Romance *a was retained in

Spanish, Sardinian, and Portuguese, reduced to [ə] in Rumanian, and deleted in French (see Table 7.66).

Of the languages exemplified here, Sardinian is considered the most **conservative** since its forms stand closest to those of the proto-language. (In fact, the Sardinian words in the examples happen to be identical with the proto-forms, but this degree of resemblance would not be maintained in a broader range of data.) In the case of the other Romance languages and changes we have discussed, the most to least conservative are: Portuguese (degemination, voicing) and Rumanian (degemination, vowel reduction); Spanish (degemination, voicing, frication); French (degemination, voicing, frication, consonant deletion, vowel reduction, apocope).

Although there is no reason to expect Proto-Romance to be identical with Classical Latin, close similarity is expected. Accordingly, the fact that our reconstructions are so close to the Latin words gives us confidence in our methods of reconstruction.

Table 7.71 Comparison of Latin and Proto-Romance forms

Latin	Proto-Romance form
rīpa	*ripa
amīca	*amika
cŭppa	*kuppa
gŭtta	*gutta

Notice that it is sometimes not possible to reconstruct all characteristics of the proto-language. For example, on the basis of our data we were not able to reconstruct vowel length (Latin had a distinction between long and short vowels) since there was no evidence of this characteristic in the cognate forms.

It is also worth noting that we are not always so fortunate as to have written records of a language we expect to be very close to our reconstructed language. In the case of the Germanic languages, for example, there is no ancient written language equivalent to Latin. We must rely completely on our reconstruction of Proto-Germanic to determine the properties of the language from which the modern-day Germanic languages descended. Furthermore, for many languages of the world we have no written historical records at all and for other languages, such as the Amerindian languages of North America, it is only very recently that we have written records.

In summary, when the forms of two or more languages appear to be related, we can, through a consideration of systematic phonetic correspondences of cognates, reconstruct the common form from which all the forms can be derived by means of phonetically plausible sound changes. Genetically related lexical forms of different languages are called cognates, the reconstructed forms, proto-forms, and a reconstructed language, a proto-language.

Internal Reconstruction

Sometimes it is possible to reconstruct the earlier form of a language even without reference to comparative data. This technique, known as **internal reconstruction**, relies on the analysis of morphophonemic variation within a single language. The key point is that the sound changes that create allomorphic and allophonic variation can be identified and then used to infer an earlier form of the morpheme. The following data are from French; because of borrowing, English exhibits a parallel set of contrasts involving [k] and [ʃ].

Table 7.72 [k] - [s] correspondence in French

maʒik	'magic'	maʒis-jẽ	'magician'
lɔʒik	'logic'	lɔʒis-jẽ	'logician'
myzik	'music'	myzis-jẽ	'musician'

The root morpheme in each row exhibits two forms, one ending in [k], the other ending in [s]. The same methods and principles used in comparative reconstruction can be applied here to reconstruct the historically earlier form of the root morpheme. If a root ending in *s is posited, no phonetically plausible change can account for the [k] in the left-hand column. By contrast, if a root-final *k is posited, the [s] can be accounted for by assuming that the *k was fronted under the influence of the high front vowel of the suffix (palatalization) and became an affricate [ts] (affrication), which was later simplified to a fricative [s] (deaffrication). All of these changes are phonetically plausible and listed in the catalogue in Table 7.3. Accordingly, internal reconstruction indicates that at an earlier point in the development of French, the root morphemes in Table 7.72 ended in the consonant *k.

The Discovery of Indo-European

The late eighteenth-century discovery that Sanskrit (the ancient language of India) was related to Latin, Greek, Germanic, and Celtic revolutionized European linguistic studies. Sir William Jones, a British judge and scholar working in India, summed up the nature and implications of the findings in his 1786 address to the Royal Asiatic Society, a part of which follows:

> The Sanskrit language, whatever be its antiquity, is of a wonderful structure; more perfect than the Greek, more copious [having more cases] than the Latin, and more exquisitely refined than either, yet bearing to both of them a stronger affinity, both in the roots of the verbs and in the forms of the grammar, than could possibly have been produced by accident; so strong indeed, that no philologer could examine them all three, without believing them to have sprung from some common source, which, perhaps, no longer exists; there is a similar reason . . . for supposing that both the Gothic and the Celtic . . . had the same origin with the Sanskrit; and the old Persian might be added to the same family.

This discovery led to several decades of intensive historical-comparative work and to important advances in historical linguistics during the nineteenth century. By studying phonetic correspondences from an ever increasing number of languages, linguists eventually ascertained that most of the languages of Europe, Persia (Iran), and the northern part of India belong to a single family, now called Indo-European. By applying the techniques of the comparative method, they began reconstructing the grammar of the proto-language from which these languages evolved, now called **Proto-Indo-European (PIE)**.

A number of individuals advanced this research. In 1814, the Danish linguist Rasmus Rask carefully documented the relationships among cognates in a number of Indo-European languages, and at the same time established the methods that would govern the emerging science of historical-comparative linguistics. He wrote:

> When agreement is found in [the most essential] words in two languages, and so frequently that rules may be drawn up for the shift in letters [sounds] from one to the other, then there is a fundamental relationship between the two languages; especially when similarities in the inflectional system and in the general make-up of the languages correspond with them.

Rask worked without access to Sanskrit. The first comparative linguistic analysis of Sanskrit, Greek, Persian, and the Germanic languages was done by the German scholar Franz Bopp in 1816. In 1822, another German, Jakob Grimm, extended Rask's observations and became the first person to explain the relationships among the cognates noted by Rask in terms of a **sound shift**, the systematic modification of a series of phonemes. Some of the correspondences on which he based his work are given in Table 7.73.

Table 7.73 Some Indo-European phonetic correspondences

Greek	Latin	English
pat<u>é</u>r	<u>p</u>ater	<u>f</u>ather
<u>t</u>reîs	<u>t</u>rēs	<u>th</u>ree
he<u>k</u>atón	<u>c</u>entum	<u>h</u>undred

The crucial observation is that where English has [f], [θ], and [h] (here, in word-initial position), Greek and Latin have [p], [t], and [k]. Grimm tabulated a series of consonant shifts for Proto-Germanic which differentiated it from other Indo-European languages. **Grimm's Law** is the name given to the consonant shifts which took place between Proto-Indo-European and Proto-Germanic.

Table 7.74 The sound shifts underlying Grimm's Law

Proto-Indo-European	p	t	k	b	d	g	bh	dh	gh
Germanic	f	θ	x	p	t	k	b	d	g

Some additional examples of the relationships captured by these shifts are given in Table 7.75. The Proto-Indo-European consonants were either maintained in Sanskrit, Greek, and Latin or in some cases underwent changes different from those found in Germanic.

Table 7.75 Some examples of the consonant shifts underlying Grimm's Law

Shift in Germanic			Sanskrit	Greek	Latin	English
p	>	f	pād-	pod-	ped-	foot
t	>	θ	tanu-	tanaós	tenuis	thin
k	>	x	çatam	hekatón	centum	hundred
b	>	p	—	—	lūbricus	slippery
d	>	t	daça	déka	decem	ten
g	>	k	ajras	agrós	ager	acre
bh	>	b	bhrātā	phrátēr	frāter	brother
dh	>	d	vidhavā	eítheos	vidua	widow
gh	>	g	hansas	khḗn	(h)ānser	goose

Although there appeared to be exceptions to Grimm's Law, they turned out to be systematic and could be traced to specific environments. For example, voiceless stops were not subject to Grimm's Law when they were immediately preceded by *s*.

Table 7.76 A systematic exception to Grimm's Law

Original *s* + voiceless stop			
Latin	st̲āre	English	st̲and [st] (not [sθ])

A particularly important discovery was made by Karl Verner, who traced a group of exceptions to Grimm's Law to the original accentual pattern of Proto-Indo-European. In a generalization that came to be known as Verner's Law, he proposed that a word-internal voiceless fricative resulting from Grimm's Law underwent voicing if the original Proto-Indo-European accent did not immediately precede it. Since stress came to be fixed on the root syllable in Germanic subsequent to the changes covered by Verner's Law, the original environment was obscured. However, Sanskrit provides direct evidence for Verner's claim since Sanskrit was very conservative in its maintenance of the original Proto-Indo-European accent. Although the English forms are complicated by other developments, the effects of Verner's Law are apparent in the following Gothic examples. In the Gothic word for *brother*, PIE *t* becomes [θ] according to Grimm's Law, whereas in the word for *father* it becomes [ð] in accordance with both Grimm's and Verner's Laws.

Table 7.77 Verner's Law

PIE	Sanskrit	Grimm's Law	Verner's Law	Gothic	
*t	bhrā́tā	*t > θ	—	[bro:θar]	'brother'
*t	pitā́	*t > θ	θ > ð	[faðar]	'father'

It should also be noted here that borrowing is an important factor which must be taken into consideration when comparative reconstruction is being carried out. For example, English has many words that do not show the effects of Grimm's Law.

Table 7.78 English words not showing the effects of Grimm's Law

Expected by Grimm's Law			Latin	English
p	>	f	ped-	pedestrian
t	>	θ	tenuis	tenuous
k	>	h	canalis	canal

The apparent failure of Grimm's Law here stems from the fact that the English words were borrowed directly from Latin or French many centuries after the sound shifts described by Grimm's Law had taken place. The task of reconstruction can often be complicated by such borrowings.

Subsequent Developments By the middle of the nineteenth century, the study of language had made great strides, especially in the field of phonetics, which opened the way for the detailed comparison of linguistic forms. One influential hypothesis at that time was that sound laws operated without exception. A group of linguists known as the Neogrammarians adopted this idea and made many important contributions to the fledgling science of linguistics by applying it to new and more complicated data. Although such factors as lexical diffusion and social pressures were more or less ignored by the Neogrammarians, their hypothesis represented an important and daring advance in the scientific study of language.

The nineteenth century also saw major advances in the classification of languages. A German scholar, August Schleicher, developed a classification for the Indo-European languages in the form of a genealogical tree. Genetic classification is discussed in much more detail in the chapter on language typology that follows.

Work in comparative reconstruction is far from finished. In particular, linguists are now considering the possibility of superfamilies. One such proposed family is Nostratic, which includes Indo-European, Afro-Asiatic (for example, Arabic, Hebrew), Altaic (for example, Japanese, Korean, Turkic), and Uralic (for example, Finnish, Hungarian). Comparative reconstruction is also playing an important role in determining the genetic relationships of the hundreds of North American indigenous languages, a topic which still remains highly controversial.

Reconstruction and Typology

Since the 1800s, when the reconstruction of Proto-Indo-European was carried out, linguists have accumulated vast amounts of information on thousands of languages. This is in part due to the explosion of studies in the field of linguistic typology, which is concerned with the investigation of structural similarities among languages that are not genetically related. Even languages that do not belong to the same family can have striking similarities. For example, in addition to shared word order patterns (see Section 2 in Chapter 8), SOV languages commonly exhibit a strong tendency toward agglutinating morphology (a type of complex affixation; see Chapter 8) and vowel harmony. Typological studies play an important role in the linguist's search for universals of language—statements which are true for all languages.

The extensive information on the languages of the world available to modern linguists was, of course, not available at the time the original reconstruction of Proto-Indo-European was undertaken. Modern linguists involved in comparative reconstruction now take a keen interest in typological studies and the role of **typological plausibility** in reconstruction has become an important topic. For example, a linguist would be very reluctant to propose a reconstruction that violated a universal property of language or that had no parallel in any known language.

Some linguists have argued that the traditional reconstruction of the PIE obstruent system (given in Table 7.79) should be rejected on the basis of typological plausibility.

Table 7.79 The traditional reconstruction of the Proto-Indo-European obstruents

p	t	$\acute{k}$	k	k^w	(voiceless stops)
(b)	d	$\acute{g}$	g	g^w	(voiced stops)
bh	dh	$\acute{g}h$	gh	g^wh	(voiced aspirated stops)
	s				

(*Note*: $\acute{k}$, $\acute{g}$, and $\acute{g}h$ are palatal stops and ^{w} indicates a labialized consonant.)

This reconstruction is typologically questionable in at least two respects. First, reconstructed forms with PIE *b are extremely rare, almost as if there were a gap in the labial system. Such a gap is very uncommon in the languages of the world. Typically if there is a missing labial stop, it is the voiceless stop that is missing, not the voiced stop. Second, the traditional reconstruction posits a series of voiced aspirated stops but no corresponding series of voiceless aspirated stops, even though some typologists have argued that all languages which have a voiced series also have the voiceless one.

Such facts have led some linguists to propose what they believe is a more typologically plausible reconstruction of Proto-Indo-European involving a voiceless stop series, an ejective series, and a voiced stop series (as well as *s as in the traditional reconstruction).

Table 7.80 A recent reconstruction of the Proto-Indo-European consonants

p	t	k̗	k	kʷ	(voiceless stops)
(p')	t'	k̗'	k'	k'ʷ	(ejectives)
b	d	g̗	g	gʷ	(voiced stops)
	s				

Not only does this reconstruction avoid the problem with the aspirated stops, it is also common for languages with an ejective series to lack the labial. From this perspective, this reconstruction seems much more plausible than the traditional one.

Both reconstructions have their supporters. In fact, however, it is difficult to come to a definitive decision on the basis of typological considerations since it is common for a proposed universal to have exceptions. For example, a few languages have been found with the characteristics attributed to Proto-Indo-European by the traditional reconstruction. These languages have labial gaps in the voiced series (for example, Amerindian languages of the Athapaskan and Caddoan families) and a voiced aspirate series but no voiceless counterpart (Madurese, an Indonesian language). Accordingly, as long as the traditional reconstruction is linguistically possible, it would not seem appropriate to reject it simply because the phonological system proposed would be a rare one.

Typological plausibility will likely continue to play a secondary role in reconstruction until linguists can draw a clear line between what is linguistically possible and what is not possible. Nevertheless, as our knowledge and understanding of language universals continues to improve, it is certain that linguists involved in the reconstruction of proto-languages will maintain an interest in typological plausibility.

7.8 LANGUAGE CHANGE AND NATURALNESS

A striking fact about language change is that the same patterns of change occur repeatedly, not only within the same language at different periods in its history but also across languages. Both the similarity of changes across languages as well as the directionality of language change suggest that some changes are more natural than others. This notion of **naturalness** is implicit in the phonetic plausibility strategy introduced in the section on comparative reconstruction.

If naturalness is a factor in language change, its manifestations should also be found in the language acquisition process and in language universals. This does seem to be the case. As a specific example, let us consider the frequently made claim that the CV syllable is the most natural of all syllable types. At least three different kinds of evidence can be brought forth in support of this claim.

First, in terms of universals, all languages of the world have CV syllables in their syllable type inventory. Second, a variety of sound changes have the effect of reducing less natural syllable types to the more natural CV type.

Table 7.81 Sound changes yielding CV syllables

Deletion						
CCV	> CV	Old English	cnēow	English	knee	/ni/
CVC	> CV	Old Spanish	non	Spanish	no	
Vowel epenthesis						
CCVCV > CVCVCV		Italian	croce	Sicilian	kiruci	'cross'

By contrast, note that such changes rarely if ever apply to a CV syllable to yield a different syllable type. Deletion of the C in a word-initial CV syllable is extremely rare, as is vowel epenthesis in a CV syllable or a sequence of CVCV syllables.

Third, in terms of language acquisition, the CV syllable type is one of the first syllable types to be acquired and many phonetic processes found in child language have the effect of yielding CV syllables, just like the sound changes listed above (see Chapter 10 on language acquisition).

Table 7.82 Phonetic processes in language acquisition yielding CV syllables

CCV→CV	tree → [tij]	(simplification of consonant clusters)
CVC→CV	dog → [dɑ]	(deletion of final consonants)

It is clear, however, that it is inappropriate to take a simplistic view of linguistic naturalness. For example, some sound changes produce less natural syllables. Thus, syncope has the effect of reducing a sequence of CVCVCV syllables to the less natural CVCCV. Usually in such cases, a different motivation can be identified, such as the preference for shorter phonological forms over longer forms. But given the complexity of human language, not to mention human behavior in general, it should not be surprising that there are many different parameters of linguistic naturalness and that these can, in turn, lead to apparently conflicting changes in language over time. It remains an important task of the linguist to identify, rank, and ultimately explain relations of linguistic naturalness. The study of language change will continue to make an important contribution to this area.

Summing Up

Historical linguistics studies the nature and causes of language change. The causes of language change find their roots in the physiological and cognitive makeup of human beings. Sound changes usually involve articulatory simplification as in the case of the most common type, **assimilation**. **Analogy** and **reanalysis** are particularly important factors in morphological change. **Language contact** resulting in **borrowing** is another important source of language change. All components of the grammar, from phonology to semantics, are subject to change over time. A change can simultaneously affect all instances of a particular sound or form, or it can spread through the language word by word by means of **lexical diffusion**. Sociological factors can play an important role in determining whether or not a linguistic innovation is ultimately adopted by the linguistic community at large. Since language change is systematic, it is possible, by identifying the changes that a particular language or dialect has undergone, to reconstruct linguistic history and thereby posit the earlier forms from which later forms have evolved. Using sets of **cognates, comparative reconstruction** allows us to reconstruct the properties of the parent or **proto-language** on the basis of **systematic phonetic correspondences**.

Studies in historical linguistics can provide valuable insights into relationships among languages and shed light on prehistoric developments. Furthermore, historical studies of language are of great importance to our understanding of human linguistic competence. In fact, it has often been stated that language change provides one of the most direct windows into the workings of the human mind. Furthermore, the study of language change contributes to our understanding of how social, cultural, and psychological factors interact to shape language. Finally, the integration of studies on language change, language acquisition, and language universals remains one of the most important challenges facing linguists today.

Key Terms

amelioration
analogy
analytic
apocope
assimilation
borrowing
comparative reconstruction
consonant deletion
consonant weakening
degemination
deletion
dialect
diphthongization
dissimilation
folk etymology
frication
fusion
genetically related
glide strengthening
Great English Vowel Shift
Grimm's Law

hypercorrection
internal reconstruction
language contact
lexical diffusion
lexical gaps
majority rules strategy
mergers
metaphor
metathesis
mutual intelligibility
nasalization
naturalness
palatalization
pejoration
phonetic plausibility strategy
phonetic sound change
phonetically conditioned change
phonological change
proto-form
Proto-Indo-European
proto-language

reanalysis	substitution
reconstruction	substratum
rhotacism	superstratum
segmental change	syncope
semantic broadening	synthetic
semantic narrowing	total assimilation
semantic shift	typological plausibility
sequential change	umlaut
sound change	Verner's Law
sound shift	vowel reduction
spelling pronunciation	weakening
splits	weakening of meaning

Sources

The advanced textbooks by Anttila and Hock (cited below) provide much more detailed discussions of most of the major topics in this chapter. They are also excellent sources for references relating to particular topics. Hock is particularly important for providing detailed discussions of syntactic change and the role of typology in reconstruction.

Overviews of historical linguistics as it applies to the development of English are presented in the books by Williams, Pyles and Algeo, Baugh and Cable, and Millward cited below.

The catalogue of sound changes is adapted from catalogues proposed by Theo Vennemann in the article "Linguistic Typologies in Historical Linguistics" in *Società di linguistica italiana* 23:87–91 (1985) and a book entitled *Preference Laws for Syllable Structure and the Explanation of Sound Change* (Amsterdam: Mouton de Gruyter, 1988). Section 2 has also benefited from unpublished material (particularly the manuscript "Linguistic Change") kindly made available by Theo Vennemann (University of Munich) to the author during his stay in Munich from 1980–1985.

The data on vowel laxing in Canadian French are from Douglas C. Walker's book *The Pronunciation of Canadian French* (Ottawa: University of Ottawa Press, 1984). The data on word order in Old and Middle English come from the book by Joseph Williams cited below. The examples of English loanwords in Gwich'in (Loucheux) are given in *Dene Yati* 1 (1): (1985), published by the Dene Language Terminology Committee, Yellowknife, the Northwest Territories. The discussion of borrowing and semantic change in English draws on materials in the book by Williams.

Figure 7.11 depicting lexical diffusion of the stress change in English nouns derived from verbs is taken from the book by Jean Aitchison cited below. Aitchison's remarks are based on the article by M. Chen and W. Wang, "Sound Change: Actuation and Implementation" in *Language* 51: 255–81 (1975). The data on the realization of [s] as [h] in Spanish were provided by Herbert Izzo of the University of Calgary.

The Germanic cognates used to illustrate family relationships are based on Leonard Bloomfield's classic work *Language* (New York: Holt, Rinehart and Winston, 1933). The data on sound change in Muskogean come from Mary Haas's book *The Prehistory of Languages* (Amsterdam: Mouton, 1969). The quote from Jones is taken from *A Reader in Nineteenth-Century Historical Indo-European Linguistics*, edited and translated by Winfred P. Lehmann (Bloomington: Indiana University Press, 1967) and the quote from Rask is taken from Holger Pedersen's book *The Discovery of Language: Li*   *Science in the Nineteenth Century* (Bloomington: Indiana Universit   1959).

Question 2 is based on data provided by Dr. George Patterson, whose generosity we hereby acknowledge. The data for Questions 3 and 4 are from F. Columbus's *Introductory Workbook in Historical Phonology* (Cambridge, Mass.: Slavica Publishers, 1974). Question 10 is based on data provided by David Bellusci. The data for Question 18 are drawn from *Source Book for Linguistics* by W. Cowan and J. Rakušan (Philadelphia: John Benjamins, 1987).

Recommended Reading

Aitchison, Jean. 1985. *Language Change: Progress or Decay?* New York: Universe Books.

Anttila, Raimo. 1989. *Historical and Comparative Linguistics*. Amsterdam and New York: John Benjamins.

Arlotto, Anthony. 1972. *Introduction to Historical Linguistics*. Lanham, New York and London: University Press of America.

Baugh, Albert C., and Thomas Cable. 1978. *A History of the English Language*. Englewood Cliffs, N.J.: Prentice-Hall.

Hock, Hans Henrich. 1986. *Principles of Historical Linguistics*. Berlin, New York, and Amsterdam: Mouton de Gruyter.

Jeffers, Robert J., and Ilse Lehiste. 1979. *Principles and Methods for Historical Linguistics*. Cambridge, Mass.: MIT Press.

Millward, C. M. 1989. *A Biography of the English Language*. New York: Holt, Rinehart and Winston.

Pyles, Thomas, and John Algeo. 1982. *The Origins and Development of the English Language*. 3d ed. New York: Harcourt Brace Jovanovich.

Williams, Joseph. 1975. *Origins of the English Language: A Social and Linguistic History*. New York: The Free Press.

Questions

1. Identify the following sound changes with reference to the catalogue of sound changes provided in Table 7.3. In each pair of examples, focus on the segment(s) in bold only. The form on the left indicates the original

segment(s) before the change and the form on the right indicates the segment(s) after the change. Note that * stands for a hypothetical representation.

a) Sanskrit	sneha	Pali	sineha	'friendship'
b) Old English	hlāf	English	loaf	
c) Latin	iuvenis [j]	Italian	giovane [dʒ]	'young'
d) English	triathlon	dialect	triath[ə]lon	
e) Latin	vidua [dw]	Spanish	viuda [wd]	'widow'
f) Sanskrit	sapta	Pali	satta	'seven'
g) Latin	turtur	English	turtle	
h)	*venré	Spanish	vendré	'I will come'
i) Italian	mundo	Sicilian	munnu	'world'
j) Old French	cire [tˢ]	French	cire [s]	'wax'
k) Latin	pān-	French	pain [ɛ̃]	'bread'
l) Latin	mulgēre	Italian	mungere	'to milk'
m) Latin	pacāre [k]	Italian	pagare	'to pay'
n) Old Spanish	maduro	Spanish	maduro [ð]	'mature'
o) Latin	peccātum [kk]	Spanish	pecado [k]	'sin'
p)	*honōsis	Latin	honōris	'honor (gen sg)'
q) English	rage	French	rage [ʒ]	'rage'
r) English	coffee	Chipewyan	[kaθi]	
s) Latin	mare	Portuguese	mar	'sea'
t) Latin	vīcīnitās	Spanish	vecindad	'neighborhood'
u) Gothic	Þliuhan [θ]	English	flee	
v) Old English	(ic) singe	English	(I) sing	
w) Latin	summa	Spanish	suma	'sum, gist'
x) Latin	ōrnāmentum	Old French	ornement [ə]	'ornament'
y)	*lūsi	Old English	lȳs [y]	'lice'

2. *i*) Describe the difference between the two French dialects in the following data given in phonetic transcription. (The symbol *y* represents a high front rounded vowel, while *ø* represents a mid front rounded vowel.)

   ii) What should change would you posit here? Why?

   iii) State the sound change in the form of a rule.

	Standard French	*Acadian French*	
a)	okyn	otʃyn	'none'
b)	kør	tʃør	'heart'
c)	ke	tʃe	'wharf'
d)	kɛ̃:z	tʃɛ̃:z	'fifteen'
e)	akyze	atʃyze	'accuse'
f)	ki	tʃi	'who'
g)	kav	kav	'cave'
h)	kɔr	kɔr	'body'
i)	kurir	kurir	'run'
j)	ãkɔ:r	ãkɔ:r	'again'

3. *i)* What sound changes differentiate Guaraní from its parent language, Proto-Tupí-Guaraní, in the following data?
    ii) State these changes in rule form.
    iii) Some of the rules must be crucially ordered. Indicate which rule must be ordered before which rule, and explain its reason.

	Proto-Tupí-Guaraní	*Guaraní*	
a)	jukir	juki	'salt'
b)	moajan	moajã	'push'
c)	puʔam	puʔã	'wet'
d)	meʔeŋ	meʔẽ	'give'
e)	tiŋ	tʃĩ	'white'
f)	potiʔa	potʃiʔa	'chest'
g)	tatatiŋ	tatatʃĩ	'smoke'
h)	kɨb	kɨ	'louse'
i)	men	mẽ	'husband'

4. *i)* Describe the three changes that took place between Proto-Slavic and Bulgarian in the following data. (The symbol ˘ over a vowel indicates that it is short.)
    ii) State these changes as rules and indicate, as far as possible, the order in which they must have applied.
    iii) Show the derivation of Bulgarian form from Proto-Slavic form for the word 'adroit'.

	Proto-Slavic	*Bulgarian*	
a)	gladŭka	glatkə	'smooth'
b)	kratŭka	kratkə	'short'
c)	blizŭka	bliskə	'near'
d)	ʒeʒĭka	ʒeʃkə	'scorching'
e)	lovŭka	lofkə	'adroit'
f)	gorĭka	gorkə	'bitter'

5. Determine all the sound changes required to derive the later form from the proto-form. Where possible, give the chronology of the sound changes.

a)	*feminam	Old French	femme (final e = [ə])	'woman'
b)	*lumine	Spanish	lumbre	'fire'
c)	*tremulare	Spanish	temblar	'tremble'
d)	*stuppam	Spanish	estopa	'tow'
e)	*populu	Rumanian	plop	'poplar'

6. Taking into consideration the Great Vowel Shift, give all the changes necessary to derive the Modern English forms from the Old English forms. (*Note:* Assume, simplifying somewhat, that the Old English forms were pronounced as they are written.)

	Old English	*Modern English*	
a)	brōde (sg acc)	brood	[bruwd]
b)	cnotta (c = [k])	knot	[nat]
c)	wīse	wise	[wajz]
d)	hlǣfdige	lady	[lejdij]

7. Place names are often subject to spelling pronunciation. Transcribe your pronunciation of the following words and then compare your pronunciation with that recommended by a good dictionary. Do you think any of your pronunciations qualify as spelling pronunciations?

   a) Worcestershire
   b) Thames
   c) Edinburgh (Scotland; compare Edinburgh, Texas)
   d) Cannes (France)
   e) Newfoundland

8. Compare the Old English singular and plural forms:

Singular	*Plural*	
bōc	bēc	'book(s)'
āc	ēc	'oak(s)'

   Although the Old English words have an umlaut plural (as in Old English gōs/gēs 'goose/geese'), the Modern English forms do not. Explain how the change in plural formation could have come about.

9. As evident in the following sentence, Shona, a modern Bantu language, has SVO word order.

   mwana   anotengesa   miriwo
   child   sells   vegetables
   'The child sells vegetables'

   By contrast, Shona's morphology reflects a different pattern as evident in the following examples.

   mwana   ano**mu***ona*
   child   **him** + *see*
   'The child sees him'

   mukadzi   ano**va***batsira*
   woman   **them** + *help*
   'The woman helps them'

   What do these examples indicate about earlier Shona or possibly Proto-Bantu word order?

10. All of the following English words at one time had meanings that are quite different from their current ones. Identify each of these semantic changes

as an instance of narrowing, broadening, amelioration, pejoration, weakening, or shift.

	Word	Earlier meaning
a)	moody	'brave'
b)	uncouth	'unknown'
c)	aunt	'father's sister'
d)	butcher	'one who slaughters goats'
e)	witch	'male or female sorcerer'
f)	sly	'skilful'
g)	accident	'an event'
h)	argue	'make clear'
i)	carry	'transport by cart'
j)	grumble	'murmur, make low sounds'
k)	shrewd	'depraved, wicked'
l)	praise	'set a value on'
m)	ordeal	'trial by torture'
n)	picture	'a painted likeness'
o)	seduce	'persuade someone to desert his or her duty'
p)	box	'a small container made of boxwood'
q)	baggage	'a worthless person'
r)	virtue	'qualities one expected of a man'
s)	myth	'story'
t)	undertaker	'one who undertakes'
u)	hussy	'housewife'
v)	astonish	'strike by thunder'
w)	write	'scratch'
x)	quell	'kill'

11. Look up the following words in a good dictionary. Discuss any semantic changes that have affected the underscored portions since Old English. Do you think speakers of Modern English have reanalyzed any of these forms in terms of folk etymology?

   a) wed<u>lock</u>
   b) witch<u>craft</u>
   c) stead<u>fast</u>
   d) after<u>ward</u>

12. The following line is from *Troilus and Criseyde V* by Geoffrey Chaucer.
His lighte goost ful blisfully is went.
[hɪs liçtə gɔːst fʊl blɪsfʊlli ɪs went] ([ç] is a voiceless palatal fricative.)
'His light spirit has gone very blissfully.'

   a) How has the meaning of the word *ghost* changed since Chaucer's time?
   b) Describe the changes that have taken place in the pronunciation of *light* and *ghost*.

13. Consider the following lyrics from the Middle English song "Sumer Is I-cumen In." Compare the Middle English lyrics with the Modern English translation and answer the questions that follow.

Original text
Sumer is i-cumen in;
Lhude sing, cuccu!
Grōweþ sēd, and blōweþ mēd,
And springþ þe wude nū.

Transcription
[sumər ɪs ikumən ɪn
lu:də sɪŋg kuk:u
grɔ:wəθ se:d and blɔ:wəθ me:d
and sprɪŋgθ ðə wudə nu:]

Translation
'Summer has come in;
Loudly sing, cuckoo!
Seed grows and meadow blooms
And the wood grows now.'

    i) What affix converted the adjective *loud* into an adverb in middle English?

    ii) What accounts for the difference between the Middle English and Modern English pronunciation of the vowel in *loud*?

    iii) What other words in this poem reflect this general shift?

    iv) How has the relative ordering of the subject and verb changed since this was written?

    v) How has the third person singular present tense suffix changed since Middle English?

14. The following Cree words were borrowed from French as the result of contact between the two groups on the Canadian prairies. (Notice that the French determiner was not treated as a separate morpheme and was carried along with the borrowed word.) What types of considerations could one plausibly assume played a role in the borrowing of these words into Cree?

	Cree	*French*	
a)	labutōn	le bouton	'button'
b)	lībot	les bottes	'boots'
c)	lamilās	la mélasse	'molasses'
d)	lapwīl	la poêle	'frying pan'
e)	litī	le thé	'tea'

15. The following Latin roots are found in words that have been borrowed into English. Since these words were borrowed after Grimm's Law had applied, they do not show its effects. All of these roots, however, do have Germanic cognates that did undergo Grimm's Law. On the basis of your knowledge of this law and the meaning of the borrowing, try to determine the Modern English (Germanic) cognate for each root. Consult a good dictionary if you need help. (*Note*: Focus on the portion of the Latin word in bold only; vowel changes must also be taken into consideration.)

	Latin root	Related borrowing	English cognate
a)	**ped**is	pedestrian	_foot_
b)	**nep**os	nepotism	
c)	**pisc**is	piscine	
d)	**ten**uis	tenuous	
e)	**corn**u	cornucopia	
f)	**duo**	dual	
g)	**ed**ere	edible	
h)	**gen**us	genocide	
i)	**ager**	agriculture	

16. Attempt to reconstruct the Proto-Germanic form for each pair of cognates. Focusing on the vowels, describe the changes that affected the Old English forms.

	Gothic	Old English	
a)	kuni	cyn	'kin'
b)	badi	bed	'bed'
c)	dōmjan	dœman	'to judge'
d)	sōkjan	sœcan	'to seek'
e)	bugjan	bycgan	'to buy'
f)	nati	net	'net'

17. Reconstruct the Proto-Romance form for each set of cognates. Give all the changes necessary to derive each of the modern forms from the proto-forms. (Refer to Section 7.7).

	Spanish	Sardinian	Rumanian		
a)	vida	bita	vită	(ă = [ə])	'life'
b)	sí	si	şi	(ş = [ʃ])	'yes'
c)	riso	rizu	rīs		'laugh'
d)	miel	mele	miere		'honey'
e)	hierro	ferru	fier		'iron'
f)	piedra	pedra	piatră	(ă = [ə])	'stone'
g)	hierba	erva	iarbă	[ă = [ə]]	'grass'
h)	oso	ursu	urs		'bear'
i)	roto	ruttu	rupt		'broken'
j)	lecho	lettu	—		'bed'

8 THE CLASSIFICATION OF LANGUAGES

*Everything it is possible for us to analyze depends
on a clear method which distinguishes the similar
from the not similar.*

Linneus *Genera Plantarum* (1754)

O ne of the most striking facts about the linguistic situation in the world today is its diversity. There are thousands of different languages, each with its own sound patterns, vocabulary, and syntactic rules. However, underlying this diversity are important similarities that allow linguists to group languages into a relatively small number of families and types. This chapter is concerned with methods of classification as well as with some of the major findings within this branch of linguistic analysis.

There are essentially two ways to go about classifying languages. One system of classification analyzes languages in terms of their structural characteristics. This results in the grouping together of languages with similar sound patterns and grammatical rules. A second system classifies languages according to their genetic relationships. Languages that developed historically from the same ancestor language are grouped together and are considered to be genetically related. In the first part of this chapter, we describe some of the ways in which languages can be classified structurally, and point out some of the characteristics most commonly found in the languages of the world. We then present the genetic groupings proposed for some familiar languages and conclude by examining some less well-known languages.

8.1 STRUCTURAL VERSUS GENETIC RELATIONSHIPS

Linguists estimate that there are between four thousand and eight thousand different languages presently spoken by the more than five billion people in the world. These figures are imprecise primarily because it is often difficult to determine whether two linguistic communities speak different languages or merely different dialects of the same language. Part of this difficulty arises from the fact that there is simply not enough information about a large number of languages. For example, it is only recently that linguists have come to know a great deal about the indigenous languages of Africa and North America, and many of the languages of South America, New Guinea, and Australia are still relatively unknown.

One test that linguists use to decide whether two varieties of speech should be considered different languages or different dialects of the same language relies on the criterion of **mutual intelligibility**. Mutually intelligible varieties of a language can be understood by speakers of each variety. According to this criterion, the English of Melbourne, the English of Milwaukee, and the English of London qualify as dialects of the same language. If two speakers cannot understand one another, then linguists normally conclude that they are speaking different languages. The Italian of Florence and the French of Paris are examples of varieties of speech that are not mutually intelligible.

Political, cultural, social, historical, and religious factors often intervene in the determination of linguistic boundaries. For example, Serbians and Croatians often say that they speak different languages. However, even though their history, religion, and spelling systems differ, Serbians and Croatians actually speak mutually intelligible dialects of the same language, which linguists call Serbo-Croatian. In contrast, we often speak of Chinese as if it were a single language, even though it is actually a number of separate, mutually unintelligible languages (Cantonese, Mandarin, Hakka, and so on), each with a host of dialects.

In addition to the problems presented by these nonlinguistic considerations, complications also arise when we try to divide a continuum of mutually intelligible dialects whose two end points are not intelligible. Dutch and German, for example, are mutually intelligible around the border area between Germany and Holland; however, the Dutch of Amsterdam and the German of Munich are not. Similarly, Palestinian Arabic and Syrian Arabic are mutually intelligible, but Moroccan Arabic and Saudi Arabian Arabic are not.

Even if we adopt the conservative estimate that there are only four thousand languages in the world, this is still a very large number. It is therefore desirable to develop a system for classifying languages into smaller groups. This sort of language classification is normally done either in terms of genetic relationships or in terms of structural characteristics.

Languages that are considered to be genetically related are grouped into families whose members are all assumed to have descended from the same ancestor language. This ancestor may be attested (that is, texts written in this language have been discovered or preserved, as in the case of Latin and its descendants), or it may be a reconstructed protolanguage for which no original texts exist (as is the case for Proto-Indo-European). This type of genetic classification is discussed further in Section 8.3.

Although genetically related languages often share structural characteristics, they do not necessarily bear a close structural resemblance. For example, Latvian and English are genetically related (both are descended from Indo-European), but their morphological structure is quite different. An English sentence such as *It has to be figured out* can be expressed in Latvian by a single word.

1. jāizgudro
     jā -iz -gudro
  (one) must out figure (it)
  'One must figure it out.'

Of course, Latvian and English are very distantly related, and languages that are more closely related will typically share a larger number of structural similarities. On the other hand, it is also necessary to recognize that even languages that are totally unrelated may share some structural similarities. Thus, English and Swahili, which are unrelated, both employ subject-verb-object word order in simple declarative sentences.

> 2. Maria anampenda Anna.
> 'Maria likes Anna.'

The next section examines some of the ways that languages can be grouped together on the basis of structural characteristics.

8.2 STRUCTURAL CLASSIFICATION

The classification of languages according to their structural characteristics is known as **linguistic typology**. A typical study in typology might group together languages that have similar word order patterns, word structure, or phonological systems. An important area of research within the study of linguistic typology involves the search for language universals—structural patterns and traits that occur in all or most human languages. Patterns or traits that occur in all languages are called **absolute universals**, while those that simply occur in most languages are known as **universal tendencies**. Many of the generalizations formulated in the study of linguistic typology involve **implicational universals**—principles that specify that the presence of one trait implies the presence of another (but not vice versa). For instance, languages with fricative phonemes (such as /f/ and /s/) will also have stop phonemes (such as /p/ and /t/), although the reverse is not necessarily true.

Another way to analyze linguistic universals is through **markedness theory**. Within this theory, **marked** traits are considered to be either more complex and/or universally rarer than **unmarked** characteristics. In addition, a marked trait is typically found in a particular language only if its unmarked counterpart also occurs. Thus, markedness theory is closely related to the study of implicational universals. An example involving vowel nasality will help illustrate these points.

Phonetically, oral vowels can be considered less complex than nasal vowels: recall that oral vowels allow the airstream to exit only through the mouth, while nasal vowels allow air to escape from both the mouth and the nose. Cross-linguistically, we find that all languages have contrasting oral vowels, while only some languages have contrasting nasal vowels. Moreover, even in the languages which have both, there are usually fewer nasal vowels than oral ones. Thus, nasal vowels (which are considered to be marked) are both phonologically more complex and rarer than oral vowels.

The following sections present some of the typological classifications and universals that have been proposed in the areas of phonology, morphology, and syntax.

Phonology

Phonological systems are usually classified on the basis of phonemic contrasts rather than by listing entire phonetic inventories. The listing of many allophones can lead to a confused picture of the relationships among phonological systems, but phonemic analysis allows the relevant contrasts to emerge. However, it should not be forgotten that the phonetic realizations of phonemes vary a great deal from language to language.

Vowel Systems Languages are often classified according to the size and pattern of their vowel systems. The most common vowel system has five phonemic contrasts, and shows two high vowels, two mid vowels, and one low vowel (see Figure 8.1). The front vowels are unrounded and the back vowels are rounded; the low vowel is unrounded. About half of the world's languages, including Basque, Hawaiian, Japanese, Spanish, and Swahili, have such a system.

```
i        u

e        o

     a
```

Figure 8.1 The most common vowel system

The majority of the world's other languages have vowel systems with three, four, six, or seven different vowels (disregarding contrasts based on length or nasalization, which can double or triple the number of phonemic vowels). Languages with fewer than three, or more than nine distinctive vowels are rare. Some typical vowel systems are presented in Figure 8.2.

```
i   ɨ   u        i                i       u

e       o        e       o        e   ə   o

    a                a                ʌ

                                      a
```

Six vowel   Four vowel   Seven vowel
system   system   system
Gilyak (Russia)   Navaho (Arizona)   Geez (Ethiopia)

Figure 8.2 Common vowel systems

Analysis of many languages has led to the discovery of a number of universal tendencies in phonological structure. Generalizations about universal tendencies in vowel systems can be made in terms of the phonological characteristics of vowels. Some of these tendencies are listed here along with a description of the most frequently occurring vowels.

- The most commonly occurring vowel phoneme is /a/, which is found in almost all of the languages of the world. Almost as frequent as /a/ are /i/ and /u/.
- Front vowel phonemes (/i, ɛ, æ/) are generally unrounded, while non-low back vowel phonemes (/o, ʊ/) are generally rounded.
- Low vowels (/æ, ɑ/) are generally unrounded.

Although English has an above average number of vowels, these phonemes all comply with the above tendencies. Thus, English has only front unrounded vowels, all the low vowel phonemes are unrounded, and all of the back, non-low vowels are rounded. The English vowel system can be represented as in Figure 8.3.

i   u

ɪ   ʊ

e   ʌ   o

ɛ   ɔ

æ   a   ɑ

Figure 8.3 The English vowel system

The relationship among contrasting vowel types (such as oral and nasal vowel phonemes and long and short vowel phonemes) can also be expressed in terms of implicational universals, since the presence of one vowel phoneme type implies the presence of another (but not vice versa).

- If a language has contrastive nasal vowels, then it will also have contrastive oral vowels. For example, French contrasts different nasal vowels (/lɔ̃/ 'long' and /lã/ 'slow'), and contrasts oral vowels with nasal vowels (/la/ 'weary' and /lã/ 'slow'). Predictably, French also contrasts different oral vowels, as in /klo/ 'shut' and /klu/ 'nail'. English shows contrasts among oral vowels but does not contrast nasal vowels with oral vowels. There are no contrasts in English like /bɑt/ and /bɑ̃t/.
- If a language has contrasting long vowels, then it will also have contrasting short vowels. For example, Finnish shows contrasting long vowels and, predictably, contrasting short vowels (see Table 8.1). The reverse is not necessarily the case. English shows contrasting short vowels but does not contrast long vowels with short ones.

Table 8.1 Finnish vowel contrasts

Long versus long	/viːli/	'junket'	/vaːli/	'election'
Short versus short	/suku/	'family'	/suka/	'bristle'
Short versus long	/tuli/	'fire'	/tuːli/	'wind'

Consonant Systems It is not particularly fruitful to classify languages according to the number of consonants that they contain, since the consonant inventories of languages may range from as few as eight consonant phonemes (in Hawaiian, for example) to more than ninety. !Kung, a language spoken in Namibia, has ninety-six consonant phonemes. (The symbol *!k* represents a type of click.) Nevertheless, a number of claims can be made about the consonant systems that occur in human language.

- All languages have stops. The most common stop phonemes in language are /p, t, k/. Very few languages lack any one of these, and there are no languages that lack all three. If any one of these three stops is missing, it will probably be /p/; for example, Aleut, Nubian, and

Witchita have no /p/ phoneme. The most commonly occurring phoneme of the three is /t/.

- The most commonly occurring fricative phoneme is /s/; few languages lack it. If a language has only one fricative, it is most likely to be /s/; for example, it is the only fricative found in Nandi (a language of Kenya) and Weri (a language of New Guinea).
- Almost every known language has at least one nasal phoneme; in cases where a language has only one nasal phoneme, that phoneme is usually /n/. (The only nasal phoneme in Arapaho is /n/.) If there are two contrasting nasals, they are normally /m/ and /n/.
- The majority of languages have at least one phonemic liquid. However, a small number of languages have none at all (Blackfoot, Dakota, and Efik, which is spoken in Nigeria, and Siona, which is spoken in Ecuador). English, of course, has two: /l/ and /r/.

Consonant phonemes are also subject to various implicational universals.

- If a language has voiced obstruent phonemes (stops, fricatives, or affricates), then it will also have voiceless obstruent phonemes. The reverse is not necessarily true, since Ainu (a language of northern Japan) has only voiceless obstruent phonemes /p, t, k, tʃ, s/.
- Sonorant consonants are generally voiced. Very few languages have voiceless sonorants; those that do always have voiced sonorants as well. For example, Burmese contrasts voiced and voiceless nasals and laterals.
- If a language has fricative phonemes, then it will also have stop phonemes. There are no languages that lack stops; however, there are some languages that lack fricatives. For example, Gilbertese (Gilbert Islands), Kitabal (eastern Australia), and Nuer (southeastern Sudan) have no fricatives.

Prosodic Universals Languages can also be classified according to their prosodic, or suprasegmental type. Languages in which pitch distinctions are phonemic are called tone languages. (The phonetics and phonology of tone were introduced in Chapters 2 and 3.) A great many of the world's languages are tone languages. Mandarin, for instance, has four contrastive tones (see Table 8.2). The other Chinese languages, as well as many Southeast Asian languages like

Table 8.2 Tone contrasts in Mandarin

mā	'mother'	high tone
má	'hemp'	low rising tone
mǎ	'horse'	falling rising tone
mà	'scold'	high falling tone

Burmese and Vietnamese, are also tone languages. A few tone languages are also found in Europe; for example, in one of the dialects of Latvian a three-way tonal distinction is made (see Table 8.3). As noted in the chapter on phonetics, tones are of two types, *level* tones and *contour* tones. Tone languages most often contrast only two tone levels (phonologically high and low), although contrasts involving three tone levels (such as high, low, and mid tones) are not uncommon. Hardly any language contrasts more than five levels of tone.

Table 8.3 Tone contrasts in Latvian

loks	[lùoks]	'arch, bow'	falling tone
loks	[lūoks]	'green onion'	level (high) tone
loks	[lûoks]	'window'	rising falling (broken) tone

Various suprasegmental universals have been proposed for tone languages.

- If a language has contour tones (such as rising or falling tone), then it will also have level tones (such as high, mid, or low tone). Burmese, Crow, Latvian, and Mandarin are examples of languages that fit this pattern. In contrast, languages with contour tones but no level tones (for example, Dafla, spoken in northern India) are very rare.
- If a language has complex contour tones (such as rising-falling or falling-rising), then it will also have simple contour tones (like rising or falling). Both the Mandarin and Latvian examples fit this pattern.

Differences in stress, discussed in Chapter 2, are also useful in classifying languages. Fixed stress languages are those in which the position of stress on a word is predictable. For example, in Mayan, stress always falls on the last syllable of a word; in Polish, Swahili, and Samoan, stress falls on the penultimate (second to last) syllable of a word, while in Czech, Finnish, and Hungarian, the stressed syllable is always the first syllable of a word. In free stress languages, the position of stress is not always predictable. Free stress is also called phonemic stress because of its role in distinguishing between words. Russian is an example of a language with free stress (see Table 8.4).

Table 8.4 Stress contrasts in Russian

múka	'torture'	muká	'flour'
zámok	'castle'	zamók	'lock'
rúki	'hands'	rukí	'hand' (genitive singular)

Syllable Structure All languages permit V and CV syllable structures (where V stands for a syllabic element and C for a non-syllabic element). These structures are assumed to be unmarked, since they appear in all languages. However, the universality of the CV structure is not merely due to its structural simplicity; the syllable structure VC appears to be equally 'simple', but it is not found universally. The presence of an onset (as in a CV syllable) is apparently more valued than the presence of a coda (as in a VC syllable), perhaps because an onset may help to signal the beginning of a new syllable.

Onsets in a given language are frequently structured differently from codas. For example, in English, a nasal + stop sequence is permitted in a coda (in a word like *hand*), but not in an onset (there are no English words that begin with the sequence *nd*). However, Swahili has precisely the opposite restrictions: the *nd* sequence is permitted in onset position (in words like *ndizi* 'banana'), but not in coda position since Swahili syllables are coda-less—they can only end in vowels.

Two implicational universals referring to syllable structure are presented below. Both deal with the relative complexity of permitted onsets and codas.

- If a language permits sequences of consonants in a syllable onset, then it will also permit single consonants or zero consonants in an onset.
- If a language permits sequences of consonants in a syllable coda, then it will also permit single consonants or zero consonants in a coda.

Morphology

Both the word and the morpheme are universally valid linguistic categories. However, there are systematic differences in the ways in which individual languages combine morphemes to form words. Four types of systems are usually distinguished, although no language fits any of these types perfectly.

The Isolating Type A language is **isolating** or **analytic** to the extent that its words consist of a single morpheme. Because most words consist only of a root, there are few bound morphemes (affixes). Categories such as number and tense are usually expressed by a free morpheme (a separate word). In Mandarin, for instance, tense is indicated by a free morpheme whose position with respect to other elements is variable.

> *3.* Ta chi fan le.
> he eat meal past
> 'He ate the meal.'
> Ta chi le fan.
> he eat   past meal
> 'He ate the meal.'

Other languages that are predominantly isolating include Cantonese, Vietnamese, Laotian, and Cambodian.

The Agglutinating Type An **agglutinating** language makes extensive use of words containing two or more morphemes (a root and one or more affixes). In such languages, each affix is clearly identifiable and characteristically encodes a single grammatical contrast. Turkish words can have a complex morphological structure, but each morpheme has a single clearly identifiable function. In the words in Table 8.5, for instance, *-ler* marks plurality, *-de* indicates 'in', and *-den* corresponds to 'from'.

Table 8.5 Affixes in Turkish

ev	'house'
ev-ler	'houses'
ev-ler-de	'in the houses'
ev-ler-den	'from the houses'

The Fusional Type Words in a **fusional** or an **inflectional language** are also complex. However, in contrast with agglutinating systems, fusional affixes often mark several grammatical categories simultaneously. In Russian, for example, a single inflectional affix simultaneously marks the noun's gender class (masculine, feminine, or neuter), its number (singular or plural), and its grammatical role (subject, direct object, and so on). The ending *-a*, for instance, can be used to indicate that a noun belongs to the feminine gender class, is singular, and functions as subject. (As noted in Chapter 4, such affixes are called portmanteau morphemes.)

4. Ptits-a pela.
'(A) bird sang.'

If you look again at the noun paradigms for Russian given in the chapter on morphology, you will see that this situation is typical of the entire case system in that language.

The Polysynthetic Type In a **polysynthetic** language, long strings of affixes or bound forms are united into single words, which may translate as an entire sentence in English. The use of portmanteau morphemes is common, although the extent to which this happens varies from language to language. Polysynthetic structures can be found in many native languages of North America, including Inuktitut, Cree, and Sarcee. The following example is from Inuktitut.

5. Qasuiirsarvigssarsingitluinarnarpuq.
qasu-iir -sar   -vig   -ssar
tired not cause-to-be place-for suitable
-si -ngit -luinar   -nar   -puq
find not completely someone 3rd sg.
'Someone did not find a completely suitable resting place.'

Most languages, including English, do not belong exclusively to any of the four categories. English employs analytic patterns in many verbal constructions, where each notion is expressed by a separate word. Future time, for instance, is indicated by a free morpheme, rather than an affix, in structures such as *I will leave*. In contrast, English exhibits considerable agglutination in derived words, such as *unwillingness*, which consist of a series of morphemes, each with a clearly definable meaning and function. The English pronoun system, on the other hand, is largely fusional since a single form can be used to indicate person, number, gender, and case. The word *he*, for instance, is used to express a third person, singular, masculine subject.

Implicational Universals A variety of generalizations can be made about word structure in human language.
- If a language has inflectional affixes, it will also have derivational affixes. For example, English not only has inflectional affixes such as the past tense *-ed* and possessive *-'s*, but it also contains derivational affixes like *un-* (*unhappy, unwanted*) and *-ly* (*quickly, slowly*).
- If a word has both a derivational and an inflectional affix, the derivational affix is closer to the root (DA = derivational affix; IA = inflectional affix), as illustrated in Table 8.6.

Table 8.6 The ordering of derivational and inflectional affixes

English
friend-ship-s   *friend-s-ship
  root DA IA   root IA DA

Turkish
iʃ   -tʃi   -ler   *iʃ   -ler   -tʃi
work   -er   *pl.*   work   *pl.*   -er
root   DA   IA   root   IA   DA

- If a language has only suffixes, it will also have only postpositions. (As noted in Chapter 5, postpositions are the equivalent of prepositions in languages that place the head at the end of the phrase.) Turkish, for example, has only suffixes; as expected, it also has postpositions rather than prepositions. This is illustrated in the following sentence.

6. Ahmet Ayʃe itʃin kitab-ɨ aldɨ.
   Ahmet Ayʃe for book-Ac bought
   'Ahmet bought a book for Ayʃe.'

Syntax

Because we lack detailed descriptions for most of the world's languages, much of the work on syntactic universals has been restricted to the study of word order as it occurs in simple declarative sentences such as *The men built the house*. Patterns are classified in terms of the relative ordering of the subject (S), direct object (O), and verb (V). The three most common word orders (in descending order of frequency) are SOV, SVO, and VSO.

7. SOV   (Turkish)
   Hasan økyz-y aldɨ.
   Hasan ox-Ac bought
   'Hasan bought the ox.'
8. SVO   (English)
   The athlete broke the record.
9. VSO   (Welsh)
   Lladdodd y ddraig y dyn.
   killed   the dragon the man
   'The dragon killed the man.'

All three of these word order patterns place the subject before the direct object. It has been suggested that the subject appears at a relatively early point in the utterance because it usually encodes the topic; that is, it indicates what the rest of the sentence is about.

While patterns that place the subject before the direct object are by far the most frequent in human language, they are not universal. There are a few VOS languages, the best-known example of which is Malagasy, the language of Madagascar.

10. VOS   (Malagasy)
    Nahita ny mpianatra ny vehivavy.
    saw   the student   the woman
    'The woman saw the student.'

As well, there are a very few OVS languages, all of which seem to be spoken in the Amazon basin of South America.

11. OVS (Hixkaryana)
    Toto jahosije kamara.
    man grabbed jaguar
    'The jaguar grabbed the man.'

Implicational Universals Sometimes, the order of elements within one kind of structure has implications for the arrangement of elements in other structures. Some of these implicational universals are stated here.

- If a language has VSO word order, then it will have prepositions rather than postpositions. Languages of this type include Berber (spoken in Morocco), Classical Hebrew, Maori (spoken in New Zealand), Maasai (spoken in Kenya), Welsh, and Irish.

12. VSO   (Irish)
Chonaic mé mo mháthair.
saw   I my mother
'I saw my mother.'

sa teach
in house
'in the house'

- If a language has SOV word order, then it will probably have postpositions rather than prepositions. Languages with this structural pattern include Basque, Burmese, Hindi, Japanese, Korean, Quechua, Turkish, and Guugu Yimidhirr, an aboriginal language of Australia.

13. SOV   (Guugu Yimidhirr)
Gudaa-ngun jarrga djindaj.
dog-Erg   boy   bit
'The dog bit the boy.'

juwaal nganh
beach from
'from the beach'

- In languages with VSO word order, adjectives and relative clauses usually follow the noun that they modify.

14. VSO   (Hebrew)
wajxal ʔĕlohim bajjom   haʃʃəviʕi məlaxto ʔaʃer ʕɔsɔ
and-ended God   on-the-day the-seventh his-work that he-did
'And God finished the work that he did on the seventh day.'
- Languages with SOV order will usually place both adjectives and relative clauses before the noun they modify.

15. SOV   (Japanese)
atarashii kutsu
new   shoes

[Yamada-ga katte iru] saru
Yamada-N keep pres. monkey
'the monkey which Yamada keeps'

Grammatical Hierarchies Implicational universals are often stated in terms of hierarchies of categories or relations. One of the most important hierarchies of this type refers to the grammatical relations of subject and direct object (see Chapter 5).

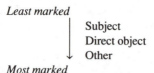

Least marked
    Subject
    Direct object
    Other
Most marked

Figure 8.4 Hierarchy of grammatical relations

Hierarchies represent degrees of markedness, with the least marked option at the top and the most marked at the bottom. According to the hierarchy in Figure 8.4, then, a process that applies only to subjects is less marked than a process that applies to direct objects, and so on. Given the definition of markedness outlined at the beginning of Section 2, this entails that if a particular phenomenon applies to direct objects, it should also apply to subjects. The converse, however, need not be true: it would not be surprising to find a process that applies to subjects but not direct objects.

Among the many typological phenomena that comply with this hierarchy is verb agreement, first mentioned in Chapter 4. As the following examples show, there are languages in which the verb agrees with just the subject and there are languages in which it agrees with both the subject and the direct object. (3 = 3rd person, sg = singular, pl = plural)

16. Agreement with subject only (Spanish):
    Subject
    Juan   parti-ó.
    Juan   leave-3/sg/pst
    'Juan left.'

17. Agreement with subject and direct object (Swahili):
    Subject   *Direct object*
    Juma a- li- wa- piga watoto
    June 3/sg pst-3/pl hit children
    'Juma hit the children.'

As predicted by the hierarchy, however, there are no languages in which the verb agrees with just the direct object.

Explaining Universals

At present, linguists are a long way from explaining why linguistic universals exist. Nonetheless, a number of interesting proposals have been made, and it is worthwhile to consider a sampling of them here.

Phonology Perceptual factors play a role in shaping phonological universals. Vowel systems (discussed earlier in the chapter) develop so as to keep vocalic phonemes as different from each other as possible. A three vowel system such as the one in Figure 8.5 allows for plenty of "space" around each vowel, which may make each easier to distinguish from the others. It may also be the case

i   u

   a

Figure 8.5 A three vowel system

that front vowels are normally unrounded, and back (nonlow) vowels are normally rounded because these vowel types are easier to perceive. Similarly, the fact that /s/ is the most commonly occurring fricative may have to do with its acoustic prominence: varieties of /s/ are inherently louder than other kinds of fricatives.

It has been recently suggested that consonant systems, like vowel systems, are shaped in response to articulatory markedness relations. For example, articulatorily basic obstruents such as [p], [t], and [k] are universally used before more complex articulations such as [tɬ] and [qʷ] come into play. Table 8.7 shows the set of obstruents that is exploited first cross-linguistically.

Table 8.7 Obstruents found cross-linguistically

p	t	k	?
b	d	g	
f	s		h
	tʃ		

Languages tend to have consonant systems that consist of about 70 percent obstruents and 30 percent sonorants, no matter what the total size of their consonant inventories may be. These figures appear to reflect the kind of space that is available for consonant contrasts: more distinctions can be made among obstruents than among sonorants. There are, for example, no nasal fricative consonants, because the air pressure needed to force air through the narrow articulatory opening characteristic of fricatives cannot be built up when so much air is flowing through the nasal passage at the same time. The number of obstruent consonants in any language is thus potentially larger than the number of sonorant consonants. This is just one example of how considerations involving articulatory complexity can play a role in the shaping of consonant systems.

Morphology Other types of explanations may be appropriate for morphological universals. For example, the fact that languages with suffixes but no prefixes always have postpositions has a historical explanation. In these languages, some postpositions became attached to a preceding word and were thereby converted into suffixes. Because suffixes in such languages have evolved from postpositions, the link between the two elements can be traced to their common origin.

The requirement that derivational affixes occur closer to the root than inflectional affixes has another type of explanation. As noted in the morphology chapter, processes such as derivation form new words, while inflection marks the subclass (plural, past tense) to which a word belongs. Given that a word must be formed before its subclass can be determined, it follows that derivational processes will precede inflection. This is reflected in word structure, where derivational affixes appear closer to the root than inflectional markers. In Figure 8.6, the verbal root *treat* is converted into a noun by the affix *-ment* before the plural inflectional marker is added.

Syntax At least some syntactic universals may be explainable in terms of the way that the human brain processes sentence structure. Consider in this respect Table 8.8, which presents a summary of word order patterns based on the

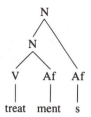

Figure 8.6

Table 8.8 Word order patterns

Phrase type	Pattern A	Pattern B
VP	*verb*-object	object-*verb*
NP	*noun*-adjective	adjective-*noun*
	noun-relative clause	relative clause-*noun*
PP	*preposition*-NP	NP-*postposition*

implicational universals discussed earlier. In order to explain why the word order properties in each column co-occur in most languages, we must use the notion of head introduced in the chapter on syntax. As you may recall, the head is the obligatory category around which a phrase is organized. Thus, V is the head of VP, N is the head of NP, and P is the head of PP. By re-examining the data in Table 8.8, you will notice an interesting generalization: the word order patterns in the left column place the head (in italics) first while those in the right column place it last. It has been suggested that syntactic structures are easier to produce and understand if the head is always uniformly at the beginning or the end of phrases; this may explain why word order patterns co-occur in the manner illustrated.

This preference cannot be absolute since there are many languages that do not observe a uniform head-first or head-last order. In English, for example, the verb typically comes at the beginning of the VP and the preposition at the beginning of the PP, but nouns occur in the middle of NPs.

18. [NP the new *book* about fitness]

The study of linguistic typology and language universals is a relatively new field within linguistics. There is obviously much still to be learned about linguistic universals, and it must be admitted that some of the current work is speculative and incomplete. No doubt many interesting new facts will eventually come to light.

8.3 GENETIC CLASSIFICATION

The world's languages can be grouped into a relatively small number of language families. However, genetic classification is sometimes difficult for a number of reasons.

Perhaps the biggest problem is simply the amount of data that must be collected before linguists can be confident about the status of a number of groups of languages. It is only in the last two decades, for example, that enough information has been accumulated to propose a detailed classification of the languages of Africa.

In many cases, linguists face the problem of establishing the tests or criteria to be used in proposing genetic relationships. There is some disagreement over the degree of similarity that should exist among languages before a genetic relationship can be proposed. This issue arises because unrelated languages will often share structural characteristics (that is, be typologically similar). This is particularly likely to occur if languages have been in contact long enough to have borrowed a large number of words, sounds, morphemes, or syntactic structures from one another.

Additional difficulties stem from the fact that genetically related languages need *not* be typologically similar. This is especially true if the relationship is a distant one, as is the case with English and Russian. Russian is highly inflectional, has an extensive case system, and has quite free word order, while English is only marginally inflectional, has virtually no case marking, and has fixed word order. Yet, both belong to the Indo-European family.

To complicate matters further still, linguists also disagree as to the number of cognates that must be uncovered before a genetic relationship between languages can be established. The more distant the genetic relationship between languages, the less likely it is that a large number of obvious cognates will be found. Sound changes, for example, can obscure similarities between cognate words. English and Latin are related (though distantly), but the similarity between cognates like Latin *unda*, meaning 'wave', and English *water* is certainly not striking.

Research is hampered as well by the fact that words that may be excellent indicators of a genetic relationship can drop out of the lexicon. For example, Old English had a word *leax* ('salmon') which was cognate with German *Lachs* and Yiddish *lox*, but this lexical item has since been lost from the English lexicon.

Nevertheless, languages that are genetically related do share many similarities, particularly if their common ancestor is not too distant. Some language families contain many hundreds of languages; in other cases, only one language may remain to represent a family; in still other cases, families have become extinct. The following sections present some information about the makeup and membership of a few of the language families represented in the world today.

The Indo-European Family

With only about a hundred languages, Indo-European is not a large family in terms of total number of languages. However, it is the largest language family in the world in terms of total number of speakers: there are about 1.7 billion native speakers of an Indo-European language. Living Indo-European languages can be assigned to one of the nine branches illustrated in Table 8.9.

Table 8.9 Main branches of the Indo-European family

Germanic
Celtic
Italic
Hellenic
Albanian
Armenian
Baltic
Slavic
Indo-Iranian

Germanic The organization of the Germanic family of languages is illustrated in Table 8.10. (In this and other tables, parentheses are used to indicate languages that no longer have any speakers. The tables are intended to exemplify

Table 8.10 The Germanic family

(East Germanic)	North Germanic	West Germanic
(Gothic)	Icelandic	German
	Faroese	Dutch
	Norwegian	Frisian
	Danish	English
	Swedish	Afrikaans
		Yiddish

the membership and organization of language families, not to provide an exhaustive list of the languages in each family.) As Table 8.10 indicates, the Germanic branch of Indo-European can be divided into three subbranches. The East Germanic branch included Gothic, the oldest Germanic language for which written texts exist (dating from the fourth century A.D.). Gothic and any other languages belonging to this branch of Germanic have long been extinct. The North Germanic (or Scandinavian) branch originally included Old Norse, a dialect of which was spoken by the Vikings, and Old Icelandic. From it, descended Icelandic, Faroese (spoken on the Faroe islands, north of Scotland), Swedish, Danish, and Norwegian.

The West Germanic branch includes German, Dutch, Afrikaans, Frisian, and English. Afrikaans is descended from the Dutch spoken by seventeenth-century settlers in South Africa (the Boers). Frisian is spoken on the north coast of Holland, and on the Frisian islands just off the coast, as well as on the northwestern coast of Germany. English descended from the speech of the Angles, Saxons, and Jutes, Germanic tribes that lived in northern Germany and southern Denmark (in an area just east of the Frisians) before invading England and settling there in A.D. 449.

Celtic The Celtic branch of Indo-European (see Table 8.11) has two main subbranches: Insular and Continental (now extinct). One representative of the latter subbranch, Gaulish, was once spoken in France but has long been

Table 8.11 The Celtic family

	Insular	(Continental)
Brythonic	Goidelic	
Welsh	Irish [= Irish Gaelic]	(Gaulish)
Breton	Scots Gaelic	
(Cornish)	(Manx)	

extinct. The Insular subbranch can be subdivided into two groups of languages: Brythonic and Goidelic. Brythonic languages include Welsh and Breton (which is spoken in northwestern France), as well as Cornish, which was formerly spoken in Britain but is now extinct. The Goidelic branch contains

Irish (or Irish Gaelic), which is still spoken natively in the western parts of Ireland, and Scots Gaelic, which is native to some of the northwestern parts of Scotland (especially the Hebrides Islands) and, to a lesser extent, Cape Breton Island in Nova Scotia.

Italic The Italic family originally consisted of a variety of languages spoken in the area corresponding roughly to modern-day Italy. The Italic languages that are presently spoken are all descended from Latin, the language of the vast Roman Empire, and are called Romance languages. It is customary to divide this language family into an Eastern group (consisting of Italian and Rumanian) and a Western group consisting of all the other Romance languages with the exception of Sardinian (which stands alone). The Western group is further divided into Ibero-Romance (Spanish, Portuguese, and Catalan) and Gallo-Romance, which includes the Romance languages spoken in France and Switzerland. These divisions are illustrated in Table 8.12.

Table 8.12 The Romance family

Eastern	Western		
	Ibero-Romance	Gallo-Romance	
Italian	Spanish	French	Sardinian
Rumanian	Portuguese	Occitan	
	Catalan	Romansch	

Hellenic The Hellenic branch of Indo-European has only one living member, Greek. Nearly all modern Greek dialects are descended from the Hellenistic Koine, a dialect based on Attic Greek, which was the speech of Athens during the Golden Age of Greek culture (500 to 200 B.C.).

Albanian The Albanian branch of Indo-European has only one member, Albanian, which is spoken not only in Albania, but also in parts of what was Yugoslavia, Greece, and Italy.

Armenian The Armenian branch also has only one member, Armenian. This language is concentrated in Armenia (between the Black Sea and the Caspian Sea, in the area known as the Caucasus) and in northeastern Turkey.

Baltic The Baltic branch contains only two surviving languages, Latvian and Lithuanian. Both are spoken in the Baltic countries just northeast of Poland. Lithuanian has an elaborate case system, which resembles the one posited for Proto-Indo-European.

Slavic The Slavic branch of Indo-European can be divided into three sub-branches: East, South, and West. The East Slavic branch is made up of Russian, Ukrainian, and Byelorussian (or White Russian); the latter is spoken in Byelorus, just east of the northern half of Poland. The South Slavic branch includes Bulgarian, Macedonian, Serbo-Croatian, and Slovenian. The latter three languages are all spoken in what was Yugoslavia. Both Macedonian and

Bulgarian are unlike other Slavic languages in having lost most of their case endings. The West Slavic branch includes Czech (the language of the Czech Republic), Slovak (the language of Slovakia), and Polish. The organization of the Slavic group of languages is represented in Table 8.13.

Table 8.13 The Slavic family

East Slavic	South Slavic	West Slavic
Russian	Slovenian	Czech
Ukrainian	Serbo-Croatian	Slovak
Byelorussian	Macedonian	Polish
	Bulgarian	Sorbian

Indo-Iranian   The Indo-Iranian branch of Indo-European is divided into Iranian and Indic subbranches. The Iranian subbranch contains about two dozen different languages, including Modern Persian (also called Farsi and spoken in Iran), Pashto (the principal language of Afghanistan), and Kurdish (found in Iran, Iraq, Turkey, and Syria). Other Iranian languages are spoken in Pakistan, Central Asia, and China.

There are about thirty-five different Indic languages. Most of the languages spoken in Pakistan, Bangladesh, and northern India belong to this branch of Indo-European. Some of the most widespread (in terms of number of speakers) are Hindi-Urdu, Bengali, Punjabi, Marathi, and Gujarati. Although Hindi and Urdu are varieties of the same language, they have totally different writing systems and are associated with different cultures; Urdu is spoken principally in Pakistan by Muslims while Hindi is spoken primarily in India by Hindus.

Less well known as an Indic language is Romany, or Gypsy. It is believed that the Gypsies were an entertainment caste in India who were invited to perform in the Middle East sometime in the Middle Ages. They never returned to India, but traveled instead to Turkey and, eventually, Europe. Romany contains many borrowed words—particularly from Greek, which was spoken in Turkey at the time of their stay. Table 8.14 depicts the organization of

Table 8.14 The Indo-Iranian family

Iranian	Indic
Persian [= Farsi]	Hindu-Urdu
Pashto	Bengali
Kurdish	Punjabi
	Marathi
	Gujarati
	Romany [= Gypsy]

Indo-Iranian. The map in Figure 8.7 illustrates the geographic location of the Indo-European families identified in this chapter.

Some Other Families

Although no introductory text could undertake to present a comprehensive survey of the world's language families, some further discussion of this topic is warranted in order to illustrate the extraordinary diversity of human language.

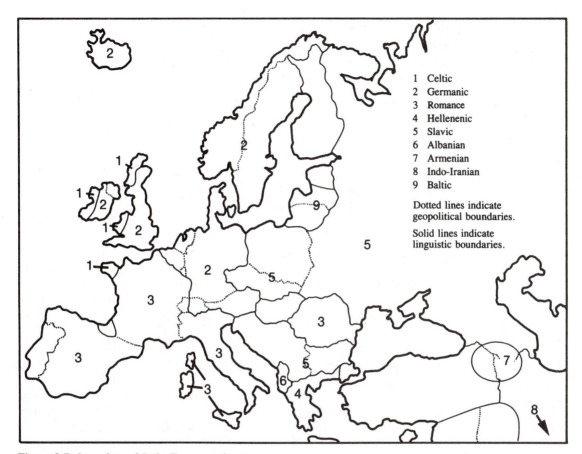

Figure 8.7 Location of Indo-European languages

Altaic The Altaic family stretches from Turkey to China in a continuum of languages. Altaic languages are also found in Siberia and East Asia. The membership of the Altaic family (see Table 8.15) is still very much in dispute, but it probably includes at least three branches: Turkic, Mongolian, and Tungusic. Recent scholarship has collected substantial evidence that Korean and Japanese are also members of the Altaic family. However, dissenting scholars argue that the similarities between Japanese, Korean, and the other languages in this proposed family are primarily typological, and that there are few reliable cognates encompassing the complete spectrum of the proposed Altaic family.

The Turkic languages of the Altaic family, spoken by more than eighty million people, include Turkish, Uzbek, Azerbaijani, Tatar, Uighur, Kazakh, and Yakut. The Mongolian languages are spoken by around ten million people, primarily in Mongolia and China, while the Tungusic languages are found in central Siberia and Mongolia. The number of speakers of Tungusic languages probably does not exceed one million people.

Altaic languages are usually agglutinating, often with several suffixes in the same word. They normally employ SOV word order and typically use

Table 8.15 The Altaic family

Turkic	Tungusic	Mongolian		
Turkish	Evenki	Khalkha	Korean	Japanese
Uzbek	Chakar	Buriat		
Azerbaijani				
Tatar [= Tartar]				
Uighur				
Kazakh				
Yakut				

postpositions rather than prepositions. Many Altaic languages have vowel harmony, a phonological phenomenon in which all vowels of a word share certain features, such as [round] or [back]. They are usually not tone languages.

Uralic The Uralic family (see Table 8.16) contains about twenty languages and has about twenty-two million speakers. Uralic languages are spoken in a band across the northern part of the temperate zone of Europe, all the way from northern Norway to Siberia. Uralic has two major branches: Samoyedic and Finno-Ugric. The Samoyedic branch contains a handful of languages spoken in northern Russia, particularly in areas around the Ural Mountains and also in Siberia.

The most widely spoken Finno-Ugric language is Hungarian. Other Finno-Ugric languages are Finnish, Lapp or Lappish, Estonian, Livonian, Karelian, and Mordvin or Mordva. Uralic languages are primarily agglutinating, and most have postpositions with SOV or SVO word order. The nouns often have many cases (Finnish has fifteen) that appear to have developed historically from postpositions that became attached to nouns as suffixes. Uralic languages are normally not tonal.

Table 8.16 The Uralic family

Finno-Ugric		Samoyedic
Finnic	Ugric	
Livonian	Vogul	Nganasan
Estonian	Ostyak	Selkup
Finnish	Hungarian	Nenets
Vodian		Enets
Vepsian		
Karelian		
Lapp/Saame		
Mordvin		
Cheremis		
Votyak		
Komi		

Caucasian The languages that are normally grouped together as Caucasian have not yet been assigned to families in a definitive way. These languages are primarily spoken in northeastern Turkey and between the Black Sea and the Caspian Sea, in and around the Caucasus Mountains. The best evidence so far points to three distinct language families—Northwest Caucasian, Northeast Caucasian, and South Caucasian (see Table 8.17).

Table 8.17 The Caucasian languages

The South Caucasian (Kartvelian) family
Georgian
Svan
Laz-Mingrelian

The Northwest Caucasian family
Kabardian [= Circassian]
Abkhaz

The Northeast Caucasian family
Chechen
Lezghian
Avar

South Caucasian (sometimes called Kartvelian) consists of Georgian, Svan, and Laz-Mingrelian. Northwest Caucasian contains Circassian (or Kabardian) and Abkhaz, while Northeast Caucasian consists of about two dozen languages; of these, Chechen, Lezghian, and Avar have the largest number of speakers. Altogether there are about thirty-five languages in the three separate families, with a total of approximately five million speakers.

Although no genetic relationship has been proven to exist among these three families, they do seem to share a number of areal features (probably brought about through mutual borrowing): many Caucasian languages have glottalized consonants, complex consonant clusters, a large consonantal inventory, and very few vowel phonemes.

Dravidian There are twenty-three Dravidian languages (see Table 8.18), which are primarily found in the southern half of India. About a hundred and fifty

Table 8.18 The Dravidian family

North Dravidian	Central Dravidian	South Dravidian
Kurukh	Telugu	Tamil
Malto	Kolami	Malayalam
	Gondi	Kannada
		Toda
		Tulu
		Kodagu

million people are native speakers of a Dravidian language. The most widely spoken languages in this family are Telugu, Tamil, Kannada, and Malayalam. Dravidian languages are normally SOV. They are agglutinating and nontonal, and usually have initial stress.

Austro-Asiatic The Austro-Asiatic family of languages (see Table 8.19) consists of about a hundred and fifty languages with approximately forty million speakers. The Munda branch of Austro-Asiatic includes languages spoken in central and northeastern India, such as Santali and Mundari. Mon-Khmer is the largest branch of Austro-Asiatic and contains languages such as Cambo-

Table 8.19 The Austro-Asiatic family

Munda	Mon-Khmer	Nicobarese
Santali	Vietnamese	Car
Mundari	Cambodian [= Khmer]	Nancowry
Ho	Mon	
	Khasi	
	Bahnar	

dian (also called Khmer) and many other languages of Cambodia, Vietnam, Burma, and southern China. Other Austro-Asiatic languages are spoken in Malaysia and on the Nicobar Islands (northwest of Sumatra). Some Austro-Asiatic languages are tonal (for example, Vietnamese) and some are characterized by large and complex vowel systems. Word order is generally SVO or SOV.

Sino-Tibetan In terms of numbers of speakers, the Sino-Tibetan family (see Table 8.20) is the largest language family after Indo-European. There are about

Table 8.20 The Sino-Tibetan family

Tibeto-Burman	Sinitic	
	Northern	Southern
Burmese	Mandarin	Wu
Tibetan		Cantonese
Sharpa		Hakka
		Hsiang
		Kan
		Northern Min
		Southern Min

three hundred Sino-Tibetan languages, with a total of approximately seven hundred million speakers. There are two major branches: the Tibeto-Burman branch and the Sinitic branch. To the first branch belong the Tibetan languages, Burmese, and many other languages spoken in northeastern India, Nepal, Burma, and Tibet. The Sinitic branch contains the languages that we call Chinese. Although a number of these languages are mutually unintelligible, they are usually called "dialects," primarily because the same writing system is used across China and can be understood by speakers of different Chinese languages (see Chapter 13). The Sinitic languages can be divided into two groups: Northern and Southern. The Northern branch contains Mandarin, which has dialects spoken in Peking (Beijing), Szechuan, and Nanking. The major Southern Sinitic languages are Wu (with dialects in Shanghai and Suchow), Cantonese, Hakka, Hsiang, Kan, Southern Min, and Northern Min.

Sino-Tibetan languages are usually tonal. They are also normally isolating languages, having many monomorphemic (and usually monosyllabic) words. Consonant clusters are normally avoided; word order is SVO or SOV.

Austronesian The Austronesian family contains over nine hundred languages divided into numerous subgroups and spoken over an area that extends from

Hawaii to Easter Island, New Zealand, Southeast Asia, and Madagascar, off the coast of Africa. The single largest grouping within the Austronesian family consists of the Malayo-Polynesian languages, which are found throughout Polynesia, Micronesia, Melanesia, Indonesia, and in some areas of mainland Southeast Asia.

One feature characteristic of Austronesian languages is the frequent use of reduplication; many of these languages also use infixes. Verb-initial sentence structure is also common, especially among the approximately one hundred Austronesian languages of Formosa (Taiwan) and the Philippines. Some of the subdivisions within the Austronesian family along with a small sample of their member languages are given in table 8.21.

Table 8.21 The Austronesian family

Formosan	Malayo-Polynesian			
	Eastern		Central	Western
	South Halmahera/ West New Guinea	Oceanic		
Amis	Saparan	Fijian	Soboyo	Tagalog
Bunun	Buli	Tongan	Seho	Cebuano
Paiwan	Sawai	Tahitian	Koba	Bontok
Puyuma	Sekar	Samoan	Bia	Ilokano
Rukai	Onin	Maori		Malay
Seediq	Ansus	Hawaiian		Balinese
Atayal		Ponapean		Malagasy
Tsou		Gilbertese		Javanese
		Mandak		Chamorro

Some work currently in progress seeks to link the Austronesian family with the Kam-Tai family (which includes Thai, Laotian, and many other languages of Southeast Asia) to form a still larger Austro-Tai family. However, this relationship is still tentative, and other research suggests that Austronesian is genetically linked to the Austro-Asiatic family of Southeast Asia and India (see above).

Australian Recent studies have established that all of the aboriginal languages of Australia belong to one Australian family. There are about two hundred such languages, but many have very few speakers. There are currently only about thirty thousand speakers of aboriginal Australian languages.

The majority of Australian languages are spoken in Arnhem Land (north central Australia) and the northern part of Western Australia. The languages with the largest number of speakers are Mabuiag (seven thousand speakers on the Torres Straits Islands, north of Australia) and the Western Desert Language (four thousand speakers in Western Australia).

Australian languages are characterized by simple vowel systems, and are not tone languages. Nouns are normally marked for case, sometimes in unusual and intricate ways, and word order is sometimes very free.

Afro-Asiatic Afro-Asiatic languages (see Table 8.22) are spoken primarily across the northern half of Africa and in the Middle East. There are about two

Table 8.22 The Afro-Asiatic family

(Egyptian)	Cushitic	Berber	Chadic	Semitic
(Coptic)	Somali	Tuareg Tamazight Shilha	Hausa	(Babylonian) Amharic Hebrew Aramaic Arabic

hundred and fifty Afro-Asiatic languages and a hundred and seventy-five million speakers of these languages. Afro-Asiatic has five main branches of which one, the Egyptian branch, no longer contains any living languages. Old Egyptian, once spoken by the ancient Pharaohs, has long been extinct. Its descendant, Coptic, is now used only as the liturgical language of the Coptic church. The remaining branches are highly distinct from each other.

Another branch of Afro-Asiatic is Cushitic, whose member languages are spoken in the Sudan, Ethiopia, Somalia, and Kenya. A third branch, Berber, includes several languages of Algeria, Morocco, and Niger, such as Tuareg and Tamazight. Still another branch of Afro-Asiatic, Chadic, contains many of the languages of Chad and Nigeria, such as Hausa. These languages, unlike other Afro-Asiatic languages, are tonal.

The fifth and largest branch of Afro-Asiatic (in terms of number of speakers) is the Semitic branch. Many (now extinct) languages mentioned in the Bible were of Semitic origin, such as Babylonian (also known as Assyrian or Akkadian), Canaanite, Moabite, Classical Hebrew, and Aramaic.

Classical Hebrew has not been spoken as a native language for millenia, although it has been maintained as a written language by Hebrew scholars. Modern Hebrew (or Israeli) is not directly descended from Classical Hebrew; rather it was created (or re-created) at the beginning of this century by regularizing some aspects of Classical Hebrew and adding new vocabulary. Modern Hebrew has only had native speakers for the past century.

Still another Semitic language, Arabic, has several varieties, not all of which are mutually intelligible. Varieties of Arabic are spoken all across North Africa and throughout the Middle East. All of these are descended from Classical Arabic, which was the language of Mohammed, the founder of Islam, and is the language of the Koran, the holy book of Islam.

The Semitic languages are characterized by a system of consonantal roots. Most roots consist of three consonants with vowels being inserted to indicate various inflectional and derivational categories. For example, Arabic has the root *k-t-b* (denoting the concept of writing) from which a variety of words can be formed, including *kitābun* 'book', *kātibun* 'writer', *kataba* 'he had written', and *jaktubu* 'he will write'. The Semitic languages frequently have pharyngeal or pharyngealized consonants.

Niger-Kordofanian Most of the languages spoken in Sub-Saharan Africa, about nine hundred, belong to the Niger-Kordofanian family of languages (see Table 8.23). In all, there are approximately a hundred and eighty million speakers of these languages. Two major branches exist: the Kordofanian

Table 8.23 The Niger-Kordofanian family

Kordofanian	Niger-Congo					
	West Atlantic	Mande	Gur	Kwa	Adamawa	Benue-Congo
Koalib	Wolof	Mandinka	Dogon	Yoruba	Sango	Efik
Katla	Fulani			Nupe	Gbaya	Tiv
				Igbo		Swahili
				Ijo		Zulu
				Ewe		Ganda
				Twi		Shona
				Kru		Kikuyu
						Kongo

branch and the Niger-Congo branch. The Kordofanian branch includes only a handful of languages spoken in the Sudan, such as Koalib and Katla. Niger-Congo, on the other hand, is much larger and can be divided into six smaller branches: West Atlantic, Mande, Gur, Kwa, Adamawa, and Benue-Congo.

The West Atlantic branch of Niger-Congo contains west coast languages such as Wolof (Senegal) and Fulani (Guinea). The Mande branch also contains many West African languages. The Kwa branch contains several Nigerian languages, such as Yoruba, Nupe, and Igbo (or Ibo), as well as Ewe (Ghana and Togo) and Twi (also called Fante, spoken in Ghana). The Adamawa branch includes languages such as Sango and Gbaya, spoken in Nigeria, Zaire, and the Central African Republic.

The Benue-Congo branch is the largest branch within Niger-Congo. The largest group of languages within this branch is the Bantu group. There are more than a hundred Bantu languages, with more than fifty-five million speakers. Some of the principal Bantu languages are Swahili (Tanzania and Kenya), Zulu (South Africa), Ganda (Uganda), Shona (Zimbabwe), and Kongo (Zaire).

Niger-Kordofanian languages are typically SVO and usually have tone systems (with the notable exception of Swahili). The Bantu languages are usually agglutinating with verb-subject and verb-direct object agreement. Languages in the Bantu group also exhibit a complex system of noun classes, each of which is marked by a distinctive set of prefixes.

Nilo-Saharan The Nilo-Saharan family is found primarily in eastern and central Africa and includes approximately one hundred and twenty languages, with about thirty million speakers. Some of the languages in this family are Maasai, Luo (both spoken in Kenya), Nubian (Sudan), Kanuri (Nigeria), and Songhai (Niger and Mali). Nilo-Saharan languages generally have tonal systems, and nouns are usually marked for case.

Khoisan The Khoisan family is quite small, containing only about thirty languages, spoken by a hundred and twenty thousand speakers. The majority of Khoisan languages are spoken in the southern and southwestern areas of Africa. Some Khoisan languages are Hottentot [=Nama], !Kung, and Sandawe (one of only two Khoisan languages spoken in eastern Africa). Khoisan languages have unusual click sounds in their consonantal systems. These clicks have been borrowed by a few neighboring Bantu languages, such as Zulu and Xhosa.

Figure 8.8 illustrates the location of the language families we have been considering.

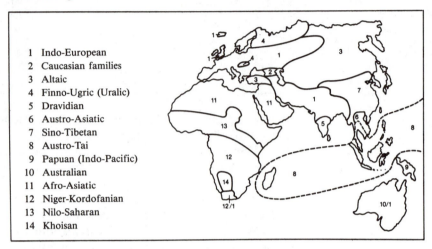

1 Indo-European
2 Caucasian families
3 Altaic
4 Finno-Ugric (Uralic)
5 Dravidian
6 Austro-Asiatic
7 Sino-Tibetan
8 Austro-Tai
9 Papuan (Indo-Pacific)
10 Australian
11 Afro-Asiatic
12 Niger-Kordofanian
13 Nilo-Saharan
14 Khoisan

Figure 8.8 Location of some Old World language families

The Americas

Contrary to popular belief, not all native American Indian (or Amerindian) languages belong to the same family. Although many of the relationships are still unclear, it appears that there are a number of different families of Amerindian languages. The major language families found in North and Central America are exemplified in Table 8.24. Their geographic location is indicated in Figure 8.9.

Table 8.24 North and Central American families

Language family	Some member languages
Eskimo-Aleut	Inuktitut
Athapaskan	Navaho, Western Apache, Hupa, Kutchin
Wakashan	Makah, Nootka, Nitinat
Salish	Flathead, Spokan, Kalispel, Coeur d'Alene
Klamath-Sahaptin	Nez Perce, Sahaptin, Klamath
Penutian	Patwin, Wintu, Nomlaki
Algonquian	Cheyenne, Potawatomi, Shawnee, Micmac
Siouan	Crow, Winnebago, Omaha
Iroquoian	Seneca, Mohawk, Oneida, Cherokee
Caddoan	Caddo, Witchita, Pawnee
Muskogean	Choctaw, Koasati, Mikasuk
Hokan	Diegueno, Yuma, Mohave
Coahuiltecan	Comecrudo, Cotoname, Pakawa, Carrizo
Uto-Aztecan	Northern Paiute, Snake, Comanche
Otomian-Pame	Otomi, Pame, Pirinda, Mazahua
Mayan	Huastecan, Cholan, Maya, Tzeltal, Tojolabal
Chibchan	Talamanca, Rama-Corobici, Cueva-Cuna

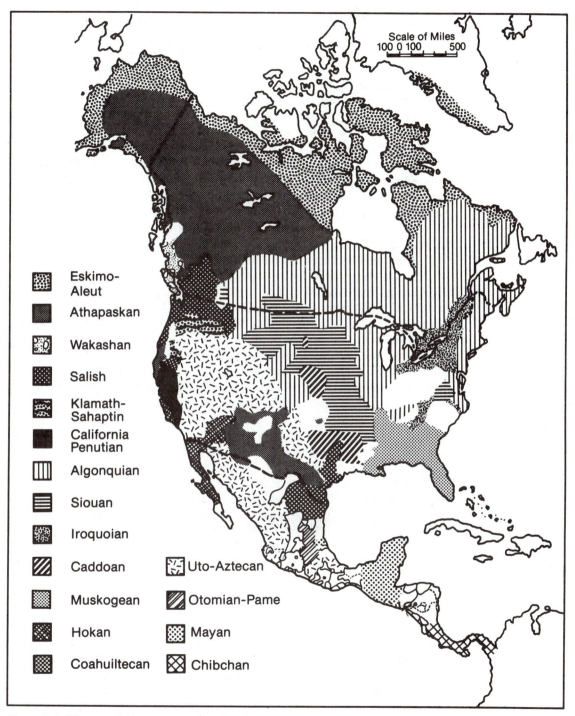

Figure 8.9 North and Central American families

In South America there are presently about eleven million people who speak an Amerindian language. There are at least six hundred different Amerindian languages spoken in South America, but our knowledge of these languages is often minimal. Some linguists estimate that there may be more than a thousand South American Amerindian languages, most of which belong to one of three families: Andean-Equatorial, Ge-Pano-Carib, and Macro-Chibchan.

The Andean-Equatorial family contains languages that are found throughout South America and may have as many as ten million speakers all together. The principal language in this family is Quechua, which has more than six million speakers. Dialects of Quechua are spoken in Peru, Ecuador, and Bolivia. This was the language of the Inca empire, which reached its height in the sixteenth century A.D., before being destroyed by the Spanish conquistadors. Other languages belonging to this family are Aymara (Peru), Arawak (Surinam), and Guarani (the major language of Paraguay). Some Andean-Equatorial languages lack laterals entirely.

The Ge-Pano-Carib family is also spread over much of South America. Some of the languages belonging to this family are Carib (Surinam), Bororo (Brazil), Witotu (Peru), and Mataco (Argentina). Languages of the Ge-Pano-Carib family often lack laterals; the dominant word order in these languages is usually SOV.

Languages of the Macro-Chibchan family are found in Central America and the northwestern part of South America. Some languages belonging to this family are Cuna (Panama), Cayapa (Ecuador), Epera (Columbia), and Warao (Venezuela). Macro-Chibchan languages generally have SOV word order.

Language Isolates

Although linguists have succeeded in placing many hundreds of the world's languages into families, there are still many other languages that cannot be so classified. A language that is not known to be related to any other living language is called an **isolate**. Basque, which is spoken in northern Spain and southern France, is such a language. Examples of other language isolates throughout the world include Ainu (northern Japan), Burushaski (Pakistan), Kutenai (British Columbia), Gilyak (Siberia), Taraskan (California), and Yukagir (Siberia).

Summing Up

The focus of this chapter is on the criteria that linguists use to classify languages and on the enormous linguistic diversity found throughout the world. Linguists sometimes attempt to classify languages solely in terms of their structural similarities and differences (that is, in terms of their **linguistic typology**), without regard for **genetic relationships**. Work in this area is primarily responsible for the discovery of linguistic **universals**, which help to identify the necessary properties of human language. The other major type of classificatory work in linguistics is concerned with establishing language families— groups of languages that are descended from a common source. While research in this area is hampered both by the large number of languages involved and the scarcity of the available data, a sizeable portion of the world's several thousand languages have been placed in families. Although there is little likelihood of ever being able to show that all human languages descended from a common source, work in this area can shed light on the nature of language change as well as on the movement of peoples throughout the world.

Key Terms

absolute universals	linguistic typology
agglutinating	linguistic universals
Amerindian	marked
analytic	markedness theory
animate	mixed
areal classification	polysynthetic
genetic classification	related
grammatical hierarchies	structural classification
head	universal tendencies
implicational universals	unmarked
isolate	word order
isolating	

Sources

The section on linguistic typology draws on data from the books by Bernard Comrie and Joseph Greenberg cited below. Other material for this section comes from *Tone: A Linguistic Survey*, edited by V. A. Fromkin (New York: Academic Press, 1978); John Hawkins's article "On Implicational and Distributional Universals of Word Order" in *Journal of Linguistics* 16: 193–235 (1980); Merrit Ruhlen's book *A Guide to the Languages of the World* (Language Universals Project: Stanford University, 1976); and the four-volume series *Universals of Human Language*, edited by J. Greenberg (Stanford, Calif.: Stanford University Press, 1978).

The section on language families is based on Bernard Comrie's book *The Languages of the Soviet Union* (London: Cambridge University Press, 1981); Joseph Greenberg's *The Languages of Africa* (Bloomington: Indiana University Press, 1966); the book by Merrit Ruhlen cited previously; and C. F. and F. M. Voegelin's *Classification and Index of the World's Languages* (cited below). The maps used to illustrate the geographic location of language families are adapted from those found in *The Origins and Development of the English Language* by T. Pyles and J. Algeo (New York: Harcourt Brace Jovanovich, 3d ed., 1982). The data for Questions 1 to 3 are found in the book by Merrit Ruhlen, cited above. The data for Question 4 were kindly provided by Dr. Leslie Saxon.

Recommended Reading

Comrie, Bernard. 1989. *Language Universals and Linguistic Typology*. 2nd ed. Chicago: University of Chicago Press.

Croft, William. 1990. *Typology and Universals*. New York: Cambridge University Press.

Greenberg, Joseph, ed. 1966. *Universals of Language*. 2d ed. Cambridge, Mass.: M.I.T. Press.

Hawkins, Peter. 1984. *Introducing Phonology*. London: Hutchinson.

Voegelin, C. F. and F. M. Voegelin. 1977. *Classification and Index of the World's Languages*. New York: Elsevier.

Questions

1. Which universal tendencies are manifested in the following two vowel systems?

   a) *Afrikaans* (South Africa) (y and ø are front rounded vowels)

   ```
   i        y              u

                    ə    o

   ɛ       ø              ɔ

                 a
   ```

   b) *Squamish* (Washington State)

   ```
   i                u

             ə

             a
   ```

2. The presence of some phonemes predicts the presence of some other phonemes in terms of implicational universals. Do the vowel systems and consonant systems below comply with the implicational universals?

   a) *Maltese Arabic*

   ```
   i       u       i:      u:

   e       o       e:      o:

        a              a:
   ```

   b) *Awji* (North New Guinea)

   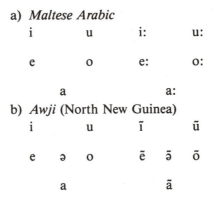

   ```
   i       u       ĩ      ũ

   e   ə   o       ẽ   ə̃   õ

        a              ã
   ```

c) *Tahitian* (Tahiti)

p   t   ?

f   h

v   r

m   n

d) *Palauan* (Palau Islands)

        t   k   ?

b

   ð

   s

m   ŋ   l   r

e) *Nengone* (Loyalty Islands, South Pacific)—Stop system only

pʰ tʰ tʰ   kʰ ?

b   d   ɖ   g

m   n   ɲ   ŋ

m̥ n̥   ŋ̥

(*Note*: ʈ and ɖ are retroflex consonants; [̥] marks a voiceless nasal; [ɲ] represents a palatal nasal.)

f) *Mixe* (South Mexico)

p   t   k ?

     d   g

     ts tʃ

     s   x h

v   ɣ

m   n

3. Morphological phenomena can be classified into four types: analytic, polysynthetic, agglutinating and fusional. Which type does each of the following languages belong to? (recip = reciprocal; caus = cause; indic = indicative or statement)

a) *Swahili*

ha -tu -ku-wa -pat-an -ish -a.
neg-1pl-pst-3pl-get-recip-caus-indic
'We didn't get them to agree with each other.'

b) *Latvian*

las-u	las-ām	rakst-u	rakst-ām
read-	read-	write-	write-
1sg/Prs	1pl/Prs	1sg/Prs	1pl/Prs
'I read'	'we read'	'I write'	'we write'

c) *Japanese*

gakusei-wa   homer-are -na -i.
student-Top praise-Pass-Neg-Prs
'The student is not praised.'

4. Analyze the following data from Latvian. Single out each morpheme and identify its meaning. Are any implicational universals reflected in the data? If so, describe how they are reflected.

  a) lidotājs   'aviator (nominative)'
  b) lidotāju   'aviator (accusative)'
  c) lidotājam   'to the aviator (dative)'
  d) lidot   'to fly'
  e) rakstītājs   'writer (nominative)'
  f) rakstītāja   'writer's (genitive)'
  g) rakstīt   'to write'

5. Consider the following data from Dogrib, an Athapaskan language spoken in Canada's Northwest Territories. Does Dogrib comply with all the word order tendencies noted earlier in Section 2.2?

  a) ʔeji done   mbehtʃi seèle ha.
     that person truck   fix   will
     'That person is going to fix the truck.'
  b) tʃeko   se-xè   ʔande ha.
     the child me-with go   will
     'The child will go with me.'
  c) done   dʒõ nàdèe
     person here lives-relative clause marker
     'the person who lives here'

6. Do the following data from Malagasy comply with all the word order tendencies for head-initial languages?

  a) amin' ny restauranta
     'to the restaurant'
  b) labiera lehibe
     beer   large
     'large beer'
  c) Entin' ny labiera ny mpiasa.
     brings the beer the waiter
     'The waiter brings the beer.'

7. To which families do the following languages belong?

a) Gujarati	j) Yuma
b) Hakka	k) Korean
c) Saame	l) Kabardian
d) Uzbek	m) Koasati
e) Sandawe	n) Hungarian
f) Huastecan	o) Flathead
g) Faroese	p) Telugu
h) Twi	q) Javanese
i) Santali	r) Navajo

8. Make a list of up to fifteen languages spoken by friends and acquaintances and identify the language family to which each belongs.

9 BRAIN AND LANGUAGE

The goal of neurology is to understand humanity
Wilder Penfield

In this chapter we will be concerned with the understanding of how language is represented and processed in the brain. This field of study is called neurolinguistics. Although the study of the relationship between brain and language is still in its infancy, much has already been learned about which parts of the brain are involved in various aspects of language production and comprehension. The field of neurolinguistics has also done much to deepen the way we think about the nature of linguistic competence.

The chapter provides a brief survey of brain structure and the methods that are currently available to study the brain. This is followed by a discussion of the different types of language disturbance that result from brain damage and by a discussion of how phonology, morphology, syntax, and semantics may be represented in the brain. The chapter concludes by reviewing the current answers to the important neurolinguistic question: Where is language?

9.1 THE HUMAN BRAIN

Contained within your skull is about 1,400 grams of pinkish-white matter. It may be the most complex 1,400 grams in the galaxy. For most of human history, however, the role of the brain as the center of mental life remained completely unknown. Even the Greek philosopher Aristotle believed that its primary function was to cool the blood.

We now know much more about the structure and functioning of the brain. But in many ways we are still quite like Aristotle, finding it hard to believe that this wrinkled mass of nerve cells could be the stuff that dreams, fears, and knowledge are made of. Nevertheless it is, and the task of brain science (or **neuroscience**) is to understand how the breadth and depth of human experience is coded in brain matter.

The brain is composed of nerve cells or **neurons** that are the basic information processing units of the nervous system. The human brain contains about ten billion neurons that are organized into networks of almost unimaginable complexity. This complexity results from the fact that each neuron can be directly linked with up to ten thousand other neurons. But the brain is not simply a mass of interconnected neurons. It is composed of structures which seem to play specific roles in the integrated functioning of the brain. The following sections provide a brief overview of these structures.

The Cerebral Cortex

The brain encompasses all the neurological structures above the spinal cord and appears to have evolved from the bottom up. The lower brain structures are shared by almost all animals. These structures are responsible for the maintenance of functions such as respiration, heart rate, and muscle coordination that are essential to the survival of all animals. As we move farther away from the spinal cord, however, we begin to find structures that have developed differently in different species. At the highest level of the brain, the **cerebral cortex**, the differences are most pronounced. Reptiles and amphibians have no cortex at all, and the progression from lower to higher mammals is marked by dramatic increases in the proportion of cortex to total amount of brain tissue. The human brain has the greatest proportion of cortex to brain mass of all animals.

In humans, the cortex is a grey wrinkled mass that sits like a cap over the rest of the brain. The wrinkled appearance results from the cortex being folded in upon itself. This folding allows a great amount of cortical matter to be compressed into the limited space provided by the human skull (in much the same way as the folding of a handkerchief allows it to fit into a jacket pocket). It has been estimated that up to 65 percent of the cortex is hidden within its folds.

It is the human cortex that accounts for our distinctness in the animal world and it is within the human cortex that the secrets of language representation and processing are to be found. The remainder of our discussion of brain structure, therefore, will focus on the features of the cerebral cortex.

The Cerebral Hemispheres

The most important orientation points in mapping the cortex are the folds on its surface. The folds of the cortex have two parts: **sulci** (pronounced /sʌlsaj/; singular: **sulcus**), which are areas where the cortex is folded in, and **gyri** (singular: **gyrus**), which are areas where the cortex is folded out toward the surface.

Figure 9.1 shows a human brain as seen from above, illustrating the many sulci and gyri of the cortex. A very prominent feature is the deep sulcus (in this case called a **fissure** because of its size) which extends from the front of the brain to the back. This fissure is known as the **longitudinal fissure**. It separates the left and right **cerebral hemispheres**. In many ways, the cerebral hemispheres can be considered to be separate brains and indeed are often referred to as the left brain and the right brain. There are two main reasons for this: the first reason is that the hemispheres are almost completely anatomically separate. The main connection between them is a bundle of nerve fibers known as the **corpus callosum**, whose primary function is to allow the two hemispheres to communicate with one another.

The other reason for considering the hemispheres to be separate brains is that they show considerable functional distinctness. In terms of muscle move-

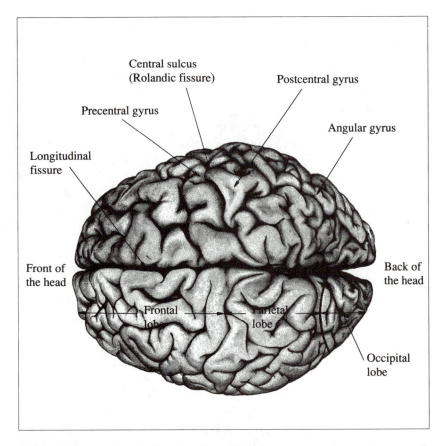

Figure 9.1 The cerebral hemispheres seen from above the head. Note the many fissures and gyri of the cortex and the prominence of the longitudinal fissure, which separates the left and right hemispheres.

ment and sensation, each hemisphere is responsible for half the body—oddly enough, the opposite half. Thus the left hemisphere controls the right side of the body and the right hemisphere controls the left side of the body. These **contralateral** (contra = opposite, lateral = side) responsibilities of the cerebral hemispheres account for the fact that people who suffer damage to one hemisphere of the brain (as a result of a stroke or accident) will exhibit paralysis on the opposite side of the body.

The hemispheres also show functional distinctness with respect to higher cognitive functions. In general, the left hemisphere seems to excel in analytic tasks such as arithmetic, whereas the right hemisphere excels in tasks which require an overall appreciation of complex patterns such as the recognition of familiar faces and melodies.

Despite the fact that the hemispheres show such specialization, we should be cautioned against sweeping generalizations about left brain versus right brain abilities or strategies. In all probability, complex mental activities involve the coordinated functioning of both hemispheres. The representation of language in the brain provides a useful example of this.

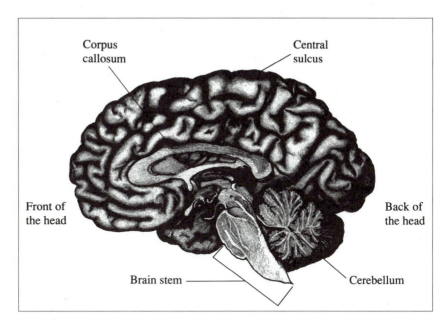

Figure 9.2 The left hemisphere seen from the inside. In this picture the corpus callosum has been cut so that one hemisphere may be separated from the other. Note how the grey cortex caps the lower structures (the brain stem and cerebellum) which are whitish in color.

Most right-handed individuals have language represented in the left cerebral hemisphere and are therefore said to be left **lateralized** for language. But not every aspect of language is represented in the left hemisphere of right-handers. Adults who have had their left cerebral hemispheres surgically removed lose most, but not all, of their linguistic competence. They typically lose the ability to speak and process complex syntactic patterns but retain some language comprehension ability. Clearly, it must be the right hemisphere that is responsible for whatever language processing ability remains.

It has also been reported that right-handed patients who suffer damage to the right cerebral hemisphere exhibit difficulty in understanding jokes and metaphors in everyday conversation. These patients are able to provide only a literal or concrete interpretation of figurative sentences such as *He was wearing a loud tie*. They frequently misunderstand people because they cannot use loudness and intonation as cues to whether a speaker is angry, excited, or merely joking. Thus the right hemisphere has a distinct role to play in normal language use.

Finally, a consideration of language representation in the brains of left-handers makes matters even more complex. Contrary to what might be expected, few left-handers have a mirror image representation for language (that is, language localization in the right hemisphere). Rather, they tend to show significant language representation in both hemispheres. Thus left-handers are generally less lateralized for language.

To sum up, although the left and right hemispheres have different abilities and different responsibilities, complex skills such as language do not always fall neatly into one hemisphere or the other. Research into why this is the case constitutes an important part of neuroscience. This research promises to reveal much about the cerebral hemispheres and about the individual representations and processes that comprise language.

The Lobes of the Cortex

We have seen that the cerebral hemispheres make distinct contributions to the overall functioning of the brain. In addition, each hemisphere contains substructures which appear to have distinct responsibilities. The substructures of the cortex in each hemisphere are called **lobes**. Like the hemispheres, the lobes of the cortex can be located with reference to prominent fissures, sulci, and gyri, which are useful as orientation points in much the same way that rivers and mountain ranges are useful in finding particular locations on a map. As can be seen in Figure 9.3, the **central sulcus** (also called the fissure of Rolando)

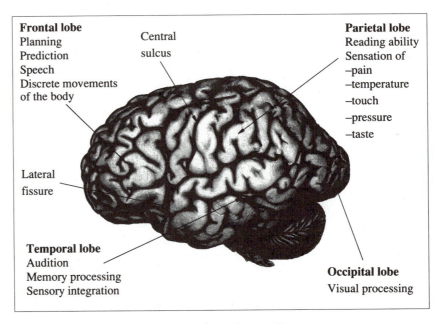

Frontal lobe
Planning
Prediction
Speech
Discrete movements
of the body

Central
sulcus

Parietal lobe
Reading ability
Sensation of
–pain
–temperature
–touch
–pressure
–taste

Lateral
fissure

Temporal lobe
Audition
Memory processing
Sensory integration

Occipital lobe
Visual processing

Figure 9.3 The left hemisphere seen from the outside

extends from the top of the cortex to another groove known as the **lateral fissure** (also called the Sylvian fissure). These two fissures are important in the delineation of the cerebral lobes. The **frontal lobe** lies in front of the central sulcus and the **parietal lobe** lies behind it. The **temporal lobe** is the area beneath the lateral fissure. The fourth lobe, the **occipital lobe**, is not clearly marked by an infolding of the cortex, but can be identified as the area to the rear of the **angular gyrus** (which has been found to play an important role in reading).

Figure 9.3 shows the left hemisphere of the brain. It indicates the location of each lobe and its specialized functions. Assuming that this is the brain of a right-hander, it is also possible to identify those areas of the cortex that have a particular role to play in language processing, as we will see.

9.2 INVESTIGATING THE BRAIN

Imagine that you could open the top of a living human being's skull and observe the brain while the individual is engaged in activities such as reading, writing, watching a baseball game, or having a heated argument. What would you see? The answer is—nothing! To the outside observer, the working brain shows no evidence of its activity. This is clearly a problem for the field of neurolinguistics, which requires the use of special investigative techniques to uncover the secrets of where and how language is processed in the brain. In addition, these special techniques must meet the ethical requirements of research with human subjects. While other neuroscientists are able to do much of their research using animal subjects, this option is not available to neurolinguists.

Imposing as they may be, the problems of investigating the processing of language in the brain are not insurmountable. Recent decades have seen a number of technological advances which have greatly facilitated the investigation of the question: What is going on in the brain when people are engaged in language behavior? In the following sections, we discuss some of the techniques of neurolinguistic investigation.

Autopsy Studies

Until recently the only way to study the brain was through **autopsy studies**. This technique was most often carried out with patients who were admitted to the hospital displaying a neurological disorder. Careful observations were made of a patient's behavior, and subsequent to his or her death, the brain was examined to determine which areas were damaged. By comparing the area of brain damage and the type of disorder the patient displayed while alive, neurologists could develop theories about the role of the damaged brain parts in normal brain functioning.

A famous example of this type of analysis comes from the work of Paul Broca, a nineteenth-century French neurologist. In 1860, Broca observed a patient who had been hospitalized for over twenty years in Paris. For most of his hospitalization, the patient was almost completely unable to speak, but appeared to understand everything that was said to him. Toward the end of his life (he died at age 57) the patient also developed a paralysis of the right arm and leg. Immediately after his death (as a result of an unrelated infection) Broca examined the brain. It showed severe damage (called a **lesion**) in the lower rear area of the left frontal lobe. Broca concluded that because the patient was unable to speak, this part of the frontal lobe must normally be responsible for speech production. Since that time, many other autopsy studies have supported Broca's conclusions. This lower rear portion of the left frontal lobe is now called **Broca's area** (see Figure 9.4 which shows this and other language processing areas of the left hemisphere). As will be discussed in Section 3, the impairment of the ability to speak as a result of brain damage is called **Broca's aphasia**.

Images of the Living Brain

Autopsy analysis has been and continues to be an important tool in the understanding of the brain. But an autopsy can only be carried out after the patient's death. Therefore, whatever information it reveals about the nature and extent of the patient's brain damage can no longer be of any use in treating the patient.

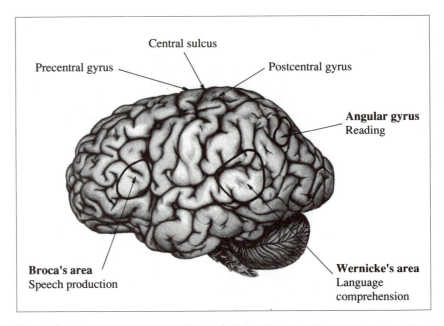

Central sulcus

Precentral gyrus

Postcentral gyrus

Angular gyrus
Reading

Broca's area
Speech production

Wernicke's area
Language
comprehension

Figure 9.4 Language processes in the left hemisphere. Damage to Broca's area is usually associated with nonfluent speech and difficulty processing complex syntactic patterns. Damage to Wernicke's area is usually associated with comprehension disturbances. Damage to the area around the angular gyrus results in reading impairment.

Computerized Axial Tomography (also called **CT scanning**) is a relatively new technique which uses a narrow beam of X-rays to create brain images that take the form of a series of brain slices. CT scans have offered neuroscientists their first opportunity to look inside a living brain. However, like autopsy, CT scanning provides a static image of the brain. It is most useful in identifying brain lesions and tumors.

Recently a number of new techniques have emerged that also make it possible to study the brain in action. One such technique is the **cerebral blood flow** study. The technique capitalizes on one of the brain's many interesting properties—it is extremely hungry for oxygen. Although the brain accounts for only about 2 percent of total body weight, it consumes about 20 percent of the oxygen the body uses while at rest. This oxygen is, of course, carried to the brain by the blood. In the cerebral blood flow technique, the subject inhales a gas that contains a radioisotope (such as Xenon 133) which enters the bloodstream and is monitored with a radioisotope detector. The detector is attached to a computer that produces images of how much blood is going to particular parts of the brain. Then, the subject is asked to engage in various sorts of cognitive activities. The neuroscientists observe the relationship between the subject's activity and the cerebral blood flow.

Cerebral blood flow studies have greatly increased our knowledge of where language processing takes place in the brain. It has been found, for example, that when subjects speak, much blood flows to the left hemisphere of the cortex and to Broca's area in particular. When subjects read, much blood flows to the occipital lobe (because it is responsible for visual processing), to the angular gyrus (which has a special role to play in reading), and to other areas of the left hemisphere. These observations support the view that the left hemisphere is primarily responsible for language and that there are specific language areas within the left hemisphere.

Learning from Hemispheric Connections and Disconnections

In the techniques that have been described, information about language representation in the brain is gained through an investigation of the brain itself. In this section, we review an alternate approach—one which examines behavior that can be associated with a particular brain hemisphere.

Dichotic Listening Studies Dichotic listening studies have been extremely important in the accumulation of the knowledge we possess about the specialization of the cerebral hemispheres. The technique capitalizes on the property of the brain that we have discussed above, namely, that each hemisphere is primarily wired to the opposite side of the body (including the head). So, most of the input to your right ear goes to the left hemisphere of your brain. Now, if the left cerebral hemisphere is indeed specialized for language processing in right-handers, these individuals should process language better through the right ear.

If you are right-handed, you will most probably be able to verify this by observing the difference between holding a telephone receiver to your right ear and holding it to your left ear during a conversation. When the receiver is held to the right ear, it will appear that the speech is louder and clearer. This phenomenon is known as the **right ear advantage (REA)**. In the laboratory technique, stereo earphones are used and different types of stimuli are presented to each ear. In general, the right ear shows an advantage for words, numbers, and Morse code, whereas the left ear shows an advantage for the perception of melodies and environmental sounds such as bird songs.

Split Brain Studies If the left hemisphere is wired to the right ear, why is it possible to understand speech presented to the left ear? There are two reasons for this. The first is that the auditory pathways to the brain are not completely crossed—there are also secondary links between each hemisphere and the ear on the same side of the body. The second is that after the right hemisphere receives information from the left ear, that information can be transferred to the left hemisphere via the corpus callosum—the bundle of fibers that connects the two hemispheres.

Evidence concerning the crucial role that the corpus callosum plays in normal brain functioning comes from the study of patients who have had this pathway surgically severed as a treatment for severe epilepsy. Studies that have investigated the effects of this surgery on cognition are referred to as **split brain experiments**. They have provided dramatic illustrations of what happens when the hemispheres cannot communicate with one another.

It appears from the behavior of split brain patients that although the right hemisphere does show some language understanding, it is mute. In one of the many split brain experiments, a patient is blindfolded and an object (for example, a key) is placed in one hand. When the key is held in the right hand, the patient can easily name it, because the right hand is directly connected to the left hemisphere, which can compute speech output. However, when the key is placed in the left hand, the patient cannot say what it is. The right hemisphere, which receives information from the left hand, knows what is there, but it can neither put this into words nor transfer the information across the severed corpus callosum to the left brain.

Split brain experiments have presented new and important knowledge about the functioning of the brain. In terms of overall investigative methodology, however, they are not quite as exotic as they seem. In fact, the logic of split brain experiments is identical to the logic employed by Broca in 1860. In both cases the researcher endeavors to learn how the normal brain works by examining which functions are lost as a result of the brain damage. In the case of split brain studies, the damage is surgically induced. In the case of Broca's patient, disease caused an experiment in nature. In the following section, we return to these experiments in nature and examine what they reveal about language representation in the brain.

9.3 APHASIA

Occasionally, humans suffer damage to particular parts of their brains. The most common cause of such brain damage is a **stroke** (also called a **cerebrovascular accident**). A language deficit caused by damage to the brain is called **aphasia**. The study of aphasia is by far the most important tool in the investigation of language in the brain. By observing and documenting the varieties of aphasic symptoms, neurolinguists have the best chance of identifying the major components of language in the brain.

In general, the amount and type of aphasic disturbance that a patient will exhibit depends on how much the brain is damaged and where it is damaged. There are many varieties of aphasia. In the following sections, we will describe some of the more important types.

C.S. Moss was a psychologist who became aphasic subsequent to a stroke. He later wrote a book about the experience entitled *Recovering with Aphasia*. The following is an excerpt from that book:

> I recollect trying to read the headlines of the *Chicago Tribune* but they didn't make any sense to me at all. I didn't have any difficulty focusing; it was simply that the words, individually or in combination, didn't have meaning, and even more amazing, I was only a trifle bothered by that fact. . . .
>
> The second week I ran into a colleague who happened to mention that it must be very frustrating for me to be aphasic since prior to that I had been so verbally facile. [I] later found myself wondering why it was not. I think part of the explanation was relatively simple. If I had lost the ability to converse with others, I had also lost the ability to engage in self-talk. In other words, I did not have the ability to think about the future—to worry, to anticipate or perceive it—at least not with words.
>
> It took a great deal of effort to keep an abstraction in mind. For example, in talking with the speech therapist I would begin to give a definition of an abstract concern, but as I held it in mind it would sort

of fade, and chances were that I would end up giving a simplified version rather than the one at the original level of conception. It was as though giving an abstraction required so much of my added intelligence that halfway through the definition I would run out of energy available to me and regress to a more concrete answer.

A consideration of Moss's recollections leads to some provocative questions about the relationship between language and thought. Is it possible that the ability to think about the future is dependent on language? Does language support abstract thought?

The type of aphasia that Moss reports involves a mixture of deficits—speaking, listening, reading, and writing. Some other forms of aphasia, however, are much more specific. In these more specific forms, particular skills are lost, and others remain intact. The study of the specific aphasias can tell us much about the building blocks of language in the brain.

Nonfluent Aphasia

Nonfluent aphasia (also called **motor aphasia**) results from damage to parts of the brain in front of the central sulcus. Recall that an important part of the frontal lobe is concerned with motor activity and that the bottom rear portion of the frontal lobe (Broca's area) is responsible for the articulation of speech (see Figure 9.4). Not surprisingly, therefore, nonfluent patients show slow effortful speech production (hence the term *nonfluent*). The most severe form of nonfluent aphasia is **global aphasia**. In this type of aphasia, the patient is completely mute. Of the less severe forms, **Broca's aphasia** is the most important.

The speech of Broca's aphasics is very halting. Patients have great difficulty in accurately producing the needed phonemes to say a word. For example, a patient who wishes to produce the sentence in *1a* would be likely to produce the utterance in *1b*.

> *1. a*) "It's hard to eat with a spoon."
> *b*) . . . har eat . . . wɪt . . . pun

The ellipsis dots (. . .) between the words in *1b* indicate periods of silence in the production of the utterance. Sentences produced at this slow rate tend to also lack normal sentence intonation. This is a common characteristic of the speech of Broca's aphasics and is called **dysprosody**. Note how the patient simplifies the consonant clusters in the words *hard* and *spoon* and changes the /θ/ to /t/ in the word *with*. The speech errors that result from these sorts of phonemic errors are called **phonemic paraphasias**.

It is tempting to think that the impairment of speech production in Broca's aphasia is caused by the fact that Broca's area is adjacent to the motor strip that controls movement of the facial muscles. The problem with this hypothesis is that damage to Broca's area usually only produces mild weakness of the muscles on the opposite side of the face and no permanent damage. Yet, for some reason, even people who can still control the muscles used in speech cannot use language properly after damage to Broca's area. This suggests that Broca's area has a language specific responsibility.

Returning to the utterance in *1b*, note that the patient also omits a number of words that would normally be used in this utterance. The words that are omitted are: *it*, *is*, *to*, *a*—the sorts of words that we too would be likely to omit if we were writing a telegram (for example, *I will meet you in the airport lounge*→ *Meet you in airport lounge*). These 'little words' are often called **function words** (Section 4.3) and their omission in the speech of Broca's aphasics has been referred to as **telegraphic speech**. (We will return to the problem of determining which items belong to the set of function words in Section 5.)

One possible account of the speech of Broca's aphasics is that it results from an economy of effort. Speech production is very effortful for these patients so they use as few words as possible because, like telegram writers, they are 'paying' by the word. But there are other characteristics of their linguistic abilities that point to a deeper cause—the disturbance of syntactic competence.

In addition to omitting function words, Broca's aphasics tend to omit inflectional affixes such as *-ing*, *-ed*, and *-en* in words such as *running*, *chased*, and *broken*. They also show difficulty judging the grammaticality of sentences. For example, given sentences such as the ones in *2*, Broca's aphasics will not always be able to determine which ones are grammatical and which ones are not.

> 2. *a*) The boy ate it up.
> *b*) *The boy ate up it.
> *c*) *Boy ate it up.
> *d*) The boy ate up the cake.

Finally, a close examination of the comprehension of Broca's aphasics offers further support to the view that there is a syntactic component to the disorder.

> 3. *a*) The mouse was chased by the cat.
> *b*) The dog was chased by the cat.
> *c*) The cat was chased by the mouse.

Broca's aphasics tend to interpret sentences such as *3a* correctly. In a sentence such as this, knowledge about the behavior of cats and mice helps the patient to guess correctly at the meaning of the sentence. For sentences such as *3b*, however, in which knowledge of the world is not a reliable guide to comprehension, patients are unsure about the meaning. Finally, Broca's aphasics tend to interpret a sentence such as *3c* as though it had the same meaning as *3a*. When we read a sentence like *3c*, we recognize it as describing an unlikely event, but our interpretation is driven by the syntax of the sentence, not by our knowledge of the world. Many Broca's aphasics appear not to have this ability.

These sorts of observations have lead many neurolinguists to reconsider the traditional view that Broca's aphasia is simply a production deficit. The possibility that Broca's aphasia also involves some central disturbance of syntactic competence is intriguing and may lead to a deeper understanding of how syntactic knowledge is represented in the brain. We will return to this question in Section 5.

A final point about Broca's aphasia is of a less technical nature but is of great importance to the understanding of the syndrome as a whole. Unlike patients such as C.S. Moss, Broca's aphasics are acutely aware of their language deficit and are typically very frustrated by it. It is as though they have complete understanding of what they should say, but to their constant dismay, find themselves unable to say it. This plight of Broca's aphasics is consistent with our understanding of the role of the frontal lobe, which is usually the site of lesion in the syndrome. Broca's area of the frontal lobe plays an extremely important role in language; however, it does not seem to be involved in the semantic relationships between words and the relationship between units of language and units of thought. The neurological basis of these meaning relationships remains almost entirely unknown. From the analysis of nonfluent aphasia in general and Broca's aphasia in particular, however, we suspect that these semantic relationships are the responsibility of areas of the brain that lie behind the central sulcus—in the temporal and parietal lobes of the brain (see Figure 9.3). This suspicion is supported by the type of language deficits associated with damage to the temporal-parietal lobes.

Fluent Aphasia

The type of aphasia which results from damage to parts of the left cortex behind the central sulcus is referred to as **fluent aphasia** (or **sensory aphasia**). This type of aphasia stands in sharp contrast to nonfluent aphasia. Fluent aphasics have no difficulty producing language, but have a great deal of difficulty selecting, organizing, and monitoring their language production.

The most important type of fluent aphasia is called **Wernicke's aphasia**. The syndrome is named after the German physiologist, Carl Wernicke, who in 1874 published a now famous report of a kind of aphasia that was almost the complete opposite of Broca's aphasia. It was determined from autopsy data that this type of aphasia was associated with a lesion in the temporal lobe just below the most posterior (rear) portion of the lateral fissure. In severe cases, the lesion could also extend upward into the lower portion of the parietal lobe. This area of the brain is now known as Wernicke's area (see Figure 9.4).

In contrast to Broca's aphasics, Wernicke's aphasics are generally unaware of their deficit. Their speech typically sounds very good: there are no long pauses; sentence intonation is normal; function words are used appropriately; word order is usually syntactically correct. The problem is that the patient rarely makes any sense. The following is a conversation between an examiner (E) and a Wernicke's patient (P).

4. *E*: How are you today, Mrs. A?
   P: Yes.
   E: Have I ever tested you before?
   P: No. I mean I haven't.
   E: Can you tell me what your name is?
   P: No, I don't I . . . right I'm right now here.
   E: What is your address?
   P: I cud /kʌd/ if I can help these this like you know . . . to make it. We are seeing for him. That is my father.

The patient in this conversation produces a number of errors. But note that most of these errors are different in kind from the errors of Broca's aphasia. While the patient is able to produce some well-formed structures (for example, *No, I don't*), these structures appear intermittently amidst various unrelated fragments. Not only are these constructions unrelated to each other, they are unrelated to the examiner's questions. It appears that the patient has no understanding of the questions being asked.

This patient displays a significant but not severe form of Wernicke's aphasia. Her speech appears to result from a semi-random selection of words and short phrases. In very severe cases of this syndrome, phonemes are also randomly selected and the result is speech that has the intonational characteristics of English but actually contains very few real words of the language. This is termed **jargonaphasia**.

The type of deficit found in Wernicke's aphasia leads us to a greater understanding of the role of the temporal-parietal area of the brain known as Wernicke's area and to a deeper consideration of the nature of language comprehension. Wernicke's aphasia is primarily a comprehension deficit. But as we have seen, when comprehension breaks down, most of what we call language ability breaks down with it. Patients cannot express themselves because they cannot understand what they have just said and use that understanding in the planning of what to say next. In a very real sense, these patients have lost contact with themselves (and therefore with the rest of the world). Wernicke's patients can't have coherent trains of thought—the brain damage does not allow the elements of the train to be connected.

In summary, our discussion of fluent and nonfluent aphasia has demonstrated how normal language use is a marriage of content and form. In the case of nonfluent aphasia, form is compromised but the content of language remains relatively intact. In contrast, fluent aphasia is characterized by a rapid flow of form with little content.

9.4 ACQUIRED DYSLEXIA AND DYSGRAPHIA

Reading and writing involve a complex array of perceptual and motor skills. In this section we will consider impairments of reading and writing which are caused by damage to the brain. The impairment of reading ability is called **acquired dyslexia** (or acquired **alexia**). The impairment of writing ability is called **acquired dysgraphia** (or acquired **agraphia**). In both cases the term *acquired* indicates that the patient possessed normal reading and/or writing ability prior to brain damage and distinguishes the syndromes from developmental dyslexia and developmental dysgraphia, which deal with disturbances of reading and writing development in children.

Reading and Writing Disturbances in Aphasia

Acquired dyslexia and dysgraphia typically accompany the aphasic syndromes which we considered in Section 3. Most Broca's aphasics show writing disturbances that are comparable to their speaking deficits. In other words, a patient who cannot pronounce the word *spoon* will also not be able to write it correctly. The resulting error in writing (for example, *poon*) is called a **paragraphia**. In spontaneous writing, Broca's aphasics also tend to omit function words and inflectional affixes. Finally, while the silent reading of Broca's aphasics is very good, their reading aloud shows the same telegraphic style as their spontaneous speech. These observations reinforce the view that the deficit in Broca's aphasia is much more than a speech articulation deficit. It is a production deficit at a very deep level of language planning.

Wernicke's aphasics also show reading and writing deficits that match their deficits in speaking and listening. The writing of Wernicke's aphasics is formally very good. They typically retain good spelling and handwriting. Their written production, however, like their speaking, makes little sense. Reading comprehension is also severely impaired in Wernicke's aphasia. Like C.S. Moss, patients can see the letters and words, but cannot make any sense of them. Again the conclusion to be drawn is that Wernicke's aphasia, like Broca's aphasia, is a central disturbance of language competence—the knowledge that underlies language functioning. In such cases of central language disturbance, whatever impairment the patient has in listening and speaking will be matched in reading and writing.

Acquired Dyslexia as the Dominant Language Deficit

In addition to the reading and writing deficits that accompany aphasia, there are many cases in which the disruption of reading and writing ability is the dominant symptom. This typically follows damage in and around the angular gyrus of the parietal lobe. An analysis of these types of disabilities has led to some very interesting theories about the nature of reading (at least in English).

Before we proceed to discuss two contrasting types of acquired dyslexia, it might be worthwhile to reflect on the abilities involved in the reading of words. Up to this point in the chapter you have read over five thousand words. Some of these words (such as the function words) are very familiar to you and you probably recognized them as wholes. But others, such as *angular gyrus* are words that you probably read for the first time. How then could you know how to pronounce them? Many theorists believe that readers maintain a set of spelling-to-sound rules that enables them to read new words aloud. These rules are important in the development of reading ability and in the addition of new words to our reading vocabulary.

Phonological dyslexia is a type of acquired dyslexia in which the patient seems to have lost the ability to use spelling-to-sound rules. Phonological dyslexics can only read words that they have seen before. Asked to read a word such as *blug* aloud, they either say nothing or produce a known word that is visually similar to the target (for example, *blue* or *bug*).

Surface dyslexia is the opposite of phonological dyslexia. Surface dyslexics seem unable to recognize words as wholes. Instead they must process all words through a set of spelling-to-sound rules. This is shown by the kinds of errors they make. Surface dyslexics do not have difficulty reading words such as *bat* that are regularly spelled. They read irregularly spelled words such as *yacht*, however, by applying regular rules and thus producing /jatʃt/. The most interesting aspect of surface dyslexics' reading ability is that they understand what they produce, not what they see. For example, a surface dyslexic would be likely to read the word *worm* as /wɔrm/ (and not /wɜrm/). When asked what the word means, the patient would answer: the opposite of cold.

Data from acquired dyslexia allow researchers to build models that specify the components of normal reading ability and their relationship to each other. Clearly, this type of analysis plays a very important role in the development of our understanding of language, the mind, and the brain.

9.5 LINGUISTIC THEORY AND APHASIA

Looking at aphasia in terms of linguistic theory gives us a new perspective on language in the brain. Linguistic theory has been traditionally concerned with the structure of language, not with how it is used in the processes of listening, speaking, reading, and writing. In contrast, the traditional way of looking at aphasia has been in terms of what the patient can and cannot do. The involvement of theoretical linguists in the study of aphasia has caused a minor revolution in the field. Aphasia researchers have begun to think about the deficit in terms of the loss of knowledge representations such as semantic features, phonological rules, and perhaps syntactic tree structures. Theoretical linguists have also found that the study of aphasia offers an important area for testing theoretical distinctions such as the one between derivational suffixes and inflectional suffixes. In this section, we will look at some of the areas in which the marriage of theoretical linguistics and neurolinguistics has been most fruitful. This fruitfulness has usually meant an increase in the sophistication of the questions that are asked about aphasia. It has also meant the discovery of new and often bizarre aphasic phenomena.

Features, Rules, and Underlying Forms

In the area of phonology, we have found that the phonemic paraphasias of Broca's aphasics usually differ from the target phoneme by only one distinctive feature (recall sentence *1*: 'with' → [wɪt]) and can therefore be easily described by phonological rules. Observations such as these lead us to believe that phonological features and rules might be good tools to characterize how language is represented and produced.

In the area of morphology, the study of aphasia has offered empirical support for the theoretical distinction between inflection and derivation. As we have discussed, Broca's aphasics show a sensitivity to this distinction in their omission of affixes in speech. Inflectional affixes are commonly dropped, but derivational affixes are usually retained. Perhaps most interesting is the tendency of some aphasics to produce underlying forms of morphemes in reading and repetition. Asked to repeat the word *illegal*, for example, some aphasics will produce *inlegal*, using the underlying form of the negative prefix rather than the allomorph that should occur before a base beginning with /l/. Again, errors such as these point to the possibility that phonological processes such as nasal assimilation and the notion of underlying form are not only an elegant way to represent linguistic competence but are also relevant to the processing of language in the brain.

The study of aphasia also stands to shed light on the nature of semantic representations. Most of the work in this area has concentrated on the many subvarieties of acquired dyslexia. In a syndrome known as **deep dyslexia**, patients produce reading errors, which are systematically related to the word that they are asked to read (in the sense that they share some semantic features but not others). Given the word *mother*, for example, a deep dyslexic is likely to read *father*.

The detailed study of semantic deficits associated with brain damage has also led to some very surprising discoveries. Most aphasics and dyslexics find abstract words much more difficult to process than concrete words. But there have been reports of concrete word dyslexia in which the patient shows exactly the opposite problem (having difficulty with concrete words such as *table*). There has even been a report of a patient who shows a selective inability to read words that refer to fruits and vegetables.

Agrammatism

In Section 3, we observed that many theorists now believe that Broca's aphasia involves a central syntactic deficit. The syndrome that is characterized by telegraphic speech has been given the name **agrammatism**—to indicate that grammatical ability has been lost. Agrammatism is the aphasic disturbance that has been most studied by linguists. As was discussed in Section 3, it is characterized by the omission of function words such as *it*, *is*, *to*, and *a*, the omission of inflectional affixes, and by comprehension deficits in cases where the correct interpretation of a sentence is dependent on syntax alone.

In recent years, many linguists have become involved in the problems of characterizing the agrammatic deficit. These problems have raised both specific questions such as: What exactly is a function word? and general questions such as: Is it possible to lose syntax? The involvement of linguists has also generated cross-linguistic studies of agrammatism that provide interesting insights into the interaction between characteristics of the syndrome and characteristics of particular languages.

Function Words

Intuitively, function words are grammatical words that can be distinguished from content words such as nouns, verbs, and adjectives. In terms of formal syntax, however, they are quite heterogeneous. They include pronouns, auxiliaries, determiners, and prepositions—items that do not fall into any single syntactic category. Much of the recent work in this area by linguists has concentrated on working out what exactly the so-called function words have in common. Some researchers have suggested that they form a phonological group—they are all words that do not normally take stress. Others have pointed to the fact that function words do not normally take affixes and therefore form a morphological group. Still others have suggested that syntactic theory should be modified so that all the words that are lost in agrammatism fall under the heading functional category (this would involve changing the status of prepositions, which are currently treated as lexical categories—see Chapter 5).

Whatever the outcome of this debate, it is clear that neurolinguistic evidence has presented a new set of challenges to the field of formal linguistics. One of these challenges is to build bridges between normal and pathological linguistic competence by finding units of analysis that are appropriate to both.

The Loss of Syntactic Competence

Another, much more general, challenge is to define what it means to possess syntactic competence such that we can speak of its loss. This challenge has forced researchers to address the question: What is the essence of syntactic knowledge? Is it the hierarchical arrangement of elements? Is it the representation of abstract entities such as traces?

Some researchers have suggested that agrammatism involves the loss of the ability to form hierarchical representations. They claim that agrammatics interpret sentences as strings of content words and assign thematic roles to nouns (as opposed to NPs) according to a default strategy such as: The first noun is the agent. This strategy works reasonably well for simple sentences in which the first noun can be assigned the thematic role of agent and the second noun can be assigned the role of theme as in sentence *5a*. It results in miscomprehension, however, for sentences such as *5b* and *5c*, where the first NP does not have the role of agent.

5. *a*) The girl kissed the boy.
    b) The girl was kissed.
    c) It was the girl that the boy kissed.

Other researchers have argued that agrammatism does not involve the loss of syntactic competence, but rather an alteration of that competence. They have claimed that agrammatics show hierarchical arrangements of elements but can no longer represent the traces that indicate an NP's position in deep structure. As a result, they are unable to recognize that the subject NP bears the theme role since they do not realize that it is the complement of the verb in deep structure (see Chapter 6).

Agrammatism in Other Languages

Data from other languages has suggested that the original characterization of agrammatism as a syndrome in which function words and inflectional affixes are lost may not reflect the true nature of this deficit, but rather reflects the fact that such deletions are possible in English.

In English, affixes are typically attached to a stem that is itself a free form. The past form of the verb *watch*, for example, is created by the addition of *-ed*; the third person singular is created by the addition of *-s*. However, not all languages work this way. In Semitic languages, such as Hebrew, the stem is typically a string of three consonants, which is unpronounceable in its uninflected form. Inflections are produced by inserting vowels into this triconsonantal 'skeleton'. For example, the Hebrew root for the verb to write is /ktv/. The masculine third person present form of the verb is /kɔtɛv/ and the masculine third person past form is /katav/. If Hebrew agrammatics simply 'lose' inflectional affixes the way they do in English, they should not be able to produce any verbs. As it turns out, Hebrew agrammatics do produce verbs, but instead of dropping inflectional forms, they choose randomly among them. This sort of evidence has provided a convincing argument against the view that agrammatic language results from a simple economy of effort. Rather, it seems that it is a linguistic deficit that involves the mis-selection of linguistic forms. It is only in languages such as English, where the stem is also a legal free form, that the agrammatism is characterized by affix omission.

9.6 WHERE IS LANGUAGE?

In this chapter we have outlined some important findings that have greatly increased our understanding of the types of language disturbances that result from damage to the brain, as well as our understanding of the association between specific areas of the brain and particular language functions. We have seen that Broca's area plays a crucial role in the articulation of speech and in the ability to create syntactic representations. Wernicke's area plays a key role in language comprehension, and the area surrounding the angular gyrus plays a special role in reading.

On the other hand, we have seen that, in an important sense, normal language use involves the integrated functioning of the entire cortex. Even right-handers who are strongly left lateralized for language show some language deficit in cases of damage to the right hemisphere. Finally, virtually all forms of aphasia are accompanied by word-finding difficulties. This observation suggests that the storage and retrieval of word forms may be diffusely represented in the brain.

There is, therefore, no simple answer to the question: Where is language? Even if there were, the task of neurolinguistics would be far from done, for the truly important question concerning language in the brain is not Where is it? but What is it? Indeed, the answer to the first question may have little to do with the answer to the second question. Consider, by analogy, the goal of understanding government: To what extent does the knowledge that Congress is to be found in Washington advance the understanding of how the federal government works?

Ultimately, the goal of neurolinguistics is to understand, in neurological terms, what language is. The field of neurolinguistics is still a long way from being able to specify how syntax is coded in brain matter, or even how a word is represented. Nevertheless, as our discussion of agrammatism has revealed, recent work by neurolinguists has resulted in important new perspectives on the nature of language competence.

Summing Up

This chapter is concerned with how language is represented and processed in the human **brain**. **Dichotic listening** studies and **split brain** studies have shown that the **left hemisphere** of the brain carries most of the responsibility for language processing in right-handed individuals. **Neuroscientists** have also used **autopsy** studies, **Computerized Axial Tomography**, and **cerebral blood flow** studies to determine the relationship between particular areas of the left hemisphere and specific language functions. It has been found that **Broca's area** is primarily responsible for speech production, **Wernicke's area** is primarily responsible for language comprehension, and the area surrounding the **angular gyrus** plays an important role in reading. Most of our knowledge concerning language representation in the brain comes from the study of **aphasia**—language disturbance resulting from damage to the brain. **Neurolinguists**, trained in both linguistics and neuroscience, carefully examine the manner in which linguistic competence is affected by brain damage. Their goal is to increase our understanding of how linguistic knowledge is coded in brain matter and how this knowledge is used in the process of language comprehension and production.

Key Terms

acquired dyslexia	agrammatism
acquired dysgraphia	agraphia

alexia
angular gyrus
aphasia
Broca's aphasia
Broca's area
central sulcus
cerebral hemisphere
cerebral cortex
Computerized Axial Tomography
contralateralization
corpus callosum
deep dyslexia
dichotic listening
dysprosody
fluent aphasia
frontal lobe
function words
global aphasia
gyri
jargonaphasia
lateral fissure
lesion

lobes
longitudinal fissure
motor aphasia
neuron
neuroscience
nonfluent aphasia
occipital lobe
paragraphia
parietal lobe
phonemic paraphasia
phonological dyslexia
right ear advantage
sensory aphasia
specialization
split brain
sulci
surface dyslexia
telegraphic
temporal lobe
Wernicke's aphasia
Wernicke's area

Sources

David Caplan's 1987 book *Neurolinguistics and Linguistic Aphasiology*: *An Introduction* is an excellent introduction to neurolinguistics. A more practical approach to aphasia and its treatment is to be found in the Rosenbek et al book *Aphasia*: *A Clinical Approach*.

The discussion of agrammatism was drawn from the rich literature that includes M-L. Kean's edited volume *Agrammatism* (New York: Academic Press, 1985) and Yosef Grodzinsky's challenging proposals in *Theoretical Perspectives on Language Deficits* (Cambridge, Mass.: MIT Press, 1990). An alternative approach to Grodzinsky's is well represented in David Caplan and Nancy Hildebrandt's book *Disorders of Syntactic Comprehension* (Cambridge, Mass.: MIT Press, 1988).

C. S. Moss's autobiographical account of his aphasic experience is to be found in *Recovery with Aphasia* (Urbana, Ill.: University of Illinois Press, 1972). Another book that offers an experiential perspective on aphasic disturbance is Howard Gardner's *The Shattered Mind* (New York: Knopf, 1975).

The material on acquired dyslexia is drawn from the volumes *Deep Dyslexia* and *Surface Dyslexia* (see Recommended Reading), as well as Y. Zotterman's book *Dyslexia*: *Neuronal, Cognitive and Linguistic Aspects* (Oxford: Pergamon Press, 1982).

Recommended Reading

Caplan, D. 1987. *Neurolinguistics and Linguistic Aphasiology*. New York: Cambridge University Press.

Coltheart, M., J. Patterson, and J. C. Marshall, eds. 1980. *Deep Dyslexia*. London: Routledge & Kegan Paul.

Patterson, K. E., J. C. Marshall, and M. Coltheart, eds. 1986. *Surface Dyslexia*. Hillsdale, N.J.: Erlbaum.

Rosenbek, J. C., L. L. Lapointe, and R. T. Wertz. 1989. *Aphasia: A Clinical Approach*. Boston: College-Hill Press.

Segalowitz, S. 1983. *Two Sides of the Brain*. Englewood Cliffs, N.J.: Prentice-Hall.

Questions

1. What distinguishes the human brain from a nonhuman brain?

2. State two reasons for considering the cerebral hemispheres to be two separate brains.

3. What are the relative advantages and disadvantages of the various techniques used to investigate the brain? Consider ethics, cost, intrusiveness, and type of information yielded.

4. Following is an unlabelled diagram of the left hemisphere. Choose four contrasting colors and color each lobe of the cortex. Use arrows to point to the central sulcus, the lateral fissure, and the angular gyrus. Finally, use a pencil to indicate areas of lesion that would result in Broca's aphasia, Wernicke's aphasia, and acquired dyslexia. Label these lesions.

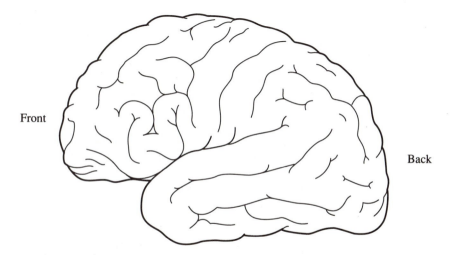

Front   Back

5. What do dichotic listening tests tell us about the specialization of the cerebral hemispheres? Can you think of any other types of stimuli that would present similar results?

6. Do you think it is possible to learn how the normal brain functions by studying brain-damaged patients? What can the study of aphasia tell us about normal language competence?

7. Contrast the differences in behavior between fluent and nonfluent aphasics. What could explain these differences?

8. Describe the differences between phonological and surface dyslexia.

9. Reread the introduction to Section 3. What do you think Moss's account tells us about the relationship between language and thought?

10. Many researchers have claimed that agrammatism involves a loss of syntactic knowledge. Imagine a type of aphasia that involves a loss of phonological knowledge. How would patients with this type of aphasia behave?

10 LANGUAGE ACQUISITION
The Emergence of a Grammar

Human brains are so constructed that one brain
responds in much the same way to a given trigger as
does another brain, all things being equal. This is why
a baby can learn any language; it responds to triggers
in the same way as any other baby.

D. Hofstadter

One of the most intriguing phenomena studied by linguists is children's acquisition of language. Fascination with this issue dates back to at least the seventh century B.C., when the Egyptian Pharaoh Psammetichus had two infants brought up in complete isolation in an attempt to determine the type of language they would learn on their own. The Pharaoh had hoped that the children's utterances would provide some clues about the origin of language. The story is that the children were brought up by an old shepherd couple, who were instructed not to speak to them (or, who were mute, depending on which version you hear). After some years, the children were heard to utter *bekos*, and the Pharaoh concluded that the original language of humankind was Phrygian, since the Phrygian word for 'bread' is *bekos*. It has been pointed out that it is not surprising that children raised in an environment of sheep cries would produce the syllable *be*.

Fortunately for all concerned, the study of language acquisition has advanced considerably since the Pharaoh's time, and linguists have been able to develop a variety of research strategies that allow linguistic development to be investigated in a more acceptable and fruitful way. Some of these strategies are discussed briefly in Section 10.1. Most of the rest of the chapter is devoted to outlining what has been learned about children's acquisition of the phonological, morphological, semantic, and syntactic systems of their language. We conclude with a brief examination of the contribution of the linguistic environment to language acquisition, the relationship between the emergence of language and cognitive development, and the possible existence of inborn linguistic principles.

10.1 THE STUDY OF LANGUAGE ACQUISITION

Although we commonly refer to the phenomenon of linguistic development as 'language acquisition', the end result of this process is actually a *grammar*—the mental system that allows people to speak and understand a language. There are at least two reasons for believing that the development of linguistic skills must involve the acquisition of a grammar.

First, as noted in Chapters 1 and 5, mature language users are able to produce and understand an unlimited number of novel sentences. This can only happen if, as children, they have acquired a system of productive grammatical rules that are applicable to novel cases. Simple memorization of a fixed inventory of words and sentences would not equip the language learner to deal with previously unheard utterances—a basic requisite of normal language use.

A second indication that children acquire grammatical rules is found in their own utterances. For example, rather than simply memorizing all the regular and exceptional past tense forms for English verbs, children formulate a general rule that adds *-ed* to the verb stem. This rule produces forms such as *doed, *leaved, and *goed in addition to washed, walked, and so forth. Such errors provide clear signs of children's attempts to construct grammatical rules.

Because language acquisition involves the emergence of a grammar, its study is closely tied to the type of linguistic analysis with which we have been concerned in preceding chapters. Indeed, linguists and psychologists studying language acquisition must often look to the study of phonology, syntax, and other components of the grammar for help in identifying and describing the rules and categories that children acquire during the first years of life.

Methods

A good deal of research on the acquisition of language is concerned with **developmental** phenomena. These include children's initial and intermediate hypotheses about particular linguistic structures, the kinds of errors they make, and the order in which different forms or structures are mastered. Investigators concerned with these problems draw on two basic methods—naturalistic observation and experimentation. Although both methods provide valuable information about the nature of the language acquisition process, they do so in different ways.

The Naturalistic Approach In the naturalistic approach, investigators observe and record children's spontaneous verbal behavior. One type of naturalistic investigation is the so-called diary study, in which a parent keeps daily notes on a child's linguistic progress. A variant of the diary study involves a trained researcher visiting individual children on a regular basis and recording a sample of utterances (perhaps one hour every second week over a period of five months). In both cases, notes are taken about the context in which children's speech occurs, the toys they are playing with, the pictures they are looking at, and the like.

The Experimental Approach In experimental studies, researchers typically make use of specially designed tasks to elicit linguistic activity relevant to the phenomenon that they wish to study. The children's performance is then used to formulate hypotheses about the type of grammatical system they are employing. Experimental studies usually employ tasks that test children's comprehension, production, and imitation skills.

One widely used method for testing children's comprehension involves supplying them with an appropriate set of toys and then asking them to act out the meaning of a sentence such as *The truck was pushed by the car*. Another method makes use of a question-and-answer format in which a child is read a sentence such as *John promised Tom to go home* and is then asked, *Who is going to go home?* In either case, the child's responses provide insights into the type of grammatical rules being used to interpret sentences.

In a typical production task, the child is shown a picture and asked to describe it. Although production tasks are useful for eliciting individual words, there are many structures, such as passives, which are hard to elicit even from adults. Moreover, because children's ability to comprehend language is often more advanced than their ability to produce sentences of their own, production tasks can provide an overly conservative view of linguistic development.

Both comprehension and production tests are often used in conjunction with imitation tasks. Although one might think that imitation would be excessively easy, it has been found that children's ability to repeat structures reflects the state of their current grammatical knowledge and that a form that has not been mastered will probably not be repeated properly. Thus, a child who has not yet acquired the auxiliary verb *be* will repeat the sentence *Mommy is talking* as *Mommy talking*.

By using naturalistic observation together with experimental techniques, linguists and psychologists have made significant progress in the study of the language acquisition process. Much of this chapter is devoted to a survey of this progress, beginning with the development of speech sounds.

10.2 PHONOLOGICAL DEVELOPMENT

From birth, children are exposed to a variety of noises in their environment. Before they can begin to acquire language, they must first separate nonspeech noises from speech sounds. The rudiments of this ability seem to be present at birth, since even newborns respond differently to human voices than to other sounds. Within two months of birth, infants can even recognize their mother's voice.

From about one month, children exhibit the ability to distinguish among certain speech sounds. In one experiment, infants were presented with a series of identical syllables consisting of the string [ba]. These were followed by an occurrence of the syllable [pa]. A change in the children's sucking rate (the normal reaction to a new stimulus) indicated that they perceived the difference between the two syllables and, therefore, were able to distinguish between [p] and [b].

Despite this early sensitivity to distinctions among speech sounds, the ability to distinguish between meaningful words is not yet present. The emergence of this ability has been examined in a task in which children are presented with two toy animals named *bok* and *pok* and are asked to respond to sentences such as *Show me pok*. To respond correctly, children must not only hear the difference between [p] and [b] but also recognize that this difference is linguistically significant—that it is used to distinguish between words in their language. Children under eighteen months have little success in this type of task.

Babbling

Even before children master the phonemic contrasts of their language, they begin to develop the articulatory movements needed to produce these distinctions in speech. The emergence of articulatory skills begins around three or four months of age, when children start to produce cooing and babbling sounds. As Table 10.1 illustrates, there are similarities in the babbling produced by children from different linguistic communities. (The data in the table

Table 10.1 Cross-linguistic similarities in babbling

Frequently found consonants			Infrequently found consonants			
p	b	m	f	v	θ	ð
t	d	n	ʃ	ʒ	tʃ	dʒ
k	g		l	r	ŋ	
s	h	w j				

come from a study of children acquiring Hindi, Japanese, English, Arabic, Mayan, and Luo.) Such cross-linguistic similarities suggest that early babbling is independent of the particular language to which children are exposed. In fact, even deaf children babble, although their articulatory activity is somewhat less varied than that of hearing children. Moreover, it is known that children who for medical reasons are unable to babble can later develop normal pronunciation. All of this suggests that babbling precedes but is not actually part of the language acquisition process.

The Developmental Order

Babbling increases in frequency until the age of about twelve months, at which time children start to produce their first understandable words. Babbling may overlap with the production of real words for several weeks before dying out. By the time children have acquired fifty words or so, they begin to adopt fairly regular patterns of pronunciation.

Language acquisition researchers have expended a good deal of effort trying to determine the order in which speech sounds are mastered in production and perception. Although this work has been hindered by difficulties in determining precisely when a contrast has been acquired, as well as by a shortage of reliable data from a sufficiently broad range of languages, some general trends seem to exist.

- As a group, vowels are acquired before consonants (by age three).
- Stops tend to be acquired before other consonants.

- In terms of place of articulation, labials are acquired first, followed, with some variation, by velars, alveolars, and alveopalatals. Interdentals (such as [θ] and [ð]) are acquired last.
- New phonemic contrasts manifest themselves first in word-initial position. Thus, the /p/-/b/ contrast, for instance, will be manifested in pairs such as *pat-bat* before *mop-mob*.
- All other things being equal, a sound that occurs in many different words will be acquired before a sound (like [ð] in English) that occurs in relatively few words.

By age two, the average English-speaking child can produce the following inventory of consonant phonemes.

Table 10.2 Consonant inventory at age two

Stops			Fricatives	Other
p	b	m	f	w
t	d	n	s	
k	g			

By age four, this inventory is considerably larger and includes the following sounds.

Table 10.3 Consonant inventory at age four

Stops			Fricatives		Affricates		Other	
p	b	m	f	v	tʃ	dʒ	w	j
t	d	n	s	z			l	r
k	g	ŋ	ʃ					

Still to be acquired at this age are the interdental fricatives [θ] and [ð] and the voiced alveopalatal fricative [ʒ].

Early Phonetic Processes

The phonetic processes responsible for the speech patterns of young language learners are far from arbitrary. For the most part, these processes simplify phonological structure by creating sound patterns that can be articulated with a minimum of difficulty. Such patterns are typified by syllables consisting of a consonant and a vowel. Stop consonants are preferred to fricatives and alveolars to palatals. Especially difficult are the fricatives [θ] and [ð]; [θ] is frequently pronounced as [f] or [t] and [ð] as [v] or [d]. Liquids too are difficult, and it is not unusual to find [l] and [r] replaced by [w].

Substitution One of the most widespread phonetic processes in child language involves substitution—the systematic replacement of one sound by another. Common substitution processes include **stopping**, the replacement of a fricative by a corresponding stop; **fronting**, the moving forward of a sound's place of articulation; **gliding**, the replacement of a liquid by a glide; and **denasalization**, the replacement of a nasal stop by a nonnasal counterpart. These processes are illustrated with the help of English examples in Table 10.4.

Table 10.4 Substitution in early speech

Process	Example	Change
Stopping (continuant → stop)	sing → [tɪŋ]	s → t
	sea → [tij]	s → t
	zebra → [dijbrə]	z → d
	this → [dɪt]	ð → d, s → t
	shoes → [tuwd]	ʃ → t, z → d
Fronting	shoes → [su:z]	ʃ → s
	John → [dzɑn]	dʒ → dz
	cheese → [tsi:z]	tʃ → ts
	goat → [dowt]	g → d
	mouth → [mʌwf]	θ → f
Gliding	lion → [jajn]	l → j
	look → [wʊk]	l → w
	rock → [wɑk]	r → w
	story → [stowij]	r → w
Denasalization	spoon → [buwd]	n → d
	jam → [dæb]	m → b
	room → [wuwb]	m → b

Syllable Simplification   A second type of process in children's speech involves the systematic deletion of certain sounds resulting in simpler syllable structure. In the data in Table 10.5, typical of the speech of two- and three-year-old children, consonant clusters have been reduced by deleting one or more segments. In all of these patterns, the weaker segment in the cluster is deleted. Thus, stops are retained over all other consonants, and fricatives are retained over liquids.

Table 10.5 Reduction of consonant clusters

/s/ + stop—(strategy: delete /s/)
  stop → [tɑp]
  small → [mɑ:]
  desk → [dɛk]
stop + liquid—(strategy: delete liquid)
  try → [taj]
  crumb → [gʌm]
  bring → [bɪŋ]
fricative + liquid—(strategy: delete liquid)
  from → [fʌm]
  sleep → [sijp]
nasal + stop—(strategy: delete nasal)
  bump → [bʌp]
  tent → [dɛt]

Another common deletion process in two-year-old children involves the elimination of final consonants. Initial consonants, in contrast, are typically retained if they precede a vowel.

1. dog → [dɑ]
   bus → [bʌ]
   boot → [buw]

Both the reduction of consonant clusters and the deletion of final consonants have the effect of simplifying syllable structure, bringing it closer to the CV pattern that is universally favored by children and that is the most widely found pattern in language.

Assimilation   Still another widespread phonetic process in children's language is assimilation—the modification of one or more features of a phoneme under the influence of neighboring sounds. In the following examples, initial consonants have been voiced in anticipation of the following vowel.

2. tell   [dɛl]
    pig   [bɪg]
    push   [bʊs]
    soup   [zuwp]

In the next set of examples, a word-final consonant is devoiced in apparent anticipation of the silence following the end of an utterance.

3. have   [hæf]
    big   [bɪk]
    tub   [tʌp]
    egg   [ɛk]
    bed   [bɛt]

Assimilation is also observed in children's tendency to maintain the same place of articulation for all of the vowels or consonants in a word. This can lead to the pronunciation of *doggy* as [gɑgij] (with two velar stops) or as [dɑdij] (with two alveolar stops).

Production versus Perception

All of the examples presented in the previous section involve production. An important question that arises at this point is whether children can perceive phonemic contrasts that they cannot yet make. According to one study, a child who would not produce a distinction in his own speech between *mouse* and *mouth*, *cart* and *card*, or *jug* and *duck* was, nonetheless, able to point to pictures of the correct objects in a comprehension task. This suggests that this child's ability to perceive the phonemic contrasts in question exceeded his ability to produce them.

Another indication that children's perceptual abilities are more advanced than their articulatory skills comes from their reaction to adult speech that fails to respect the normal phonemic contrasts. The following report describes one such incident:

> One of us, for instance, spoke to a child who called his inflated plastic fish a *fis*. In imitation of the child's pronunciation, the observer said: "This is your *fis*?" "No," said the child, "my *fis*." He continued to reject the adult's imitation until he was told, "That is your fish." "Yes," he said, "my *fis*."

The child's reaction to the adult's imitative pronunciation of *fish* shows that he could perceive the difference between [s] and [ʃ] even though he could not yet produce it himself.

10.3 MORPHOLOGICAL DEVELOPMENT

As is the case with the sound pattern of language, the details of morphological structure emerge over a period of several years. Initially, the words of English-speaking children seem to lack any internal morphological structure. Affixes are entirely absent and most words consist of a single root morpheme. Gradually, inflectional and derivational morphemes appear, marking an increased capacity for word formation.

In a language such as English, which has many examples of irregular inflection (*men* as the plural of *man*, *ran* as the past of *run*), children often begin by simply memorizing forms on a case-by-case basis without regard for general patterns or rules. Thus, they may initially produce the correct plural form for *man* and the correct past tense for *come*. As they subsequently observe the generality of *-s* as a plural marker and *-ed* as a past tense marker around age 2;6 (two years, six months), they may incorrectly add these suffixes to the irregular forms—producing words such as **mans* and **runned*. (Errors that result from the overly broad application of a rule are called **overgeneralizations**.)

For a period of several months, the overgeneralized forms and their correct counterparts may co-occur in children's speech. Even occasional mixed forms such as *felled*, a blend of *fell* and *falled*, may be used before children come to distinguish between inflected forms that follow a general rule and those that must be treated as exceptions.

Table 10.6 The development of affixes

Stage 1: case-by-case learning
Stage 2: overuse of general rule
Stage 3: learning of exceptions to the general rule
Stage 4: production of adult forms

A Developmental Sequence

From the early work on language acquisition, it has been clear that the development of bound morphemes and nonlexical categories (such as determiners and auxiliaries) in English takes place in an orderly sequence with relatively little variation from child to child. In a pioneering study of this phenomenon, the more or less invariant developmental sequence in Table 10.7 was found in three children between the ages of twenty and thirty-six months.

Table 10.7 Typical developmental sequence for English-speaking children

1. *-ing*
2. plural *-s*
3. possessive *-'s*
4. *the, a*
5. past tense *-ed*
6. third person singular *-s*
7. auxiliary *be*

An interesting feature of this developmental sequence is that it seems to be unrelated to the frequency of the different morphemes in the speech heard by children. As Table 10.8 shows, the determiners *the* and *a* were the most frequent grammatical morphemes in the children's environments, yet were acquired

Table 10.8 Typical relative frequency of morphemes in parental speech

1. *the, a*
2. *-ing*
3. plural *-s*
4. auxiliary *be*
5. possessive *-'s*
6. past tense *-ed*
7. third person singular *-s*

relatively late. The prepositions *in* and *on*, on the other hand, were less frequent than the determiners and the plural ending, but were acquired before either.

Determining Factors What determines the order of acquisition of minor lexical categories and bound morphemes? Research on a variety of languages suggests that several factors are involved.

1. Occurrence of the morpheme in utterance-final position Children show a greater tendency to notice and remember elements that occur at the end of the utterance than those found in any other position. All other things being equal, this favors the learning of suffixes over prefixes.

2. Syllabicity Children seem to take greater notice of morphemes such as *-ing* and *on*, which constitute syllables, than the plural or possessive suffix *-s*, which is a single consonant.

3. A straightforward relation between form and meaning Whereas the word *the* functions only as a determiner, the portmanteau verbal ending *-s* simultaneously represents three linguistic categories: third person, singular, and present (nonpast) tense. This type of morpheme is difficult for children to acquire.

4. Lack of exceptions Whereas all singular nouns form the possessive with *-'s*, not all verbs use *-ed* to mark the past tense (*saw*, *read*, *drove*). Such exceptions hinder the language acquisition process.

5. Lack of allomorphic variation Whereas the affix *-ing* has the same form for all verbs, the past tense ending *-ed* has three major allomorphs—/t/ for verbs such as *chase*, /d/ for forms such as *crave*, and /əd/ for verbs such as *recite*. This type of allomorphic variation, which also occurs with the plural, possessive, and third person singular affixes in English, slows morphological development.

6. Clearly discernible semantic function Whereas morphemes such as *in*, *on*, and the plural *-s* appear to express easily identifiable meanings, some morphemes (such as the third person singular *-s*) appear to make no contribution to the meaning of the sentence. Acquisition of this latter type of morpheme is relatively slow.

The status of the English morphemes whose developmental order we have been considering is indicated in Table 10.9; as before, morphemes are listed in order of emergence. As you can see, the morphemes that are acquired first generally exhibit more of the properties just discussed than those that emerge at a later point.

Table 10.9 Factors affecting development

Morphemes	Factors					
	1	2	3	4	5	6
-ing	+	+	+	+	+	+
plural *-s*	+	±	+	+	−	+
possessive *-'s*	−	±	+	+	−	+
the, a	−	+	+	+	−	−
past tense *-ed*	+	±	+	−	−	+
third person singular *-s*	+	±	−	+	−	−
auxiliary *be*	−	±	−	+	−	−

Morpho-phonemic Rules

As children's productive and perceptual abilities improve, they start to gain command of morphophonemic rules, including those responsible for allomorphic variation of the sort associated with the English plural (/s/ in *hats*, /z/ in *pens*, /əz/ in *judges*) and the past tense (/d/ in *played*, /t/ in *taped*, /əd/ in *hunted*). Initially, even allomorphic variation as straightforward as the *a/an* alternation in English can cause difficulty for language learners, and it is not unusual to hear children aged two to three produce utterances such as *an cucumber*.

A well-known technique for studying the development of morphophonemic rules is to present children with nonsense words and then ask them to form plurals or past tense forms. If the children have mastered rules for allomorphic variation, they ought to be able to add appropriate endings even to words they have never heard before. In a classic experiment, children were shown a picture of a strange creature and told "This is a wug." A second picture was then presented and the children were given the following type of question.

4. Now, there's another wug. There are two of them.
   Now, there are two . . . ?

Children who knew the plural formation rule were able to respond with the form /wʌgz/. Table 10.10 indicates the average scores attained by preschoolers (aged four to five) and first graders (aged five and a half to seven) on specific nonsense words in this experiment. As you can see, the various allomorphs of the plural are acquired at different times. Particularly problematic is the /əz/ allomorph, which is needed in the last four nonsense words in the table. Even first-grade children fail to produce the correct form of the plural here in well over half the cases studied.

Table 10.10 Percentage of correct responses on wug test

		Preschoolers	First graders
/s/	heafs	79%	80%
/z/	wugs	76	97
	luns	68	92
	tors	73	90
	cras	58	86
/əz/	tasses	28	39
	gutches	28	38
	kashes	25	36
	nizzes	14	33

Word Formation Rules

Like inflectional morphemes, English derivational affixes and compounding appear to be acquired in a more or less fixed order. This was illustrated in a study of the six word formation processes in Table 10.11. Children were given

Table 10.11 Word formation processes

Type	Example
Agentive -er	teacher (= one who teaches)
Noun-noun compounds	bird house
Adjectival -y	dirty
Instrumental -er	eraser (= something to erase with)
Adverbial -ly	quickly, quietly

sentence frames that required the formation of a new word for a real or made-up root. For the agentive -er, for example, a typical frame would be *A person who teaches is called a. . . .* As Table 10.12 shows, not all word formation

Table 10.12 Percentage correct for made-up roots

Construction	Preschool	Early school	Middle school
Agentive -er	7%	63%	80%
Compound	47	50	65
Adjectival -y	0	30	55
Instrumental -er	7	35	45
Adverbial -ly	0	13	20

processes were equally easy for the children. The crucial factor in determining the order of emergence of these word formation processes seems to be productivity. The two processes that apply most freely in English (the formation of a noun by the addition of the agentive affix -er to a verb and compounding) were the first to emerge. On the other hand, morphemes such as -ly that can apply to only a restricted set of adjectival roots (*quiet/quietly* but **red/redly*, **fast/fastly*) seem to be mastered at a much later age.

Even the subtlest properties of word formation seem to be acquired in the preschool years. One such property involves the fact that an inflectional suffix such as the plural cannot occur inside compounds (compare **dogs catcher* with *dog catcher*). In one study, children as young as three years of age produced compounds that obeyed this constraint. Thus, when asked a question such as *What do you call someone who eats cookies?*, they responded by saying *cookie eater* rather than **cookies eater*.

Of course, the acquisition of word formation processes is not entirely error-free. Three- and four-year-old children, for example, have been observed to make word order errors in compounds, producing forms such as **breaker bottle* (for *bottle breaker*) and **builder wall* (for *wall builder*). However, such errors typically disappear by age five.

10.4 DEVELOPMENT OF WORD MEANING

By age eighteen months or so, the average child has a vocabulary of fifty words or more. Over the next months this vocabulary grows rapidly, sometimes by as much as ten or twelve words a day. The words in a typical vocabulary of a two-year old are in Table 10.13. As Table 10.13 shows, noun-like words are

Table 10.13 Typical vocabulary of a two-year-old child

Objects
body parts: cheek, ear, foot, hand, leg, nose, toe
food: cookie, cereal, drink, egg, fish, jam, milk
clothes: boot, clothes, dress, hat, shirt, shoes, socks
household: bag, bath, bell, bottle, box, brush, chair, clock, soap, spoon, water, watch
animals: bear, bird, cat, cow, dog, horse, sheep

Properties
bad, dirty, fat, good, more, nice, poor, sweet

Actions and events
bring, burn, carry, catch, clap, come, cut, do, dry, fall, get, give, go, kick, kiss, knit, look, meet, open, pull, push, ring, shut, sit, sleep, speak, sweep, tickle, wag, warm, wash

Other
away, down, now, up, no, yes, thank you, goodbye

predominant in the child's early vocabulary, with verb- and adjective-like words being the next most frequent category types. Among the most frequent individual words are expressions for displeasure or rejection (such as *no*) and various types of social interaction (such as *give* and *bye-bye*). Over the next few years, continued rapid expansion of this vocabulary takes place so that by age six most children have mastered about five thousand different morphemes. These developmental trends are found in all linguistic communities and therefore appear to be universal.

Acquisition of Word Meaning

A major factor in lexical development is the child's ability to use contextual clues to draw inferences about the category and meaning of new words. From around seventeen months of age, for instance, children can use the presence or absence of determiners to distinguish between proper nouns (names) and common nouns. Two-year-old children who are told that a new doll is a *dax* will identify a similar doll as a *dax* as well. However, if they are told that the new doll is *Dax*, they will restrict use of the new word to the doll they have actually been shown.

Children are also able to use the meaning of other words in the sentence as well as their understanding of the nonlinguistic context to form hypotheses about new words. In one experiment, for example, three- and four-year-old children were asked to act out the meaning of sentences such as "Make it so there is *tiv* to drink in this glass (of water)." The only clues to the interpretation of the nonsense word *tiv* come from the meaning of the sentence and from the child's understanding of the types of changes that can be made to a glass of water. Not only did more than half the children respond by either adding or removing water, some even remembered what *tiv* "meant" two weeks later!

The meanings that children associate with their early words sometimes correspond closely to the meanings employed by adults. In many cases, however, the match is less than perfect. The two most typical semantic errors involve overextension and underextension.

Overextension In cases of **overextension**, the meaning of the child's word overlaps with that of the corresponding adult form, but also extends beyond it. The word *dog*, for example, is frequently overextended to include horses, cows, and other four-legged animals. Similarly, *ball* is sometimes used for any round object, such as a balloon, an Easter egg, a small stone, a plastic egg-shaped toy, and so on.

The Basis for Overextension A major issue in the study of language acquisition is whether children's overextensions are the result of similarities in the appearance (shape, size, texture) or the function of the objects to which the overextended word refers. The evidence collected to date suggests that perceptual properties are the critical factor in children's first hypotheses about word meanings. As a result, children often overextend a word to include a set of perceptually similar objects that they know to have diverse functions. One child, for example, used the word *moon* for the moon, grapefruit halves, a crescent-shaped piece of paper, a crescent-shaped car light, and a hangnail. Another child used the word *money* for a set of objects ranging from pennies to buttons and beads. If you consider the examples of overextension given in Table 10.14, you will see that they too are more plausibly explained in terms of perceptual similarities than a shared function.

Table 10.14 Examples of overextension

Word	First referents	Subsequent extensions
tick tock	watch	clocks, gas-meter, fire hose on a spool, scale with round dial
fly	fly	specks of dirt, dust, small insects, child's toes, crumbs of bread
quack	duck	all birds and insects, flies, coins (with an eagle on the face)
candy	candy	cherries, anything sweet
apple	apples	balls, tomatoes, cherries, onions, cookies
turtle	turtles	fish, seals
cookie	cookies	crackers, any dessert
kitty	cats	rabbits, any small furry animal
box	boxes	elevators

Children seem to overextend more in their production than in their comprehension. A child who overextends the word *dog* in his or her own speech, for example, may well point only to dogs when asked by an adult to find the dogs in the picture shown in Figure 10.1. This suggests that children sometimes deliberately overextend words in production to compensate for their limited vocabulary.

Underextension While overextensions are the most frequent type of word-meaning error in early language, children also frequently employ **underextension** by using lexical items in an overly restrictive fashion. For example, at the age of nine months, one child restricted her use of the word *car* to a particular situation. She used it only for cars moving on the street as she watched out of the window, not for cars standing still, for cars in pictures, or for cars she rode in herself.

Figure 10.1 Picture used for animal identification tasks

Another type of underextension is the use of a word to name a specific object without extending it to other members of that class. Thus, *kitty* might be used to refer to the family pet, but not to any other cats. Or, the word *dog* might be used for collies, spaniels, and beagles, but not for Chihuahuas.

Underextension errors often reflect children's propensity to focus on prototypical or core members of a category. As noted in Chapter 6, the potential referents of many words differ in terms of how well they exemplify the properties associated with a particular concept. Thus, among the potential referents of the word *dog*, collies and spaniels have more of the properties associated with the concept 'dog' (long hair, relative size, type of bark, and so on) than do Chihuahuas. While the preference for a prototype can be overruled by factors such as the presence of a nontypical category member in the child's everyday experience (in the case of dogs, a Chihuahua as a family pet), it is clear that the internal structure of fuzzy and graded concepts can have an important influence on semantic development.

Spatial and Dimensional Terms

English has many words that are used to express spatial relations (such as *in*, *on*, and *behind*). Although syntactically similar (most are prepositions), these words differ from each other in terms of their semantic complexity. Notice, for example, that the relation expressed by *on* and *in* does not depend on the speaker's viewpoint: if two marbles are on a box, then they are on it no matter where the speaker is standing. However, matters are more complicated in the case of the relations expressed by *behind* and *in front of* since we would say that the marbles are behind the box only if the box is between us and the marbles. If we stand on the opposite side of the box, the marbles would then appear to be in front of the box. Matters are slightly simpler when the object with respect to which the marbles are situated has an inherent front and back (such as a television). In this case, we can ignore our own position and focus on the marbles' location with respect to the front part of the television.

These considerations seem to be directly reflected in the order in which words expressing spatial relations are acquired.

Table 10.15 Order of acquisition for words expressing spatial relations

Step	Words	Description
1	in, on, under, beside	independent of speaker's perspective
2	behind, in front of	used with objects with inherent fronts and backs
3	behind, in front of	used with objects without inherent fronts or backs

Interestingly, this developmental order has been observed in a number of languages (Italian, Turkish, and Serbo-Croatian) other than English. This suggests that the considerations that determine the semantic complexity of spatial words are universal and therefore are manifested in the acquisition of all languages.

Dimensional Terms Like words referring to spatial relations, terms describing size and dimensions are also acquired in a relatively fixed order, depending on their generality. The first dimensional adjectives to be acquired, *big* and *small*, are the most general in that they can be used for talking about any aspect of size (height, area, volume, and so on). In contrast, the second group of adjectives to emerge, *tall*, *long*, *short*, *high*, and *low*, can only be used for a single dimension (height-length). The remaining modifiers (*thick-thin*, *wide-narrow*, and *deep-shallow*) are still more restricted in their use since they describe the secondary, or less extended dimension of an object. For instance, the dimension of a stick that we describe in terms of width or thickness is almost always less extended than the dimension that we describe in terms of height or length, which tends to be the more salient dimension.

Table 10.16 Order of acquisition for dimensional adjectives

Step	Words	What they describe
1	big-small	any aspect of size
2	tall-short, long-short, high-low	a single dimension
3	thick-thin, wide-narrow, deep-shallow	a secondary dimension

The importance of the salient dimension in the development of adjectives is underlined by a peculiar error that has been observed in children's early use of the modifier *big*. When asked to choose which of the following two figures is the 'big one', children between the ages of three and five tend to choose figure 10.2b over 10.2a.

Figure 10.2

Although figure *a* is larger in overall area, figure *b* is greater on the vertical dimension. The fact that children take *b* to be bigger suggests that height is more salient to them than is overall area.

10.5 SYNTACTIC DEVELOPMENT

Like phonological and morphological development, the emergence of syntactic rules takes place in an orderly sequence. Beginning with the production of one-word utterances near the end of the first year of life, children gradually master the rules for sentence formation in their language. Some of the milestones in this developmental process are considered here.

The One-Word Stage

As noted earlier, children begin to produce one-word utterances between the ages of twelve and eighteen months. A basic property of these one-word utterances is that they can be used to express the type of meaning that would be associated with an entire sentence in adult speech. Thus, a child might use the word *dada* to assert (among other things) 'I saw daddy's hat', *more* to mean 'Give me more candy', and *up* to mean 'I want up'. Such utterances are called **holophrases**.

A striking feature of holophrastic utterances is children's skill in communicating complex messages with a single word. This skill seems to be based on a strategy of choosing the most informative word that applies to the situation being commented upon. A child who wanted a candy, for example, would say *candy* rather than *want* since the former word is more informative in this situation. Similarly, a child who notices a new toy would be more likely to say *toy* than *see*, thereby referring to the most novel feature of the situation he or she is trying to describe.

Table 10.17 lists some of the semantic relations that children commonly try to express during the one-word stage.

Table 10.17 One-word utterances

Semantic relation	Utterance	Situation
Agent of an action	dada	as father enters the room
Action or state	down	as child sits down
Object of an action	door	as father closes the door
Location	here	as child points
Recipient	mama	as child gives mother something
Recurrence	again	as child watches the lighting of a match

The Two-Word Stage

Within a few months of their first one-word utterances, children begin to produce two-word utterances of the sort shown in Table 10.18.

Table 10.18 Patterns in two-word speech

Child's utterance	Adult form	Semantic relations
Baby chair	The baby is sitting on the chair.	agent-location
Doggie bark	The dog is barking.	agent-action
Ken water	Ken is drinking water.	agent-object
Hit doggie	I hit the doggie.	action-object
Daddy hat	Daddy's hat	possessor-possessed

It is unclear whether children in the two-word stage have acquired syntactic categories such as noun, verb, and adjective. As the following utterances show, words that belong to separate categories in the adult language (the adjective *busy* and the verb *push*) can occur in identical patterns in the two-word stage. This makes it difficult to determine whether the child is treating them as separate categories.

5. Mommy busy.
   Mommy push.

Another problem is that the inflectional affixes that distinguish among syntactic categories in adult English (such as the plural and the past tense) are absent from the speech of children in the two-word stage. While this does not show that children lack lexical categories, it makes it very difficult to demonstrate that they possess them. For this reason, many linguists and psychologists prefer to describe children's utterances in terms of the semantic relations that they express (as in Table 10.18) rather than the syntactic categories of adult speech.

The Telegraphic Stage

After a period of several months during which their speech is limited to one- and two-word utterances, children begin to produce longer and more complex grammatical structures. Some representative utterances from the first part of this period are given in the following example.

6. Chair all broken.
   Daddy like this book.
   What her name?
   Man ride bus today.
   Car make noise.
   Me wanna show Mommy.
   I good boy.

At first, these utterances lack bound morphemes and most nonlexical categories. Because of their resemblance to the style of language found in telegrams, this acquisitional stage is often dubbed **telegraphic**. Over a period of several months, affixes, determiners, and auxiliary verbs emerge.

A noteworthy feature of the telegraphic stage is that children make virtually no word order errors. As the previous examples illustrate, adult word order patterns are employed even though individual words may not have the appropriate endings. In languages with variable word order (such as Korean and Russian), children use the various word order patterns in roughly the same proportion as adults do.

Because of the diversity and sophistication of the utterances produced during the telegraphic stage, there is general agreement that this period is characterized by the emergence of powerful grammatical devices. Foremost among these are the phrase structure rules, which regulate the order and composition of syntactic units. If you reconsider the examples in *6*, you will see evidence for the S rule (as in *Daddy like this book*) as well as for an XP rule that forms structures consisting of a head (especially a V) and a complement (*like this book, ride bus, show Mommy*). Modifiers, including adjectives like *good* and adverbs like *today*, also exist during this period.

As already noted, determiners, auxiliaries, and other non-lexical categories are conspicuously absent from the telegraphic stage. Since these are the types of words that occur in specifier positions, children's speech gives the impression that XP categories are acquired in steps, with heads and complements emerging before specifiers. Table 10.19 summarizes the development of phrase structure.

Table 10.19 The development of phrase structure

Stage	Approx. age	Developments
Holophrastic	1–1.5 yrs	single word utterances; no structure
Two-word	1.5–2 yrs	early word combinations; presence of syntactic categories unclear
Telegraphic	2–3 yrs	emergence of the S rule and the part of the XP rule that yields heads and complements
Later	3 yrs up	emergence of non-lexical categories, including those used as specifiers (Det, Aux)

Later Development

In the years following the telegraphic stage, children continue to acquire the complex grammar that underlies adult linguistic competence. To date, acquisition studies have dealt with only a few aspects of this later development. Some of the findings on particular English constructions are reviewed in this section.

Negation Children seem to acquire basic patterns of negation involving *no* and *not* in three stages during the second and third years of life.

Stage 1 (approximately eighteen to twenty-five months) The use of *no* at the beginning of the sentence.

    7. No the sun shining.
        No sit there.
        No dog bite you.
        No money.
        No Mom sharpen it.
        No Fraser drink all tea.

Stage 2 (approximately twenty-six to forty-two months) Negative elements (usually *no*) now occur sentence-internally, but children still do not have productive mastery of auxiliary verbs. Forms like *can't* and *don't* occur occasionally, but *can* and *do* are not found. This suggests that children do not yet have command of auxiliary verbs and are treating *can't* and *don't* as simple negative morphemes.

8. I no singing song.
   The sun no shining.
   Don't sit there.
   Dog no bite you.
   We can't talk.
   I no want envelope.
   I no taste them.

Stage 3 (after forty-two months) The forms *not* and *n't* now appear sentence-internally with auxiliary verbs, as in adult speech.

9. I'm not singing a song.
   The sun isn't shining.
   The dog won't bite you.
   It's not cold.
   I don't have a book.

Inversion   In the very early stages of language acquisition, children signal *yes-no* questions by means of rising intonation alone. (Recall that auxiliary verbs are a relatively late development.)

10. See hole?
    I ride train?
    Ball go?
    Sit chair?

Even after individual auxiliary verbs appear in child language, there is often a delay of a few months before they undergo Inversion and appear at the beginning of the sentence in *yes-no* questions. In one study, for example, a young boy began using the auxiliary verb *can* at age two years, five months, but did not employ it in an inversion pattern until six months later.

An interesting error in children's early use of Inversion in both *yes-no* and *wh* questions is exemplified in *11*.

11. *Can* he *can* look?
    What *shall* we *shall* have?
    Did you *did* came home?

In these sentences, the auxiliary verb occurs twice—once to the left of the subject (in the position that it occupies after Inversion) and once to the right (in the VP specifier position it occupies in deep structure). It has been suggested that this pattern reflects an error in the application of the Inversion transformation in that a copy of the moved auxiliary is left behind in the specifier position within VP.

Experimental work has shown that this type of error is more likely in a sentence such as *12* with a complex subject NP.

12. [The girl who is crying] should leave→
    *Should [the girl who is crying] should leave?

This presumably happens because the subject NP stands directly between the auxiliary's deep structure position and the position to which it is moved in surface structure. As such, its complexity can interfere with the Inversion operation.

Wh Questions *Wh* questions emerge gradually between the ages of two and four. For many children, the following three stages are involved.

Stage 1 Children produce both *yes-no* questions and *wh* questions, but Inversion is not possible since auxiliary verbs are not yet acquired. The first *wh* words to be acquired are typically *what* and *where*, followed by *why*; *how* and *when* are relatively late acquisitions.

13. Where that?
    What me think?
    Why you smiling?
    Why not me drink it?

Stage 2 Auxiliary verbs make their appearance and undergo Inversion, but only in *yes-no* questions. *Wh* questions continue to be formed without Inversion.

14. *Yes-no* questions (with Inversion):
    Did Mommy pinch her finger?
    Can't you fix it?
    Do I have it?
    Will you help me?
    Is Mommy talking to Robin's grandmother?

15. *Wh* questions (no Inversion):
    What I did yesterday?
    Why kitty can't stand up?
    Where I should put it?
    Where I should sleep?
    Why you are smiling?

Stage 3 Inversion is applied in *wh* questions as well as *yes-no* questions.

16. Where did my mitten go?
    Where should I sleep?
    Why are you smiling?

For some children, Inversion in *wh* questions develops in two substages, appearing first in affirmative structures and later in negative ones. In these cases, children who are able to produce the affirmative constructions in *16* above will still use ill-formed negative sentences such as the following.

17. Why you can't sit down?
    Why kitty can't stand up?

Even after children have learned subject-verb Inversion, they often make mistakes involving tense and agreement, such as those in 18.

18. Did I caught it?
What did you doed?
Does lions walk?

The Interpretation of Sentence Structure (advanced)

As noted in Chapter 6, the interpretation of sentences draws heavily on information about how words are hierarchically organized to form phrase structure. In this section we will briefly consider some aspects of the acquisition of two interpretive phenomena that rely on information about syntactic structure.

Thematic Roles In Chapter 6, we saw that thematic roles are assigned to particular (deep structure) positions in accordance with the following generalizations.

19. A P assigns its role (location, source, or goal) to an NP complement.
A V assigns its theme role to an NP complement.
A V assigns its agent role to the subject.

Children learning English are able to associate thematic roles with particular structural positions at a very early point in the acquisition process. By the time their average utterance length is two words, they are able to respond correctly about 75 percent of the time to comprehension tests involving simple active sentences such as *20*, in which the truck is the agent and the car is the theme.

20. The truck bumped the car.

However, correct comprehension of the corresponding passive structure in *21* emerges much later.

21. The car was bumped by the truck.

As the following data show, children have a great deal of difficulty with passive constructions up to age seven or so.

Table 10.20 Comprehension of passive constructions

Group	Percentage correct
Nursery school	20
Kindergarten	35
Grade 1	48
Grade 2	63
Grade 3	88

Thematic role assignment in passive structures is complicated by the fact that the NP bearing the theme role occurs in the subject position while the agent (marked by the preposition *by*) appears after the verb.

22. Passive sentence:
The car was bumped by the truck
Theme   *Agent*

Active sentence:
The truck bumped the car.
Agent   *Theme*

Thus, passive sentences are almost mirror images of their active counterparts in that the agent occurs after the verb and the theme before it rather than vice versa. Significantly, the most common error made by children is to assume that the first NP is the agent and the second NP the theme. This suggests that they are overgeneralizing the thematic role pattern found in active sentences and have not yet learned the special properties of passive constructions.

As the data in Table 10.20 show, children realize around age five or six that treating the first NP as agent and the second NP as theme is not always appropriate, but they are confused about how they should interpret passive structures. The scores for this period (around 50 percent correct) suggest that responses are based on guessing. Finally, around age seven, children's scores begin to rise dramatically, indicating that they have begun to acquire the special properties associated with thematic role assignment in the passive construction.

Pronominals and Reflexives In Chapter 6, we saw that a reflexive pronoun (*himself*, *herself*, and so on) must have an antecedent in the minimal clause containing it. Thus, *23* can only have the interpretation in which *himself* refers to Gary.

23. Sam said that [s Gary slapped *himself* on the wrist].

In contrast, a pronominal (*him*, *her*) in this position can refer only to Sam or to someone not mentioned in the sentence.

24. Sam said that [s Gary slapped *him* on the wrist].

In terms of language acquisition, there is some reason to believe that children are able to interpret reflexives correctly before pronominals. Thus, children between the ages of three and five correctly interpret *himself* as Gary. However, they tend to misinterpret *him* by allowing it to refer to Gary too. It is not until age seven or so that language learners are able to interpret pronouns correctly in this type of structure.

10.6 DETERMINANTS OF LANGUAGE ACQUISITION

In the preceding sections, we have seen that children acquire the grammar for their language over a period of several years. While it is relatively easy to describe the order in which children acquire various phonemic contrasts, morphemes, and syntactic rules, it is much more difficult to explain *how* they do this. The sections that follow outline some of the skills and abilities that may help children acquire the categories and rules that make up the grammar of their language.

The Role of Imitation and Correction

At one time, it was widely believed that children learn language by simply imitating the speech of those around them. We now know that this cannot be true, since many utterance types produced by children do not closely resemble structures found in adult speech. Plural forms such as *foots* and negative constructions such as *No the sun shining* are obvious examples of structures that are unique to child language. As noted earlier, such utterances reflect children's attempts to construct grammatical rules, not the imitation of adult speech.

The importance of imitation to language acquisition is placed in further doubt by the fact that children are typically unable to imitate structures that they have not yet learned. Thus, a child who has not yet acquired the Inversion rule for *wh* questions will "imitate" sentence *25a* by producing *25b*.

25. *a*) What have you seen? (*model*)
    b) What you have seen? (*child's imitation*)

Findings like these suggest that children process the speech they hear in terms of their current grammatical system.

This is not to say that imitation plays no role in language learning. While many children rarely attempt to repeat the utterances they hear, some language learners do seem to make selective use of imitation. They imitate new words in constructions they have already learned and repeat novel constructions that contain words already familiar to them. Such selective imitation suggests that children do not blindly mimic adult speech, but rather exploit it in very restricted ways to improve their linguistic skills.

Another common assumption is that parents provide children with direct linguistic training by correcting ill-formed utterances. This assumption has not been supported by studies of actual interactions between parents and children. Instead of correcting children's speech, parents react to the meaning of children's utterances. In one case, a parent reacted to the utterance *Mama isn't boy, he's a girl* by responding *That's right*.

Even when adults do attempt to correct children's grammatical errors, their efforts seem to have little effect. The following actual exchange between a child and his mother is typical in this regard.

26. *Child*: Nobody don't like me.
    Mother: No, say "Nobody likes me."
    Child: Nobody don't like me.
    [*Exchange is repeated eight times.*]
    Mother: No, now listen carefully; say "Nobody likes me."
    Child: Oh! Nobody don't LIKES me.

A more subtle form of correction occurs when adults repeat a child's immature utterance, making the adjustments needed for it to be grammatical in the adult language.

27. *Child*: Daddy here.
    Mother: Yes, Daddy is here.
    Child: Boy chasing dog.
    Mother: Yes, the boy is chasing the dog.
    Child: Him go.
    Mother: Yes, he is going.

A recent study of upper-middle-class families in the United States suggests that mothers are more likely to revise their children's utterances if they are ungrammatical. It is not yet known whether this practice is common in other groups or whether it actually helps in children's acquisition of language.

The Role of Parental Speech

Linguistic development obviously depends in crucial ways on the child's linguistic experience. Children who are exposed to English learn to speak English, those exposed to Spanish learn Spanish, and so on. Moreover, children who are not exposed to language do not develop linguistic skills beyond the babbling stage.

A good deal of recent work has been devoted to the search for a possible relationship between language acquisition and the type of speech that is typically addressed to young language learners. Such speech is often called **caregiver speech** or **Motherese**. A valuable product of this research has been the discovery that speech addressed to young children has special properties that could well heighten its comprehensibility. Phonologically, for example, caregiver speech is known to consist of clearly articulated utterances with pauses between phrases and exaggerated intonation contours to signal questions, imperatives, and statements. Parental speech also tends to concentrate on the here and now, consisting primarily of statements relating to the child's current surroundings, activities, and needs. The following examples help illustrate this.

28. That's right, pick up the blocks. (*said as the child is picking up a box of building blocks*)
    That's a puppy. (*said as the child is looking at a young dog*)
    The puppy's in the basket. (*said as the child is examining a puppy in a basket*)

It seems reasonable to suppose that exposure to this type of language makes it easier for children to match forms (morphemes, words, and phrases) with meanings, and thereby to acquire the vocabulary and structure of their language.

Table 10.21 lists some features commonly found in the speech of middle-class English-speaking mothers to their children.

Table 10.21 Some features of English motherese

Phonetic
Slower speech
Higher pitch
Exaggerated intonation and stress
Longer pauses

Lexical and semantic
More restricted vocabulary
Concrete reference to here and now

Syntactic
Fewer incomplete sentences
Shorter sentences
More commands and questions

Conversational
More repetitions
Fewer utterances per conversational turn

Although potentially helpful, it is not clear that these phenomena are actually crucial to the language acquisition process. In some cultures, for instance, children are not considered to be potential conversational partners until

LANGUAGE ACQUISITION   385

they are fluent speakers. Little speech is addressed directly to them, although they do spend a lot of time with their mothers and are exposed to a good deal of conversation among adults. The fact that these children seem to learn language in a normal fashion indicates that exposure to the speech style typical of middle-class mothers in North American society is not necessary for language acquisition.

We also know that parental speech has highly selective effects on child language. In one widely cited study, the speech of fifteen mothers to their daughters (aged one year to two years and three months) was analyzed. It was found that there were correlations between only some aspects of caregiver speech and child speech. For instance, the number of *yes-no* questions in parental speech was positively correlated with the rate at which auxiliary verbs developed. This was presumably because auxiliaries occur in the salient sentence-initial position in *yes-no* questions (*Can Jennifer go?*). However, many other features of parental speech seem not to influence child language. For example, the relative frequency of bound morphemes in parental speech apparently has no direct effect on their order of acquisition.

In and of itself, parental speech cannot explain how language acquisition occurs. However, research into caregiver speech may contribute to this goal in less direct ways by helping determine the types of linguistic experience that are most valuable to children. This in turn will help identify the types of mechanisms and strategies involved in language acquisition.

The Role of Cognitive Development

Cognitive development is the name given to the emergence of the various mental abilities and skills that make up the human intellect. Because there are dramatic changes in children's linguistic abilities and in their other cognitive skills during the first years of life, it is tempting to think that the two are somehow linked. Indeed, prominent psychologists have suggested both that cognitive development shapes language acquisition (a view put forward by the Swiss psychologist Jean Piaget) and that language acquisition is crucial to cognitive development (a position associated with the Russian psychologist Lev Vygotsky).

There are many suggestive similarities between language acquisition and cognitive development. During the first two years of life, for example, several cognitive advances that could facilitate language acquisition take place. One of these involves the development of **object permanence**, the ability to recognize that objects have an existence independent of one's interaction with them. Prior to the development of this ability, children seem to assume that an object ceases to exist when it moves out of sight, and that it is a different entity when it reappears. They therefore do not know where to look for an object that they observe being hidden. From their perspective, it has apparently simply ceased to exist. The emergence of object permanence around age eighteen months generally coincides with the beginning of a period of rapid growth in the child's vocabulary. The relative timing of these two events suggests a possible connection: children do not learn the names for objects until they understand that those objects have an independent existence.

During the first twenty-four months of their lives, children also acquire the ability to classify objects and actions. They seem to understand that certain things are eaten, others can be sat upon, still others serve as toys, and so on.

It is conceivable that these classification skills may also help to create linguistic categories such as noun and verb. It has also been suggested that a general ability to arrange and order elements with respect to each other plays a role in children's attempts to organize words into sentences.

Still another link between cognitive development and language acquisition involves seriation, the ability to arrange elements (such as sticks) in order of increasing or decreasing size. Children who are unable to perform this type of task typically describe the objects on which they are working simply as *long* or *short*. In contrast, children who are capable of seriation (aged five and older) use comparative terms such as *longer* and *shorter*. Here again, there is an apparent connection between an aspect of language (the comparative suffix for adjectives) and a more general cognitive skill (seriation).

Just as cognitive development may influence language acquisition, so may the emergence of linguistic skills have an effect on cognition. At the very least, language seems to provide its users with an enhanced capacity for complex reasoning. It is also conceivable that language may help draw children's attention to certain conceptual distinctions that would otherwise develop more slowly. For instance, in the course of being exposed to words such as *father*, *mother*, and *brother*, children may make discoveries about family relationships that might otherwise develop more slowly.

Some Special Cases Considerations such as these notwithstanding, there is reason to think that language acquisition and other types of cognitive development are to a very significant degree independent of each other. A rich source of evidence for this conclusion comes from the study of children with particular types of mental deficits, including those whose general cognitive development is quite good but whose language is deficient in some respect.

One such child is the much discussed Genie, who was kept in a small room with virtually no opportunity to hear human speech from around age two to age thirteen. After many years of therapy and care, Genie's nonlinguistic cognitive functioning was described as relatively normal and her lexical and semantic abilities as good. In terms of syntax and morphology, however, many problems remained, as evidenced in the following sample utterances.

Table 10.22 Some of Genie's utterances

Utterance	Meaning
Applesauce buy store	'Buy applesauce at the store.'
Man motorcycle have	'The man has a motorcycle.'
Want go ride Miss F. car	'I want to go ride in Miss F.'s car.'
Genie have full stomach	'I have a full stomach.'
Mama have baby grow up	'Mama has a baby who grew up.'

As these examples show, Genie makes word order errors (the second example above) and her speech does not contain nonlexical categories or affixes.

Another pattern of disability was observed in Rick, a severely retarded fifteen year old whose performance on a variety of nonlinguistic tasks suggests that his general cognitive level is that of a preschool child. Yet, as the following examples illustrate, Rick's speech shows signs of syntactic and morphological sophistication—with appropriate use of affixes, nonlexical categories, and word order.

29. She must've got me up and thrown me out of bed.
She keeps both of the ribbons on her hair.
If they get in trouble, they'd have a pillow fight.
She's the one that walks back and forth to school.
I wanna hear one more just for a change.

Case studies such as these suggest that certain aspects of language (in particular, morphology and syntax) are independent of nonlinguistic types of cognitive development. This in turn implies that the mental mechanisms responsible for the acquisition of those parts of the grammar are relatively autonomous and that their operation neither follows from nor guarantees general cognitive development.

The Role of Inborn Knowledge (advanced)

Although both cognitive development and exposure to the speech of others are clearly crucial to language acquisition, other factors must also be involved. Apes have many of the cognitive skills of two-year-old children, but they do not acquire language even when they are exposed to speech. This suggests that there is something about the human mind that equips it to acquire language. A very influential view among linguists is that children are born with advance knowledge of the type of categories and rules that are found in the grammar of any human language. They would therefore know, for example, that the words in the language they are acquiring will belong to a small set of syntactic categories (N, V, and so on), and that there will be rules of a certain sort to create larger phrases (NP, VP, S), although they would have to learn from experience the precise nature of elements within each phrasal category. The set of inborn categories and principles common to all human languages is called **Universal Grammar (UG)**.

Of course, not every feature of a language's grammar can be inborn. In the case of phrase structure, for example, UG stipulates that an XP constituent can include a head X and its complements, but it does not specify the relative order of these elements. This differs from language to language, so that a child acquiring English must learn that Vs and Ps precede their complements while a child acquiring Japanese must learn that heads follow their complements. As noted in Chapter 5, Universal Grammar includes a parameter (set of options) for word order. As illustrated in Table 10.23, these options include head-initial order versus head-final order. (We ignore the positioning of specifiers for the purposes of this illustration.)

Table 10.23 The word order parameter

Stipulated by UG	Resulting options
XP→X, Complement	XP→X Complement (head-initial)
	XP→Complement X (head-final)

The view that certain grammatical knowledge is inborn is known as **nativism**. Although nativism has roots in philosophy that date back thousands of years, its popularity in linguistics is due largely to the theories of Noam

Chomsky, a linguist at the Massachusetts Institute of Technology. Chomsky's basic claim is that the grammars for human language are too complex and abstract to be learned on the basis of the type of experience to which children have access. He therefore concludes that significant components of the grammar must be inborn.

To illustrate this, we must consider a relatively complex example involving the notion of c-command introduced in the chapter on semantics. As you may recall, c-command is defined as follows.

30. NP_a c-commands NP_b if the first category above NP_a contains NP_b.

The c-command relation plays a crucial role in the statement of a number of linguistic principles, including the following constraint on reflexive pronouns (in English, pronouns ending in *self*).

31. Principle A: A reflexive pronoun must have an antecedent that c-commands it.

The C-Command Requirement is responsible for the interpretation of sentences such as *32*.

32. The boy's father hurt himself.

The antecedent for *himself* in *32* is *the boy's father*, not *the boy*; that is, the sentence must be taken to mean that the father of the boy is both the person who was hurt and the person who did the hurting. This fact follows from Principle A, provided that we assume that sentence *32* has the structure depicted in Figure 10.3. In Figure 10.3, there is only one category that stands

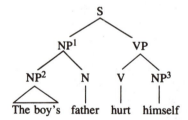

Figure 10.3

above the NP *the boy's father*—namely S. Since this phrase also contains the reflexive pronoun, NP^1 c-commands *himself* according to our definition and can therefore serve as its antecedent in accordance with the C-Command Requirement. The same is not true of *the boy* (NP^2) since the first category above it does not contain the reflexive. This means that NP^2 does not c-command the reflexive and cannot serve as its antecedent.

There are two major reasons for believing that the C-Command Requirement must be inborn. First, the notion of c-command is quite abstract. It is not the type of concept that we would expect young children to discover simply by listening to sentences. Since we also know that parents do not give children formal language lessons, it makes sense to think that c-command is an inborn notion that does not have to be discovered or taught.

Second, the C-Command Requirement seems to be universal. There appear to be no languages in which the equivalent of English *himself* can refer to the boy rather than the boy's father in structures such as *32*. The universality of this principle would be explained if it were innate and hence part of the advance or inborn linguistic knowledge of all human beings.

The claim that children are born with abstract linguistic principles is controversial, and research on alternatives continues. However, the hypothesis that the grammar is genetically structured is an exciting and intriguing development in linguistics. It is one of the many areas in the field of language acquisition where important breakthroughs remain to be made.

Summing Up

This chapter has been concerned with the problem of how children acquire the grammar of their first language. Research in this area deals with two major issues: the nature of the **developmental** sequence leading to the emergence of mature linguistic competence and the factors that make it possible for children to acquire complex grammatical rules. We have seen that over a period of several years children gradually acquire different subsystems of the grammar (**phonology, morphology, syntax**, and so on). In many cases, acquisition will involve a number of intermediate stages, each of which marks a successively closer approximation to the adult grammar. A number of factors are known to contribute to the child's acquisition of language, including the properties of parental speech, the effects of general cognitive development, and (possibly) inborn linguistic knowledge. We look to future research for deeper insights into the precise role of these and other factors.

Key Terms

caretaker speech	one-word stage
denasalization	overextension
developmental sequences	overgeneralizations
diary study	Principle A
experimental approach	stopping
fronting	telegraphic
gliding	two-word stage
holophrases	underextension
motherese	universal grammar
nativism	word formation rules
naturalistic approach	

Sources

Pioneering work on infant perception is reported in "Developmental Studies of Speech Perception" by P. Eimas in *Infant Perception*, edited by L. Cohen and P. Salapatek (New York: Academic Press, 1975). The cross-linguistic data on babbling are summarized and discussed in *Phonological Acquisition and Change* by J. Locke (cited below). Differences between children's production and perception of speech sounds are discussed in *The Acquisition of Phonology: A Case Study* by N. Smith (London: Cambridge University Press, 1973); the "*fis* phenomenon" is reported in "Psycholinguistic Research Methods" by J. Berko and R. Brown in *Handbook of Research Methods in Child Development*, edited by P. Mussen (New York: John Wiley & Sons, 1960). David Ingram's *Phonological Disability in Children* (cited below) contains many useful examples of early phonetic processes.

The pioneering work on the developmental order for English bound morphemes and lexical categories was done by R. Brown and reported in his book *A First Language: The Early Stages* (Cambridge, Mass.: Harvard University Press, 1973). The cross-linguistic data on the factors determining morphological development come from "Universal and Particular in the Acquisition of Language" by D. Slobin in *Language Acquisition: The State of the Art*, edited by E. Wanner and L. Gleitman (London: Cambridge University Press, 1982). The original "*wug* test" was done by J. Berko and is reported in her article "The Child's Learning of English Morphology" in *Word* 14: 150–77 (1958). The work on the development of derivational affixes and compounding in English is from "Recent Research on the Acquisition of English Morphology" by B. Derwing and W. Baker in *Language Acquisition*, edited by P. Fletcher and M. Garman (London: Cambridge University Press, 1979).

The data on the acquisition of the prohibition against inflection within compounds is from "Level-Ordering in Lexical Development" by P. Gordon in *Cognition* 21:73–93 (1985). Word order errors within compounds are reported in "Coining Complex Compounds in English: Affixes and Word Order in Acquisition" by E. Clark, B. Hecht, and R. Mulford in *Linguistics* 24:7–29 (1986).

The sample fifty-word vocabulary in Section 4 is from p. 149 of the book by Ingram, cited below. The differences in the type of words in children's early vocabulary were first noted by K. Nelson, "Structure and Strategy in Learning to Talk" in *Monographs of the Society for Research in Child Development* 38, no. 149, 1973.

The "*dax* experiment" on proper and common nouns is reported by N. Katz, E. Baker, and J. Macnamara in their article "What's in a Name? A Study of How Children Learn Common and Proper Nouns" in *Child Development* 45: 469–73 (1974); the "*tiv* experiment" is from "The Child as Word Learner" by S. Carey in *Linguistic Theory and Psychological Reality*, edited by M. Halle, J. Bresnan, and G. Miller (Cambridge, Mass.: MIT Press, 1978). The literature on spatial and dimensional terms is reviewed in *Psychology and Language* by H. Clark and E. Clark (cited below).

The data on the acquisition of passive structures come from a study by E. Turner and R. Rommetveit, reported in their article "The Acquisition of Sentence Voice and Reversibility" in *Child Development* 38: 650–60 (1967). The data on the development of negatives and question structures are based on the classic article by E. Klima and U. Bellugi, "Syntactic Regularities in the Speech of Children," in *Psycholinguistic Papers*, edited by J. Lyons and R. Wales (Edinburgh: Edinburgh University Press, 1966).

The role of correction in language development is examined in "Derivational Complexity and the Order of Acquisition in Child Speech" by R. Brown and C. Hanlon in *Cognition and the Development of Language*, edited by J. Hayes (New York: John Wiley & Sons, 1970) and in "Brown and Hanlon Revisited: Mothers' Sensitivity to Ungrammatical Forms" by K. Hirsh-Pasek, R. Treiman, and M. Schneiderman in *Journal of Child Language* 11: 81–88 (1984). The relationship between *yes-no* questions in parental speech and the development of auxiliaries is discussed by E. Newport, H. Gleitman, and L. Gleitman in their article, "Mother, I'd Rather Do It Myself: Some Effects and Noneffects of Maternal Speech Style" in *Talking to Children*, edited by C. Snow and C. Ferguson (London: Cambridge University Press, 1977).

General reviews of the role of cognitive development in language acquisition can be found in the book by D. Ingram (below). The description of Genie and of Rick is based on "Abnormal Language Acquisition and the Modularity of Language" by S. Curtiss in *Linguistics: The Cambridge Survey*, Vol. 2, edited by F. Newmeyer, 96–116 (New York: Cambridge University Press, 1988).

Recommended Reading

Clark, Herbert and Eve Clark. 1977. *Psychology and Language*. New York: Harcourt Brace Jovanovich.

De Villiers, Jill and Peter de Villiers. 1978. *Language Acquisition*. Cambridge, Mass.: Harvard University Press.

Ingram, David. 1989. *First Language Acquisition: Method, Description and Explanation*. New York: Cambridge University Press.

Locke, John. 1983. *Phonological Acquisition and Change*. New York: Academic Press.

Owens, Robert. 1984. *Language Development: An Introduction*. Columbus, Ohio: Charles E. Merrill.

Piattelli-Palmarini, Massimo, ed. 1980. *Language and Learning: The Debate between Jean Piaget and Noam Chomsky*. Cambridge, Mass.: Harvard University Press.

Wanner, Eric and Lila Gleitman, eds. 1982. *Language Acquisition: The State of the Art*. London: Cambridge University Press.

Questions

1. One piece of evidence that children acquire and overgeneralize a grammar is their production of forms like *doed*, *leaved*, and *goed*.

i) From recollections of your experience with children, give some more examples for this fact other than the past tense rule.

ii) What might we expect a young child to use in the place of the following adult words? Justify your choice in each case.

a) fish (plural)
b) went
c) mice
d) ate
e) has
f) geese
g) brought
h) hit (past tense)
i) himself
j) women

2. In one naturalistic study, a search for passive structures in a sample of 18,000 utterances from sixty children yielded only nineteen examples produced by twelve of the children.

a) Does this mean that the other forty-eight children had not yet mastered the passive structure?
b) How are the disadvantages of the naturalistic method exemplified here?

3. The following transcriptions represent the pronunciation of a two-year-old child. Indicate which phonetic processes have applied in each case.

a)	skin	[kɪd]	h)	tent	[dɛt]
b)	spoon	[buwn]	i)	teddy	[dɛdij]
c)	zoo	[duw]	j)	brush	[bʌt]
d)	John	[dɑn]	k)	bump	[bʌp]
e)	bath	[bæt]	l)	play	[pwej]
f)	other	[ʌdə]	m)	breakfast	[brɛkpəst]
g)	Smith	[mɪt]	n)	cheese	[tʃijs]

4. Drawing on the phonetic processes posited for the preceding exercise, predict one or more plausible immature pronunciations for each of the following words.

a)	show	e)	juice
b)	please	f)	thumb
c)	spit	g)	zebra
d)	under	h)	ring

5. Based on the discussion in Section 3 about the developmental sequence for morpheme acquisition, consider the acquisition in other languages of the morphemes corresponding to those listed in Table 10.7. Would you predict that these morphemes would be acquired in exactly the same order as their English equivalents? Why or why not?

6. Each of the following utterances is from the speech of a child in the two-word stage. Identify the semantic relation expressed by each of these utterances.

Intended meaning	Child's utterance
a) Jimmy is swimming	Jimmy swim.
b) Ken's book	Ken book
c) Daddy is at work.	Daddy work
d) You push the baby.	push baby
e) Mommy is reading.	Mommy read

7. Consider the following data from Jordie, a two and a half-year-old child, in light of the list of morphemes in Table 10.7.

Intended meaning	Jordie's utterance
a) Where's my blanket?	Where my blanket?
b) It goes right here, Mommy?	Go right here, Mommy?
c) It's running over.	Running over.
d) Here, it goes here.	Here, go here.
e) No, that's mine.	No, that mine.
f) Dinosaurs say gronk.	Dinosaur say gronk.
g) There's more.	There more.

   i) Which of the morphemes in Table 10.8 are missing in Jordie's sentences but present in the equivalent adult utterance?

   ii) List the morphemes that are present in both the adult interpretations and in Jordie's speech.

8. Now consider the following utterances from a child named Krista.

Intended meaning	Krista's utterance
a) My name is Krista.	Mine name Krista.
b) My last name is Pegit.	Last name Pegit.
c) The tape is right there.	Tape right there.
d) Daddy's book	Daddy book.
e) I've got a book.	I'm got a book
f) Read me a story.	Read me story.
g) I'll do it.	I'm do it.
h) He went outside.	He went outside.
i) Open the gate, please.	Open a gate, please.
j) That's gramma's house.	Gramma's house.
k) Smell the flowers.	Smell flowers.
l) Shoes on.	Shoes on.
m) The wee boy fell down.	Wee boy fell down.
n) That's my ball.	That's mines ball.

   i) Which morphemes are missing in Krista's speech, but present in the adult interpretations?

   ii) Krista uses the past tense twice in the above utterances. Do you think this is evidence that she has acquired the past tense morpheme? Why or why not?

iii) Comment on Krista's difficulty with possessive pronouns.

iv) Do you think she has acquired possessive -'s? Why or why not?

9. The allomorphic variation associated with the 3rd person singular verbal ending -*s* is identical to that found with plural -*s*.

i) Make up a test parallel to the one discussed in Section 3.

ii) If possible, give your test to children between the ages of three and seven. Are your results similar to the ones discussed in the chapter?

10. The following utterances were produced spontaneously by Holly, aged three years.

a) I learned about loving moms.

b) Put him in the bathtub.

c) We eated gummy snakes.

d) Thank you for giving these books us.

e) I don't know.

f) He bited my finger. (When corrected, she said: He bitted my finger.)

g) I runned in the water.

h) I rided on a elephant.

i) Has Holly acquired the past tense morpheme? How do you know?

ii) What is the evidence in Holly's speech that she has learned the XP rule? the S rule?

iii) Can you safely conclude that at this point in Holly's development she has acquired lexical and nonlexical categories? What is the evidence that she has acquired the category noun? the category verb?

11. The following sentences were uttered by a child aged two and a half.

a) What's this is called?

b) Mom, what these is called?

c) Did you don't go to school today?

d) You gonna don't go to school?

Considering these four sentences, describe the child's current knowledge of the Inversion transformation.

12. Consider the following speech sample from a child.

a) What Evan will read?

b) Where Evan will read?

c) Why you see seal?

d) Why she want to?

i) Determine the stage of development of this child in terms of his acquisition of question structures.

ii) What do we expect to happen next?

13. Consider the following examples of overextensions, all of which have actually been observed in children's speech. What is the basis for each of these overextensions?

Word	First referent	Overextensions
a) sch[s]	sound of a train	music, noise of wheels, sound of rain
b) bow-wow	dog	sheep, rabbit fur, puppet
c) baby	baby	people in pictures
d) sizzo	scissors	nail file, knife, screwdriver, spoon
e) policeman	policeman	mailman, sailor, doctor
f) strawberry	strawberry	grapes, raspberry
g) fireworks	fireworks	matches, light, cigarette
h) Batman	Batman logo on a T-shirt	any logo on a T-shirt

14. Since children have a tendency to focus on the prototypical members of categories in the acquisition of words, how might you expect children to underextend the following words? What members of the category might you expect children not to include?

    a) car   d) flower
    b) tree   e) table
    c) ball   f) shoe

15. As mentioned in this chapter, children acquire certain spatial terms like *behind* and *in front of* relatively late. They also acquire words like *those*, *this*, *here*, and *there* relatively late. What do all of these words have in common that delays their acquisition?

16. Studies of hearing children growing up in homes with nonspeaking deaf parents show that children cannot learn language from radio or even television.

    a) Can you think of any reasons for this?
    b) What are the implications of these findings for our understanding of the type of experience that is required for language acquisition?

11 SECOND LANGUAGE ACQUISITION

The study of languages . . . should be joined to that of objects, that our acquaintance with the objective world and with language . . . may progress side by side. For it is people we are forming and not parrots.

Comenius, 1657

In the last chapter, we introduced some of the theories about how children acquire a first language and outlined the different stages through which children pass during the language acquisition process. Unlike the first language (L1) learner, the second language (L2) learner already has an established language system for communicating. Cognitively more mature, L2 learners do not approach a second language in the same manner as they do a first. These facts alone justify setting L2 acquisition apart from L1 acquisition and treating it as a separate field of study. The term **applied linguistics** is often used to refer to L2 research, in that it is directly concerned with the application of linguistic theory to second language teaching and learning.

At the outset, it is necessary to define some of the terminology indispensable to a discussion of L2 acquisition. The term **second language** is used to mean a language that is learned after the first or native language is relatively established. It is not applicable to the case of a child learning two languages simultaneously during a bilingual upbringing. The L2 acquisition process also includes learning a new language in a foreign language context (studying English in Japan) as well as learning a new language in the host environment (learning French in France). The term second language may refer to a second, third, fourth, or even fifteenth language.

Some L2 researchers make a strong distinction between L2 learning and L2 acquisition. They define *learning* as a deliberate, conscious attempt to master a language. In contrast, they define the term *acquisition* as a less deliberate, subconscious process of mastering language, and often associate it with the manner in which children acquire language. Other researchers maintain that learning and acquisition are distinct types of cognitive behavior, and that learned and acquired knowledge are totally unrelated. In this chapter, however, the two terms will be used interchangeably. Second language acquisition is taken here to involve both conscious and subconscious processes regardless of the age of the learner and the language learning environment.

11.1 QUESTIONS AND ISSUES

Is learning a second language at all similar to the way we learn a first language? What is the effect of age on the language learning process? How is the L2 learner's progress affected by the language learning environment and the type of linguistic input he or she receives? These are just a few of the many questions to which L2 researchers are committed to finding answers. The results of some of their efforts will be discussed in this section.

The Optimal Age Issue

It has long been claimed that the older the learner, the less successful he or she will be at learning a second language. The role of age in learning second languages is a controversial issue in L2 research.

Among the traditional conceptions of L2 learning is the idea that children learning second languages in natural environments learn more easily and more proficiently than do adults under similar circumstances. This widely held belief has led to the idea that there is an optimal age or a critical period for L2 acquisition, which ends around the age of puberty. There are basically three considerations that are relevant to this idea: biological, cognitive, and affective.

Proponents of the biological argument believe that a child's brain is more "plastic" and, consequently, should be more receptive to certain aspects of language acquisition, especially in the area of pronunciation. Some researchers claim that pronunciation is dependent on early maturing neural circuits that control the brain and organs used for speech, while higher-order language functions, such as the development of semantic relations, are more dependent on late maturing neural circuits. This is in part why some researchers claim that after puberty, languages have to be learned through a conscious, labored effort, and that foreign accents cannot be overcome easily after this time. This idea continues to be controversial, however, since the biological evidence is too scanty to support a satisfactory explanation for the alleged superiority of children over adults in L2 learning.

The cognitive argument is that the adult's superiority in the domain of abstract thought should give adults the edge over children in L2 acquisition. This has implications for adolescents and adults, who generally learn the second language in a formal setting where the emphasis is on the conscious learning of language structures and grammatical rules. However, dependence on conscious rule knowledge may also impede the natural process of L2 acquisition.

Affective or emotional differences between children and adults are also reputed to have a crucial influence on second language learning. While adolescents are learning to think more abstractly, they are also experiencing the familiar adolescent feelings of self-consciousness and anxiety. Children are generally less inhibited about mimicking sounds than are adults, and this may positively affect their pronunciation. Normally, children do not have negative attitudes toward the second language culture, and they usually have a strong desire to be part of a group or community, which enhances their desire to learn the language.

While "the younger the better" is still a popular recommendation for potential L2 learners, this assumption is still being investigated. The biological,

cognitive, and affective arguments conflict regarding the optimal time for
learning a second language. Nevertheless, studies support the idea that the
number of years of exposure to the second language and the starting age of the
learner affect the ultimate level of success, especially regarding pronunciation.
Although young children may initially learn more slowly than adults, they
eventually surpass them.

The Role of Linguistic Input

Two factors crucial to L2 acquisition are the kind of language and the type of
language learning environments to which an L2 learner is exposed. The language that learners hear serves as their learning model, and the environment in
which they hear it affects how they view the second language and how they
learn it.

Foreigner Talk and Teacher Talk As pointed out in Chapter 10, a great deal of
attention has been concentrated on the language heard by the child and the way
in which this language becomes more complex as the child matures. L2 researchers maintain that a special type of language input, not unlike caregiver
speech, also exists for L2 learners. They have labeled this language **foreigner
talk** or **teacher talk** depending on the situation. Both caregiver speech and
foreigner or teacher talk are characterized by simplification of the linguistic
code.

When speaking to L2 learners, native speakers may choose simple word
order and more common vocabulary items. They formulate explanations or
questions carefully and attempt to produce well-formed utterances by avoiding
false starts, slips of the tongue, unfinished sentences, and hesitations. They
modify vocabulary by employing frequently used words, and avoiding idiom-
atic expressions such as *He flew off the handle* in favor of *He got angry.*
Vocabulary that might be unfamiliar is often paraphrased, such as *hold on very
tightly* for the verb *cling.*

The excerpt in *1a* exemplifies language that might be used by a teacher to
native speakers of English in a classroom. The excerpt in *1b*, by way of comparison, illustrates what happens when the same teacher speaks to nonnative
speakers of English in an ESL (English as a second language) situation.

1. *a*) (non-ESL situation) . . . I didn't recognize her at first sight.
    b) (same teacher in ESL situation) . . . I didn't know who she was
    when I first saw her.

While it is clear that many native speakers employ similar kinds of foreigner
talk, it is not clear how such modifications affect the L2 learner's developing
grammar, or whether the effects are positive or negative.

Some researchers maintain that the best way to improve an L2 learner's
linguistic ability is through **comprehensible input**, input a little beyond the
learner's linguistic competence. Such input is indispensable for language acquisition since, in order to acquire language most effectively, learners must
understand a large portion of the language presented to them and must also be
challenged by a more difficult structure. They can acquire the latter within the
communicative context by using their extralinguistic knowledge. From this
perspective, it appears that oversimplification of the linguistic code might have

a negative effect on the L2 learner's progress. More research is needed before we can understand the precise effects of foreigner or teacher talk on L2 acquisition and the exact nature of comprehensible input.

The Language Learning Environment

L2 learning can take place in different environments: natural, formal, or a combination of both. Learning a second language in the host country or in an immersion program involves natural environments because the focus is on communication. Learning a second language in a classroom situation or in any situation where a prescribed course of study is followed involves formal environments. The combination of a formal and a natural environment might entail studying the second language in a classroom in the host country.

Language learners who return from studying a second language in the host country generally outperform students who have been exposed only to formally structured classroom situations. Living in the L2 country provides a natural environment for communicating that is rarely found in a classroom. Contacts with native speakers can also help to break down social and cultural barriers.

In the classroom or formal environment, L2 learners do not have much time for spontaneous conversation about daily events. They are usually occupied with drills, translation, and grammar, while only part of the class time is free for conversation and language games.

Natural and formal language learning environments offer different benefits. While natural environments enhance communication skills, formal environments allow for learning of explicit rules. Allowing for formal language study tends to satisfy curiosity about language at the same time as it caters to individual language learning strategies. Such strategies can be strongly pronounced in adults who have developed specific learning styles over the years. As well, adults usually express a preference for structured language learning as opposed to the more natural environment, at least in the initial stages. Once they have established a solid base in the second language, they often choose an immersion program as the next step.

Comparing L1 and L2 Acquisition

L2 researchers are divided over whether L1 and L2 acquisition are similar. There are numerous factors that must be considered when making such a comparison: age (cognitive, physiological, and affective maturity), the language learning environment, and the respective characteristics of the L1 and L2 systems being compared.

Theoretical Viewpoints Theories that compare L1 and L2 acquisition can be roughly divided into two camps: nativist and nonnativist. Proponents of nativism believe that certain components of grammatical knowledge are innate, in that humans are said to be born with a genetically determined set of abstract linguistic principles known as Universal Grammar (UG). Other theorists view L2 acquisition as the acquisition of a complex cognitive skill, and are concerned exclusively with cognitive processes and information processing, paying little attention to linguistic issues.

In Chapter 10, the tenets of a Universal Grammar approach to L1 acquisition were outlined. Some research in UG suggests that L2 learners have access to at least some of the innate principles and parameters of the inborn UG involved in L1 acquisition. This not only explains how L2 acquisition is possible, it helps account for why some of the errors that occur during this process often resemble those that occur during L1 acquisition.

In contrast, non-nativist-oriented research argues that L1 acquisition for children and L2 acquisition for adults are fundamentally different. They believe that UG is not available to L2 learners, at least not to adults. Adult L2 acquisition is perceived to be more like general learning and problem solving. Compared with children acquiring their first language, adult L2 learners meet with less success, often speak with an accent and a non-native-like grammar. According to some linguists, this should not happen if L2 learners have access to the same UG as children acquiring their first language. Non-nativists argue that instead of UG, adult L2 learners draw on a combination of L1 knowledge and general problem-solving systems unique to each individual. If correct, this would account for the variation in how adults acquire a second language.

In the sections to follow, we will examine some research studies that compare L1 acquisition with L2 acquisition by children and adults in the areas of morphology, syntax, and phonology. The research findings we present concentrate on speakers of other languages learning English as a Second Language (ESL), a reflection of the current focus of North American L2 research.

L1 and L2 Morpheme Acquisition Both L1 and L2 learners appear to acquire morphemes in specific orders. When the L1 and L2 orders are compared, however, several differences are apparent. In spite of these, some researchers claim that since there seems to be a universal order of acquisition for morphemes, both L1 and L2 acquisition are guided by universal mechanisms. Other investigators are more skeptical. They point out that the bulk of evidence on L2 grammatical morpheme acquisition is based on learners of English as a second language in North America. There is very little cross-linguistic evidence to support claims regarding natural acquisition orders for learners of other languages. To date, insufficient research has been done to explain similarities or differences between L1 and L2 acquisition orders.

Transitional Constructions In the domain of English syntactic development, specifically the learning of negation and interrogatives, L1 and L2 acquisition appear to share similar characteristics. Both L1 and L2 learners tend to negate externally at first (*No smoke*), then to negate internally (*I no smoke*), ultimately followed by the correct form (*I don't smoke*).

The acquisition patterns for *wh* questions and *yes-no* questions are similar. Question acquisition begins with repeating an utterance with rising intonation (*I ride car?*), followed by use of *wh* words sentence-initially without inverting the auxiliary (*Where are you going?*). Finally, verbs are inverted correctly for both *wh* and *yes-no* questions. Both L1 and L2 learners continue for some time to make mistakes in tense and agreement.

These different stages of syntactic development consist of **transitional constructions** and are said to make up **developmental sequences.** While many of the stages in L1 and L2 acquisition appear to be similar, some researchers have found that L2 learners produce a wider variety of forms in a single developmental phase. Other have noted that the transitional constructions produced by L2 learners do not necessarily exist in their native language. Some researchers use these findings to support the idea that there are universal mental mechanisms involved in learning a second language, although more cross-linguistic evidence is needed to confirm these claims.

Researchers have also discovered that **routines** and **patterns** are employed by both L1 and L2 learners in the early stages of language acquisition. In L1 research, it has been noted that children often produce unanalyzed stretches or chunks of speech that are considerably beyond their developing rule system in terms of complexity. Routines are defined as whole utterances that are error free and appear to be learned as unanalyzed wholes, similar to the way a single word is learned. For instance, a child may say *Lookit* or *It's my turn* in order to participate in play activities. Patterns are partially analyzed utterances with open slots for a word or phrase such as *Gimme* _____or *D'you wanna* _____? The child may not segment the words correctly at first, not realizing that *Gimme* ('Give me') is in fact two words and not one.

It appears that L2 learners rely more heavily on routines and patterns than L1 learners. Thrust into the communicative situation, the L2 learner needs these devices to allow social interaction despite minimal linguistic competence. Routines such as *How do you do* or *Happy to meet you* are typical of the chunks learned in the initial L2 learning stages. By using routines and patterns, L2 learners can begin communication in the second language before acquiring the structures of that language. Some linguists even believe that the early memorization of routines and patterns is central to the acquisition of rule-governed language.

11.2 THE STUDY OF SECOND LANGUAGE ACQUISITION

The field of L2 research, as we know it today, is less than twenty years old. To a great extent, it has followed a pattern of research similar to that of L1 acquisition, borrowing and adapting many of the L1 research techniques. Like L1 research (see Chapter 10), L2 research employs both naturalistic and experimental studies. When conducting experimental studies, researchers typically make use of several kinds of tasks.

The **structured communication task** involves testing L2 learners' knowledge of a specific second language structure such as negation or *wh* questions. For example, hoping to elicit a negative construction, the researcher asks *Do you have a pet elephant?* and the subject may answer *No, I don't.* Such a task is commonly used in experimental studies. A **nonstructured communication task** is simply natural conversation between the researcher and L2 learner, with no special focus on a particular language structure. It is most often used in longitudinal studies, in which large amounts of dialogue data are collected from the same subject or group of subjects over an extended period of time.

In a **linguistic manipulation task**, the subject's attention is directed to the language forms themselves. For example, asking an L2 learner to change the proper nouns to a pronoun in the sentence *Jeremy and Jessica competed for first place* requires the subject to manipulate certain elements.

The results from these different tasks may not be directly comparable. Communicative tasks require a less conscious approach than do linguistic manipulation tasks, which require a conscious focus on a linguistic detail, a process rarely engaged in when conversing naturally.

In order to obtain a complete picture of the L2 acquisition process, it is necessary to combine the findings from both naturalistic and experimental studies, keeping in mind that differences in the tasks may affect the results. Studies conducted on a wide range of different languages are also needed in the quest for universals of second language acquisition. For example, in order to discover more about the universal processes involved in the acquisition of complex sentence structures such as relative clauses, many languages and language types must be considered.

In the sections to follow, we will examine several aspects of the L2 learner's development as investigated by recent studies. The research findings we present concentrate on learning English as a second language, a reflection of the current focus of L2 research.

Phonological Development

Many studies have been done in the area of L2 phonological development. Children acquiring a language in the second language environment are likely to achieve a nativelike pronunciation whereas adults are not. While it is possible for adults to acquire a nativelike accent, it is more often the exception than the rule.

The phonological domain is an area where a learner's first and second language clearly interact. It has been postulated that the L2 elements that are similar to those in the L1 repertoire will be replaced by those elements in the early stages. However, L2 sounds that do not exist in the L1 will follow their own course of development, in much the same way as sounds develop in the native language. While L2 phonological acquisition may be similar to L1 acquisition in this regard, it is very different in other respects. L2 learners must produce complex phonetic sequences from the very beginning. Their first attempts at pronunciation are not restricted to labial and alveolar stops and low vowels, which are often predominant in the early stages of L1 acquisition.

Because L1 and L2 phonological systems interact, pronunciation errors may systematically reflect the structure of each learner's respective native language. For example, a German speaker using English may say *I am sat* instead of *I am sad*, applying the final consonant devoicing rule of German. Korean speakers may tell you that they saw a *ship in the field* when they actually saw a *sheep*, since Korean has only lax vowels in closed syllables. These examples are cases of **interference** or **negative transfer**, the inappropriate use of an L1 structure in the L2 system. Further examples are given in Table 11.1.

Such errors usually arise in the early stages of L2 acquisition in the phonological, syntactic, and morphological domains. Instances of transfer from the phonological domain are generally not as easily modified as those in the areas of syntax and morphology. Many people who come from various L1 backgrounds and have lived in the second language culture for a long time master the second language syntax and lexicon, but may not lose their accents.

Table 11.1 Some cases of phonological interference (negative transfer)

Spanish→English:	Maria likes meeting me at [ɛ]school. (epenthetic vowel inserted before word-initial consonant cluster in Spanish)
Japanese→English:	Mik[ɯ] [dzɯ]riv[ɯ]es[ɯ] a big[ɯ] [tsɯ]ruck[ɯ]. (epenthetic vowels create consistent CV syllables in Japanese; /d/ and also /t/ become the affricates /dz/ and /ts/ respectively before the phoneme /ɯ/)
German→English:	I ha[f] foun[t] somethin[k] in the gar[t]en. (syllable-final consonant devoicing in German; the closely related word *Garten* 'garden' carried over from German)
Swedish→English:	She told a funny [j]oke. (no alveopalatal /dʒ/ in Swedish; articulatorily similar palatal /j/ consistently substituted for it)
French→English:	[d]is is [ʁ]eally [fãtastik]. (no /ð/ in French; /d/ consistently substituted for it; French speaker substitutes French uvular [ʁ] for English retroflex r; closely related word [fãtastik] is used instead of English 'fantastic')
English→French:	Elle a pe[r]d[uw] la cr[ej] *instead of French* [ɛl a peʁdy la kʁɛ] (English speaker substitutes English retroflex *r* for French uvular [ʁ]; English substitutes the vowel [uw] for French [y] since English has no front rounded vowels, and the English tense vowel [ej] for French [ɛ], since English does not have lax vowels in final position in monosyllabic words)
English→Japanese:	Obasan wa shinbun o jonde imasu. My aunt is reading the newspaper. Where intended utterance is: Grandmother is reading the newspaper Oba:san wa shinbun o jonde imasu. (no long versus short vowel contrasts in English as in Japanese)

Morphological Development

In their efforts to study the L2 acquisition of grammatical morphemes, L2 researchers were inspired by Roger Brown's classic longitudinal study of child L1 learners. They wanted to determine whether there also exists a common order of acquisition among L2 learners of various language backgrounds. The performance of child and adult L2 learners has been investigated independently, as age is considered a crucial factor.

Child L2 Morpheme Acquisition Data have been obtained from both cross-sectional and longitudinal studies of children learning English from more than twenty-two language backgrounds, including Afghani, Arabic, Chinese, Greek, Hebrew, Italian, Japanese, Korean, Persian, Spanish, Thai, Turkish, and Vietnamese. It has been found that these children showed a similar order of acquisition regardless of their first language. The emphasis in some research of this type has been on establishing a developmental order for groups of morphemes, rather than for the individual morphemes themselves. Figure 11.1 indicates the groups of morphemes that some researchers have found to make up different developmental stages.

Group 1	Case contrasts in pronouns *(he-him, they-them, she-her)*	

Group 2	Singular copula *('s / is)*	Singular auxiliary *('s / is)*
	Plural auxiliary *(are)*	Progressive *(-ing)*
	Plural *(-s)*	

Group 3	Past irregular *(went)*	Conditional auxiliary *(would)*
	Possessive *('s)*	Plural *(-es)*
	Third person singular *(-s)*	

Group 4	Perfect auxiliary *(have)*	Past participle *(-en)*

Figure 11.1 Child L2 grammatical morpheme acquisition

Adult L2 Morpheme Acquisition Using many of the same morphemes, L2 researchers decided to investigate the possibility that adults, like children, acquired these morphemes in an invariant order. With the help of structured oral communication tasks, another study concluded that adults from at least sixteen different language groups acquired eleven grammatical morphemes in more or less the same order. When we compare the order of acquisition for adults and children for eight of the grammatical morphemes in question, it is obvious that, in spite of some differences, the acquisition sequence is remarkably similar, regardless of the subject's age or language background (see Figure 11.2). (The groupings for child L2 learners correspond to those illustrated in Figure 11.1.) Many researchers have suggested that frequency of occurrence in the speech of native speakers may explain the order of morpheme acquisition, but to date this claim has not been substantiated. An alternative explanation involves the notion of communicative impact, which predicts that L2 learners will learn morphemes according to their relative importance for understanding a message. For example, the plural affix *-s* is one of the first morphemes learned. This morpheme marks plural number, which is very important to the meaning of an utterance such as *The girls came over.* (Many girls are coming as opposed to only one.) This plural marker is learned prior to the possessive *'s* (for example, *Jed's car*), perhaps because the possessive relation can be inferred from the word order and so need not be marked morphologically. When learners are communicating, they usually focus on content and not on form. Therefore, only the semantically more important items receive priority in the initial stages of grammatical morpheme acquisition.

Although these explanations are still only speculative, many researchers suggest that the invariant order of morpheme acquisition is evidence for Uni-

	Child L2 learners	Adult L2 learners
Group 1	plural (-s) progressive (-ing)	progressive (-ing) singular copula ('s/is)
Group 2	singular copula ('s/is) singular auxiliary ('s/is) articles (the, a) past irregular (went)	plural (-s) articles (the, a) singular auxiliary ('s/is) past irregular (went)
Group 3	3rd person singular (-s) possessive ('s)	3rd person singular (-s) possessive ('s)

Figure 11.2 L2 acquisition patterns for children and adults

versal Grammar. Other researchers caution that results from longitudinal studies on morpheme acquisition do not concur with the results from these cross-sectional studies, and that a child's or adult's first language may affect acquisition order. For example, a native speaker of Japanese has some difficulty acquiring the English definite/indefinite article (the/a) contrast since Japanese does not make this distinction.

Syntactic Development

The study of L2 acquisition of syntax has concentrated mainly on negation, question structures, and relative clauses. The following research is based on both oral and written language production.

Negation Regardless of native language background, L2 learners appear to learn basic English sentence negation in four steps, as shown in Table 11.2.

It must be noted that the steps toward the mastery of negation are not so clearly delineated for every L2 learner. To some degree, variation depends on the native language of the L2 learner. Spanish L1 speakers, for instance, tend to spend more time on the first step of external negation since their language contains many sentences structurally similar to those used in the first stage. For example, *No estudio mucho*, which translates as 'I don't study a lot', literally means 'not (I) study much'. Some L2 learners also exhibit a preference for either *no* or *not* in the initial stages.

Questions Research on the development of *wh* questions and *yes-no* questions is based on studies of children, adolescents, and adults with different language backgrounds. The acquisition of these two question types will be discussed together.

The *wh* question in English requires the speaker to perform two operations. First, the speaker must place a *wh* word (*what, why, who, where, when,* or *how*) at the beginning of the sentence. Second, it is necessary to invert the auxiliary verb and the subject. For example, in order to form a *wh* question in

Table 11.2 Negation structures

Stage 1	External negation	No your sitting here. No smoke. No happy. Not cold.
Stage 2	Internal negation: *No* occurs inside the negated phrase. *Don't* may appear but is considered as an unanalyzed unit or chunk. (The learner is not conscious of the two units *do* and *not*.)	I no can sing. She no come tomorrow. I don't can explain.
Stage 3	Auxiliary verbs may be used. *No* or *not* are used correctly with main and auxiliary verbs.	You not doing it. I won't try. No, I didn't.
Stage 4	The target language structure is acquired: the use of auxiliaries is consistently correct, and the construction (*no* + verb) disappears. Tense and agreement are marked, but not always perfectly.	He doesn't know he won. I didn't felt it.

response to the statement *Henrietta will sing a song,* the speaker will make the following changes.

2. *a*) Prepose *wh* word. (What Henrietta will sing?)
   b) Invert subject and auxiliary verb. (What will Henrietta sing?)

During the first stage in the development of questions, the learner's interrogative structure is marked by rising intonation with no inversion or initial *wh* words. The acquisition of *wh* questions and *yes-no* questions is a gradual process, and the stages given in Table 11.3 may overlap. They do not always emerge in this order, and some L2 learners, depending on their native language, may linger at one stage longer than at others or may develop a different stage. German L1 speakers, for example, often invert the main verb, producing questions such as *Sing you those songs?* until they learn to insert *do*. This is probably because main verbs as well as auxiliaries may undergo inversion in German.

Relative Clauses Relative clauses are one of the most widely investigated structures in L2 syntactic research. In the sentence *The locals who were watching the rodeo were shocked by the accident,* a sentence is embedded within an NP. The embedded sentence *who were watching the rodeo* modifies the N *locals* and is called a restrictive relative clause (RC) because it tells us exactly which locals were shocked by the accident.

Relative clauses are complex structures and vary considerably across languages according to their location in a sentence and in their different syntactic forms. The following examples illustrate variation in word order in restrictive relative clauses (see Chapter 5). Compare sentence *3a* from a head-initial language (the relative clause occurs after the head noun) with *3b*, from a head-final language (the relative clause occurs before the head noun). The bracketed phrases are relative clauses and modify the underlined head in the NP.

Table 11.3 Question structures

Stage 1	Rising intonation, no inversion. Some *wh* questions such as *What this?* appear at this stage but they seem to be learned as chunks.	Mickey is painting?
Stage 2	True production of *wh* questions begins. The auxiliary is usually omitted, so there is no subject-auxiliary inversion.	What you study? What the time? What you doing?
Stage 3	Auxiliaries such as *is, are,* and *was* appear, but are not yet inverted systematically with the subject.	Where is the woman? Are you a teacher? What she is singing?
Stage 4	For *wh* questions, the verbs *is, are,* and *was* tend to be regularly inverted. The auxiliaries *do* and *am* are still omitted at this stage, although inversion with *do* may begin for *yes-no* questions.	Who are they? What he saw? Do you work in the school?
Stage 5	The auxiliaries *do, am,* and *has* are acquired and correctly inverted with subjects in *wh* questions. However, the *do* in *yes-no* questions may still be misformed.	Where do you live? When are you leaving? Do he see that?

3. *a*) Head-initial: Spanish

          N   RC   VP

       La mujer [que está pintando el cuarto] está cantando.

       'The woman [who is painting the room] is singing.'

    b) Head-final: Japanese

       RC   N   VP

       [Heja- o penki de nutte iru] onna - ga utatte imasu.

       [room-Ac painting being] woman - Nom singing is.

       'The woman who is painting the room is singing.'

As you recall from Chapter 5, different languages may have different head positions (initial versus final). In English and Spanish, the head precedes the relative clause, whereas in Japanese, the head follows the relative clause. L2 researchers who maintain a UG perspective propose that the head position found in one's native language may have an effect on the L2 acquisition of complex structures such as relative clauses.

Recent cross-linguistic studies on the L2 acquisition of English relative clauses indicate significant differences in acquisition patterns between the Japanese and Spanish speakers. Spanish speakers are more successful than the Japanese, who produce fewer relative clauses in both oral and written English. UG researchers suggest that the Spanish speaker's success may be attributable to their reliance on their head-initial L1 structure for working out the grammar of English required for relative clause formation. In contrast, Japanese speakers need to establish a new head-initial position for English and to lose the L1 head-final order. Further studies using many other languages are needed in order to confirm such phenomena cross-linguistically.

11.3 METHODS OF ANALYSIS

The research studies discussed here reveal that L2 learners, whether children or adults, follow a developmental route, experimenting with their linguistic knowledge. Achieving fluency in a second language is evidently a creative process, one of trial and error, revision and reconstruction.

The notion of L2 learning as a dynamic cognitive process was not always accepted among applied linguists and psychologists. It was once believed that language learning was basically a process of forming automatic habits. This view influenced a school of linguistic analysis whose particular interest was in the errors produced by L2 learners.

Contrastive Analysis

Seeking to improve L2 teaching methodologies, early researchers came to believe that by comparing and contrasting the learner's native language with the second language, new insights could be gained into the language learning process. This approach is known as **contrastive analysis (CA)**. It was claimed that the errors produced by the learner would occur at those points at which the two languages were dissimilar.

Consider, for example, the English-speaking L2 learner who wants to say *I am ten years old* in French. The correct structure is *J'ai dix ans* (literally, 'I have ten years'). It can be predicted that many students will produce *Je suis dix ans* ('I am ten years'), substituting the verb *être* ('to be') for *avoir* ('to have'), a direct translation of the English form. This illustrates the idea behind comparing L1 and L2 language structures so that potential trouble spots can be predicted and focused on in the L2 lesson.

In time, many researchers questioned the theoretical and practical relevance of CA. They discovered that not all errors could be predicted from the source language. Some errors were unique and did not reflect the L1 structure. The L2 learner's language could be quite variable according to context and situation, and CA did not take this into account. Moreover, the anticipated improvements in teaching methodology were not forthcoming. Whether or not teachers could predict errors seemed to have little to do with the effectiveness of their teaching.

Error Analysis

From the CA perspective, any errors in L2 production, especially those that evidently involved negative transfer, were viewed as evidence of the L2 learner's incompetence with the second language. In time, however, L2 researchers and teachers began to view the learner as a creative participant in his or her language development. This, in turn, affected their view of the L2 learner's errors. An approach known as **error analysis (EA)** saw errors as indicators of the learner's current underlying knowledge of the second language, or as clues to the hypotheses that a learner may be testing about the second language. In this sense, errors provide us with insights into the language system that L2 learners are acquiring and using at a particular period. Such an L2 system is called **interlanguage**.

Interlanguage is viewed as a dynamic system since it changes constantly as the learner progresses through a theoretically infinite number of states of grammatical development along a continuum. The learner starts with the native language and continuously revises and extends rules until fluency in the second language is attained. Each L2 learner's interlanguage is unique. As learners progress toward nativelike proficiency in the second language, their interlanguage is characterized by fewer and fewer errors.

Proponents of EA claim that a careful study of a large corpus of spoken and written errors committed by L2 learners provides data that can help teachers determine the L2 learner's development. They therefore concentrate their efforts on the description and classification of various kinds of errors, with an explanation of these errors as their ultimate goal.

Error Types Research on L2 learners' interlanguage has resulted in the identification of several types of errors. Such errors fall roughly into two categories: interlingual and developmental. **Interlingual** errors are the result of L1 interference, implying that some structure from the native language has been transferred to the second language, as in the example above of English speakers learning how to talk about their age in French.

When L2 errors cannot be accounted for on the basis of the first language, they are considered to be **developmental**; that is, to result from the manner in which the language acquisition mechanisms themselves operate. These errors arise from a mismatch between the L2 learner's grammar and that of the native speaker. Such errors are considered developmental because they represent evidence of the learners' attempts to acquire language based upon their hypotheses about the language they are learning.

A comparison of adult and child L2 learners shows that adults tend to exhibit more first language influence in their errors than do children. The adult errors that reflect the L1 structure generally comprise about 30 percent of the total number of errors, the remainder being developmental. Allowing for problems in identifying the causes of errors, the percentages suggest that L1 interference is not the prime cause of learner errors.

It must be noted that because of the ambiguous nature of many errors, the distinction between interlingual and developmental errors is not always clear. When an L2 learner uses the double negative in English (*I don't know nothing about it*), it may be difficult to determine whether this is a developmental error or whether the learner has picked up a structure from a nonstandard dialect or whether the learner's native language allows double negatives.

Within the interlingual and developmental categories, errors can also be classified according to the grammatical subsystem involved: phonology, syntax, morphology, and semantics. Errors can be further classified as errors of omission, addition, or substitution (the L2 learner may omit certain items, add unnecessary ones, or exchange one element for another). Items may also be misordered or misformed either phonologically or morphologically. Table 11.4 provides one example of how errors may be classified by creating an error taxonomy. Whether these errors are classifiable as interlingual or developmental can be determined only by comparing the relevant L1 and L2 structures and by examining the errors within the corpus of the data from which they were extracted, namely, the discourse produced by the L2 learner.

Many researchers argue that comparative taxonomies focus too much on the error tokens themselves and not enough on the communicative effect of

Table 11.4 Taxonomy of interlanguage errors

Grammatical subsystem	Sample error	Description	Category
Morphology	He was call.	Omission	Developmental: past participle form not acquired
	Why didn't you came to work?	Addition	Developmental: double marking of past tense
Syntax	What this is?	Misordering	Developmental: misordering of the verb
Phonology	Man is eborubing. (evolving)	Substitution and addition (/b/ substituted for /v/, /r/ substituted for /l/; /u/ added)	Interlingual: phonological interference from Japanese
Semantics	She is a sensible person.	Substitution (*sensible* for *sensitive*)	Interlingual: French lexical interference (French *sensible* = English *sensitive*)

these errors. What effects do certain types of errors have on a reader or listener? What kinds of errors result in total miscommunication between the L2 learner and the native speaker?

The Communicative Effect Taxonomy Several taxonomies of communicative effect have subsequently been developed by having native English speakers make judgments about the comprehensibility of sentences with different types of errors. Apparently, errors that significantly hinder communication involve word order as in *4*, connectors as in *5*, and other features of sentence organization.

  4. *a*) Marcella amused that movie very much. (produced utterance)
     b) That movie amused Marcella very much. (intended utterance)
  5. *a*) She will be rich until she marries. (produced utterance)
     b) She will be rich *when* she marries. (intended utterance)

However, in the sentence *My husband not here*, communication is not impeded even though the verb is missing. Nor does the following error in verb complement affect intelligibility: *My doctor suggests me to take a vacation*. It is understood that the speaker meant 'My doctor suggests that I should take a vacation'.

Determining the effect of learners' errors is a complex and problematic task. The way in which native speakers respond to these errors will vary according to their age, their educational level, and the extent of their communication with foreigners. Also, perceptions of errors may vary according to the context in which they are presented (informal or formal), and whether the errors are being read or heard.

Although the development of taxonomies is important in error analysis, merely describing an error does not provide an explanation that would lend insight into L2 acquisition strategies. Focusing on such taxonomies is not conducive to considering language development as a dynamic process. Furthermore, most error analysis data come from cross-sectional study samples, not from longitudinal studies, which better capture an evolving interlanguage.

Researchers working in interlanguage theory strive to account for both systematicity and variability in the development of the L2 learner's interlanguage. Such research has led to conversational analysis and a consideration of the role of discourse in L2 acquisition. Thus far, data from longitudinal studies indicate that L2 learners slowly and gradually incorporate rules into their personal interlanguage systems, which they are continuously revising. More data must be gathered and an adequate theoretical model developed before the above methods of error analysis can further enhance our understanding of the L2 acquisition phenomenon.

11.4 THE LEARNER

During the past decade of L2 studies, researchers have realized that there is a need to focus more sharply on how L2 learners master the complexities of a new grammatical system. They have subsequently examined in greater detail the kinds of strategies learners may use as well as their personality characteristics. Both are crucial to the development of L2 theory and teaching methodologies.

Language Learner Strategies

At present, there are numerous definitions of the term **strategy**. In this chapter, we define strategies as the mental processes involved (1) in forming and testing hypotheses about linguistic input, and (2) in using linguistic knowledge in communicative situations. Although an elaborate taxonomy of learner strategies has been developed, we will consider only three types that are particularly relevant to language learning: learning strategies, production strategies, and communication strategies.

Learning Strategies are the ways in which language learners process language input and develop linguistic knowledge. These processes may be subconscious (unplanned) or conscious (deliberate). Recall the overgeneralization shown by children when learning to form the past tense (as when the past tense of *go* is produced as *goed*). This is also evidenced in L2 acquisition, as was illustrated in the section on error analysis. The process of overgeneralization is considered to be a subconscious one; the L2 learner is unwittingly relying on prior knowledge and extending it to create new language forms.

The memorization of prefabricated or formulaic speech, such as the routines and patterns employed by L1 and L2 learners (*I dunno, I can't speak English*), is another subconscious learning strategy. The learner frequently hears these patterns used in a communicative situation and absorbs them without analyzing the separate components. Although the process is unobservable, the patterns themselves are the observable products of the related and conscious strategy of pattern imitation. The imitation of certain language patterns is often encouraged in L2 classrooms as a teaching technique.

Production Strategies are employed by L2 learners when attempting to use their learned linguistic knowledge in communication. Production strategies may include the preplanning or rehearsing of utterances as well as the correction of utterances.

Preplanning in production involves choosing the components of the utterance (nouns, verbs, adjectives and adverbs, affixes and inflections, and their corresponding phonetic realizations) with a communicative objective in mind. Correcting or monitoring strategies are a part of the rehearsing aspect of production. Learners use a monitoring strategy when they correct what they want to say just before they say it or immediately afterwards.

Communication Strategies, like production strategies, serve communicative needs. However, they differ in that they are used when L2 learners lack the appropriate linguistic knowledge to say what they want to say. A communication strategy is usually a conscious plan instigated to fulfill an immediate communicative need. For example, an L2 learner may want to say *The teacher made the child go home*, but he or she does not know the causative form *make*, and therefore uses his or her available knowledge to say *She asked the child to go home*. In many cases, the result may be a slight modification of the original intent of the message, but the central idea is conveyed.

Communication strategies encompass a host of substrategies, which involve paraphrasing, substituting one word for another (such as *animal* for *giraffe*), borrowing from the native language (transfer), or avoiding certain structures altogether by changing the topic of conversation. L2 learners make use of such strategies to keep a conversation going. Understandably, the use of communication strategies is more prevalent in a natural environment than in a formal environment. The memorization of tourist "survival language" for on-the-spot communication is a familiar example of a popular communication strategy.

L2 versus L1 Learner Strategies Language learner strategies include learning, production, and communication strategies, among many others. Many L2 learners employ similar strategies: they overgeneralize, they transfer certain aspects of their native language, and they simplify various L2 structures as they subconsciously or consciously test their hypotheses about the second language. We have seen that some of these strategies are similar to those applied by children during the L1 acquisition process as they infer rules and draw conclusions about the language they hear. Not unlike children, L2 learners often need a **silent period** (a period of aural exposure to the language) so that incoming information may be processed and stored in memory. Once stored, it is ready for use in spontaneous production, and ultimately becomes a permanent part of the L2 repertoire.

L2 strategies, however, differ from those employed by L1 learners due to the L2 learner's cognitive maturity, longer attention span, and greater memory capacity. L2 learners may have a different drive to communicate depending on their language learning environment. Strategies will also vary according to the cognitive makeup and personality of the learner.

Personality

A person who appears hopeless at language is not necessarily lacking in the appropriate intellectual ability; it may be a personality trait that inhibits him: he may be resisting what seems to him an encroachment on his personality.

W. E. Lambert

Many psychologists argue that personality is inseparably related to our cognitive or learning style. L2 researchers have tried to isolate and investigate several personality traits that they believe to have implications for success or failure in learning a second language. Aptitude, motivation, attitude, and empathy are a few of the many traits studied for their potential effects on the language learning process.

Aptitude Whether an L2 learner is an adult or a child, it is assumed that some people have a special talent, a knack, or an aptitude for learning a second language. Aptitude involves having verbal intelligence (familiarity with words and the ability to reason analytically about verbal materials). Questions remain concerning the effect of aptitude on L2 success and the accuracy with which varying degrees of aptitude can be measured to account for the rate of development or eventual success or failure in L2 learning.

Motivation In L2 acquisition, motivation is described as the need or desire the learner feels to learn the second language. Two kinds of motivation have been cited with respect to how they affect language acquisition: integrative motivation and instrumental motivation.

Integrative motivation is defined as a desire to achieve proficiency in a new language in order to participate in the life of the community that speaks the language. Someone motivated in this sense exhibits a sincere and personal interest in the people and the culture represented by the group.

Instrumental motivation is identified as the desire to achieve proficiency in a new language for utilitarian reasons, such as getting a job or a promotion. Thus, it reflects the practical value and advantages of learning a new language.

Both types of motivation may influence the rate and quality of L2 acquisition, each being more effective under specific conditions. In fact, most situations involve both types of motivation. For example, English-speaking civil servants working in New York City might be motivated to improve their Spanish proficiency by the prospect of a salary increase. In addition, working in a predominantly Spanish-speaking community, they might be motivated by the desire to understand better the people they serve. In this case, they are both instrumentally and integratively motivated.

There is no doubt that motivation plays a critical role in determining the success or failure of L2 learners. Still unresolved are the problems of measuring motivation and its different manifestations to determine its exact effects.

Attitude L2 learners' attitudes are said to reflect their beliefs or opinions about the second language and culture, as well as their own culture. Some researchers believe that attitude and motivation are closely related. They claim that integrative and instrumental motivation reflect the basic attitude of the language learner toward learning languages and toward the second language culture. For example, an English-speaking American's positive attitude and desire to understand Hispanic Americans will lead to high integrative motivation to learn Spanish. The extent to which learners prefer their own language over the one they are learning is an important attitudinal factor.

Negative attitudes may lead to decreased motivation and in all likelihood failure to attain proficiency. In an L2 learning situation, projecting a positive attitude is also a necessary ingredient for keeping communication lines open, which in turn inevitably leads to the acquisition of better communication skills.

Empathy Empathy has been defined as the ability to put oneself in someone else's shoes. An empathic L2 learner has the capacity for participation in another's feelings or ideas, to project his or her personality into the personality of another. Some researchers propose that empathic people will be favorably predisposed to learning languages in a natural environment. They may more easily emulate a nativelike pronunciation since they are purportedly less inhibited than others. Furthermore, because of their sensitivity to others, empathic people may be better at picking up nuances of word meaning and their implications in different linguistic contexts. While these suppositions are not unreasonable, they remain as suppositions since their implications are extremely difficult to quantify.

11.5 TEACHING METHODOLOGIES

The field of applied linguistics has been influenced by theoretical trends in linguistics, psychology, and sociology. This influence is reflected in the various methodologies and approaches in second language teaching over the years. A brief look at some of the approaches prevalent before the 1960s as well as the most recent developments will help to outline the often divergent directions of L2 teaching and learning philosophies and to focus on what can be expected in the future.

Grammar Translation Method

The most traditional method for L2 teaching is the **grammar translation method**, which has its roots in the way in which Latin and Greek have been taught for centuries. This method emphasizes reading, writing, translation, and the conscious learning of grammatical rules. Its primary goal is to develop literary mastery of the second language. Memorization is the main learning strategy and students spend their class time talking "about the language" instead of "in the language." The curriculum requires the memorization of paradigms, patterns, and vocabulary, with translation being used to test the acquired knowledge. Consequently, the role of L1 is quite prominent.

Such an approach satisfied the needs of traditional humanist education for many years, until World War II created a greater demand for L2 speakers with highly developed speaking and listening skills. Today, the grammar translation method is still popular in many education systems and makes up some part of many L2 curricula.

Direct Method

The **direct method**, which originated in the seventeenth century, was revived in the 1900s as an alternative to grammar translation. Advocates of this method believe that adult L2 learners can learn a second language in essentially the same manner as a child. Therefore, if possible, the teacher should try to create a natural learning environment within the classroom. Instead of explicit grammar instruction, the major emphasis is on communicating. Classes are carried out totally in the second language with absolutely no reliance on the first language or on any form of translation. The expectation is that through question and answer dialogues, the second language will gradually be acquired. Problems have arisen with such an approach because adults do not in fact learn exactly like children, and they express the need for explicit instruction in grammar and other aspects of the second language.

Audiolingual Method

Neither grammar translation nor the direct method was based on any particular linguistic or psychological theory. Searching for an alternative to these two approaches, preferably one with a strong theoretical foundation, L2 teachers and researchers turned to the linguistic and behaviorist learning theories of the 1950s. These two theories provided the foundation for the **audiolingual method**.

The audiolingual method in some sense represents a return to the direct method, as its main goal is to develop nativelike speaking ability in its learners. Translation and reference to L1 are not permitted. Underlying this approach, however, is the notion that L2 learning should be regarded as a mechanistic process of habit formation.

In classrooms and language laboratories, students are conditioned to respond correctly to either oral or written stimuli. Since proponents of this method assume that language is a set of conditioned habits, students are not granted time to think about their responses but are required to respond immediately to a model utterance. Language learning is not viewed as a creative, cognitive process but as mechanical mimicry.

Audiolingual learning comprises dialogue memorization and pattern drills, thus ensuring careful control of responses. None of the drills or patterns are to be explained, since knowledge of grammatical rules would only obstruct the mechanical formation of habits. The audiolingual method enjoyed a long period of popularity, but is rarely used today in its entirety.

Eventually, work in cognitive psychology and transformational grammar undermined the view that linguistic behavior was based on habit formation and could be effectively learned through rote memorization exercises. Cognitive psychologists maintain that the mind is an active agent in the language learning process, and is not just passively influenced by environmental factors. Language must be taught and learned as a functional system applicable in communicative contexts, and not as a series of drills or abstract rules. This approach is presently manifested to some degree in communicative language teaching.

Communicative Language Teaching

During the past decade, the development of **communicative language teaching methods**, an approach that seeks to produce communicatively competent language learners, has been heralded as the future direction for L2 researchers and teachers. While it appears that the notions behind communicative competence are replacing the underpinnings of audiolingualism and grammar translation, the transition has not been entirely smooth.

Misinterpretation of the concept of **communicative competence** itself is in part responsible for the confusion. Becoming communicatively competent does not simply entail having the ability for spontaneous self-expression. While it includes having grammatical knowledge of the system, it also extends into a more abstract domain: knowledge of the appropriateness of language use. This domain includes sociocultural knowledge, paralinguistic (facial and gestural) and proxemic (spatial) knowledge, and sensitivity to the level of language use in certain situations and relationships, depending on whether they are formal or casual. Merely knowing how to produce a grammatically correct sentence is not enough. A communicatively competent person must also know how to produce an appropriate, natural, and socially acceptable utterance in all contexts of communication. *Hey, buddy, you fix my car!* is grammatically correct but not as effective in most social contexts as *Excuse me, sir, I was wondering whether I could have my car fixed today.*

In the past, most methodologies have concentrated on grammar, vocabulary, and pronunciation. Now, with the focus shifted to the learners and how they might learn to use language, many teachers are at a loss to understand the exact constituents of a communicative language teaching approach or method. Communicative language teaching has become an umbrella term to cover many approaches that purport to be communicative in design. In many cases, this approach emphasizes content and not form. By providing the student with authentic communicative activities involving relevant themes and topics, the experiential aspect of L2 learning is emphasized. It is assumed that if the students interact with second language speakers using real-life subject matter, the language will be acquired subconsciously.

Since language always operates within a sociocultural context, many people also believe that such a context should be an integral part of any communicative method. L2 researchers and teachers have realized too that any L2 method must be founded on psycholinguistic insights about the cognitive processes involved in acquiring a second language. More research is needed in the area of learner strategies in order to improve our current understanding of the language learning process and to develop better teaching methods.

The Role of the Teacher The teacher who chooses a communicative methodology must be prepared to play a new part in the classroom. Throwing out a one-way communication line is no longer sufficient. Rather, the teacher must adopt several roles: a mediator in a group-dynamic situation, a catalyst for ideas, a facilitator of communication, an advisor and organizer. The teacher must cultivate an awareness of individual learner differences, which vary with the L2 learner's age, sex, background, and socioeconomic status. This awareness must extend to choosing teaching materials that are truly communicative in nature. Students need real-life problems to solve in the second language, such as calling an airline and asking for flight times or having dinner at someone's home in the L2 culture. These activities can be simulated in the classroom or can actually be carried out in the community. Role-playing (with specific instructions) as well as self-awareness activities that concentrate on personal feelings, opinions, and attitudes of the L2 learner are invaluable stimuli for productive communication.

Multiple Methodologies L2 teachers and researchers are realizing that one method alone will not satisfy the demands of language learners of different ages, different learning styles, diverse backgrounds, and varying degrees of motivation. Today we see the emergence of a variety of new communicative approaches that are being used primarily in adult L2 education. These recent approaches take into consideration that more than cognitive factors need attention in the L2 acquisition process. Their orientations are subsequently more holistic or humanistic. They attempt to provide a nonthreatening environment where teacher and classmates provide support to each L2 learner. In this manner, one can deal with the complex affective aspect of the learner's personality, an aspect that has often been overlooked in the past.

Total physical response is the most widely publicized of these approaches. It takes into consideration the silent period deemed necessary for some L2 learners. During the first phase of total physical response, students are not required to speak. Instead, they concentrate on obeying simple commands in the second language. These commands eventually become more complex. For example, *Walk to the door* becomes *Scratch your head while you walk to the door at the back of the classroom.* Students later become more actively involved, verbally and creatively. The objective of this approach is to connect physical activity with meaningful language use as a way of instilling concepts. Proponents claim that it is very effective in the initial to early intermediate stages of L2 acquisition.

In the **community counseling** classroom, L2 learners are told that they are part of a group and not a class. This group identification supposedly reduces potential anxieties and provides a great deal of emotional support to the learner. The teacher is seen in the role of a counselor, while the students are clients. A client begins communication in his or her native language, the counselor translates, and the client repeats the utterance. Then another client picks up the conversation, which is then continued by another, and so forth. The conversation proceeds in this fashion with the counselor intervening to translate. The session is taped so that linguistic rules and certain utterances may be explained later.

Students who learn via the **natural approach** are also not expected to communicate verbally in the second language from the outset. They spend class time involved in communicative activities such as problem-solving tasks and language games, often working in pairs. Students may, however, respond using their native language and can decide for themselves when they are ready for the second language. Errors are ignored unless communication is impaired. Formal explanations and grammar exercises are completed outside the classroom environment. Teachers using this approach claim that rapid acquisition of listening and speaking skills is enhanced, as there is a tremendous amount of comprehensible input available to the students during their silent period.

11.6 THE IMMERSION APPROACH

Over the last decade, **immersion** programs have become increasingly popular as a way of teaching children a second language, especially for Spanish in the United States and French in Canada. In this context, immersion means that students are instructed in most of their courses and school activities in the second language. Instruction is usually begun in the second language and eventually incorporates the native language.

The main objective of any immersion program is that all students acquire a high level of proficiency in oral, listening, and literacy skills. Attempts to achieve literacy in the second language prior to achieving literacy in the native language have been quite successful in both the United States and Canada. Moreover, immersion has exerted a positive influence on the L2 learner's attitude toward the L2 culture.

Fundamental to an immersion program is the belief that normal children have the inherent capacity to learn a second language without jeopardizing their native language expertise. The success rate of immersion programs to date has convinced parents and educators that such a belief is valid.

Total Immersion

Total immersion involves the instruction of all subjects in the second language, including physical education and extracurricular activities. Early total immersion begins in kindergarten with no in-class use of the native language until the second or third year in school. At that time, treated as any other subject, L1 language arts in the native language may be taught for one hour a day. As the grade level increases, so does the degree to which the native language is used. In the case of French immersion in Canada, instruction in English language arts is eventually increased to a maximum of 50 percent of total daily instruction time, the remaining instruction being in French.

Both native and second language skills are carefully monitored during the immersion program. In the beginning stages, immersion students may experience some problems with their native language, particularly in spelling and reading (in which they have received less instruction). Eventually, they catch up with monolingual speakers in all subject areas.

Partial Immersion

Partial immersion involves instruction in the second language for half the school day and in the native language for the other half. Early partial immersion begins in kindergarten. The language of instruction in the morning or afternoon may differ with each grade from year to year. Compared with their monolingual peers, partial immersion students' performance in the native language is generally poorer for several years into the immersion program. When their L2 skills are compared with those of the total immersion students at the same grade level, partial immersion students are also less proficient.

Since immersion programs provide greater exposure to the second language than any other type of language teaching program, it is not surprising that they produce better results. For the same reason, early total immersion programs have a higher success rate than do early partial programs. Students from early total immersion programs invariably develop a more nativelike command of the second language than do students from other immersion programs.

Even though immersion students become highly proficient in listening and literacy skills, their production skills are often flawed, since many immersion students develop a type of interlanguage with their classmates. In a situation where communication among nonnative speakers of a second language is the primary goal, many errors are unheeded and uncorrected, thereby becoming a part of the immersion students' L2 system. This deficiency need not persist, however. If immersion is complemented by more formal instruction and drill of complex language structures, production skills may be greatly enhanced.

Summing Up

This chapter focuses on some of the major issues and questions that concern L2 researchers, linguists, and teachers in the field of **second language acquisition**. L2 acquisition may take place in a **natural** or **formal environment** or a combination of both. In their attempts to discover more about the L2 acquisition process, researchers have compared various L1 and L2 processes, relying to a great extent on L1 research methods. Findings in the areas of morpheme acquisition and syntactic development suggest that both L1 and L2 learners share similar **transitional constructions** and **learner strategies**. Learner strategies include **learning**, **production**, and **communication** strategies and substrategies.

Contrastive analysis and **error analysis** have both contributed to the attempt to learn more about the L2 learner's **interlanguage**. The study of interlanguage promises to provide greater insight into the L2 acquisition process.

Over the past decade, there has been a great deal of research in the areas of personality and **cognitive style.** Attitude and motivation are considered to be important requisites for success in L2 acquisition.

L2 teaching methodologies have, to varying degrees, been influenced by linguistics and psychology. The shift in focus to the learner as a communicator has spawned numerous teaching methodologies and approaches within the domain of **communicative language teaching**. The contributions of many source disciplines, including linguistics, neurolinguistics, psychology, sociology, and pedagogy are needed before we are able to understand fully the mystery of what happens inside the L2 learner's mind.

Key Terms

audiolingual method
communication strategy
communicative language teaching
community counselling
comprehensible input
contrastive analysis
developmental errors
direct method
error analysis
foreigner talk
grammar translation method
immersion

instrumental motivation
integrative motivation
interference
interlanguage
interlingual errors
learning strategy
linguistic manipulation task
metacognitive strategy
natural approach
negative transfer
nonstructured communication task
patterns

production strategies   structured communication task
routines   target language
silent period   teacher talk
speech community   total physical response

Sources

Research reported on morpheme acquisition and syntactic development is drawn from Bailey et al. in H. Dulay. M. Burt, and S. Krashen (cited below), R. Ellis (cited below), and B. van Patten's "Processing Strategies and Morpheme Acquisition" in *Universals of Second Language Acquisition,* edited by F. Eckman, L. Bell, and D. Nelson (Rowley, Mass.: Newbury House, 1985); and *Linguistic Perspectives on Second Language Acquisition,* edited by S. M. Gass and J. Schachter (Cambridge: Cambridge University Press, 1989).

Discussions of contrastive analysis, error analysis, and interlanguage are based on E. Tarone's *Variation in Interlanguage* (London: Edward Arnold Press, 1988), S. P. Corder's *Error Analysis and Interlanguage* (Oxford: Oxford University Press, 1981), and T. van Els et al. (cited below) as well as from *Theories of Second Language Learning* by Barry McLaughlin (Baltimore: Edward Arnold Press, 1987). Examples of communicative effect errors were adapted from H. Dulay, M. Burt, and S. Krashen (cited below) and S. Johannson's "Problems in Studying the Effect of Learners' Errors" in *Studies in Second Language Acquisition* 1:41–52 (1975).

Arguments for the critical period hypothesis come from S. Krashen, M. Long, and R. Scarcella's *Child-Adult Differences in L2 Acquisition* (Rowley, Mass.: Newbury House, 1982) and T. van Els et al. (cited below). Research on foreigner talk and teacher talk is drawn from *Classroom Oriented Research in Second Language,* edited by H. Seliger and M. Long (Rowley, Mass.: Newbury House, 1983). The notion of comprehensible input is presented in detail in S. Krashen's *Principles and Practices in Second Language Acquisition* (Oxford: Pergamon Press, 1982).

The presentation of learner strategies is drawn largely from R. Ellis (cited below). The literature on personality and cognitive styles is reviewed in H. Brown's *Principles of Language Learning and Teaching* (Englewood Cliffs, N.J.: Prentice-Hall, 1980). The quote on personality is taken from W. E. Lambert's "Psychological Approaches to the Study of Language, Part II: On Second Language Learning and Bilingualism" in *Modern Language Journal* 47: 114 (1963).

Language teaching methodologies are reviewed in T. van Els et al. (cited below) and in H. Hammerly's *Synthesis in Second Language Teaching* (N. Burnaby, B.C.: Second Language Publications, 1982).

Information on immersion is drawn from M. Swain's "French Immersion: Early, Late, Partial" in *Canadian Modern Language Review* 34: 577–85 (1978),

F. Genesee's "Bilingual Education of Majority-Language Children: The Immersion Experiments in Review" in *Applied Psycholinguistics* 4: 1–46 (1983), and M. A. Snow and R. Shapira's "The Role of Social-Psychological Factors in Second-Language Learning" in M. Celce-Murcia (ed.) (cited below).

Recommended Reading

Celce-Murcia, M., ed. 1985. *Beyond Basics: Issues and Research in TESOL*. Rowley, Mass.: Newbury House.

Chaudron, C. 1988. *Second Language Classrooms*. New York: Cambridge University Press.

Ellis, R. 1985. *Understanding Second Language Acquisition*. Oxford: Oxford University Press.

Hatch, E. M. 1983. *Psycholinguistics: A Second Language Perspective*. Rowley, Mass.: Newbury House.

Larsen-Freeman, D. 1986. *Techniques and Principles in Language Teaching*. Oxford: Oxford University Press.

McLaughlin, B. 1987. *Theories of Second Language Learning*. Baltimore: Edward Arnold Press.

Scarcella, R. C., and R. L. Oxford. 1992. *The Tapestry of Language Learning*. Boston: Heinle and Heinle.

van Els, T., T. Bongaerts, G. Extra, C. van Os, and A-M. Janssen-van Dieten. 1984. *Applied Linguistics and the Learning and Teaching of Foreign Languages*. R. R. van Oirsouw, trans. London: Edward Arnold Press.

White, L. 1989. *Universal Grammar and Second Language Acquisition*. Amsterdam: John Benjamins Publishing Company.

Questions

1. The following data represent a conversation between native speakers of English (NS) and beginning nonnative speakers (NNS). Note any instances of what you perceive to be foreigner talk. In what ways do the native speakers ask nonnative speakers questions? Do you think that asking questions in this way provides a good model for L2 learners? Why or why not?

   a) NS: Did you like New York?
        Did you like New York? New York, did you like it?
      NNS: Yes, I like.
   b) NS: When do you go to, uh, Maine? You say you fish in Maine, right?
      NNS: Yeah, right.
      NS: When? When do you go there?
   c) NS: Do you know anyone in California?
      NNS: (silence)

NS: Do you know anyone in Los Angeles?
NNS: Sorry?
NS: Do you have a friend in Los Angeles?
NNS: Oh! Yeah, I have.

2. Your friend has decided to study Russian as a second language. She is twenty-four years old and lives in Montreal. What factors would you recommend that she consider when undertaking such a venture?

3. Discuss some of the advantages and disadvantages of natural and formal language learning environments for adult L2 learners based upon what you know about adult L2 acquisition and perhaps from personal experience.

4. The following interlanguage sentences containing relative clauses were spoken by adult Farsi speakers learning English.

   a) Ryan liked the girl that her father was the teacher.
   b) Nazli saw the accident that the train caused it.
   c) Sara patted the dog that growled.
   d) She saw the man that her friend gave him a gift.

   Note that c) is different from the others. Describe the interlanguage patterns shown by the above data. What can you guess about relativization in Farsi? How might a Universal Grammar approach to these data explain this phenomenon?

5. In Spanish, sentences are negated by placing *no* 'not' before the (first) verb. As well, subject pronouns may be omitted. Given these facts, predict what types of errors a Spanish speaker in the early stages of learning English might make in negating the following utterances.

   a) I can see.
   b) The children like cookies.
   c) She is standing by the window.
   d) Fred likes to play the piano.

6. Contrastive analysis and error analysis represent two approaches to dealing systematically with the L2 learner's errors. Which approach do you feel would be most advantageous for discovering more about the kinds of errors L2 learners are likely to make when learning the phonology of a second language?

7. The following utterances were produced by an adult Arabic speaker learning English. Examine the underlined instances of verbal agreement. How do they differ from standard English? Explain the effect of this speaker's interlanguage.

   a) She <u>give</u> me every morning a free coffee.
   b) She <u>know</u> why he late.
   c) <u>There is many</u> things to see.

d) <u>Many customs</u> I don't know what <u>it means</u>.

e) When <u>he stay</u> one more year, he can be citizen.

8. Tape record a conversation (at least thirty utterances) with an L2 learner with his or her permission. Write down everything said in the conversation, eliminating imitations and repetitions. Choose one specific aspect of the data such as tense, pluralization, articles, and so on, and describe it.

   i) Identify the errors made.

   ii) Determine which errors can be considered as interlingual errors, and which can be considered developmental errors.

   iii) What percentage (approximately) of the errors are interlingual errors?

   iv) What other types of errors remain, and what do they suggest?

   v) Discuss the implications of your findings in terms of what you know about learner strategies.

9. A Mandarin-speaking child learning English has written the following paragraph. Describe what is happening in terms of his interlanguage development, paying particular attention to verb tense and the use of definite and indefinite articles.

   In 1985 a boat full with gold sailing from China to America disappeared in middle of the ocean. The captain of the boat is John. He had a son name David. His mother give him the sword that his father had used. David had promise his mother he will find his father. The next day, David and the his partner Chris had gone to middle of the ocean. Chris and David are grow up together. They each have a magic crystal. It has seven magic power. The day was a raining day. They are start to go, but suddenly the sea water fly in the air, and there is strong light under the ocean. They saw those creatures. "They all looks like sharks," said Chris.

10. The following data were elicited through a nonstructured communication task (natural conversation) from intermediate level L2 learners of different language backgrounds who were learning English as a second language. Explain how the italicized forms differ from standard English usage. Do you see a predictable relationship between these interlanguage forms and standard usage? Can you determine any strategies these learners appear to employ with respect to word use?

    a) I had a *discuss* with my teacher.

    b) You get sick very *easy*.

    c) Martin is a *physics*.

    d) The dog is stopped to *breath*.

    e) You have to *trip* to Canada.

    f) She can't finish her *educated*.

11. Think of people you know who have successfully learned a second language and those who have earnestly tried and failed. Consider their per-

sonalities. In your opinion, what are the most important characteristics for learning a second language?

12. If you were to design a second language program whose goal was to teach adult immigrant students basic communication skills (sometimes referred to as "survival English"), what would be the main features of your program? Which teaching methodology or combination of methodologies would you choose? Justify your choices.

13. If you were planning an immersion program for a school system, at what age would you recommend it begin? Defend your decision on the basis of what you know about child and adult differences and similarities in learning a second language.

12 LANGUAGE IN SOCIAL CONTEXTS

*. . . it is clear that
the causes on which
linguistic facts depend
must be social in nature . . .*

Antoine Meillet

This chapter treats a variety of social contexts in which one can examine both the use of language and the impact of extralinguistic factors on language. The topics range from regional variation in language through social variation in language to studies of language use in interaction. The goal is to convey the fact that a speech community is highly complex and structured. A reading of this chapter should leave an awareness that the reality of language in social contexts is not one of proper speech versus all other speech but of a set of complementary speech varieties that constitute the structured speech community. In promoting this awareness, the chapter also reveals the analytical techniques and theoretical assumptions that underlie the topics examined.

12.1 FUNDAMENTAL CONCEPTS

The subdiscipline of linguistics that treats the social aspects of language is called **sociolinguistics**. In this chapter, this label will be used to refer to all research about language in social contexts. Such research ranges from the very limited and localized context of a single conversation to studies of language use by whole populations. Given these quite diverse areas of research interest, it might be assumed that many sociolinguists do not share the same fundamental concepts or goals. This is to some extent true.

Despite the fact that there are a number of ways of approaching the study of language in social context, there are nevertheless certain terms and concepts that are common to most of them. All sociolinguistic studies concern language in a social context, treating speakers as members of social groups. The group isolated for study is called the **speech community**. Depending on the study, the speech community may have as few members as a family or as many members as China. The important characteristic is that the members of the speech community must, in some reasonable way, interact linguistically with other members of the community; they may share closely related language varieties, they may share attitudes toward linguistic norms, or they may be part of a single political entity.

The term **speech variety** or **language variety** refers to any distinguishable form of speech used by a speaker or group of speakers. The distinguishing characteristics of a speech variety may be lexical, phonological, morphological, or syntactic; usually they are a combination of all of these. We will be interested in speech varieties of three types: social speech varieties (also called **social dialects** or **sociolects**), regional speech varieties (or **regional dialects**), and functional speech varieties (or **registers**). Sociolects are again subdivisible into several smaller categories, largely as a function of the type of social group that shares the particular speech variety. Most often, one thinks of sociolects in terms of the socioeconomic status of speakers. Other sociolects, however, may be associated with ethnic, sex, occupational, or age groups. In most speech communities, there is a single speech variety called the **standard**, which is perceived by members of the community to be higher in status and more correct than the others.

While sociolects are defined by the linguistic differences associated with definable social groups in a single geographic area, regional dialects are associated with the linguistic traits shared by social groups in a single geographical area. Clearly the variety spoken by any single speaker, the **idiolect**, will be jointly determined by the sociolect and regional dialect appropriate to that individual.

Besides the interspeaker differences in speech associated with the geographical area and the social characteristics of the speaker, there are intraspeaker differences associated with the speech situation: who is being spoken to, the subject of the conversation, who else may be listening, and so on. Thus, while most speakers are limited to a single sociolect and geographical dialect, a fluent speaker must employ a variety of registers.

12.2 SOCIAL DIFFERENTIATION OF LANGUAGE

Social differentiation of language, in its broadest sense, refers to correlations between variation in language use and a speaker's membership in various social groups.

Social Stratification

As noted above, it is possible to correlate differences in how people speak with their membership in various social groups. Perhaps the most frequently invoked social correlate of language differentiation is socioeconomic status (SES). SES is associated with the income level, type of occupation, type of housing, educational level, and similar characteristics of speakers. Sociolinguistic investigations which focus on SES usually involve large random surveys of urban populations. They typically require respondents to read aloud passages, word lists, and sets of minimal pairs. They also attempt to elicit speech that more closely resembles natural (unaffected) language by asking respondents to tell a story about some interesting experience. The data obtained from these surveys are then subjected to quantitative analysis, which may involve statistical methods.

Approaches to the study of linguistic differentiation in the speech community that proceed from the assumption that SES is an important (or the most important) correlate of differences in language usage generally arrive at (or proceed from) a view of vertical variation which is referred to as the **social stratification** of language. It is probably fair to say that most sociolinguistic studies over the past two decades or so have been concerned with this vertical variation of language and that most have viewed it as a function of the speaker's membership in a particular socio-economic class.

Stratification of language, while widespread in the world, is probably not universal. It is, on the other hand, reasonable to claim that social differentiation of one sort or another is universal. Underlying this claim is the belief that there are always differences in speech communities and that these differences correlate with the existence of social groups within the community. These social groups may be functions of the socioeconomic status, gender, age, ethnicity, or other characteristics of their members.

Other Ways of Studying Social Differentiation

Two alternative approaches which are challenging the traditional methodology are **social network analysis** and **Principal Components Analysis**.

Social Network Analysis A sociolinguist using the social network approach does not rely on large random samplings of a population but, rather, examines first-hand from the perspective of a participant-observer the language use of a preexisting social group. Just as more traditional sociolinguists may assume that social stratification exists and that this has significance for the interpretation of data, researchers using the social network approach also make certain assumptions. These researchers attach importance to the nature of the relationships (and resulting interactions) of a speaker and interpret linguistic variation in terms of the kinds and densities of relationships the individual enjoys in various groups.

The density of a network is related to the potential for communication among members of the network and can be either closeknit or looseknit. A person's social network will consist of everyone in every group in which the person plays some role. Closeknit networks, which typically characterize speakers of the highest and lowest SES groups, exert a great deal of peer pressure on speakers. They are thus associated with language maintenance, since speakers in such a network, in that they interact with the same relatively limited set of people in a number of different kinds of relationships, reinforce each other's speech habits. Closeknit networks among the high SES groups reinforce either a standard speech variety or one with high status. Closeknit networks among low SES groups are loci for nonstandard speech varieties.

Social networks have been likened to a Chinese fan (as in Figure 12.1), in which each group is both separate but at the same time exhibits overlap with other groups and all groups converge on the person at its center. Thus the nature and frequency of interactions in the family group will differ from those among fellow workers, members of the same sports team, neighbors, and the like. In a sense, such studies can lend weight to the notion that we 'talk like those we talk to', more especially where those interactants are in a closeknit network.

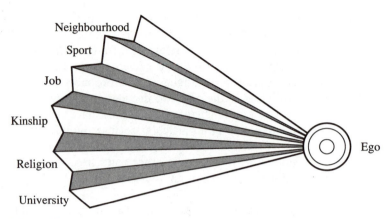

Figure 12.1 Social networks

Principal Components Analysis The newest technique to challenge the traditional approach is Principal Components Analysis (PCA). This approach has been used in studies of the Sydney, Australia, and St. John's, Newfoundland, speech communities. PCA is highly quantitative. It uses statistical techniques that allow the investigator to examine a large number of linguistic variants, to compare speakers with similar linguistic characteristics (displayed on graphs in clusters) and, only as a last step, to determine what social similarities are shared by these linguistically categorized groups of speakers. A particular 'Principal Component' is a set of variables (such as the phonological ones in Table 12.2 below) which can be shown statistically to give the best account of the data. Groups of people who share particular linguistic features are categorized in terms of those sets of linguistic features rather than with respect to preconceived sociological features. Given the lack of *a priori* assumptions about the relevance of particular social categories, the results of PCA studies are seen by the investigators as more reliable pictures of social differentiation than was possible using traditional methodologies. In the section below on nonstandard phonological features we consider some of the results of the PCA study of St. John's, Newfoundland.

The Social Stratification of English

The United States is distinctive in that, instead of a national standard there are a small number of regional varieties that are regarded as correct in their areas. We term this variety or varieties *Standard English*. These varieties differ principally in their phonology, and hardly at all in their written form. It is relatively easy to tell an educated Bostonian from an educated Charlestonian by listening to even their most careful speech; it is virtually impossible to distinguish the two on the basis of written works. Varieties other than the standard are termed *nonstandard*. This term is to be preferred to the designation *substandard*, which suggests some inherent inferiority of these varieties. In fact, the selection of standard and nonstandard varieties of English and other languages has to do with historical facts about who spoke which variety when; it has nothing to do with anything intrinsic to the varieties. Were English history a bit different, Cockney English might be standard English in Great Britain, and prescriptivists would have great fun criticizing those speakers who actually pronounce written *h*'s.

Nonstandard Grammatical Features Certain features of nonstandard varieties of English are often singled out by prescriptivists as demonstrating the inherent illogic or lack of systematicity of nonstandard varieties. An oft-cited grammatical feature of this sort is the so-called double negative, seen in sentence *1a*.

1. a) She don't know nothing.
   b) She doesn't know anything.
   c) She knows something.

A prescriptivist asserts that the two negations in the first sentence (*-n't* and *no-*) cancel each other out. Thus, the speaker in *1a* has supposedly uttered an affirmative sentence with the meaning of *1c*. Anyone who hears the sentence in *1a*, however, knows that its meaning is the same for the nonstandard speaker as the meaning of *1b* is for the speaker of the standard. (Of course, proponents of this view refuse to carry it to its logical conclusion and accept *She don't never know nothing* as a negative sentence because of its three negatives.) The nonstandard and standard negative sentences differ from the affirmative sentence in the same two ways: both verbs are marked as negative and both indefinite pronouns are marked differently from the pronoun in the affirmative sentence. When the verb is negated in Standard English, an indefinite pronoun in the verb phrase is also negated, by changing *some-* to *any-*. In the nonstandard variety, negating the verb causes the pronoun to be negated by changing *some-* to *no-*. Both varieties mark negation twice and thus are equally logical.

There is another nonstandard feature in *1a*—the verb *do*, which co-occurs with the subject pronoun *she*. This sort of usage and the similar one seen in nonstandard *She know* are also condemned by prescriptivists. These two sentences violate the Standard English subject-verb agreement rule, which requires present-tense English verbs with third person subjects to have a special ending (*-s*). An examination of the morphology of Standard English verbs and a look at the historical development of these forms, however, show that over time all but the third person singular ending *-s* has been lost in the present tense. A nonprescriptivist view of those nonstandard varieties that lack a special ending in this form would hold that they have simply carried this particular linguistic change to its logical conclusion by eliminating the last remaining inflectional ending in the present tense.

Double negation, subject-verb agreement, and a number of other grammatical features are, of course, fairly superficial aspects of language. Trivial as some of these features may seem to some, the following letter (which appeared in numerous North American newspapers) attests to their enduring importance for others.

Dear Ann Landers:
I have been dating a young man for several years. Dan is everything a girl could want. Well, almost. He is kind, nice looking, considerate, fun to be with, and he makes good money. The only drawback is Dan's grammer. For example, he says, "I seen," "youse," and "have went." I bite my tongue when he makes these awful mistakes, especially in front of my friends. I don't want to be ashamed of him, Ann, and I don't want to embarrass him either, but I'm afraid one day I might.

Is there a chance that we can have a good marriage in spite of this?
I am 26 and a college graduate. Dan is 27 and attended trade school. I
do love him, but I fear I'll be a nagging wife—or worse yet, a silent wife
who is ashamed of her husband's grammer. Please hurry your answer.
He is waiting for mine.

—York, Pennsylvania

Dear York:
Dan sounds too good to discard. Ask him if he wants to be corrected—
when the two of you are alone, of course. Incidentally, you misspelled
the word grammar throughout your letter. It is AR, dear. Perhaps you
and Dan are not so far apart as you think.

Nonstandard Phonological Features The entities of interest to sociolinguists
are called sociolinguistic **variables**. These variables are speech sounds that do
not occur uniformly across a speech community or, occasionally, even in the
speech of an individual. For instance, a particular variable may be realized one
way in one speech variety and a different way in another speech variety. Similarly, a variable might be rendered one way by speakers when they are speaking carefully and another way in a more casual speaking style.

Perhaps the most widespread phonological variable in English is (ng). We
use parentheses to set off sociolinguistic variables, thus distinguishing them formally from phonemes and phones. Since (ng) is a variable, it is not always realized the same way in speech. Its two realizations are [n] and [ŋ]. The same word
might be pronounced with one or the other realization by the same speaker or by
different speakers: *swimming* might thus be realized as [swɪmɪn] or as [swɪmɪŋ].
These realizations do not occur randomly in speech. There are well-established
correlations between the two realizations of (ng) and such extralinguistic factors as the socioeconomic status and sex of speaker, the relative formality (or
informality) of the speech situation, its physical location, and the nature of the
particular lexical item. The variable tends to be realized as [ŋ] by speakers of
higher socioeconomic status, by females, and in formal situations. Words such
as *analyzing* (in general, formal vocabulary) are pronounced more frequently
with [ŋ] than with [n], while words such as *chucking* are more often heard with
[n] than with [ŋ]. One study even showed that in school situations, more [ŋ]'s
were heard in the classroom and more [n]'s were heard on the playground.

Other English sociolinguistic variables often discussed in the literature are
listed in Table 12.1 with their realizations. These three variables differ from the
variable (ng). Use of the nonstandard varieties of (th) and (dh) will bring highly
negative judgments of the speakers. Use of the nonstandard variety [n] for
(ng), while not approved, will not result in such severe judgments. The status
of postvocalic [r], the (r) variable, varies radically by geographic area, as we

Table 12.1 Some English sociolinguistic variables

Variable	Phonetic realization
(th)	[θ], [tθ], or [t]
(dh)	[ð], [dð] or [d]
(r)	[r] or [Ø] (*zero*)

have seen. No single realization is standard in all areas of the United States. Use of the [r] will be regarded as correct in Los Angeles and stigmatized in Maine.

Often the existence of competing realizations of a single variable is indicative of a sound change in process. Thus, black speakers in Hillsborough, North Carolina, exhibit variation in the realization of (r); the community is in the process of change from non-[r]-pronouncing to [r]-pronouncing.

The St. John's study mentioned above isolated some five consonantal and eight vocalic variables in the speech of its 120-person sample. Various statistically based groupings of these variables constituted particular Principal Components. Any one variable might appear in more than one Principal Component (PC) (along with other variables) but each PC was a set of variables linked to (and defining) some group of speakers. Principal Component 1 [PC1] was expressed in terms of the nonstandard realizations of each of the six variables given in Table 12.2.

Table 12.2 Phonological variables in Newfoundland English PC1

Variable	Word	Phonetic realization
(e)	bay	a) standard diphthongal [ej]
		b) nonstandard monophthongal [e:]
(o)	boat	a) standard diphthongal [ow]
		b) nonstandard monophthongal [o:]
(θ)	three	a) standard interdental fricative [θ]
		b) nonstandard alveolar stop [t]
(l)	mole	a) standard dark [ɫ]
(post-		b) Irish-like clear [l]
vocalic)		c) vocalic [ɣ] (mid-back unrounded)
(or)	bore	a) standard [ɔr]
		b) nonstandard [ar]-like pronunciation
(ð)	them	a) standard interdental fricative [ð]
		b) nonstandard alveolar stop [d] or flap [D]

Speakers evidencing high values (i.e., high percentages of occurrence) of the *nonstandard* realizations of the variables in table 12.2 turned out almost exclusively to be older males. There were no correlations with socioeconomic status or religion.

Principal Component 2 [PC2], on the other hand, consisted of another grouping of variables.

Table 12.3 Phonological variables in Newfoundland English PC2

Variable	Word	Phonetic realization
(ing)	fishing	a) standard [ɪŋ]
		b) nonstandard or casual [ɪn]
(ð)	them	a) standard interdental fricative [ð]
		b) nonstandard alveolar stop [d] or flap [D]
(θ)	three	a) standard interdental fricative [θ]
		b) nonstandard alveolar stop [t]

Speakers with high values of the *standard* realizations of the variables in Table 12.3 clustered together and showed a greater proportion of women than men and also a higher proportion of the uppermost SES groups than did other clusters of speakers. This is consistent with other findings which tend to show standard features occurring more in the speech of women and persons of higher socioeconomic status and less in the speech of men and persons of lesser socioeconomic status.

Language and Gender

Using the words *language* and *gender* in the same context can lead to confusion. Linguists use the word *gender* as the label for certain ways languages may subcategorize their lexicons. The word does not ultimately refer to sex. In popular usage, however, and in other social sciences *gender* refers to social distinctions drawn between men and women. In the following section, *gender* used by itself will have this sociological sense and the term *grammatical gender* will be used when referring to internal language categories. Any discussion of language and sex implies that observed differences between the speech of men and women are biological rather than social. It is far from clear at the present stage of research what correlations can be made between the (biological) sex of an individual and his or her speech.

There is a considerable literature on the general topic of language and gender, which may be taken as including all of the following:

- differences in language use associated with the gender (or sexual orientation) of the speaker or addressee (person spoken to)
- differences in language use associated with the gender (or sexual orientation) of the referent (person spoken about)
- efforts to alter the language with respect to ways gender is or is not encoded

Two different, but not necessarily contradictory, views have been advanced as to the relationship between language and gender. One view, which has characterized much sociolinguistic research in this area, holds that gender differences in language are simply a reflection of the way society works. Another view, one often associated with some feminists, claims that, far from merely reflecting the nature of society, language serves as a primary means of constructing and maintaining that society. The continued use in English, for instance, of male forms (such as *chairman*) in a generic sense (as we will see below) excludes women and is seen as perpetuating a social order in which women are invisible. Thus attitudes as to how people should talk and, indeed, how they are to regard their own status within society are formed by language and continue to be reinforced unless language changes (or is altered).

There is certainly truth in both of these views. Clearly language does mirror society with respect to what is seen as important and even normal. On the other hand, if groups (whether gender, ethnic, or other) are marginalized by the ways they are categorized or labelled by language, then this issue must be addressed and certain aspects of the language may need to be changed in order to include rather than exclude particular groups. In the following sections we will explore some specific types of gender differentiation in language and will examine some efforts to remove sexist language from English. The correlation between sexual orientation of speaker and language use is treated below.

Gender-Exclusive Differentiation refers to the radically different speech varieties men and women possess in a particular society. In some societies, a woman or a man may not normally be allowed to speak the variety of the other gender. It is in this sense that the varieties are gender-exclusive. A society in which this is the norm is typically one in which the roles assigned the sexes are rigid, and in which there is little social change.

This phenomenon has been observed in some Amerindian societies but is no longer as widespread as it probably was in the remote past. A study of Koasati (a Muskogean language spoken in Louisiana) showed that members of this speech community possess different verb forms based on the gender of the speaker. Two of these differences are described in Table 12.4. If the women's

Table 12.4 Gender-exclusive verb forms in Koasati

W	M	
kã	kas	'he is saying'
lakawhôl	lakawhós	'lift it!'

form ends in a nasalized vowel, the men's form has final [s] and no nasalization. Where the women's form has falling pitch-stress (marked ˆ) on its final syllable and ends in a short vowel followed by [l], the men's form shows high pitch-stress (marked ʹ) and [s] for the [l]. (W stands for woman and M for man.) In traditional Koasati society, women and men normally used the forms appropriate to their sex, but they were not forbidden the use of forms associated with the other sex. In quoting a member of the opposite sex, a Koasati used the form appropriate to the person being quoted.

Gender-exclusive differentiation has assumed an even more radical form in some societies. The most extreme form, and a rarity, is one in which the gender of the speaker and that of the addressee are both encoded in the language. In Biloxi (an extinct language of the Siouan family), the following forms (each meaning 'carry it!') were found (see Table 12.5). Singular and plural refer to the number of addressees.

Table 12.5 Examples of gender-exclusive differentiation in Biloxi

	Singular	Plural
M to M	kikankó	kítakankó
M or W to W	kitkí	kítatkí
W to M	kitaté	kítatuté

Gender-Preferential Differentiation is much more common in the languages of the world than is gender-exclusivity. This phenomenon is reflected in the relative frequency with which men and women use the same lexical items or other linguistic features. If, as is often asserted, female English speakers use words such as *lovely* and *nice* more often than do male speakers, we can claim that English speakers exhibit gender-preferential differentiation. Women have also been shown to possess a greater variety of specific color terms than men in North American society. If this is true, it is probably due to the tasks traditionally performed by women. There is no evidence to show that women have more acute color perception than do men. Men are reputed to possess larger lexicons in areas associated with traditional male activities (such as particular occupations and sports). These examples may appear stereotypical, but they do reflect the sometimes subtle, sometimes blatant, differences between the activities of members of the two genders. It is not the language that is sexist but the attitudes of its speakers.

Other differences between men's and women's language in North American society are seen in women's more frequent use of politeness formulas. There are a number of ways in which requests (or commands) can be mitigated in English. Instead of simply saying to someone *Open the window!* we might say *Please open the window! Would you please open the window? Could you open the window? Would you mind opening the window? Do you find it stuffy in here?* and so on. These are all less direct ways of requesting than the straightforward command and, it is claimed, would more likely be employed by women. Since we are discussing gender-preferential usage here, we must emphasize that all of the above ways of phrasing a request are available to all speakers but, it is asserted, are not equally selected by male and female speakers.

Talking about men and women, the most obvious way in which sex differences with respect to a referent are manifested in English is through grammatical gender. The use of English pronouns is instructive in this regard. We do not employ *he*, for instance, to refer only to males. In Standard English, it is used as a generic third person singular pronoun when the sex of the referent is unknown or irrelevant. Thus, we occasionally still hear sentences such as *Did everyone turn in* his *assignment today?* even if the entire group of referents consists of women. However, we more often hear utterances such as the following: *No one can with impunity take the law into* their *own hands* (asserted by former Mayor Koch of New York City) and *Why don't we go to our first caller and see what* their *concerns are?* (from a television talk-show host). In these sentences, we have instances of singular (gender-indefinite) *they*, which is widespread in colloquial English and which denotes an indefinite individual of unspecified gender. For speakers who utter sentences of this sort, the pronouns *she* and *he* are reserved for reference to individuals whose gender is known.

English nouns, though not overtly marked for gender like those in Latin, Russian, or many other languages, do distinguish between women and men. Generally in English, nouns referring to occupations are at once both masculine and generic. There occasionally are female forms for the names of occupations (*sculptress*, *actress*, *usherette*) but these have evolved to connote more than just the sex of the practitioner of the occupation. Many observers feel that these and similar forms trivialize the women so labeled. A woman who acts in films pointedly identified herself as an *actor* in an interview, not as an *actress*. She said that *actor* connoted for her someone who was serious about the craft, while *actress* did not.

The element *-man* has come under considerable scrutiny in the recent past with respect to its reference. The pervasiveness of male-referential forms used generically (as in *chairman*, *postman*, and *mankind*) disturbs many observers, who feel that such language not only reflects discriminatory historical values but also perpetuates them.

This concern has resulted in moves to eliminate discriminatory forms from the language. In many instances, the suffix -*man* has been changed to gender-neutral -*person*. Other morphological processes have resulted in the creation of new forms (a *postman* becomes a *letter carrier*, and a *fireman* becomes a *fire fighter*). Changes have also come about in the use of pronouns. In many cases, regulations, laws, and the like have been rewritten to eliminate discriminatory masculine forms, replacing them with forms such as *he/she* or generic *they*. Whatever the future holds, many people's sensitivity to the ways in which the gender of referents is (or is not) encoded in language has been heightened over the past few years.

Replacement of sexist nouns with gender-neutral ones and a few adjustments in the use of third-person pronouns contribute, of course, to the creation of a less biased language. Advocates of the view (discussed earlier) that language does not merely mirror society but rather molds it would point to further and more wide-ranging examples of sexism which should be reformed. Deferential uses of language by women (the use of politeness formulas or hedges, for example) would be supplanted by more assertive behavior. Unequal treatment of men and women in various areas of the language would be levelled out. For, in this view, as long as these inequalities exist, they reinforce the status quo and leave women as a marginalized group.

Euphemism

Euphemism is the avoidance of words that may be seen as offensive, obscene, or somehow disturbing to listeners or readers. Items that are euphemized are said to be tabooed. The word **taboo** was borrowed from the Tongan language and, in its most general sense, refers to a prohibition on the use of, mention of, or association with particular objects, actions, or persons. As originally used in Polynesia, *taboo* had religious connotations, but in sociolinguistics it now denotes any prohibition on the use of particular lexical items. Taboo and euphemism are thus two faces of the same coin.

In the English-language speech community, the most obvious taboos are not religious but sexual. Despite a recent tendency toward the relaxation of some prohibitions on the use of explicit terms relating to sex, many such taboos still exist. These long ago gave rise to the use of euphemisms (often technical terms of Latin and Greek origin) in ordinary conversation. They enabled speakers to avoid the more earthy colloquial lexical items.

The first item in the taboo list in Table 12.6 is an example of the lengths to which Victorians went in order to avoid mention of anything they felt to be suggestive. *Leg* was seen to be too explicit a reference to the body, particularly the female body, and thus was replaced by the more generic term *limb*. This

Table 12.6 Taboos and euphemisms relating to sex

Tabooed word	Euphemism
leg	limb
cock	rooster
breast	bosom
fuck	copulate, make love

was the language fashion during an age when women wore floor-length dresses and piano legs were covered out of modesty on the part of their owners. *Rooster* is a North American euphemism for older *cock*. It is derived from the verb *roost* and replaced a word that had come to be used to denote 'penis'.

Another set of taboos in the English-speaking world have to do with excrement (see Table 12.7). The word *toilet* is an interesting example of a euphemism that, after long use, has itself come to be taboo. It came to be used in French in the past as a euphemism for the word meaning *restroom*.

Table 12.7 Taboos and euphemisms relating to excrement

Tabooed item	Euphemism
shit	poop
fart	break wind
piss	pee
toilet	convenience, facility, commode

It originally meant 'little towel'. English speakers who avoid a word such as *toilet* in the late twentieth century might be deemed prudish, but they do nevertheless exist.

Slang

Slang is a label that is frequently used to denote certain informal or faddish usages of nearly anyone in the speech community. The term was first attested in English in the mid-eighteenth century, used in reference to "special vocabulary used by any set of persons of a low or disreputable character; language of a low and vulgar type" (according to the *Oxford English Dictionary*). Nowadays, it is often applied to aspects of the language of adolescents or others who are perceived as speaking nonstandard varieties of the language.

Slang exists alongside jargon and argot as members of a class of speech varieties of limited usage in the speech community. Each of these last two mentioned varieties, whether characteristic of an occupational or social group, is confined to a comparatively small number of speakers and is obscure to outsiders. Slang, while it may be fleeting and subject to rapid change, is more widespread and more familiar to large numbers of speakers. Particular 'slangs', however, are very much associated with membership in groups and, when used in the presence of another member of the same group, serve as an affirmation of solidarity with other members.

Studies have shown that slang usage is abundant, creative, and socially important in high schools, colleges, and universities. High school students often divide themselves into groups, each distinguished from the other by clothing and hair styles, the kinds of music they listen to, and their slang. It is sometimes reasonable to speak of a tripartite division of high school students into a (1) 'leading crowd' (called Jocks, Preppies, Collegiates, or Soc's [sowʃəz]), (2) a 'rebellious crowd' (termed Burnouts, Hoods, or Greasers) and (3) those who belong to no particular group (Lames). A study of one high school, carried out in the early 1980s, showed students being aware of some seven groups: (1) Jocks, (2) Freaks (or Heads), (3) Punks (or Rockers), (4) Snobs, (5) Preppies, (6) Brown-Noses (or Homework Gang), and (7) Nerds (or Hosers). There were links and similarities between some of the groups (Jocks and Preppies), and other 'groups' (Brown-Noses and Nerds) were said to consist of students not belonging to any of the first five categories. The slang of Freaks and Punks had, among other characteristics, numerous terms for drugs. The Jocks and Preppies had many of the exaggerated characteristics of California 'Valley Girl' speech (for example, extreme shifts in pitch or frequent use of *like*) in their slang.

A study of slang at a major university (U.C.L.A.) produced a dictionary that included details of syntax and word formation as well as some indications of the origins of many of the slang expressions.

Table 12.8 Origins of U.C.L.A. slang

Slang expression	Meaning	Origin
homeboy	'very close male friend'	Black English
mazeh	'gorgeous guy'	Hebrew
happa	'half-Asian person'	Japanese
have missile lock	'concentrate on'	popular film

The students were also found to use particular word formation processes in producing slang.

Table 12.9 Processes of word formation in U.C.L.A. slang

Slang	Meaning	Source	Process
sucky	'awful'	suck	derivation [V→A]
mazehette	'gorgeous girl'	mazeh	derivation [N→N]
gork	'nerd'	geek + dork	blending
cas [kæʒ]	'all right'	casual	clipping
T.F.A.	'great!'	Totally Fucking Awesome	acronym
fake-bake	'tanning salon'	fake + bake	compounding

In addition to these morphological techniques of word formation, there was substantial use of the semantic technique of metaphor, in which an existing lexical item is replaced by another that suggests an image similar to that associated with the item replaced. Often the new coinage can be seen as more dramatic than the original. A typical instance of this process is seen in the phrase *blow chunks* 'vomit'. This replaces the older phrase *throw up* with a new phrase that has greater impact. Although speakers of this slang can also be expected to exhibit phonological variability with respect to (ing) in their usual speech, they consistently realize (ing) as [ɪn] in the slang word *bitchin'* 'good, excellent' so that there is no **bitching* alternating with it.

Interestingly, the slang items gathered in this study had a relatively limited semantic range. That is, the overwhelming majority of forms referred to comparatively few concepts. Many concerned the appearance of males (most were flattering, such as *hoss* 'stud; muscular male'; only a few were not: *eddie* 'ugly guy'). A large proportion of the terms referring to women were denigrating (as, *wilma* 'ugly girl', or *turbobitch* 'crabby female'). Some descriptive labels were gender-neutral (e.g., *studmuffin* both 'strong, muscular person' and 'cute person; achiever' and *gagger* 'disgusting person or thing'). Other frequently attested semantic domains in the U.C.L.A. slang included every aspect of university life, sexual relations, and other bodily functions.

Jargon and Argot

The terms **jargon** and **argot** are often used almost interchangeably to refer to 'obscure or secret language' or 'language of a particular occupational group'. Since the term *argot* arose in the seventeenth century as the label for a speech variety used by French beggars and street merchants and later was applied to the secret language of criminals, we will use it to denote 'secret language'. It is a label for speech varieties associated with social groups whose members wish to or must conceal themselves or some aspects of their communication from nonmembers. We will use jargon as the label for 'vocabulary peculiar to some field; occupational sociolect'.

'Gay Lingo' Language used by members of the male homosexual community is, in historical perspective at least, an example of an argot. It was either used covertly or its use in public was not meant to be understood by nongays. The lexicon of this argot covers a variety of concepts but is particularly rich in terms denoting sexual practices, categories of homosexuals, physical appearance, and matters of taste, among others.

Table 12.10 Some words from 'gay lingo' which have attained wider usage in the speech community

butch	'(of a woman) very "masculine"; (of a man) macho'
camp	'a playful appreciation of the ridiculous or kitsch'
come out	'disclosing one's homosexuality'
(in the) closet	'relating to the concealing of one's homosexuality (or other trait) from public knowledge'

Only *butch* preserves most of the original notion in nongay casual speech. The other three terms, though clearly arising in the gay subculture, have gained wider usage. Thus one can now refer not only to a 'closet homosexual' but, in an age that increasingly frowns on the use of tobacco, to a 'closet smoker'. While a homosexual can 'come out', so can anyone else who wishes to acknowledge some aspect of his or her identity that has previously been masked. The notion of camp has become so well-known that a philosopher wrote an essay on it and it frequently appears in discussions of art and entertainment. These words are excellent examples of the fact that argots, jargons, and, especially, slang are productive sources of lexical items that later become part of the linguistic resources of the wider speech community.

'Hacker Jargon' Practitioners of many professions are often accused by others of having obscure jargons that deny communicative access to nonmembers of the group. Although jargons may offer effective and efficient ways of communication within the group, they are confusing to outsiders. One contemporary jargon that is notably unclear to the noninitiate, but nevertheless important and increasingly influential in the language, is hacker jargon. Hackers are perhaps best defined as 'particularly enthusiastic and resourceful computer users and programmers'. Their jargon is characterized by a substantial vocabulary associated with computers, but also evidences unusual rules both in its syntax and word formation. The word *hardware* 'the computer or its attachments', for instance, provided via reanalysis of *-ware* the neologism *software* 'instructions, applications that are distinct from the computer and require use of the computer in order to function'. Over time the use of *-ware* has been further extended so that hackers have coined terms such as those in Table 12.11.

Table 12.11 Some instances of *-ware* in hacker jargon

freeware	'software provided without fee by its developer'
shareware	'software for which the developer requires a voluntary payment of a small fee by the user'
guiltware	'shareware which contains a message detailing how much effort the developer has put into it and implying that the user should immediately pay the fee'
crippleware	'shareware which has some important functionality removed, so as to entice the user to remit the fee in order to receive a fully functional version'
crudware	'large quantities of low-quality freeware available from users' groups'
postcardware	'freeware for which the developer's only requested payment is a postcard from the user's hometown'
happiware	'freeware which contains a message stating the developer hopes it will make the user happy'
vaporware	'products (software or hardware) announced far in advance of their appearance, which may never take place'
wetware	'the human brain; human beings such as programmers'

Hackers, of course, very often use computers for communication. In so doing they have adapted some features of face-to-face interaction to this electronic medium. Thus an e-mail (electronic mail) message may be filled with typed utterances such as *<groan>* or *<chortle>*. These usages may then be transferred into the hackers' verbal interaction so that they actually say 'groan' in the course of speaking. There are also numerous 'emoticons'—use of standard keyboard characters to convey the emotions or attitudes of the communicator, such as ;-) 'a smile and a wink' or :-('a frown or anger'. LISP, a programming language, uses a *p* suffix to denote functions resembling questions. A LISP programmer may then appropriate this (normally written) usage in his or her speech and utter *'Foodp?'* which means perhaps 'Do you want to eat?' All of the examples in this paragraph are instances of usage from one type of language being adapted for use in another. Hackers offer in microcosm an example of a very resourceful use of the devices available to speakers of the language and an indication of ways in which language changes.

Politics and Language

In countries with substantial populations speaking different languages, there may be a need for more than one standard language. Such countries often have designated official languages, which are recognized by the government for national or regional use. In Canada, French and English are official languages; in Finland, Finnish and Swedish are official languages; in Belgium, French and Flemish (Dutch) are similarly recognized. Countries with numerically significant localized minorities sometimes assign quasi-official status to the languages of these peoples. In such situations, the local language may be used on street signs, in the local media and, occasionally, even in local schools and

administrative bodies. Examples of this type of limited local linguistic autonomy abound—in, for instance, the Inuit language in Canada, the Sámi (Lapp)
language in Norway, and the Romansch language in Switzerland.

On a global scale, English has increasingly become the chief international
language of communication. In many countries, this is perceived to present a
threat to indigenous languages. English is by far the most common second
language in the world. The more English is used for communication between
persons who speak it as a second language, the less their own languages are
used, and the less useful they may become for modern communication. It is to
avoid the loss of their indigenous languages that many governments take action
either by limiting the use of foreign languages (such as English) or by requiring
the use of some indigenous language. Thus, we have the examples of both
France and Quebec restricting the use of English and encouraging the use of
French in business and technology. A more extreme example is Ireland, where
the use of the Irish language is promoted, although it is spoken by only about
five percent of the country's population.

Multilingualism There is a great deal of variation in nations of the world with
regard to language situations. At one extreme are countries such as Iceland and
Portugal in which almost everybody speaks the same language. (Although this
situation is limited to a very few relatively small countries, most Americans
seem to think of this as the normal situation.) Next are countries such as the
United States and Spain in which there is one dominant language spoken by a
good-sized majority of the nation, but in which there are notable linguistic
minorities. Then there are countries such as Canada and Belgium in which the
great bulk of citizens are speakers of one of two major languages. At the other
extreme are countries such as India, which had twenty-four major languages
and hundreds of minor ones. (The designations *major* and *minor* are determined by number of speakers and legal position in the nation.)

Just as there are many language situations among the nations of the
world, so there are many language policies adopted by these nations. One such
policy, much favored, is to recognize only a single language for most official
and educational purposes. This is the policy in Poland, Malaysia, and Senegal,
among many others. It is important to note that the connotations of this policy
may be very different depending upon the existing linguistic situation. Thus, in
Poland, the national language, Polish, is spoken natively by the vast majority
of the population. In Malaysia, the national language, Bhasa Malay is spoken
natively by the largest single ethnic group in the country, but there are significant minorities whose languages, Chinese and Tamil, have little official
status. This creates the potential for tension between speakers of Chinese and
Tamil on one side and Bhasa Malay on the other. In Senegal, a large percentage
of the population speaks Wolof natively, but the national language is French,
spoken natively by almost none of the population. This situation reflects the
relative prestige of the two languages and the legacy of French colonial rule
of Senegal.

In the United States, the preponderant portion of the population speaks
English natively, and this is the *de facto* national language. However, the

Supreme Court decision in *Lau* vs. *Board of Education* and policies emitting from both the legislative and executive branches of the government have established safeguards for speakers of minority languages. Thus, voting materials must be made available in significant minority languages, and school boards must plan for the education of non-English-speaking children in ways that take into account their differing native languages.

Canada, Belgium, and South Africa, among others, follow a policy of absolute legal equality between two languages. While this sometimes is better followed in theory than in practice, it does provide a method by which two ethnic groups may live in a single political entity without either imposing its language on the other. In Canada and Belgium, this policy has provided a framework for continued political unity, which would have been seriously endangered if a single language policy had been pursued. The Republic of South Africa follows an unusual version of this policy in that the two official languages, Afrikaans and English, are each spoken natively by a small minority of the country's population. Switzerland is the only nation to attempt the policy of legal equality with more than two languages, German, French, and Italian all having equal status in Switzerland. Romansch, a Romance language, also has a legal status, albeit more restricted.

Nations such as India and the Philippines, in which a large variety of languages are spoken by significant groups, have opted for a national language-regional languages policy. In this arrangement, a single language, often the largest single language (e.g., Tagalog, in the Philippines) is chosen as the national language. All citizens of the country are expected to be able to function in that language. At the same time, other languages are recognized as official in specific geographical areas of the country. India follows this policy but has two national languages, Hindi and English; twelve other languages have official status in particular states, while Sanskrit and Sindhi have official status but no designated territory.

12.3 DIALECTOLOGY

The term **dialectology** is used to refer to the study of regional dialects. Modern dialectology got its start in Europe about a century ago as a result of the interest of historical linguists in observing the spread of sound change. This early work was principally concerned with phonology. Later work has considered other aspects of language, but phonology is still the greatest area of concentration, with the lexicon in second place. Dialectologists have been comparatively less interested in morphology and syntax.

Methods

Dialectologists gather data from speakers in a variety of ways. Originally, aspects of speech were recorded by hand on worksheets in interviews and then subjected to analysis. Today, dialectologists use sophisticated interviews and record speakers' utterances on tape, thus lending greater accuracy to their work. Many dialectologists use computers for quantitative analysis or visualization of their data.

The work of dialectologists may be published in the form of articles, but may take the form of a dialect atlas. A dialect atlas contains numerous maps that exhibit regional variation in a language. These maps may plot features that characterize a particular group of speakers or they may, for instance, be used to show features that separate one group of speakers from another. The computer-generated map in Figure 12.2 is designed to show similarities in

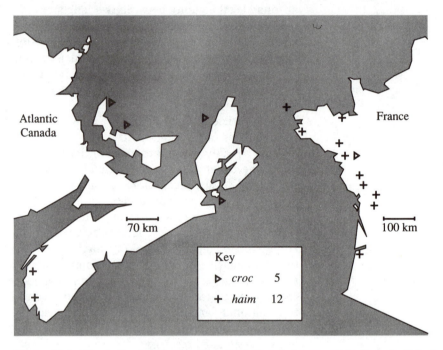

Figure 12.2 Words for 'fishhook' [Standard French *hameçon*] in French dialects of Atlantic Canada and western France (Péronnet and Arsenault, 1990)

shared vocabulary between French-speaking fishing villages in Atlantic Canada and France, thus demonstrating the probable geographical origins of the settlers of the Maritime villages.

Sometimes it is possible to discern clear boundaries between speakers of one dialect and speakers of another. These boundaries are represented on maps by means of lines called **isoglosses**. The latter may be drawn with respect to one feature (generally phonological or lexical) but the more significant boundaries occur in the form of bundles of isoglosses. These lines are meant to indicate that, with respect to the feature or features in question, people on one side share one variant while those on the other share a different one.

The following are examples of lexical items elicited in dialect surveys. The questions are adapted from some used in actual surveys in different parts of North America. Respondents might be asked to circle the form they ordinarily used in each instance or to respond verbally to the question. These examples also illustrate the rural bias of much of traditional North American dialectology.

Table 12.12 Sample questions from some North American English dialect surveys

Definitions for the terms sought	Possible responses
Walking diagonally across a lot or an intersection	kitty-corner(ed), catty-corner(ed), going catty-wampus, caper-corner(ed), catty-wompsum, antigoglin, bias-ways
Children's nicknames for one who tattles	tongue tattler, tattle-tale, tattle-box, tittle-tattle, squealer, rat, fink
Tired, exhausted	fagged out, perished, beat up, (plumb) tuckered (out), used up, done up, done in, petered out, give out, whipped, pooped, all in, bushed, wore (slam) out
Group of trees in open country	grove, motte, bluff, chênière, chenier, clump
Calls to horses (when getting them from pasture)	ku-jack!, co-jack!, kope!, curp!, curph!, quop!, quopy!, quoby!, quowa!, whistling

Early dialectologists typically surveyed large areas. They also believed that isolated rural speech was likely to be purer and of more interest than urban speech. They therefore emphasized rural and small-town speakers over urban

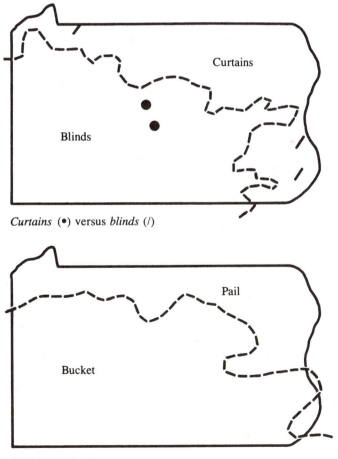

Curtains (•) versus *blinds* (/)

Pail versus *bucket*

Figure 12.3 Dialect areas in Pennsylvania

ones. Thus, the *Linguistic Atlas of the Eastern United States*, with more than 2,500 informants, had only twenty-five from New York City. More recently, a number of sociolinguists have been interested in intensive studies of urban areas. William Labov interviewed well over 100 speakers from a single area of New York City. Similarly, there has been a change of emphasis from the written questionnaires of the early dialect studies to attempts to record speech in the most natural possible form.

English in North America

Dialect differences in Europe often have hundreds of years of history. By the time of Alfred the Great (ninth century A.D.), there were already several distinct varieties of Old English, and some of these distinctions can be followed through to distinctions in Modern English varieties in Great Britain. Dialect differences in North America originated much more recently. Although there was some tendency for speakers of a single English dialect to settle together in North America, the net effect of immigration was a geographical mixing of English dialects and thus a leveling of dialect differences. The major geographical dialects of North American English, therefore, have histories of only a few hundred years of separation at most.

Within the United States alone, there are several major regional dialects. These are illustrated in Figure 12.4. The main dialect areas in the eastern United States are the Northern, Midland, and Southern regions. They are distinguished from each other primarily in terms of particular phonological and lexical features. The distinctions among these regions tend to become less obvious as one moves to the west. This reflects the historical pattern of migration from east to west in North America in which dialectal differences have become blended.

American English Generally speaking, the study of American dialectology has proceeded like the settlement of the United States itself, from east to west. The most extensively published studies and the most certain generalizations concern the Eastern Seaboard and adjoining states. Here we find three major dialect areas: Northern, encompassing the area north of a line running westward from central New Jersey through northern Pennsylvania; Southern, including those areas south and east of a line starting at the Atlantic at the southern border of New Jersey and heading westward almost to West Virginia, and then heading south through North Carolina and South Carolina; and Midland, including the area between the Northern and Southern areas. The Northern dialect area contains Eastern New England (Maine, New Hampshire, Rhode Island, and eastern Massachusetts and Connecticut) as a major sub-area. The Midland dialect is divided into Northern Midland (Pennsylvania, southern New Jersey, northern Maryland, and northern West Virginia) and Southern Midland (southern West Virginia, western Virginia, western North Carolina, and northwestern South Carolina). Studies have been made of the westward extensions of these dialects, but the situation is more complicated and less well studied than along the Eastern Seaboard.

Northern English The Northern dialect is set off by the use of such vocabulary terms as *pail* rather than *bucket*, *angleworm* for *earthworm*, and *pit* rather

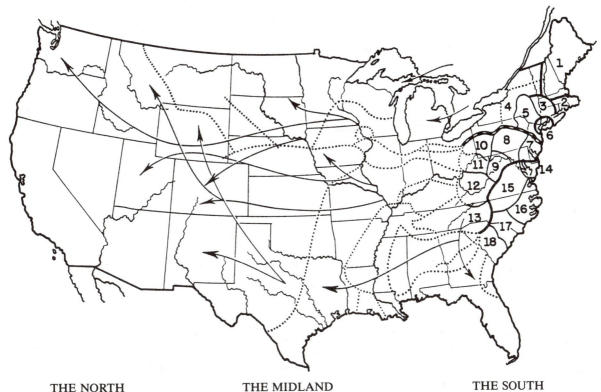

THE NORTH

1. Northeastern New England
2. Southeastern New England
3. Southwestern New England
4. Inland North
5. The Hudson Valley
6. Metropolitan New York

THE MIDLAND

North Midland

  7. Delaware Valley (Philadelphia)
  8. Susquehanna Valley
10. Upper Ohio Valley (Pittsburgh)
11. Northern West Virginia

South Midland

  9. Upper Potomac & Shenandoah
12. Southern West Virginia &
    Eastern Kentucky
13. Western Carolina & Eastern
    Tennessee

THE SOUTH

14. Delmarva (Eastern Shore)
15. The Virginia Piedmont
16. Northeastern North Carolina
17. Cape Fear & Peedee Valleys
18. The South Carolina Low Country

Figure 12.4 Regional dialects of American English. Eastern dialects are numbered. Other (more tentative) dialect boundaries are indicated by dotted lines. Arrows indicate direction of major migrations.

than *seed* in a cherry. Phonologically it has a phonemic distinction between the vowels in *morning* and *mourning*, /s/ in *greasy*, and /uw/ in *root*. Eastern New England is set off from the rest of the Northern dialect by the loss of postvocalic /r/ (i.e., in such words as *barn*, *four*, and *daughter*) and the use of /a/ for /æ/ in words such as *aunt*, *bath*, and *half*.

Midland English The Midland dialect is distinguished by vocabulary items such as *skillet* for frying pan, *blinds* for window shades, and *poke* for a paper sack. Phonologically it retains postvocalic /r/ and has /θ/ finally in *with*.

Northern Midland is distinguished by *run* for a small stream and /a/ in *frog*, *hog*, and *fog*, which do not rhyme with *dog*. Southern Midland has *redworm* for *earthworm*, *pack* for *carry*, and /a/ for /aj/ in words such as *write* and *ride*.

Southern English Southern English is marked by the loss of postvocalic /r/, /z/ in *Mrs.*, and the use of *tote* for *carry* and *snap beans* for *string beans*. It shares with Southern Midland the use of *you-all* for the second person plural pronoun, /juw/ in words such as *news* and *due*, *shucks* rather than *husks* for the coverings of corn, and *might could* for *might be able to*.

12.4 MIXED LANGUAGES

No natural language is in any sense 'pure' or free from all influence from other languages and cultures. Some languages in the world are, however, mixtures composed of elements from many sources. This very quality of being 'mixed' rather than the product of one clear historical evolution lends a unique character to these languages.

Pidgins

The term **pidgin** is used by linguists as the label for speech varieties that develop when speakers of two or more different languages come into contact with each other and do not know each other's language. A pidgin is not the native language of any group. Where pidgins still exist their use may be confined to the marketplace or similar domain. There are numerous theories as to why and how pidgins have come about. Some pidgins have been called 'trade languages' or 'trade jargons' and have clearly arisen as the result of contact between people who were seeking to do business with each other. Sailors have been ascribed a particular role in the genesis of certain pidgins. Some scholars have claimed that jargons called 'nautical English' or 'maritime French' served as the basis for later pidgins in various parts of the world. Clearly, sailors did at least play an important role in spreading major colonial languages (English, French, Spanish, Portuguese, and Dutch) throughout the world, but it is unclear that their jargons formed the basis for resulting pidgins.

There is some evidence to support the claim that pidgins may have arisen as a result of the apparently quite normal tendency for speakers in contact situations to 'simplify' their speech both syntactically and lexically. Linguists use the term *foreigner talk* for such simplified registers. This term is used to describe the way an adult native speaker of English attempts to communicate with a non-English speaker, relying on simple concepts and avoiding more complicated syntactic devices such as embedded clauses or passives. Foreigner talk is similar to *baby talk*, which is the label for the simplified register adults use to talk with babies.

However they may have arisen, pidgins typically present a syntactic structure that is comparatively simple and exhibit certain characteristic relationships to their source languages. They normally reflect the influence of the higher status (or dominant) language in their lexicon and that of the lower status language in their phonology (and occasionally syntax). For example, the following sentence from the Hawaii Pidgin English spoken by Philippine laborers in Hawaii prior to 1930 consists of English words, but has the verb in initial position (where it occurs in Philippine languages):

2. wok had dis pipl
   work hard these people
   'These people work hard.'

Pidgins are an important subset of a larger group of languages termed **lingua francas**. These are 'third' languages that are used for communication among speakers of different languages. The name derives from a medieval trade language (called Lingua Franca) used in the Mediterranean region and based largely on Romance languages (Italian, French, and Spanish) but also containing elements of Greek, Arabic, and Turkish. In the modern world, it is fair to say that English is the most important lingua franca, since it is used as a means of communication for purposes of business among large numbers of people who do not otherwise share a common language.

Creoles

A **creole** is a language that, having originated as a pidgin, has become established as a first language in some speech community. In most instances, creoles that have become established as first languages in particular countries continue to exist alongside the standard (higher status) language that was originally pidginized. The standard language usually serves as the language of education and administration. The creole, not having the stabilizing base of a written tradition and likely subject to the influence of the standard, tends to change more rapidly over time.

Typically, different varieties of the creole emerge, some resembling the standard more than the others. The standard may serve as a source for new lexical items in the creole. In such situations, the creole may develop varieties that to greater or lesser extents resemble the standard. Those varieties that show the greatest lexical influence from the standard and are otherwise most similar to the standard are labelled **acrolects**. Those which evidence the least influence from the standard are called **basilects**. Varieties between these two extremes are called **mesolects**.

Along with most pidgins, most creoles have existed in a relatively narrow belt between the Tropics of Cancer and Capricorn (see Figure 12.5). There are a number of them in the West Indies, the East Indies, and West Africa. Two important and opposing views on the origin and development of these creoles are the notions of **relexification** and the **language bioprogram** hypothesis. Both of these theories are based on the fact that creoles the world over show remarkable similarities in their grammars, such as SVO word order.

In brief, the relexification hypothesis holds that creoles either (1) all go back to a single historical source (such as the sixteenth-century West African slaver's jargon Pidgin Portuguese or the original Lingua Franca) and have essentially retained the grammar (syntax) of that pidgin, but have undergone changes in their vocabulary (relexification) in different subsequent linguistic and cultural contexts, or (2) may have more than one historical source, but still are largely re-formed over time through the replacement of lexical items while the comparatively simple grammars remain relatively unchanged.

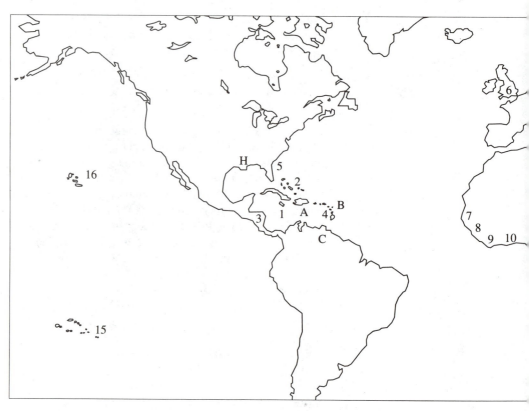

Figure 12.5 Some English- and French-based pidgins and creoles of the world

The language bioprogram hypothesis holds that similarities among creoles are not the result of historical transmission from an original 'proto-pidgin' grammar, but reflect linguistic universals both in terms of first language acquisition and with respect to processes and structures that are putatively innate in the human brain. A pattern of similar innovations in the development of the first generation of creoles has been observed that, it is claimed, can only be explained in terms of a theory of linguistic universals. These innovations include, for example, the use of various preverbal particles to indicate notions such as completeness, ongoing action, and the like. In the following sentence from Hawaiian Creole, for example, the particle *stei* (from English 'stay') is used to indicate an action currently taking place:

3. ai no kea hu stei hant insai dea
     I no care who stay hunt inside there
     'I don't care who's hunting in there.'

Pidgins are seen as structurally deficient in many respects and inadequate as input to children acquiring their first language. Children are thus said to be thrown back on their innate language bioprogram to provide a basic structure for the creole. This produces a generation of speakers of a language that can serve as the basis for further generations of learners and can, for instance,

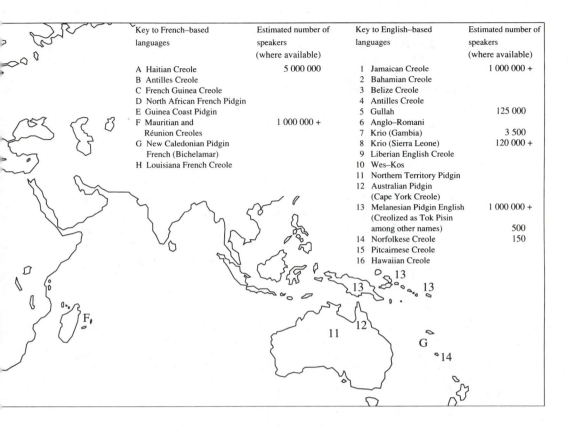

Key to French–based languages	Estimated number of speakers (where available)	Key to English–based languages	Estimated number of speakers (where available)
A Haitian Creole	5 000 000	1 Jamaican Creole	1 000 000 +
B Antilles Creole		2 Bahamian Creole	
C French Guinea Creole		3 Belize Creole	
D North African French Pidgin		4 Antilles Creole	
E Guinea Coast Pidgin		5 Gullah	125 000
F Mauritian and	1 000 000 +	6 Anglo–Romani	
Réunion Creoles		7 Krio (Gambia)	3 500
G New Caledonian Pidgin		8 Krio (Sierra Leone)	120 000 +
French (Bichelamar)		9 Liberian English Creole	
H Louisiana French Creole		10 Wes–Kos	
		11 Northern Territory Pidgin	
		12 Australian Pidgin (Cape York Creole)	
		13 Melanesian Pidgin English (Creolized as Tok Pisin among other names)	1 000 000 +
		14 Norfolkese Creole	500
		15 Pitcairnese Creole	150
		16 Hawaiian Creole	

undergo the sorts of lexical changes mentioned above in which it may come to resemble the original higher status language more.

Cape York Creole Among the English-based creoles of the world is Cape York Creole (CYC), spoken in the northern tip of Australia opposite Papua-New Guinea. The data from this creole in Tables 12.13 to 12.15 will help to illustrate the fact that creoles are not simply deformed or bastardized languages but, in fact, have interesting characteristics of their own that are not shared with the standard.

Table 12.13 Singular pronouns in Cape York Creole

First person	ai, mi
Second person	ju
Third person	i, im

CYC has developed categories of pronouns not seen in Standard English. Differences from Standard English include the fact that in the third person there is no three-way gender distinction and that all of these pronouns can serve as a subject. Only *mi*, *ju*, and *im*, however, can serve as objects. This is reminiscent of the Standard English pronouns *me* and *him*, which serve as objects. The main difference between the CYC pronominal system and that of

Standard English lies in the nonsingular forms. CYC exhibits two nonsingular categories: dual and plural. The forms for second and third person are shown in Table 12.14. The form *-pela* derives from English *fellow*. It occurs in several

Table 12.14 Dual and plural pronouns in Cape York Creole (second and third person)

Dual, second person	jutu(pela)
Dual, third person	tupela
Plural, second person	ju(pela)
Plural, third person	ol, dempela

realizations, *-fela* being the acrolectal form. In the first person, a further distinction is made between *inclusive* and *exclusive* pronouns. Inclusive pronouns *include* the speaker and addressee ('you and I'), while exclusive pronouns *exclude* the addressee but include the speaker and someone else. These pronominal categories are realized in CYC in the forms in Table 12.15, all of which are first person, nonsingular.

Table 12.15 Dual and plural pronouns in Cape York Creole (first person, nonsingular)

Dual, inclusive	jumi, jumtu	(speaker plus one addressee)
Dual, exclusive	mitu	(speaker plus one other, not the addressee)
Plural, inclusive	mipela, wi	(speaker plus addresses)
Plural, exclusive	mitupela, wi	(speaker plus others, not addressees)

The following example illustrates the semantic differences among some of these categories. Assume that they are uttered in a situation in which three persons (A, B, and C) are present.

4. *a*) If A says to B *jumi go nau*, A is saying that the two of them will go but not C.
   b) If A says to B *mitu go nau*, A is saying that A and C will go but not B.
   c) If A says to B and C *mipela go nau*, A is saying that all three of them will go.

It should be apparent from these few examples that creoles, far from being less than a standard, are capable of distinctions not found in the standard. The existence of a dual category of number alongside those of plural and singular, for example, affords CYC speakers a precision not available to speakers of Standard English. The dual is often seen in languages spoken in small-scale, mainly agricultural societies in which it is useful to be able to designate items as occurring in pairs. The distinction between inclusive and exclusive pronouns is widespread in languages of the world, being present in many Amerindian languages, for example. Note how, in the foregoing translations, English can only somewhat clumsily paraphrase the ideas expressed by these CYC pronouns. These distinctions are, however, important to CYC speakers—and probably to speakers of neighboring indigenous languages—and thus are incorporated into the pronominal system. Like other English-based creoles, CYC shares a number of features with Standard English but has its own linguistic system and its own history.

12.5 SPEECH SITUATIONS

Speech situations are social situations in which there is use of speech. They are the main locus for research by interactional sociolinguists. The methods of description and analysis of speech situations differ markedly from the techniques we have previously examined in this chapter. A speech situation consists of a number of components. In analyzing a speech situation, the sociolinguist seeks to specify how each of these components is realized. Once this has been done, an understanding of the how, what, and why of the interaction is achieved.

In Table 12.16, the components of the speech situation have been mnemonically arranged to form the acronym SPEAKING. These notions become more concrete in the context of a specific example. Consider the following situations, which might occur in a university.

Table 12.16 Components of the speech situation arranged mnemonically

S	The setting and scene of a speech situation, distinguishing between the physical locale and the type of activity
P	The participants, often characterized by terms such as addresser, addressee, speaker, performer, audience, questioner, answerer, caller, interviewer, interviewee, and so on
E	The ends, including both functions and outcomes
A	The act sequence, including the content and form of speech
K	The key, tone, mood, or manner, distinguishing among serious, facetious, formal, sarcastic, and so on
I	The instrumentalities, including the "channel" (verbal, nonverbal, face to face, written) and "code" (the language and/or variety used)
N	The norms of interaction and interpretation (the basic rules that seem to underlie the interaction)
G	The genre, any one of a class of named speech acts (greeting, leave-taking, lecture, joke, and so on)

Setting, Scene A classroom could be the setting and might accommodate a number of scenes, among them a lecture, tutorial, club meeting, or conversation.

Participants The different scenes provide for a number of possible relationships between interactants: teacher-student, leader-member, addresser-addressee, among others.

Ends Among the numerous possible functions might be the instructional (in a lecture), the consultative (in a tutorial), and the interactional (in a friendly conversation). The outcomes could include whatever has been learned in the lecture or tutorial, the plans for a party in the club meeting, or the sharing of gossip in the conversation.

Act sequence The content and form might vary from the structured lecture material, to the question and answer or problem solving of the tutorial, to the agenda of the meeting, to the small talk of the conversation.

Key The mood would range from the comparative formality of the lecture to the relative informality (even jocularity) of the conversation.

Instrumentalities All the situations would be face to face, mostly verbal (aside from appropriate nonverbal aspects such as the raising of a hand for recognition and the performance of written tasks). The variety of English would likely be Standard English in the lecture but might contain significantly more nonstandard features in the conversation. Recalling the sociolinguistic variable (ng) from Section 12.2, we might expect to hear it realized as [ŋ] in the lecture but as [n] more often in the conversation.

Norms The norms would vary considerably from situation to situation. The rights (or status) of participants would differ markedly. In the lecture, tutorial, and, perhaps to a lesser extent, the club meeting, the teacher (or leader) would control the situation. He or she might do most of the talking and generally determine the course of the interaction. Other participants would normally be required to secure the permission of the leader in order to speak. In the conversation, there would be greater equality between participants.

Genre A lecture can be termed a genre in itself. It is recognizable by its form, limited number of topics, speaker-audience format, and relative formality. A tutorial would include questions and answers, among other acts. A conversation consists of a number of possible speech acts (or genres). Among these might be an initial greeting (*Hi!*), a concluding leave-taking (*Bye!*), and intervening narratives (including perhaps a joke). Thus, it can be seen that genre is a component that can be understood on more than one level. A lecture can be a genre but so can a greeting or a joke, which is included in the lecture.

As we can see from these examples, speaking in social contexts involves more than simply being able to form grammatical sentences. Sociolinguists claim that speakers possess communicative competence, or underlying knowledge of the linguistic system combined with knowledge of the rules (or norms) for the appropriate use of language in speech situations. In interactional sociolinguistics, the concern is not so much with the grammaticality of utterances but rather with their appropriateness. The next section treats this matching of language with situation in its discussion of the concept of functional speech variety, or register.

Register

The form that talk takes in any given context is called a **register**. Different registers may be characterized in phonological, syntactic, or lexical terms. A register is also a function of all the other components of a speech situation discussed in the previous section. A formal setting may condition a formal register, characterized by particular lexical items, greater adherence to the rules of Standard English, absence of stigmatized sociolinguistic variables, and so on. An informal setting may be reflected in a less formal register that exhibits casual vocabulary, more nonstandard features, greater instances of stigmatized variables, and so on. Registers can also be categorized in terms of their relative explicitness.

Two good friends discussing a matter well known to both do not need to make every detail of their conversation explicit. Each may correctly assume that the other knows basically what the conversation is about. Such an assumption can result in the appropriate use of pronouns and elliptical sentences, both of which are less explicit (more implicit) than nouns or full sentences. The speakers' shared background knowledge will fill in the blanks. Similarly, shared knowledge in an ongoing situation, such as experienced by spectators at a hockey game, means that one fan can refer to the goalie as *he* (perhaps pointing as well) and be understood by another. A university lecture (or a textbook) is, on the other hand, a scene that requires both a formal and an explicit register, since new and unfamiliar concepts are being introduced and explained.

The following examples of some registers of spoken and written language are mainly differentiated from each other in terms of relative formality and explicitness.

5. "This is close to a charge. Call it yourself. No, he did move over on him!"

This was uttered by a color commentator describing an instant replay in a basketball game. It was understandable in context and appropriately implicit. Only one noun was used in the quotation, and it is a technical term in basketball. The referents of the pronouns (other than the audience-directed "yourself") were entirely context-bound. It was reasonable to assume that anyone who could see the telecast could interpret their meanings.

6. "That's what I ought to look like is like that."

This sentence is again entirely context-bound (and maximally implicit) in its meaning. It was appropriate, however, when uttered. Its speaker and addressee both understood what *that* refered to. Its syntax is also consistent with its informality.

7. "In those pants you really look like a zhlub."

Again, the interpretation of the precise reference is limited to the context in which the sentence was uttered. Also, the use of an ethnic slang term *zhlub* (meaning 'gauche or coarse person' in Yiddish) signals an informal register.

8. "Wilt thou have this man to be thy wedded husband. . . ."

Lexical, morphological, and syntactic archaisms signal this formal (and ritualized) register.

9. "Pellagra is characterized by cutaneous, mucous membrane, CNS, and gastrointestinal symptoms."

This quotation from a medical handbook illustrates features of a formal register (in the written channel) by its fully formed sentence, high degree of explicitness, use of the passive, and the presence of medical sublanguage.

10. "Bruins Harpooned"

This appeared as a caption to a graphic on a television newscast. Its elliptical form is obviously derived from the style of newspaper headlines. It is appropriate to the written channel of communication and illustrates the importance of shared knowledge in the interpreting of elliptical utterances. A hockey fan would know that the caption refers to the defeat of the Boston Bruins by the Hartford Whalers.

11. "Time to go bye-bye."

The minimal syntax and choice of lexical items characterize this utterance as one that might be directed by a parent to a child. It is an example of a simplified register called baby talk (termed *motherese* in Chapter 10). Baby talk is widespread, perhaps even universal, in speech communities in the world. In English, it is specifically characterized by its limited lexicon, simple syntax, and relatively high pitch. In these respects, it is most similar to the registers we use to speak to a pet or a lover and is thus both nonthreatening and nurturing. With respect to its simplified grammar and lexicon, baby talk resembles the foreigner talk register mentioned in the discussion of the genesis of pidgins.

The preceding quotations are a small sample of the variety of registers available to English-speakers. All competent speakers of the language are able to produce at least a few registers, thereby making their speech appropriate for particular speech situations.

Forms of Address

One aspect of speech that has been productively analyzed by interactional sociolinguists is that of address term usage. This phenomenon has been observed in a variety of languages and cultures. It seems clear that all languages have address forms and specific rules that determine their appropriate use. Every time speakers call someone or refer to him or her by name, they indicate something of their social relationship to or personal feelings about that individual. A person might be on first-name terms with a friend but not with an uncle or a mother. A grandparent might be addressed by a pet name coined in childhood, but an employer might be called "Ms. Costello" and might address the employee by first name. There is nothing unusual about these examples. Not everyone functions with precisely this assortment of address forms, but they are probably quite representative of general usage in our society.

Compared to most of the world's languages, English has a relatively simple system of address terms, such as those shown in Table 12.17. Address terms can be used reciprocally or nonreciprocally. In the first case, speakers address each other with the same type of term (FN or TLN). This is a sign of a symmetrical social relationship in which both parties have the same status (friends, colleagues, and so on). In the case of nonreciprocal usage, there is an asymmetrical relationship, one in which the difference in status between participants is marked. Thus, one person might use FN, and the other TLN. This is typical of a doctor-patient or teacher-student relationship.

Table 12.17 Types of address terms in English

Term	Example
First name (FN)	Jane!
Title + last name (TLN)	Mr. Simpson!
Title alone (T)	Nurse!
Last name (LN)	Smith!
Kinterms (KT)*	Granny!

*Alone or with FN or LN, as appropriate

In English, and other languages as well, it is also possible to avoid address terms altogether when participants are unsure which term to use. This practice is called **no-naming**. In the case of English speakers, it results in participants using *you* while scrupulously avoiding terms such as FN or TLN. A familiar example of this occurs in the university setting when students no-name an instructor if unsure whether to call him or her by a more specific address term.

Other European languages have one complication that has been largely missing from our language since the seventeenth century: the choice of two pronouns in the second person. On one level in the grammars of these languages, choosing between these two pronouns (*tu* and *vous* in French) is a function of the number of people being addressed—singular versus plural. These pronouns, however, also encode the sociolinguistic dimensions mentioned above. Thus, the form *tu* is like our FN in connoting friendship or intimacy when used mutually and in connoting lower status of the addressee when used nonreciprocally. The form *vous* used with a singular addressee is similar to our TLN in these respects. The details of these usages vary from language to language, but these broad outlines are indicative of the general tendencies.

Outside Europe and other areas where European languages dominate, these overall patterns still hold but often in complex systems with vast numbers of address forms. In many instances, we also have to take into account not only the second person pronouns, but first and third person pronouns as well. In many languages (especially those in highly traditional, stratified societies), there are a number of first person singular pronouns. In Thai, for example, there are seventeen different forms that translate English *I*. Their appropriate use is based on the status of the speaker, that of the addressee, and the relationship between the two. In the same language, there are a further seventeen second person forms and eleven third person forms. In addition, there are numerous categories of nouns that can be used in direct address. The rules for deciding which form is appropriate are complex and require the participants to have some knowledge about each other's status. Given these complications and the possibility that selecting an inappropriate form might be rude or insulting, there is also a provision for no-naming. The forms in Table 12.18, all equivalent to English *you*, are but a small sample of the set of address terms available in the Bangkok speech community.

Table 12.18 Some Thai address terms

Speaker	Addressee	Term
friend/kin/spouse	friend/kin/spouse	/nii/
adult/superior	child/inferior	/nuu/
Buddhist monk	superior monk	/pradeedprakhun/
inferior/non-monk	superior/monk	/t^{h}an/

Discourse and Text

Language used in naturally occurring situations takes many forms. Any bit of talk produced by a speaker, which is distinct from other bits of talk from the same speaker and from other speakers in a speech situation, is an **utterance**. An utterance may be realized as a single sentence ('*I have to leave now*'), an elliptical sentence ('*Time to go*'), a sequence of sentences (as in a long response to a question), or a single word ('*Yes*'). Any utterance will also be analyzable in terms of the components of SPEAKING and thus will have, in addition to a particular form, an appropriate speaker and hearer, function, and so forth. The set of utterances produced by a speaker can be referred to as that speaker's **discourse**. The written (or transcribed) version of any utterance or body of discourse is called a **text**. The field that deals with the organization of texts, ways in which parts of texts are connected, and the devices used for achieving textual structure is **discourse analysis**.

Discourse analysis is very much a multidisciplinary field. Its practitioners are drawn from linguistics, anthropology, sociology, philosophy, psychology, computer science, and other disciplines. Linguists working in this area tend to focus on the nature of the language used in texts, particularly on those devices that provide a structural framework to texts and those that provide the cohesion necessary for a text to be perceived as an organized whole.

Discourse Markers In either spoken or written discourse, the 'utterer' produces not only strings of nouns, verbs, adjectives, adverbs, and the like, but, as well, makes use of forms called **discourse markers** to provide structure. One scholar who is concerned with this phenomenon of naturally occurring language use has defined discourse markers as 'sequentially dependent elements that bracket units of talk'. By this she means that these markers occur over the length of a bit of discourse, separating one 'unit of talk' from a previous one. The bits of talk are themselves defined by the markers. In English alone there are a number of such discourse markers. Not all of them have received a great deal of study, and there remains much work to be done in order to reach a full understanding of what all of the markers are and how they function. Similar phenomena in other languages remain to be treated.

Two typical discourse markers in English are *well* and *y'know*. In *12* we see an example of the use of *well* as a discourse marker.

> *12. Speaker A*: Did you enjoy your trip to the mountains?
> *Speaker B*: Well, it rained the whole time, so we had to stay indoors and never got to do anything.

In this instance *well* serves to introduce a response that is possibly contrary to what might have been expected. It also avoids the most direct possible answer to the *yes-no* question posed by speaker A: *No!* English speakers tend to soften negative responses to such questions by using a hedge such as *well*, as seen in *13*.

> *13. Speaker C*: Could you type this letter for me before you leave?
> *Speaker D*: Well, I was really planning to get an early start on my weekend so I thought I'd leave a few minutes early.

A discourse marker such as *y'know* can be used to appeal to knowledge shared by speaker and addressee, to involve the addressee more in the interaction, to test whether the addressee does in fact share the knowledge, or a combination of these.

> *14.* Say, I saw Betty last week. Y'know, the girl who used to live across the street?
> *15.* I was driving to Drumheller on Sunday and saw this incredible coulee on the way. Y'know, that's a sort of canyon where there's been a lot of erosion?

In *14* the speaker apparently assumes that the addressee knows or recalls the girl in question. In *15* the speaker assumes that the addressee does not share (or may not share) the information (what a coulee is) and thus uses *y'know* to bracket off the unit of talk that provides the clarification.

The long list of discourse markers in English includes such forms as *oh*, *I mean*, *anyway*, coordinating conjunctions (*and*, *but*, *or*), temporal adverbs (*then*, *now*), and others. Although speakers are not usually aware of them, they are essential and their use provides organization to discourse (especially spoken discourse).

Textual Cohesion While discourse markers bracket off units of talk and do provide some element of cohesion, there are other linguistic resources that are more typically thought of as the primary **cohesive devices** in English. Table 12.19 provides a list of some of these devices.

Table 12.19 Textual cohesion in English

(1) Reference (anaphoric):
    I know <u>Grant</u>. <u>He</u> drives a red car.
(2) Reference (cataphoric):
    It's awfully dry, <u>this toast</u>.
(3) Lexical cohesion (substitution):
    Speaker G: Do you know <u>San Francisco</u> at all?
    Speaker H: I've never been to <u>the place</u>.
(4) Ellipsis:
    Speaker E: Do you speak French?
    Speaker F: No.

In examples (1), (3), and (4) in Table 12.19 there are two sentences, either uttered by one speaker or by two speakers in sequence. Cohesive devices are not limited, however, to operating between sentences. Most of these can function within one sentence, as we see in example (2). In examples (1), (2), and (3) the underlined elements are the ones that exhibit cohesion; one underlined constituent presupposes the other. The more usual type of pronominal reference in English is **anaphoric**, in which the noun or noun phrase occurs earlier in the text than the pronoun with which it is coreferential. In the less frequent **cataphoric** reference, a pronoun is coreferential with a noun or noun phrase that occurs later in the text. In both of these (which are subcategories of **endophoric** or **textual reference**) one must know (or be able to find) the coreferential noun or noun phrase in order to be able to decode the pronoun. This link between the pronoun and the constituent with which it is coreferential is the cohesive tie between parts of the same text. Similarly, in example (3) *San Francisco* and *the place* refer to the same thing, and understanding the second phrase requires one to have access to the first. One phrase has been substituted for the other and the two utterances are thus linked.

In example (4) the minimal utterance in response to a *yes-no* question can only be interpreted by the speakers' knowledge that this one word replaces (or stands for) a fuller response ('*No, I don't speak French*') which, however, would probably be heard as stilted and thus inappropriate here. Another possible response would be '*No, I don't.*' This is also elliptical, since decoding it requires knowledge of the preceding utterance.

These are a few instances of cohesive devices in English. Other languages possess similar ones for the creation of texts. It is possible to observe these, as was the case with discourse markers, in written as well as spoken discourse. They are some of the most important and obvious linguistic means for connecting language and situation.

Summing Up

The field of **sociolinguistics** treats the social aspects of language use. This chapter focuses on three principal types of **speech variety: regional dialects, sociolects,** and **register,** along with a number of related phenomena. **Dialectology** deals with regional variation in language. All varieties of a language are dialects, but in all communities, one variety, the **standard,** has more prestige than the others. In many countries, the linguistic picture is complicated by the existence of multilingualism. Sociolects of any language may reflect **social stratification** and **social differentiation,** as well as the age and sex of their users. Among many speakers, **taboo** forms are replaced by **euphemisms.** Some segments of any population develop secret languages or **argots,** while **sublanguages** are associated with specialized professions, and **play languages** with children. The interaction of different linguistic groups may give rise to **pidgins,** mixed languages without native speakers. **Creoles** arise when pidgins are learned as native languages. Finally, speech situations are reflected in the use of **registers,** linguistic variants that are appropriate in a given situation.

Key Terms

acrolect	mesolect
anaphoric	no-naming
argot	norms
basilect	participants
cataphoric	pidgin
cohesive device	politeness formula
creole	Principal Components Analysis
dialectology	regional dialect
discourse markers	register
discourse analysis	relexification
endophoric	scene
ends	setting
euphemism	slang
gender-exclusive differentiation	social network analysis
gender-preferential differentiation	social stratification
genre	speech variety
interactional sociolinguistics	speech situation
isogloss	standard
jargon	taboo
key	text
language bioprogram	textual reference
lingua franca	utterance

Sources

Underlying the discussion of the social network approach are Lesley Milroy, *Language and Social Networks* (Oxford: Blackwell, 1980), Lesley Milroy, *Observing and Analysing Natural Language* (Oxford: Blackwell, 1987), and Jeremy

Boissevain, *Friends of Friends: Networks, Manipulators and Coalitions* (Oxford: Blackwell, 1974). Figure 12.1 comes from the latter. Background for the discussion of Principal Components Analysis and the later treatment of phonological variables in Newfoundland English came from a paper, "Problems in the Analysis of Sociolinguistic Variability: From Social to Linguistic Groupings," presented by Sandra Clarke at the 19th Annual NWAVE conference, held at the University of Pennsylvania, October 1990. The source for the section on nonstandard grammatical features, and, indeed, an underlying inspiration for sections dealing with the social stratification of English is William Labov's article "The Logic of Nonstandard English" in *Report of the Twentieth Annual Round Table Meeting on Linguistics and Language Studies*, edited by James E. Alatis, 1–43 (Washington: Georgetown University Press, 1970).

General sources on language and gender are David Graddol and Joan Swann, *Gender Voices* (Oxford: Blackwell, 1989), Dennis Baron, *Grammar and Gender* (New Haven: Yale University Press, 1986), and Robin Lakoff, *Talking Power: The Politics of Language* (New York: Basic Books, 1990). Some of the terminology used in the language and gender section was adapted from Anne Bodine's article "Sex Differentiation in Language" in *Language and Sex: Difference and Dominance*, edited by Barrie Thorne and Nancy Henley, 130–51 (Rowley, Mass.: Newbury House, 1975). The Amerindian examples in this section were taken from Mary Haas's article "Men's and Women's Speech in Koasati" in *Language* 20:142–49 (1944).

Some concepts in the discussion of slang were derived from Penelope Eckert, *Jocks and Burnouts: Social Categories and Identities in the High School* (New York: Teachers College Press, 1989). The study of language use in a high school mentioned in the text is from Janet P. Bowes, "Teenage Labelling: 'Are You a Jock or a Freak?'" in *Calgary Working Papers in Linguistics*, No. 9:7–16 (1983). Slang examples in Tables 12.8 and 12.9 are from Pamela Munro, ed., *U.C.L.A. Slang: A Dictionary of Slang Words and Expressions Used at U.C.L.A. U.C.L.A. Occasional Paper in Linguistics* #8 (1989).

The examples of 'gay lingo' in Table 12.10 and some of the accompanying discussion are derived from Wayne Dynes, *Homolexis: A Historical and Cultural Lexicon of Homosexuality, Gai Saber Monograph No. 4* (1985). The discussion of 'hacker jargon' and the examples in Table 12.11 are adapted from the "Jargon File," version 2.2.1 (15 Dec 1990), an on-line publication.

General background for the discussion of contemporary methodologies in dialectology was adapted from Alan R. Thomas, ed., *Methods in Dialectology* (Clevedon: Multilingual Matters, 1988). The map in Figure 12.2 is taken from Louise Péronnet and Paul-André Arsenault, "Linguistic Atlas of French Maritime Terminology: Computerized Maps," *Journal of English Linguistics* 22 (1): 25–29 (1990). Material in Table 12.12 is adapted from Alva L. Davis, Raven I. McDavid, Jr., and Virginia G. McDavid, eds., *A Compilation of the Work Sheets of the Linguistic Atlas of the United States and Canada and Associated Projects*, 2d edition (Chicago: University of Chicago Press, 1969).

General discussion of the nature and origins of pidgins and creoles is adapted from Peter Mühlhäusler, *Pidgin and Creole Linguistics* (Oxford: Blackwell, 1986) and Derek Bickerton's article "The Language Bioprogram Hypothesis" in *The Behavioral and Brain Sciences* 7:173–221 (1984). Material on Cape York Creole is derived from the article "Cape York Creole" by Terry Crowley and Bruce Rigsby in *Languages and their Status*, edited by Timothy Shopen, 153–207 (Cambridge, Mass.: Winthrop Publishers, 1979). The map showing the distribution of some English- and French-based Creoles and pidgins is from Ian F. Hancock's article "A Survey of the Pidgins and Creoles of the World" in *Pidginization and Creolization of Languages*, edited by Dell Hymes, 509–23 (Cambridge, Mass.: Cambridge University Press, 1971) and from Ian F. Hancock's article "Repertory of Pidgin and Creole Languages" in *Pidgin and Creole Linguistics*, edited by Albert Valdman (Bloomington: Indiana University Press, 1977).

The components of SPEAKING and the inspiration for the section in which they appear derive from Dell Hymes's article "Models of the Interaction of Language and Social Life" in *Directions in Sociolinguistics: The Ethnography of Communication*, edited by J. Gumperz and D. Hymes, 35–71 (New York: Holt, Rinehart and Winston, 1972). The section on register is inspired partially by M.A.K. Halliday, *Language as Social Semiotic* (London: Edward Arnold, 1978). Another source on register is Hywel Coleman, ed., *Working with Language: A Multidisciplinary Consideration of Language Use in Work Contexts* (Berlin: Mouton de Gruyter, 1989). An underlying source for the section on address terms is the article by Roger Brown and Albert Gilman, "The Pronouns of Power and Solidarity" in *Style in Language*, edited by Thomas A. Sebeok, 253–76 (Cambridge, Mass.: MIT Press, 1960). The discussion and examples of Thai address terms are taken from Angkab Palakornkul's work *A Sociolinguistic Study of Pronominal Strategy in Spoken Bangkok Thai* (Dissertation: University of Texas, 1972).

Underlying the sections on text and discourse is Michael Stubbs, *Discourse Analysis: The Sociolinguistic Analysis of Natural Language* (Oxford: Basil Blackwell, 1983). Discussion of discourse markers is based on Deborah Schiffrin, *Discourse Markers* (London: Cambridge University Press, 1987). Treatment of cohesive devices is derived from M.A.K. Halliday and Ruqaiya Hasan, *Cohesion in English* (London: Longman, 1976).

Question 4 was suggested by data in W. N. Francis, *Dialectology: An Introduction* (London: Longman, 1983).

Recommended Reading

Allan, Keith, and Kate Burridge. 1991. *Euphemism and Dysphemism*. New York: Oxford University Press.

Chambers, J.K., and Peter Trudgill. 1980. *Dialectology*. London: Cambridge University Press.

Coates, Jennifer. 1986. *Women, Men and Language*. London and New York: Longman.

Fasold, Ralph. 1984. *The Sociolinguistics of Society*. Oxford: Blackwell.

————. 1990. *The Sociolinguistics of Language*. Oxford: Blackwell.

King, Ruth. 1991. *Talking Gender: A Guide to Nonsexist Communication*. Toronto: Copp Clark Pitman.

Saville-Troike, Muriel, 1989. *The Ethnography of Communication: An Introduction*. 2d ed. Oxford: Blackwell.

Questions

1. Based on your knowledge of your speech community, design a simple questionnaire (along the lines of the sample in Table 12.12) testing for particular lexical items. If you live in a rural community, you might explore items similar to those in the table. If you live in a city, look, for example, at names for types of buildings or houses, streets, sidewalks, the spaces between streets and sidewalks, and so on.

2. Choose a particular field of endeavor (for example, farming, computers, or weaving) and, either by using secondary sources or by interviewing people, discover and describe the unique features of its jargon.

3. Find two English speakers who grew up in areas different from you. Determine what lexical items they use for the following notions:

   a) first meal of the day (morning)
   b) midday meal (weekdays)
   c) evening meal (weekdays)
   d) large, formal meal (weekend)
   e) mid-morning or midday first meal (weekends)
   f) meal midway through an evening work shift
   g) late afternoon quick meal

   Contrast their terms with yours. Does anyone have more than one term for any one of these notions? Under what conditions do they use these different terms? Did they volunteer any other meal names besides those elicited? In what ways do your findings provide evidence for social, regional, or situational differentiation of language?

4. English exhibits considerable variation (from region to region, from speaker to speaker in the same region, and even in the speech of individuals) with respect to the pronunciation of the vowel associated with the letters *oo* in the following sets of words. Most speakers of North American English use /uw/ or /ʊ/ in these words, but the vowel /ʌ/ also occurs in some. Examine these three groups and determine which vowel you use. If possible, contrast your pronunciation with that of a speaker of another variety of English. In which group(s) does the pronunciation appear to be

most stable (uniform)? In which is the least uniformity seen? Are there any correlations between variations in pronunciation of *oo* in these words and the regional origin of speakers?

   a) pool, fool, mood, loop, boon, doom, loose
   b) good, foot, book
   c) hoof, roof, soot, room, coop, hoop

5. Carefully examine how your local newspaper, radio, or television uses language with respect to matters of gender. Point out any instances of gender-biased or of gender-neutral language. Pay particular attention to the coverage of sports and note to what extent the nature and amount of language used is biased or not.

6. Monitor the speech in your community, and determine whether there are any sociolinguistic variables such as the (ing), (ð), and (θ) discussed in the chapter. If so, how are they reflected in speech? (*Hint*: You might examine the realizations of the phonemes /t/ and /d/ in words such as *sitting* and *reading*.)

7. Groups of people even as small as one's family can share linguistic features that set them off from other groups and provide a measure of solidarity. Consider your own family's sociolect and point out any lexical or other features that you believe to be unique. Contrast these with similar items from the family sociolects of two other students.

8. List and classify (both semantically and morphologically) as many slang words from your community as you can. Do all groups of adolescents in a particular community or school share the same slang? How do their ways of speaking differ? How are they alike?

9. In early Modern English, there were two functioning second person pronouns: *thou* and *ye*. *Thou* was used by social superiors to inferiors (including parents to children) and *ye* was used by the inferior in addressing the superior. *Thou* has been lost from general use in our language. Only *ye* (in the form *you*) has survived. In view of the discussion of address terms in this chapter, what has caused this change?

10. Choose a contemporary English-language play or film. Transcribe and examine some dialogue, if no published version is available for you to consult. List and discuss the discourse markers used in the dialogue. Point out how they may be used to achieve temporal sequencing of related events, involvement of the addressee or audience, or interjecting the speaker's own point of view. Try to compare this fictional dialogue with real-life conversations. Show how the play or film resembles or fails to resemble naturally occurring talk.

11. Consult with a speaker of another language regarding cohesive devices in his or her language. Using reference items listed above under Sources, try to determine some types of such devices used in that language. Look

specifically for the two types of reference mentioned, ellipsis and substitution as shown in Table 12.19. Are all of these exhibited in the other language? Do they appear to work in much the same way as in English? What other devices does your consultant suggest you consider?

For the Student Linguist

WHEN LANGUAGE GOES BAD

Nothing shows more clearly how many rules and norms we have about language use than when something goes awry. The following example, from Tom Stoppard's *Rosencrantz and Guildenstern are Dead,* would probably be an interactional sociolinguist's worst nightmare.

In case you haven't read the play or seen the movie, Rosencrantz and Guildenstern (who you may recall as two minor characters from *Hamlet*) are killing time and decide to play a game. The rules of the game are actually straightforward. Unfortunately for the poor interactional sociolinguist, the guys aren't too consistent with their application of the rules. Thus, some of the statements they make about the game (e.g., "cheating") aren't scored as part of the game while others are (e.g., "I hadn't started yet.").

The speech norms seem even more dubious when you look at Rosencrantz and Guildenstern's decisions about what does (and does not) count as a synonym, as a *non sequitur*, or as rhetoric. However, it's surprising to me that many of the components of this speech situation are relatively easily identifiable in spite of this being such an absurd discourse. After you've identified the components, you might want to experiment with making just one or two of them absurd (choosing different ones than Stoppard did) while keeping the others logical, and see if there's any sort of system or pattern to effective humor. Then again, too much analysis always kills a joke. Maybe you should just rent the video, make some popcorn, and put off your homework for tonight.

ROS: We could play at questions.
GUIL: What good would that do?
ROS: Practice!
GUIL: Statement! One-love.
ROS: Cheating!
GUIL: How?
ROS: I hadn't started yet.
GUIL: Statement. Two-love.
ROS: Are you counting that?
GUIL: What?
ROS: Are you counting that?
GUIL: Foul! No repetitions. Three-love. First game to . . .

ROS: I'm not going to play if you're going to be like that.
GUIL: Whose serve?
ROS: Hah?
GUIL: Foul! No grunts. Love-one.
ROS: Whose go?
GUIL: Why?
ROS: Why not?
GUIL: What for?
ROS: Foul! No synonyms! One-all.
GUIL: What in God's name is going on?
ROS: Foul! No rhetoric. Two-one.
GUIL: What does it all add up to?
ROS: Can't you guess?
GUIL: Were you addressing me?
ROS: Is there anyone else?
GUIL: Who?
ROS: How would I know?
GUIL: Why do you ask?
ROS: Are you serious?
GUIL: Was that rhetoric?
ROS: No.
GUIL: Statement! Two-all. Game point.
ROS: What's the matter with you today?
GUIL: When?
ROS: What?
GUIL: Are you deaf?
ROS: Am I dead?
GUIL: Yes or no?
ROS: Is there a choice?
GUIL: Is there a God?
ROS: Foul! No *non sequiturs,* three-two, one game all.
GUIL: (*seriously*) What's your name?
ROS: What's yours?
GUIL: I asked you first.
ROS: Statement. One-love.
GUIL: What's your name when you're at home?
ROS: What's yours?
GUIL: When I'm at home?
ROS: What home?
GUIL: Haven't you got one?
ROS: Why do you ask?
GUIL: What are you driving at?
ROS: (*with emphasis*) What's your name?
GUIL: Repetition. Two-love. Match point to me.
ROS: (*seizing him violently*) WHO DO YOU THINK YOU ARE?
GUIL: Rhetoric! Game and match!

13 WRITING AND LANGUAGE

Outside of a dog, a book is a man's best friend;
inside of a dog, it's too dark to read.

Groucho Marx

Speaking and writing are different in both origin and practice. Our ability to use language is as old as humankind, and reflects biological and cognitive modification that has occurred in the evolutionary history of our species. **Writing**, the symbolic representation of language in storable graphic form, is a comparatively recent cultural development, having occurred within the past five thousand years and only in certain parts of the world. The contrast between speech and writing comes into sharper focus when we consider that spoken language is acquired without specific formal instruction, whereas writing must be taught and learned through deliberate effort. There are entire groups of people in the world today, as well as individuals in every literate society, who are unable to write. While spoken language comes naturally to human beings, writing does not.

13.1 TYPES OF WRITING

As different as they are, speech and writing share one major characteristic: just as spoken language shows an arbitrary link between sound and meaning, the various symbols and techniques used in written language show an arbitrary link between symbol and sound. All writing can be grouped into two basic types, called logographic and phonographic, depending on the technique of linguistic representation they use.

Logographic Writing

The term **logographic** (from Greek *logos* 'word') refers to a type of writing in which symbols represent morphemes or even entire words.

Logograms Logographic writing is the oldest type of genuine writing. Ancient Mesopotamian cuneiform inscriptions, Egyptian hieroglyphics, and primordial Chinese characters were all highly logographic in their early stages. In fact, all writing systems maintain some logographic writing. Conventional abbreviations such as &, %, $, and the like are logographic, as are the symbols for numerals. To a certain extent, logographic writing can be read independently of its language of origin. For example, the Arabic numbers 1, 2, 7, 10, and so on can be read in any language.

Phonographic Writing

No writing system is purely logographic, however. Nor can it be, since using a separate symbol to write each word in a language is simply too cumbersome. Throughout human history, writing systems have always evolved signs that represent some aspect of pronunciation. In **phonographic** writing (from Greek *phōnē* 'sound'), the symbols represent syllables or segments.

Syllabic Writing As the name suggests, **syllabic** writing employs signs to represent syllables (a set of syllabic signs is called a **syllabary**). Languages with relatively simple syllabic structures such as CV or CVC (Japanese and Cree, for example) are well suited to this type of writing, since they contain a relatively limited number of syllable types. In Japanese, the word *kakimashita* '(s/he) wrote' can be written with the five syllabic signs か ka, き ki, ま ma, し shi, and た ta: かきました .

Alphabetic Writing Alphabetic writing represents consonant and vowel segments. Unlike the International Phonetic Alphabet, which is devised expressly to represent details of pronunciation, ordinary alphabets generally ignore nonphonemic phenomena. Thus, the spelling of the English words *pan* and *nap* represents the phonemes /p/, /n/, and /æ/, but ignores consonant aspiration, vowel nasalization, stress, and other subphonemic variation. As we will see in Section 13.4, some spelling systems also express certain morphophonemic alternations.

Writing systems emerged and spread around the earth over a long period of time. The next sections trace the development of some writing systems from their pictorial origins.

13.2 THE HISTORY OF WRITING

It is surprising that we cannot say with certainty how a comparatively recent cultural phenomenon like writing originated. We do know that writing developed in historically recorded stages, the earliest of which involves direct representation of objects and which is sometimes called *prewriting*.

Prewriting

Figures and scenes depicted on cave walls and rock faces in the Americas, Africa, and Europe twelve thousand years ago or perhaps even earlier may have been forerunners of writing. Some of these petroglyphs (scenes painted on stone) may represent a type of protoliterate stage that did not evolve into a full-fledged writing system.

These drawings depict a wide range of human and animal activity, and may even have been intended for purposes of linguistic communication. Some of them were doubtless a form of religious magic to guarantee a successful hunt or other benefits. Perhaps some were purely esthetic expression. Some illustrations, such as those depicting the phases of the moon, may have been part of some form of record keeping. Figure 13.1*a* shows a pair of elk from a rock-wall drawing in Sweden dating from the Old Stone Age (early paleolithic) period, perhaps as far back as 20,000 B.C. Figure 13.1*b* shows an incised eagle bone from Le Placard, France, that dates back some thirteen thousand to fifteen thousand years. The incisions, which vary subtly, have been analysed as a record of lunar phases.

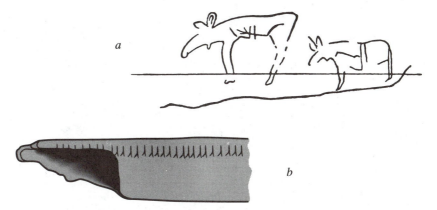

Figure 13.1 *a*. Early paleolithic drawing, Sweden; *b*. Le Placard eagle bone

Pictorial records thus link the origins of writing with the history of representative art.

An even more direct connection links the origin of writing with record keeping. It has been suggested that the idea of writing had its origin in small clay tokens and counters that were used in record keeping and business transactions in the ancient Middle East. These small, fire-baked pieces of clay were apparently used for thousands of years before writing emerged. Counters representing cattle and other goods were stored on shelves or in baskets. Eventually, people began to make an impression of the tokens on soft clay tablets rather than storing and shipping the tokens themselves. This may have led to the idea that other objects and events in the world could be represented symbolically.

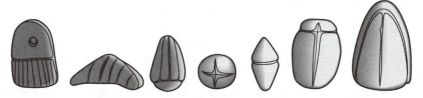

Figure 13.2 Ancient Mesopotamian tokens

Pictograms

Whatever their purpose, there is no doubt that pictures were among the precursors of the written word. Early writing systems all evolved from pictorial representations called **pictograms** or picture writing. Each pictogram was an image of the object or objects (and, in some cases, concepts) it represented, and, as far as we know, offered no clues to pronunciation. This kind of communication has been found among people throughout the ancient and modern

world. Figure 13.3 is an example of Amerindian picture writing taken from a
record kept by a Dakota named Lonedog; these pictures served as a kind of
memory aid and not as a detailed record of events.

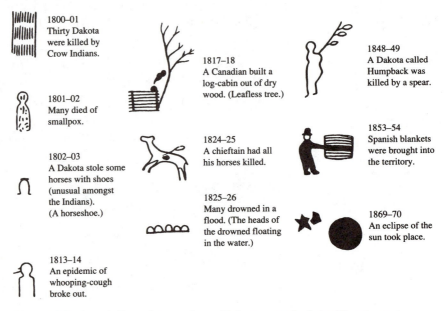

1800–01
Thirty Dakota
were killed by
Crow Indians.

1801–02
Many died of
smallpox.

1802–03
A Dakota stole some
horses with shoes
(unusual amongst
the Indians).
(A horseshoe.)

1813–14
An epidemic of
whooping-cough
broke out.

1817–18
A Canadian built a
log-cabin out of dry
wood. (Leafless tree.)

1824–25
A chieftain had all
his horses killed.

1825–26
Many drowned in a
flood. (The heads of
the drowned floating
in the water.)

1848–49
A Dakota called
Humpback was
killed by a spear.

1853–54
Spanish blankets
were brought into
the territory.

1869–70
An eclipse of the
sun took place.

Figure 13.3 Amerindian pictography: a Dakota record of significant events

Pictograms are still used today, and they reflect the memory-aid nature of
this form of prewriting. Signs indicating roadside services or information in
parks are all pictographic in nature. The International Olympic Committee has
developed a standardized set of pictograms to indicate sporting events.

Figure 13.4 Contemporary pictograms: Olympic signs for sporting events

A contemporary and very sophisticated development of pictographic writing, **Blissymbolics** (originally called semantography), was developed by Charles K.
Bliss. It makes use of a number of recombineable symbols that represent basic
units of meaning, as the following example illustrates.

'person'   'forward'   'building'   'visitor'

Figure 13.5 Blissymbolics

Though Blissymbolics was intended as a means of international, cross-linguistic communication by its inventor, its primary use today is as a means of augmentative communication for nonspeaking individuals. The Blissymbolics Communication Institute of Toronto sets the standard for the training and application of Blissymbols for this specialized purpose.

As we consider developments that emerge from pictographic representation, it is important to remember that pictograms are not writing in any sense of the word. They do not represent any linguistic elements such as segments, syllables, morphemes, or words, nor are they associated with rules for presenting any of these elements in sequence that parallel syntactic rules. Finally, pictograms typically lend themselves to more than one interpretation, and so provide only limited clues about their intended meaning.

13.3 THE EVOLUTION OF WRITING

The earliest known pictographic writing came from Sumeria, from where it spread to surrounding areas about five thousand years ago. The inherently ambiguous pictograms came to represent abstract notions by extending their use to include concepts felt to be associated with them. A pictogram of the sun could also mean 'light' or 'heat' and even 'energy', an arrow, 'to run', and a foot, 'to go', 'to stay', or 'to bring'. It is possible that by the time such symbols appear, we are encountering writing in its logographic form.

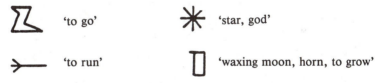

'to go'   'star, god'

'to run'   'waxing moon, horn, to grow'

Figure 13.6 Sumerian logograms

Although its evolution was gradual, we can state with some certainty that Sumerian writing was logographic because, from a fairly early stage, it was written in a consistent linear order that would appear to reflect the order of words in speech. We cannot say with certainty at what date pictures began to be read as words, but once this practice had taken hold, the stage was set for the evolution to phonographic writing.

Rebuses and the Emergence of Writing

A major development in the history of writing took place around 3000 B.C. with the first use of Sumerian symbols to represent sound rather than just meaning. Known as the **rebus principle**, this innovation allowed a sign to be used for any word that was pronounced like the word whose meaning it originally represented. In the following inscription of an economic transaction, for example, the symbol in the upper left-hand corner, originally used to represent the word *gi* 'reed', here represents a homophonous word with the meaning 'reimburse'.

Figure 13.7 Sumerian rebus inscription (c. 3000 B.C.)

Thanks to the rebus principle, concepts that could not be directly depicted by a pictogram/logogram could be represented in writing. Thus, the sign for the word *ti* 'arrow', ➤—, was also used for the word *ti* 'life', and the sign for the word *mu* 'tree', ⊶⟩, could also stand for the word *mu* 'name' and the suffix -*mu* 'my'.

Towards Syllabic Writing

Once the breakthrough towards phonographic writing had been made, it did not take long (in historical terms) before syllabic writing began to emerge. Within about 500 to 600 years, signs that clearly represent not just homophonous words, but parts of words—specifically, syllables—had become well established in Sumerian writing. Typically, the Sumerians overlapped their syllabic signs in order to use them more efficiently. Thus, a word like 'kir' would be represented by the syllabic signs for 'ki' and 'ir' in sequence. Without this overlapping technique, a special sign for 'r' would have had to be employed. Figure 13.8 illustrates this with Sumerian cuneiform signs, which are discussed in more detail in the following section.

ki + ir = kir

Figure 13.8 Overlapped Sumerian syllabic signs

Sumerian writing never developed into a pure syllabary. Logographic elements were interspersed with syllabic ones, and in addition, many syllabic signs were used to represent syllables with other pronunciations as well.

Cuneiform Over the centuries, Sumerian writing was simplified and eventually produced with the use of a wedge-shaped stylus that was pressed into soft clay tablets. This form of writing, initiated in the fourth millennium B.C., has come to be known as **cuneiform** (from Latin *cuneus* 'wedge'). In time, a change in writing practices led the cuneiform signs to be rotated ninety degrees to the left. This resulted in their bearing even less resemblance to their pictographic origins than before. Figure 13.9 illustrates this development in two forms.

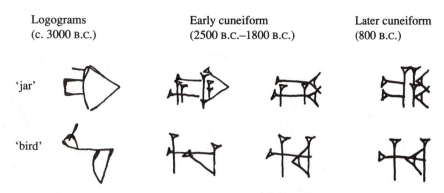

Figure 13.9 Changes in cuneiform writing

The cuneiform system was borrowed by the Elamites and Akkadians in the third millenium B.C., a little later by the Persians, and in the second millennium B.C. by the Hittites far to the north in the ancient region of Anatolia (Modern Asian Turkey).

Cuneiform writing persisted until about the first few centuries of the Christian era in some areas, and then disappeared from use, not to be rediscovered until the nineteenth century. It was first deciphered from Old Persian texts, a breakthrough that led to the deciphering of Akkadian, Sumerian, and Hittite, among other languages that employed it. This script was used for thousands of years but then was generally replaced by more efficient systems of writing employed by the Semitic peoples of the Eastern Mediterranean.

Another Middle Eastern Writing System: Hieroglyphics

At about the time Sumerian pictography was flourishing, a similar system of pictorial communication was in use in Egypt. The Egyptian signs have become known as **hieroglyphics** (meaning 'sacred inscriptions' in Greek). The earliest texts display about five hundred such symbols. Like Sumerian pictograms, the hieroglyphic signs at first represented objects, but later they became logographic in that they began to be associated with words.

Egyptian hieroglyphics developed into a mixed system of both word writing and phonographic writing. For example, the sign for a lute was a picture of a lute: ; this represented the word itself: *nfr*. Only the consonants of words represented by hieroglyphics are known with certainty. The Egyptians did not represent the vowels, which can only be partially reconstructed from transcriptions in Greek and other languages that were made much later. Eventually, the sign came to be disassociated from the word it represented, and thanks to the rebus principle (Section 3.1) was used to transcribe other words that consisted of or included these sounds, such as the word for 'good', whose consonants were also *nfr*.

These symbols eventually came to be used to represent the consonant phonemes of words by application of what is called the **acrophonic principle** (from Greek *akros* 'extreme'): sounds are represented by pictures of objects whose pronunciation begins with the sound to be represented. In this way, the first consonant of a word-sign came to be what the sign stood for. For example, the hieroglyph for 'horned viper' is read logographically as <u>f(V)t</u>; this sign is also used to represent the phoneme /f/ in spellings such as 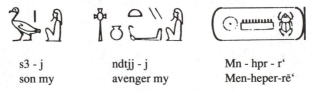 *fen* 'pleasant'. As we will see, this principle was crucial in the development of true alphabets. In Egyptian writing, however, it was only part of a system that mixed logographic and phonographic elements. Figure 13.10 shows some hieroglyphics.

s3 - j   ndtjj - j   Mn - hpr - rʿ
son my   avenger my   Men-heper-rēʿ

Figure 13.10 Egyptian hieroglyphics (c. 2000 B.C.)

Hieroglyphics continued in decreasing use down to Christian times. By the second century A.D., Egyptian began to be written with Greek letters, and by the third century A.D., hieroglyphics had been replaced by the Greek alphabet.

The Emergence of Alphabets

In the Middle East, alphabetic writing was slowly emerging from mixed writing systems over a long period. Building on this tradition, the Semitic peoples of ancient Phoenicia (modern Lebanon) had devised a writing system of twenty-two consonantal signs as early as 1000 B.C. This system was written horizontally, right to left, without variation in the placement of the letters, as had been common in earlier scripts. It was ultimately to lead to the development of many alphabetic writing systems, including both the Greek and Latin alphabets.

The pictorial (and eventually logographic) origins of the Phoenician alphabet are evident in a number of its symbols. The development of logograms for a stylized ox's head, throwing stick, and wavy flow of water are shown in Figure 13.11, along with the corresponding letter names.

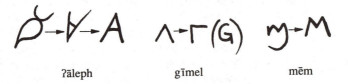

ʔāleph   gīmel   mēm

Figure 13.11 Pictorial and logographic origins of some signs in the Phoenician alphabet

These symbols eventually came to be used to represent the consonant phonemes of words by application of the acrophonic principle. In this way, *ʔāleph* was used to represent the glottal stop; *gīmel*, a /g/; and *mēm*, an /m/. Some of the symbols of the Phoenician alphabet had developed from Egyptian hieroglyphics, and, as in hieroglyphic writing, vowels were not represented (see Figure 13.10).

The Phoenicians were a trading people, and their alphabetic writing spread to adjacent countries and beyond. Eventually, the Greeks acquired and adapted the Phoenician alphabet.

The Greek Alphabet The Greeks developed the Phoenician writing system into a full alphabet: each sign represented one phoneme and all phonemes were recorded by a sign. The Greeks were aware that some of the Phoenician symbols represented consonant sounds that were not found in Greek. Some of these symbols were adapted to represent Greek vowels, and other unneeded consonant signs were dropped. Figure 13.12 illustrates the evolution of the Classical Greek and ultimately the Latin alphabet from the original Phoenician consonantal signs.

Symbols			Greek			Latin	
Phoenician	Name	Phonetic value	Early	Classical	Name	Early	Monumental (Classical)
	'Aleph	'		A	Alpha	A	A
	Beth	B		B	Beta		B
	Gimel	G		Γ	Gamma		C
	Daleth	D		Δ	Delta		D
	He	H		E	Ĕpsilon		E
	Waw	W			Digamma		F
							G
	Zayin	Z		Z			H
	Ḥeth	Ḥ		H	Ēta		
	Teth	Ṭ		θ	Theta		I
	Yod	Y		I	Iota		(J)
	Kaph	K		K	Kappa		K
	Lamed	L		Λ	Lambda		L
	Mem	M		M	Mu		M
	Nun	N		N	Nu		N
	Samekh	S					
	'Ayin	'		O	Ŏmicron		O
	Pe	P		Π	Pi		P
	Sade	S					
	Qoph	Q					Q
	Reš	R		P	Rho		R
	Šin	SH—S		Σ	Sigma		S
	Taw	T			Tau		T
				Y	Upsilon		V
				X	Chi		X
				Ω	Ōmega		Y
							Z

Figure 13.12 Evolution of the Greek and Latin alphabets

Phoenician *ʔāleph*, as we have seen, represented a glottal stop. Since Greek had no glottal stop phoneme, the *ʔāleph* was employed to represent the vowel /a/ in Greek. Phoenician ⋀ (*h*) was used to represent the Greek vowel /e/. Other signs were added to the system by the Greeks, such as ϕ /f/, X /x/, Ψ /ps/, and Ω /ō/.

The Phoenician names for the letters (*aleph, beth, gimel, daleth,* and so on) were maintained by the Greeks (as *alpha, beta, gamma, delta,* and so on), but the pictorial origins had been lost and the names carried no other meaning. The writing system itself gained its name from the first two letters of the series: alphabet.

The Roman Alphabet When Greek colonists occupied southern Italy in the eighth and seventh centuries B.C., they took their alphabet with them. It was in turn taken up and modified by the Etruscan inhabitants of central Italy, a non-Latin-speaking people who were a political and cultural power before the rise of Rome. It is believed that the Romans acquired their alphabet through the Etruscans. As the Romans grew in power and influence during the following centuries, first as masters of Italy and later of Europe, the Roman alphabet spread throughout the Empire.

Under the Romans, the Greek/Etruscan alphabet was again modified, this time with some symbols influenced by the Etruscans. The Γ in Greek writing developed into both *C* for the phoneme /k/ and *G* for /g/. The oldest inscriptions also retained *K* for /k/ in some words, but it was generally replaced by *C*. Similarly, *Q* was retained before /u/. Roman script also employed Greek *U, V, X, Y,* and *Z* and moved *Z* to the end of the alphabet. The symbols ϕ, Θ, Ψ, and Ω were among those discarded, and *H* was converted back to a consonant symbol.

Some subsequent changes were made in the alphabet as it was adapted by various peoples of the Roman Empire. In English, for example, *W* was created from two juxtaposed *V*'s. Spanish employs a tilde (˜) over *n* (ñ) to signify a palatal nasal, as in *año* /año/ 'year', and French uses a cedilla under the *c* (ç) to indicate the dental fricative /s/, as in the spelling of *français* /frãsɛ/ 'French'.

Other Developments, East and West

A great number of alphabetic systems evolved and flourished in addition to the Greek and Latin traditions. In this section, we briefly present some of these that are of historical significance or interest.

Runic Writing Germanic tribes occupying the north of Italy developed an early offshoot of the Greek/Etruscan tradition of writing into a script known as Runic writing. This system emerged shortly after the beginning of the Christian era, and its developments were eventually found as far north as Scandinavia. Runic writing persisted until the sixteenth century in some areas before giving way to the Latin alphabet.

Figure 13.13 illustrates some signs from one of the oldest known Runic inscriptions, which dates from about the third century A.D. The angular style of the letters arose because the alphabet was carved in wood or stone, neither of which readily lends itself to curved lines. The script is read from right to left.

ⲓ✝ⲋⲀⲨⲓⲟ Ⲁⲏ Haragasti 'the warrior's guest'
(? epithet for the god Odin)

Figure 13.13 Runic script

Cyrillic Script Another offshoot of the Greek script was created for the Slavic peoples in the ninth century A.D. The Greek missionary brothers Constantine (Cyril) and Methodius introduced a writing system for the translation of the Bible that is now known as **Glagolitic** script. A later development, which combined adaptations of Glagolitic letters with Greek and Hebrew characters, has come to be known as the **Cyrillic** alphabet. The current Russian, Byelorussian, Ukrainian, Serbian, Macedonian, and Bulgarian alphabets, as well as those used to represent many non-Slavic languages spoken in the former Soviet Union, have evolved from this early Cyrillic script. Some examples of its development and adaptation are given in Figure 13.14, followed by a short passage in contemporary Russian Cyrillic, which is transliterated for its letter values.

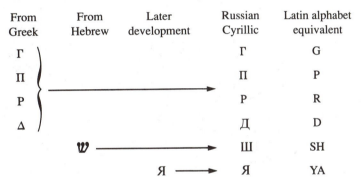

From Greek	From Hebrew	Later development	Russian Cyrillic	Latin alphabet equivalent
Г			Г	G
П			П	P
Р			Р	R
Δ			Д	D
	ש		Ш	SH
		Я	Я	YA

Мы все учились понемногу
Чему-нибудь и как-нибудь ...

mɨ vse utʃilis' ponemnogu
tʃemu-nibud' i kak-nibud'...

We all pick up our education
In bits and pieces as we can ...
Pushkin, *Eugene Onegin*, I.5

Figure 13.14 Contemporary Russian Cyrillic transliterated

Two Semitic Alphabets Both Arabic and Hebrew are written with alphabets that descend from or are closely related to Phoenician script. Both are essentially consonant-writing systems (vowels are indicated with optional marks), and both are written from right to left.

The contemporary Arabic alphabet is the most widespread of all the descendents of Middle Eastern writing except the Latin alphabet. Its earliest inscription dates back to the fourth century A.D. In the latter half of the seventh century, this script was used to write the sacred text of Islam, the Koran, and accompanied the rapid spread of Islam over the next centuries. It contains twenty-eight consonants (vowels are indicated by diacritics above the consonants), and is written from right to left. An interesting feature of this alphabet is the fact that twenty-two of its twenty-eight signs have different forms, depending on their position in (or outside of) a word. Figure 13.15 shows this variation for the forms of the letters *b* and *k* in initial, medial, and final position, as well as their forms when written in isolation.

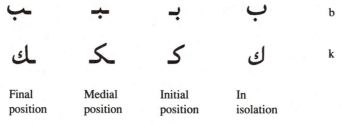

Final position	Medial position	Initial position	In isolation

Figure 13.15 Variation in two Arabic letters according to position

The resemblances among the signs shown in Figure 13.16 demonstrate the clear link between Phoenician script and the Hebrew and Arabic scripts.

Letter name	Phonetic value	Phoenician	Modern Hebrew	Modern Arabic
'Āleph	'A			
Bêth	B			
Gimel	G			
Dāleth	D			
Hē	H			
Wāw	V			
Zayin	Z			
Ḥēth	CH			
Ṭēth	T			
Yōdh	Y			
Kaph	K			

Letter name	Phonetic value	Phoenician	Modern Hebrew	Modern Arabic
Lāmadh	L			
Mêm	M			
Nūn	N			
Sāmekh	S			
'Ayin	A			
Pê	P			
Ṣādê	TS			
Qōph	Q			
Rêš	R			
Šîn	SH			
Tāw	T			

Figure 13.16 The Phoenician, Hebrew, and Arabic alphabets

Other Descendants of Middle Eastern Systems Early Middle Eastern scripts gave rise to Aramaic, Old Hebrew, and South Arabic syllabaries, which, in turn, led to a host of further writing systems eventually stretching across the Near East and North Africa from India to Morocco. Figure 13.17 illustrates this widespread diffusion on a time scale.

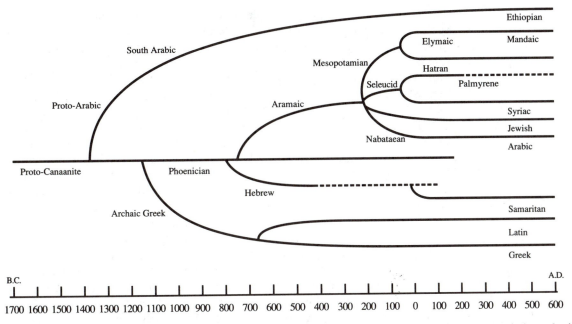

Figure 13.17 Development of writing systems (dotted lines indicate that the line of development is hypothetical)

13.4 SOME OTHER WRITING SYSTEMS

While writing systems that originated in the ancient Middle East have spread throughout the world, other writing systems—some of which may or may not have been influenced by Middle Eastern developments—have emerged as well. This section examines some of these.

Chinese Writing

The Chinese system of writing developed out of pictograms that eventually came to represent morphemes (most of which are also words). The oldest inscriptions are the oracle texts, written on animal bones and tortoise shells and dating back to about twelve hundred B.C. These include many recognizable drawings, such as ⊙ 'sun' and 🌙 'moon'. A change toward more symbolic signs began at an early date as more abstract notions were symbolized, such as ⌣ 'above' and ⌢ 'below'. Signs were also combined to extend meanings metaphorically. For example, the sign for 'to tend' 牧 is derived from 牛 'cow' and 攴 'hand and whip'. 'To follow' 从 is two men in sequence, and so on. As the system became more and more logographic, the characters became more abstract. Figure 13.18 shows the historical development of the sign for 'dog'.

Figure 13.18 Historical development of the Chinese symbol for 'dog'

Application of the rebus principle and historical sound change over many centuries, together with the natural evolution to more abstract signs, has led to the current Chinese writing system. From one perspective, this system can be said to be syllabic. This is the case because most native Chinese words are monosyllabic, so the signs that represent them represent syllables. However, the system is not a true syllabary in that more than one sign may represent the same syllable, and this often in an incomplete manner.

The units of contemporary Chinese orthography are called **characters**. Many monosyllabic words are represented in true logographic fashion by a character that consists of a single symbol. For example, the Mandarin words for 'hand' [ʃow] and 'horse' [ma] are written 手 and 馬, respectively (omitting tones). However, the overwhelming majority of the characters (one estimate is 99 percent) consist of two parts.

The main component of a multielement character is called the **phonetic determinative**. It provides information about the pronunciation of the corresponding morpheme. Although about 4,000 different phonetic determinatives are used in Chinese writing, they represent pronunciation very imperfectly. For example, phonetic determinatives do not provide all the information needed to pronounce Chinese. Tone, which is contrastive in Chinese (see Chapter 2), is not represented at all, and many phonetic determinatives indicate only part of the morpheme's pronunciation. The determinative 敖, for instance, is used for a wide variety of words ending in *ao* without regard for whether the initial consonant is *j*, *n*, *r*, or some other element. Furthermore, due to sound changes over the last centuries, about one-third of all phonetic determinatives provide little or no useful information about current pronunciation. Finally, because Chinese has many homophones, even the most informative phonetic determinatives can be used for many different words.

Chinese characters also include a semantic component, called the **radical** or **key**, which provides clues about the morpheme's meaning. There are about 200 different radicals in contemporary Chinese writing. Table 13.1 provides examples of some of the characters that can be formed by combining phonetic determinatives with radicals.

Table 13.1 Some Chinese characters

Phonetic determinatives

	Semantic radical	A 敖 (*áo*)	B 參 (*cān*)	C 堯 (*yáo*)	D 甫 (*fǔ*)
1	亻 'person'	傲 (*ào:* 'proud')	傪 (*cān:* 'good')	僥 (*jiāo:* 'lucky')	俌 (*fǔ:* 'help')
2	扌 'hand'	攃 (*ào:* 'shake')	摻 (*shān:* 'seize')	撓 (*náo:* 'scratch')	捕 (*bǔ:* 'catch')
3	木 'wood'	橃 (*ào:* 'barge')	椮 (*shēn:* 'beam')	橈 (*náo:* 'oar')	楠 (*fú:* 'trellis')
4	氵 'water'	潵 (*ào:* 'stream')	渗 (*shèn:* 'leak')	澆 (*jiāo:* 'sprinkle')	浦 (*pǔ:* 'creek')

Notice that only the phonetic determinative in column A provides complete information (ignoring tone) about the pronunciation of the four morphemes it represents. The other determinatives supply helpful, but incomplete, information about pronunciation. The determinative *yao* (column C), for instance, has a pronunciation that rhymes with that of the four morphemes it helps to represent.

The usefulness of the information supplied by the radicals also varies. Thus, the characters in row 1 represent morphemes whose meaning is at best indirectly associated with that of the radical ('person'), but the radicals in rows 2, 3, and 4 are much more informative. For example, the characters in row 2 all denote actions involving the hand while those in row 3 refer to things made of wood and those in row 4 all have something to do with water.

Although neither phonetic determinatives nor semantic radicals alone are sufficient to identify the morpheme that they represent, they are more than adequate when used in conjunction with each other. Despite its complexities—one authority has described the system as 'outsized, haphazard, inefficient, and only partially reliable'—Chinese writing provides its users with an effective way to represent the words and morphemes of the language. Moreover, the lack of efficiency in signs is offset by wide readability of the literary script among diverse peoples of differing (though related) Chinese languages. Although a speaker of Mandarin and a speaker of Cantonese may pronounce the word for 'fire' differently—[xwo] and [fɔ] respectively (tones are omitted)—they can read it from the same character 火 since no alphabetic representation is employed.

Calligraphy is an ancient and respected art in China, and Chinese writing exists in a number of styles. In recent times, the script has been written from left to right along a horizontal axis, although newspapers and older texts begin in the right-hand margin and read downwards. The Communist government of the People's Republic of China has introduced simplified characters (some newly invented) as a way of promoting literacy. At the same time, a system of writing Mandarin with a modified Latin alphabet, called **pinyin**, has also been introduced in the People's Republic. Pinyin is used as a subsidiary system for writing such things as street signs, addresses, and brand names, as well as a means of teaching children how to pronounce characters.

Japanese Syllabics

Modern Japanese is written with the help of two syllabaries. These systems, known as **katakana** and **hiragana**, were developed by modifying Chinese characters that were once used for their phonetic value in writing Japanese. Figure 13.19 shows the development of three Japanese hiragana and katakana symbols from the original Chinese characters.

Original characters	宇	加	久	比	利	呂
Katakana	ウ	カ	ク	ヒ	リ	ロ
Hiragana	う	か	く	ひ	り	ろ
Transcription	u	ka	ku	hi	ri	ro

Figure 13.19 Evolution of some katakana and hiragana symbols

The next Figure, 13.20, provides a more complete inventory of the two Japanese syllabaries along with their phonetic values. As you can see, katakana is more block-like and hiragana is more rounded.

Although Japanese can be written exclusively with either syllabary, everyday writing involves a mixture of Chinese characters (called **kanji** in Japanese), in addition to hiragana and katakana. Kanji symbols are typically used to represent all or part of a word's root. The character 人, for example, represents the Japanese root morpheme *hito* 'man'. Although this character is used with

Katakana chart

COLUMN LINE	A	I	U	E	O
SINGLE VOWEL	ア A	イ I	ウ U	エ E	オ O
K	カ KA	キ KI	ク KU	ケ KE	コ KO
S	サ SA	シ SHI	ス SU	セ SE	ソ SO
T	タ TA	チ CHI	ツ TSU	テ TE	ト TO
N	ナ NA	ニ NI	ヌ NU	ネ NE	ノ NO
H	ハ HA	ヒ HI	フ HU	ヘ HE	ホ HO
M	マ MA	ミ MI	ム MU	メ ME	モ MO
Y	ヤ YA		ユ YU		ヨ YO
R	ラ RA	リ RI	ル RU	レ RE	ロ RO
W	ワ WA				ヲ O
N			ン N		

Hiragana chart

COLUMN LINE	A	I	U	E	O
SINGLE VOWEL	あ A	い I	う U	え E	お O
K	か KA	き KI	く KU	け KE	こ KO
S	さ SA	し SHI	す SU	せ SE	そ SO
T	た TA	ち CHI	つ TSU	て TE	と TO
N	な NA	に NI	ぬ NU	ね NE	の NO
H	は HA	ひ HI	ふ HU	へ HE	ほ HO
M	ま MA	み MI	む MU	め ME	も MO
Y	や YA		ゆ YU		よ YO
R	ら RA	り RI	る RU	れ RE	ろ RO
W	わ WA				を O
N			ん N		

Figure 13.20 Hiragana and katakana syllabaries and their phonetic values (voicing, vowel length, and gemination are not indicated here)

the same meaning in Chinese, its pronunciation is completely different in that language ([rən] in Mandarin). An interesting complication in the use of kanji arose from its logographic nature. A symbol like 山, which represents the root morpheme meaning 'mountain', is read in some contexts as the Japanese pronunciation /san/ of the original Chinese word, although in other contexts it is read as the Japanese word /yama/. These variations in the reading of kanji must also be mastered to become literate in Japanese.

In mixed writing, affixes are represented by hiragana symbols. The phrase *in the man's car*, for example, can be written as in Figure 13.21, with the roots 'man' and 'car' represented with kanji, and the possessive morpheme *no* and the locative suffix *de* written with hiragana.

hito no   kuruma de

人 の   車 で

man Gen   car Loc
kanji hiragana   kanji hiragana

Figure 13.21 A phrase written in kanji/hiragana

In theory, the same phrase could just as well be written entirely with hiragana (Figure 13.22), but mixed writing is the normal practice in Japanese.

ひ と の く る ま で
hi to no ku ru ma de

Figure 13.22 Phrase from figure 13.21 written in hiragana

The katakana syllabary is used to write onomatopoeic words as well as words borrowed into Japanese from other languages. In addition, it is employed in advertising and telegrams.

Finally, it should be noted that the Latin alphabet, *romaji* in Japanese, is also making inroads in Japan. It is not unusual to see all four writing systems used together, especially in advertising.

ほんのり 甘味 さらっと あと 味
(honnori amami saratto ato aji)
'Subtle sweetness and light after taste.'

_____ -- Hiragana
~~~~~ -- Katakana
===== -- Kanji

トマト の 新しい ジュース です
(tomato no atarashii juusu desu)
'It's a new tomato juice.'

Figure 13.23 Kanji, hiragana, katakana, and romaji in a Japanese advertisement

Korean Writing

Korean was once written with Chinese characters, which had been introduced in the first centuries A.D. Korean suffixes, however, could not be easily represented by Chinese writing. Various devices were tried to alleviate this problem but inadequacies persisted. Finally, King Sejong (1419–1452) commissioned an alphabetic script, called **Hangul**, consisting of eleven vowels and seventeen consonants that, after some modifications over the centuries, became the standard Korean writing system. The uniqueness of Hangul resides in the fact that alphabetic symbols are grouped together in units to represent the syllables of individual morphemes. Figure 13.24 shows how a set of symbols are grouped to form words.

Hangul symbols

ㅂ   ㅜ   ㄹ   ㄱ   ㅗ   ㅣ

/p/   /u/   /l/   /k/   /o/   /i/

Grouped symbols

불   고기

'fire' /pul/   'meat' /koki/

Written form

불고기

'barbecued meat' *pulkoki*

Figure 13.24 Korean Hangul

American Scripts

A number of major civilizations developed on the American continents. Two of these, the Mayans of the Yucatan and the Aztecs of Mexico, employed complex writing systems. In both systems, we can see the evolution of pictograms that leaned toward phonetic word signs, just as did the Egyptian hieroglyphics illustrated in Section 13.3. Mayan symbols are called glyphs. Some were read as word signs (logograms). But the writing systems relied on other uses of the signs as well. The rebus principle was employed, sometimes only partially, as in the Mayan use of the sign for a smoking bundle of pine, 🔥 /taaʒ/, to represent the locative preposition /ta/. Mayan signs could be combined for their phonetic value alone in a form of syllabic writing. Glyphs that mix syllabic writing with logographic representation are also found.

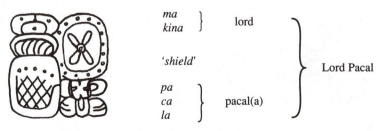

Figure 13.25 Mayan hieroglyphics

The Cherokee Syllabary Some American writing systems do not date back to a distant ancestor but have been more recently invented. After the colonization of North America by Europeans, a number of scripts were developed to provide native peoples with a form of written communication. In one well-known case, the Cherokee leader Sikwayi (Sequoia) devised a syllabic script for the use of his tribe, in which each symbol was either based on the shapes of English letters or newly invented. This orthography was ultimately reduced to eighty-five signs, and books and a newspaper of the Cherokee nation were published in it. In 1903, the script was supplanted by the Latin alphabet.

Sign	Value	Sign	Value	Sign	Value	Sign	Value	Sign	Value
Ꭰ	*a*	Ꭱ	*e*	Ꭲ	*i*	Ꭳ	*o*	Ꭴ	*u*
Ꭶ	*ga*	Ꭸ	*ge*	Ꭹ	*gi*	Ꭺ	*go*	Ꭻ	*gu*
Ꭽ	*ha*	Ꭾ	*he*	Ꭿ	*hi*	Ꮀ	*ho*	Ꮁ	*hu*
Ꮃ	*la*	Ꮄ	*le*	Ꮅ	*li*	Ꮆ	*lo*	Ꮇ	*lu*
Ꮉ	*ma*	Ꮊ	*me*	Ꮋ	*mi*	Ꮌ	*mo*	Ꮍ	*mu*

Figure 13.26 Some Cherokee syllabic symbols

The Cree Syllabary Professional linguists have often played a role in the development of American scripts, as have missionaries. The syllabic script of the Cree Indians was the creation of a missionary, J. Evans, in the nineteenth century. It was employed for religious literature, and by 1861, the entire Bible appeared in the Cree syllabary. Today, in somewhat modified form, the same script is used by Cree speakers across Canada.

Cree morphemes are made up of syllables that combine one of ten initial consonants with one of seven vowels (i, ī, ē, a, ā, o, ō); each of these combinations (ā, tʃā, kā, nā, mā, pā, and so on) is represented by a single symbol. Each consonant may also end a syllable, and so must be represented by a separate symbol. Because of this, the Cree system is not wholly syllabic. As in many syllabaries, the symbols are not combinations of those that represent individual sounds; there is no connection, for instance, between the symbols for the syllable ki ᑭ and the syllable i ᐃ.

A striking feature of the Cree syllabary is its phonetic symbolism. The vowel of a syllable is indicated by the direction its symbol faces. Symbols that face 'south' (downward on the printed page) contain ē, 'north' (upward) contain i or ī, 'east' (facing right) contain o or ō, and 'west' or left-facing syllables contain a or ā. Finally, vowel length is indicated by a superposed dot, as in sī, ᓰ. Such regularity is not found in all syllabic systems.

The syllables of Plains Cree, a variety of Cree spoken in Western Canada, are represented with the following symbols (other dialects use slightly different ones).

Δ	*i*, *ī*	▽	*ē*	▷	*o*, *ō*	◁	*a*
Λ	*pi*, *pī*	V	*pē*	>	*po*, *pō*	<	*pa*
∩	*ti*, *tī*	U	*tē*	⊃	*to*, *tō*	C	*ta*
Γ	*ci*, *cī*	⏗	*cē*	↲	*co*, *cō*	Ⴑ	*ca*
P	*ki*, *kī*	٩	*kē*	₫	*ko*, *kō*	Ⴆ	*ka*
Γ	*mi*, *mī*	⊓	*mē*	⅃	*mo*, *mō*	L	*ma*
σ	*ni*, *nī*	⌀	*nē*	₰	*no*, *nō*	₳	*na*
⸝	*si*, *sī*	⟍	*sē*	⟋	*so*, *sō*	⟍	*sa*
⸕	*yi*, *yī*	⟋	*yē*	⟍	*yo*, *yō*	⸜	*ya*

Finals

ˈ *p* ′ *t* ‑ *c* ⟍ *k* ‹ *m* ˄ *s* ⟩ *n* ● *y* ○ *w* ▪ *h* ˟ *hk* ₠ *l* ₃ *r*

Figure 13.27 Western Cree syllabary

The examples in Figure 13.28 illustrate the use of the Cree syllabary.

₫ Λ nīpi 'leaf'   σ Λ nipi 'water'   ⸕ Λ sīpi 'river'

Figure 13.28 Three words in Western Cree syllabary

Some Other American Scripts The Cree syllabary, appropriately modified, is used by the Inuit of Baffin Island to represent their language, which is unrelated to Cree.

Alphabetic scripts based upon modified Roman letters were also used among the Algonquian tribes for various periods of time. Occasionally, some Roman letters were assigned new phonetic values.

A word-writing system developed by the Alaskan Inuit toward the end of the nineteenth century in time evolved into a partially syllabic system, though it did not become fully syllabic. A number of different systems are in use in different regions of Alaska, and in some, tendencies toward alphabetization are discernible.

African Scripts

In the past several centuries, societies in Central Africa have also produced syllabic scripts, which have either developed in stages from pictograms to refined syllabaries or have been invented by one or several individuals. Although the idea of writing appears to have been imported into these societies, the development of the various systems was indigenous.

The first Sub-Saharan African writing seems to have been that of the Vai peoples in the region of Sierra Leone and Liberia. In the nineteenth century, a native of the area developed a syllabary from a picture communication system. The system grew to consist of 226 syllabic signs plus a few word signs. Vai writing appears to have spawned a number of imitations throughout the area.

The writing of the Bamum people in the Cameroons was invented at the end of the nineteenth century by a native leader. The current seventy syllabic signs show tendencies toward alphabetization.

The only sure example of alphabetic writing developed in modern times among African peoples is the Somali alphabet. The originator, acquainted with Arabic and Italian, devised an alphabet composed of nineteen consonants and ten vowels. The letter symbols appear to have been independently invented, but their names are based on those used for the letters of the Arabic alphabet, and are listed and recited in the same order.

Indian Scripts

A pictorial script appears to have had an independent origin in Northern India, where inscribed seals, pottery, and copper tablets dating back to the third millennium B.C. have been unearthed. The system seems to have consisted of about 250 signs such as 〒, ⊞ , and ⩜, but died away long before another writing system, seemingly derived from Semitic, was employed in the middle of the first millennium B.C. to record the ancient Sanskrit language.

The date of the first appearance of Indian Sanskrit signs cannot be ascertained, but they resemble Aramaic and appeared as a full system of writing in the edicts of Ashoka (who ruled from 272 to 231 B.C.). They were set down in two types of writing: Kharosthi and Brahmi. The former continued in use until about the fifth century A.D. in Northern India. The Brahmi script gave rise to all later varieties of Indian writing.

One of these varieties, a cursive type called the Gupta script, was later employed to write Tocharian, Saka, and Turkish manuscripts discovered in eastern Turkestan. In India, it evolved into the Devanagari script, which became the most widespread type of writing in the subcontinent and that was used to record the voluminous literature of the Sanskrit language. Inscriptions in Devanagari are found throughout Southeast Asia, Indonesia, and as far afield as the southern Philippines. Figure 13.29 shows Devanagari and some of the many other scripts found in India and Southeast Asia.

Figure 13.29 *a.* Devanagari; *b.* Gurmukhi script; *c.* Modern Malayalam script; *d.* Modern Thai script

Varieties of Indian writing were carried abroad by Buddhist missionaries and influenced writing systems in Tibet and Central and Southeast Asia. The Dravidian peoples of Southern India also developed a number of scripts under the influence of the Northern varieties. Another ancient India script, called Pali, gave rise to a number of Southeast Asian writing systems, including Thai and Cambodian.

The examples cited in this chapter only touch on the variety of writing systems past and present that scholars have investigated. The index of one standard work lists 470 scripts. Many of these are historically related, but the number nonetheless testifies to human ingenuity and creativity in devising writing systems.

13.5 ENGLISH ORTHOGRAPHY

The set of conventions for representing language in written form is called an **orthography**. English employs an alphabetic orthography in which symbols are used to represent individual consonant and vowel segments rather than syllables or words. In this section, we will consider the nature and history of English orthography as well as the relationship between writing and reading.

Irregularities

A frequently expressed complaint about English orthography is that it does not establish a one-to-one relationship between symbols and phonological segments. Table 13.2 lists some well-known examples of this.

Table 13.2 Some problems with English orthography

Problem	Example
1. Some letters do not represent any segment in a particular word.	through, sign, give, palm
2. A group of two or more letters can be used to represent a single segment.	think /θ/, ship /ʃ/
3. A single letter can represent a cluster of two or more segments.	saxophone /ks/, exile /gz/
4. The same letter can represent different segments in different words.	on /ɑ/, bone /ow/, one /wʌ/
5. The same segment can be represented by different letters in different words.	/uw/ in rude, loop, soup, new, sue, to, two

The following excerpt from a poem by Richard Krogh vividly illustrates the extent to which English orthography departs from the principle of one symbol, one segment.

> Beware of heard, a dreadful word
> That looks like beard and sounds like bird.
> And dead; it's said like bed, not bead;
> For goodness sake, don't call it deed!
> Watch out for meat and great and threat
> (They rhyme with suite and straight and debt).
> A moth is not a moth in Mother,
> Nor both in bother, broth in brother.

Historical Factors The relationship between symbol and segment in English orthography has not always been so indirect. In fact, the spelling system used throughout England during the Old English period provided a regular set of direct symbol-segment relationships. The foundation for today's system, it lacked the symbols 'j', 'v', and 'w', but made use of four symbols that are not part of our current alphabet.

Table 13.3 Old English symbols not found in Modern English spelling

Symbol	Name	Segment(s) represented
æ	ash	[æ]
ð	eth	[θ] and [ð]
þ	thorn	[θ] and [ð]
ƿ	wynn	[w]

The relationship between symbol and segment in English orthography was significantly disturbed in the Middle English period as the phonological pattern of the language began to change. To see an example of this, we need only consider the Great Vowel Shift, which dramatically altered the pronunciation of long vowels—converting /i:/ into /aj/, /e:/ into /i:/, and so on (see Chapter 7). Because Old English orthography used the same symbol for long and short vowels, complications arose when the former vowels changed. Thus, the letter 'i', which had formerly been used only to represent short /i/ and long /i:/, ended up representing short /i/ and /aj/ (the end result of the Great Vowel Shift for /i:/). This practice continues today, as exemplified in the spelling of *hid* and *hide*. There are many comparable pairs of words involving these and other vowel pairs: *sane/sanity*, *divine/divinity*, *please/pleasant*, and so on.

Additional complications arose following the invasion of England by French-speaking Normans in the eleventh century. The use of English in official documents declined and regional orthographies developed in the absence of a national standard. To make matters worse, scribes, who were trained primarily to write French and Latin, introduced a number of conventions from those languages into English spelling. Among those that have survived are the use of 'ch' rather than 'c' for /tʃ/ (*cheese*, *chin*, etc.), 'th' rather than thorn and eth for /θ/ and /ð/ (*bath* and *they*), and 'c' rather than 's' for /s/ (*grace*, *ice*, *mice*).

Towards the end of the fifteenth century, yet another trend developed—the spelling of words in a manner that would reflect their etymological origin. An enduring example of this influence is found in the spelling of the words *debt*, *doubt*, *receipt*, and *salmon* (formerly spelled *dette*, *doute*, *receite*, and *samon*), all of which were given a silent consonant to make them look more like the Latin words from which they descended.

By the 1500s, English orthography had become increasingly irregular and idiosyncratic, with many different spellings in use for the same word. The word *pity*, for example, could be spelled *pity*, *pyty*, *pitie*, *pytie*, *pittie*, and *pyttye*. As printing presses came into greater use and books became more widely available, the need to reform and regularize English orthography became apparent. In the late 1500s and early 1600s, a number of individuals (most notably Richard Mulcaster and Edmond Coote) formulated and published spelling rules, which were gradually adopted by printers and other literate speakers of English. Although these rules retained many of the indirect letter-segment relationships discussed above, they at least had the effect of stabilizing English spelling. By the 1700s, English orthography was more or less fixed.

The vast majority of the spelling conventions introduced during this period are still in use today. One of the most famous, proposed by Mulcaster in 1582, involves the use of the silent *e* at the end of words such as *name*, *same*, *mate*, and so on to indicate a preceding long (tense) vowel. After the loss in the fourteenth century of the [ə] which this letter originally represented, word-final *e* had been used haphazardly and, prior to Mulcaster's proposal, was added to the end of almost every word that would otherwise end in a single consonant. Although the effects of this practice can be seen in the modern spellings of words such as *have*, *done*, and *gone*, the primary function of silent *e* in the modern system is to signal a preceding long vowel, as Mulcaster proposed.

Obstacles to Reform

Over the years, there have been numerous proposals for the reform of English orthography, including those put forward by Benjamin Franklin, George Bernard Shaw, and Noah Webster. Far-reaching reforms, however, are unlikely for a variety of reasons. For one thing, they would require a long and difficult period of transition. As the following letter to *The Economist* by M. J. Shields illustrates, reform would not be painless even if it took place over a period of many years.

> For example, in Year 1 that useless letter 'c' would be dropped to be replased either by 'k' or 's', and likewise 'x' would no longer be part of the alphabet. The only kase in which 'c' would be retained would be the 'ch' formation, which will be dealt with later. Year 2 might reform 'w' spelling, so that 'which' and 'one' would take the same konsonant, wile Year 3 might well abolish 'y' replasing it with 'i' and iear 4 might fiks the 'g-j' anomali wonse and for all.
>
> Jenerally, then, the improvement would kontinue iear bai iear with iear 5 doing awai with useless double konsonants, and iears 6 - 12 or so modifaiing vowlz and the rimeining voist and unvoist konsonants. Bai iear 15 or sou, it wud fainali be posibl tu meik ius ov thi ridandant leterz 'c', 'y' and 'x' - bai now jast a memori in the maindz of ould doderers - tu replais 'ch', 'sh' and 'th' rispektivli.
>
> Fainali, xen, after sam 20 iers ov orxogrephkl riform, we wud hev a lojikl, kohirnt speling in ius xrewawt xe Ingliy spiking werld . . .

People who knew only the reformed spelling system proposed in this letter would have difficulty reading books written in traditional orthography. Those who wished to read any of the millions of books or articles currently in print would therefore have to either learn the traditional spelling system or have the documents that interested them transliterated into the new orthography.

A second factor militating against serious orthographic reform has to do with the dialectal variation found within English. Because English is spoken in more parts of the world than any other language, it has many different dialects. Any attempt to establish an orthography based on a principle of one segment, one symbol would result in serious regional differences in spelling. For instance, speakers of Boston English would write *far* as *fa* since they do not pronounce syllable-final [r]. Speakers of some dialects would write both *tin* and *thin* as *tin* since they have no /t/-/θ/ distinction. Moreover, while most speakers would have identical spellings for *cot* and *caught* (since these words are homophonous in their speech), speakers of other dialects would spell the words differently to reflect the fact that they pronounce them differently.

Other Considerations Even if considerations relating to practicality and dialectal variation did not rule out major reforms to our orthography, there might still be reasons for retaining at least some of the current irregular spelling conventions.

One advantage of our contemporary system is that it often indicates derivational relationships among words. For instance, if the words *logic* and *logician* or *sign* and *signature* were spelled phonetically, it would be difficult to perceive the relationship between them since the root is pronounced differently in each case.

1. logic [lɑdʒɪk] logician [lɑdʒɪʃn̩]
    sign [sajn]   signature [sɪgnɪtʃr̩]

There are many other such cases where English orthography ignores differences in pronunciation, so that a morpheme can have the same or nearly the same spelling in different words.

Examples such as these show that English orthography does not simply try to represent phonemic contrasts. In some cases at least, it ignores morphologically conditioned alternations among phonemes to provide a single representation for the variants of a morpheme. This has led some people to conclude that English orthography is a type of morphophonemic spelling system, in that it is more sensitive to morphophonemic factors than to phonemic ones. Once this fact is taken into account, it is possible to see the usefulness of orthographic conventions that allow *c* to stand for either /k/ (*electric*) or /s/ (*electricity*) and *t* to represent /t/ (*react*) or /ʃ/ (*reaction*).

Table 13.4 Some pronunciation differences not represented by English

electri**c** - electri**c**ity	[k] and [s] represented as *c*
inser**t** - inser**t**ion	[t] and [ʃ] as *t*
righ**t** - righ**t**eous	[t] and [tʃ] as *t*
bom**b** - bom**b**ard	Ø and [b] as *b*
dam**n** - dam**n**ation	Ø and [n] as *n*
impre**ss** - impre**ss**ion	[s] and [ʃ] as *ss*
alle**ge** - alle**g**ation	[dʒ] and [g] as *g*; [ɛ] and [ə] as *e*
resi**gn** - resi**g**nation	Ø and [g] as *g*; [aj] and [ɪ] as *i*
ch**a**ste - ch**a**stity	[ej] and [æ] as *a*
prod**u**ce - prod**u**ctive	[uw] and [ʌ] as *u*
pl**ea**se - pl**ea**sant	[ij] and [ɛ] as *ea*

Morphological considerations are reflected in English orthography in other ways as well. Consider in this regard the spelling of the following words.

2. lapse   mess
    dense   crass
    house   kiss
    mouse   miss

Although these words all end in the phoneme /s/, this segment cannot be represented as a simple 's'. Instead, the 's' is either doubled (when immediately preceded by a lax vowel, as in the second column) or followed by an 'e' (all other cases). This reflects a general rule of English orthography, which reserves word-final 's' for inflectional suffixes (particularly, the plural and the third person singular). Thus, the single 's' is permitted in the word *laps* (the plural of *lap*) but not in *lapse*.

Another example of morphological influence is found in the rule that prohibits a final 'll' in polysyllabic words—*plentiful, excel, repel*, and so on. As the following examples show, this rule is systematically suspended for two types of morphological pattern: compounds (the first column) and derivations consisting of a prefix and its base (the second column).

3. baseball   unwell
   spoonbill   resell
   landfill   recall

Yet another morphologically influenced rule of English orthography converts a post-consonantal 'y' to an 'i' in front of a suffix.

4. carry   carri-ed
   merry   merri-ly
   marry   marri-age
   candy   candi-es
   beauty   beauti-ful

The existence of rules and practices such as these demonstrate that English orthography is much more than a system for phonemic transcription. Its intricacies can be understood only through the careful study of the history and structure of the linguistic system that it seeks to represent.

Impact on Reading

The three types of writing systems described earlier in this chapter each represent different types of linguistic units—words in the case of logographic systems; syllables in the case of syllabaries; and consonants and vowels in the case of alphabets. Because of these differences, each orthography places different demands on readers. We know that different parts of the brain are used for reading word-based writing systems and segment-based orthographies (syllabaries and alphabets). Because phonological structure is largely irrelevant to logographic writing, people suffering from Broca's aphasia (see Chapter 9) typically do not lose the ability to write and read logograms. However, the use of syllabaries and alphabets can be severely disrupted by this type of brain disorder. There are reports of Japanese patients suffering from Broca's aphasia who are unable to use hiragana or katakana (the Japanese syllabaries), but retain mastery of kanji (the word-based writing system that is also in use in Japan).

Further information about the relationship between language and writing systems comes from the study of the congenitally deaf. Because such people have never heard speech, they have little or no understanding of the phonological units that alphabets represent. Significantly, congenitally deaf individuals have a great deal of difficulty learning to read English. Even after many years of instruction, their reading remains poor and few attain college-level skills in this area.

The type of linguistic unit represented by an orthography also has an effect on how children with normal hearing learn to read. Each system has its own advantages and disadvantages. Children learning Chinese characters, for instance, have little difficulty understanding what each symbol represents, but it takes them many years to learn enough symbols to be able to write and read all the items in their vocabulary. (Knowledge of several thousand separate symbols is required just to read a newspaper.) Even educated people typically know only a few thousand characters and must often use dictionaries for new or unfamiliar ones.

This problem does not arise in syllabic and alphabetic orthographies. Because languages have far fewer syllables and phonemes than morphemes or words, the entire inventory of symbols can be learned in a year or two and then used productively to write and read new words. This is the major advantage of phonographic orthographies over word-based writing systems.

There is reason to think that children find syllabaries easier to master than alphabets. Children learning syllabaries (such as Japanese) are reported to have fewer reading problems initially than children learning alphabetic orthographies. Although at least some difficulties encountered by children learning to read English may be due to the complexity of English spelling conventions, Italian and German children learning to use their relatively regular alphabetic orthographies also have reading problems.

The advantage of syllabaries over alphabets for young readers apparently stems from the fact that children have less difficulty identifying syllables than phonemes. One study revealed that 46 percent of four year olds and 90 percent of six year olds can segment words into syllables. In contrast, virtually no four year olds and only about two-thirds of all six year olds can segment words into phoneme-sized units. Since learning to read involves an understanding of the types of units represented by written symbols, it therefore stands to reason that syllabaries will generally be easier for young children to learn.

Of course, it must be remembered that syllabaries may have disadvantages of other sorts. While syllabic writing is feasible for languages such as Japanese that have a relatively small number of syllable types, it would be quite impractical in English where there are dozens of different syllable structures. Ultimately, an orthography must be judged in terms of its success in representing language for the purpose of reading and writing. There is no doubt that an alphabetic orthography is superior to a syllabary for representing the phonological structure of English.

Summing Up

The development of writing has been one of humanity's greatest intellectual achievements. From **pictograms** and **logograms**, the graphic representation of language has developed through **syllabic** writing to the **alphabet**. This was achieved through the discovery of the relationship of sign to sound. Eventually, this discovery resulted in the reduction of the number of signs required to symbolize a language in written form.

Many of the large number of writing systems found throughout the modern world owe their origin directly or indirectly to the Semitic writing systems of the eastern Mediterranean. As the idea of writing spread, new forms of the signs were independently invented and sound-symbol correspondences were altered in accordance with language structures. Some writing systems derived from the Graeco-Phoenician tradition are today scarcely recognizable as such, since so little remains of the original signs. In cases where the entire system was invented, perhaps only the idea of writing is traceable to the early traditions.

In all cases, the historical line of development is clear. There seems to be no evidence of a culture that has developed an alphabet and then followed this with the development of, for example, a logographic script. But this cultural line of development does not imply that earlier forms of writing are inferior to alphabetic writing. In the case of languages such as Japanese or Cree, the syllabic writing system is as well suited to the phonological structure of the language as an alphabetic script.

Key Terms

acrophonic principle	logographic writing
alphabetic	orthography
character	Phoenician script
cuneiform	phonetic determinative
Cyrillic script	phonographic writing
Glagolitic script	pictograms
Hangul	radical
hieroglyphic	rebus principle
hiragana	runic writing
kanji	syllabary
katakana	syllabic

Sources

Comprehensive surveys of the development of writing and of the world's writing systems are found in Jensen, Gelb, and DeFrancis (all cited below). The idea that writing may have originated in record keeping with clay tokens is taken from Schmandt-Besserat (cited below). The following figures are adapted: from Jensen, 13.1a, 13.3, 13.6, 13.10, 13.13, 13.26, 13.29; from Alexander Marshack, *The Roots of Civilization* (New York: McGraw-Hill, 1972), 13.1b; from Schmandt-Besserat, 13.2; from DeFrancis (see further references to origins of these figures therein), 13.7 (p. 76), 13.8 (p. 82), 13.12 (p. 180), 13.16 (p. 168), 13.25 (p. 127), copyright ©1989 by the University of Hawaii Press; from M. W. Green, "Early Cuneiform," in Senner (cited below), 13.9 (p. 45); from Sampson (cited below), 13.11; from Frank Moore Cross, "The Invention and Development of the Alphabet," in Senner (cited below), 13.17 (p. 89). Figures 13.9 and 13.17 are copyright ©1989 by the University of Nebraska Press and reprinted by permission. The sport pictograms in Figure 13.4 are courtesy of the Olympic Trust of Canada, ™Official Mark ©Canadian Olympic Association, 1972. Figure 13.5 is courtesy of the Blissymbolics Communication Institute, Exclusive licensee, 1982, and is derived from the symbols described in the work, *Semantography*, original copyright C. K. Bliss 1949.

Reference to Arabic writing is from James A. Bellamy, "The Arabic Alphabet," in Senner (cited below). John DeFrancis (University of Hawaii), Robert Fisher (University of Toronto/York University), and Brian King (University of British Columbia) all provided insightful and helpful comments (especially regarding Chinese writing), so many, in fact, that we were not able to make use of all of them here. Their views are not necessarily those reflected in the chapter. The discussion of Chinese writing is derived from DeFrancis (cited below), as is Table 13.1 (p. 107); Figure 13.18 was taken from Jerry Norman, *Chinese* (New York: Cambridge University Press, 1988); Chinese characters were provided by Kazue Kanno. The presentation of Japanese writing also owes to DeFrancis, as well as to M. Shibatani, *The Languages of Japan* (Cambridge: Cambridge University Press, 1990); Figure 13.19 is also adapted from Shibatani (p. 127). The hiragana and katakana charts (Figure 13.20) are adapted from Len Walsh's *Read Japanese Today* (Tokyo, Japan: Charles E. Tuttle, 1971); examples of Japanese writing were provided by Kazue Kanno. Presentation of the Cree syllabary is adapted from D. Pentland, *Nēhiyawasinahikēwin: A Standard Orthography for the Cree Language* (Saskatoon: Saskatchewan Indian Cultural College, 1977). The examples of Northern Indian pictorial script are from John Marshall, *Mohenjo-Daro and the Indus Civilization* (London: 1931).

The discussion of the history of English spelling is based on *A History of English Spelling* by D. G. Scragg (New York: Barnes & Noble, 1974). The examples of spelling rules sensitive to morphological structure come from the book by D. W. Cummings cited below. Data on children's ability to segment words into syllables and phonemes comes from I. Y. Liberman, reported in Gibson and Levin (cited below).

Recommended Reading

Cummings, D. W. 1988. *American English Spelling*. Baltimore, Md.: The Johns Hopkins University Press.

DeFrancis, John. 1989. *Visible Speech: The Diverse Oneness of Writing Systems*. Honolulu: University of Hawaii Press.

Gelb, I. J. 1952. *A Study of Writing*. Chicago: University of Chicago Press.

Gibson, E., and H. Levin. 1975. *The Psychology of Reading*. Cambridge, Mass.: MIT Press.

Gleitman, L., and P. Rozin. 1977. "The Structure and Acquisition of Reading I: Relations Between Orthographies and the Structures of Language." In *Toward a Psychology of Reading*. Edited by A. Reber and D. Scarborough, 1–53. Hillsdale, N.J.: Erlbaum.

Jensen, H. 1970. *Sign, Symbol and Script*. G. Unwin, trans. London: George Allen and Unwin.

Sampson, G. 1985. *Writing Systems: A Linguistic Introduction*. Stanford, Calif.: Stanford University Press.

Schmandt-Besserat, Denise. 1989. "Two Precursors of Writing: Plain and Complex Tokens." In *The Origins of Writing*. Edited by W. M. Senner, 27–42. Lincoln, Neb.: University of Nebraska Press.

Senner, W.M., ed. 1989. *The Origins of Writing*. Lincoln, Neb.: University of Nebraska Press.

Wallace, Rex. 1989. "The Origins and Development of the Latin Alphabet." In *The Origins of Writing*. Edited by W. M. Senner, 121–36. Lincoln, Neb.: University of Nebraska Press.

Questions

1. Suppose you are the user of a pictographic writing system that can already represent concrete objects in a satisfactory way. Using the pictographic symbols of your system, propose extensions of these symbols to represent the following meanings.

   a) hunt   f) cook
   b) cold   g) tired
   c) fast   h) wet
   d) white   i) angry
   e) strength   j) weakness

2. Suppose you are constructing a syllabary system for English, and are trying to write the following words in your syllabary system. Do you encounter any problem? If yes, explain why.

foe	law	shoe
slaw	slow	slowly
lee	day	daily
sue	pull	shop
ship	loop	food
lock	shock	unlock
locked	shocked	pulled
shops	locker	shod
float	splint	schlock

3. Examine the spelling and the pronunciation of the following words. Do you think English orthography has any advantage? If yes, explain why.

   a) hymn   hymnal
   b) part   partial
   c) recite   recitation
   d) reduce   reduction

e) design   designation
f) critical   criticize   criticism
g) analogue   analogous   analogy

4. After discussing the forms in Question 3, consider the following forms. Does the spelling system treat all cases of allomorphic variation the same way?

a) invade   invasion
b) concede   concession
c) assume   assumption
d) profound   profundity

5. Briefly outline the advantages and disadvantages of the three major types of writing systems.

14 ANIMAL COMMUNICATION

As I listened from a beach-chair in the shade
To all the noises that my garden made,
It seemed to me only proper that words
Should be withheld from vegetables and birds.

W. H. Auden

Communication—the passing on or exchange of information—distinguishes what is living from what is nonliving in nature. Communication is found even in the apparently passive world of plants; trees, for example, have been found to pass on information about advancing predators by means of chemical signals. Animals communicate among themselves and with humans so effectively that they are frequently held to use "language". From the linguist's point of view, however, not just any communication qualifies as language as it is defined in this book.

A question which therefore interests many linguists is whether animals make use of any system of communication that genuinely resembles or approximates human language. Just as the use of communication sets what is living apart from what is nonliving, the use of language is often said to set humans apart from all other animals. If animals are able to communicate with a system that is structured like human language, then language as we know it is not the unique property of our species, and we will have to look for other ways of defining humanness. This chapter investigates the ways in which animal communication is like human language and the ways in which it is different.

14.1 NONVOCAL COMMUNICATION

One of the most striking things about animal communication is the variety of means by which it is carried out. Animals communicate not only with sounds but with scent, light, ultrasound, visual signs, gestures, color, and even electricity. From the slime mold to the giant blue whale, all animals appear to have some means of communication. Some nonvocal modes of communication are described here.

Scent Chemically based scent communication is used by species as different as molds, insects, and mammals. Chemicals used by animals specifically for communicative purposes are called **pheremones**. The slime mold signals its reproductive readiness through the release of a pheremone. Dogs and other canines leave a urine-based pheremone as an identification mark to stake out their territory, and many nonhuman primates have specialized scent glands for the same purpose.

Light Probably the best known light user in North America is the firefly or lightning bug. This small flying beetle uses light flashes in varying patterns to signal its identity, sex, and location.

Electricity Certain species of eels in the Amazon River basin communicate their presence and territoriality by means of electrical impulses at various frequencies. Each species signals at a specific frequency range, and the transmitting frequencies, like those of radio and television stations, do not overlap.

Color The color—or color patterns—of many animals plays an important role in their identification by members of their own species and other animals. The octopus changes color frequently and this coloring is used for a wide range of messages, including territorial defense and mating readiness.

Facial expression These are specific types of gesture that communicate meaning. When a male baboon yawns, bares its fangs, and retracts its eyebrows, it is indicating a willingness to fight. A wide variety of facial expressions is found among chimpanzees, a number of which are shown in Figure 14.1. Experiments

Figure 14.1 Some chimpanzee facial expressions: *a.* anger; *b.* fear-anger; *c.* affection; *d.* frustration-sadness; *e.* playfulness

have shown that humans can classify the meanings of these expressions quite accurately. For example, when humans draw back the corners of their mouths into a smile, they are generally indicating cooperation. A nonhuman primate's smile also indicates nonaggressiveness.

Posture This is a common communicative device among animals. Dogs, for example, lower the front part of their bodies and extend their front legs when they are playful. They lower their whole bodies to the ground when they are submissive. Postural communication is found in both human and nonhuman primates as well.

Gesture A gesture may be defined as active posturing. Humans wave their arms in recognition or farewell, dogs wave their tails in excitement, and cats flick their tails when irritated. Many birds perform elaborate gestures of raising and lowering the head or racing back and forth across the water in their mating rituals.

14.2 COMMUNICATION STRUCTURE

Underlying this bewildering variety of communicative methods are certain common elements. An understanding of these is necessary for comparing the differences and similarities among communicative systems. Communication relies on using something to stand for something else. Words are an obvious example of this: you do not have to have a car, a sandwich, or your cousin present in order to talk about them—the words *car*, *sandwich*, and *cousin* stand for them instead. This same phenomenon is found in animal communication as well. Instead of fighting over territory, for example, many animals produce sounds or make gestures that threaten and intimidate intruders—the message replaces the attack. Birds utter warning calls that represent the presence of a threat. A threatening animal or human need not be seen by other birds before they take flight—the message replaces visual perception of the threat.

Each of these things that stand for other things is technically known as a **sign**. The sign is a unit of communication structure that consists of two parts: a **signifier**, be it a word, a scent, a gesture, or an electrical frequency, and something **signified** that exists in the real world, and which is mentally represented by the sign—the sign's conceptual content. The real world can be thought of as either external, mental, or emotional, and so what is signified by a sign can be as diverse as a tree, an abstract idea, a perception, or a feeling. Because their content is conceptual, all signs are associated with some **meaning**, such as 'danger' or 'item of furniture with legs and a flat top'. Individual instances of signs are called **tokens**. For example, in the sentence *The baby threw the rattle* there are five word tokens, but only four signs; *the* occurs twice as a token, but it is the same sign in both instances. Figure 14.2 illustrates these distinctions.

The study of signs is known as **semiotics**. Semiotics is a field of study that links many diverse disciplines, among them linguistics, anthropology, philosophy, zoology, genetics, literary study, and computer science. Since an understanding of signs is essential for understanding how messages are transmitted, the next section examines their structure in more detail.

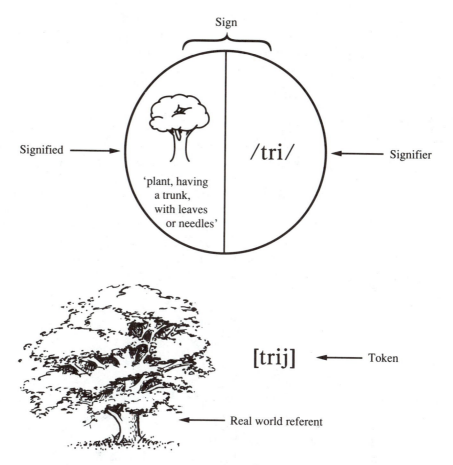

Figure 14.2 A sign

The Signifier A signifier is that part of a sign that stimulates at least one sense organ of the receiver of a message. The phonological component of the word *tree*, represented as /tri/ and pronounced [trij] is a typical linguistic signifier. A signifier can also be a picture, a photograph, a sign language gesture, or one of the many other words for *tree* in different languages.

The Signified The signified component of the sign refers to both the real world object it represents and its conceptual content.

The first of these is the real world content of the sign and its *extension* or *referent* (Chapter 6) within a system of signs such as English, avian communication, or sign language. In our example, the referent is represented by a drawing since there is no room to include a real tree between the pages of this book. (Of course, the signifier [trij] could also have a picture of a tree as its referent.) It is easiest to think of referents as concepts or persons or things, but they may be ideas or feelings as well.

The signified component of a sign also evokes an *intension* (Chapter 6) to users of the system in question. A word for 'tree' evokes concepts that probably include 'plant', 'having a trunk', and 'bearing leaves or needles' in the minds of speakers of any language who are familiar with trees. Animals appear to conceptualize in terms of classes or categories as well. Certain monkeys, for example, distinguish among various types of predators on the basis of size, shape, and motion (see Section 14.5).

Types of Signs

Signs can be divided into three basic types, depending on (1) whether the signifier naturally resembles its referent, (2) whether the signifier is directly (causally) linked with the referent in a physical or mechanical sense, or (3) whether signifier and referent are arbitrarily associated.

Iconic Signs **Iconic** signs, or *icons*, always bear some resemblance to their referent. A photograph is an iconic sign; so too is a stylized silhouette of a female or a male on a restroom door. A baboon's open-mouth threat is iconic, resembling as it does the act of biting. Onomatopoeic words like *buzz*, *splat*, and *squish* in English and their counterparts in other human languages are also iconic in that they somewhat resemble what they signify.

Figure 14.3 Some iconic tokens: *a*. open-mouth threat by a Japanese macaque (*Macaca fuscata*); *b*. park recreation signs; *c*. onomatopoeic words in English

Icons are widespread in the communication systems of all animals; many postures and gestures that are critical to animal communication are iconic, as are the postures and gestures used by humans. Human linguistic communication, however, does not make extensive use of iconic signs.

Indexical Signs An **indexical** sign, or *index*, fulfills its function by pointing out its referent, typically by being a partial sample of it. Indexes are not arbitrary, since their presence has in some sense been caused by their referent. For this reason it is sometimes said that there is a causal link between an indexical sign and its referent. The track of an animal, for example, points to the existence of the animal by representing a part of it. The presence of smoke is an index of fire.

Most important for our discussion here is a specific kind of indexical sign called a **symptomatic** sign, or *symptom*. Symptomatic signs spontaneously convey the internal state or emotions of the sender and thus represent the sender in an indexical manner. For example, the fact that our body temperature rises when we are ill is a spontaneous reflection of our internal state. When someone steps on our foot and we cry out, the cry is a spontaneous reflection of our internal state and thus constitutes a symptomatic sign.

Since symptomatic signs are spontaneous, we do not consider them to be deliberately selected by the sender for purposes of communication. We do not choose to cry out in pain in the same way as we might, for example, decide to call our dwelling place a *house*, *home*, *dwelling*, or *residence* in the appropriate circumstances. As forms of communication, symptomatic signs are therefore used primarily by the receiver of a message to assess the internal state of the sender. Since senders do not deliberately choose to send the signal, the message is assumed to be essentially out of their control.

Symbolic Signs **Symbolic** signs bear an arbitrary relationship to their referents and in this way are distinct from both icons and indexes. Human language is highly symbolic in that the vast majority of its signs bear no inherent resemblance or causal connection to their referents, as the following words show. No phonological property of the words in Figure 14.4 gives you any hint as to

```
hana    = ?
prozor  = ?
talo    = ?
kum     = ?
berat   = ?
```

Figure 14.4 Arbitrary sound-meaning correspondence in language

their possible meaning. (*Hana* means 'flower' or 'nose' in Japanese, *prozor* is 'window' in Serbo-Croatian, *talo* is 'house' in Finnish, *kum* means 'sand' in Turkish, and *berat* means 'heavy' in Indonesian.)

We encounter many other symbolic signs in everyday life. The hexagonal shape of a stop sign is symbolic; it bears no inherent connection with the message it helps to communicate. The colors used in traffic signals are symbolic as well; red has no more inherent connection with the act of stopping than yellow.

Mixed Signs Signs are not always exclusively of one type or another. Symptomatic signs, for example, may have iconic properties, as when a dog opens its mouth in a threat to bite. Symbolic signs such as traffic lights are symptomatic in that they reflect the internal state of the mechanism that causes them to change color. Still, we classify a sign according to its major property: if it resembles its referent, it is iconic; if it is linked to its referent in some causal way or provides some partial sample of it, it is indexical (and symptomatic if it spontaneously expresses some internal state), and if its relationship to its referent is arbitrary, it is a symbol.

Signals All signs can act as **signals** when they trigger a specific action on the part of the receiver, as do traffic lights, words in human language such as the race starter's "Go!", or the warning calls of birds. Typically, a signal releases more energy in the receiver than it takes for the transmitter to send it. For example, the simple release of a mating pheremone into the wind by a female moth (a symptomatic sign and also a signal) can cause the male to fly as much as six kilometers in search of her. Signals are very common in animal communication, but only a limited subset of human linguistic activity consists of signaling.

Sign Structure

No matter what their type, signs show different kinds of structure. A basic distinction is made between **graded** and **discrete** signs.

Graded Signs Graded signs convey their meaning by changes in degree. A good example of a gradation in communication is voice volume. The more you want to be heard, the louder you speak along an increasing scale of loudness. There are no steps or jumps from one level to the next that can be associated with a specific change in meaning.

Gradation is common in many forms of communication. The hands of most clocks move in a graded manner, as does the needle of an automobile speedometer. Many animal signals, such as the barking of dogs, are graded as well. A goose has essentially one type of honk, which may become louder and faster as it takes off in flight, but does not become another kind of honking. The gradually increasing fear in the facial expression of the monkey depicted in Figure 14.5 is also a graded sign.

Figure 14.5 Some graded signs: the facial expressions *a*, *b*, and *c* of the macaque monkey represent just three points on a continuum expressing fear; *a*. is a neutral face; *b*. expresses slight fear; and *c*. expresses extreme fear. Each expression grades into the next. The hands of the clock in *d*. express minutes in a graded manner.

Discrete Signs Discrete signs are distinguished from each other by "step-wise" differences. There is no gradual transition from one sign to the next. The phonemes of human language are good examples of discrete signs. Contrasting stop and fricative phonemes in English are perceived as either voiced or voiceless—there is no intermediate category. The digital displays of watches are discrete as well, since they progress from one minute (or even second) to the next with no gradation. Traffic lights, too, are discrete signs; there is no gradual shifting from green to yellow to red. Some examples of discrete signs are given in Figure 14.6.

All three kinds of signs—*iconic*, *symbolic*, and *symptomatic*—may be graded or discrete. The gradual baring of its fangs by a threatening canine is

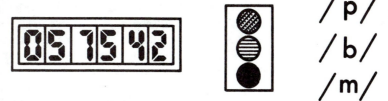

Figure 14.6 Some discrete tokens

iconic and graded. A photograph is iconic and discrete. Morse code is symbolic and discrete, but a slowly dimming light that signals the beginning of a theatrical performance is symbolic and graded. Symptomatic signs, too, may be discrete (the traffic light again) or graded (the crying of a child or the act of blushing).

It is possible for a discrete sign to be internally graded, and even to slip over into another type by degrees. Human crying, for example, is interpreted by experimental subjects as becoming gradually more like screaming as the audible intake of breath between sobs becomes shorter and shorter. Figure 14.7 illustrates this

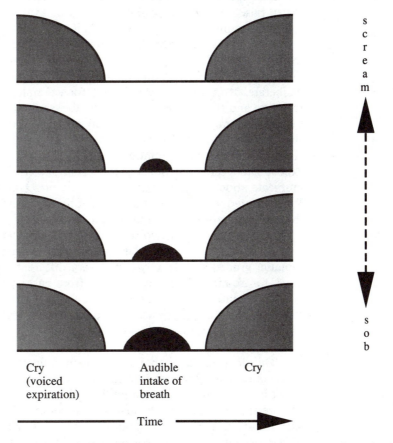

Figure 14.7 The graded continuum from sobbing to screaming (the height of the stippled and blackened areas represents the audibility of the vocalization and the width its time): both sob and scream are discrete signs, even though each grades into the other.

phenomenon. At the extreme ends of the continuum, there is no difficulty interpreting the sound as one or the other, although it is difficult to say precisely when a 'sob' becomes a 'scream'. Thus we can say that 'sobbing' and 'screaming' are discrete symptomatic signs, but each of them is internally graded, and their gradations overlap. The same is true of many vocalizations in animal communication.

A View of Animal Communication

Most animal language, it is claimed, shows little arbitrariness. It is said to be largely symptomatic and not deliberate, conscious, or symbolic. For example, if a monkey gives a certain cry in the presence of danger, it is assumed that the monkey is spontaneously signaling its fear by vocalizing but is not deliberately warning other group members of the danger. The vocalization is interpreted and used by other members of a group for their own benefit.

In the past, the acquisition of communicative systems by animals was said to be largely devoid of learning and experience. Rather, it was claimed that the systems are rather strictly limited by genetic inheritance, and in this sense radically unlike human language, the acquisition of which requires exposure to a mature system. This limitation certainly appears to be true in some cases. When raised in isolation, animals as diverse as the fox, the elephant seal, the cat, and certain monkeys develop the full range of vocalizations typical of their species. However, as we see in Section 14.4, the situation can be more complex than this.

It is further claimed that animal communication is neither conscious nor deliberate. It is not widely believed, for example, that a monkey assesses a situation and then deliberately chooses to warn others of danger by selecting a token from a repertoire of meaningful sound symbols at its disposal. The term **stimulus-bound** is also used to describe animal communication, since it is often claimed that animal communication occurs only when it is triggered by exposure to a certain stimulus or for certain specific ends. Animals do not communicate about anything but the here and now. As the philosopher Bertrand Russell noted, "No matter how eloquently a dog may bark, it cannot tell you that its parents were poor but honest."

With respect to structure, animal communication is said to show few traces of discrete structuring beyond the obvious fact that one group of symptomatic, graded signals may sound very different from another. Whining in dogs, for example, is clearly different from barking, but both are assumed to be symptomatic. Combining and recombining of discrete units of structure such as phonemes, morphemes, and words are not characteristic of the way animals communicate. Dogs do not combine whines and barks to make novel messages.

This does not mean that animal communication consists of random emotional outbursts. Nor does it mean that animal communication does not show structure. Animal communication is both complex and organized. Evolutionary pressure has guaranteed that animal communication is optimally in tune with the survival requirements of each species. The electrical communication of Amazonian eels is an excellent means of communication in muddy waters. The danger whistle of a small, tree-dwelling primate is ideal for nocturnal communication in dense forest. Small jungle frogs in South America communicate by sticking out their long and colorful legs, ideal for sending messages in the dim and noisy jungle. But jungle frogs do not try new combinations of leg movements in order to come up with an original message, any more than the electric eel recombines frequencies in order to signal something it has never conveyed before. Animal communication appears to be severely limited in the messages it can convey.

Recent work on animal communication has often focused on its relationship to human linguistic communication. The next sections examine communication among several kinds of animals and compare it with human language.

14.3 THE BEES

I have no doubt that some will attempt to "explain" the performances of the bees as the results of reflexes and instincts. . . . for my part, I find it difficult to assume that such perfection and flexibility in behavior can be reached without some kind of mental processes going on in the small heads of the bees.

August Krogh, *Scientific American*

The System

Forager bees display a remarkable system of communicating the location of a food source to other bees in their hive. When a food source has been discovered, the forager flies back to the hive and communicates information about it by performing special movements (which humans call *dancing*) before other members of the hive. The dancing conveys information about the location of the food source, its quality, and its distance from the hive.

Distance Distance is conveyed by one of three different dances performed on the wall or floor of the hive (some species have only two different dances, and so may be said to have a different "dialect"). In doing the round dance, the bee circles repeatedly. This indicates a food source within five meters or so of the hive. The sickle dance indicates a food source from five to twenty meters from the hive. It is performed by the bee dancing a curved figure-eight shape. The tail-wagging dance indicates distances further than twenty meters. In this dance, the bee wags its abdomen as it moves forward, circles to the right back to its starting point, repeats the wagging forward motion, and circles left. The cycle then begins again.

Direction The round dance does not communicate direction, presumably since the food source is so close to the hive. The direction of more distant food sources is indicated in the other two types of dance.

As the bee performs the sickle and tail-wagging dances, it is simultaneously indicating the direction of the food source. Bees orient themselves in flight relative to the angle of the sun. When the dancing is performed on the vertical wall of the hive, it is apparently "understood" that the top of the hive wall represents the current position of the sun in the sky. During the sickle dance, the angle of the open side of the figure eight relative to the hive's vertical alignment indicates the direction of flight toward the food source relative to the sun. When the bee performs the tail-wagging dance, the angle of its wagging path relative to the hive's vertical angle indicates the path of flight toward the food source relative to the sun. Figure 14.8 illustrates the dances and their manner of indicating the direction of the food source.

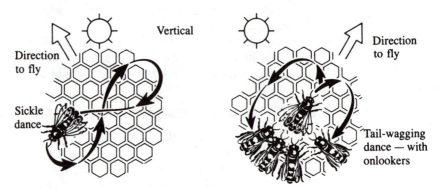

Figure 14.8 Bee dancing

Quality Quality of the food source is indicated by the intensity of the dancing and the number of repetitions of the circling movements. As the food source is depleted, the dance is performed with less vivacity.

Other Factors These messages are not communicated with perfect accuracy, nor are they the only ones involved in bee communication. Bees also leave a hive-specific pheremone trace at the site of the food source, thereby directing their fellow foragers to the precise location. The bees also carry back traces of the food source odors, which further aid other bees in the search. A whole complex of communicative modes operating on different channels—a **constellation**—is employed in bee communication.

Bees and Humans

How does bee communication compare with human language? The three patterns that the bees dance are in no way inherently connected with the messages they communicate and so are symbolic in nature. The communication of direction is iconic, and in this sense may be comparable to a human gesture. It is, however, a very sophisticated iconicity mixed with a symbolic element, since the bees are able to transfer the horizontal flight path to a vertical representation on the hive wall. The expression of food source quality is, in all probability, symptomatic: the more stimulated a bee is by the quality of the food source, the faster it dances.

The total communicative constellation involves other passive sources of communication as well, such as pheremones and food source samples. The performance even involves audience participation. During its dancing, the returning bee is expected to provide samples from the food source. If it fails to, it may be stung to death.

Bee communication, then, like human language, shows symbolic, iconic, and symptomatic traits, as well as interaction between sender and receiver of the messages. But there is a major difference between the two systems of communication. The topic of bee communication is severely constrained. Bees communicate only about food sources. Furthermore, their potential for communication is very limited. Only certain locations of food sources can be conveyed. Bees cannot communicate the notion of up or down. They can be easily tricked into communicating the wrong direction of the food if a strong light source is placed in an incorrect position with relation to the food. They can also be tricked into giving the wrong information about distance to the food source if they are forced to walk or stop several times on route. This indicates that they gauge distance by time. The bees show no means of assessing varying information and of communicating this fact. Their system of communication appears to be closed ended and limited to a specific number of facts about a specific type of information.

It also appears that bee language is largely innate—that is, there is very little need for a new forager bee to be exposed to the system in the presence of other bees. Foragers on their first flight perform the appropriate dances, although they refine their performance to some extent with time and exposure to other dancing. Their flight orientation to the sun is imperfect at first, but it develops within a few hours.

The innateness of bee dancing has been tested by cross-breeding Austrian bees, which do not perform the sickle dance to express intermediate distance of the food source from the hive, with Italian honeybees, which do. The results of such experiments further support a genetic interpretation of bee communication. In a cross-breeding experiment, the bees that bore a physical resemblance to their Italian parent performed the sickle dance to indicate intermediate distance 98 percent of the time. The bees that bore a physical resemblance to their Austrian parent performed the round dance to indicate intermediate distance 96 percent of the time; they did not perform the sickle dance at all. The dance pattern used in a specific situation appears to be inherited from a certain parent along with other more obvious genetic traits.

In 1948, when the Danish physiologist August Krogh made the statement quoted at the beginning of this section, he struck at the widely accepted notion that animal behavior was either the result of some kind of conditioning or, in some ill-defined way, instinctive. Much has been learned since then about the enormous quantity of information imparted by genetic transfer. It is now possible to state with a fair degree of certainty that the complex and sophisticated behavior of bees and other equally remarkable insects is in all probability largely genetically predetermined and, unlike human language, it relies very little on exposure to the mature system in order to be acquired.

14.4 THE BIRDS

How intelligent is a creature that can amuse himself for fifteen minutes by uttering, over and over, the following sounds: uhr, uhr, uhr, Uhr, URH, URH, Wah, Wah, wah, wah, wah.

Jake Page (on his Amazon Parrot)

Bird Vocalization

Birds, as Jake Page later found out, can do a lot more than utter sounds over and over. Even the parrot, which has been labeled for years as nothing but a stimulus-bound mimic, has been shown to have some capacity for meaningful labeling (although it took a test parrot four years to acquire a vocabulary of eighteen nouns). The parroting of trained birds is nothing more than a non-intentional response to an external stimulus arrived at through repetitive conditioning. Natural communication among birds is far more interesting than the performances of trained ones, and efforts to understand how birds communicate have shed light on parallels in human linguistic communication.

Bird vocalization can be divided into two types, **call** and **song**. Calls are typically short bursts of sound or simple patterns of notes. Songs are lengthy, elaborate patterns of mostly pitched sounds.

Calls Calls serve very specific functions in the bird community. They typically warn of predators, coordinate flocking and flight activity, express aggression, or accompany nesting or feeding behavior. The cawing of crows is a typical call. It seems to convey a generalized mobilization to possible danger. When a crow hears cawing, it flies up to a tree if it is on the ground, or flies higher in a tree—or to another tree—if it is already in one. (If there are crows in your neighborhood, you can test this yourself, as cawing is easy to imitate.)

In some birds, individual calls are associated with specific activities; a danger call is quite different from a call given when birds are grouped in flight. A flight call is generally short, crisp, and easy to locate by other group members. The honking of geese in flight is a typical example of this sort of call. Because it is loud and easy to locate, it is well suited to enable the bird flock to stay together. The call given by small birds when larger avian predators threaten them is very different. It is typically thin and high-pitched. This kind of sound is difficult to locate, and so can be given as a warning without revealing the position of the caller. Such functional utility is typical of bird calls, and in fact, calls that serve the same communicative purpose are often remarkably similar among different species of birds.

Songs Birdsong is different from calling. Although calls are produced year round, singing is largely seasonal. Furthermore, it is generally only male birds that sing.

The main purposes of song are, as far as we know, to announce and delimit the territory of the male and to attract a mate. Birds establish territory for breeding purposes and defend it vigorously. Across the United States, it is a common sight in the spring to see a pair of red-winged blackbirds (*Agelaius phoeniceus*) team up to drive away a male of their species that has strayed into their territory. The use of song enables male birds to establish and maintain this territory without constant patrolling and fighting. Moreover, once a bird has established its territory, its song serves to attract and maintain contact with a mate. It follows that birdsong is unique from species to species, and even varies to some degree from bird to bird within the same species, since its purposes require species and individual recognition.

In some species, songs are nothing more than a successive repetition of calls. In others, songs consist of complex patterns of pitches—sometimes called syllables—that form longer repeated units or themes. The sometimes elaborate complexity of song structure reflects individual variation among the singers, and, as pointed out previously, serves a specific purpose. Figure 14.9 shows a

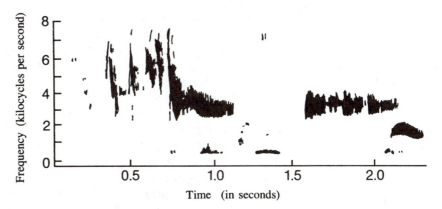

Figure 14.9 Spectrograph of a robin song

spectrograph (an acoustic recording that shows pitch and intensity of sound) of the song of the European robin (*Erithacus rubecula*). Note how the different subsections of the song are distinct and recognizable. There is also some evidence that sections of a song are combined in different orders by certain birds. There is no evidence that recombination is associated with different meanings.

Avian Dialects There is evidence for both song and call dialects among bird species. Researchers even speak of avian isoglosses, lines that can be drawn on a map to indicate shared characteristics among dialects, and that are based on variations in the melody of song syllables or themes (see Figure 14.10). The reason for the existence of dialects is still unclear; it may be no more than a reflection of individual avian variation in song and call learning. If it is, we are led to an intriguing issue in the relationship of bird vocalization to human language—the question of how bird vocalizations are acquired.

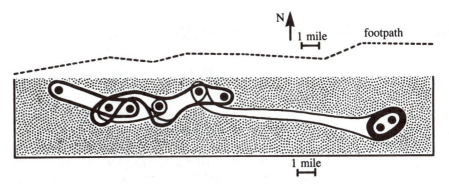

Figure 14.10 Avian isoglosses: call patterns of male Hill Mynas (Shaded area indicates forested hills; unshaded is open plain.)

Birds and Humans

The acquisition of call and song by birds shows interesting parallels with recent hypotheses about the acquisition of language by human children (see Chapter 10). Though a great deal of bird vocalization—particularly calls—appears to be innate, there is much that appears to be acquired. Studies of avian dialects have shown that birds reared in the same nest acquire different song dialects when they live in different dialect areas. It also appears to be the case that singing ability is lateralized in the left brains of birds, as is linguistic ability in humans. Still more significant for linguistic study is the fact that some birds must acquire the species-specific characteristics of their song within a certain time-span or critical period.

A number of bird species do not develop fully characteristic songs if they are prevented from hearing them during the early stages of their lives. The chaffinch (*Fringilla coelebs*) is one such bird. If chaffinches are reared in isolation, they sing, but replicate only in a general way the typical song of the species. If young chaffinches are reared away from fully developed singers, but with other young chaffinches, the entire experimental "community" develops an identical song. Finally, chaffinches that have been exposed to only some part of the fully developed song (those that are captured in the autumn of the first year of life) will, the following spring, develop a song that is partially typical but not completely well formed.

These experiments indicate that there are some songbirds that have both an innate and a learned component in their song. The innate component predisposes them to perform a general song that is extremely simplified. This has been called a **template** or a blueprint. Only exposure to the fully formed song of the species will enable them to produce the correct song. (Exposure to other song causes some species to imitate in this direction; other species simply do not acquire anything they are exposed to unless it is their own species-characteristic song.) Finally, it is clear that certain birds do not acquire their characteristic song in a brief span of time, but that several seasons of exposure are required. The evidence from songbird studies, while not transferable directly to humans, gives strong support to the idea that a combination of innate and learned components is one way that the acquisition of complex behavior takes place in nature.

14.5 NONHUMAN PRIMATES

Some animals share qualities of both man and the four-footed beasts, for example, the ape, the monkey, and the baboon.

Aristotle, *On Animals*

Fascination with nonhuman primates goes far back in human history. Their social behavior has long been seen as an amusing (and sometimes instructive) parody of human behavior. Since the establishment of the fact that we are closely related genetically to these animals—some 99 percent of our genetic matter is shared with chimpanzees and gorillas—the resemblance of their behavioral, social, and communicative traits to ours has been seen as more than an amusing counterpart to human activity. Recently, the question of our shared cognitive, and especially linguistic ability, has become more important; it is thought that a better understanding of nonhuman primates may shed light on the evolution of human social and cognitive abilities.

Primates form a large class of mammals, which range from the tiny tarsier to the imposing mountain gorilla. Some are nocturnal, some diurnal in their activity cycle. Some are solitary, some form part of complex social groups. Many are tree-dwelling, but many are ground-dwelling. Some are quadrupeds, and some show periods of bipedal locomotion. Figure 14.11 shows one widely accepted classification of primates.

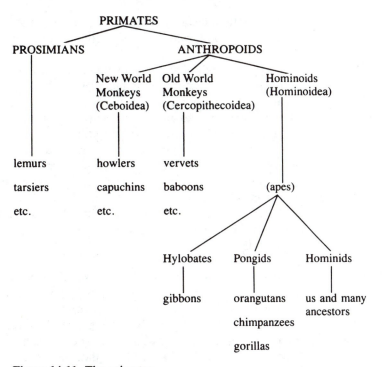

Figure 14.11 The primates

The prosimians are an evolutionarily early group found on the island of Malagasy, in Sub-Saharan Africa, and in Southeast Asia. New World Monkeys range from Mexico through South America. Among them are the only primates with prehensile (grasping) tails. Old World Monkeys include the many tree- and ground-dwelling species of Africa and the Far East. The larger nonhuman primates—baboons, chimpanzees, and gorillas—are not native to North and South America. Baboons, large, mainly ground-dwelling primates, are found from central to northern Africa. They show a high degree of social organization, intelligence, and aggressiveness. The hominoids include the agile gibbons, solitary orangutans (both found only in Southeast Asia), the large but peaceful gorillas, chimpanzees, and humans.

The validity of studies of communication among captive primates has been criticized because the animals' social existence is highly limited and compromised in zoos. Studies of nonhuman primate communication have largely left the zoo and laboratory and moved into the animals' natural habitat. While careful observation of nonhuman primate communication is still the basis of this work, the use of playback experiments, in which tape recordings of natural calls are played back over hidden loudspeakers, has led to a greater understanding of the communicative systems of these animals.

In the next section, we first turn our attention to nonhuman primate communication in the wild. It is there that we can gain an initial understanding of how forms of nonhuman primate communication resemble or differ from our own in terms of function and structure.

Some Functions of Nonhuman Primate Communication

Although the societal existence of even the most gregarious nonhuman primate is relatively simple when compared to that of humans, primates communicate for many different reasons.

Typical nonhuman primate communication serves to mark and announce territory, to warn other group members of danger, to seek or maintain contact with a mate or other members of the species, and to interact with members of the troop or species in various ways we can call "socializing". Socializing vocalizations are particularly important in mother-child bonding and in primate groups with a complex and hierarchical social structure. In these groups, it is important to know which members have a higher or lower rank so that group members can behave accordingly in their presence. Vocalization is a key factor in maintaining this behavior.

As we briefly survey some aspects of the structure of nonhuman primate communicative systems, we will also refer to the ways in which structure and function are linked.

Prosimian Communication

Prosimian communication shows a small repertoire of sounds that are patterned into discrete groups. The lemur (*Lemur catta*) of Madagascar is a typical prosimian with respect to its vocal communication system. It has been described as making essentially two types of vocalization, noises and calls, each of which shows some grading. The vocalizations appear to be symptomatic. They are classified in Table 14.1; quasi-phonetic descriptions like *spat* should be interpreted as onomatopoeic. Each graded set of sounds is used in a circumscribed range of situations. The calls, in particular, are limited to threat or fear encounters. They seem to form a graded series, ranging from the *light spat* to the *bark* in intensity.

A small repertoire of distinct vocalizations is the norm among prosimians. The slow loris (*Nycticebus coucang*), an Asian prosimian, is reported to have no more than five calls.

Table 14.1 Lemur vocalization

Noises		Calls	
Sound	Context	Sound	Context
single click	in response to strange objects	light spat (yip)	when driving off threatening inferiors
clicks, grunts	during locomotion, or for friendly greeting	spat	when crowded or handled roughly
purr	while grooming	bark	when startled

Monkeys

The study of communication among the many varieties of New and Old World Monkeys is too vast for this chapter. An oversimplified picture reflects what most researchers agree is primarily a symptomatic system, but one that shows a larger number of signs, with more gradation among them, than does the communication of prosimians.

One study of the Bonnet Macaque (*Macaca radiata*), a South Asian monkey, presents a system of twenty-five different basic patterns that are used in various social interactions, including contact, agonistic encounters, foraging, greeting, sexual contact, and alarm giving. These vocalizations are determined by correlating observation with spectrographic analysis; descriptive labels are also given to the vocalizations, such as *whoo*, *rattle*, *growl*, *whistle*, and *bark*. These basic patterns are described as grading into each other. It is also claimed that they occur in combinations. There is no evidence, however, that these recombinations mean anything novel when they occur.

The communication systems of many monkeys appear to be genetically determined. This has been established by raising newborns in isolation. However, this statement cannot be made for all monkeys. In some cases, input from the adult system appears to be required. The study of one small monkey has suggested that not all monkey vocalizations are symptomatic, and that experience and learning can play a role in the acquisition of the communicative system.

The East African vervet monkey (*Cercopithecus aethiops*) is said to have three distinctive and arbitrary calls that announce the presence of either eagles, snakes, or large mammals posing a threat. These calls are associated with different responses by the monkeys. When they hear the eagle call, the monkeys look up or run into the bushes. The snake call causes them to look down at the ground near them. The mammal alarm sees them run up into the trees, or climb higher in a tree if they are already in one.

These findings, which appear to have been well established by playback experimentation since they were first reported in 1967, suggest that not all non-human primates rely strictly on symptomatic signals to communicate or to trigger behavior in other monkeys. It is claimed rather that the vervets assess the potential danger situation and then choose a specific call with a clearly defined referent to announce the danger. Furthermore, each call is a vocalization signifier that is arbitrarily linked with its referent. Other monkeys respond appropriately to the calls without necessarily observing the danger themselves. All this taken together suggests a cognitive ability for classification of objects in the world and an ability to link this classification system to arbitrary sounds for purposes of intentional communication (see Figure 14.12).

The vervet may not be an isolated case. Goeldi's Monkey (*Callimico goeldii*), found in South America, is cited as having five different alarm calls, three of which are used when terrestrial predators approach, and two of which have been heard in the presence of large birds. Such observations support the claim that monkeys have the cognitive capacity to associate perceptual categories with vocalizations.

The acquisition of these signals among vervets is interesting. Infant vervets appear to distinguish innately among broad classes of mammals, snakes, and birds, but they also give the "eagle call" when other birds appear and the "leopard call" when other terrestrial mammals appear. Adults distinguish between leopards and less dangerous mammals, and eagles and less dangerous birds (as well as between snakes and sticks), and it is claimed that this ability

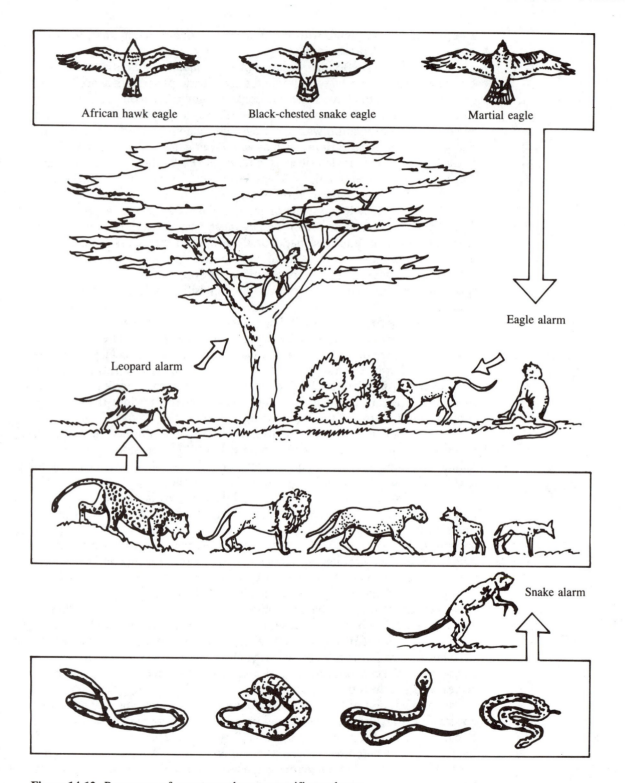

Figure 14.12 Responses of vervet monkeys to specific predators

must be perfected through experience. This once again suggests that a mixture of innate components and learning is typical of the way communication systems are naturally acquired.

Gibbons, Orangutans, and Chimpanzees

Since the higher primates are close genetic relatives of humans, it is natural to expect their vocal communication to resemble that of humans. Perhaps surprisingly, communication among the higher primates does not show much indication of discrete vocal signs that could be interpreted as resembling human words. Rather, the communication systems of these animals are made up of groups of graded vocal signs.

Gibbons and Orangutans Gibbons display an interesting form of vocal interaction known as duetting. **Duetting**, the interchange of calls in a patterned manner between two members of a species, is found among certain birds, bats, and even antelopes. Duetting is, however, atypical of primate communication—among the hominoids, only gibbons perform it. Recent playback experiments show that duetting among gibbons serves to maintain spacing among territories much as does birdsong (see Section 14.4). Playback of duetting within a gibbon's territory will cause it to approach the apparent source of the vocalizations, possibly with the intent of driving the intruders out. Playback of singing and duetting from outside a group's territory only infrequently evokes a response. Recognition of individuals does not appear to play a role in these vocalizations.

Unlike gibbons, which live in family groups, orangutans largely keep to themselves (except for mother-child pairs). Among the solitary forest males, loud calls serve a territorial and spacing function. These calls also identify the individuals who produce them. High-ranking males approach calls, presumably to confront the intruder, while low-ranking males stay away from areas where they hear the calls of high-ranking males. These calls are, in other words, indexes, which stand in for the individual animals themselves, and orangutans must identify and assess each of these calls before acting on them.

Chimpanzees Chimpanzees vocalize with a number of graded calls. As many as sixteen types have been reported. Some of these appear to show rather specific referents. Chimps typically hoot to signal location (a sound that carries well in dense forest). Hooting is also used in greeting or when chimps are excited about something. Another typical vocalization is known as rough grunting and is given in the presence of a favorite food source. A recent experiment has led to the claim that transmission of signs from one generation to the next plays a role in the acquisition of certain signs among chimpanzees.

"Language" in the Wild? Especially among highly socialized species, nonhuman primate vocalizations all show a great deal of variation. There is every indication that their vocalizations form part of a constellation of communicative acts including gesture, posture, gaze (eye "pointing"), and the expression of affect, all of which must be interpreted by other troop members. The obvious complexity of communication systems among these animals suggests that the level of mental activity devoted to communicative behavior is quite high.

Despite the high degree of intelligence and social organization these animals demonstrate, there is very little evidence for arbitrary relationships between sound and meaning among apes. Even more significantly, there is no evidence of recombining various sections of a message to form new messages. Nothing that parallels the phonemic or morphological recombination of human language has been discovered in the natural communication systems of nonhuman primates.

It is possible that the lack of parallels with human linguistic communication in species closely related to our own may be due to the nature of their social organization. The small groups or family units typical of chimpanzees and gorillas living in a food-rich environment may not have required the development of any other mode of communication. What has evolved is suited to their needs. This does not mean, however, that our near-relatives do not possess any of the cognitive abilities necessary for using a system of communication akin to human language. There is some evidence, for example, of left hemisphere development of the type associated with human linguistic ability. A number of recent experiments with nonhuman primates have attempted to determine the extent—if any—of their linguistic abilities.

14.6 TESTING NONHUMAN PRIMATES FOR LINGUISTIC ABILITY

Much attention has been paid in recent years to nonhuman primates that are supposedly able to communicate with humans through the use of sign language.

Controlled testing of the possible shared linguistic abilities of nonhuman primates and humans goes back to 1948, when two psychologists attempted to train Viki, a young chimpanzee, to say meaningful words in English. With great effort, Viki learned to approximate the pronunciations of a few words like *cup* and *papa* over a period of fourteen months. But the experiment was doomed to failure from the start, because the vocal fold structure and supralaryngeal anatomy of the chimpanzee is unsuited for producing human sounds.

Chimpanzee vocal folds are fatty and less muscular than those of humans, and the neurological pathways between the brain and vocal folds are less developed than in humans. The chimpanzee's epiglottis extends well up into the throat cavity, which lessens the range of sounds it can produce. Finally, the whole larynx-tongue linkage rests higher in the chimpanzee throat, which results in limitations on its humanlike sound production as well. In short, the chimpanzee is unsuited for human speech, and concentrating effort on teaching it to articulate words was distracting from the more provocative question: to what extent is the chimp capable of linguistic behavior?

Some Experiments

An experiment conducted from 1965 to 1972 by Allen and Beatrice Gardner with a young female chimpanzee named Washoe created a new perspective on nonhuman primate linguistic abilities. The Gardners attempted to raise Washoe much as a human child would be raised, and to teach her American

Sign Language (Ameslan), on the assumption that it was a genuinely linguistic form of communication (of which there is no doubt). Given the known manual dexterity of chimpanzees, it was felt that sign language might provide a window on chimpanzee linguistic abilities.

Washoe The Gardners' reports claim that Washoe communicates intentionally with arbitrary signs in a creative manner, and thus shows the rudiments of human linguistic ability. Washoe learned to produce approximately 130 signs over a period of three years. (She recognized many more.) Most significantly, it is claimed that Washoe spontaneously combined these signs to form novel utterances. She is reported to have signed *water bird* on seeing ducks. Washoe also is said to have spontaneously produced *baby in my cup* when her toy doll was placed in her drinking cup and she was asked "What's that?"

Washoe was the first but not the only chimpanzee to be taught sign language. The results have suggested to some linguists that chimpanzees show greater ability to associate arbitrary tokens with referents than was believed earlier, and that they demonstrate rudimentary syntactic behavior. Other chimps, gorillas, and an orangutan that have been taught Ameslan since the pioneering Washoe experiment are reported to have performed even better.

Nim Still other experiments in teaching chimpanzees sign language have produced contradictory results. The achievements of a chimpanzee named Nim have been interpreted by his teachers as consisting of frequent repetitions of a small number of all-purpose signs (*Nim*, *me*, *you*, *eat*, *drink*, *more*, and *give*) that were largely appropriate to any context. These signs are said to have made up almost 50 percent of Nim's production. Furthermore, there are no reports of his engaging in creative combining of signs. It is also claimed that all of the signing chimps and gorillas are unconsciously cued by their trainers (there is more on this phonemenon in a later section).

Nonsigning Experiments

Much of the criticism leveled at Washoe's performance centered on the relative informality of her training and claims that Ameslan is a loose communicative system that does not require a strict adherence to syntactic rules. Two very different experiments with chimpanzees attempted to forestall such criticism.

Lana A chimpanzee called Lana was trained to fulfill her needs for food, fresh air, grooming, and entertainment (in the form of slide shows) by requesting these from a computer-controlled apparatus. Communication with the computer was carried out by means of a simple but syntactically rule-governed language of nine arbitrary symbols. The symbols were on buttons that lit up and activated the computer when pressed. Any deviation from the syntactic rule system invented for the experiment failed to get the desired responses from the computer. Human experimenters communicated directly with the chimpanzee through use of the same symbols. Lana learned to label and to request food and other amenities through the computer.

The experiment with Lana was criticized because she was said to have learned simple reflex associations among symbol, sequence, and reward, and was consequently not displaying linguistic abilities. There was no evidence that she had acquired the rules underlying the sequences, and so could not be said to have displayed linguistic abilities.

Sarah Another now-classic experiment involved training a young female chimp named Sarah to manipulate arbitrary plastic symbols in a predetermined manner in order to obtain rewards. Sarah had to learn to use word order correctly, since only the order in Figure 14.13 would obtain a banana.

Figure 14.13 Arbitrary symbols used in experiments with the chimpanzee Sarah

She also seemed to show sensitivity to more abstract words such as *if/then* in sentences like the one in Figure 14.14.

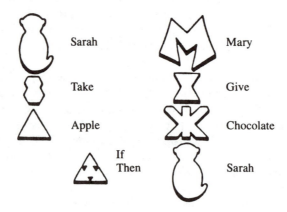

Figure 14.14 A "sentence" understood by Sarah

But was Sarah learning aspects of human language or was she, too, trained? Humans who are taught similar skills perform them as well as Sarah but find it difficult to translate them into human language. They approach the exercise of moving plastic symbols around to obtain a reward as a puzzle that is not necessarily associated with language. It has been suggested that Sarah was performing the same kind of puzzle-solving and not demonstrating human-like linguistic capacities.

These studies have led to a resurgence of interest in human-animal communication. Language-using dogs, cats, pigs, and even turtles have been reported for thousands of years. The basis of much of the current criticism of all of these experiments rests on the performance of a horse in Germany at the turn of this century.

The Clever Hans Controversy

When I play with my cat, who is to say that my cat is not playing with me?

Michel de Montaigne, *Essays*

In 1904, a Berlin school teacher named Wilhelm von Osten claimed to possess a horse that showed evidence of a humanlike capacity to think. His horse, Clever Hans (*der kluge Hans*), could supposedly calculate and convey messages by tapping out numbers or numbered letters of the alphabet with a front hoof or by nodding his head. Experimentation by a skeptical scientist, Oskar Pfungst, eventually showed that Clever Hans was not so much a creative thinker as a careful observer. The horse perceived cues that indicated he had performed correctly. For example, von Osten involuntarily moved his head very slightly when a correct answer had been reached. This movement was outside the normal perceptual range of human observers (less than five millimeters), but the horse had learned to associate it with the correct answer. When observers did not know the answer to a question, or when Clever Hans was blindfolded, he failed to perform his miracles.

Clever Hans's performance resulted from **dressage**, a type of interaction between trainer and animal that depends on the animal's interpreting subtle cues given by the trainer. The Clever Hans phenomenon is an excellent example of dressage, which need not involve conscious communication on the part of humans. The highly developed perceptual ability displayed by Clever Hans is common to many animals. Many scientists believe that chimpanzees and gorillas that use sign language and perform other languagelike tasks are demonstrating nothing more than the Clever Hans phenomenon.

The position is explained as follows. Human trainers want very much for their animal charges to succeed. This desire is translated into involuntary actions, which can be seized on by the animal due to its keen perceptual abilities; it is these cues that determine the animal's performance. A typical example of this is pointed out in Washoe's signing of *baby in my cup*, which has been recorded on film (*First Signs of Washoe*). A careful examination of this interchange shows that the human repeatedly holds out the object to be signed and then points rapidly at the cup. Probably none of this cueing was intentional on the human's part.

Some so-called linguistic activity may be the result of factors other than the Clever Hans effect. Some reports of creative signing, such as Washoe's *water bird*, are dismissed as reflex signing that shows no intention of forming combination on the part of the chimp. Reports of the gorilla Koko's wit (she occasionally produces the opposite sign of the one requested, such as *up* for 'down') are also considered to be exaggerated or simply wishful thinking by researchers.

Some reports of linguistic behavior are attributed to inaccurate or nonsystematic observing. (If Washoe answered *what's that* with any noun sign, the answer was considered correct.) Other reports are attributed to over-optimistic interpretation of signs. (Koko is reported to intentionally produce "rhyming" signs—those that are very similar to the one asked for or expected.) In short, those who do not view chimpanzee signing and symbol manipulation as linguistically relevant claim that this behavior is more simply explained as arising from straightforward response-reward association and/or from dressage, and not a reflection of linguistic competence. As one researcher noted, training two pigeons to bat a ping-pong ball across a net does not mean that the birds know the rules of ping-pong.

The Great Ape Debate

We believe that . . . there is no basis to conclude that signing apes acquired linguistic skills.

Mark S. Seidenberg and Laura Petitto

When these projects [Washoe, Lana, Sarah, and Nim] are taken together, it can be seen that chimpanzees are within the range of language behavior of humans and therefore have the capacity for language.

Roger Fouts

Researchers involved with the chimpanzees and gorillas who are being taught to sign attest to the emotional bonds they form with them, and also emphasize that even in human language, such bonds are a prerequisite to normal communication. They strongly insist that apes do communicate spontaneously and creatively with humans. Roger Fouts, who has spent many years in close contact with Washoe and other chimpanzees, puts the case this way.

> I reject the notion that there is some ultimate cut-and-dried criterion that distinguishes language from all other social and cognitive behaviors, or that distinguishes human communication and thought from that of all other species.

It is important to emphasize that most researchers sympathetic to the idea that apes show human linguistic abilities employ a broader definition of language than many of their critics. For these researchers, language use includes socialization and the use of communicative constellations.

For many linguists critical of these projects, a definition of language that rests on its social or functional aspects is unacceptable. In much current linguistic thinking, language is viewed as independent of the purposes it serves. This view, sometimes called the *linguistic autonomy hypothesis*, equates language with grammar—the "mental system that allows humans to form and interpret the words and sentences of their language," to quote from Chapter 1 of this text. It follows from this definition that linguistic ability in nonhuman primates can only be claimed to exist if the animals show, at the very least, spontaneous and intentional symbolic signs that are manipulated in a rule-governed manner.

Symbol Use All researchers who support the claim that nonhuman primates can employ intentional symbolic communication deny that cueing is a major factor in the apes' abilities, although most admit that it might be present on occasion. In order to refute charges of the Clever Hans effect, researchers employ a strict form of experimentation.

Primate sign-language researchers try to avoid cueing by the use of a **double-blind test**. In this test, the ape is shown objects or pictures of objects that are invisible to a second human researcher. The ape's signing is then recorded by this researcher, and interpreted by a third one. In this way, unintentional cueing is said to be avoided.

Critics of this research claim that even double-blind tests can be affected by human-animal interaction. First, the apes must be taught to perform the task. During this process they may be conditioned to provide certain responses. Secondly, it is difficult to avoid any human-animal interaction during these tests, and this could lead to subliminal cueing. As we have also seen, many claims for symbolic behavior on any ape's part have been dismissed as stimulus-response conditioning—the mere aping of behavior in order to obtain a reward. We still have no way of knowing whether Washoe's use of a sign sequence like TIME-EAT indicates that she has a concept of time.

Ongoing work with two chimpanzees named Sherman and Austin has led to their exchanging signed information about classes of objects such as 'tool' and 'food'. These experiments are claimed to have circumvented any reliance on the Clever Hans effect and shown that signing apes can communicate about whole referential classes of items rather than be bound to simple stimulus-response association with individual items such as 'banana' and 'ice cream'.

Careful control of experiments has convinced some linguists that limited symbol use has been exhibited by some apes, perhaps even up to the level of a two-year-old human child. But some linguists who allow that a level of symbolic signing has been achieved have also denied this is a critical feature for defining language. Rather, rule-governed, creative symbol combinations and syntactic behavior are said to be the critical features.

Creative Signing? A feature of language that sets it apart from most animal communication is its creativity—the fact that humans can use language to create novel messages. Sign researchers claim that such creativity is present in the many instances of novel combinations signed by the animals.

An early and famous instance of alleged creative signing was Washoe's WATER BIRD, which she signed on seeing a duck in the water for the first time. Such alleged compound signing behavior has been noted in various signing apes. Some of the gorilla Koko's novel combinations are provided in Table 14.2.

Table 14.2 Some sign combinations produced by Koko

Compound	Referent
MILK CANDY	rich tapioca pudding
FRUIT LOLLIPOP	frozen banana
PICK FACE	tweezers
BLANKET WHITE COLD	rabbit-fur cape
NOSE FAKE	mask
POTATO APPLE FRUIT	pineapple

Critics say either that such combinations are accidental or that the ape produces the two signs independently of each other and thus does not display true compounding. There is no doubt that Washoe signed both WATER in the presence of water, and BIRD in the presence of the bird, but there is no consistent indication from her other output that she has a rule of compound formation.

It has been claimed that in more recent and carefully controlled experiments with a pygmy chimpanzee (*Pan pansicus*) named Kanzi, statistically significant differences in the spontaneous ordering of symbols has been observed. The conclusion that has been drawn from this is that Kanzi has exhibited a form of grammatical rule. For example, Kanzi frequently used combinations of signs that link two actions, such as CHASE HIDE, TICKLE SLAP, and GRAB SLAP. In fifty-four out of eighty-four cases, the first sign corresponded to the invitation to play and the second to the type of play requested.

Is There Syntax? Claims for syntactic behavior among signing apes have also been made. Even though it has been claimed that the general (though loose) syntax of Ameslan is copied by the apes, reports on the signing chimp Nim showed that the animal had no consistent word-order patterning. In fact, Nim's syntactic output was structurally incoherent. His longest sentence is reported as GIVE ORANGE ME GIVE EAT ORANGE ME EAT ORANGE GIVE ME EAT ORANGE GIVE ME YOU.

Koko is said to have developed her own word order in noun phrases—the adjective consistently follows the noun it modifies. But it is difficult to prove claims for syntactic behavior in animal signing, since all signing forms constellations with facial expression and gestures and so may be said to reduce the need for rigorous syntax. Koko, for example, can sign a meaning like "I love Coca-Cola" by hugging herself (the sign for *love*) while signing COCA-COLA at the same time with her hands.

In spite of what is now considered to be the disappointment of the earlier studies (possibly because too much was expected of them), some controlled experimentation continues. Recently, the pygmy chimpanzee Kanzi is reported to have produced significant (though not wholly consistent) differences in the placement of animate agents in sign combinations. When another chimpanzee named Matata was grabbed, Kanzi produced GRAB MATATA, but when Matata performed an action such as biting, Kanzi produced MATATA BITE.

Lingering Doubts As we have seen, supporters of language use among apes have not yet proved to the satisfaction of their critics that genuine symbolic behavior is occurring, much less anything resembling rule-governed creativity in compounding or syntactic patterning.

Researchers who see the results of ape studies as positive evidence for linguistic ability in these animals claim that their opponents keep raising the stakes every time a chimp or a gorilla accomplishes something that could be interpreted as linguistic behavior. Possible evidence of symbol use or creative signing as evidence of linguistic ability is dismissed by these opponents as unsurprising or irrelevant. Supporters of ape studies note that such critics are motivated by a long tradition of viewing animals as "organic machines" that are locked into specific behavioral and communicative repertoires by their genetic inheritance, and that can therefore only respond automatically to a given situation with a narrow range of signs. Their own view, they claim, is at once more ancient and more modern in granting animals a certain as yet unknown degree of intentionality and cognitive ability in their behavior.

In general, recent experiments have established more convincingly than earlier ape studies that symbol use and referential behavior form part of the cognitive makeup of some nonhuman primates. Taken together with naturalistic studies, they help circumvent the claim that all evidence of symbol use among nonhuman primates is caused by the Clever Hans phenomenon.

Nonetheless, questions about creative sign combination and use of syntax still remain. Kanzi's alleged rules have been equated with those of a two-year-old child. But the major difference between a chimpanzee and a child at that point in their lives is that the elementary grammar of a two year old is the first hint of a full system that is rapidly developing and that will be in place in a matter of a few more years. While Kanzi's communicative behavior constitutes interesting evidence for a chimpanzee's awareness of the world, it does not unequivocally imply a system of grammar. It has been noted, for example, that Kanzi's "rules" are often bound up with a natural order of action or relationships (as when the sign GRAB precedes the sign SLAP).

The apparent lack of rule-governed behavior among signing apes (especially in the realm of syntax) remains to critics of these experiments the linguistic hurdle that the animals have not overcome. It is certain that apes do not show syntactic behavior to any degree that humans do (for example, embedding is completely lacking) and many linguists claim that without such behavior, the apes cannot be said to be using language. Syntax, in the strict linguistic sense, means a system of rules capable of producing a sentence of potentially infinite length (even though in practice this is never required). There is no evidence that primates have shown this ability.

Implications

Critics of the ape studies have at this time carried the day. Funding sources for ape-human research have dried up, and most of the subjects have lost their privileged relationships with humans and been returned to zoos. But the severe reaction to the apparent failure of ape-human linguistic communication research has had positive effects on the field as well. Recent trends—the number of experiments on animal cognition in the wild, and the more carefully controlled experiments with apes like Kanzi—are leading us slowly closer to new ideas on this age-old issue.

The real significance of these experiments in ape-human linguistic communication goes far beyond popular enthusiasm about what an ape might say to us if it could talk. It has often been pointed out that an animal's view of the world must be totally unlike our own. It is perhaps not surprising that apes appear to communicate largely about their fundamental emotions and such basic needs as food and play.

In time, this research may help illuminate what is truly unique about human linguistic ability. As we have seen, many linguists claim that there is no connection between the communicative behavior of nonhuman primates and the complex structures of human language. The opposing view claims that the capacity for true grammatical activity can be found in nonhuman primates. This implies that what we call language arises out of a cognitive difference in *degree* and not in *kind* between humans and these animals. The optimistic view is that such research may ultimately shed light on the evolutionary origins of our species and its language use by demonstrating the degree of shared cognitive abilities between ourselves and our nearest genetic relatives.

14.7 COMPARING COMMUNICATION SYSTEMS: DESIGN FEATURES

Throughout this chapter, we have emphasized the distinction between communication and language. In this final section, we will compare human linguistic communication with what we have learned about systems of animal communication.

The Features

Differences and similarities between human language and natural animal communication systems can be highlighted by comparing essential characteristics of the systems. These characteristics are called **design features** and are set up (perhaps unfairly) with reference to human language. Since this book emphasizes the essentially mental nature of linguistic ability, the design features that follow do not include the traditional references to vocal-auditory transmission. What is emphasized is the nature of the semantic and organizational structuring of each system.

1. Interchangeability All members of the species can both send and receive messages.

This is obviously true of human language. It is not the case with bee dancing (performed only by foragers) or birdsong (performed only by males). Nonhuman primate vocalizations appear to be interchangeable.

2. Feedback Users of the system monitor what they are transmitting.

Humans monitor their linguistic output and correct it. It is debatable whether bees do so when they dance, or whether birds monitor their calls. It is not known whether birds monitor their song; it is likely that they do.

3. Specialization The communication system serves no other function but to communicate.

Human language represents reality—both external (real world) and internal (states, beliefs)—symbolically in the mind. Speech serves no purpose other than to convert language into sound for transmission purposes. Symptomatic tokens are unspecialized. Crying is a symptomatic signal that may be interpreted by someone else and thus function communicatively, but its primary purpose is physiological (the clearing of foreign matter from the eye, the release of emotional tension). Bee dancing and birdsong, on the other hand, appear to be specialized communicative activity. Alarm calls of any species may be symptomatic but at the same time are specialized for different types of predators.

4. Semanticity The system conveys meaning through a set of fixed relationships among tokens, referents, and meanings.

Human language conveys meaning through arbitrary symbols. Bee dancing conveys meaning, but within a very limited range, as do bird calls and song, along with nonhuman primate vocalizations. The range of meaning is broader and more subtle in nonhuman primate vocalizations. Although we cannot claim to know the minds of such near relations as chimpanzees and gorillas, it appears that the range of meanings suggested by their behavior in the wild does not approach the vastness of human semanticity (see Feature 8).

5. Arbitrariness There is no natural or inherent connection between a token and its referent.

This is overwhelmingly true of human language, with the possible exception of a few onomatopoeic terms. Bee dancing shows some arbitrariness, since there is no obvious connection between the form of the dance and the distance from the hive. Expressions of food source quality and direction are not arbitrary, however. Many bird calls are highly suited for their purpose, such as danger calls, which are difficult to locate, and in this sense are not arbitrary. Most nonhuman primate vocalization appears to be equally adaptive. Arbitrariness has, however, been claimed for vervet alarm calls.

6. Discreteness The communication system consists of isolatable, repeatable units.

Human language shows distinctive features, phonemes, syllables, morphemes, words, and still larger combinations. Bee dancing may be thought of as consisting of two (or three) discrete types, but these dances are not recombinable. There is some evidence for subunits in birdsong. They are also present in primate call systems.

7. Displacement Users of the system are able to refer to events remote in space and time.

Bee dancing shows displacement. No evidence for displacement is found in bird calls or songs. Baboons occasionally produce threat and fight vocalizations long after an aggressive encounter, but there is no evidence that this is reflecting displacement; it probably reflects a slow winding down of the animal's affective state. Among apes, it is not yet clear whether some degree of displacement is a feature of either their communication in the wild or the systems they have learned from humans. Nonhuman primates do not appear to communicate about imaginary pasts or futures, which humans are able to do with language.

8. Productivity New messages on any topic can be produced at any time.

This is obviously true of human language. Bees show limited productivity. Bird calls show none. Birdsong shows evidence of recombination (the songs of laughing gulls are well documented in this respect), but it is doubtful whether these recombinations transmit novel messages. This is also true of recombination in the calls of certain monkeys (such as macaques).

9. Duality of patterning Meaningless units (phonemes) are combined to form arbitrary signs. These signs in turn can be recombined to form new, meaningful larger units. In human language, phonemes can be combined in various ways to create different symbolic tokens: *spot*, *tops*, *opts*, and *pots*. These tokens in turn can be combined in meaningful ways: *Spot the tops of the pots.*

There is no evidence of this type of patterning in any known animal communication system.

10. Tradition At least certain aspects of the system must be transmitted from an experienced user to a learner.

This is obviously a factor in the acquisition of human language. It is possibly present in a very limited way in bee communication, and it is definitely present in the acquisition of birdsong for some species. The situation for nonhuman primates is unclear.

11. Prevarication The system enables the users to talk nonsense or to lie.

Undoubtedly, this property is found in human language. There are specialized mimics found among birds, fishes, and even insects. A few examples of animal deception have been noted among the arctic fox and among vervets, but it is not clear whether this is normal species-specific behavior or the acts of a few isolated individuals. The question of intentionality is crucial here. Current work with birds suggests that some species learn as many songs as possible and use this repertoire to maintain territorial advantage by "impersonating" other species. This may well be purely genetically determined behavior, but, in any event, it is highly complex.

12. Learnability A user of the system can learn other variants.

Humans can learn a number of different languages. Bees are limited to their own genetically specified dialect. Bird calls are apparently limited in this same way. As noted previously, some birds learn songs of other species, but this may well be simply mimicry. Nonhuman primates seem restricted to their own systems.

13. Reflexiveness The ability to use the communication system to discuss the system itself.

No evidence exists that any other species writes grammars or linguistics textbooks.

Tables 14.3 and 14.4 summarize this survey of design features.

Table 14.3 Summary of design features for bees and birds

Design feature	Bees	Birds
1. Interchangeability	no; foragers only	no; only males sing
2. Feedback	?	?
3. Specialization	yes	yes
4. Semanticity	yes—very limited	yes—limited
5. Arbitrariness	yes, for expressing distance	yes, though highly adaptive
6. Discreteness	in a limited way	yes, in song
7. Displacement	yes	no
8. Productivity	yes—very limited	possibly
9. Duality of patterning	no	no
10. Tradition	possibly, but highly limited	yes, limited
11. Prevarication	no	possibly
12. Learnability	no	possibly
13. Reflexiveness	no	no

Table 14.4 Summary of design features for nonhuman primates and humans

Design feature	Nonhuman primates	Humans
1. Interchangeability	yes	yes
2. Feedback	probably	yes
3. Specialization	in part	yes
4. Semanticity	yes	yes
5. Arbitrariness	limited confirmation; selectively adaptive	yes
6. Discreteness	in call systems	yes
7. Displacement	no	yes
8. Productivity	possibly	yes
9. Duality of patterning	no	yes
10. Tradition	possibly	yes
11. Prevarication	possibly	yes
12. Learnability	no	yes
13. Reflexiveness	no current evidence	yes

Summing Up

This brief overview of animal communication systems emphasizes that human language is one communication system among the many that life forms on this planet employ. Communication can be described with reference to the **sign**, which is composed of two components, a **signifier**, and that which is **signified**. Signs may be **iconic**, **symbolic**, or **indexical** (the latter including the **symptomatic** sign), and structured as **graded** or **discrete** types. Most animal communication has traditionally been viewed as symptomatic, though studies of communication among birds and bees suggest symbolic signs are used. A significant innate component may interact with some exposure to the communication system, especially among birds. Nonhuman primate communication consists of graded series of vocalizations and appears to show little arbitrariness.

Experiments with nonhuman primates have created controversy over whether chimpanzees and gorillas have shown symbolic behavior and a capacity for linguistic behavior. Many researchers have dismissed the work as an example of **dressage** or the Clever Hans phenomenon.

Human language and systems of animal communication share certain **design features**. Humans, however, lack many communicative skills that animals possess. We are hopelessly inadequate at following scent trails, a feat that prosimians accomplish with ease; cannot change color for communicative purposes with the facility of an octopus; and are not as gifted as horses and many other mammals at assessing and interpreting subtle body gestures. Humans do possess an ability to symbolize that far exceeds that of bees and even (allowing for the most generous interpretation possible of recent experiments) our nearest relatives, chimpanzees and gorillas. Human language is also more flexible and productive in manipulating these symbols than any known animal communication system. Language is as suited for—and indeed as much a part of—human life patterns as the communication systems of our fellow creatures are for their modes of existence.

Key Terms

arbitrariness	graded (sign)
call	iconic
Clever Hans	indexical
design features	interchangeability
discrete (sign)	learnability
displacement	prevarication
double-blind test	productivity
dressage	prosimian
duality of patterning	referent
duetting	reflexiveness
feedback	semanticity

semiotics	spectrograph
sign	stimulus-bound
signal	symbolic
signified	symptomatic
signifier	template
song	token
specialization	tradition

Picture Credits

Chimpanzee facial expressions in Figure 14.1, and monkey facial expressions in Figure 14.5, are adapted from S. Chevalier-Skolnikoff's "Facial Expression and Emotion in Nonhuman Primates" in *Darwin and Facial Expression*, edited by P. Ekman, 11–90 (New York: Academic Press, 1973). Park information signs in Figure 14.3 are courtesy of Alberta Recreation and Parks. Figure 14.7 is adapted from D. Todt's "Serial Calling as a Mediator of Interaction Processes: Crying" in *Primate Vocal Communication*, edited by D. Todt, D.P. Goedeking, and D. Symmes, 88–107 (Berlin: Springer-Verlag). Bee dancing (Figure 14.8) is adapted from K. von Frisch's *The Dance Language and Orientation of Bees*, p. 57 (cited in sources) and reprinted by permission. The spectrograph of the robin song (Figure 14.9) is from *Bird-Song* by W. H. Thorpe (cited in sources) copyrighted and reprinted with the permission of Cambridge University Press. Avian isoglosses in Figure 14.10 are from Paul Mundinger's "Microgeographic and Macrogeographic Variation in Acquired Vocalizations of Birds" in *Acoustic Communication in Birds*, vol. 2, edited by D. E. Kroodsma, E.H. Miller, and H. Ouellet, 147–208 (New York: Academic Press, 1982) and reprinted by permission. Figure 14.12 illustrating the response of vervet monkeys to predators is taken from *Animal Language* by Michael Bright with the permission of BBC Enterprises Ltd. (cited in sources). Tokens used in the Sarah experiments (Figures 14.13 and 14.14) are taken from D. Premack and A. J. Premack as cited on p. 179 in E. Linden's *Apes, Men, and Language* (Baltimore, Md.: Pelican Books, 1974).

Sources

The theory of semiotics outlined in this chapter is drawn from several recent works on semiotics, including T. Sebeok's *Contributions to the Doctrine of Signs*, Studies in Semiotics 5 (Bloomington: Indiana University Press, 1976), *I Think I Am a Verb* (New York: Plenum Press, 1986), and U. Eco's *Semiotics and the Philosophy of Language* (Bloomington: Indiana University Press). Bee communication is drawn from K. von Frisch's "Dialects in the Language of the Bees" in *Scientific American* 202 (2): 78–87 (1962) and his work *The Dance Language and Orientation of Bees*, translated by C. E. Chadwick (Cambridge, Mass.: Harvard University Press, 1967). Bird vocalization is based largely on W. H. Thorpe's *Bird-Song* (Cambridge, Mass.: Cambridge University Press, 1961). Jake Page's parrot is reported in *Science* (1982). Lemur vocalizations in

Table 14.1 are drawn from A. Jolly's *Lemur Behavior* (Chicago: University of Chicago Press, 1966). Vervet communication is drawn from R. M. Seyfarth and D. L. Cheney's "How Monkeys See the World," edited by Snowden et al. (cited below). Creative signing by Koko is reported in F. Patterson and E. Linden's work *The Education of Koko* (New York: Holt, Rinehart and Winston, 1981). The reference to cultural transmission of signs among chimpanzees is drawn from Michael Tomasello's "Cultural Transmission in the Tool Use and Communicatory Signaling of Chimpanzees?" in Parker and Gibson (cited below), pp. 274–311; some of the material on invented rules by the pygmy chimpanzee Kanzi is drawn from Patricia Marks Greenfield and E. Sue Savage-Rumbaugh's "Grammatical Combination in *Pan paniscus*," also in Parker and Gibson, pp. 540–76; this volume contains a number of other articles relevant to the question of nonhuman primate cognitive and linguistic abilities. Some exercise material is drawn from various articles in *How Animals Communicate*, edited by Thomas A. Sebeok (Bloomington: Indiana University Press, 1977).

Recommended Reading

Bright, Michael, 1984. *Animal Language*. London: British Broadcasting Corporation.

Cheney, Dorothy L., and Robert M. Seyfarth. 1991. *How Monkeys See the World*. Chicago: University of Chicago Press.

de Luce, Judith, and Hugh T. Wilder, eds. 1983. *Language in Primates: Perspectives and Implications*. New York: Springer-Verlag.

Hockett, Charles. 1960. "The Origin of Speech." *Scientific American* 203 (3): 88–96.

Lieberman, Philip. 1984. *The Biology and Evolution of Language*. Cambridge, Mass.: Harvard University Press.

Parker, Sue Taylor, and Kathleen Rita Gibson. 1990. *"Language" and Intelligence in Monkeys and Apes: Comparative Developmental Perspectives*. Cambridge, England: Cambridge University Press.

Sebeok, Thomas A., and Jean Umiker-Sebeok. 1980. *Speaking of Apes*. New York: Plenum Press.

Sebeok, Thomas A., and Robert Rosenthal, eds. 1981. *The Clever Hans Phenomenon: Communication with Horses, Whales, Apes, and People*. Annals of the New York Academy of Sciences 364. New York: The New York Academy of Sciences.

Snowden, C.T., C.H. Brown, and M.R. Petersen, eds. 1982. *Primate Communication*. London: Cambridge University Press.

Thorpe, W. H. 1974. *Animal Nature and Human Nature*. Garden City, N.Y.: Doubleday.

Questions

1. The following signs are all symptomatic.

   a) Dogs wag their tails when happy, cats flick their tails when irritated.
   b) An octopus, when showing aggressive behavior, becomes bright red.
   c) The Canada goose shows aggressive intentions by opening its mouth, coiling its neck, and directing its head toward an opponent. When it is unlikely to attack, its mouth is closed, its head is horizontally extended, and its head is directed away from an opponent.
   d) Tree leaves change color in the fall.
   e) The presence of stratocumulus clouds accompanies good weather.

   i) Explain why we can say that each case involves a symptomatic sign.
   ii) Signs in some cases may be iconic or symbolic in addition to being symptomatic. Identify which cases contain mixed signs, and which sign is the primary sign.

2. Find two examples each of *iconic*, *symbolic*, and *indexical* signs you encounter in the course of a day. Is it possible to classify unambiguously each sign as to type? If not, state why in each case.

3. What do the following chimpanzee facial expressions convey? Using a mirror, try to imitate the facial expressions; does this make it easier for you to label them? What characteristics of the signs lead you to your conclusion in each case?

a)   b)   c)

4. Observe an animal in a zoo or at home for at least one-half hour. Try to discover at least three unambiguous signs the animal employs to communicate. Describe each one in terms of both *signifier* and *signified*. (A good way to do this is to note carefully the context in which the sign is given, who it addresses, and what the receiver's response is to the communication.)

5. Add two columns to the list of design features presented in Tables 14.3 and 14.4. For one column, take the perspective of a researcher who believes that apes show true linguistic ability in their signing, and fill in the column from this point of view. Fill in the other column from the perspective of

a researcher who does not believe such ability has been shown. Be sure to comment on each design feature.

6. Now that you have been exposed to both sides of the ape language issue, summarize your own conclusions about it. Do you believe that human language is different in degree or in kind from the communicative behavior of the great apes? Why?

Answers to question 3: a) submission; b) excitement, perhaps affection; c) desiring, perhaps mixed with frustration.

15 COMPUTATIONAL LINGUISTICS

Contrary to popular belief, computers are not smart. In fact, they are only as smart as the human beings that teach them, no more and no less. Computers have no magical powers to do anything they are not explicitly told to do. They cannot guess, except when told how to guess. They cannot think, except when human programmers tell them very explicitly how to reason. But they can remember, and this they do exceptionally well. Furthermore, they can count. This they do remarkably well and remarkably fast too.

One of the central questions in computational linguistics is this: what would a computer program have to contain to enable the computer to analyze or create spoken or written sentences and paragraphs correctly? This is something that we humans achieve effortlessly. However, consider the amount and type of information that a computer would have to know about language in order to understand a simple sentence like this:

1. Many elephants smell.

First, the computer would have to understand the meaning and use of each of the words. For example, the word *many* can occur only with countable nouns, as in *many elephants*. The word *many* cannot occur with uncountable nouns, as in **many money*. A countable noun can appear in such phrases as *one elephant* or *two elephants*, whereas an uncountable noun cannot, as in **one money* or **two moneys*. Some words of this type, such as *most*, can appear both with countable nouns, as in *most elephants*, and uncountable nouns, as in *most money*. A computer would have to know that the *-s* at the end of *elephants* means that the word is plural. This being the case, the verb *smell* has to be in the plural form. The sentences **Many elephants smells* and **Many elephant smells* are not grammatical English sentences.

In addition to this grammatical knowledge about *many* and about agreement between subject and verb, there is a great deal of other information people have about sentence *1*. We know that elephants are animals and we know that animals smell, so we know that elephants are likely to be smelly. This is called *real world knowledge* as distinct from *grammatical knowledge*. For example, although flies are animals too, they do not smell with the same intensity as elephants. Furthermore, when analyzed carefully, the verb *smell* has two uses. One is the intransitive use in which the subject of the sentence, in this case *elephants*, is what is smelly, as in *Many elephants smell bad*. The other is the transitive use, in which the elephants are doing the smelling, as in *Many elephants smell their food*. The meaning of the two verbs is different even though they are spelled the same, and the function of the subject *elephant* is different in the two interpretations.

What sort of knowledge about pronunciation would a computer need to know to utter this sentence? The rules of pronunciation, like the rules of grammar, are different for each language. They are likely to vary within the same language depending on many factors. For example, the word *elephant* has the letters *ph* in the middle. English speakers know that this *ph* is to be pronounced with the phoneme /f/, as in *telephone* or *emphatic*. However, what about the words *upholstery* or *upheaval*? Why are these words not pronounced with an /f/ for the letter *ph*? Both words consist of the prefix *up-* and a base. In the case of *upholstery*, the word came from Old English *up-* and *-holden*, and it appears that this internal structure continues to determine the phonemes in pronunciation, even in Modern English. Of course, there is more to pronunciation than just converting letters to sounds, as shown in Chapters 2 and 3, and in later sections of this chapter.

These examples are sufficient to illustrate the quantity and variety of information that humans know about language. We take this knowledge for granted. Until we try to write computer programs to understand or generate even the most simple sentences, there is no need to pick apart the knowledge about language that we possess. However, computers are only as capable as the humans that program them, so it is the task of the linguist to spell out this knowledge for the computer. This is a major undertaking, involving all aspects of knowledge of language.

Computational linguistics is a relatively new discipline that lies in the intersection of the fields of linguistics and computer science. It is but one of many new hybrid disciplines involving computers that require computational expertise as well as a background in another field. The term *computational linguistics* covers many subfields. It sometimes refers to the use of computers as a tool to understand or implement linguistic theories. This means that linguists and computer scientists can gain a better understanding of the scientific and research questions by using computers. On the other hand, the term is sometimes used to refer to working systems or applications in which linguistic knowledge is needed. In this case, the questions and issues are usually ones of software engineering as well as of theory.

This chapter is organized around subfields of linguistics that are discussed in other chapters in this book: phonetics and phonology, morphology, syntax, and semantics. There is also a section on computational lexicology. The first part of the chapter shows how each *linguistic* subfield is used as the basis for a *computational linguistic* subfield. The second part of the chapter shows some ways in which these various subsystems are combined to create computer systems that use language.

15.1 COMPUTATIONAL PHONETICS AND PHONOLOGY

The Talking Machine: Speech Synthesis

At the 1939 World's Fair in New York, a device called a vocoder was displayed. The machine, developed by scientists at Bell Laboratories, reconstructed the human voice by producing a sound source which was then modified by a set of filters. The values for the filters were derived from the analysis of human speech. The vocoder system consisted of a source of random noise for unvoiced sound, an oscillator to give voicing, a way to control resonance, and some switches to control the energy level. This was to simulate the vowel sounds and fricatives (see Chapter 2). Then there were controls for the stop consonants /p,b/, /t,d/, and /k,g/. An amplifier then converted the modified source signal into sound that resembled the human speech it was originally modeled after.

The vocoder was nicknamed the Talking Machine. It was a crude device, but it demonstrated that good speech synthesis could indeed be achieved, given the right values for the major frequencies, and the right methods of concatenating and modifying adjacent values. Early systems used different technology from that used today, but the principles remain the same. The goal is to replicate the wave forms that correctly reflect those of human speech in order to produce speech which, at the very least, will be intelligible and aesthetically pleasing and, in the ultimate, could not be distinguished from the speech of a human being.

Chapter 2 gave a summary of articulatory phonetics, that is, how sounds are made when humans speak. Chapter 3 covered some aspects of sound systems. Speech recognition and speech synthesis rely on a detailed knowledge of acoustic phonetics as well as articulatory phonetics, although there are correlations between the acoustic and articulatory properties of sounds. Acoustic phonetics is the study of the structure of the wave forms that constitute speech. As explained in Chapter 2, the lungs push a stream of air through the trachea. The air stream is modified first at the glottis and then by the tongue and lips.

Each sound can be broken down into its fundamental wave forms, as shown in Figure 15.1. The figure shows a spectrographic analysis or **spectrogram** of the words *heed*, *hid*, *head*, *had*, *hod*, *hawed*, *hood*, and *who'd* as spoken by a British speaker. The diagrams give a visual representation of the duration of the utterance on the horizontal axis, and the different frequencies in the wave form on the vertical axis. The main frequencies, or **formants**, show up because they have more intensity than other frequencies. Note the different locations of the formants along the frequency dimension for the different vowels. The sound /h/ is only slightly visible as fuzzy lines across the spectrum because /h/ is a voiceless fricative with little or no glottal constriction (see Chapter 2, Section 2.5). The acoustic effect is weak "white noise" resembling fuzz or static. The /d/ is a stop, so there is just a low frequency "voice bar" resulting from the vibrations in the glottis, but there are no vowel formants for the period of closure since the air flow is blocked. This shows up as blank space on the spectrogram. For speech synthesis, the first three formants are the most critical for identifying different vowels. The others add some refinement to the sound, but they do not determine intelligibility or naturalness with the same significance as the first three formants.

Since different vowels are composed of different frequencies, in theory all a speech synthesizer would have to do is replicate those vowel sounds, put in a few consonants, and string them together just as letters are strung together to make words and sentences. Unfortunately, the matter is not so simple, since sounds are not fixed. Rather, they vary according to the segments that surround them. Effects occur on adjacent segments and across groupings, sometimes as far as six phonemes away. For example, Figure 15.2 shows the same

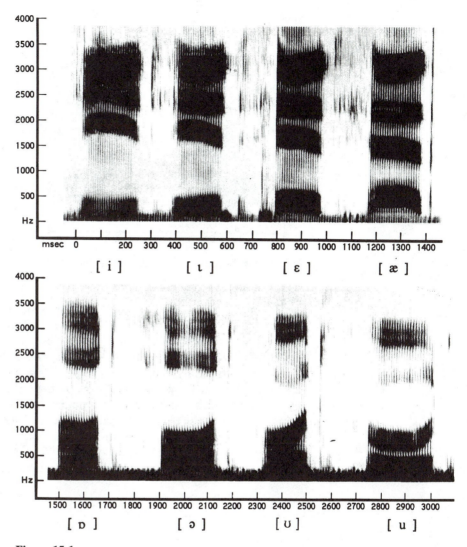

Figure 15.1

phonemic vowel /æ/, but notice the rises and slumps in the formants. The
figure shows how adjacent consonants can modify vowels. Similarly, vowels
modify consonants. Nasal sounds modify entire chunks of speech. On top of
these local changes, there are changes to entire phrases based on suprasegmental features such as stress and intonation (see Chapter 2, Section 2.9).

Many steps are involved in achieving speech synthesis, and there are many
different choices in ordering these steps. The text to be spoken has to be analyzed syntactically, semantically, and orthographically. Pronunciations for exceptional words such as *have*/hæv/ or *four*/fɔr/ must be found. These words
do not follow the predictable letter-sound correspondences of English: *have*
does not rhyme with *nave* or *rave*, and *four* does not rhyme with *sour* or
glamour. Contrastive sounds need to be assigned based on the letters and based

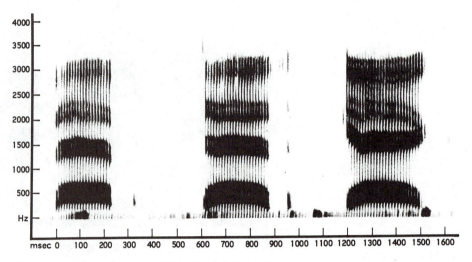

Figure 15.2 Spectrograms of the words *bab*, *dad*, *gag*

on other information about the word. After the correct phoneme is chosen, a system must look at the environment to see which allophone of the phoneme to choose. For example, to return to Figure 15.2, if the system were trying to pronounce *bab* /bæb/, the vowel /æ/ corresponding to the labial onset and labial offset would be chosen, since labials tend to lower adjacent formants.

A syntactic analysis of a sentence permits a system to identify words that might go together for phrasing. This is particularly important for noun compounds in English. As many as six nouns can be strung together, and the pronunciation of the compound can change the listener's interpretation of the meaning. For example, the expression *Mississippi mud pie* could have two interpretations, depending on its structure. The most likely interpretation is shown in Figure 15.3, where the mud pie is Mississippi style. Alternatively, the

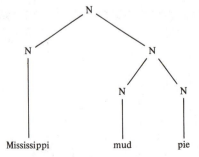

Figure 15.3

pie could be made of mud from Mississippi, in which case the structure of the expression is different, as shown in Figure 15.4, and so is the pronunciation. Syntactic analysis can also determine the part of speech for noun/verb pairs that are spelled the same but pronounced differently, such as the verb *record* /rəkɔ́rd/ and the noun *record* /rékərd/. Finally, parentheticals will be identified, as in these sentences:

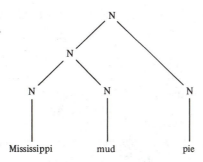

Figure 15.4

2. Here are the apples, as you can see.
3. He said, although I don't believe it, that he was a good driver.

Parentheticals are typically pronounced at a lower pitch and loudness. When pronounced with main phrase intonation, they are difficult to understand. Finally, a semantic analysis of a sentence, and of a text, gives an idea of focus and stress. These features must be translated into duration (length), pitch, and loudness in order for synthetic speech to sound completely natural.

Given advances in computer technology, along with advances in electronics and acoustics, intelligible speech synthesis has already been achieved. However, everyone who has seen popular science fiction films knows that even now, synthetic speech still sounds synthetic. In addition to the syntactic and semantic issues raised above, a number of difficult problems remain, such as incorporating intonational variety into the rules to eliminate the droning quality of synthesized speech, and improving individual sounds.

Speech Recognition or Speech Analysis

As we have seen, speech consists of very complex wave forms changing rapidly across time and in subtle ways, which can affect the perception of a message. The task of speech recognition is to take these wave forms as input and decode them. This is exactly what we humans do when listening to speech. The wave form that reaches the ear is a continuous stream of sound; we segment the sound into words, phrases, and meaningful units so we can determine the meaning of the utterance. The task of a speech recognition system is to teach a computer to understand speech, whether the system models human mechanisms or not.

Even though human beings have no trouble decoding speech wave forms, computers do. The problems are immense. First of all, as shown in Chapter 2, Section 2.10, speech sounds are modified by adjacent sounds in natural speech. The faster and more informal the speech, the more sounds are merged and dropped. Guessing what sounds have been dropped based on faulty and limited input is an extremely difficult task. Knowledge of context, of syntactic structure, of probabilities of occurrence are helpful, but the problem is still not solved.

Since decoding of continuous speech presents such problems, some systems impose the requirement that words be pronounced slowly, and separated by a slight pause. The pause gives a clear cue that the word has ended, so a system has much less guesswork to do. Also, if the speech is said more slowly, fewer sounds will be dropped. In addition to the constraint of pronouncing words in isolation, limiting a system in its vocabulary means that the recognition machine will have less guesswork to do. Finally, yet another way to reduce the guesswork is to require that an individual user "train" the system to be tailored to his or her voice alone. Anyone who is skilled at recognizing voices can attest to the fact that no two people sound alike. The purpose of "training" a computer is to familiarize it with the unique and distinguishing features of the user's voice.

Another very difficult problem for speech recognition is what is called the "cocktail party effect," such as that of being in a crowded room. Even though there is much noise from other people, from music, or from the street, humans manage to filter out the background noise and pick out a particular sound or conversation to listen to. Everyone has had the experience of not hearing a sound, such as a leaking faucet, until someone points out the sound, and the annoying sound then becomes the only one to be heard. Whatever mechanisms were used to suppress the noise of the faucet were deactivated when brought to the listener's attention. Computer recognition systems cannot distinguish the speech signal from the noise, so they perform poorly in noisy environments. Thus, another condition—a reasonably quiet environment—must be imposed on systems in order for them to function adequately.

Each of these constraints can be imposed to result in more reliable systems, but the overall research problem still remains: how can humans be so adept at decoding speech yet computers cannot be easily taught to do so?

15.2 COMPUTATIONAL MORPHOLOGY

Morphology is the study of the internal structure of words, covering such topics as affixation, compounding, and infixation (see Chapter 4). Most research in computational morphology arose as a by-product of developing natural language processing systems. Looking up words in a computational dictionary for these systems turned out to be more complicated than met the eye, precisely because of morphological processes that can conceal the base word. For example, if a dictionary has the word *book*, the word *books* would not be found by a simple search. Unless a system is explicitly told that *book* is related to *books* by a productive and regular rule of inflectional morphology, it would not be able to infer that those words are related. Thus, a program needs to include the rule of pluralization in English as well as other rules in order to recognize or generate the morphological permutations of words.

Morphological Processes

Most morphologically conditioned changes in written English involve spelling, with some changes in stems. Examples are *stop/stopped*, *sing/sang*, and *tolerate/tolerant*. In general, morphological variations in English are not as opaque as in other languages. Some languages, such as German, have very productive compounding, whereas others have infixation and reduplication, or complex stem changes. Words altered by morphological processes cannot be easily recognized by a natural language processor unless they are properly related to their bases for lexical lookup.

Implementing Morphological Processes: Method One Broadly speaking, there are two approaches to computational morphology. Historically, the first was called a stemming or stripping algorithm. An algorithm is a set of rules for solving a problem; the term was first used in mathematics to describe the rules for solving mathematical problems. Since algorithmic procedures usually involve a sequence of repeated steps, the term is naturally suited to computer programs in general, and to programs for computational linguistics in particular. In the stemming or stripping algorithm, affixes are recursively stripped off the beginnings and ends of words, and base forms are proposed. If the base form is found in the base-form dictionary, then the word is analyzable. Successful analyses provide information about the internal structure of the words as well as whatever other information is produced by the rule for a given affix, such as part of speech change, inherent semantic changes (e.g., *-ess* is + feminine), or other information (e.g., abstract, Latinate, singular, plural). Most of these systems are sensitive to constraints on affix ordering such as described in the chapter on morphology. Inflectional affixes occur outside of derivational affixes, and there may be some derivational affixes that occur outside of other derivational affixes.

Two different types of dictionaries are possible with the stemming method: word-based and stem-based. A word-based system has a dictionary with words only. For word generation, all input to morphological rules must be well-formed words, and all output will be well-formed words. For word analysis, all proposed stems will be words. The word-based system has proven to be very useful for projects that use large machine-readable dictionaries, since dictionaries list words, not stems. A machine-readable dictionary is a dictionary that appears in computer form, such as that available in spelling checkers or thesauruses. Machine-readable dictionaries have definitions, pronunciations, etymologies, and other information, not just the spelling or synonyms. (See Section 15.4 for more on machine-readable dictionaries.)

Table 15.1 presents an example of the type of analyses given by a word-based stemming system. To analyze *conceptualize* as an infinitive verb (v form(inf)),

Table 15.1 Input word: conceptualize

Analysis	Part of speech	Features
concept	N	num(sing)
-ual	A	
-ize	V	form(inf)

first *conceptual* must be analyzed as an adjective (adj). This would be done by a rule stating that the suffix *-ize* can attach to certain adjectives to create verbs. *Conceptual* can be analyzed as an adjective if *concept* can first be analyzed as a singular noun (n num(sing)). This would be done by a rule for *-ual* stating that the suffix *-ual* can attach to certain nouns to create adjectives. *Concept* is stored in the dictionary as a singular noun, so this lexical lookup serves as the final step of the analysis. The analyses shown here actually result from recursive calls to the morphological rules. Each rule has conditions that restrict its operation. In this example, the *-ual* rule states that the base must be a singular noun. The condition for the *-ize* rule is that the base must be an adjective.

Since each condition is met, an analysis is possible. The word *conceptualize* is deemed a well-formed infinitive verb.

How would the system analyze a more complex form? Consider the analyses in Table 15.2 of the word *conceptualizations*, which is based on the pre-

Table 15.2 Input word: conceptualizations

Analysis	Part of speech	Features
concept	N	num(sing)
-ual	A	
-ize	V	form(inf)
-ation	N	num(sing)
-s	N	num(plur)

vious example. In this example, the suffix *-ation* attaches to infinitival verbs. Notice that when *-ation* attaches to *conceptualize*, there is a spelling change. If no spelling rules were written, then the word **conceptualizeation* would be allowed by the system. Finally, the plural marker *-s* is attached to the noun. For the plural suffix *-s*, there is no change in the part of speech, but only in the number feature of the word from singular to plural. Observe that these examples illustrate a word-based system. Both the dictionary entry, in this case *concept*, and the complex words *conceptualize* and *conceptualizations* are well-formed words of English.

How would this system differ if it were stem-based? For this example, the morpheme *-cept* might be listed in a stem dictionary, due to its presence in other words in English, such as *reception*, *conception*, *inception*, and *perception*. Since *-ceive* and *-cept* are related in a regular way, this relationship might also be given in the stem dictionary, or the words could be related by rule. Consider again *conceptualizations*, analyzed down to a stem in Table 15.3. In

Table 15.3 Input word: conceptualizations

Analysis	Part of speech	Features
con-		
-cept	N	num(sing)
-ual	A	
-ize	V	form(inf)
-ation	N	num(sing)
-s	N	num(plur)

this example, the prefix *con-* attaches to *-cept*. The point was made earlier that a word-based morphology system can use a regular dictionary as its lexicon, but no such convenience exists for a stem-based system. In order for stem-based morphology to get wide coverage, a large dictionary of stems is required. (More on this topic is found in the section on computational lexicology later in this chapter.)

Implementing Morphological Processes: Method Two The other common approach to computational morphology, the two-level approach, is fundamentally different from the stemming approach. This results in basic differences in computational properties. Both systems contain a lexicon or dictionary, although two-level morphology *requires* a stem-based lexicon. Both systems have rules, but the rules are very different. In two-level morphology, the rules define correspondences between surface and lexical representations; they specify if a correspondence is restricted to, required by, or prohibited by a particular environment. *Lexical* roughly corresponds to *underlying*, whereas *surface* usually means *orthographic* but sometimes *phonemic*. In Figure 15.5, the lexical

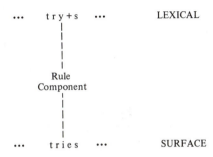

Figure 15.5

representation of *try* followed by the +*s* is compared with a surface representation *tries*.

Lexical and surface representations are compared using a special kind of rule system called finite-state transducer. Simply put, the rules would decide whether the lexical *y* could correspond to the surface *i* based on information the rules have already seen. The rules that compare lexical and surface form move from left to right, so when a successful correspondence is made, the rule moves along. One of the claimed strengths of this method is that, since the procedure moves from left to right, it accurately reflects the way that people process words. Since people hear and read English from left to right (i.e., the beginning of the word is encountered before the end), a system that incorporates this directionality might be an actual model of processing. The primary drawback of the two-level system is that it requires a specialized stem dictionary, complete with restrictions on the stems so that not all affixes attach without restrictions. For example, a dictionary would need to include -*cept* or -*mit* (for *transmit*, *submit*, *permit*, and so on).

Some Problems in Computational Morphology

Compounding is a particularly thorny problem since it tends to be so productive that compounds are often not listed in a dictionary. The word *bookworm*, for example, does not appear in Webster's Seventh New Collegiate Dictionary. A good morphological analyzer should be able to analyze *bookworm* as shown in Table 15.4. However, what about a word like *accordion*?

Table 15.4 Input word: bookworm

Analysis	Part of speech	Features
book	N	num(sing)
worm	N	num(sing)

The analysis in Table 15.5 shows *accordion* to be composed of the noun *accord* plus the noun *ion*. This is obviously incorrect because *accordion* is not a compound analogous to *bookworm*. Since *accordion* does not ever have this analysis, it might be marked as an exception to morphological decomposition.

Table 15.5 Input word: accordion

Analysis	Part of speech	Features
accord	N	num(sing)
ion	N	num(sing)

A related problem arises due to overenthusiastic rule application. Table 15.6 presents an analysis of *really*. Here *really* is analyzed as [*re-* [*ally-* verb]verb],

Table 15.6 Input word: really

Analysis	Part of speech	Features
re-		
ally	V	form(inf)

meaning "to ally oneself with someone again." This analysis is correct, although highly improbable. Cases like *really* bring up a difficult issue. Should a word like *really* be specially marked in the dictionary as a nonanalyzable word, an exception to the rules that would apply to regular formations like *reapply*, *redo*, and *reduplicate*? Or should the rules be allowed to apply freely? What about a word like *resent*, which could either be [*re-*[*sent*verb]verb] as in *He didn't get my letter, so I resent it* and [*re- sent*verb] as in *Did he resent that nasty comment*? The spelling of this word is truly ambiguous, so a decision about its analyzability requires knowledge of syntactic and semantic features in the sentence and context. Usually the decision is driven by practical concerns. A system that is designed to implement a theory, but that does not need to perform well on a task that applies the theory would probably allow the rules to apply freely. A system that needs to perform accurately on large texts would probably mark *really* and *resent* as nonanalyzable words, even though strictly speaking they are not.

15.3 COMPUTATIONAL SYNTAX

Research in computational syntax arose from two sources. One was the practical motivation resulting from attempts to build working systems to analyze and generate language. Some of these systems, such as machine translation and database query systems, are discussed in Section 15.6. The other source was a desire on the part of theoretical linguists to use the computer as a tool to demonstrate that a particular theory is internally consistent. In this case, less value was given to efficiency or broad coverage since this was not the goal. The emphasis was instead on theory testing and on formal issues in natural language analysis. Ideally, builders of practical systems should take more advantage of theoretical insights, and linguistic theoreticians should pay more attention to practical problems. This has been the case in recent research on parsing, although this is a fairly new friendship.

Natural Language Analysis

Parsers and Grammars Chapter 5 showed how sentences can be analyzed by rules into substructures such as noun phrases, verb phrases, prepositional phrases, and so on, as shown in Figure 15.6. Given a system of rules, an ana-

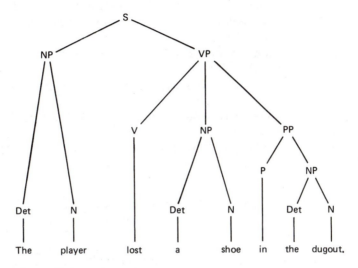

Figure 15.6

lyzer will be able to break up and organize a sentence into its substructures. A grammar can be viewed as the set of rules that define a language. These rules can be of different shapes or formats, which give them different properties. A **parser** is the machine or engine that is responsible for applying the rules. A parser can have different strategies for applying rules. Chapter 5, Section 5.4 showed how the rules for sentence structure differ between languages. These differences are reflected in the grammars for these languages, although the parser that drives the grammars can remain constant.

Determinism vs. Nondeterminism Any time a syntactic parser can produce more than one analysis of the input sentence, the problem of backtracking is raised. For example, if the beginning of the sentence in Figure 15.7 is read word

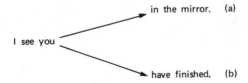

Figure 15.7

by word, there is more than one possible ending. In choice (a), the word *you* is the object of the main verb *see*. For (b) the word *that* has been left out, as is permitted in English, so the word *you* is the subject of the clause *you have finished*. If the parser follows path (a), and if that path turns out to be the wrong one, how can the situation be rectified to get the right analysis? Or can choices be controlled so that a parser never has to undergo the time-consuming task of going back and starting over?

The term **nondeterministic** may refer to going back or backtracking if the first analysis turns out to be impossible. It may also mean following multiple paths in parallel, meaning that both analyses are built at the same time but on separate channels. The term **deterministic** means that the parser has to stick to the path it has chosen. There have been many proposals about controlling the backtracking of parsers. The problem is a serious one since the number of alternatives increases as the coverage of a system increases. The result is that as an analyzer improves, it also becomes more and more cumbersome because each time it is presented with more and more options.

Top-Down vs. Bottom-Up Parsing Consider the following phrase structure rules for English:

> 4. *a*) S → NP VP
>   *b*) NP → (Det) (A) N (PP)
>   *c*) VP → V (NP) (PP)
>   *d*) PP → P NP

There are two ways to build an analysis of a sentence, using just these rules. This section illustrates the principles of what is called *top-down* and *bottom-up* parsing. Working systems may not function exactly like this, but the principles are the same.

In addition to the rules in *4*, we also need to give some lexical items, or **terminal nodes**, for each category or **nonterminal**.

> 5.   N → Curly
>   V → sat
>   P → on
>   Det → the
>   N → grass

Generally speaking, a nonterminal is not a word in the language. Rather, it is a category or a phrase, such as N or NP. A terminal can be thought of as a word (although sometimes a terminal is a part of a word or several words). In top-down parsing, the analyzer always starts with the topmost node, in this case S, and finds a way to expand it. The only rule in the set *4* for S is shown in Figure 15.8. Both NP and VP are nonterminal nodes. The next rule to apply

Figure 15.8

is the NP expansion rule and then the VP expansion rule. The results are shown in Figure 15.9. Although N is a nonterminal, it has no expansions, so the next rule to apply would be the VP rule. If the subject of the sentence had been *the batter*, then the NP would have been expanded to Det and N. This process

Figure 15.9

continues until no more expansions could apply, and until all the lexical items or words in *5* occur in the correct position to match the input sentence *Curly sat on the grass*. Top-down parsers suggest a hypothesis that a proposed structure is correct until proven otherwise.

In contrast, bottom-up parsers take the terminals (words) of a sentence one by one, replace the terminals with proposed nonterminal or category labels, and then reduce the strings of categories to permissible structures. For the same example, the analysis would be built as follows: first the word *Curly* would be assigned the category N; then *sat* would be assigned to V, and so on. The partial analysis up to this point is shown in Figure 15.10. None of the rules in *4*

Figure 15.10

permit the combination of N and V; none permit V and P nor P and Det to combine. But the NP rule does combine Det and N to build up a structure, as shown in Figure 15.11. This continues until the structure of a sentence is built.

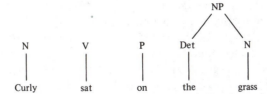

Figure 15.11

It has been proposed that the building of the structure from the terminal nodes up to the topmost S node from left to right reflects the way human beings process sentences more accurately than the top-down approach, but this is a controversial issue.

Generative Capacity (advanced) The term *generative* in this context refers to formal properties of grammars as mathematical systems. It does not refer to language generation, which is discussed below. Recall that a grammar consists of a set of rules that describe a language. Assume also some finite set of symbols, *V*, the vocabulary of a language. For English, examples of *V* would be:

6. V_L = [*player, shoe, child, lost, a* . . .]

In the vocabulary V are other symbols and categories, such as N and *Det*. Formally, a language L over V is a finite set of strings of symbols taken from V. Informally, a language consists of strings from the vocabulary. Of course, a sentence is more than just a string of words, as shown in Chapter 5. Furthermore, the set of strings is greater than the set of well-formed sentences, as sentences 7 to 9 show. Even though the vocabulary V may be a finite list, the language L may be a finite or infinite. This is because of recursion, a very powerful property of natural languages. The application of a finite number of recursive rules results in languages that can contain an infinite number of well-formed strings.

The following sentences consist of vocabulary from the set in 6. While 7 is a well-formed sentence in English, 8 and 9 are not.

7. A child lost a shoe.
8. *child shoe a.
9. *Lost a shoe a child.

Although 9 is not in the language L for English, it could be found in the language L for Spanish, given the same vocabulary.

10. Perdió un zapato un niño.
    lost   a shoe a child

The grammar of English would give a correct description of 7, but not 8 or 9. On the other hand, the grammar of Spanish would allow both 7 and 9, but not 8. The goal of an implemented grammar is exactly the same. An **implementation** is simply a practical system. The grammar rules are programmed into a computer, and the computer program then decides if the string is permitted in the language. If the string is permitted, it then has the task of giving the sentence the correct description.

Natural languages (as opposed to computer languages) are highly complex, so discovering the correct grammar for a given language is an extremely difficult task. The complexity and subtlety of natural languages continue to present a challenge to linguists. There are many competing theories of what the "correct" grammar of natural languages will be like. Even the grammar for English, a very well-studied natural language, is not at all well-understood. One issue that all theories agree upon, however, is that a grammar should have certain properties. Grammars should give a correct description of the following:

A. The strings of a language L
B. The structures corresponding to the strings in L

Property A is called **weak generative capacity**. Property B is called **strong generative capacity**. (Generative here does not mean "create" but rather "describe.")

To explain, Figure 15.6 shows an analysis in which the first two words *the* and *player* are joined into a noun phrase (NP). The verb phrase (VP) is described by the grammar as consisting of a verb (V), followed by a noun phrase (NP), followed by a preposition phrase (PP). These three constituents are immediately dominated by the VP node. What if a different grammar were to claim a different structure for this sentence? Consider the structure in Figure 15.12. This analysis makes different claims about the structure of the sentence, but the actual string of words stays the same. The tree in Figure 15.12

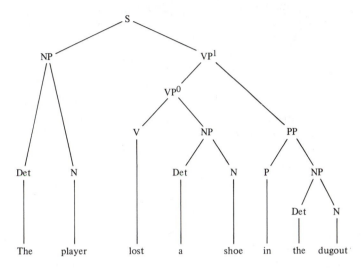

Figure 15.12

has two levels of verb phrase. One is VP^1, which dominates everything in the predicate of the sentence. The other is VP^0, which dominates only the main verb and the direct object. The grammar generating the structure in Figure 15.12 differs in strong generative capacity from the grammar for Figure 15.6. However, both grammars may have the same weak generative capacity since they both have the ability to describe the string *The player lost a shoe in the dugout*.

Role of Syntax and Semantics The preceding section dealt with syntactic analyzers, but it is important to note that the division between what should be handled by the syntactic component of a system and what is properly in the semantic component is a matter of great debate. For example, some systems might claim that selections of prepositions by verbs, often considered a syntactic property, is actually dependent on the semantic category of the verb. For example, not all verbs can take the instrumental, as in the reading of *11* in which *the stick* was used to hit the dog.

11. He hit the dog with a stick.

If a different verb is substituted for *hit*, would the sentence be semantically or syntactically ill-formed?

12. ?He told his story with a stick.

Some systems assume that a syntactic analysis precedes a semantic one, and that the semantics should be applied to the output of syntactic analyses. This is the position of the earliest transformational models, which was incorporated into many computational systems. Some systems perform syntactic and semantic analyses hand-in-hand. Other systems ignore the syntactic, viewing it as a second-step derivative from semantic analyses.

Natural Language Generation

What Is Generation? To utter a sentence, a speaker first must decide on goals, plan the information to be included, and then express that information in a sentence of his or her language. The language generation problem is often viewed as the reverse of the language analysis problem, but this is not accurate. In the same way, the generation of speech, discussed in Section 15.6, is in no way simply the reverse of speech recognition. Certain problems are the same, but many are not.

Language generation has been the underling of computational linguistics. The reason for this may be that it is a more difficult area to work in than language analysis. For language analysis, the linguist is given a set of data (i.e., strings of the language) with which to work. For language generation, the linguist has ideas and plans that need to be turned into language. A language generator must be able to make decisions about the content of the text, about issues of discourse structure, and about cohesion of the sentences and paragraphs. In contrast, a language analyzer might be invoked to make proposals about discourse and content, but the raw material upon which guesses are based is already there. For the language generator, only concepts and ideas are available to work with. Choices of words (lexical items) and syntactic structures are part of decisions to be made in building a text.

As with syntactic analyzers, there are two approaches to generation: top-down and bottom-up. In the top-down approach, first a very high-level structure of the output text is determined, along with very abstract expressions of meaning and goal. Then lower levels are filled in progressively. Subsections are determined, and examples of the verbs with their subjects and objects, if any, are proposed. This is refined, until the prefinal stage when lexical items are chosen from the dictionary. After all sentences have been decided upon, and after all lexical items have been inserted, there is a component to "smooth" and provide low-level coherence to the text. This component makes sure that pronouns are used correctly, for example, and that connecting phrases such as *in the preceding paragraph* or *on the other hand* are used correctly. In contrast, the bottom-up approach builds sentences from complex lexical items. First, words to achieve the goals are hypothesized. Then sentences are composed, and finally high-level paragraph and text coherence principles are applied.

The Generation Lexicon The lexicon is just one link in many difficult steps involved in generating natural and cohesive text for an underlying set of goals and plans. Imagine that you have determined an underlying message, plan, or goal. In order to figure out how to translate the underlying message into some actual words in a language, your generation system will have to figure out such matters as what verbs to pick and how to pick the subjects and objects, if any, for those verbs.

Suppose you want to express how fast time is going by in your life. You might use the verb *elapse*. *Elapse* is said to be a one-place predicate or a one-place verb. It is intransitive, so it takes just one argument, the subject. (The term *argument* here refers to grammatical dependents of a verb.) If you want to talk about baseball, you need to describe the action. You might use the verb *hit*. *Hit* is transitive; it takes two arguments. *Hit* is also often used with an instrumental, a phrase that tells what the subject hit *with*, as in *with a stick* in sentence *11*. In this case, *hit* can take three arguments. Finally, a verb like *give* takes an agent, theme, and goal, and those three arguments can be expressed as a subject, object, and indirect object, indicated by *to* as in *13*. Alternatively, *give* can undergo what is called Dative Movement, as in *14*, in which case the indirect object *dog* appears next to the verb and is not preceded by the preposition *to*.

13. He gave a stick to the dog.
14. He gave the dog a stick.

Often verbs with very close meanings take different numbers of arguments and in different order. For example, *give* can also mean *donate*, but *donate* does not permit the same alternations as *give*.

15. He donated a stick to the dog.
16. *He donated the dog a stick.

A system must be capable of deciding what the meaning to be conveyed is, and then it must be capable of picking very similar words to express that meaning. The lexicon or dictionary must supply items to instantiate the link between meaning and words.

The design and content of the generation lexicon is one of the most difficult areas in language generation. The lexicon needs to contain many different types of information, such as syntactic facts about verbs, facts about usage and focus, and facts about types of modifiers. Building lexicons for generation is one of the goals of computational lexicology, as discussed in the following section.

15.4 COMPUTATIONAL LEXICOLOGY

Since phrases, sentences, and paragraphs are composed of words, computer systems need to contain detailed information about words. The section on morphology dealt with the structure and analyses of word forms, but there is more to know about words than this.

Computational linguists are realizing that an analyzer or generator is only as good as its dictionary or lexicon. The lexicon is the repository of whatever information a particular system needs. The individual words in the lexicon are called lexical items. Chapter 5, Section 5.2, shows how lexical insertion occurs in syntactic structure. For example, in order for a bare structure such as Figure 15.13 to be "filled out" with real words, a program would need to have a

Figure 15.13

match between a word marked Det in the lexicon and the slot in the tree requiring a Det. The same goes for any part of speech, such as noun, verb, or adjective. Given the items in *5*, a valid match for Figure 15.13 would be Figure 15.14. Figure 15.15 would not be a valid match. Notice that the preposition *on*

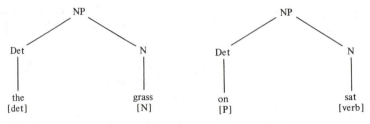

Figure 15.14   **Figure 15.15**

occurs under the determiner node, and the verb *sat* occurs under the noun node. At the very least, the condition of matching part of speech has to be met.

A computer program would need to know more than just part of speech to analyze or generate a sentence correctly. Subcategorization, that is, the number of arguments a verb can take, must be considered (see Chapter 5). Knowledge of thematic roles, such as agent, theme, and goal, is also needed (see Chapter 6, Section 6.2). A syntactic analyzer would also need to know what kinds of complements a verb can take.

> *17.* I decided to go.
> *18.* *I decided him to go.
> *19.* *I persuaded to go.
> *20.* I persuaded him to go.

The verb *decide* can take the infinitive *to go* as in *17*, but it cannot take an NP object and then the infinitive, as in *18*. The verb *persuade* is the opposite. It cannot take the infinitive *to go* as in *19*, but it must have an NP object before the infinitive, as in *20*.

The lexicon needs to know about the kinds of structures in which words can appear, about the semantics of surrounding words, and about the style of the text. For example, sentence *21* is strange in meaning, but the structure is fine.

> *21.* I broke the concept.

The verb *break* is transitive and so can take an object, but the problem here is the type of noun; *concept* is [+abstract], but *break* requires a [+concrete] noun. Only concrete objects are breakable, unless the meaning is metaphorical as in *The disease broke his will to live.* (See Chapter 6 for more discussion of semantics.)

What does a computational lexicon look like? So far the list of information includes:

> *22.* Lexical Item
>   1. Part of Speech
>   2. Sense
>   3. Subcategorization
>   4. Semantic Restrictions

Keeping in mind that a computational lexicon has to contain as much information as possible in order to correctly analyze and generate phrases, sentences, and text, the following are also needed:

22. (continued)
   5. Pronunciation
   6. Context and Style
   7. Etymology
   8. Usage (e.g., taboos)
   9. Spelling (including abbreviations)

The task of collecting all the important information for every existing word in the English language is awesome. In addition, given that the kind of information needed cannot be found in conventional dictionaries, how are computational lexicons built? There are several approaches. One is to hand-build a lexicon specifying only those features that a given system needs and using only the lexical items that are most likely to occur. For example, assume that an analyzer is reading the *Wall Street Journal*, and assume that the sentence to be analyzed is *His interest is high this month.* If the analyzer is to assign a meaning to this sentence, it has to know at least the information below.

   Word: interest-1
   1. Part of Speech: Noun
   2. Inherent Semantic Features: [+concrete], . . .
   3. Context: Financial

In just this usage, there is no reason to know about the abstract meaning of *interest* as "attention" or "concern." The lexical entry for this other sense would include the information below.

   Word: interest-2
   1. Part of Speech: Noun
   2. Inherent Semantic Features: [+abstract], . . .
   3. Context: Emotional

Most words have many different senses, and sometimes the different senses have very different grammatical behavior. Every time a new word is added to the lexicon, if a new feature is also added, then the dictionary builder has to go back through the lexicon and modify every word to match the new expanded word. When *interest-2* was added to the dictionary, new features had to be added, namely that *interest-1* does not have a context "Emotional" and that *interest-2* does not have a context "Financial." One of the major problems in building computational dictionaries is extensibility. The problem is how to add new information, and modify old information, without starting over each time.

   Another option in building large lexicons is to use two resources: the power of the computer and the data of machine-readable dictionaries. A machine-readable dictionary (MRD) is a conventional dictionary, but it is in machine-readable form (i.e., on the computer) rather than on the bookshelf. MRDs are useful in building large lexicons because the computer can be used to examine and analyze automatically information that has already been organized by lexicographers, the writers of dictionaries. Unfortunately, the type of information that is needed by a computational dictionary is not always easy to find in a conventional dictionary. However, with some clever approaches to exploiting the hidden information in conventional MRDs, it appears that many important facts can be pulled out and put into a computational lexicon. This work is still in its earliest stages, so it is uncertain how far it can be pushed, but it is an important line of research in computational linguistics.

For example, the knowledge that a word has a sense that is [+ human] is needed in a computational lexicon for both syntactic and semantic reasons. Webster's Seventh New Collegiate Dictionary, which has about seventy thousand headwords, has just over a thousand nouns that are defined in terms of the word *person*. Some examples are given below:

> *accessory*
> > a *person* not actually or constructively present but contributing as an assistant or instigator to the commission of an offense—called also accessory before the fact
>
> *acquaintance*
> > a *person* whom one knows but who is not a particularly close friend
>
> *intellectual*
> > a very intelligent or intellectual *person*
>
> *scatterbrain*
> > a giddy heedless *person*: FLIBBERTIGIBBET
>
> *unbeliever*
> > one that does not believe: an incredulous *person*: DOUBTER, SKEPTIC

Notice that each word can have other senses. *Accessory*, for example, can mean an object or device that is not essential but that enhances the main object. A program has been written to extract these words. The headwords are then marked [+ human], and synonyms such as *flibbertigibbet*, *doubter*, and *skeptic* can also be marked as [+ human] in one sense.

Although this approach is appealing, caution is in order. In the first place, lexicographers are people, and dictionaries are huge undertakings written by many different contributors. Therefore, there is less internal consistency than would be ideal. Finally, and most seriously, there is the problem that most words have more than one sense. Keeping track of which senses have which features is not an easy task. Furthermore, the decision on what is a sense is also not clear-cut. The problem of extensibility enters into play again. Even with all these restrictions, however, using machine-readable dictionaries as a resource for constructing large lexicons looks very promising.

Another approach to building large lexicons for natural language analysis and generation is **corpus analysis**. The larger the corpus, or text, the more useful it is, since the chances of covering the language as it actually is used increase. In addition to size, a good corpus should include a wide variety of types of writing, such as newspapers, textbooks, popular writing, fiction, and technical material. As an example of the way large corpora (the plural of corpus) are useful, consider the verb of movement *flounce*. The definitions given for the verb in Webster's Seventh New Collegiate Dictionary are:

flounce 1

> to move with exaggerated, jerky motions
> to go with sudden determination
> to trim with flounces

These definitions tell nothing about likely subjects. Looking at corpus data will yield this information. From a large corpus, about twenty occurrences of the verb *flounce* were extracted. Thirteen had subjects that were female, as in sentences *23* and *24*.

> *23.* Carol flounced out to the kitchen for an apron.
> *24.* She flounced off with a following of hens behind her.

Four had subjects that were clothing:

> *25.* The white cashmere dressing-gown flounced around her.

One had *horses* as the subject, and the other subjects were pronouns. The point is that, given a good parser, it would be possible to extract automatically all the subjects of a given verb, and then to look for properties of those subjects. For *flounce*, that information would appear in the lexicon as:

> *Word: flounce-1*
> *1.* Part of Speech: Verb
> *2.* Subcategorization: Intransitive
> *3.* Semantic Restrictions: female human subject
>
> *Word: flounce-2*
> *1.* Part of Speech: Verb
> *2.* Subcategorization: Intransitive
> *3.* Semantic Restrictions: clothing subject

Using computers to extract linguistically useful information from dictionaries and texts for the purpose of constructing large lexicons is a new field within computational linguistics. It holds great promise in providing a solution to the difficult but fundamental problem of building computational lexicons out of already existing resources. At this point, clever programs give large and comprehensive lists of words with a potential characteristic, but human judgments are still necessary. If the computer is viewed as a tool to be used in collecting lists of words, then the endeavor is successful. If the goal is to view the computer as the only tool, and to eliminate the human judge, then computational lexicon builders still have a long way to go.

15.5 COMPUTATIONAL SEMANTICS

So far in this chapter, we have focused on structure: the structure of sentences and words. However, in order to understand what a word, sentence, or text means, a computer program has to know the semantics of words, sentences, and text. This section treats briefly some of the semantic representations and processes that have been proposed in computational linguistics.

Semantic issues were touched on in the preceding section. The lexical item contains a field for semantic information, including such information as what kind of semantic features a verb requires for its subject or which thematic roles a verb requires or permits. The semantic fields for the two senses of *flounce* are:

Word: flounce-1
Semantic Restrictions: female human subject
Word: flounce-2
Semantic Restrictions: clothing subject

Although the semantics of words is an important component of any language system, there is yet a broader issue: the semantics of sentences and paragraphs.

Two approaches to semantics and language analysis have been proposed: syntactically based systems and semantically based systems. Considering for the moment the analysis of sentences, in the first approach the sentence is assigned a syntactic analysis, much in the way outlined in Chapter 5 and earlier in this chapter. A semantic representation is built after the syntactic analysis is performed (see Figure 15.16). The problems arise in getting from one repre-

Syntactically Based Systems

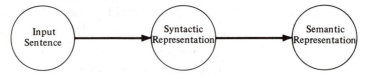

Figure 15.16

sentation to the other. This is sometimes called the mapping problem. However, in the semantically based system, first a semantic representation is built. Sometimes there is no syntactic analysis at all (see Figure 15.17). Consider a response to the question *Who got the coffee today?*

26. The new student went.

Semantically Based Systems

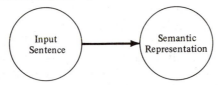

Figure 15.17

A syntactic analysis of the sentence would show that *the new student* is the first NP directly dominated by S (see Figure 15.18). From there, the parser might guess that the subject is *the new student*. This is often true in English, although it is not always the case. Still, nothing is said about the fact that the subject is the actor (i.e., the one who performs the action) with a verb like *go*. Compare this to the intransitive version of the verb *open*.

27. The door opened.

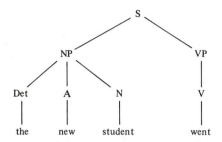

Figure 15.18

In this case, the subject *door* is not performing an action. Something or someone opened the door. A syntactically based system obtains this knowledge about a sentence after a structure is built.

In contrast, a semantically based system builds a semantic representation first. For sentence *26*, it might look something like the one in Figure 15.19.

```
Go  −  Actor
          NP
went      the new student
```

Figure 15.19

The word order is not important. The semantic representation of related sentences might be the same.

28. John gave the book to Mary.
29. John gave Mary the book.
30. The book was given to Mary by John.

The mapping into the various syntactic forms of what is basically the same sentence occurs after the semantic representation is decided upon. Semantically based systems have been used for text and discourse analysis, such as for understanding stories.

Both approaches still need to accomplish the same goal, namely that of assigning word meaning, sentence meaning, and text meaning. The problem of semantic representation will not be covered here. However, it must be mentioned that determining matters like reference, as in *31*, and scope, as in *32* to *34*, are part of what needs to be achieved.

31. I saw him in the bookstore.
32. Pregnant women and children get out first.
33. Ripe apples and peaches make a good fruit salad.
34. Every person speaks two languages.

For *31*, is this a specific bookstore or just some bookstore? For *32*, what is the scope of *pregnant*? Is it *pregnant women and pregnant children*? This is unlikely. But in *33*, the likely interpretation is *ripe apples and ripe peaches*. Finally, in *34*, does every person speak the same two languages? Or different languages?

Pragmatics

The word *meaning* itself has many meanings. In addition to word meaning, logic, paragraph meaning, and so on, it has also been loosely applied to the field of **pragmatics**. Pragmatics is the study of how language is used in communication. Consider the following telephone conversation.

> *35.* Caller: Is George at home?
> Answer: Yes.

This dialogue is amusing because the answerer has broken some basic conversational principles. The caller is not really asking the literal question *Is George at home?* although the semantic analysis of the sentence would indicate that this is a request for information about whether or not George is at home. The syntactic form of the question requires the answers *yes* or *no*, but nothing else. The dialogue in *36* does not have the amusing quality of *35*.

> *36.* Caller: Are you tired?
> Answer: Yes.

Conversational principles (see Chapter 6) require that an answer be as informative as possible. This is not the case in *35*. Another example of conversational principles is illustrated in *37* and *38*.

> *37.* Sue got on the horse and rode into the sunset.
> *38.* Sue rode into the sunset and got on the horse.

Why is *38* strange? The coordinating conjunction *and* should just be a simple joining of two like parts. The nouns from *33*, for example, could be reversed with no strange result (the scope problem remains unsolved, however):

> *39.* Ripe peaches and apples make a good fruit salad.

The reason for the problem in *38* is that the word *and* is often given a temporal interpretation. This may not be part of the meaning of *and* but rather a matter of how it is used.

Whether pragmatics is a subfield of semantics is controversial, but there is no disagreement on the fact that knowledge of pragmatic principles is necessary to understanding and generating language.

15.6 PRACTICAL APPLICATIONS OF COMPUTATIONAL LINGUISTICS

The previous sections of this chapter have shown how the use of computers has forced linguists to formulate rigorous statements of theory and facts, because all of the implicit knowledge that humans have about language has to be made explicit. Theories become testable in a concrete way. Implementations of practical systems tend to force researchers (and students) to understand a particular language process in very detailed terms. Since related skills are needed both for linguistic analysis and for programming, the field of computational linguistics has flourished. This section discusses some specific types of computer systems that involve using linguistically sophisticated programs.

An **application** can be defined as the use to which a program or set of programs is put, for example, a payroll application, an airline reservation application, or a word processing application. Most early applications in computational linguistics fell into three categories: indexing and concordances, machine translation, and information retrieval. Other applications included speech synthesis and recognition and database applications.

Indexing and Concordances

Indexing means finding, identifying, and usually counting all occurrences of a certain word in large texts. This application of computers to language study does exactly what computers are best at doing: locating a word, recording the location by line or sentence number, and counting how many times it appears. The examples of the use of the word *flounce* in the lexicology section were extracted from text using an indexing program. The program searched text on the computer to find any occurrence of the string *flounce*, *flouncing*, *flounced*, or *flounces*. When the string was found, the computer program took out the sentence and saved it in a separate file. A tally was kept of each time a targeted word was found.

A concordance tells which words occur near other words. Concordance and indexing programs are used widely in literary analysis. Some authors seem to favor using certain words in the context of other words. Concordance programs can find these relationships. A concordance program could tell, for example, how many times the word *she* occurred next to *flounce*.

Perhaps the most widely used word count was performed by Henry Kucera and Nelson Francis in 1962 on a corpus of one million words. The corpus is referred to as the Brown corpus since the work was completed at Brown University. Kucera and Francis took fifteen different texts and wrote a program to count the number of times each word appeared. The ten most frequent words of English are:

the	69,971
of	36,411
and	28,852
to	26,149
a	23,237
in	21,341
that	10,595
is	10,099
was	9,816
he	9,543

The numbers after the words indicate how many times they appeared in the one million words. Word frequency lists such as this have been useful to psycholinguists who need to pay attention to frequency when designing experiments.

These early applications are still very useful, but they are not linguistic in nature. They used the power of the computer to count and categorize words, so the results were of use to the linguist, but they did not rely on any linguistic knowledge. For example, to find *flounce*, the related words *flounced*, *flounces*, *flouncing* also had to be looked for. Early systems were not endowed with morphological knowledge, so they could look only for the exact string given. The program could not figure out that *flounce* and *flouncing* were related forms. Furthermore, all occurrences of the strings *flounce*, *flounces*, and so on were pulled out, without regard to part of speech. Since the goal was to look at subjects of verbs, it was necessary to distinguish between the verb *flounce* and the noun *flounce* as in *The women always flounce out* and *The chair had a lacy flounce around the bottom*. Notice the implications of this: two of the top ten most frequent words are forms of the verb *be*, but since the system counts only strings, the forms *is* and *was* are counted separately. The inability of early systems to relate words had other problems. For example:

Minute	53
Min	5
Min.	1
Min,	1

are probably all variations of the word *minute*, although this would have to be verified by checking the original text. The count of *minute* is 53, but it really should be 60.

Most current concordance and indexing programs have solved some of the easier problems such as abbreviations, but most of the harder problems still remain. First of all, morphological knowledge is needed in order to relate various forms of the same word to just one base word. Second, syntactic knowledge is needed in order to figure out the part of speech of the word in the sentences and in order to figure out the arguments of the verbs, such as subject and object. Finally, semantic knowledge is needed to know the thematic roles of the arguments and to know which meaning of a word is intended.

Text Retrieval

Most libraries have abstracts of articles available by computer. Anyone who has ever tried to search for articles on a particular topic has had the frustrating experience of having to wade through masses of irrelevant material to find what was wanted. For example, when the word *morphology* was searched in the Library Index of Book Titles, the following titles were among those returned:

> Principles of Polymer Morphology
> Image Analysis and Mathematical Morphology
> Drainage Basin Morphology
> French Morphology

If a linguistically sophisticated program had been used to retrieve these titles, it is likely that they would have been divided according to the semantic subject field. Thus a chemist would not get titles on French, just as a linguist would not get titles on chemistry.

What linguistic expertise could text retrieval systems use? Again, as with indexing and concordance, the three critical subareas are computational morphology, syntax, and semantics. For example, someone wanting to know about the theory of light might want to find all references to the word *light* in an encyclopedia. This is not an unreasonable request, since there are now several encyclopedias available on compact disc, which can be read by a drive attached to a personal computer. The user can search through the text in ways that cannot easily be done with encyclopedias in book form. Searching for the string *light* anywhere in the text might give *lightening*, *enlightenment*, and *light-*

hearted, but also *delight* and *candlelight*. On the other hand, if the user searches only for *light* surrounded by blanks, then words like *lighting* or *lights* would be missed. Without a parser and semantics, there is no clue about the nature of the word *light* when it is found in the text. The problem appears simplistic, but it is far more complex than meets the eye.

Machine Translation

The purpose of a machine translation system is the same as that of any translation system: taking text written or spoken in one language and writing or speaking it in another (see Figure 15.20). Translation poses challenging

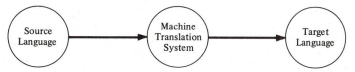

Figure 15.20

problems both for the human translator and for the machine attempting to do what the human does. Projects in machine translation in the 1940s and 1950s spawned much of the early research in computational linguistics. Consider the written case first, and think of a single institution like the United Nations. Every day millions of words need to be translated from one language to another. Add to that other political and scientific institutions, plus businesses and publishers. This results in an overwhelming need for help in translation since the process, when done correctly, is time-consuming and mentally demanding. Since computers are suited to tasks requiring memory, it would seem that, with careful programming, the problem of translating by computer could be solved.

This was the thinking of computer scientists and linguists, but the problems turned out to be far more difficult than was imagined. Much government money was poured into the machine translation task from the late 1940s to the early 1960s, but results were slow to emerge due to the complexity of unforeseen problems. The subtlety of language, the nuances and lack of precision, caused problems because computers are suited to mathematical computation where subtleties do not prevail. Funding agencies became disillusioned, and although most researchers were still hopeful, they were humbled by the difficulties encountered in early years.

Researchers are now more realistic about their goals. Rather than attempting to build full-fledged machine translation systems that automatically convert a text from one language to another, some projects are aiming toward machine-assisted translation. In these projects, the computer is viewed as a tool to aid the translator. The computer makes suggestions, but the human translator makes final decisions. Other projects are developing ways to take texts and pass them through a preprocessor. A preprocessor is a system that looks at sentences and figures out which ones might present problems. The computer can identify the problem, and then ask the original writer to clarify. Take the first example in this chapter:

40. Many elephants smell.

Since this sentence is ambiguous as explained earlier, it might be sent back to the writer to be clarified.

Machine translation applications encompass many aspects of computational linguistics. For this reason, the venture is one of the more challenging to researchers. In addition, the notion of a machine that is capable or nearly capable of mimicking a very complex and subtle human activity constitutes an intriguing enterprise.

The source language needs to be analyzed syntactically and semantically. Lexical items need to be matched. This is a particularly difficult task. Not only do words in one language often not exist in another, but sometimes several words are used for one. One example involves the German words *essen* and *fressen*. Both words mean *eat* in English, but the verb *essen* is used for humans, whereas *fressen* is used for animals. If the system made the mistake of using *fressen* for people, it would be an insult. An example from Spanish concerns a missing word, as shown in *41* and *42*. Sentence *43* gives the word-by-word translation of the Spanish in *42*.

41. The elephants slept but didn't snore.
42. Los elefantes durmiéron pero no roncaron.
43. *The elephants slept but not snored.

The word-by-word translation of *42* is not English. What's wrong? In English, in a negative sentence without an auxiliary verb, the properly inflected form of the verb *do* needs to be inserted. Since *41* is in the past tense, and since the subject is plural, the correct form is *did*. There is no word for *did* in the Spanish version of the same sentence. Just as the human translator has to know this fact, so does the machine translation system. If the input language were Spanish and the input sentence were *42*, then the English generation system would need to know to insert the verb *do*, properly inflected, and not to inflect the main verb. The difficulties increase with languages that are fundamentally different in nature, such as English and Japanese, or Spanish and Finnish, or French and Chinese.

If the machine translation system is required to take spoken language as input and give spoken language as output, then the system becomes even more complex, as shown in Figure 15.21.

Figure 15.21

Speech Recognition

A speech recognition system takes spoken language as input and understands it (see Figure 15.22). The result could be the written text of what was said, or it could be orders to another machine. For example, a smart typewriter equipped with a recognition device will take orders to delete a line. The typewriter follows orders, but the words *delete line* will not be written. Speech recognition is a process that humans perform effortlessly, but teaching computers to recognize speech has turned out to be more difficult than was origi-

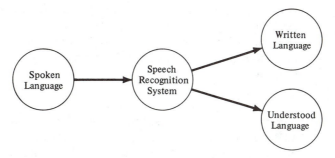

Figure 15.22

nally thought. Some of the linguistic problems involved were outlined in the sections on computational phonetics and phonology.

What are some applications that would benefit from a speech recognition system? One that has been explored is in the area of medical record keeping. Writing down details of examinations is time-consuming; often doctors leave out critical information due to these time pressures. With a speech recognition system, the doctor would simply talk while doing an examination. The speech would automatically and instantly be translated into text, which could be printed out immediately. In this way, the doctor could examine the report with the patient there to make sure everything has been covered. Medical terminology is fairly controlled, so the computer would have an advantage in guessing words. The examination room is relatively quiet, reducing the problem of background noise. Finally, a speech recognition system would allow the doctor to use both hands while speaking. Medical records could immediately go into a central library, which could be referred to by researchers studying symptoms and diagnoses. Last but not least, no one would ever have to struggle to read the doctor's illegible handwriting!

Such a system would have to be absolutely perfect. However, it is easier to correct an error in a report than to write one. Other applications that have been explored include quality control devices for inspecting assembly lines. For example, a worker would be able to say words like *pass* or *fail*, and the machine would then know whether to accept the part or refuse it. A very important application of speech recognition is in developing aids for the physically disabled. These include devices such as voice-operated appliances, machines, and tools. Applications such as these have great promise.

Speech Synthesis

A speech synthesis system has the opposite goal from a speech recognition system (see Figure 15.23). Applications for speech synthesis systems abound. One of the most important uses is "reading" to the visually impaired. Pre-

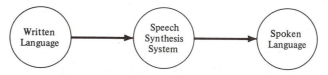

Figure 15.23

viously this required a human either to do the actual reading or to pre-record books and other material. This is not only expensive but also limiting, since what the person wants or needs to read may not be available on tape. Another important application is as a talking aid for the vocally handicapped. Communication boards and talking typewriters show the value of converting text to spoken language.

Another fairly common application is in an area called *database query*. A database is a large source of information, such as bank records, billing records, airline schedules, and theater and movie schedules. Imagine wanting to find out about ticket availability for the theater, movies, or other cultural events. This information is constantly changing as people buy tickets and as agencies release tickets. When you call, the text-to-speech machine can read the information aloud directly out of the database. No one has had to record it, which is time-consuming and expensive. Furthermore, the information is completely up-to-date. Other applications include use in machine translation systems, for robots, for expert systems, and for novel medical applications.

Summing Up

This chapter has covered the relatively new field of **computational linguistics**, which is the application of computers to the study of linguistic problems. There are two goals in computational linguistics. One is to use the computer as a tool to build programs that model a particular linguistic theory or approach. For this goal, the computer becomes a testing ground for the theory. The other goal is to build working systems that use linguistic information. The chapter covers the fields of computational phonetics and phonology, morphology, syntax, lexicology, and semantics and pragmatics. A section on **applications** presents some of the devices that have incorporated linguistic tools, such as machine translation systems and reading machines for the visually impaired.

Key Terms

application	nonterminal node
determinism	parser
generative capacity	real world knowledge
grammatical knowledge	speech recognition
implementation	speech synthesis
machine translation	terminal node
nondeterminism	text retrieval

Recommended Reading

Allen, James. 1987. *Natural Language Understanding*. Benjamin/Cummings: Menlo Park, California.

Grishman, Ralph. 1986. *Computational Linguistics: An Introduction*. Cambridge University Studies in Natural Language Processing. Cambridge University Press: Cambridge.

Journal of the Association for Computational Linguistics. 1987. Volume 13, Numbers 3–4.

King, Margaret, ed. 1983. *Parsing Natural Language.* Academic Press/Harcourt Brace Jovanovich: London.

Klatt, Dennis. "Review of text-to-speech conversion for English." *Journal of the Acoustical Society of America.* Vol. 82:3:1987.

Levinson, Stephan E. and Mark Y. Liberman. "Speech Recognition by Computer." *Scientific American.* April 1981.

Savitch, Walter J, Emmon Bach, William Marsh and Gila Safran-Naveh, eds. 1987. *The Formal Complexity of Natural Language.* New York: D. Reidel/Kluwer.

Questions

1. What kinds of problems might a computer have with these sentences?

   a) Sue bought red apples and plums.
   b) It was a large animal house.
   c) Susan baked in the kitchen.
   d) Susan baked in the sun.
   e) Susan baked.

2. What are the main uses of a text-to-speech system? What information does the computer need to know in order to pronounce these sentences in informal style?

   a) What are you doing tonight?
   b) The woman was delighted.
   c) That article misled me.
   d) That's a new car, isn't it?
   e) It was a tough test, although I did well.
   f) Can't you sing better?

3. What rules are necessary for a computer program to analyze these words? (*Hint*: First figure out the prefixes and suffixes. Refer to the chapter on morphology if necessary.)

   a) kindness
   b) kindly
   c) kindnesses
   d) nationalism
   e) countability
   f) nontransformational
   g) reusable

4. What different structures might a syntactic analyzer propose for the following sentences?

a) She saw the man with a telescope.

b) Watch dogs bark.

c) Broadcast programs like 60 Minutes.

5. Think of a word that has many different meanings, such as *bank* or *interest*. Then give information about that word using the categories in Section 15.4. Give at least two senses for each part of speech. The following example has one sense for the noun part of speech, and two senses for the verb part of speech.

WORD: bank

a) Part of Speech: Noun

b) Sense Number: 1

c) Semantic Restrictions: of a river

d) Pronunciation: /bæŋk/

e) Context and Style: normal

f) Example: The bank of the river was grassy.

WORD: bank

a) Part of Speech: Verb

b) Sense Number: 1

c) Subcategorization: transitive, requires the preposition *on*

d) Semantic Restrictions: object of preposition is either a person or thing

e) Pronunciation: /bæŋk/

f) Context and Style: informal

g) Example: I can't bank on him to do it.

WORD: bank

a) Part of Speech: Verb

b) Sense Number: 2

c) Subcategorization: transitive

d) Semantic Restrictions: object is money

e) Pronunciation: /bæŋk/

f) Context and Style: normal

g) Example: She banks her money at the local branch.

6. Give three applications of computational linguistics. How can these systems improve the quality of life for people with physical disabilities?

For the Student Linguist

ONE SECOND

Mike is driving the kids to the game. It's a simple sentence; you probably have no problem understanding it and can do so within the few seconds it takes to utter this sentence. But by now you've learned something about phonetics, phonology, morphology, and syntax, and so you can recognize that there's a lot of structure hidden inside this seemingly simple sentence. In computational linguistics we deal with the ways in which individual components of grammar interact. One place where this happens is during parsing.

I think parsing is one of the most fascinating parts of language. To illustrate how complex parsing must be, I've listed some of the steps your brain might be following as you hear this sentence. Imagine how much work you'd have to do for a more complicated sentence.

M

As soon as you hear the first sound, you're already coming up with possible words:

my	Mabel	microphone	magazine	meat
music	Midol	migraine	mine	mud
might	make	mat	miss	mice
Mike	mascara	moped	mitochondria	model

Mi

Each new sound eliminates some possibilities and makes others more likely.

my	microphone	mitochondria
might	Midol	mine
Mike	migraine	mice

Mike

Already there's a conflict: this string of sounds could be *my* plus another word (starting with [k]), or *Mike*, *microphone*, etc.

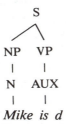

Mike is d

By now these sounds are probably identified as *Mike is . . .*, since a possibility like *My kismet . . .* is ruled out by the [d] and *my* followed by some unknown word has a low probability. So syntax can kick in, and start making tree structures. You might wonder when your brain knows it's going to get a sentence. It might assume it right away, and postulate an *S* node as soon as the first word starts. Or maybe it waits until it hears something verb-like. What do you think? Let's assume that as soon as it hears a noun or a determiner, it knows it's going to get an NP, and as soon as it gets an AUX or a verb it knows it's going to get a VP.

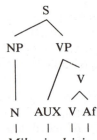

Mike is driving

The morphology component of the parser didn't have to do much with the first two words, but once it reaches *driving* it has to identify the verb stem and the affix. Meanwhile, phonology and morphology together have to rule out something like *Mike is dry . . . ving. . . .* Notice how misleading it could be to pick the first legitimate-sounding sequence as the real sequence; it's *Mike*, not *My k . . .*, it's *Mike is driving*, not *Mike is dry*. So your brain has to delay decisions a bit, until it has confirmation that it has made the right choice.

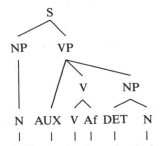

Mike is driving the kids

Now the morphology component has a dilemma. *Kids* could be plural or possessive (remember, you're hearing this, so you can't see any punctuation), so the morphology and syntax components can't tell whether the NP is complete (if it's just *the kids*) or to expect more material in the NP, waiting for whatever object follows *the kid's* or *the kids'*.

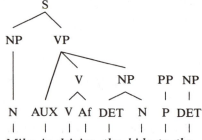

Mike is driving the kids to the

Once you hear *the*, you can rule out something like *the kid's two cars . . .* or *the kids' two cars . . .* and "close" the NP (decide that it's complete). Or can you? What if the PP following *kids* modifies it (and therefore the PP for *to the game* is a sister of the N for *kids* instead of a sister of the

NP *the kids*)? Again, the different components have to interface to determine the structure as quickly as possible without locking into an incorrect decision prematurely.

Why am I emphasizing the need to figure out when you've reached the end of some phrase? Because it might require more memory to hold a group of words as an open, active unit than to declare it a complete constituent. Sort of like having a limited amount of desk space; it's easier to file away things you know you're done with than to keep them spread all over your desk surface and in your way.

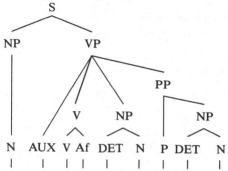

Mike is driving the kids to the game.

And finally you're done. Pretty amazing that you can do all that parsing in a few seconds, isn't it? Now you can try to explain why sentences like the following are so hard to understand. Good luck.

The dog walked past the kennel barked.

Since Sheila kept on eating the brownies burned.

The reporter that the dog that Mary owns bit last week slept late.

GLOSSARY

Ablaut A vowel alternation that marks grammatical contrasts (e.g., *sing/sang* in English) See also **Replacement**.

Absolute universals Patterns or traits that occur in all languages.

Absolutive A case assigned to the subject of an intransitive verb and the object of a transitive verb in ergative languages.

Abstract representation A representation that is to a greater or lesser degree distinct from its phonetic realization.

Accidental gaps Gaps in a language's inventory of forms that correspond to nonoccurring but possible forms.

Accusative (Ac) A case assigned to the direct object noun phrase.

Acoustic phonetics The study of the physical properties of speech sound in terms of how we hear them.

Acquired dysgraphia The impairment of already acquired writing ability.

Acquired dyslexia The impairment of already acquired reading ability.

Acrolect The creole variety that is most similar to the standard.

Acronym A word formed by taking the initial letters of some (or all) of the words in a phrase or title and pronouncing them as a word (e.g., AIDS, NASA).

Acrophonic principle A principle by which a sound is represented in writing by a picture of an object whose pronunciation begins with the sound to be represented.

Act sequence A component of the speech situation, which includes the content and form of speech.

Active (sentence) A sentence where the agent is encoded as grammatical subject of the sentence (e.g., '*The boy ate the beans*').

Adjective A lexical item that modifies a noun and heads an adjective phrase.

Adverb A lexical item that modifies a verb.

Affix (Af) A bound morpheme that modifies the meaning and/or syntactic (sub)category of the stem in some way (e.g., *un-* and *-able* in *unreadable*).

Affricate A non-continuant consonant characterized by a slow release of its closure (e.g., [tʃ] and [dʒ]).

Agent A thematic role borne by the entity that performs an action (e.g., '*the boy*' in the sentence '*The boy ate the beans*').

Agglutinating (language) A language that makes extensive use of polymorphemic words (i.e., words containing a root and one or more affixes) and in which each grammatical contrast is typically encoded by a separate, clearly identifiable morpheme (e.g., Turkish).

Agrammatism A language disorder involving the loss of minor lexical categories and affixes, usually associated with Broca's aphasia.

Agraphia Loss of the ability to write caused by brain damage.

Agreement A relationship between elements, where a property of one word requires a corresponding form of another.

Alexia See **Acquired dyslexia**.

Algorithm A set of rules for solving a problem. The term was first used in mathematics to describe the rules for solving mathematical problems.

Allomorph A variant form of a morpheme (e.g., in English /-əz/, /-z/, and /-s/ are allomorphs of the plural morpheme /z/).

Allophone A predictable variant of a phoneme (e.g., [t] and [tʰ] are allophones of the phoneme /t/ in English).

Alpha rules Phonological rules stated in a conventional formula in which variables (α, β, etc.) are introduced for the value of distinctive features.

Alphabetic (writing) A system of writing in which symbols represent consonant and vowel segments.

Alternating stress A stress pattern in which multiple stresses fall at regular intervals.

Alveolar ridge A small ridge that protrudes from just behind the upper front teeth within the oral cavity (also called the *alveolum*).

Alveopalatal (sound) A sound produced in the area between the palate and the alveolar ridge where the roof of the mouth rises sharply (also called **Palatoalveolar**) (e.g., [ʃ], [ʒ]).

Ambisyllabic segment A segment that can be simultaneously part of two adjacent syllables.

Amelioration A semantic change where the meaning of a word becomes more positive or favorable (e.g., the meaning of *knight* used to be 'boy').

Amerindian (language) An indigenous language of North or South America (e.g., Cree, Haida).

Analogy An inference that if two things are alike in some respects they must be alike in others (e.g., since *mow* and *know* are alike in that they are both verbs, by analogy with *mowed,* the past tense of *know* should be *knowed*).

Analytic (language) A language in which words are typically made up of a single morpheme (also called an **Isolating language**) (e.g., Cantonese).

Anaphoric reference A referential relationship between a noun phrase and a pronoun occurring later in the text.

Angular gyrus A language center in the brain that lies behind Wernicke's area and is responsible for converting a visual stimulus into an auditory form and vice versa.

Animate In some languages, a class consisting of nouns, most of which have living referents.

Antecedent The NP on which a pronoun depends for its interpretation (e.g., *John* in *John hurt himself*).

Anterior (sounds) Sounds articulated in front of the alveopalatal region (e.g., [p], [d], [z] and so on).

Antonyms Words or expressions that are opposites in some component of their meanings (e.g., *hot* and *cold*).

Aphasia Language loss caused by damage to the brain.

Apocope The loss of a word-final vowel (e.g., Middle English [na:mə]→ Modern English [nejm]).

Arbitrariness A property of communication whereby there is no natural or inherent connection between a sign and its referent.

Archaisms Lexical items that are survivors of forms previously more widely used (e.g., Newfoundland English *drite* meaning 'dryness in the air').

Arcuate fasciculus The bundle of nerve fibers connecting Wernicke's area and Broca's area.

Areal classification A classification of languages that identifies characteristics shared by languages in geographical contact.

Argot The language of any social group whose members want to conceal the content of their communication from some other group (sometimes called **Cant**).

Articulatory phonetics The study of the physical production of speech sounds.

Aspiration The release of air through the oral cavity caused by a delay in the voicing of a vowel following the release of a voiceless stop.

Assimilation The modification of one or more features of a sound under the influence of neighboring elements (e.g., *Banff* is often pronounced [bæmf]).

Association lines Lines that link a phonetic or phonological representation on one tier to representations on another tier (e.g., the lines connecting a tonal representation to the vowel pronounced on that tone).

Audiolingual method A method of second language teaching based on the notion that second language learning should be regarded as a mechanistic process of habit formation.

Autosegmental phonology An approach that sees phonology as comprising several 'tiers', each of which consists of a separate arrangement of segments.

Auxiliary verb (Aux) A verb that serves as the specifier of a main verb (also called a **Helping verb**) (e.g., *has* in *He has left*).

Back (a) **(sound)** A sound made with the tongue retracted. (b) **(of the tongue)** The hindmost part of the tongue that lies in the mouth.

Backformation A word formation process that occurs when a word whose structure is apparently similar to that of a derived form undergoes a process of "deaffixation" (e.g., *resurrection→resurrect*).

Base A word to which an affix is added.

Basilect The creole variety that is least similar to the standard.

Bilabial (sound) A sound made with both lips (e.g., [p], [b]).

Binary (features) Features that are considered to be either wholly present or wholly absent in the articulation of a sound (e.g., [±voice], [±coronal], etc.).

Blade (of the tongue) The part of the tongue that lies just behind the tip.

Bleeding (rule ordering) A rule ordering where the first operates so as to make the following rule inapplicable.

Blend A new word that is created from parts of two already existing lexical terms (e.g., *breakfast + lunch → brunch*).

Blissymbolics A contemporary development of both pictographic and ideographic writing, intended as a means of international, cross-linguistic communication for non-speaking individuals.

Body (of the tongue) The main mass of the tongue.

Borrowing The acquisition of words, sounds, or rules by one language from a language with which it has contact (e.g., English has borrowed the words *government, religion,* and *science* from French).

Bound (morpheme) A morpheme that must be attached to another element (i.e., it cannot constitute a word by itself) (e.g., *-s* in *books*).

Bounded foot A foot that consists of a head and no more than one unstressed syllable.

Boustrophedon A style of writing in which lines are written alternately right to left, left to right, and so on.

Broca's aphasia Aphasia caused by damage to the lower rear portion of the left frontal lobe, characterized by poor articulation, phonemic paraphasia and agrammatism.

Broca's area An area in the frontal lobe of the left hemisphere that plays a crucial role in organizing the articulatory patterns of speech and the formation of words and sentences.

C-command A notion that is relevant to the interpretation of a pronoun and is formulated as follows: A category *A* c-commands a category *B* if the first category above *A* also dominates *B*.

Call (bird) Short bursts of sound produced by birds that typically serve to warn predators, coordinate flocking and flight activity, and so on.

Cant See **Jargon** and **Argot**.

Caretaker speech See **Motherese**.

Case An inflectional category that marks the grammatical function of an NP (i.e., subject, object, etc.) (e.g., nominative, accusative, genitive).

Cataphoric reference A referential relationship between a noun phrase and a pronoun occurring earlier in the text.

Central sulcus A sulcus that extends from the top of the cortex to the lateral fissure.

Cerebral cortex The highest portion of the brain, whose structure and development are different depending on the species (e.g., the human brain has the greatest proportion of cortex to brain mass of all animals).

Cerebral dominance The control of cognitive and perceptual functions by a particular hemisphere of the brain.

Cerebral hemisphere The left or right half of the cerebral cortex.

Cerebral plasticity Flexibility in neurological organization that is supposedly characteristic of children in the critical period for language acquisition.

Character The unit of contemporary Chinese orthography, usually consisting of two parts, a **determinative** and a **radical**.

Clause A structure consisting of an NP and a VP; also called S.

Clever Hans A horse that seemed to have a human-like capacity to think.

Clipping A word formation process whereby a new word is created by shortening a polysyllabic word (e.g., *advertisement→ad*).

Closed syllable A syllable that ends in a consonant.

Coarticulation An articulation in which phonemes overlap to a certain extent.

Coda The segments of a syllable that follow the nucleus (e.g., /n/ and /l/ in *central*).

Cognates Words that have descended from a common source (e.g., English *father*, German *Vater*, and French *père*).

Cognitive development The emergence of the various mental abilities and skills that make up the human intellect.

Cognitive style The way in which we are predisposed to process information in our environment.

Cohesive device A device that establishes a connection among two or more elements in the discourse (e.g., anaphoric reference, cataphoric reference, lexical cohesion, ellipsis, and so on).

Coinage A newly created word.

Communication strategy A strategy that serves the communicative needs of an L2 learner: a conscious plan instigated to fulfil an immediate communicative need.

Communicative competence A speaker's underlying knowledge of the linguistic system and the norms for the appropriate use of language in particular speech situations.

Communicative language teaching method (CLT) Second language teaching methods that are communicative in design, emphasizing functional language in the attempt to attain the goal of communicative competence.

Community counselling (teaching method) A method of second language teaching in which the L2 learner is considered part of a group rather than a class, and the teacher assumes the role of counsellor, allowing the student to begin communication in his or her own language.

Comparative reconstruction Establishment of a parent language by systematically comparing several daughter languages.

Complement A syntactic constituent that provides information about entities and locations implied by the meaning of the head.

Complement clause A sentence-like construction that is embedded as a sister of V (e.g., *I wonder* whether he has left).

Complementary distribution The distribution of allophones in their respective phonetic environments such that one never appears in the same phonetic context as the other (e.g., the distribution of long and short vowels in English).

Complementizer (Comp) A category that takes an S complement, forming a CP (e.g., *whether, that, if*).

Complex (word) A word that consists of two or more morphemes (e.g., *gentle-man-ly*).

Componential analysis The analysis of lexical items in terms of a finite set of semantic features.

Compounding The combination of two or more free morphemes to form a new word (e.g., *lighthouse*).

Comprehensible input The linguistic input to which the L2 learner is exposed that is slightly beyond his or her competence in the target language.

Computerized Axial Tomography A technique that uses a narrow beam of X-rays to create images of the body parts that take the form of a series of slices of the parts.

Conduction aphasia A language disorder resulting from damage to the arcuate fasciculus and characterized by severe difficulty in repeating auditory forms.

Conjugation The complete set of inflected forms associated with a verb (also called a **Verbal paradigm**).

Conjunction (C) A minor lexical category whose members serve to join categories of the same type (e.g., *and, or*).

Connotation The set of associations that a word's use can evoke.

Consonant Sounds made with a narrow or complete closure in the vocal tract; the airflow is either completely blocked momentarily or restricted so much that noise is produced.

Consonant deletion Deletion of consonants by some phonological rules.

Consonant weakening A lessening in the time or degree of a consonant's closure.

Consonantal (sounds) Sounds that are produced with some obstruction in the vocal tract, and have low acoustic energy (e.g., [p], [b], [s], and so on).

Constellation A complex of communicative modes operating on different channels.

Constituent A syntactic unit in the sentence.

Constricted glottis The phonological feature that represents the sounds made with the glottis closed.

Continuant A sound produced with continuous airflow through the mouth (includes vowels, glides, fricatives, and some liquids).

Contour tone A tone that changes pitch on a single syllable.

Contradiction A relationship between two sentences wherein the truth of one sentence entails the falsity of the other (e.g., *Harry is a bachelor; Harry is married*).

Contralateralization Control of one side of the body by the brain hemisphere on the opposite side.

Contrast To show difference(s) in form that may be related to difference(s) in meaning (e.g., the sounds [k] and [p] contrast in the words *cane* and *pain*).

Contrastive analysis (CA) An approach to L2 acquisition research that involves the comparison of the linguistic structures of the L2 learner's native language and the target language to determine their similarities and differences.

Conversational implicature A conclusion about the speaker's intended meaning based on "rules" for conversation such as the Cooperative Principle.

Conversational maxims Guidelines to satisfy the Cooperative Principle (e.g., the Maxim of Relation, Quality, Quantity, and Manner).

Conversion A morphological process that creates a new word by assigning a stem to a new lexical category without affixation (e.g., *ship* (noun)→*ship* (verb)).

Cooperative Principle A principle used in communication and according to which an utterance is assumed to be informative and relevant in the context of the communicative situation.

Coordinate structures A structure in which two or more constituents of the same syntactic category are linked together with the help of a conjunction such as *and* or *or*.

Coordinate structure constraint A constraint that prohibits affecting only one of the constituents of a coordinate structure.

Coordination test A test used for identifying constituents by coordinating two sequences of words.

Coronal (sounds) Sounds that are produced with the tongue tip or blade raised (e.g., [t], [d], [s], and so on).

Corpus callosum A bundle of nerve fibers connecting the two hemispheres of the brain.

Cortex The outside surface of the human brain (also called *grey matter*) that provides the basis for the cognitive abilities distinguishing humans from other mammals.

Cranberry morpheme A morpheme that is neither an affix nor a free morpheme and that occurs in extremely restricted contexts (e.g., *cranberry*, *huckleberry*).

Creative (use of language) A characteristic of human language that allows novel and innovative responses to new experiences and situations.

Creole A language that has developed from a pidgin to become established as a native language in some speech community.

Critical period According to some theorists, a period extending from about age two to puberty during which language must be acquired.

Cuneiform A form of writing used by the Sumerians in the fourth millenium B.C. and produced with a wedge-shaped stylus pressed into soft clay tablets.

Cycle Each application of a phonological rule when the rule applies at more than one level.

Cyrillic (alphabet) A writing system that combines adaptations of Glagolitic letters with Greek and Hebrew characters.

Dative (Dat) A case assigned to the noun phrase that specifies an indirect object or a recipient.

Declension The complete set of inflected forms associated with a noun (also called a **Nominal paradigm**).

Deep dyslexia A type of acquired dyslexia in which patients produce reading errors that are semantically related to the word that they are asked to read.

Deep structure A level of syntactic representation that results from insertion of lexical items into the tree structure generated by the phrase structure rules.

Degemination A process in which a geminate segment becomes a single segment.

Degenerate foot A metrical foot that consists only of a head (i.e., minimal foot).

Degree word A category that specifies the extent of adjectives or adverbs.

Delayed release A phonological feature that specifies affricate consonants.

Deletion A phonetic process that removes a segment from certain phonetic contexts (e.g., *parade* is often pronounced [pr̥ejd]).

Denasalization In child language, the replacement of a nasal stop by a non-nasal counterpart (e.g., [suwd] for [suwn]).

Denotation Entities that a word or a phrase refers to.

Dental (sound) A sound made with the tongue placed against, between, or near the teeth.

Derivation (a) In morphology, a word formation process by which a new word is built from a stem, usually through the addition of an affix, that changes the word class and/or basic meaning of the word. (b) The set of steps or rule applications that results in the formation of a sentence in syntax and of a phonetic representation from an underlying form in phonology.

Descriptive (analysis) An analysis that aims to describe the linguistic facts as they are.

Design features Essential characteristics of communication systems that have been established with reference to human language.

Determinative A nonphonetic symbol that indicates a composite character's meaning; used in Chinese writing and historically also found in other logographic systems, such as Egyptian and Sumerian (also called a **Radical** or a **Specifier**).

Determiner (Det) A minor lexical category whose members combine with nouns to form noun phrases and specify whether the noun is definite or indefinite (e.g., *the, a*).

Deterministic parsing A type of automatic computer parsing of language in which no backtracking is permitted.

Developmental (approach) An approach to language acquisition research that focuses on the stages children go through as they make hypotheses about particular linguistic structures.

Developmental (errors) Errors that occur in language acquisition and provide evidence of the learner's attempts to create a grammatical system based on his or her hypotheses about the target language (e.g., *why didn't he came to work?*).

Developmental sequences The stages of linguistic development that are relatively invariant across language learners.

Dialect A regional or social variety of a language characterized by its own phonological, syntactic, and lexical properties.

Dialectology A branch of linguistics concerned with the analysis and description of regional varieties of a language.

Diaphragm The large sheet of muscle that separates the chest cavity from the abdomen and helps to maintain the air pressure needed to keep the speech mechanism functioning steadily.

Diary study A type of naturalistic investigation in which a researcher keeps daily notes on a child's linguistic progress.

Dichotic listening An experiment in which the subject listens to different sounds in each ear.

Diphthong Vowels that exhibit a change in quality within a single syllable (e.g., [ej], [ow], [aw]).

Diphthongization A process where a pure vowel becomes a diphthong.

Direct method (DM) A method of second language teaching that is based on the belief that an adult L2 learner can learn language in the same manner as a child and therefore involves no grammar instruction but rather concentrates on communicating.

Direct object The NP immediately dominated by VP; the sister of V (e.g., *the budgie* in *Kate fed the budgie*).

Directionality A parameter that designates the direction of a process such as syllabification and stress assignment.

Discourse A set of utterances that constitute a speech event.

Discourse analysis The study of the organization of texts, ways in which parts of texts are connected, and the devices used for achieving textual structure.

Discourse markers Sequentially dependent elements that bracket units of talk (e.g., *well, you know*, etc.).

Discrete (tokens) Tokens that are distinguished from each other by "stepwise" differences (e.g., the digital display of a clock).

Displacement A property by which the users of the communication system are able to refer to events that are remote in space and time.

Dissimilation A process in which a sound is modified so that it becomes less like another neighboring sound (i.e., the opposite of assimilation) (e.g., *fifths* may be pronounced as [fɪfts]).

Distinctive feature A feature that serves to distinguish contrastive forms (e.g., the feature [voice] is distinctive in English because it underlies the contrast between /p/ and /b/, /t/ and /d/, etc.).

Dominate A structural relation in which there is a path in the tree from a node *A* to a node *B* (e.g., S dominates NP and VP).

Dorsal features Phonological features that specify the position of the tongue body (e.g., [high], [low], [back], etc.).

Dorsum The body and back of the tongue.

Double-blind test A test in which a subject's responses are interpreted independently by someone other than the administrator of the test.

Downdrift A tonal phenomenon in which each high tone is lower than the preceding high tone, but higher than the low tone that immediately precedes it.

Dressage An interaction between a trainer and an animal in which the animal responds to very slight (sometimes subconscious) cues communicated by the trainer.

Duality of patterning A property of communication systems in which meaningless units are combined to form arbitrary signs that, in turn, are recombined to form new larger signs.

Duetting The interchange of calls in a patterned manner between two members of a species.

Dysprosody One of the characteristic properties of Broca's aphasia, where intonation is completely absent.

Elsewhere Any linguistic environment other than some specifically restricted environment.

Elsewhere allomorph An allomorph that occurs in other than some specifically restricted environment.

Endocentric compounds Compound words in which one member identifies the general class to which the meaning of the entire word belongs (e.g., *dogfood* is a type of food in English).

Endophoric reference See **Textual reference**.

Ends A component of the speech situation, which shows the function and the outcome of the speech.

Entailment A relation between two sentences wherein the truth of the second necessarily follows from the truth of the first, but the reverse is not necessarily the case (e.g., the truth of *The wolf killed the bear* entails the truth of *The bear is dead*).

Environment The phonetic context in which a segment occurs.

Epenthesis The phonetically motivated insertion of a sound between segments (e.g., *film* may be pronounced as [fɪləm]).

Ergative (Erg) In ergative languages, a case marker used for the subject of a transitive verb but not the subject of an intransitive verb.

Error analysis (EA) An approach to L2 research that involves the listing and classification of the learner's errors in an attempt to discover developmental patterns.

Euphemism A word or phrase that is less direct than the taboo word it replaces and is considered to be more socially acceptable (e.g., *passed away* for *died*).

Exclusive A type of first person plural pronoun whose referents do not include the addressee.

Exocentric compounds Compound words in which the category of the compound does not follow from the category of either member (e.g., *redneck*).

Experimental approach A method of studying first language acquisition that makes use of specially designed tasks to elicit linguistic activity.

Extension The set of entities that a word picks out in the world (e.g., the extension of *the current Queen of England* is Queen Elizabeth II).

Extrametricality The invisibility of peripheral entities to phonological rules such as stress assignment.

Extrinsic rule ordering A rule ordering that must be specified by the analyst independently of any general principles.

Feature (a) **(Phonetic)** The smallest nonreduceable building block of linguistic structure. (b) **(Phonological)** See **Distinctive feature**. (c) **(Semantic)** See **Semantic feature**.

Feature hierarchy A representation of how features are related to each other.

Feedback A property of communication in which users of the system monitor what they are transmitting.

Feeding (rule order) A rule ordering where the first rule makes the application of the following rule possible.

Field dependence A learning style in which the learner operates holistically, perceiving the "field" as a whole rather than in terms of its component parts.

Field independence A learning style in which the learner operates analytically, perceiving the "field" in terms of its component parts rather than as a whole.

First person The speaker (or speakers) as opposed to listeners and outsiders.

Flap A sound made by striking a point of articulation as an articulator passes across it (as in the alveolar flap of English).

Flapping A phonetic process in which an alveolar stop is pronounced as a voiced flap between vowels, the first of which is generally stressed (e.g., [bʌ́tɾ] → [bʌ́Dɾ]).

Fluent aphasia An aphasia caused by damage to parts of the left cortex behind the central sulcus, where the patients can produce their language, but have a great deal of difficulty selecting, organizing, and monitoring their language production.

Folk etymology The reanalysis of a word by the speakers of a language, typically reflecting the confusion of forms that are phonetically and/or semantically similar (e.g., *berfrey*→*belfry*).

Foreigner Talk The speech used by native speakers in communicating with L2 learners, characterized by the use of relatively simple structures and common lexical items.

Formants The main frequencies of a sound. Formants show up as black bands on a spectrogram because they have more intensity than other frequencies.

Free form An element that may occur in isolation and/or whose position with respect to neighboring elements is not entirely fixed.

Free (morpheme) A morpheme that can be a word by itself.

Free rule application Unordered application of rules in a derivation.

Free variation The free alternation of allophones and/or phonemes in a given environment (e.g., *sto*[pˀ], *sto*[p]; /ɛ/*conomics*, /ij/*conomics*).

Frication A sound change where stops weaken to fricatives.

Fricative A consonant produced with a continuous airflow through the mouth and with a narrowed oral passage such that there is audible friction (e.g., [s], [z], [f], [v], etc.).

Front (sound) A sound made in front of the palatal region.

Frontal lobe A subsection of the cortex that lies in front of the central sulcus.

Fronting The moving forward of a sound's place of articulation (e.g., [ʃuw]→ [suw]).

Full reduplication A reduplication process in which the whole word is duplicated.

Functional categories Words whose main function is specifying grammatical relations rather than carrying semantic content.

Function words See **Functional categories.**

Fusion A morphological change where a word becomes an affix (e.g., English affixes such as *-hood*, *-dom*, and *-ly* used to be words).

Fusional languages Languages whose affixes often mark several grammatical categories simultaneously.

Fuzzy concepts Concepts that do not have precise definitions with clear-cut boundaries that distinguish them from other concepts.

Gender classification A grammatical category dividing nouns into classes often based on shared semantic and/or phonological properties (also called **Noun class**).

Gender-exclusive differentiation A type of social differentiation in which the use of some linguistic forms depends on the gender of the speakers.

Gender-preferential differentiation A type of social differentiation in which the frequency of some linguistic forms depends on the gender of the speakers (e.g., in English, the word *lovely* is more likely to be used by a woman).

Generate To form a linguistic representation by a system of rules.

Generative grammar A system of rules capable of forming or generating the potentially infinite set of sentences in a language.

Genetic classification A classification of languages according to their origin.

Genetically related (languages) Languages descended from a common parent language.

Genitive (Gen) A case assigned to the noun phrase that bears the possessive relation or some other close connection with the head noun.

Genre A component of the speech situation, which refers to any one of a class of named speech acts (e.g., greeting, leave-taking, lecture, joke, and so on).

Glagolitic A writing system introduced among Slavic peoples for the translation of the Bible by the brothers Constantine (Cyril) and Methodius in the ninth century A.D.

Glide A type of sound that is produced with an articulation like that of a vowel, but that moves quickly to another articulation or quickly terminates (e.g., [j], [w]).

Glide strengthening A sound change where a glide is changed to a corresponding affricate (e.g., [j] has become $[d^z]$ in Italian).

Gliding In child language acquisition, the replacement of a liquid by a glide (e.g., [wajd] for [rajd]).

Global aphasia The most severe form of nonfluent aphasia, where the patient is completely mute.

Glottal (sound) A sound made with a special modification of the vocal folds besides that needed for voicelessness, voicing, and whispering (e.g., [ʔ] and [h]).

Glottis The space between the vocal folds.

Goal A thematic role that describes the end point for a movement (e.g., '*Mary*' in the sentence '*Terry gave the skis to Mary*').

Graded concept A concept that is graded in terms of its typical member.

Graded (tokens) Tokens that change in quantity or degree without steps or jumps from one level to the next (e.g., voice volume).

Grammar The system of elements and rules needed to form and interpret sentences.

Grammar translation method (GTM) A method of second language teaching that emphasizes reading, writing, translation, and the conscious learning of grammatical rules, its primary goal being to develop a literary mastery of the target language.

Grammatical (sentence) A sentence that speakers judge to be a possible sentence in their language.

Grammatical hierarchy A hierarchy of grammatical relations such as subjects and objects in terms of markedness.

Grammatical utterance An utterance that speakers judge to be possible in their language.

Grammaticized concepts Concepts that are expressed as affixes or nonlexical categories.

Great English Vowel Shift A series of nonphonetically conditioned modifications to long vowels that occurred from the Middle English period to the eighteenth century.

Grid A unit that shows the strength of stresses in metrical feet.

Grimm's Law The consonant shifts that took place between Proto-Indo-European and Proto-Germanic, which were tabulated by Grimm.

Gyri Areas where the cortex is folded out toward the surface.

Hangul The standard Korean alphabetic script.

Head (of a foot) A stressed element within a foot.

Head (of a word) The morpheme that determines the category of the entire word (e.g., *house* is the head of the compound word *greenhouse*).

Head (of a phrase) The lexical category around which a phrasal category is built and that is invariably present in the phrase (e.g., N is the head of NP).

Helping verb See **Auxiliary verb.**

Hieroglyphics Egyptian pictograms that developed through logographic, syllabic, and even partially alphabetic stages.

High (sound) A sound made with the tongue raised (e.g., [i], [k], [u]).

Hiragana One of the two Japanese syllabic writing systems.

Holophrase One-word utterances that are endowed with a sentence meaning and that characterize an early stage of first language acquisition.

Homophones Two words that have an identical phonetic form but are each associated with an entirely different meaning (e.g., *sail/sale*).

Hypercorrection Overgeneralization of a particular rule of a language.

Iambic foot A bounded right-headed foot.

Icon A token that bears some resemblance to its referent (e.g., a photograph).

Ideogram A pictogram that represents an idea rather than a concrete object.

Illocutionary act An act that is performed by the speaker by virtue of producing an utterance (e.g., promising, commanding, arresting).

Immersion A method of second language teaching in which the students are instructed in most of their courses and school activities in the second language.

Implicational universals Principles that stipulate that the presence of one linguistic trait implies the presence of another, but not vice versa (e.g., languages with fricative phonemes (/s/, /z/, etc.) will also have stop phonemes (/p/, /t/, etc.) although the reverse is not always true).

Inanimate In some languages, a class consisting of nouns, most of which have non-living referents.

Inclusive A type of first person plural pronoun whose referents include the addressee.

Indexical sign Signs whose presence have in some sense been caused by their referents (e.g., the presence of smoke is an index of fire).

Infix An affix that occurs within another morpheme.

Inflection A morphological process that modifies a word's form in order to mark the grammatical subclass to which it belongs (e.g., sg. *wolf*→pl. *wolves*).

Inflectional language See **Fusional language**.

Instrumental motivation The desire to achieve proficiency in a new language for utilitarian reasons, such as getting a job or a promotion.

Instrumentalities A component of the speech situation, which includes 'channel' (verbal, written, electronic mail, etc.) and 'code' (the language and/or variety used).

Integrative motivation A desire to achieve proficiency in a new language in order to participate in the life of the community that speaks the language.

Intension A word or expression's inherent sense, the concepts that it evokes (e.g., the intension of *Prime Minister of Canada* is 'leader of the majority party in Parliament').

Interactional sociolinguistics A type of sociolinguistics that includes the subdisciplines of ethnography of communication, discourse analysis, and pragmatics.

Interchangeability A property of communication in which all users can both send and receive messages.

Intercostals The muscles between the ribs.

Interdental (sound) A sound made with the tongue placed between the teeth (e.g., [θ], [ð] as in *bath* and *bathe*, respectively).

Interfaces The interactions among the various components of grammar.

Interference The inappropriate use of an L1 structure in the L2 system.

Interlanguage The dynamic language system unique to an L2 learner as he or she passes through a number of states of grammar along a continuum, starting with the native language and ultimately approaching the target language.

Interlingual (errors) Errors made by L2 learners that are the result of L1 interference.

Internal reconstruction A technique used to reconstruct an earlier form of a language by relying on the current morphophonemic variation within that language.

International Phonetic Alphabet (IPA) A system for transcribing the sounds of speech that attempts to represent each sound of human speech with a single symbol.

Intonation Movement of pitch that is not related to contrastive differences in the meanings of forms.

Intransitive (verb) A verb that cannot take a direct object NP (e.g., *sleep, exist*).

Intrinsic rule ordering A rule ordering that is a logical consequence of the nature of the rules.

Inversion A syntactic transformation in which a constituent order is reversed.

Island A syntactic constituent in which no element can be affected by transformation (e.g., no element can be extracted from complex noun phrases).

Isogloss In a linguistic atlas, a line that separates an area in which a particular feature of pronunciation, grammar, or vocabulary is found from surrounding areas where that feature is absent.

Isolate A language that is not known to be related to any other living language (e.g., Ainu).

Isolating (language) See **Analytic (language)**.

Jargon Obscure specialized language or vocabulary peculiar to some field (see **Sublanguage**).

Jargon aphasia A severe type of Wernicke's aphasia, characterized by the poor selection of phonemes and words while retaining the normal intonation of the language.

Kanji Chinese characters used to represent word roots in Japanese.

Katakana One of the two Japanese syllabic writing systems; it is widely used in advertising and in spelling non-Japanese words.

Key A component of the speech situation that specifies the mode, such as serious, facetious, formal, sarcastic, and so on.

Labial (sound) Any sound made with closure or near-closure of the lips (e.g., [w], [b], [m], etc.).

Labiodental (sound) A sound produced with the lower lip near or touching the upper teeth (e.g., [f], [v]).

Labiovelar (sound) A sound made with the tongue raised near the velum and the lips simultaneously rounded (e.g., [w]).

Language A human communication system that is usually distinguished by mutual understanding or political boundaries.

Language bioprogram hypothesis The hypothesis that the similarities among creoles are due to Universal Grammar.

Language contact Interaction between speakers of one language and speakers of another language or dialect.

Laryngeal features Phonological features that represent laryngeal states (e.g., [voice], [spread glottis], and [constricted glottis]).

Laryngeal node A node in the feature geometry in autosegmental phonology, which dominates laryngeal features such as voicing, spread glottis, and constricted glottis.

Larynx A box-like structure made of cartilage and muscle in which the vocal folds are located, commonly known as the voice box.

Lateral fissure The major fissure that extends from front to back of the cerebral hemisphere.

Lateral fricative A lateral sound made with a narrow enough closure to be classified as a fricative.

Lateral (sound) A sound made with the sides of the tongue lowered (e.g., varieties of [l]).

Lateralization The localization of a neurological function in one side of the brain. See also **cerebral dominance**.

Lax (vowel) A vowel that is made with a relatively less constricted tongue body or root (e.g., [ɪ], [ə], [ʊ]).

Learnability A property of communication in which a user of the system can learn other variants.

Learning strategies The ways in which L2 learners process language input and develop linguistic knowledge (e.g., generalization).

Length The subjective impression of time occupied by the duration of a phone.

Lenition See **Weakening**.

Lesion The place of severe damage to the brain.

Lexical ambiguity A situation in which a single form has two or more meanings (e.g., a *trunk* is a 'piece of luggage' or an 'elephant nose').

Lexical category An open class of words distinguished on the basis of its semantic and combinatorial properties (e.g., noun, verb, adjective).

Lexical diffusion The process whereby a linguistic change manifests itself first in a few words and then gradually spreads through the vocabulary of the language.

Lexical gaps See **Accidental gaps**.

Lexical insertion The insertion of words into tree structures under the appropriate lexical category label.

Lexicalization The process whereby concepts are encoded in the words of a language.

Lexicography A branch of linguistics concerned with the principles and practice of dictionary-making.

Lexicon The speaker's mental dictionary; it contains a lexical entry for each item in his or her vocabulary as well as a set of word formation rules.

Lingua franca A language that enables communication to take place when two or more groups of people come into contact who do not share a common native language.

Linguistic competence The linguistic knowledge that enables the speaker of a language to produce and understand an unlimited number of familiar and novel utterances.

Linguistic manipulation task An experimental task in second language acquisition research in which the subject's attention is directed to the language forms themselves.

Linguistic universals Structural characteristics that occur across the languages of the world.

Linguistic typology The classification of languages according to their common structural characteristics (e.g., word order patterns).

Linguistics The study of how language is organized and used.

Liquid A consonant made with a continuous flow of air through the oral cavity but with an obstruction less than that of fricatives (e.g., [l], [r]).

Loan words Words that are borrowed from one language into another (e.g., The words *poodle* and *kindergarten* were borrowed into English from German).

Lobes Substructures of the cortex in each hemisphere.

Location A thematic role that specifies the place where an action occurs (e.g., '*the SkyDome*' in the sentence '*The athletes practiced in the SkyDome*').

Locative (Loc) Thematic role of the noun phrase that specifies place or location.

Locutionary act A speech act consisting of the utterance of a sentence with a particular meaning.

Logogram A sign that represents an entire word and is not recognizable as a picture.

Logographic (writing) A system of writing in which a sign represents an entire word.

Longitudinal fissure Deep sulcus that extends from the front of the brain to the back and separates the left and right cerebral hemispheres.

Loudness The subjective impression of a phone's volume relative to the sounds around it.

Low (sound) A sound made with the tongue lowered (e.g., [a], [ɑ], [æ]).

Machine-readable dictionary A dictionary that appears in computer form, such as that found in spelling checkers or thesauruses.

Machine translation Translating from one language, such as English, to another, such as French, using a computer.

Main (verb) A verb other than an auxiliary (*They may* win).

Major class features Phonological features that distinguish the major classes of sounds: consonant, obstruent, nasal, liquid, glide, and vowel ([consonantal], [vocalic], and [sonorant]).

Major lexical categories Lexical classes in which membership is "open" in the sense that new words are constantly being added (e.g., noun, verb, adjective).

Majority Rules Strategy A strategy used in comparative reconstruction requiring that the phoneme occurring in the largest number of cognate languages be reconstructed in the proto-language unless it can be ruled out on some other grounds.

Manner features Phonological features that represent the manner of articulation (e.g., [nasal], [continuant], [delayed release], and [lateral]).

Manner of articulation The manner in which airflow is modified by the speech organs in the production of a sound.

Marked (features) Complex or less common features or characteristics in a language.

Markedness theory The idea that whether a linguistic feature is marked or unmarked can help to understand linguistic universals.

Matrix A representation of sounds, where all the relevant distinctive features and their values are placed in an array.

Matrix (clause) The larger clause in which an embedded clause occurs (e.g., the entire bracketed sentence in [*John said* that he was leaving]).

Maxim of Manner A conversational maxim that calls for avoiding ambiguity and obscurity.

Maxim of Quality A conversational maxim that calls for making one's contribution true.

Maxim of Quantity A conversational maxim that calls for making one's contribution as informative as required.

Maxim of Relation A conversational maxim that calls for relevance.

Mergers Phonological changes where two or more phonemes collapse into a single one.

Mesolect A creole variety that falls between a basilect and an acrolect.

Metacognitive strategy A strategy employed by L2 learners where the learners are aware when they plan, monitor, or evaluate the success of a learning activity.

Metaphor A figure of speech containing an implied comparison based on the perception of a similarity between distinct objects or actions (e.g., *he grasped the idea*).

Metathesis A change in the relative positioning of sounds (e.g., *ask* may be pronounced as [æks]).

Metrical feet Elements of metrical structure consisting of a stressed syllable and an associated unstressed syllable (or syllables).

Metrics The study of stress placement.

Mid (vowel) A vowel for which the tongue is neither raised nor lowered (e.g., [ɛ], [ʌ], [o]).

Minimal foot See **Degenerate foot**.

Minimal pair A pair of linguistic forms that differ by only one element and contrast in meaning.

Minor (lexical category) A lexical class in which membership is "closed" in the sense that it is restricted to a fixed set of elements already in the language (e.g., preposition and pronoun).

Mixed type language A language that simultaneously has some characteristics of two or more morphological types such as isolating, polysynthetic, agglutinating, and fusional types.

Modifiers A class of elements that express properties of heads.

Morpheme The smallest unit of language that carries information about meaning or function.

Morphology The system of categories and rules involved in the creation and interpretation of complex words.

Morphophonemic rules Rules that account for alternations among allomorphs.

Motherese A type of speech that is typically addressed to young language learners.

Motion verbs Words that can describe motion through space (e.g., *come, go,* and *move* in English).

Motor aphasia See **Nonfluent aphasia**.

Movement test A test for identifying the syntactic constituents by moving a sequence of words.

Murmur Voiced sounds produced with the vocal folds relaxed to allow enough air to escape to produce a whispery effect (i.e., whispery voice).

Mutual intelligibility One of the criteria for deciding whether two varieties of speeches are dialects of the same language, which must be mutually intelligible.

Nasal Sound produced by lowering the velum so that the air escapes through the nasal cavity.

Nasalization Articulation of a sound with a nasal character (e.g., nasalized vowels, nasalized stops)

Native speaker A person who acquired a language at an early age without explicit instruction.

Natural approach A method of second-language teaching in which the L2 learner is free to use the second language in a naturalistic communicative environment (e.g., problem-solving tasks and language games).

Natural class Class of sounds that shares common phonological properties.

Naturalistic approach A method of studying first-language acquisition where the investigators observe and record children's spontaneous verbal behavior. (e.g., diary study).

Naturalness A hypothetical linguistic property that is simultaneously found in common sound changes, language universals, and language acquisition (e.g., CV syllable is the most natural of all syllable types).

Negative transfer See **Interference**.

New information Knowledge that is introduced into the discourse for the first time.

No-naming The strategy of avoiding address terms altogether when participants are unsure which term to use.

Node (in a feature hierarchy) Point in a feature hierarchy that represents the grouping of a feature or features.

Nominative A case assigned to the subject noun phrase.

Non-deterministic parsing A method of automatic parsing by computer in which either the computer is permitted to backtrack when an analysis fails or in which more than one analysis may be built in parallel.

Nonfluent aphasia A type of aphasia caused by damage to parts of the brain in front of the central sulcus, characterized by slow effortful speech production.

Nonlexical categories See **Functional categories**.

Nonphonetically conditioned sound change A sound change that has no motivation in the immediate phonetic environment.

Nonstandard (dialect) A variety of language that differs from the standard dialect in systematic ways.

Nonstructured communication task A task used in L2 research in which the researcher and the L2 learner are involved in natural conversation with no special focus on a particular language structure.

Nonterminal (intonation) contour A rising or level intonation that often signals incompleteness.

Nonterminal symbol The parts of a structure which are not lexical items, for example, VP, NP, Det, N. Compare with *terminal* symbol.

Norms Basic rules that seem to underlie speech interaction.

Noun (N) A major lexical category whose members typically name entities, and heads a noun phrase (e.g., *key*, *Jean*, *honesty*).

Noun class See **Gender classification**.

Noun phrase (NP) A phrase built around a noun head (e.g., *the black shroud*).

Nucleus The [+syllabic] segment that forms the core or basis of a syllable.

Number A grammatical category marking distinctions between singular, plural, and (where appropriate) dual.

Object permanence The child's realization that objects in the environment exist as independent entities with their own inherent properties—a milestone usually reached in the sensorimotor stage of development.

Oblique A case assigned to noun phrases that occur with a preposition.

Obviative A form that is used in some languages for referring to an entity (other than the speaker or the addressee) that has not been chosen as the focus of the conversation.

Occipital lobe A subsection of the cortex that is to the rear of the angular gyrus.

Old (given) information Knowledge that the speaker assumes is available to the addressee at the time of the utterance.

One-word stage A stage of first-language acquisition where children characteristically produce one-word utterances.

Onomatopoeic (word) A word whose phonetic shape resembles its referent in some sense (e.g., *buzz, splash, cock-a-doodle-doo*).

Onset The portion of a syllable that precedes the nucleus (e.g., /spl/ in *spleen*).

Open syllable A syllable without a coda.

Oral (sound) A sound produced with a raised velum allowing airflow only through the oral cavity (e.g., [o], [p], [h]).

Ordered rule application The application of a sequence of phonological rules in a certain order, especially when the order is necessary to derive the correct form.

Orthography The set of conventions for representing language in written form.

Overextension A developmental phenomenon in which the meaning of a child's word overlaps with that of the equivalent adult word, but also extends beyond it (e.g., *dog* is used to refer to other animals as well as dogs).

Overgeneralizations See **Overextension**.

Palatal (sound) A sound produced with the tongue touching or nearly touching the palate (e.g., [j]).

Palatalization A process of assimilatory change whereby a consonant anticipates a front vowel or consonant and takes on a palatal or alveopalatal place of articulation.

Palate The highest part of the roof of the mouth.

Palatoalveolar (sound) See **Alveopalatal (sound)**.

Paragraphia Writing errors made by Broca's aphasics that have characteristics corresponding to their speech.

Parameter A universal dimension along which languages may vary.

Paraphrase The relationship between two sentences with identical meanings (e.g., *The wind is tearing the canopy* and *The canopy is being torn by the wind*).

Parse To give a grammatical description of words, phrases, and sentences.

Parietal lobe A subsection of the cortex that lies behind the central sulcus.

Partial reduplication A morphological process in which part of a stem is repeated to form a new word.

Participants A component of speech situation, characterized by terms such as addressor, addressee, speaker, performer, audience, and so on.

Particle (Prt) A minor lexical category whose members are attached to VP and can occur either before or after a direct object (e.g., *he took* out *the garbage; he took the garbage* out).

Passive (sentence) A sentence whose theme is encoded as grammatical subject (e.g., The beans were eaten).

Patterns In L2 learning, partially analyzed utterances with open slots for a word or phrase (e.g., *D'you wanna* _____?).

Pejoration A semantic change where the meaning of a word becomes more negative or unfavorable (e.g., the meaning of *wench* used to be 'girl').

Performative (verb) A verb whose utterance involves the performance of an illocutionary act (e.g., *promise, warn,* etc.).

Perlocutionary act A speech act that has a particular effect on the listener (e.g., an utterance that frightens, ridicules or insults).

Person A grammatical category that typically distinguishes among the first person (speaker), second person (addressee), and third person (anyone else).

Pharyngeal (sound) A sound made by modifying airflow in the pharynx.

Pharynx The tube of the throat between the larynx and the oral cavity.

Pheremones Chemicals used for specific communicative purposes by animals.

Phoenician script An early writing system devised by the Semitic peoples of ancient Phoenicia as early as 1000 B.C., which had twenty-two consonantal signs.

Phone Any human speech sound.

Phoneme A contrastive segmental unit with predictable phonetic variants.

Phonemic paraphasia A language disorder involving the systematic substitution and deletion of phonemes (e.g., *wrench* may be pronounced as *kench*).

Phonemic (representation) A level of representation in which the predictable features of sound are left unspecified.

Phonemic transcription A type of transcription of sounds where phonetic details are ignored and only phonemic contrast is recorded.

Phonetic determinative The component of a multi-element Chinese character that provides information about pronunciation.

Phonetic Plausibility Strategy A strategy used in comparative reconstruction that requires that any process posited to account for the change of the reconstructed phoneme into the sounds observed in the data be phonetically plausible.

Phonetic sound change A sound change that affects the allophones of an already existing phoneme, but does not result in the addition, deletion, or re-arrangement of phonemes.

Phonetic transcription A type of transcription of sounds where not only phonemic differences but also phonetic details are recorded.

Phonetically conditioned (sound change) A change in a language's sound pattern that stems from the modification of a segment under the influence of a particular phonetic environment.

Phonetics The study of the inventory and structure of the sounds of language.

Phonographic writing A writing system in which a sign represents some aspect of pronunciation such as syllables and segments. See also **Logographic writing**.

Phonological change See **Phonetically conditioned (sound change)**.

Phonological class A set of elements sharing certain phonological features.

Phonological constraint A phonological restriction on morphological processes.

Phonological dyslexia A type of acquired dyslexia in which the patient seems to have lost the ability to use spelling-to-sound rules.

Phonological merger A historical change occurring in cases where two or more phonemes collapse into a single contrastive unit, resulting in a net reduction in the number of phonemes in the language.

Phonological rules Rules that relate the underlying forms of words to their phonetic forms.

Phonological shift A historical change in which a series of phonemes is systematically modified so that their organization with respect to each other changes (e.g., the Great English Vowel Shift).

Phonological sound change A sound change that results in the addition, deletion, or rearrangement of phonemes.

Phonological split A historical change in which allophones of the same phoneme come to contrast with each other, creating one or more new phonemes in the language.

Phonology The study of the elements and principles that determine how sounds pattern in a language.

Phonotactics The system and study of the arrangement of phonemes in sequence.

Phrase structure rule A rule that specifies how a syntactic constituent is formed out of other smaller syntactic constituents (e.g., S→NP VP).

Phylum In language classification, a group of related stocks of language families.

Pictogram A symbol that is an image of the object it represents and that is drawn for the purpose of communication.

Pidgin A lingua franca with a highly simplified grammatical structure that has emerged as a mixture of two or more languages and has no native speakers.

Pinyin A system of writing Mandarin with a modified Latin alphabet.

Pitch The auditory property of a sound that enables us to place it on a scale that ranges from low to high.

Place features Phonological features that represent the place of articulation. (e.g., [labial], [round], [coronal], [anterior], and [strident]).

Place of articulation The point at which the airstream is modified in the vocal tract to produce a phone (also called *point of articulation*).

Plural An inflectional category associated with nouns with more than one referent.

Politeness formulas Modifications of a simple expression so that it can convey politeness (e.g., Open the window!→Please open the window.).

Polysemy A phenomenon in which a word has two or more meanings that are at least vaguely related to each other (e.g., a *diamond* is a 'jewel' or a 'baseball field').

Polysynthetic (language) A language that makes extensive use of polymorphemic words (i.e., words made up of a root and one or more affixes) but that is more complex than an agglutinating or fusional language in terms of the number of morphemes it can combine and the type of allomorphic variation it exhibits (e.g., Chipewyan, Inuktitut).

Portmanteau (morpheme) A single morpheme that is used to encode more than one grammatical contrast (e.g., the affix *-a* in Russian *dom-a* 'house' simultaneously marks genitive case, singular number, and masculine gender).

Postposition In some languages (e.g., Korean), a minor lexical category whose members typically designate relations in space or time; they follow the NP with which they combine to form a PP.

Pragmatics The speaker's and hearer's background attitudes, beliefs, and understanding of the context of an utterance and the knowledge of the way in which language is used to communicate information.

Predicate An obligatory constituent other than the subject in a sentence.

Prefix An affix that occurs in front of its stem (e.g., *re-* in *redo*).

Preposition (P) A minor lexical category whose members typically designate relations in space or time (e.g., *in, before*); they precede the NP with which they combine to form a PP.

Prepositional phrase (PP) A phrase built around a preposition head (e.g., *in the zoo*).

Prescriptive (grammar) A grammar that aims to state the linguistic facts in terms of how they should be.

Presupposition The assumption or belief implied by the use of a particular word or structure (e.g., the verb *admit* in *Nell admitted that the team had lost* indicates that the speaker is presupposing the truth of the claim that the team lost).

Prevarication A property of communication in which the system enables the users to talk nonsense or to lie.

Primary (stress) The most prominent stress in a word (e.g., the first syllable in *telegraph* has primary stress).

Principal components analysis (PCA) An approach to studying social differentiation, where the statistical investigation of a large number of linguistic variants precedes determining what social similarities are shared among them.

Principle of compositionality The meaning of a sentence is determined by the meaning of its component parts and the manner in which they are arranged in syntactic structure.

Principle A A syntactic condition that requires all reflexives to be c-commanded by their antecedents within the same clauses.

Principle B A syntactic condition that prohibits nonreflexive pronouns from being c-commanded by noun phrases in the same clause that have the same reference.

Processes (phonetic) Articulatory adjustments that occur during the production of speech.

Production strategy A strategy employed by L2 learners when attempting to use their learned linguistic knowledge in the communication process (e.g., rehearsing, pre-planning of utterance).

Productivity In morphology, the relative freedom with which an affix combines with stems of the appropriate category (e.g., The English plural suffix *-s* is more productive than the adjectival suffix *-ous*).

Progressive assimilation The modification of one or more features of a sound due to the influence of a preceding segment (so called because the direction of the influence is "forward" to a following segment).

Pronoun (Pro) A minor lexical category whose members can replace a noun phrase and that look to another element for their interpretation (e.g., *he*, *herself*, *it*).

Prosimians A group of nonhuman primates found on the island of Madagascar.

Prosodic See **Suprasegmentals**.

Proto-form The form that is reconstructed as the source of cognate words in related languages.

Proto-Indo-European A language from which most of the languages of Europe, Persia (Iran), and the northern part of India are considered to descend.

Proto-language The reconstructed language that is presumed to be the common source for two or more related languages (e.g., Proto-Indo-European).

Prototypical members The best or the most typical example of a given concept (e.g., 'robin' can be the prototypical member of the concept 'bird').

Proximate A form that is used in some languages for referring to the entity (other than the speaker or the addressee) that has been chosen as the focus of the conversation.

Quality (of a vowel) The characteristic sound of a vowel.

Radical See **Determinative**.

Reanalysis (in morphology) A factor of language change, where a word that formerly was not broken down into component morphemes is reanalyzed as having internal structure (e.g., *hamburger* is reanalyzed as *ham* + *burger*).

Rebus A string of pictorial symbols read for their phonetic value.

Reconstruction Constructing a language by analyzing related languages.

Recursive A property of a rule or rules that allows indefinite reapplication.

Reduced (vowel) The vowel schwa [ə], so called because it often appears as a weakly articulated, unstressed variant of stressed vowels.

Reduplicative (affix) A morphological process that repeats all or part of the stem to which it is attached.

Referent The entity to which a word or phrase refers.

Reflexive pronoun A pronoun that must have a c-commanding antecedent in the same clause; in English, a pronoun ending in the morpheme *self.*

Reflexiveness A property of communication where the communication system is used to discuss the system itself.

Regional dialect A speech variety associated with a particular geographical area.

Register A speech variety used in a specific social situation.

Register tone A tone that has a stable pitch over a single syllable.

Regressive assimilation A phonological process in which one or more features of a sound are modified due to the influence of a following sound (so called because the direction of the influence is "backward" to a preceding segment).

Related (languages) See **Genetically related (languages)**.

Relational analysis A syntactic analysis in which phenomena are described in terms of grammatical relations such as subject and direct object rather than morphological patterns or the order of words.

Relative clause A sentence-like construction that is embedded within an NP and provides information about the set of entities denoted by the head noun (e.g., *The meteor* that she saw).

Relexification hypothesis The hypothesis that creoles are formed through replacement of vocabulary, with little change in grammar.

Replacement A process that substitutes one nonmorphemic segment for another (e.g., *foot/feet* and *sing/sang* in English).

Representations Graphic presentations of feature changes.

Retroflex Sounds produced by curling the tongue tip back into the mouth (e.g., American English [r]).

Rhotacism A consonant weakening where [z] or [s] changes to [r].

Rhyme A subconstituent of a syllable, which is made up of the nucleus and coda.

Right ear advantage A phenomenon where speech is louder and clearer when it is heard in the right ear than in the left ear for right-handed people.

Root (a) (of the tongue) The part of the tongue contained in the upper part of the throat. (b) In a complex word, the morpheme that remains after all affixes are removed (e.g., *mind* in unmindfulness).

Root node A node in a feature hierarchy where all major class features are grouped together.

Rounded (sound) A sound that is made with the lips protruding (e.g., [u], [w]).

Routines In L2 learning, whole utterances that are error-free and appear to be learned as unanalyzed wholes, similar to the way a single word is learned.

Rule A formal statement of a linguistic process.

Runic writing A writing system that was developed shortly after the beginning of the Christian era by Germanic tribes and lasted until the sixteenth century.

Sapir-Whorf Hypothesis The hypothesis articulated by Edward Sapir and Benjamin Whorf that the particular language people speak has a shaping influence on the way in which they think and perceive the world.

Scene See **Setting**.

Schwa The lax, mid, unrounded vowel [ə].

Second person A listener or listeners as opposed to the speaker and others.

Second language A language that is learned after the first or native language is relatively established.

Secondary (stress) The second most prominent stress in a word (e.g., the third syllable in the word *solitary* has secondary stress).

Segment An individual speech sound.

Segmental change A sound change that affects a segment.

Semantic broadening The process in which the meaning of a word becomes more general or more inclusive than its historically earlier form (e.g., the word 'aunt' used to mean only father's sister).

Semantic feature The components of meaning that make up a word's intension (e.g., *man* has the feature [+ human]; *dog* has the feature [-human]).

Semantic narrowing The process in which the meaning of a word becomes less general or less inclusive than its historically earlier meaning (e.g., the word 'meat' used to mean any type of food).

Semantic role The role that the referent of an NP plays in the event described by a sentence (also called **Thematic role**) (e.g., agent, theme).

Semantic shift A process whereby the meaning of a word changes in such a way that the word comes to refer to a new, but related, set of objects (e.g., *silly* used to mean 'weak').

Semanticity A property of communication, in which the system conveys meaning through a set of fixed relationships among signs, referents, and meanings.

Semantics The various phenomena pertaining to the meaning of words and sentences; the study of meaning in human language.

Semiotics The study of signs.

Sensory aphasia See **Fluent aphasia**.

Sentence (S) A syntactic unit consisting of a noun phrase and a verb phrase.

Sequential change A sound change that involves a sequence of sounds (e.g., assimilation, epenthesis).

Setting The physical or social environment in which a speech event occurs.

Sex-exclusive differentiation See **Gender-exclusive differentiation**.

Sex-preferential differentiation See **Gender-preferential differentiation**.

Sibilant A strident sound that is relatively higher in pitch than other stridents and has a hissing quality (e.g., [s], [z]).

Sign A unit of communication structure that consists of two parts: a signifier (such as a sequence of sounds [trij]), and something signified (such as a tree in the real world).

Signal A token that triggers a specific action on the part of the receiver (e.g., a traffic light).

Signified Objects or concepts in the real world that are expressed by the signifier.

Signifier Some physical manifestation by sounds, scent, light, ultrasound, visual signs, gestures, color, electricity, and so on, that stimulates at least one sense organ of the receiver of a message and forms a sign (e.g., a word, a photograph, a sign language gesture).

Silent period In second language learning, a period of aural exposure to the language during which the learner does not attempt to use the language orally.

Simple vowel A vowel that does not show a noticeable change in quality within a single syllable (e.g., [ɪ], [æ], [ʌ]).

Simple (word) A word that consists of a single morpheme (e.g., *flea*).

Singular An inflectional category associated with nouns with a single referent.

Sisters Two or more categories that have the same node immediately above them in a tree structure (e.g., V and the direct object NP).

Slang An informal nonstandard speech variety characterized by newly coined and rapidly changing vocabulary.

Social dialect See **Sociolect**.

Social network analysis An approach for studying social differentiation, where a sociolinguist examines first-hand from the perspective of a participant-observer the language use of a preexisting social group.

Social stratification The differentiation of language varieties along social parameters.

Sociolect A speech variety spoken by a group of people who share a particular social characteristic (e.g., ethnicity, sex, age, occupation) (also called **Social dialect**).

Sociolinguistics The study of the various phenomena pertaining to the social use of language.

Song Lengthy patterns of sounds produced only by male birds for territorial and mating purposes.

Sonorant (sounds) Sounds that have relatively greater acoustic energy (e.g., vowels, glides, liquids, and nasals).

Sound change A systematic change of sounds that took place over a long period.

(Sound) shift The systematic modification of a series of phonemes.

Source A thematic role that describes the starting point for a movement (e.g., '*Maine*' in the sentence '*The senator sent the lobster from Maine to Nebraska*').

Spatial deictics Forms whose use and interpretation depend on the location of the speaker and/or addressee within a particular setting (e.g., *this/that* and *here/there* in English).

Spatial metaphor Use of a word that is primarily associated with spatial orientation to talk about physical and psychological states.

Specialization A property of communication in which the system serves no other function but to communicate.

Specifier (in XPs) Words that typically mark a phrase boundary and help to make more precise the meaning of the head (e.g., determiners such as *the*, auxiliaries such as *will*, and degree words such as *quite* or *almost*).

Spectrogram The graphic representation of an acoustic analysis of sound produced by a machine.

Speech community A group whose members share both a particular language or variety of language and the norms for its appropriate use in a social context.

Speech situations Social situations in which there is appropriate use of language.

Speech sounds See **Phone**.

Speech variety The language or form of language used by any group of speakers on any one occasion.

Spelling pronunciation One factor in sound change, where a new pronunciation reflects the spelling of the word (e.g., *often*).

Split brain experiments Studies that have investigated the effects of surgery that severed the corpus callosum as a treatment for severe epilepsy.

Splits Phonological changes where two allophones become separate phonemes due to the loss of the conditioning environment.

Spread glottis The feature that distinguishes unaspirated from aspirated consonants.

Spreading Association of a feature to neighboring segments in autosegmental phonology.

Standard (language) The superimposed language variety of a country that is generally employed by the government and the media, and that is taught in schools and is often the only or main written language.

Stem The unit to which an affix is added (e.g., in the word *statements*, the root *state* is the stem for *-ment* while the complex form *statement* is the stem for *-s*).

Stimulus-bound (response) A response that is triggered by exposure to a particular external event.

Stock In language classification, a group of related language families.

Stop A consonant produced with a complete and momentary closure of airflow through the vocal tract (e.g., [p], [t], [k]).

Stopping In child language acquisition, the replacement of a fricative with a corresponding stop (e.g., [tuwp] for *soup*).

Strategy The mental processes involved in forming and testing hypotheses about linguistic input and in using linguistic knowledge in communicative situations.

Stray syllable adjunction The process by which extrametrical syllables are joined to the metrical foot after stress placement.

Stress clash A configuration where two stresses stand immediately next to each other on a given level.

Stressed (syllable) A syllable that is relatively prominent in an utterance, often due to the combined effects of pitch, loudness, and length (e.g., in the word *college*, the first syllable is stressed).

Strident A fricative that is distinctly noisier than other fricatives made at or near the same place of articulation (e.g., [s] vs. [θ], [z] vs. [ð]).

Structural change The output, or right side, of a transformational rule.

Structural description The input, or left side, of a transformational rule.

Structurally ambiguous The property of a string of words that is assigned to more than one syntactic structure (e.g., *I took a picture of the tourist with the camera*).

Structured communication task A task used in L2 research that involves testing an L2 learner's knowledge of a specific second language structure such as negation or interrogatives.

Subcategorization Features that divide lexical categories into subcategories by indicating their compatibility with different complement types (e.g., *put*: [_____ NP PP]).

Subject The NP immediately dominated by S; the sister of VP (e.g., *backpacks* in *backpacks are comfortable*).

Subject constraint A constraint on syntactic transformations that prohibits affecting elements in a subject phrase.

Sublanguage A speech variety associated with a particular profession that facilitates communication among members of that profession (sometimes used in an overlapping sense with **Jargon** and **Cant**).

Substitution (of sounds) Replacement of one segment with another similar sounding segment.

Substitution test The replacement of a group of words by a single word to test whether the group of words is a syntactic unit (e.g., the gang *robbed the bank*; they *robbed the bank*).

Substratum influence The influence of a less politically or culturally dominant language on a more dominant language (e.g., the influence of the speech of the indigenous population in a colonial country on the language of the conquering power).

Suffix An affix that occurs after its stem (e.g., *-s* in *tapes*).

Sulci Areas where the cortex is folded in.

Superstratum influence The influence of a more politically or culturally dominant language on a less dominant language (e.g., the influence of the

English language on the native speech of former colonial territories such as India).

Suppletion The replacement of one root by another to express an inflectional contrast (e.g., the past tense of *go* is *went*).

Suprasegmentals The intrinsic aspects of phones, such as pitch, loudness, and length.

Surface dyslexia A type of acquired dyslexia in which the patients seem unable to recognize words as wholes while retaining the ability to use spelling-to-sound rules.

Surface structure A level of syntactic representation that results from the application of whatever transformations are needed to yield the final syntactic form of the sentence.

Syllabary A set of syllabic signs, each of which represents a syllable.

Syllabic consonants A consonant that functions as a syllabic nucleus.

Syllabic (writing) A system of writing in which each sign represents a syllable.

Syllable A unit of phonological organization composed of one or more segments and minimally containing a nucleus, usually a vowel, a syllabic liquid, or a syllabic nasal.

Symbolic (tokens) Tokens that bear no inherent resemblance to their referents (e.g., the word *hair*).

Symptomatic (tokens) Tokens that spontaneously convey the internal state of the sender (e.g., a yelp of pain).

Syncope The loss of word medial vowels, often due to their appearance in an unstressed syllable next to a stressed syllable (e.g., *police* may be pronounced as [plijs]).

Synonyms Two words or expressions with identical meanings (e.g., *select* and *choose*).

Syntactic categories Categories of words or phrases defined in syntactic terms.

Syntax The various phenomena pertaining to the form and organization of sentences; the study of sentence formation.

Synthetic language A language that makes extensive use of polymorphemic words (e.g., words containing a root and one or more affixes) and often uses portmanteau morphemes (also called an **Inflectional language**) (e.g., Spanish).

Systematic gaps Non-occurring forms that would violate the phonotactic constraints of a language (e.g., in English **mtlow*).

Taboo Any social prohibition on the use of particular words or phrases.

Tap A sound made by rapidly touching the tongue tip to the back of the teeth or the alveolar ridge.

Target language A second language or a language that is learned nonnatively.

Teacher Talk The linguistic input received by L2 learners from their second language teachers, often characterized by simplification of the linguistic code.

Template The innate component that predisposes birds to perform a rudimentary version of their species-specific song.

Telegraphic The speech that is characterized by a lack of minor lexical categories and affixes (in young children aged two to four years and aphasia patients).

Temporal lobe A subsection of the cortex that lies beneath the lateral fissure.

Tense In syntax and morphology, an inflectional category indicating the time of an event or action relative to the moment of speaking.

Tense (vowel) A vowel produced with a relatively tense tongue and vocal tract musculature (e.g., [i], [e], [u], etc.).

Terminal (intonation) contour A falling intonation at the end of an utterance, which usually signals that the utterance is complete.

Terminal symbol The lexical items or prefixes, suffixes, stems, and words of a language. Compare with *non-terminal* symbol.

Text The written version of any utterance or body of discourse.

Textual reference References recovered from the text itself (e.g., anaphoric, cataphoric, lexical cohesion, and ellipsis).

Thematic role See **Semantic role**.

Theme A thematic role that describes the entity undergoing an action or a movement (e.g., '*the beans*' in the sentence '*I ate the beans*').

Third person Noun phrases (or participants) in a sentence other than the speaker and addressee(s).

Tier A level of phonological description in which only certain phonological elements are represented (e.g., a syllabic tier, a tonal tier).

Tip (of the tongue) The narrow area at the front of the tongue.

Token Individual instances of signs.

Tone Pitch differences that signal differences in meaning.

Tone language A language in which differences in word meaning can be signaled by differences in pitch.

Topic A notion that corresponds to what a sentence or group of sentences is about.

Total assimilation The assimilation of all the features of neighboring segments.

Total physical response (TPR) A method of L2 teaching in which the student is initially not required to speak, but rather carries out simple commands in the second language (e.g., *close the door*).

Trace (*t*) An empty category that is left behind when an element is moved.

Trachea The tube through which air flows between the lungs and the larynx, commonly known as the windpipe.

Tradition A property of communication whereby at least certain aspects of the system must be transmitted from an experienced user to a learner.

Transformation A rule that moves a category within a syntactic structure to create a new syntactic structure (e.g., *Wh*-**Movement**).

Transitional constructions The structures characteristic of different stages in the developmental sequence during L2 acquisition.

Transitive (verb) A verb that takes a direct object NP (e.g., *hit*, *use*).

Tree structure The hierarchical representation of a phrase or sentence.

Trill A sound made by passing air over the raised tongue tip and allowing it to vibrate for several cycles.

Trochaic foot A bounded left-headed foot.

Truth conditions The truth or falsity of a sentence with respect to the real world.

Two-word stage A stage of first language acquisition, where children normally utter two succeeding words.

Typological plausibility Plausibility of language reconstruction on the basis of whether the property of the reconstructed language is consistent with properties of actual languages.

Umlaut A sequential change, where a vowel or a glide in one syllable affects the vowel in another syllable.

Unbounded foot A foot that consists of a head and any number of unstressed syllables.

Underextension A developmental phenomenon in which a child uses a lexical item to denote only a subset of the items it denotes in adult speech (e.g., *cat* is used to refer to only one specific cat).

Underlying (form) In phonology, a form from which phonetic forms are derived by rule.

Universal Grammar The proposed set of genetically transmitted categories and principles common to all human languages.

Universal tendency Structural patterns or traits that are found in most languages (e.g., most languages have fricative phonemes).

Unmarked (features) Common and universally less complex features or characteristics in a language.

Unordered rule application The application of several rules where the order among them is irrelevant.

Utterance Any instance of language produced by a speaker.

Uvula The small flap of tissue that hangs from the velum.

Uvular (sound) A sound made with the tongue touching or near the uvula (e.g., [q], [G]).

Variable (sociolinguistic) Sounds that are realized in different ways in speech, depending on sociolinguistic factors (e.g., the progressive ending *-ing* is realized as either [ɪŋ] or [ɪn]).

Velar (sound) A sound made with the tongue touching or near the velum (e.g., [k], [g], [ŋ]).

Velum The soft area toward the rear of the roof of the mouth (also called the *soft palate*).

Verb (V) A major lexical category whose members designate actions, sensations, and states (e.g., *run*, *feel*, *seem*).

Verb complement A clause within the VP portion of a sentence (e.g., *he said* [he would leave]).

Verb phrase (VP) The phrase built around a verb head (e.g., *shoot the puck*).

Verbal hedges Discourse markers such as *perhaps* or *maybe*, that hedge a speaker's assertions.

Verner's Law A generalization made by Karl Verner, which states that a word-internal voiceless fricative resulting from Grimm's Law underwent voicing if the original Proto-Indo-European accent did not immediately precede it.

Vocal cords See **Vocal folds**.

Vocal folds A set of muscles that line the inner wall of the larynx and flare outward forming paired folds (also called **Vocal cords**).

Vocal tract The speech organs above the larynx (i.e., the oral cavity, the throat or pharynx, and the nasal cavity).

Vocalic (sounds) Vowels and liquids.

Voice In syntax and morphology, an inflectional category used to indicate the role of the subject's referent in the action described by the verb (e.g., passive versus active).

Voiceless (sound) Any sound made with the vocal folds not vibrating (e.g., [p], [s], [h]).

Voicing A state during which the vocal folds are brought close together, but not tightly closed, allowing air to pass between them causing them to vibrate.

Voicing assimilation A process where segments assimilate in voicing to neighboring segments.

Vowel A resonant, syllabic sound produced with less obstruction in the vocal tract than that required for glides.

Vowel reduction A process that converts a vowel into the short, lax segment [ə].

Weakening A type of assimilation in which a lessening in the time or degree of a consonant's closure occurs (also called **Lenition**).

Weakening of meaning A semantic change where the meaning of a word is weakened (e.g., the English word *soon* used to mean 'immediately' instead of 'in the near future').

Wernicke's aphasia A type of aphasia caused by damage to the temporal-parietal area of the brain, whose victims lose the ability to interpret while they retain the ability to produce grammatical sentences.

Wernicke's area The area of the brain involved in the interpretation and the selection of lexical items.

Wh movement A syntactic transformation where wh-phrases are moved to complementizer position.

***Wh* question** A question beginning with a *wh* word such as *who, what, where* (e.g., *Who did it?*).

Whispery voice See **Murmur**.

Word A minimal free form.

Word formation rules Rules that specify how to form one class of words out of another.

Word manufacture See **Coinage**.

Word order A linear order of words in a sentence.

Word-based morphology Morphology that can form a new word from a base that is itself a word (e.g., *re-do* and *treat-ment* in English).

Writing The symbolic representation of language in storable, graphic form.

X′ rule A phrase structure rule that deals with intermediate categories, which states that an intermediate category X′ consists of a head, X, and any optional complements.

XP rule A phrase structure rule that deals with maximal categories, which states that a maximal category XP consists of an optional specifier and an X′.

Zero derivation A morphological process that does not require any detectable phonological changes.

LANGUAGE INDEX

INDEX